Public Administration in Ethiopia

Public Administration in Ethiopia

Case Studies and Lessons for Sustainable Development

Edited by
Bacha Kebede Debela,
Geert Bouckaert,
Meheret Ayenew Warota,
and Dereje Terefe Gemechu

Editorial Team
Annie Hondeghem, Trui Steen and Steve Troupin

LEUVEN UNIVERSITY PRESS

Published with the support of
VLIR-UOS (Belgium) KU Leuven Ambo University Addis Ababa University

Published in 2020 by Leuven University Press / Presses Universitaires de Louvain / Universitaire Pers Leuven. Minderbroedersstraat 4, B-3000 Leuven (Belgium).

ISBN 978 94 6270 256 1 (Paperback)
ISBN 978 94 6166 363 4 (ePDF)
ISBN 978 94 6166 364 1 (ePUB)
https://doi.org/10.11116/9789461663634
D/2020/1869/49
NUR: 759

Layout: Crius Group
Cover design: Frederik Danko
Cover illustration: Ethiopia flag against city blurred background at sunrise, backlight (www.freepik.com/natanaelginting)

Table of Contents

Preface to the Handbook

Building an effective, inclusive, and accountable public administration has increasingly factored in the agenda of policymakers and other stakeholders, including the academia, in the effort to achieve sustainable development. This first Ethiopian Public Administration Handbook is the product of a joint effort by Ambo University, KU Leuven Public Governance Institute (Belgium) and the Addis Ababa University JOINT Project, funded by VLIR-UOS, Belgium (2018–2020). The handbook builds on the results of a TEAM project on "Strengthening Institutional Capacity to Support Public Administration and/or Development Management Programmes at Ambo University," carried out by Ambo University and KU Leuven and funded by VLIR-UOS, Belgium (2013–2018).

The handbook was coauthored by Ethiopian academics and practitioner-academics, also called "para-academics." It is built on PhD studies and conference papers, written for a series of conferences organized within the framework of the TEAM and JOINT projects by project partners and other partners, including the Ethiopian Public Administration Association (EPAA), which was created by TEAM Project in 2016. The establishment of EPAA after over five decades of public administration teaching in Ethiopia has significant implications.

The handbook addresses a wide range of timely crucial issues and will be a required reading for public administration students, practitioners, and theorists interested in public administration, public policy, and sustainable development. In fact, it not only discusses public administration in the Ethiopian context but also creates a stepping-stone for teaching and researching issues related to public administration in Ethiopia in a manner that is conducive to achieving sustainable development.

Bacha Kebede Debela
Ambo University

Geert Bouckaert
KU Leuven

Meheret Ayenew Warota
Addis Ababa University

Dereje Terefe Gemechu
Ethiopian Civil Service University

Acknowledgments

This handbook would not have possible without the incredible support of a number of institutions and individuals. First, we are exceedingly indebted to VLIR-UOS (Belgium) for funding the TEAM Project "Strengthening Institutional Capacity to Support Public Administration and/or Development Management Programmes at Ambo University" between Ambo University and KU Leuven (2013–2018) and the JOINT project "Professionalizing Ethiopian Public Administration to Support Development Practitioners" between Ambo University, KU Leuven Public Governance Institute (Belgium), and Addis Ababa University (2018–2020). An eight-year grant allowed participants to pragmatically learn from project activities, such as the organized conferences, to benefit from interaction between the partners and other stakeholders, and ultimately, to create this Ethiopian Public Administration handbook.

The Projects were awarded to Geert Bouckaert (Flemish Promoter) and Bacha Kebede Debela (local promoter-Ambo University). Beyond partner institutions, interestingly, the grant was used to connect Ethiopian PA scholars and practitioners to each other and other international PA scholars and PA professional associations, notably the International Institute of Administrative Sciences (IIAS) and the Association of African Public Administration and Management (AAPAM).

We are also grateful to the project partners – the KU Leuven Public Governance Institute, Ambo University, and Addis Ababa University – for supporting the projects, including the writing of the handbook. Furthermore, we are indebted to many individuals, especially to Martine De Koninck, Ann Hasendonckx, and Christel Maes (KU Leuven International Office); Annie Hondeghem and Trui Steen (KU Leuven Governance Institute); the KU Leuven Governance Institute secretariats, particularly to Anneke Heylen (Project financial manager) and Inge Vermeulen; and Wannes Verbeeck and Peter Verbeeck (both from VLIR-UOS) for their incredible support since 2012.

This book also exceedingly benefited from Ethiopian PA scholars and para-academics who presented the papers at the conferences organized by project partners and other collaborators. Our thanks also goes to conferences participants, who diligently discussed the papers and contributed to the improvement thereof. We are profoundly thankful to the contributors of the handbook. We owe many thanks to reviewers at the Public Governance Institute (Belgium), who provided stimulating comments and suggestions. We are grateful to Leuven University Press for publishing this handbook. We are also indebted to Leuven University Press team, which did extraordinary work in preparing the volume's publication.

Bacha Kebede Debela
Ambo University

Geert Bouckaert
KU Leuven

Meheret Ayenew Warota
Addis Ababa University

Dereje Terefe Gemechu
Ethiopian Civil Service University

About the Authors

Deribe Assefa Aga holds an MPA degree (2010) and a PhD (2016). His research interests include, inter alia, project management, gender studies, democracy, and local governance. Currently, he is an assistant professor of public management at Ethiopian Civil Service University. There he conducts research and teaches in the fields of public management, project management, and organizational behavior.

Kassa Teshager Alemu (PhD), as an associate professor of development studies. He teaches and conducts research at the Ethiopian Civil Service University. His research interests include issues related to local economic development, rural and urban development, and the role of actors in development.

Hirko Wakgari Amanta is a lecturer and researcher at Oromia State University. Currently, he is a PhD student in development studies at Addis Ababa University. His research interests include institutions, governance, and sustainable development.

Kiflie Worku Angaw is a lecturer at Dilla University. His main research interests are: public administration education and professionalization, development actors' interface and global dynamics, the political economy of development, public governance and regional integrations, development policy and public institutions and ICT in public sectors.

Frehiwot Gebrehiwot Araya (PhD) was an assistant professor at Addis Ababa University, Department of Public Administration and Development Management. She is currently serving as head of the Addis Ababa City Public Service and Human Resource Development Bureau. Her main research focuses on public policy and public finance.

Henok Seyoum Assefa (PhD) is a deputy chief executive officer at the Ethiopian Press Agency and vice president at the Ethiopian Public Administration Association (EPAA). He has been teaching and researching in the areas of public administration and policy for over ten years. His areas of research interest include social policy, governance, and media.

Wondem Meuriaw Ayalew is a lecturer of public management and policy at Assosa University and a PhD student at Addis Ababa University. His main research areas include public service delivery, public private partnership, and governance.

Bruno Broucker is a visiting professor at the KU Leuven Public Governance Institute, a higher education expert at the Institute of Tropical Medicine, and an elected member of the executive committee of the European Association for Institutional Research (EAIR). He has published several international articles and book chapters on higher education governance and policy and is lead editor of *Higher Education System Reform* (2019). ORCID: 0000-0002-6961-7098.

Bacha Kebede Debela is an assistant professor at Ambo University (Ethiopia) and president of the Ethiopian Public Administration Association (EPAA). He holds a PhD in Social sciences from KU Leuven (2017). His main research interest areas include performance management, sustainable development, local government and governance, and developing countries.

Temesgen Genie Chekol is a lecturer at Dire Dawa University, Institute of Technology, School of Civil Engineering and Architecture. His research interests are construction economics, finance, environment, and sustainable development.

Bouckaert Geert is a professor of public management at the KU Leuven Public Governance Institute, Belgium. He is past president of the International Institute of Administrative Sciences and of the European Group for Public Administration. He is a member of the UN Committee of Experts on Public Administration.

Solomon Gebreyohans Gebru is a PhD researcher at KU Leuven, Belgium, and an assistant professor of political science and former Director of Institutional Transformation and Quality Assurance at Mekelle University. He has published articles and book chapters. His PhD focuses on higher education governance in Ethiopia. ORCID: 0000-0002-1759-8884.

Tewelde Mezgobo Ghrmay (PhD) is an assistant professor at Mekelle University. His main research interests are new public management and strategic management.

Amante Gutata Goshu is a lecturer in public administration and development management at Addis Ababa University, as well as being a freelance consultant since 2008. His research interest areas are governance, urbanization, development, public policy, and marketing.

Moti Mosisa Gutema is an assistant professor of public policy, the director of the Deliverology Coordination Office at Dilla University, and a researcher at the Institute of Strategic Affairs.

Bahiru Deti Heyi (PhD) is an assistant professor at Dilla University, Ethiopia. He is chairman of the board of the Ethiopian Public Administration Association (EPAA); vice chair of Ethiopian Society for Public Administration and Management (ESPAM), African Association for Public Administration and Management Chapter in Ethiopia; and member of the Economic and Development Association of Oromia (EDAO). His research interests are in the areas of public policy, public finance administration, local government, governance, public service delivery, urban governance and management, and development management.

Annie Hondeghem is a full professor at the Faculty of Social Sciences at the KU Leuven and director of the Public Governance Institute. She is a specialist in the domain of public personnel management, policy on equal opportunities and diversity, and change management. She is also conducting research on asylum, migration, and integration. She is the editor (together with prof. James Perry) of *Motivation in Public Management (2014)*. ORCID: 0000-0002-0900-3959.

Challa Amdissa Jiru is a lecturer and a PhD student at Addis Ababa University, Department of Public Administration and Development Management. His main research interests are public sector performance management, reform, and leadership.

Dessalegn Kebede Kedida is a deputy commander and research and community service directorate director at Oromia Police College. He graduated from Oromia State University with a BA degree in HRM and holds an MBA in management from Ambo University. His research interest focuses on police human resource management practice and its development.

Aklilu Wubet Lema is a lecturer at Addis Ababa University, Department of Public Administration and Development Management. His research forces on decentralization and fiscal policy.

Adare Assefa Mitiku obtained his PhD from KU Leuven, Public Governance Institute. He is currently working for Defense Construction Enterprise – a government owned Construction Company in Ethiopia. His main research interests include leadership and governance, organizational studies, human resource policies and practices, politico-administrative relations, and training and development.

Denamo Addissie Nuramo (PhD) is an assistant professor and chair holder at Addis Ababa University, Institute of Architecture Building Construction and City Development. His research interests include sustainable built environment, construction economics, automation in the construction industry, and alternative construction materials.

Zekarias Minota Seiko is a lecturer at Ethiopian Civil Service University and PhD candidate in environment and development, Addis Ababa University. His research interests include FDI, impact evaluation, labour dynamics, climate change, and livelihoods.

Trui Steen is professor of Public Governance and Coproduction of Public Services in the Public Governance Institute at KU Leuven, Belgium. Her research includes topics such as professionalism, public service motivation, professional-citizen co-production of public services, central–local government relations and collaborative innovation in the public sector. She chairs the IIAS Study Group on Co-production of Public Services.

Hiwot Amare Tadesse is a lecturer at Ambo University. Currently she is a PhD candidate at KU Leuven University, Belgium. Her research interests include partnerships, state-society relations, governance, and the developmental state.

Defferew Kebebe Tessema is a lecturer at Addis Ababa University, Department of Public Administration and Development Management. His research focuses on local economic development and urban governance.

Steve Troupin (PhD) is a lecturer at the Public Governance Institute, KU Leuven, Belgium, and strategic projects officer at the International Institute of Administrative Sciences (IIAS). He has published in peer-reviewed journals.

Alebachew Asfaw Yimer (PhD) is an assistant professor in public management in the College of Business and Economics at Bahir Dar University. He conducts research on management in the public sector, with an emphasis on leadership, strategic management, organizational change, organizational culture, and performance management.

Belayneh Bogale Zewdie is a lecturer in the Department of Public Management, Faculty of Business and Economics, Kotebe Metropolitan University, Addis Ababa, Ethiopia.

1

INTRODUCTION

1
Public Administration in Ethiopia: Case Studies and Lessons for Sustainable Development

Bacha Kebede Debela, Geert Bouckaert, Meheret Ayenew Warota, and Dereje Terefe Gemechu

Background and Objectives

In the West, scholars have identified four public administration/management models: Public Administration, Public Management, New Public Management, and Public Governance. The Public Administration model marks the first systematic and formalized approach to public administration (Van Dooren et al., 2015) and is characterised by Weberian features such as hierarchy, continuity, impartiality, legal-rational authority, and professionalism in public administration (Cheema, 2007). The Public Management model focuses on managing the public sector and is based on private management approaches and principles (Blum & Manning, 2009; Bouckaert & Halligan, 2008). The New Public Management (NPM) was the dominant model from the late 1970s to the late 1990s (African Development Bank, 2005; Pollitt & Bouckaert, 2017). It was driven by the leading proponents of the neoliberal economic ideal, which advocates the need to reduce the size of government, apply market-type mechanisms, and implement private sector leadership principles in public sectors to improve performance (Christensen & Lægreid, 2007; Van Dooren et al., 2015). The NPM traveled across the world, including to developing countries, and was diffused by many actors, including such transnational institutions as the World Bank, the International Monetary Fund and the OECD, through their funding, research publications, and consultancy work (Andrews, 2013; Peterson, 2015).

New Public Governance (NPG) was introduced in the 2000s, partly due to the failure of NPM to deliver expected results (Pollitt & Bouckaert, 2017); to its unintended consequences, such as increased socio-structural inequalities, particularly in developing countries; and its dysfunctional effects on public sector performance and accountability frameworks (Bouckaert et al., 2010; Christensen & Lægreid, 2007). This model emphasizes vertical and horizontal interaction and partnerships, as well as mutual accountability and responsibility, between and among the state, the private sector, civil society, and citizens and stakeholders who participate in joint efforts to achieve several societal objectives (Bouckaert & Halligan, 2008; Hughes, 2012; Steen et al., 2018).

Despite the expected variation, and despite the fact that all four models are Western models, they have been introduced by developing countries. Indeed, the literature shows that there are differences in adoption and implementation of reform programmes, even in the West (Pollitt & Bouckaert, 2017), which is partly explained by the differences in politico-administrative contexts (Ongaro & Ferlie, 2019; Pollitt & Bouckaert, 2017).

Recently, some African countries such as Ethiopia, Botswana, Mauritius, Tanzania, Rwanda, South Africa, and Uganda have adopted the Asian Developmental State (DS) doctrine (Clapham, 2018; Edigheji, 2010; Evans, 2010; Mbabazi & Taylor, 2005; Taylor, 2005; Vaughan & Gebremichael, 2011). The African Union (AU) and the UN-ECA are also promoting the DS doctrine to ensure socioeconomic transformation in Africa (AU, 2014; UN-ECA, 2011). There is also a rhetoric on African consensus-oriented leadership/ pan-Africanism leadership (Jackson, 2004), which accentuates the need to "correct the historical injustice" by strengthening mutually beneficial relationships within the continent and at a global scale (AU 2014, 10–11).

Moreover, African countries, including Ethiopia, have subscribed to the United Nation's Sustainable Development Goals (SDGs), which aim to ensure "no one left behind" by 2030, an a goal also on the African Union's agenda 2063 (AU, 2014). The UN (2015) claims governments are responsible for ensuring better economic, social, and ecologal performance to safeguard the well-being of citizens. The failure to achieve sustained results on economic, social, and ecologal dimensions not only threatens the well-being of citizens but also erodes the legitimacy and trustworthiness of governments.

The UN and the AU promote strengthening institutions, partnerships, and stakeholders' participation in development programs. The UN SDGs 11, 16, and 17 are specifically related to public administration. Goal 11 focuses on inclusive, resilient, and sustainable cities and human settlements. Goal 16 and 17 focus respectively on building effective, accountable, and inclusive public administration at all levels, as well as on effective global partnership to revitalize sustainable development (UN, 2015; see also Bouckaert, 2020).

The winds of decentralization and democratization have blown in many African countries since the 1990s. However, the democratization and liberalization process has been uneven across the continent. Worse, it has been scaled back in many African countries, partly due to the divide and rule of historical colonial legacies, which destroyed African civilizations; the increasing neopatrimonialism, authoritarianism, and suppression of opposition parties by the ruling party; and the gradual shift to a single-party state in many African contexts (Southall, 2003). Secondly, as observed by Kyed and Buur (2007), the ambiguous and sometimes the contradictory relationship between the indigenous institutions (indigenous leaders) and government institutions based on Western models is also an important factor.

At the same time, higher education plays a significant role in helping countries achieve SDGs; among other things, effective PA teaching and research not only generate relevant knowledge and increase graduates' employment opportunities (Pinheiro et al., 2018) but also are crucial to strengthening institutions so they can effectively solve societal problems (Rosenbaum 2015). Bouckaert (2020) rightly claims the study of public administration should be concerned both with producing knowledge and with improving public administration and public policy (see also Ongaro, 2020). Therefore, how to ensure the relevance of PA teaching and research, how to organize PA teaching and research (Bouckaert & Jann, 2020), and how to attract competent PA students are crucial issues (Bertels et al., 2020). Accordingly, it is important to recall that the mere existence of higher learning institutions is not sufficient for national and reginal development. It also crucial to note that, as Newcomer and Allen (2015) rightly point out, PA teaching may vary in terms of missions, institutional locations, and the nature of the student population. It may also vary within countries and across regions, suggesting that effective public administration presupposes contexts that fit knowledge and solutions.

Nevertheless, while the applicability of Western theory to Africa is contestable from theoretical, policy, and managerial perspectives, most African universities rely on Western theories for teaching and research, including in the areas of public administration/management/policy. This could be due to the effect of colonialization and the fact that many Africans have got their education, among others fields in public administration, in the West (Kolisnichenko, 2015). The other fairly important factor could be the lack of sufficient publications by African scholars and practitioners. As Rugasira (2013) observes, while specific African problems have to be addressed by Africans, the contribution of African scholars to scientific publication is scarce, only 0.5 percent. As a consequence, most knowledge production on Africa comes from Western authors.

Public administration in Ethiopia can be analyzed over the three Ethiopian regimes: The Imperial regime (-1974), the Derg regime (1974-1991) and the EPRDF regime (1991-), with each having overlapping and unique features.

This book primarily focuses on the current regime but accounts for historical and sociological factors inherited from the previous regimes. The monarchical and highly centralized imperial regime introduced elements of Western public administration. The 1931 Constitution vested all ultimate legislative, executive, and judicial powers in the emperor (Clapham, 1969), who regarded himself as an elect of God and thus theoretically absolute and unchallenged (Clapham, 1969; Hiwet, 1975; Holcomb & Ibssa, 1990; Howard, 1955). The imperial parliament was instrumental in further centralization and suppression of citizens' voices (Ayenew, 2019). PA teaching in Ethiopia started during the reign of Emperor Haile Sellassie in the 1950s at Addis Ababa University.

The Derg regime was also an exceedingly centralized government and adopted Marxist and Leninist socialist ideology (Adejumobi, 2007; Hiwet, 1975; Holcomb & Ibssa, 1990).The national *shengo*, the parliament of the Derg regime, was also substantially weak; meanwhile, the president was extremely powerful (Ayenew, 2019). Since coming into power after toppling the Derg regime in the 1990s, the EPRDF has introduced a series politico-administrative reform programs. Three major reform waves could be distinguished: regionalization, federalization and local decentralization, and federalization and Democratic Developmental State (DDS) doctrine. The first wave took place under the Transitional Government of Ethiopia (1991-1995), which established fourteen regional governments and entrusted the responsibility for public services to regional governments (Debela & Troupin, 2016; Peterson, 2015). During this period, the country adopted a neoliberal economic policy (Adejumobi, 2007). The 1995 Constitution established the federal government as having nine regional states and two city administrations, with the country officially continuing the tenets of the NPM doctrine (Mengesha & Common, 2007). In 2001 the second phase of decentralization occurred (Peterson, 2015; World Bank, 2013). In the aftermath of the relatively free but contested 2005 national elections (Abbink, 2006; Ayenew, 2019), the government officially adhered to the Democratic Developmental State (DDS) doctrine (Clapham; 2018; Lefort, 2012; Vaughan & Gebremichael, 2011). In general, the post-1990s reforms have been driven both by internal and external factors (Debela, 2017; Peterson, 2015).

Overall, since the 1990s, Ethiopia has registered impressive economic growth. Among other positive developments, access to education has increased and the number of higher education institutions and the students pursuing higher education has expanded many times over. Yet, inequality has remained a critical issue. Importantly, the democratization process and inclusiveness have been rolled back significantly. In the 2015 elections, the ruling party took all the national parliamentary seats, confirming that the relationship between economic growth and sociopolitical development is not linear or automatic. Consequently and unsurprisingly, a few months after the national election the country was hit by mass protests, leading to the appointment of Prime Minister Abiy Ahemed in 2018.

Against this general backdrop, the chapters in this book analyze the contexts, processes, and results of politico-administrative reforms in post-1990 Ethiopia. The modest aim of this volume is to contribute to PA teaching and research in Ethiopia. The principal question of the handbook is: *How can we describe and explain the contexts, the processes, and the results of the post-1990 politico-administrative reforms in Ethiopia and what are the implications for sustainable development?*

From Projects and Conferences to a Handbook: How Did This Handbook Come About?

The First Project (2013-2017)

The seeds for this book were sown in 2012. That year, Geert Bouckaert (Flemish promoter) and Bacha Kebede Debela (local promoter) – with the support of Martine De Koninck (KU Leuven International Office) and Steve Troupin (KU Leuven) – developed a project entitled "Strengthening Institutional Capacity to Support Public Administration and/or Development Management Programmes at Ambo University." Geert Bouckaert submitted the proposal for funding to VLIR-UOS and the project was selected for the second-round application. Hence Geert Bouckaert and Steve Troupin came to Ambo to participate in a workshop (August 27, 2012) and to jointly formulate the proposal. At the workshop, capacity building and the relevance of PA teaching and research stood out as critical issues, which were therefore systematically incorporated into the final project proposal submitted by Geert Bouckaert; this was subsequently selected by VLIR-UOS for funding in 2013.

The First National PA Conference (2015)

While part of the project activities involved the financing of PhD studies, other elements included the holding of workshops. Thus, on September 21, 2015, the First National PA conference was organized by Ambo University and KU Leuven, in collaboration with CCRDA, in Addis Ababa. The theme of the conference was "Governance for Sustainable Development in Ethiopia." Interestingly, the participants (six universities with PA programmes and practitioners [federal and regional equivalents], among others), stressed improving capacity-building and ensuring the relevance of PA teaching and research and ultimately agreed on the need to establish an interactive structure for dialogue on PA teaching and research in Ethiopia.

Consequently, on September 29, 2016, another interesting landmark was achieved. More than five decades after the teaching of public administration had been introduced in Ethiopia; the Ethiopian Public Administration Association (EPAA) was established at a founding conference, facilitated by Ambo University, KU Leuven, and Addis Ababa University. Fifty-one delegates from thirteen institutions participated. EPAA was officially launched on February 8, 2018, at Addis Ababa University.

The Second Project (2017-2020)

In 2017, capitalizing on the ongoing project and supported by Martine De Koninck (KU Leuven International Office) and Steve Troupin (KU Leuven), Geert Bouckaert (KU Leuven), Bacha Kebede Debela (Ambo University) and Frehiwot Gebrehiwot Araya (Addis Ababa University) developed a project entitled "Professionalizing Ethiopian Public Administration to Support Development Practitioners," to be run jointly by KU Leuven Public Governance Institute, (Belgium), Ambo University, and Addis Ababa University. Geert Bouckaert (the Flemish promoter) submitted the proposal and the project was funded by VLIR-UOS and launched in 2018. Both projects were coordinated by Steve Troupin (KU Leuven), and Anneke Heylen (KU Leuven) was responsible for their financial/administrative management.

The Second National PA Conference (2018)

On September 22, 2018, the Second National PA Conference was organized on the theme of "Administrative Resilience for Sustainable Development in Ethiopia" by Ambo University and KU Leuven, in close collaboration with the International Institute of Administrative Sciences (IIAS) and the Association of African Public Administration and Management (AAPAM), in Addis Ababa. Several papers were presented and discussed by participants, including EPAA members.

The Third National PA Conference (2020)

In 2020 the third National PA Conference was organized by Ambo University, KU Leuven Public Governance Institute, and Addis Ababa University in partnership with the Ethiopian Public Administration Association (EPAA) and with the support of VLIR-UOS and the Belgian Cooperation to Development, on the theme "Strengthening Institutions for Sustainable Development in Ethiopia/Africa" in Addis Ababa, on January 24-26. Several participants, including EPAA members and the Federal Civil Service Commission Commissioner, took part in the conference and actively discussed the papers.

Based on the aforementioned projects and conferences, we invited the authors of the second and the third National PA Conference papers to submit improved versions of their papers for potential inclusion in this volume. We received twenty-six contributions, which were carefully reviewed and commented, with feedback sent to each author for revision. In the end, we received twenty-three completed chapters, the majority of them revised three times.

We believe the contributions in this book are not only helpful for PA teaching and research in Ethiopia but also witness the importance of strengthening effective, accountable, and inclusive institutions for sustainable development. Governance, institutions, and sustainable development were the core issues discussed at the three National PA conferences. Enjoy reading these chapters, and long live EPAA!

The Handbook and Its Chapters

The chapters in this handbook address a wide range of issues and are systematically clustered into five parts. Part II of the book focuses on governance, partnership, participation, and institutions. The contribution by Deribe Assefa Aga (chapter 2) is generic but arguably applies to Ethiopia. Using explanatory research design, he finds that democratic quality enhances public trust in government and that public trust in turn mediates the relationship between democracy and overall citizens' life satisfaction. Belayneh Bogale Zewdie (chapter 3) uses exploratory research and shows the challenges and prospects of the Ethiopian developmental state in promoting democratic governance. The contribution by Aklilu Wubet, Challa Amdissa, Defferew Kebebe, and Frehiwot G/hiwot (chapter 4) reveals that the federal legislature of Ethiopia has various oversight tools at its disposal, but that among them it predominantly relies only on reports and committee hearings. Therefore, in the related contribution by Challa Amdissa, Defferew Kebebe, and Aklilu Wubet (chapter 5), we learn that public-parliamentary engagement is low, partly due to exceedingly limited institutional capacity. Hiwot Amare Tadesse and Trui Steen (chapter 6), using the most-similar-case study strategy, analyze the impact of the developmental state doctrine on the functioning of multi-stakeholder partnerships for health service delivery in Ethiopia. They conclude that the state dominates and excessively controls stakeholders in health service delivery. The contribution by Bahiru Detti (chapter 7) concentrates on citizen participation and empowerment at the level of local government. He finds local residents' participation in development programs to be low and that local development programmes have not substantially empowered Ethiopian citizens. The contribution by Bacha Kebede (chapter 8) discloses that much is to be done to shattering the glass ceiling and glass walls and to increase genuine women participation in political and managerial jobs. Drawing on the new institutionalism and the political settlement approach, Hirko Wakgari (chapter 9) argues that the NPM-driven reform in Oromia National Regional State is constrained by inadequate institutional capacity (bureaucratic capacity) and an overly politicized bureaucracy and civil service. A related contribution by Tewelde Mezgobo (chapter 10) highlights that effective NPM-driven reform needs to break the one-size-fits-all path dependency, and that there is a need for a sector specific approach and clarity on the assumptions of NPM related reform tools. By comparing and contrasting the indigenous Gadaa System and Western democracy Moti Mosisa Gutema (chapter 11) reveals the difference in values and decision-making process between the two systems.

Part III is devoted to people as human resources. Henok Syeoum (chapter 12) examines meritocracy, career development, and promotion in the Ethiopian Federal Civil Service. He reveals that despite the legal frameworks, a prevalence of a mix of meritocratic and political patronage in the recruitment, career development, and promotion in the Federal Civil Service. Similarly, using historical neoinstitutionalism Bacha Kebede Debela, Geert Bouckaert, and Steve Troupin (chapter 13) finds a shift from centralized HRM to a decentralized system, a shift from seniority to merit and qualification, and the systematic use of politico-administrative reforms and reform tools to enhance the allegiance of civil servants to political executives in the Oromia National Regional State. The chapter by Alebachew Asfaw (chapter 14) examines the strategic contribution of middle managers in Ethiopian civil service organizations. He finds that mid-level managers play a significant role in the civil service and that they predominantly emphasize facilitation and mentoring roles, followed by production roles, and change orientations roles. Adare Assefa and Annie Hondeghem (chapter 15), using historical and sociological institutionalisms, examine the leadership context of the Ethiopian Civil Service. They argue that the continuous politicization of civil service and the deep-seated sociological factors have led to the use of a predominantly authoritarian leadership style in the federal civil service and yet at the same time resulted in a preference for a pragmatic leadership approach.

Part IV is devoted to performance and quality. Using Data Envelopment Analysis (DEA) reference technology Bacha Kebede Debela, Geert Bouckaert, and Steve Troupin (chapter 16) analyse the technical efficiency of tewnty-nine towns in Oromia National Regional State in ensuring the drinking water supply. They find that the majority of municipalities were inefficient and the technical efficiency of the municipality depends on DEA model specifications. The chapter by Temesgen Genie Chekol and Denamo Addissie Nuramo (chapter 17) reveals that the cost and time performance of Ethiopian Mega Sugar Construction Projects is poor. Gutata Amante (chapter 18) assesses the performance of Ethiopia on general good governance indictors and finds the performance of the country to be inconsistent; he finds improvement in adherence to the rule of law, a decline in voice and accountability, and no significant change in the regulatory quality dimensions, as well as fluctuating trends in the remaining performance indicators. Kassa Teshager and Zekarias Minota (chapter 19) on their part reveal that organizational climate and individual factors are important factors for explaining public servants' attitude and performance in federal public sectors in Ethiopia.

Part V addresses the governance of policies. Using the European University Association University Autonomy Scorecard, Solomon Gebreyohans Gebru, Annie Hondeghem, and Bruno Broucker (chapter 20) examine the institutional autonomy of Ethiopian public universities. They find the institutional autonomy of the Ethiopian higher education institutions to be low and suggest the relevance of the European University Association University Autonomy Scorecard to improve institutional autonomy and performance. Likewise, the contribution by Challa Amdissa Jiru (chapter 21) analyzes the outcome of the Ethiopian education policy since the 1990s. He reveals that Ethiopia has impressively improved access to education, but ensuring equity remains a critical challenge. The chapter by Kiflie Worku (chapter 22) is specifically on public administration education in Ethiopia. He finds several challenges, including inappropriate and inadequate PA staff educational profile and the employability challenges facing PA graduates.

The contribution by Wondem Mekuriaw (chapter 23) focuses on examining the implementation of community policing in Addis Ababa City Administration. He discovers that the implementation of community policing is modest, partly due to inadequate institutional capacity. He also point out that the government has used community policing to control citizens at grass root level. The other related study, by Dessalegn Kebede Kedida (chapter 24), explores the practices and challenges of community policing in Adama

Town Administration. Kedida discloses that limited institutional capacity, inadequate incentives for community police officers and limited community participation persist as major challenges to the implementation of community policing in the town. Finally, Bacha Kebede Debela, Geert Bouckaert, Meheret Ayenew Warota, and Dereje Terefe Gemechu (chapter 25) draw conclusions and implications for sustainable development and PA teaching and research in Ethiopia.

How to Use This Very Ethiopian Handbook

This Handbook is based on Ethiopian cases, which are researched by Ethiopian researchers, using Ethiopian (mostly primary) data. The Handbook is developed for teaching in Ethiopian PA programs by Ethiopian scholars, for Ethiopian masters and PhD students and researchers, as stepping-stones for their own research.

This Handbook invites the Ethiopian academic (PA) community, but also and even more the practitioners, to not copy-paste models that do not fit the context. The best guarantee for failure is to blindly copy-paste (Western) models, even if one can learn for a range of models. This Handbook invites practitioners and academia to push for research-based teaching using Ethiopian cases.

Seminars allow for the replication of some of the research, or at least for the critical disussion of methods, data, models, conclusions, and even recommendations.

It is our hope that this Handbook contributes to building capacity for better public governance. We hope that the volume inspires ideas to realize the SDGs in a resilient Ethiopian society, where "nobody is left behind." For this, we need a public sector that is proactively matches SDG 11 (focusing on inclusive, resilient, and sustainable cities, and human settlements), SDG 16 (building effective, accountable, and inclusive institutions, with peace and justice at all levels), and SDG 17 (on effective global partnerships with the private sector, NGOs, and citizens).

References

Abbink, J. (2006). Discomfiture of Democracy? The 2005 Election Crisis in Ethiopia and Its Aftermath. *African Affairs*, 105(419), 173-199.

Adejumobi, S. A. (2007). *The History of Ethiopia*. Westport, CT: Greenwood Publishing Group.

African Development Bank. (2005). African Development Report 2005. New York: Oxford University Press.

African Union. (2014). Agenda 2063 African Union Commission Archives. https://au.int/en/agenda2063.

Andrews, M. (2013). *The Limits of Institutional Reform in Development: Changing Rules for Realistic Solutions*. Cambridge: Cambridge University Press.

Ayenew, M. (2019). *Parliament–Public Engagement in Ethiopia: Selected Notes and Case Studies on a Political Fragile State*. Addis Ababa: Forum for Social Studies.

Bertels, J., Bouckaert, G., & Jann, W. (2020). The Survey: A Long-Distance Conversation about the Future of Public Administration in Europe. In Bouckaert and Jann (eds), *European Perspectives for Public Administration: The Way Forward*, Leuven: Leuven University Press, pp. 43-70.

Blum, J., & Manning, N. (2009). Public Management Reforms across OECD Countries. *Public Management and Governance*, 2, 41-58.

Bouckaert, G. (2020). From Public Administration in Utopia to Utopia in Public Administration. In Bouckaert and Jann, *European Perspectives for Public Administration*, pp. 71–84.

Bouckaert, G., & Halligan, J. (2008). *Managing Performance: International Comparisons*. London: Routledge Taylor & Francis Group.

Bouckaert, G., & Jann, W. (2020). Introduction: The EPPA Project. In Bouckaert and Jann, European Perspectives for Public Administration, pp. 21–42.

Bouckaert, G., Peters, B. G., & Verhoest, K. (2010). *The Coordination of Public Sector Organisations*. Hampshire: Palgrave Macmillan.

Cheema, S. (2007). Linking Governments and Citizens through Democratic Governance. In D. Rondinelli (ed.), *Public Administration and Democratic Governance: Governments Serving citizens*, Geneva: Economic and Social Affairs, United Nations, pp. 29-51.

Christensen, T., & Lægreid, P. (2007). The Whole of Government Approach to Public Sector Reform. *Public Administration Review*, 67(6), 1059 1066.

Clapham, C. (1969). *Haile-Selassie's Government*. London: Longmans, Green Co.

Clapham, C. (2018). The Ethiopian Developmental State. *Third World Quarterly*, 39(6), 1151-1165.

Debela, B. (2017). *Managing Performance in Ethiopian Municipalities: A Benchlearning Approach of Urban Water Services in Oromia National Regional State* Leuven: KU Leuven, Public Governance Institute.

Debela, B., & Troupin, S. (2016). Transforming Ethiopian Public Administration for Sustainable Development: The Impact of Organisational Proliferation and Policy Coordination on Access to Drinking Water. 37th AAPAM Roundtable Conference, Zambia, Lusaka, February 29-4 March 4.

Edigheji, O. (2010). Constructing a Democratic Developmental State in South Africa: Potentials and Challenges. In O. Edigheji (ed.) *Constructing a Democratic Developmental State in South Africa: Potentials and Challenges*. Cape Town South Africa: HSRC Press, pp.1-33.

Evans, P. (2010). Constructing the 21st Century Developmental State. In Edigheji,Constructing a Democratic Developmental State in South Africapp. 37–-58.

Evils, S., Steen, T., Brandsen, T., & Verschuere, B. (2018). The Dark Side of Co-Creation and Co-Production. In Brandsen, Steen, & Verschuere (eds), *Co-Production and Co-Creation: Engaging Citizens in Public Services*. New York: Taylor and Francis, pp. 284--293.

Hiwet, A. (1975). Ethiopia: From Autocracy to Revolution. *Review of African Political Economy*, 1, n.p.

Holcomb, B., & Ibssa, S. (1990). *The Invention of Ethiopia: The Making of a Dependent Colonial State in Northeast Africa*. Trenton, NJ: The Rea Sea Press.

Hughes, O. (2012). *Public Management and Administration*. London: Palgrave Macmillan.

Jackson, T. (2004). *Management and Change in Africa: A Cross-cultural Perspective*. London: Routledge.

Kolisnichenko, N. (2015). Multiple System, Multiple Approaches: National Organizational Arrangements for the Delivery of Public Administration Education and Training. In A. Rosenbaum (ed.), *In Quest for Excellence: Approaches to Enhancing the Quality of Public Administration Education and Training*. United Nation and IASIA/IIAS, pp. 143-70.

Kyed, H. M., & Buur, L. (2007). Introduction: Traditional Authority and Democratization in Africa. In H.M. Kyed and Buur, L. (ed.), *State Recognition and Democratization in Sub-Saharan Africa*. New York: Palgrave Macmillan, pp. 1-28.'

Lefort, R. (2012). Free Market Economy, 'Developmental State' and Party-state Hegemony in Ethiopia: The Case of the 'Model Farmers.' *Journal of Modern African Studies*, 50(4), 681-706.

Mengesha, G. H., & Common, R. (2007). Public Sector Capacity Reform in Ethiopia: A Tale of Success in Two Ministries? *Public Administration and Development*, 27 (5), 367-80.

Newcomer, K. & Allen, H. (2015). Public Administration Education: Adding Value in the Public Service. In Rosenbaum, *In Quest for Excellence*, pp. 43-59.

Ongaro, E. (2020). Forms of Knowledge for the Practice of Public Administration. In Bouckaert and Jann *European Perspectives for Public Administration*, pp. 273-282.

Ongaro, E., & Ferlie, E. (2019). Exploring Strategy-Making in 'Non-New Public Management' Public Services Settings: The Case of European Union Agencies. *Administrative Sciences*, 9(1), 23.

Peterson, S. B. (2015). *Public Finance and Economic Growth in Developing Countries: Lessons from Ethiopia's Reforms*. London: Routledge.

Pinheiro, R., Šima, K., Young, M., & Kohoutek, J. (2018). University Complexity and Regional Development in the Periphery. In R. Pinheiro, Young, M. and Šima, K. (ed.) *Higher Education and Regional Development*. Cham: Palgrave Macmillan pp. 1-20.

Pollitt, C., & Bouckaert, G. (2017). *Public Management Reform: A Comparative Analysis – Into the Age of Austerity*. 4th ed. New York: Oxford University Press.

Rosenbaum, A. (2015). International Accreditation, IASIA and the International Commission of Accreditation of Public Administration Education and Training Programs (ICAPA). In Rosenbaum, (*In Quest for Excellence*, pp. 13-22).

Rugasira, A. (2013). *A Good African Story: How a Small Company Built a Global Coffee Brand*. London: Bodley Head.

Southall, R. (2003). *Democracy in Africa: Moving beyond a Difficult Legacy*, vol. 2. Capetown: HSRC Press.

Taylor, I. (2005). Botswana's Developmental State and the Politics of Legitimacy. In G. Harrison (ed.) *Global Encounters*, International Political Economy, Development and Globalization, pp. 41-62. London: Palgrave Macmillan.

United Nations (UN). (2015). Transforming Our World: The 2030 Agenda for Sustainable Development. General Assembly (70/1).

United Nations Economic Commission for Africa (UN-ECA). (2011). Economic Report on Governing Development in Africa – The Role of the State in Economic UN-ECA, Addis Ababa, Ethiopia.

Van Dooren, W., Bouckaert, G., & Halligan, J. (2015). *Performance Management in the Public Sector*. London: Routledge.

Vaughan, S., & Gebremichael, M. (2011). *Rethinking Business and Politics in Ethiopia*. Africa Power and Politics, UK Aid, Irish Aid.

World Bank. (2013). Federal Democratic Republic of Ethiopia Public Sector Reform Approach Building the Developmental State – A Review and Assessment of the Ethiopian Approach to Public Sector Reform, Report No: ACS3695, The World, USA, Washington, DC. http://documents.worldbank.org.

II

GOVERNANCE

Introduction

Situated within the broader Public Governance Model, this Part (II) focuses on democratic governance, partnership, and participation. In shifting from "administration" to "management," and from "management" to "governance," there is an increasing need to include stakeholders as citizens and as users of services and policies. This requires visions on how to include citizens, as citizens and as users, at different stages and in their different roles of "involvement," "engagement," "commitment," "participation," and even "partnerships." Even if these chapters demonstrate some gaps between intentions and reality, a reform and implementation program is emerging.

The first chapter (chapter 2) discusses the relationship between electoral democracy, public trust, and citizens' life satisfaction. The core message is that public trust in government positively mediates the relationship between electoral democracy and citizens' life satisfaction. Informed by an exploratory research design, the second chapter (chapter 3) analyzes the effect of Developmental State (DS) doctrine on the democratization process in Ethiopia. The chapter clarifies that the DS doctrine enabled the regime in power to systemically and strategically turn a multiparty parliamentary party system enshrined in the constitution into a single-party state. Chapter 4 is tasked with analyzing mechanisms and parliamentary oversight tools used by the National Parliament of Ethiopia. The chapter pinpoints that although the parliament has used different oversight tools, among them predominantly reports and committee hearings, the executive government branch overwhelmingly dominates the legislature. As a consequence, due to the non-representativeness of the parliament and other factors, the next chapter (chapter 5) shows that the parliamentary-public engagement necessary for improving democracy and governance is low. Chapter 6 reveals that the DS doctrine has constrained multistakeholder partnership development to deliver health service, confirming that the developmental state doctrine not only restrains the democratization process but also limits the space for multistakeholder engagement in development activities. Perhaps, due to the influence of DS, chapter 7 also shows that the local people's participation in development activities are inadequate. Likewise, the chapter on gender (chapter 8) clarifies that the DS doctrine cannot warrant gender equality in political executive and managerial jobs, even when the legislation supports gender parity. Chapter 9 reveals that, despite existing elements of the NPM doctrine that should in theory counteract this trend, the public service in Oromia/Ethiopia is highly politicized. Chapter 10 challenges the one-size-fits-all approach and suggests a sectorial approach to implement NPM elements. The authors have provided key conclusions and insights.

Culture makes a difference for administrating, managing, and governing. Cultures also differ across global space. As a consequence, it is necessary to also focus on administrative culture in Ethiopia to show its features and specificities. This is crucial to avoid blind copy-pasting of "solutions" coming from abroad, from regions with a different cultural background. Even if students, teachers, researchers, and practitioners need to be aware of other models, there is a need to be critical from the point of view of differences and their implications. Blind copy-pasting and uncritical teaching of models, mostly from the West, could result in a mismatch with the culture at hand. There is not much research about differences of administrative cultures and their implication for Ethiopia. Therefore, chapter 11 compares and contrasts the indigenous Gadaa system (institution) with the Western democratic system. It reveals the differences in the process and values between the two systems. The authors have provided key conclusions and insights for the public administration and democratization process in Ethiopia and demonstrated the importance of including (administrative) cultural differences.

II.1

DEMOCRATIC GOVERNANCE

2
Electoral Democracy and Citizen Life Satisfaction: The Mediating Role of Public Trust

Deribe Assefa Aga

Box 1: Key points of this chapter

The key points of this chapter, inter alia, include:

- ✓ Citizen life satisfaction or happiness is one of researchable topics in public administration and political science;
- ✓ Electoral democracy may influence citizen life satisfaction;
- ✓ Public trust mediates the positive relationship between electoral democracy and overall citizens' life satisfaction;
- ✓ This study employs multiple regression and mediation models.

Box 2: Learning objectives

Readers will gain the following insights from this chapter:

- ✓ Appreciate the importance of citizen life satisfaction or happiness in enhancing social tolerance and people's participation in economic activities;
- ✓ Explain the meanings and components of electoral democracy, public trust, and citizen life satisfaction;
- ✓ Understand the relationship between electoral democracy, public trust, and citizen life satisfaction;
- ✓ Describe the mechanism through which electoral democracy explains citizen life satisfaction.

Box 3: Abbreviations

Adj. R-sq = Adjusted R-squared (R^2)

SD = Standard deviation

SWL = Satisfaction with life

WVS-6 = World Values Survey –sixth wave

Introduction

Life satisfaction refers to "the degree to which individuals evaluate positively the quality of their life in total" (Pacek & Radcliff, 2008:268). It is often used interchangeably with "happiness" and is one of researchable topics in public administration and political science (Curini, Jou, & Memoli, 2014; Pacek & Radcliff, 2008). This is mainly because it plays an indispensable role in enhancing social tolerance and people's participation in economic activities, which may in turn contribute to economic growth in a given country. Life satisfaction, or happiness, also helps to reduce the potential for revolutionary change of governments (Inglehart 1990 as cited in Curini et al. [2014]). From a development point of view, "sustainable development" captures human well-being, social inclusion, and environmental dimensions. This implies that the quest for happiness paves the way for the quest for sustainable development (Helliwell, Layard, & Sachs, 2012). Accordingly, scholars highlight that social science should discover what enhances and what hinders life satisfaction or happiness, which is the fundamental goal of every citizen (Curini et al., 2014).

Citizens' life satisfaction is generally considered as an ultimate goal of public administration. In line with this, prior studies indicate that public administration plays a significant role in influencing whether individuals are able to make a good living and should nurture the maximization of people's satisfaction. Supporters of this argument note that genuine election is at the heart of creating governmental accountability to the citizenry, which in turn enhances life satisfaction. There is, however, an ongoing debate about the role of democratic election in the creation of the outcome forms of democracy, such as political legitimacy, public trust, and life satisfaction (Rothstein, 2009). In African context in particular, there is scant empirical literature providing explanations for how politics and public administration influence citizens' life satisfaction.

The scholarly literature has documented certain variables as predicators of life satisfaction, which may be mainly categorized into micro and macro factors. The micro factors relate to employment status, income, education, people's community ties and friendships, health, personal freedom, individual values, and demographic variables. The macro factors include the unemployment rate, inflation rate, gross domestic product per capita, and unemployment benefits (Frey & Stutzer, 2000c; Whiteley, Clarke, Sanders, & Stewart 2010). At the same time, debates over what contributes to life satisfaction receive more attention in the political culture literature. Past studies about determinants of life satisfaction that relate to government performance and political process, however, focused on macro-level factors, such as institutional conditions (Bjørnskov, Dreher, & Fischer, 2010), governance quality (Helliwell et al., 2012; Ott, 2010) and policy outputs (Pacek & Radcliff, 2008; Whiteley et al., 2010). These macro-level determinants in aggregate forms neglect the potential influence of individual-level attitudes toward government performance on life satisfaction (Curini et al., 2014).

With regard to the role of democracy in satisfaction, studies indicate that the ability to participate in the political process influences individuals' subjective well-being (Owen, Videras, & Willemsen, 2008). In the same line of inquiry, the work by Dolan, Metcalfe, and Powdthavee (2008) reveals that electoral democracy can significantly influence citizens' life satisfaction. However, the findings from such studies are not conclusive (Potts, 2016). In addition, there is little empirical work that explicates about the mechanisms through which electoral democracy influences life satisfaction (Frey & Stutzer, 2000a, 2000b; Inglehart, 2009).

Thus, this study examines whether and to what extent democratic electoral affects life satisfaction. Using data from the latest World Values Survey (WVS-6), the present study aims to investigate the mediating role of public trust in the relationship between democratic electoral quality (as a proxy measure of democracy) and citizen life satisfaction. More specifically, the study seeks to address three basic research questions, namely (1) What is the status of democratic electoral quality? (2) What is the overall citizen life satisfaction? (3) To what extent does public trust play a mediating role in the relationship between democratic electoral quality and life satisfaction?

1. Theoretical Background

This section explains conceptual definitions and the theoretical literature related to the core constructs of the study, namely electoral democracy, life satisfaction, and public rust.

1.1. Democracy

Democracy is defined as "a government in which the supreme power is vested in the people and exercised by them directly or indirectly through a system of representation usually involving periodically held free elections" (Potts, 2016:87). The popular definition of democracy is a system of government of the people, by the people, and for the people (Blind, 2007). Democratic electoral quality, which is one of the important constructs in this study, depends on the openness of nomination and selection of candidates, the degree of electoral contestation, and the inclusiveness of voting procedures. If political parties undertake the nomination and selection of candidates in a transparent manner by letting the community to participate, this enhances democratic electoral quality. Similarly, the extent to which there is choice and contestation among potential candidates for election is a good measure of democratic electoral quality. What is of interest in the inclusiveness of voting procedures is the extent to which citizens as individual voters take part in the voting process (Manion, 2006).

1.2. Life Satisfaction

Veenhoven (1996) defines "life-satisfaction as the degree to which a person positively evaluates the overall quality of his/her life as-a-whole. In other words, how much the person likes the life he/she leads."

The literature documents three theories that explain what factors drive life satisfaction (Veenhoven, 1996). The first theory is relativism, which assumes that life satisfaction varies over time because the standards against which the comparison is made simply change. This suggests that satisfaction is the result of a comparison between life-as-it-is to conceptions of how-life-should-be. In this approach, life satisfaction is the difference between people's perceptions and expectations and the course of life events that cover political, economical, and social activities. In this view, it is not possible to create lasting satisfaction, neither at the individual level, nor the societal level (Veenhoven, 1996).

The second theory is dispositional, which suggests that innate personality characteristics determine life satisfaction. According to this theory, people are born either happy or unhappy, and policy interventions have little influence in determining the level of life satisfaction or happiness (Veenhoven, 2004). It assumes that life satisfaction is a fixed disposition, implying that an improvement in society does not make people more satisfied. At the individual level, life satisfaction is a general tendency to like or dislike things, which may emanate from innate temperament as well as past life experiences. The implication of this theory is that the evaluative reaction will remain the same whether the phenomenon is good thing or bad thing. This means that the discontented will always be pessimistic while the satisfied will always see the better side of things. At the societal level, some cultures may tend to have a gloomy outlook on life, whereas others are optimistic (Veenhoven, 1996).

The third theory of life satisfaction is pragmatism, which proposes that life satisfaction is mainly the outcome of citizens' evaluation of public administration system and government efforts in enhancing economic affluence, social equality, political freedom, and access to knowledge (Veenhoven, 1996). The present study fits within the pragmatism of life satisfaction view, in which life satisfaction or happiness can be enhanced by facilitating some conditions for people (Veenhoven, 2004). Following this line of argument, the literature documents a number of empirical studies concerning factors determining life satisfaction.

Using Switzerland as a case study, Frey and Stutzer (2000a) categorize the determinants of happiness as demographic, economic, and institutional factors. Demographic factors comprise personality attributes such as age, gender, citizenship (national/foreigner), extent of foreign education, family setting, and employment status. Economic factors include both micro- and macroeconomic conditions, such as income level and inflation. Institutional factors relate to the presence of constitutional conditions deemed necessary for democracy and federalism, as well as the extent of their implementation. In a similar manner, Stutzer and Frey (as cited in Dorn, Fischer, Kirchgässner, and Sousa-Poza (2008)]) found that economic, socio-demographic, and institutional variables have a positive significant effect on general level life satisfaction. They operationalize the strength of democratic institutions as the extent of citizen empowerment through a specific institution of direct democracy. A study by Bjørnskov, Dreher, and Fischer (2008) indicates that levels of income and education tend to be positively associated with life satisfaction. In yet another individual level factor, an employed person has a higher level of satisfaction than an unemployed person.

1.3. Public Trust

The literature on trust studies identifies two types of trust. One relates to interpersonal trust, which refers to trust between people. The second one is institutional trust, which refers to people's trust in the functioning of organizational, institutional, and social systems (Wittmann Zhang & Schenker-Wicki, 2012). The present study is confined to public trust as an aspect of institutional trust.

According to Camões and Mendes (2019:2), public trust refers to the "belief in ethical values and behavior, such as fairness, equity, and the defense of civic and human rights" that citizens lean on in making a judgment on the trustworthiness of government. The concept has affective, cognitive, and behavioral dimensions. Public trust encompasses citizens' support for both process-related and outcome-related elements in the political system. The process aspects concern how decision-making processes are organized in terms of level of participation, the approach to problems and solutions, and the competence of government employees. In short, this implies "doing things the right way." Output-related elements, one of the pillars of the New Public Management movement, concern "who gets what" in politics. This aspect argues that governments should be much more output-oriented and more effective, which can be explained as "do the right things" (Christensen & Lægreid, 2005).

Sako and Helper (1998) provide a broad definition for citizens' trust in government by using three dimensions, namely (1) Competence (are public institutions capable of doing what they say they will do?); (2) Contractual (will public institutions carry out their contractual agreement?); and (3) Good-will (will public institutions make an open-ended commitment to take initiatives for mutual benefit while refraining from taking unfair advantage?).

As stated by Norris (2011), public trust reflects support for the political system, which may imply confidence in the political community, institutions, and political leaders. Similarly, Park and Blenkinsopp (2011) define public trust as citizens' subjective assessment on the extent to which a government or its public service is competent, reliable, and honest, while also meeting their needs.

Public trust in this study's context refers to citizens' general level of trust in government and its key institutions. Thus, public trust is a subjective attitudinal indicator about the degree of confidence that citizens have in state authorities and administrative branches such as the police, the courts, federal government, federal parliament, and the civil service system (Beeri, Uster, & Vigoda-Gadot, 2019).

2. Research Model and Hypotheses of the Study

This section deals with the study's conceptual framework and hypotheses. As depicted in figure 1, the study argues that public trust in government mediates the positive relationship between democratic electoral quality and life satisfaction.

2.1. Democratic Electoral Quality and Life Satisfaction

The dependent variable of this study is respondents' level of satisfaction with life, usually referred to as Satisfaction with Life (SWL), or happiness. In each WVS, respondents are asked the following question: "All things considered, how satisfied are you with your life as a whole these days?" Response categories range from "dissatisfied" (with a value of 1) to "satisfied" (with a value of 10).

Democracy is the rule of the people by the people. This is realized through free and fair elections, resulting in a government that represents the majority of citizens. Thus, people will accept a political authority if they perceive that the election is fair and free. This would in turn enhance life satisfaction (Rothstein, 2009). However, flaws in electoral processes, such as lack of clear and electoral rules, registration problems or deficiencies, unequal access to the media/public resources, and vote buying would adversely affect democracy. For instance, when citizens observe these electoral malpractices, they judge the process as undemocratic, which in turn makes people less happy (Carreras & İrepoğlu, 2013). Overall, electoral democracy may enhance high levels of political autonomy and extensive participatory opportunities, which in turn tends to increase life satisfaction. This means if people feel that they can influence political process, they should have high level of life satisfaction (Whiteley et al., 2010). In the same vein, Potts (2016) underlines that people value not only policy decisions made by the government but also the way the decisions are reached. This means that if people trust the procedure followed to reach a decision, they will be happier. Such euphoria emanates from procedural utility.

On basis of the above arguments, I propose the following research hypothesis:

Democratic electoral quality has a positive and significant effect on citizen life satisfaction.

2.2. Electoral Democracy and Public Trust

There is an ongoing debate about whether electoral democracy is an indispensable source for the creation of public trust. One argument suggests that electoral democracy enhances public trust. In electoral democracy, free and fair elections result in a government representing the majority of the citizens. It upholds the essence of democracy, which is "rule of the people by the people" (Lindberg & Lindberg, 2006; Manion, 2006). From a contrasting point of view, Rothstein (2009) argues that there is little evidence showing the positive contribution of electoral democracy in creating public trust. In this study, we argue that electoral democracy helps to create public trust in government. This leads to the next hypothesis of the study:

Democratic electoral quality has a positive and significant effect on public trust.

2.3. The Mediating Effect of Public Trust

Electoral democracy influences life satisfaction because democracy implies that government adopts policies that are closer to citizens' preferences. This should increase people's happiness (Dorn, Fischer, Kirchgässner, & Sousa-Poza, 2007). Therefore, the following hypothesis can be formulated:

Public trust plays a mediating role in the relationship between democratic electoral quality and citizen life satisfaction.

2.4. Conceptual Framework of the Study

Here, I present the study's conceptual framework, comprising its independent, mediating, and dependent variables.

Figure 1: Conceptual framework of the study

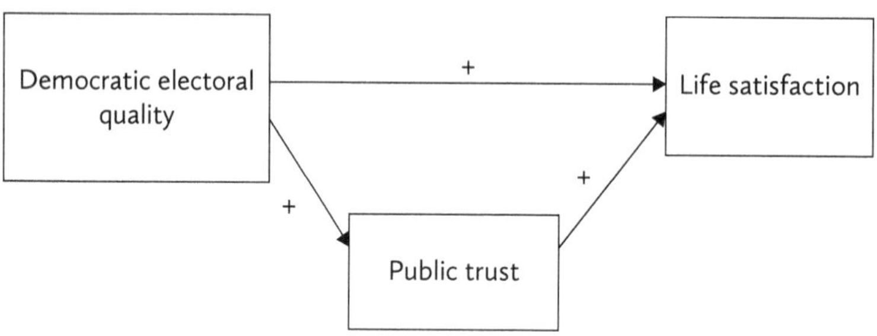

(Source: based on work by Owen et al. [2008]).

3. Research Methods

This section comprises subsections on research design, population, sample size and sampling technique, data sources, and data collection instruments. It also deals with data collection procedures, methods of data analysis, model specifications, a description of study variables, and ethical considerations.

3.1. Research Design

This research project is both descriptive and explanatory in nature. It is a descriptive study in the sense that it seeks to describe citizens' perceptions about electoral democracy as well as levels of public trust in government and life satisfaction. The study is explanatory in the sense that it investigates the effect of electoral democracy on life satisfaction. In addition, it elucidates the mediation effect of public trust in the relationship between electoral democracy and public trust.

3.2. Data Sources

This study used secondary data from the World Values Survey (WVS). The WVS provides data on sociocultural and political change worldwide. It consists of national sample surveys in over ninety countries, using a common questionnaire with variables on beliefs, values, economic development, democratization, religion, gender equality, social capital, and subjective well-being. The survey has been coordinated by the World Values Survey Association since 1981. So for, the WVS comprises six waves. Its first wave was from 1981-1984 and covered twenty-three countries, mostly developed nations. The second was undertaken from 1990-1994. A third wave of surveys was carried out in 1995-1998, this time in fifty-five nations and with increased attention being given to analyzing the cultural conditions for democracy. A fourth wave of surveys was carried out in 1999–2004 in sixty-five countries and included better coverage of African and Islamic societies, which had been under-represented in previous surveys. A fifth wave was carried out in 2005-2009 and a sixth wave, which is the latest survey, was carried out in 2010–2014 in sixty countries (see WVS website at www.worldvaluessurvey.org).

The data source for this study was WVS- 6, which covered 2010-2014. From a total of 89,565 participants covering sixty countries, 51.1 percent were female and the remaining 48.9 percent were male. In this survey, 19.1 percent of the participants (n= 17127) were from ten African countries.

3.3. Measures

For electoral democracy, nine question items ranging from V228A to V228I in WVS-6 were considered. All these items reflect the quality of election in a democratic system and respondents assessed each of the items on a Likert scale of 1-4, ranging from "very often" to "not at all often." Some items, which were stated in a positive direction, were recoded before running descriptive and inferential analyses. This was to ensure that higher values indicate better electoral democracy ratings.

In the WVS-6 questionnaire, public trust was measured by a 4-point scale from 1, for "a great deal," to 4, for "none at all." In this survey, public trust question items cover question items that range from V113 to V118, excluding

V116. But, this scale was recoded in such a way that higher values express higher levels of trust in government and its key institutions. Particular to this study, the institutions that were considered in the analysis include the police, the courts, federal government, federal parliament, and the civil service system. For the purpose of inferential statistics, a public trust index was created by computing the mean trust score from the public trust in each of the institutions measured on a 4-point scale (Cronbach's $\alpha = .851$). Such an approach is in line with the works of Beeri et al. (2019), Chevalier (2019), and Martinez-Martin (2010).

Life satisfaction, the dependent variable in this study, is coded on a 10-point scale. In each WVS, respondents are asked the following one item question: "All things considered, how satisfied are you with your life as a whole these days?" Response categories range from "completely dissatisfied" (which is assigned a value of 1) to "completely satisfied" (with a value of 10). On this scale, high scores indicate high level of life satisfaction or happiness. In the WVS-6 questionnaire, question number V23 represents life satisfaction. For analysis purposes, life satisfaction was considered as a continuous variable (Beeri et al., 2019; Chevalier, 2019; Martinez-Martin, 2010).

3.4. Reliability and Validity Test

A reliability test shows the internal consistency of items that make up a given construct, whereas a validity test confirms the accuracy of measurements. The reliability of the study's constructs was tested by using Cronbach's alpha. Following the recommendations by Field (2013), the analyses of internal homogeneity showed acceptable results, as presented in table 1.

Table 1: Number of items and Cronbach's alpha

Construct	Number of items	Cronbach's alpha
Electoral Democracy Quality	9	.737
Public trust	5	.851
Life-satisfaction	One-item	-

Source: Computed from WVS- 6 *dataset*

3.5. Methods of Data Analysis

This study employed mainly quantitative data analysis, whereby both descriptive and inferential data analysis methods were used. Descriptive analysis provides the realities as they exist using a frequency table, mean, and standard deviations (SD). Using the means or percentages of a certain response is very simple and useful for comparison purposes. For Likert scale data, analysis must take into account the distribution of responses to the question (Gundelach & Kreiner, 2004).

For Likert scale type of data with a 4-point scale, the responses for each item of the main constructs of the study were transformed from a 4 points Likert scale to a 2-point scale, in order to make the analysis process very simple and understandable. For example, response options comprising [1. a great deal, 2. quite a lot, 3. not very much, 4. none at all] were transformed to "a great deal, /quite a lot" and "not very much/none at all." Subsequently, a frequency table was used to present this type of data.

In addition to using frequency percentages (%), the composite mean was computed for each of the main constructs to show the overall findings. Though there is a debate whether to consider a Likert-scale measure as ordinal or interval, it is acceptable to assume Likert-scale as an interval scale of measurement (Martinez-Martin, 2010). In this line of methodology, Chevalier (2019) indicated that it is meaningful to produce a scale of attitudes from a Likert-scale measure when Cronbach's Alpha is greater than 0.7. Accordingly, this study considered all the three main constructs (i.e., electoral democracy quality, public trust, and life satisfaction) as continuous variables.

For all the proposed hypotheses, the study employed mediation analysis, which assumes four classical conditions as requirements (Baron & Kenny, 1986). First, the independent variable, a composite of democratic electoral quality in this case, must be associated with the outcome, life satisfaction. Second, the independent variable must be significantly related with the mediator, public trust in government. Third, there must be a significant relationship between the mediator and the outcome. Finally, the effect of the independent variable on the outcome must be significantly reduced for partial mediation, or to zero for full mediation when the mediator is entered.

4. Results

This section presents the study's findings using descriptive and inferential analysis techniques.

4.1. Profile of the Respondents

This study used secondary data from WVS- 6, which covered 2010-2012. From a total of 89,565 participants in the survey, 51.1 percent were females and the remaining 48.9 percent were male. In this survey, 19.1 percent of the participants (n= 17127) were from ten African countries.[1]

4.2. Descriptive Statistics for the Main Constructs of the Study

Table 2 reveals descriptive statistics for the main constructs of the study, namely life satisfaction, public trust, and democratic electoral quality.

As indicated in table 2, the mean life satisfaction level in our sample is around 6.82 (which represents 68.2 percent), with a standard deviation of 2.3. This suggests considerable variation in average level of life satisfaction. Computed from a 4-point Likert scale, the public trust in government and democratic electoral quality are 61 percent and 68 percent respectively.

Table 3 provides information about the descriptive statistics on the main constructs between African and other countries. Specific to African countries covered by the WVS-6 survey, the level of citizen life satisfaction is about 62 percent, which is lower than the satisfaction level of other countries (70 percent). Similarly, the performance of African countries in electoral democracy (26 percent) is below that of other countries (27 percent). Though the study did not have prior hypotheses about the level of life satisfaction and electoral democracy between African and other countries, both findings show that the differences are statistically significant ($t= -37.295$, $P<0.05$ for life satisfaction, and $t=-20.101$, $P<0.05$ for democratic electoral quality; please see appendix 3 and appendix 4). These findings indicate that the better the quality of electoral democracy in a given country, the more satisfied its citizens are with their life (Beeri et al., 2019).

4.3. Qualities of Electoral Democracy

According to Manion (2006), the qualities of electoral democracy inter alia include the openness of nomination and selection of candidates, the degree of electoral contestation, and the inclusiveness of voting procedures. This

Table 2: Descriptive statistics for all respondents

	N	Minimum	Maximum	Mean	Std. Deviation
Satisfaction with your life	88987	1	10	6.82	2.284
Public trust	88342	1	4	2.4535	.74745
Democratic electoral quality	56443	1	4	2.7062	.59317
Valid N (listwise)	56018				

Table 3: Descriptive statistics by continent: African and other countries

By Continent		N	Minimum	Maximum	Mean	Std. Deviation
African	Satisfaction with your life	17033	1	10	6.23	2.473
	Democratic electoral quality	13961	1	4	2.6190	.58984
	Public trust	16820	1	4	2.4425	.75956
	Valid N (listwise)	13,859				
Other Countries	Satisfaction with your life	71954	1	10	6.95	2.215
	Democratic electoral quality	42483	1	4	2.7349	.59147
	Public trust	71523	1	4	2.4560	.74455
	Valid N (listwise)	42,158				

subsection examines whether elections across the world fulfill democracy characteristics as presented in table 4.

The findings in table 4 show that the majority of the respondents (more than 60 percent) had good perceptions about the counting of votes, fairness of election officials, coverage of elections by the media, and availability of a genuine choice in the elections. Contrary to this, they replied that opposition candidates lack freedom to participate and voters are threatened with violence at the polls.

4.4. Public Trust in Government

Public trust refers to the degree to which citizens evaluate how well the political system is performing (Kim, 2005). Table 5 shows public trust in government.

Table 4: Qualities of electoral democracy

	Not often/ Not at all often	Fairly often/ very often
	%	%
Votes are counted fairly	35.2%	64.8%
Opposition candidates are prevented from running	38.3%	61.7%
TV news favors the governing party	56.9%	43.1%
Voters are bribed	51.0%	49.0%
Journalists provide fair coverage of elections	38.9%	61.1%
Election officials are fair	42.2%	57.8%
Rich people buy elections	53.2%	46.8%
Voters are threatened with violence at the polls	30.9%	69.1%
Voters are offered a genuine choice in the elections	33.0%	67.0%

N= valid response rates ranges from 49,826 to 53,300
Composite mean: 2.7062 (on the basis of a 4-point Likert scale from the original questionnaire)
Source: Computed from 2014 *WVS dataset*

Table 5: Public trust in government and its institutions

	Not very much/None at all	Quite a lot/A great deal
	%	%
Trust: The police	44.0%	56.0%
Trust: The courts	45.4%	54.6%
Trust: The government	53.7%	46.3%
Trust: Parliament	60.3%	39.7%
Trust: The Civil service	52.5%	47.5%

As reported in table 5, a large number of citizens had low trust in parliament, the federal government, and the civil service system. In relative terms, they had a moderate trust in the police and the courts.

4.5. Correlations between the Main Constructs

Correlation analysis shows the association between variables. In this regard, table 6 presents the findings from the correlation analysis for the main constructs of the study, namely electoral democracy, public trust, and life satisfaction.

The results of correlation analysis (table 6) indicate that both electoral democracy and public trust have a positive and significant correlation with life satisfaction. This shows that life satisfaction (happiness) can be advanced by further democratization (Veenhoven, 2008).

4.6. Towards Explaining Life Satisfaction

The central issues of this study are to examine the effect of electoral democracy on life satisfaction and to investigate whether public trust plays a mediating role between electoral democracy and life satisfaction. Accordingly, table 7 displays results from the mediation analysis, which entailed performing a series of regression analyses that capture all the three hypotheses of the study.

In model 1 of table 7, the result indicates that democratic electoral quality has a positive significant effect on the dependent variable, life satisfaction ($\beta = 0.415$, $P < .001$). Thereby, hypothesis 1 is confirmed and step 1 of the mediation analysis is fulfilled. The result of model 2 in table 7 shows that the composite of democratic electoral quality has a significant positive effect on public trust ($\beta = 0.375$, $P < .001$), showing that step 2 of the mediation analysis is also satisfied.

Model 3 in table 7 entails performing step 3 and step 4 of the mediation analysis at the same time. Step 3 confirms that public trust in government, the mediator variable, is significantly related to life satisfaction ($\beta = 0.280$, $P < .001$). Once public trust (the mediator variable) is entered into the regression model, the effect of democratic electoral quality on life satisfaction is reduced from $\beta = 0.415$ to $\beta = .310$, which is step 4 of the mediation analysis. This represents a 25.3 percent reduction. This confirms the significance of the indirect effect of democratic electoral on life satisfaction through its positive relationship with public trust. Thereby, public trust partially mediates the relationship between democratic electoral and life satisfaction.

Table 6: Correlations

	Electoral Democracy	Public trust	Life Satisfaction
Electoral Democracy	1		
Public trust	.308**	1	
Life Satisfaction	.102**	.133**	1

Notes: **. Correlation is significant at the 0.01 level (2-tailed). N is greater than 56,000

Table 7: Regression statistics for the effect of public trust as a mediator between electoral democracy and life-satisfaction

	Model 1	Model 2	Model 3
	Life satisfaction	Public trust	Life satisfaction
Electoral Democracy	0.415***	0.375***	0.310***
	(0.0163)	(0.00488)	(0.0171)
Public trust			0.280***
			(0.0140)
_cons	5.726***	1.367***	5.344***
	(0.0452)	(0.0135)	(0.0490)
adj. R-sq	0.011	0.095	0.018

Notes: N= 56090, Standard errors in parentheses, * $p<0.05$, ** $p<0.01$, *** $p<0.001$

5. Discussion

This study has shown that electoral democracy contributes to life satisfaction. In other words, citizens' assessment on electoral democracy influences their level of life satisfaction.

It also explicates that public trust partially mediates the positive relationship between electoral democracy and life satisfaction. These findings have both theoretical and practical implications. From a theoretical point of view, the study contributes to the existing literature focusing on the unsolved issue of what explains life satisfaction. More specifically, the finding that electoral democracy has a significant positive effect on life satisfaction is in line with democratic theory, which states political structures and processes have significant effects on citizens' quality of life and their sense of subjective well-being (Whiteley et al., 2010).

Contrary to the prior proposition that government has less effect on happiness (Headey and Wearing, 1992 as cited in Ott [2011]), the current study confirms that political factors and government are the sources of happiness. This shows that collective conditions in a nation (in this case, electoral democracy) explain happiness beyond the effect of individual differences in terms of employment, income, personality, education, gender, social relations, and age.

In a practical sense, the study highlighted the importance of making elections free, fair, and inclusive, as this would enhance both public trust and citizens' life satisfaction. This would require a concerted action by politicians, policy makers, public managers, and the public at large. Democratic electoral quality, which is one of the important constructs in this study, reflects the openness of nomination and selection of candidates, the degree of electoral contestation, and the inclusiveness of voting procedures. When political parties undertake the nomination and selection of candidates in a transparent manner by letting the community participate, this enhances democratic electoral quality. Similarly, greater degrees of choice and contestation among potential candidates for election improve democratic electoral quality. Furthermore, the extent to which citizens as individual voters actively take part in the election process would promote the inclusiveness of voting procedures.

5.1. Limitations of the Study

The study has some limitations that should be considered when interpreting its findings. First, this study used a cross-sectional data set, not a longitudinal one. As a result, the study does not reveal the changes in the relationship between electoral democracy, public trust, and life satisfaction over a period of time. In addition, a cross-sectional research design could not establish a cause and effect relationship. Second, the findings are based on subjective ratings instead of objective data with regard to the main constructs of the study. However, multiple scale items were used to measure each construct except life satisfaction, in order to consider all possible information on the constructs.

The third limitation concerns the use of parametric inferential analyses for the Likert scale of measurement. This study, however, employed multiple items to capture important aspects of the constructs, just as applied by the prior studies (Beeri et al., 2019; Chevalier, 2019; Martinez-Martin, 2010). The fourth limitation relates to the small value of coefficient of determination (i.e., adj. R-sq is lower than 10 percent), which poses a question on the explanatory capacity of the model. In this regard, future research could attempt to identify other potential mediators and moderators that influence the relationship between electoral democracy and life satisfaction.

Conclusions

The study of life satisfaction is of great importance, as it influences people's personal life as well as their level of participation in political and economic affairs. This study aimed to examine whether and how electoral democracy influences citizens' life satisfaction. Accordingly, this study demonstrated that electoral democracy has both direct and indirect effect on life satisfaction. In other words, the findings indicated that democratic election significantly enhances public trust in government. Chiefly, the study underlines that public trust mediates the positive relationship between electoral democracy and overall citizens' life satisfaction.

The study showed that political factors in terms of electoral democracy and public trust have significant effect on life satisfaction. This shows that not only demographic factors (age, gender, citizenship [national/foreigner], level of education, family setting, and employment status) and economic factors (such as income level and inflation) but also political factors significantly explain citizen life satisfaction or happiness.

Thus, politicians and election officials need to uphold democracy principles and electoral qualities so as to improve life satisfaction. This can be achieved by government policy that requires making election process (pre-election period, the election period, and post-election period) free, fair, and inclusive.

In addition to electoral democracy, public trust is of importance in influencing life satisfaction. As clearly suggested by Welch, Hinnant, and Moon (2005), government and its institutions can enjoy a high level of public trust by adopting ICT-based public service delivery, improving their administrative rules, making its process more transparent, and reducing public officials' discretionary power. Building public trust would in turn have a positive effect on life satisfaction.

Acknowledgements

The author would like to thank the anonymous reviewers for their helpful comments and suggestions that improved the quality of this paper. The author is also indebted to Bacha Kebede Debela (PhD) who provided me with very useful journal articles and for his encouragement throughout the research process.

Notes

1. These countries are Algeria, Ghana, Libya, Morocco, Nigeria, Rwanda, South Africa, Zimbabwe, Tunisia, and Egypt

References

Baron, R. M., & Kenny, D. A. (1986). The Moderator–Mediator Variable Distinction in Social Psychological Research: Conceptual, Strategic, and Statistical Considerations. *Journal of Personality and Social Psychology*, 51(6), 1173.

Beeri, I., Uster, A., & Vigoda-Gadot, E. (2019). Does Performance Management Relate to Good Governance? A Study of Its Relationship with Citizens' Satisfaction with and Trust in Israeli Local Government. *Public Performance & Management Review*, 42(2), 241-279.

Bjørnskov, C., Dreher, A., & Fischer, J. A. (2008). Cross-Country Determinants of Life Satisfaction: Exploring Different Determinants across Groups in Society. *Social Choice and Welfare*, 30(1), 119-173.

Bjørnskov, C., Dreher, A., & Fischer, J. A. (2010). Formal Institutions and Subjective Well-being: Revisiting the Cross-country Evidence. *European Journal of Political Economy*, 26(4), 419-430

Blind, P. K. (2007). Building Trust in Government in the Twenty-first Century: Review of Literature and Emerging Issues. Paper presented at the 7th Global Forum on Reinventing Government Building Trust in Government, United Nations, Vienna.

Camões, P. J., & Mendes, S. M. (2019). Do Citizens Trust the Civil Service Differently? Comparing the Determinants of Confidence in Political-administrative Institutions. *International Journal of Public Administration*, 42(14), 1234-1244.

Carreras, M., & İrepoğlu, Y. (2013). Trust in Elections, Vote Buying, and Turnout in Latin America. *Electoral Studies*, 32(4), 609-619.

Chevalier, T. (2019). Political Trust, Young people and Institutions in Europe. A Multilevel Analysis. *International Journal of Social Welfare*, 28(4), 418-430.

Christensen, T., & Lægreid, P. (2005). Trust in Government: The Relative Importance of Service Satisfaction, Political Factors, and Demography. *Public Performance & Management Review,* 28(4), 487-511.

Curini, L., Jou, W., & Memoli, V. (2014). How Moderates and Extremists Find Happiness: Ideological Orientation, cCtizen–Government Proximity, and Life Satisfaction. *International Political Science Review,* 35(2), 129-152.

Dolan, P., Metcalfe, R., & Powdthavee, N. (2008). Electing Happiness: Does Happiness Affect Voting and Do Elections Affect Happiness? *Discussion Papers* 08/30, Department of Economics, University of York.

Dorn, D., Fischer, J. A., Kirchgässner, G., & Sousa-Poza, A. (2007). Is it Culture or Democracy? The Impact of Democracy and Culture on Happiness. *Social Indicators Research,* 82(3), 505-526.

Dorn, D., Fischer, J. A., Kirchgässner, G., & Sousa-Poza, A. (2008). Direct Democracy and Life Satisfaction Revisited: New Evidence for Switzerland. *Journal of Happiness Studies,* 9(2), 227-255.

Field, A. (2013). *Discovering Statistics Using IBM SPSS statistics.* Thousand Oaks, CA: Sage.

Frey, B. S., & Stutzer, A. (2000a). Happiness, Economy, and Institutions. *The Economic Journal,* 110 (466), 918-938.

Frey, B. S., & Stutzer, A. (2000b). Happiness Prospers in Democracy. *Journal of Happiness Studies,* 1 (1), 79-102.

Frey, B. S., & Stutzer, A. (2000c). Maximising Happiness? *German Economic Review,* 1(2), 145-167.

Gundelach, P., & Kreiner, S. (2004). Happiness and Life Satisfaction in Advanced European Countries. *Cross-cultural Research,* 38(4), 359-386.

Helliwell, J., Layard, R., & Sachs, J. (2012). *World Happiness Report.* https://worldhappiness.report/ed/2012/.

Inglehart, R. (2009). Democracy and Happiness: What Causes What? In B. Radcliff & Dutt, A. (eds), *Happiness, Economics and Politics: Towards a Multi-Disciplinary Approach,* 256. Chelthenham, UK: Edward Elgar.

Kim, S.-E. (2005). The Role of Trust in the Modern Administrative State: An Integrative Model. *Administration & Society,* 37(5), 611-635.

Lindberg, S. I., & Lindberg, S. (2006). *Democracy and Elections in Africa*: Baltimore: Johns Hopkins University Press.

Manion, M. (2006). Democracy, Community, Trust: The Impact of Elections in Rural China. *Comparative Political Studies,* 39(3), 301-324.

Martinez-Martin, P. (2010). Composite Rating Scales. *Journal of the Neurological Sciences,* 289(1-2), 7-11.

Norris, P. (2011). *Democratic Deficit: Critical Citizens Revisited.* Cambridge, UK: Cambridge University Press.

Ott, J. C. (2010). GoodGovernance and Happiness in Nations: Technical Quality Precedes Democracy and Quality Beats Size. *Journal of Happiness Studies,* 11(3), 353-368.

Ott, J. C. (2011). Government and Happiness in 130 Nations: Good Governance Fosters Higher Level and More Equality of Happiness. *Social Indicators Research* 102(1), 3-22.

Owen, A. L., Videras, J., & Willemsen, C. (2008). Democracy, Participation, and Life Satisfaction. *Social Science Quarterly*, 89(4), 987-1005.

Pacek, A., & Radcliff, B. (2008). Assessing the Welfare State: The Politics of Happiness. *Perspectives on Politics*, 6(2), 267-277.

Park, H., & Blenkinsopp, J. (2011). The Roles of Transparency and Trust in the Relationship between Corruption and Citizen Satisfaction. *International Review of Administrative Sciences*, 77(2), 254-274.

Potts, J. C. (2016). Democracy and Happiness: A True Correlation? *Journal of Arts and Humanities*, 5(3), 86-92.

Rothstein, B. (2009). Creating Political Legitimacy: Electoral Democracy versus Quality of Government. *American Behavioral Scientist*, 53(3), 311-330.

Sako, M., & Helper, S. (1998). Determinants of Trust in Supplier Relations: Evidence from the Automotive Industry in Japan and the United States. *Journal of Economic Behavior & Organization*, 34(3), 387-417.

Veenhoven, R. (1996). Developments in Satisfaction-Research. *Social Indicators Research*, 37(1), 1-46.

Veenhoven, R. (2004). Happiness as a Public Policy Aim: The Greatest Happiness Principle. In A. Linley & S. Joseph (eds), *Positive Psychology in Practice*. Hoboken, NJ: John Wiley and Sons.

Veenhoven, R. (2008). Healthy Happiness: Effects of Happiness on Physical Health and the Consequences for Preventive Health Care. *Journal of Happiness Studies*, 9(3), 449-469.

Welch, E. W., Hinnant, C. C., & Moon, M. J. (2005). Linking Citizen Satisfaction With E-government and Trust in Government. *Journal of Public Administration Research and Theory*, 15(3), 371-391.

Whiteley, P., Clarke, H. D., Sanders, D., & Stewart, M. C. (2010). Government Performance and Life Satisfaction in Contemporary Britain. *The Journal of Politics*, 72(3), 733-746.

Wittmann Zhang, X., & Schenker-Wicki, A. (2012). Trust and Control across Three Emerging Economies. Presented at British Academy of Management Conference 2012, Cardiff, September 11-13, 2012.

Appendixes

Appendix 1: Sex of the respondents

		Frequency	Percent	Valid Percent	Cumulative Percent
Valid	Male	43782	48.9	48.9	48.9
	Female	45691	51.0	51.1	100.0
	Total	89473	99.9	100.0	
Missing	Missing; Unknown	40	.0		
	No answer	51	.1		
	Total	91	.1		
Total		89565	100.0		

Appendix 2: No. of respondents by continent

		Frequency	Percent	Valid Percent	Cumulative Percent
Valid	Other countries	72438	80.9	80.9	80.9
	African	17127	19.1	19.1	100.0
	Total	89565	100.0	100.0	

Appendix 3: Independent Samples Test for mean life satisfaction by continent

Group Statistics

	By Continent	N	Mean	Std. Deviation	Std. Error Mean
Satisfaction with your life	African	17033	6.23	2.473	.019
	Other Countries	71954	6.95	2.215	.008

Independent Samples Test

	t-test for Equality of Means						
						95% Confidence Interval of the Difference	
	T	Df	Sig. (2-tailed)	Mean Difference	Std. Error Difference	Lower	Upper
Satisfaction with your life	-37.295	88985	.000	-.720	.019	-.758	-.682

Appendix 4: Independent Samples Test for democratic electoral quality by continent

Group statistics

	By Continent	N	Mean	Std. Deviation	Std. Error Mean
Democratic electoral quality	African	13961	2.6190	.58984	.00499
	Other Countries	42483	2.7349	.59147	.00287

Independent Samples Test

	t-test for Equality of Means						
						95% Confidence Interval of the Difference	
	T	Df	Sig. (2-tailed)	Mean Difference	Std. Error Difference	Lower	Upper
Democratic electoral quality	-20.101	56441	.000	-.11590	.00577	-.12720	-.10460

3

Status, Challenges, and Prospects of the Ethiopian Developmental State (Emphasis on Democratic Governance)[1]

Belayneh Bogale Zewdie

Box 1: Key points of the chapter

- ✓ The debate on democratic governance vs. development seems a "false choice" and a sequencing fallacy.
- ✓ There exists a considerable gap between form and reality when it comes to democratic governance in Ethiopia.
- ✓ The bottlenecks include the dispute between a shared vision and the quest for nations, nationalities, and people's self-determination; the hostile relationship between the government and media, political opposition, and civil societies; the poor performance of some governance indicators.
- ✓ The achievements in HDI Ethiopia has made in the ten years since it shift toward the developmental state model are undisputed. The policy and strategic commitments and constitutional guardianship of democratic governance are positive factors.
- ✓ Dealing with such a state demands appropriate innovation and a pragmatic approach in order to deepen the democratic governance agenda in the context of the developmental state.

Box 2: Reading this chapter will give you insight in

- ✓ Conceptualization of the developmental state;
- ✓ Characteristics of the developmental state;
- ✓ Gray areas in the Ethiopian "democratic developmental state" model; and
- ✓ Challenges and prospects of democratic governance in the Ethiopian developmental state.

Box 3: Abbreviations

EPRDF = Ethiopian People Revolutionary Democratic Front
FDRE = Federal Democratic republic of Ethiopia
GTP = Growth and transformation Plan
HEP = Higher Education Proclamation
HDI = Human Development Index
SAP = Structural Adjustment program
TPLF = Tigrayan People's Liberation Front
TVET = Technique and vocational education and training
UN = United Nations
UNDP = United Nations Development Program
USA = United States of America
WB = World Bank

1. Introduction

Nowadays the terms "governance" and "democracy" are accepted as the nucleus of development politics. Bad governance is being increasingly regarded as one of the root causes of all evil within our societies. Major donors and international financial institutions are also basing their development assistance on the condition that reforms that ensure "democratic governance" are carried out (WB, 1992; UNESCAP, n.d; WB, 2013). On top of this, the concept of democratic governance has been widely recognized as prerequisite for successful nation-building and socioeconomic progress.

The concept of democratic governance has received increasing attention in Africa over the last three decades. The importance of the concept for African development is related to three major issues (WB, 2013). Firstly, it is related to the need to create the basic extra-economic conditions necessary for the growth of the African economy, such as effective public administration, an independent and functioning judiciary, a transparent financial system, and accountability. Secondly, the concept is related to the common developmental challenges of Africa, such as accountability, rule of law, freedom of expression and association, and legitimate and inclusive governments. Improving these factors may be considered as a significant move toward African renewal. Thirdly, the adoption and continuous improvement of the market-oriented system in Africa has been prescribed as a key to development.

In line with this, according to government reports, Ethiopia has achieved encouraging development results, maintaining an economic growth rate of 10 percent over the last ten years. The international community has also recognized that there has been growth, though there is not much agreement on the rate (statistics). It has also been reported that the country has come to enjoy the fastest improvement in the Human Development Index among the Least Developed Countries (IIAG, 2015; Bekele & Regassa, 2012). Moreover, the government claims that it is determined to accelerate and maintain this development result while strengthening its democratic governance agenda. It has set for itself a challenging goal of creating a "democratic developmental state" and building a green economy (MoFED, 2010; Bekele & Regassa, 2012). Additionally, the county has also the ambition to become a middle-income state by 2025. In short, Ethiopia, a self-declared developmental state, seeks to construct a developmental state while also deepening its democratic governance.

The country has recently launched a set of coordinated comprehensive development plans, called the Growth and Transformation Plan (GTP) I and II. The first phase, which lasted for five years from 2010/11 to 2014/15 (MoFED, 2010), has come to a conclusion, leading to the kick-off of the second phase as of the 2015/16 budget year. The idea of the developmental state calls for such coordinated development plans, which identify the development priorities of the country and the respective roles of each sector, so as to facilitate the achievement of the national goals.

The concept of constructing a developmental state while also deepening democracy and good governance, as stimulating as it is to those who value a democratic developmental state, poses a set of challenges. It evokes the question as to whether pressing the democratic governance agenda impedes or facilitates development. The issue of whether there is a relationship of priority, or primacy, between development and democratic governance has not been resolved (Bekele & Regassa, 2012) and has evoked difficult questions and lengthy debate among development scholars. These questions are raised in different forms in different contexts and lead to smaller, local, and context-specific issues that need to be raised and discussed.

Hence, there has to be continuous rhetoric and discourse within the academic community and practitioners in the field so as to attain conceptual clarity. To this end, the author of this chapter strongly believes that this chapter will serve to provoke thought and stimulate discussions. Especially in Ethiopian context, where the culture of boldly discussing politics is not yet very deep, the importance of this chapter is self-evident.

2. Objectives of the Review

The general objective of this chapter is to explore the status, challenges, and prospects of good governance in a developmental state, with particular emphasis on the Ethiopian context. Specifically;

- To come up with conceptual clarity regarding the developmental state;
- To portray the characteristics of the developmental state model;
- To point out the gray areas in the Ethiopian democratic developmental state model; and
- To discuss the challenges and prospects of democratic governance in the Ethiopian developmental state.

3. Materials and Methods

By way of desk review, the chapter attempts to point out the status, challenges, and prospects of democratic governance under the Ethiopian developmental state model, examining national legal, strategic, and policy documents (such as the Growth and Transformation Plan I and II and different related programs) and various publications and prior studies in this area. Hence, the reviewer looked into the literature on the developmental state in general and the Ethiopian state in particular. The overall goal of the review is to provoke thoughts and to stimulate discussions.

4. Conceptualizing Developmental State

The concept of a developmental state is not utterly new to the literature in politics, development studies, and economics. While the term has been used to refer to state-led economic planning as experienced in the countries of East Asia and some other countries that have worn the label since the 1970s, a serious attempt at conceptualizing it is said to have begun with the work of Chalmers Johnson in the 1980s (Johnson, 1982). In his analysis of Japanese development in the 1970s, Johnson created the foundations for the model of the developmental state. He first used the term to describe strong interventionist policies that led to sustained, rapid industrialization and long-term economic development. For example, in the period that began with the Second World War and continued up to the 1980s, the economy of Japan was shaped by a political ideology that privileged raising income levels and sustaining industrial growth.

But it was the small East Asian "tigers"—Korea, Taiwan, and Singapore—that became the archetypal instantiations of the model (Amsden, 1989; Wade, 1990). The East Asian "tigers" managed to change their position in the world economic hierarchy, moving from "underdeveloped" to "developed" in the course of two generations. This kind of shift is not only unprecedented among twentieth-century developing countries. It is exceptional even in the broader context that includes the historical experience of Europe and the Americas (Evans and Heller, 2018).

In the context of Africa, Mckinsey (2010) labeled Botswana and Mauritius as the "African Lions" to demonstrate the two states as the African version of successful developmental states. In Ethiopia, the term is increasingly being used and dominating political discourse.

4.1. Meaning of Developmental State

There is no agreed definition of the developmental state; rather, the discussion and debate on it is a work in progress. However, just like many other social science concepts, it can be defined and conceptualized in diverse ways (Jaleta, 2015). A developmental state may be defined as a state wherein the government is closely involved in macro- and microeconomic planning in order to grow the economy. It has generally been observed that successful developmental states are able to advance their economies much faster than regulatory states that use regulations to manage the economy. As an example, according to Hollander (2011), it took the USA and United Kingdom approximately fifty years to double their economy while it took China, which is a developmental state, approximately ten years to achieve the same goal. However, this argument seems simplistic, since the contexts and periods of the Chinese and the aforementioned western countries economic doubling time were quite different.

A developmental state is often defined in terms of its ideological orientation (i.e., promoting the ideal and agenda of developmentalism) and its institutional arrangements (i.e., its institutional capacity to formulate and implement its policies and programs), whereby the state has to build efficient and effective institutions to achieve its developmental goals. Standard descriptions also maintain that a developmental state is a state with instincts to resist external demands (e.g., multinational corporations) and oppress internal resistance (from groups focused on transient political gains or short–term profits, i.e., local political and business elites) (Bekele & Regassa, 2012).

This latter description suggests that a developmental state ought to have the capacity to control internal strife and build consensus among citizens on the national developmental agenda by drawing attention to the long-term benefits for all (Zenawi, 2006; Bekele & Regassa, 2012). An economic report on Africa holds that a developmental state is "one that has the capacity to deploy its authority, credibility and legitimacy in a binding manner to design and implement development policies and programs for promoting transformation and growth, as well as for expanding human capabilities" (ECS & AU, 2011, p. 7). Ideally, therefore, a developmental state needs to be a persuasive state with the competence to mobilize people and resources around its development plan (Zenawi, 2006). In other words, a democratic developmental state requires a shared vision and national consensus as preconditions for success. Peter Evans refers to it as a state with institutional design meant to advance the transformative role of the state "rather than constraining the state," a state with the capacity to formulate and implement its development goals in an authoritative and binding fashion resulting in improved economic performance (Evans, 1995).

The developmental state is also referred to as an autonomous/independent state, with a decidedly interventionist bent, as it seeks to monitor and control the economy. In this sense, it can even be viewed as a model of capitalism that nonetheless differs from a minimalist state or other species of interventionist states such as the regulatory state and the welfare state (Wade, 1990; Edigheji, 2005; Bekele & Regassa, 2012). The late prime minister of FDRE, Melese Zenawi, contrasted the developmental state with weak states (which easily bow to the pressure mounted on them by the business or political elite) or predatory states (which tend to be extractive and exploitative of public resources for private purposes) (Zenawi, 2006).

A developmental state is, therefore, a state that is and seeks to be a strong player in the economy of a nation with a view to enhancing economic development. It is a state that promotes macroeconomic stability and establishes an institutional framework that provides law and order, effective administration of justice and peaceful resolution of conflicts (Mkandawire, 2001). The aspiration of developmental states is chiefly catching up with the advanced world by breaking out of a path dependency that has not led to the economic transformation needed to overcome poverty. In words of Bekele and regassa (2012) "the goals are articulated as achieving development (mainly to mean economic growth) without necessarily treading upon the neoliberal tradition" (p. 10). Their aspiration is to facilitate, if not dictate, economic transformation and capacity building while cautiously controlling internal and external market forces.

4.2. Characteristics of a Developmental State (in the Ethiopian Context)

In order to understand the concept of a developmental state, it is helpful to highlight some of the characteristics of the model. Developmental states generally ***put strong emphasis on technical education and the development of numeracy and computer skills*** within the population. This technically oriented education is strategically used to improve the capacity of government structures, particularly the bureaucracy (Amsden, 1989). What emerges out of this strategy is that the political and bureaucratic layers are populated by extremely educated people who have sufficient analytical tools to be able to take leadership initiatives, based on sound scientific basis.

In Ethiopia, a review of policy and strategic documents demonstrates the critical role of education in the overall development endeavors. As such, the country's Education and Training Policy provides a definition of education that is strongly rooted in the purpose and role it plays in human life in general. Similarly, the HEP sets objectives for higher education that include the promotion and enhancement of research focusing on knowledge and technology transfer consistent with the country's priority needs (FDRE, 2009). This objective not only emphasizes the importance of technology transfer, it also implies the identification of priority areas for the country. A similarly adequate policy focus has been given for TVET providers and related institutions, which are meant to be strengthened to become "centers for technology capabilities' accumulation and transfer" (Ibid, 2009: 55) However, the ever-increasing rate of graduate unemployment and the deteriorating quality of higher education is becoming a cause of concern in the country.

The other characteristic of a developmental state is the centrality of a ***development-oriented political leadership bound together by a powerful economic and political ideology focused on development*** (Fritz and Menocal, 2006; Pempel, 1999, Waldner, 1999). The circumstances that give rise to a development-oriented political leadership can be quite diverse. According to Waldner (1999), this leadership grows out of a political context characterized by the absence of pressure, which gives these leaders scope to construct institutions conducive to economic development. Other analysts suggest that a development-oriented leadership evolves from of a clear consensus within the governing elites, both administrative and political, over the scope and direction of development (Leftwich, 2010). The final factor is the interests of political survival and legitimacy, which push political elites toward a developmental orientation.

However, given the relatively polarized politics and the heterogonous nature (multiethnic, multilingual, and multicultural) of Ethiopia, where the quest for the rights of nations, nationalities, and people is the center of political discourse, engendering a development-oriented political leadership with lesser pressures is quite difficult. The experience of East Asian countries also suggests the importance of clear consensus and shared vision between different elites as an instrument to build a development-oriented leadership. However, at least as far as the reviewer is concerned, the Ethiopian state lacks this virtue. Worse, part of the political leadership has been accused of rent-seeking and predatory bandit behavior, which is a clear obstacle for the creation of development-oriented elite.

Compared to other developing regions, the ***autonomy, capability, and effectiveness of the permanent executive*** in the East Asian developmental states are quite impressive. This may be traced back to the presence of a bureaucracy in the Weberian tradition, which prioritizes meritocratic recruitment, provides promotion incentives, shows rationality, and guarantees high levels of prestige and legitimacy to bureaucratic officials (Meyns and Musamba, 2010; Wong, 2004). Onis supports this observation: "Rigorous standards of entry not only ensured a high degree of bureaucratic capability, but also generated a sense of unity and common identity on the part of the bureaucratic elite. Hence the bureaucrats were imbued with a sense of mission and identified themselves with national goals which derived from a position of leadership in society" (Onis, 1991: 114). Such a bureaucracy exhibits uncommon levels of autonomy and effectiveness when it is obviously free from unproductive interference from the political leadership. As a result, decision-makers and technocrats were able to effectively formulate economic policy and employ innovation in public service delivery (ECA and AUC, 2011; Pempel, 1999).

Nonetheless, the Ethiopian public sector lacks these key manifestations of a developmental bureaucracy. There is also evidence of recruitment and promotion based on political patronage in some key public agencies. In the words of Mebratu (2015):

> *"......the civil service in Ethiopia today is actually being re-politicized. Thus, understanding of Ethiopian efforts to adopt reforms—in the context of developmental paradigm—provides key perspectives and experiences to end hiding behind development if there is actual need to transform civil service institutions and save them from being simple cogwheels that conclusively carry out the wishes of politicians."*

A production-oriented private sector working closely with an interventionist government has been at the center of the rapid building of a successful developmental state. Based on long-term institutionalized alliances among political power, the financial sector, and industrial capital, these state-private sector partnerships were crafted on the principle of reciprocity, such as connecting subsidies to performance, and acted as an incentive for productivity (Caldentey, 2008; Wade, 2010). Nonetheless, the reality on the ground demonstrates that the majority of Ethiopian business is characterized by short-term investments that are seeking for short-term returns and "hot money". This makes profit, particularly short-term profit, a significant factor in the investment decision-making process.

The other characteristic of the developmental state is the ***existence of performance-oriented governance***. Developmental states are found to enjoy support because they are associated with promoting rapid economic growth and providing economic benefits to both the ruling elites and the general public. Hence due attention is given to performance orientation and the delivery of services (performance legitimacy) to citizens rather than to the ballot (electoral legitimacy) (Johnson as cited by Musamba, 2010). In Ethiopia, state legitimacy is achieved through the ballot; however, the main shortcoming is that society has, arguably, not reached an equilibrium stage where the feedback mechanism between voting patterns and the delivery of services reinforce each other. Moreover, there is emerging criticism of the Ethiopian government related to election frauds and suppressive laws that "has narrowed the political arena". Critics often also accuse the regime of having room only for weak, fragile, and puppet political oppositions.

To conclude, developmental states tend to manifest the following traits: economic nationalism (skepticism about neo-liberalism), strong government bureaucracy, and production oriented private sector, prioritization of economic growth over political reform, performance legitimacy, and focus on technical education. Successful developmental states have used the aforementioned traits to transform their economies and be globally competitive, to reduce poverty and inequality in their societies and by and large to enhance quality of life. In this regard, Ethiopia, a self declared democratic developmetal state, lucks most of the manifestations of successful developmental states.

4.3. The Genesis of the Developmental State in Ethiopia

The first attempt to adopt a developmental state in Ethiopia dates back to the early twentieth century. Reformist intellectuals of 1920s like *Negadras* Gebre Hiwot Bykedagne, *Blatten* Geta Hiruy W/Silassie, Dr. Martin Workneh, and Ato Kebede Michael were passionate about the Japanese development model. In October 1931, the imperial government of Ethiopia sent a group of government officials and intellectuals to Japan to study different aspects of that country's development for use as a development model (Zewde, 2002). The first Ethiopian Constitution of 1931 directly modeled Japan's Meiji constitution of 1890 (Zewde, 1990).

However, Ethiopia's attempt to adopt the Japanese development state model was not successful for various reasons. The most notable one is the fact that the Ethiopian intellectuals did not conduct an in-depth study of the Japanese model (Jaleta, 2015). The imperial government's commitment was also not up to the required level. The model was not supported by the objective reality of the then Ethiopia due to the great deal of difference between the two countries (Zewde, 1990). Some other external factors that contributed to the unsuccessful attempt to adopt the Japanese model included the Italian invasion and occupation of Ethiopia from 1936 to 1941 and the eruption of the Second World War in 1939 (Jaleta, 2015). Additionally, this attempt to join the first generation of developmental state was aborted by the feudo-capitalist orientation of the empire after the Second World War and its successor – the socialist military dictatorship.

In the contemporary Ethiopia, there is no agreement on the exact time when Ethiopia officially embraced the developmental state model. There are authors, for example Gebremichael (2013), who argue that certain elements of the developmental state were observed in the 1995 constitution. For others, the revival of the developmental state in Ethiopia has been affected by multiple interconnected factors. According to Clapamn (2013), the 2001 crisis within the TPLF and the resultant split of the party was one of the factors. The divisions within the party, among others, emanated from differences in ideology, on development strategies and the war with Eritrea. The victorious group then came up with its revisionist idea, declaring its commitment to building a developmental state (Clapham, 2013). Another factor was the surprising emergence of strong contestants for office in the 2005 national elections. EPRDF had admitted that its programs were not well-received by the people and that the party was forced to come up with new national development-oriented programs to win the hearts of the electorate. To this effect, the late Meles Zenawi's government instituted the idea of a democratic developmental state, as a rebrand to their earlier ideology of a revolutionary democracy (Negash, 2012). Moreover, the ideological pitfalls of the neoliberal paradigm, which had led Africa into another economic dead-end and into a state of fragile, unstable democracy, were another source of pressure (Zenawi, 2011). Hence, the reemergence of the developmental state in Ethiopia is a result of contentious twists and turns in search of an alternative path of development that fits the reality of the country.

Jaleta (2015) claims that the Ethiopian model is drawn from South Korea, Taiwan, and China, that is, on the belief that the path to accelerated economic growth is through a strong developmental state that creates policy space, encourages and directs investments, and promotes a strong work culture and ethics among the population. The Ethiopian developmental state model reveals an emulation of the Chinese model, in that there is a de facto one-party state that prioritizes economic development over the democratization process (Jaleta, 2015). Although Ethiopia is a self-declared "democratic" developmental state, the country is facing sharp criticisms on its commitment to real democratic governance.

4.4. Grey Areas in the Ethiopian "Democratic Developmental State"

It is helpful to think of the developmental state as a state-led capital development process and a conscious effort at finding a short-cut to the advanced capitalist mode of development. In this sense, one notes that the developmental state model stands in stark contrast to the "Revolutionary Democratic State," which can be seen as a Marxsism-Leninism inspired doctrine in which the stopover in capitalism is temporary as the state is meant to steadily but inexorably head into a planned socialist economic system (Bekle & Regassa, 2012).

However, the Ethiopian approach toward development has been characterized by the doctrinal confusion of the democratic developmental state and revolutionary democracy. Though the country is a self-declared democratic developmental state, the ruling coalition uses the two doctrines interchangeably as if they are one and the same. Hence, there has to be a clear position on what the democratic developmental state is and what it is not, so as to shed light on the gray area.

The other gray area in the Ethiopian developmental state model is the quest for ideological hegemony and strategic policy-making, which contrasts with constitutionally recognized multiparty electoral democracy. Developmental states generally believe that they will attain state legitimacy through delivery of services to citizens (Edigheji, [2005]; Musamba [2010]), rather than through the ballot. As it has been mentioned above, most successful developmental states are found to enjoy support because they are associated with promoting rapid economic growth and providing economic benefits to both the ruling elites and the general public. Article 56 of the Federal Democratic Republic of Ethiopia constitution stated that legitimacy is achieved through the ballot (FDRE, 1995). However, the main shortcoming is that Ethiopian society, arguably, has not reached an equilibrium stage where the feedback mechanism between voting patterns and service delivery reinforce each other. Additionally the scheme on how to reconciling the constitutionally granted multi party democracy and that of hegemonic performance legitimacy sentiment in developmetal state model is not clear. That's why critiques often accuse the regime for having room only to weak, fragile and puppet political oppositions.

5. Governance in a Developmental State

By governance we mean the manner in which power is exercised by governments in the management of a country's social and economic resources. "Good" governance is the exercise of power by various levels of government in an effective, honest, equitable, transparent, and accountable manner (Smith, 2007; WB, 2003).

Good governance has eight major characteristics (UN, 2007; UNESCAP, n.d). It is participatory, consensus-oriented, accountable, transparent, responsive, effective and efficient, equitable and inclusive, and follows the rule of law. It assures that corruption is minimized, the views of minorities are taken into account, and that the voices of the most vulnerable in society are heard in decision-making. It is also responsive to the present and future needs of society.

Diagram 1: Characteristics of Good governance (UN, 2007; UNESCAP, n.d)

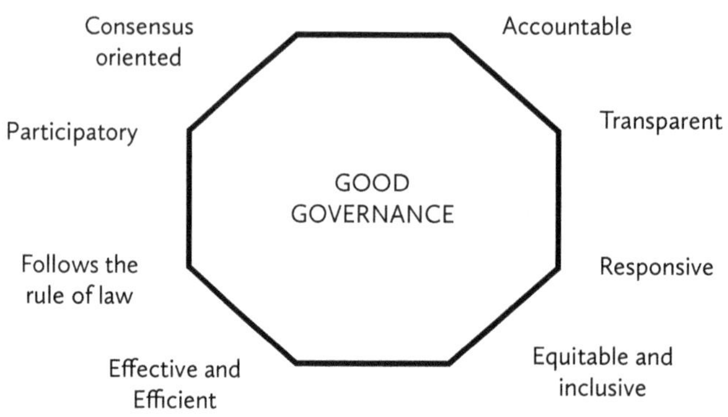

5.1. The Ethiopian Governance Status

The government claims that Ethiopia is an emerging democracy departing from its authoritarian past. There are appreciable formal attempts at capacity-building as the basis of installing the culture of democratic governance. There is also evidence that there are considerable improvements in some indicators of democratic governance. Nevertheless, the reality on the ground, on some key indicators of democratic governance, remains utterly opposed to the formal rhetoric in official documents. The reality of Ethiopia's democratic status, based on some key indicators of democratic governance, is highlighted in the subsequent paragraphs.

Based on the Ibrahim Index of African Governance (IIAG), which measures the quality of governance in African countries on an annual basis by compiling data from diverse global sources, Ethiopia demonstrates notable progress at the overall governance level. Since 2011, as one of the top ten improvers on the continent, Ethiopia has shown steady improvement in overall governance. In 2015, Ethiopia ranked thirty-first in Africa and sixth out of the thirteen countries in its geographical region (IIAG, 2015). The same index indicated that the country has registered a considerable improvement of performance in safety and rule of law and in human development in particular.

Despite the surge in the overall governance status of Ethiopia, the index score of 48.6 (out of 100) is lower than the African average (50.1). Moreover, the progress is not comprehensive, with the country showing weakening performance in some subcategories and indicators (IIAG, 2015). The performance in some specific governance indicators was also reported as deteriorating. For example, the lowest indicator under the safety and rule of law subcategory was seen in accountability, with a score of 43.8. Similarly the county has performed poorly and slipped in score in human rights and participation. Particularly, the indicator "Free & Fair Elections" has fallen by 11.1 points since 2011 (IIAG, 2015). Transparency International in its 2016 corruption perception index also ranked Ethiopia 108th out of 176 countries, indicating a high degree of corruption. As per the report, the country is overwhelmed with corruption, which permeates all sectors, with land as a particularly important sector of corruption (Transparency International, 2016).

5.2. Challenges of Democratic Governance in the Ethiopian Developmental State

The challenges of good governance in a developmental state are many and varied. Creating an inclusive responsive state with efficient and effective institutions and accountable and transparent government that is based on rule of law while making the government the leader of the economy is not something one can do easily. Accordingly, the summary of the most critical challenges of building good governance in the Ethiopian developmental state are as follows:

a) Harmonizing the ethno-linguistic based federal system and the quest of nations, nationalities, and peoples with the need to install a shared vision and national consensus;
b) Overcoming the historical legacy of feudalism, authoritarianism, and inequality;
c) Forming a capable state with an efficient bureaucracy, meritocratic public service system, and overcoming turnover and poor skill levels (Mebratu, 2015);
d) Dismantling and fighting corruption and rent-seeking behavior, which is deep-rooted in the current system;
e) The prevailing hostile relationship between the government and media, political opposition, and civil societies is an area of concern that impedes democratic governance in Ethiopia. Several reports (for example, APRM Ethiopian Report, 2011; Kelsall, 2013), have noted that journalists and publishers are being harassed and prosecuted for alleged violations of press and counterterrorism legislations (the Mass Media and Freedom of Information Proclamation of 2008, and the Anti-Terrorist Proclamation of 2009). There is also an apparent challenge with regard to civil society organizations. Civil society organizations have been pressed firmly in line with the government's policy through the 2009 Charities and Societies Proclamations, which restrain the scope of their activities and funding. The same holds true for the opposition parties. As of today (UNECA, 2012 cited in Jaleta, 2015), the ruling coalition does not seem to have a genuine belief that opposition parties can play positive roles in building democratic governance and national consensus. Hence, living under a constitutional democracy with the duty of protecting and enforcing human rights by harmonizing the relationship between collective and individual, and civil/political and economic/socio-cultural rights is a trillion-dollar assignment given the aforementioned track records.
f) Confronting the external elements that constrain the freedom of the developmental state to achieve its objectives (Zenawi, 2006).These challenges need to be met as we seek to build a democratic developmental state in Ethiopia. They remain as challenges in spite of the fact that, owing to the collapse of the "Washington Consensus" and the emergence of new global players, their toll might not be as large as it once was (Bekele & Regassa, 2012).
g) The challenges of democratically mobilizing people and resources for the developmentalist project and winning popular trust. As this sort of

mobilization towards the realization of vision set has to be carried out voluntarily in democratic state, it puts heavy burden on the government to strike the delicate balance.

Moreover, institutional capacity building of the public sector should be stressed here. Currently public institutions are strongly influenced by the ruling elite. From the point of view of equal representation, the higher positions in many governmental departments are assigned according to an ethnic-based quota system. Willingly or unwillingly, the bureaucrats are expected to operate in conformance with their ethnic affiliation rather than in pursuit of the goals of their organization. Because of this, instead of transparency, the desire to fulfill the wishes of the political agenda introduces the temptation for corruption that has become endemic in the functioning of the Ethiopian bureaucracy (Asayehegn, 2012). Therefore, if the Ethiopian government desires to use the state as a very important medium to tackle the chronic developmental problems (beyond empty promises and short-term political advantages to sustain power), it needs to improve the capability of its public administration sector and keep the permanent executive/the bureaucracy politically neutral.

5.3. Prospects of Democratic Governance in Ethiopia

The sharp focus of the Ethiopian government on economic development and the clarity of goals (eradication of poverty and becoming a middle-income country by 2025) manifest the ideological orientation of the government toward developmentalsim. In this regard, the government has been working on important plans that have brought significant economic growth and poverty reduction in the country. These plans are the Sustainable Development and Poverty Reduction Program (SDPRP), followed by the Plan for Accelerated and Sustainable Development to End Poverty (PASDEP) (from 2005–2010), the Growth and Transformation Plan One (from 2011 to 2015) (MoFDD, 2010), and the current Growth and Transformation Plan Two. Despite the weak capacity of institutions (the capacity of the executive, availability and strength of the central planning, the quality of public enterprises to control the commanding heights, availability of national consensus and shared vision, etc. are all elements to be further explored), there has been an encouraging success story. For instance, poverty in Ethiopia is reducing at one of the fastest rates in the world. The percentage of the population living below the poverty line declined from 44 percent in 2000 to 29 percent in 2010 and to 23.5 percent in 2016 (UNDP, 2017).

The government has also set its vision on building a democratic state, a system of good governance and social justice based on the blessing and full participation of citizens. This commitment is clearly expressed in the country's higher-level policies and national strategic plans. For instance, the vision of the GTP is "to become a country where democratic rule, good governance and social justice reign, upon the involvement and free will of its peoples…." (MoFED, 2010). Likewise in the same document, the economic vision is expressed as building an economy exhibiting sustainable economic development and securing social justice and increasing per capita income of the citizens.

Besides ideological orientation and national polices and strategies, the constitution (the supreme low of the land) itself can be seen as prospectively important for building good governance. To directly quote the preamble of FDRE constitution:

> *"We, the Nations, Nationalities and Peoples of Ethiopia: Strongly committed, in full and free exercise of our right to self-determination, to building a political community founded on the rule of law and capable of ensuring a lasting peace, guaranteeing a democratic order, and advancing our economic and social development; Firmly convinced that the fulfillment of this objective requires full respect of individual and people's fundamental freedoms and rights, to live together on the basis of equality and without any sexual, religious or cultural discrimination;…."* (FDRE constitution, Preamble)

The explicit recognition of the whole range of human rights set in international human rights conventions in what constitutes one-third of the corpus of the constitution shows the country's commitment, at least in principle, to democratic values and the principles of good governance.

The investment and remarkable development in economic infrastructure is promising. Thousands of kilometers of roads have been built to connect all sates and districts (*Woredas*) of the country. The Ethio-Djibouti rail is also operational while other networks are in the pipeline. There is an astonishing boost in mobile phone subscribers. Despite the restrictive government, there is also growing private media. As the economy is booming, the expansion of higher education and production of a university-trained work force in the country holds great promise and returns. All this will significantly increase the flow information (Jaleta, 2015), commodities, human capital, and the like, thus helping create a more enlightened citizenry. Having enlightened citizens is, in turn, an important tool to build democratic governance.

6. Conclusion

In this desk review, an attempt has been made to explore the status, the challenges, and the prospects of democratic governance in a developmental state by reflecting on the case of Ethiopia. It is far beyond the scope of this chapter to pretend to solve the puzzle that has preoccupied the subject of the relationship between the developmental state and democratic governance. The review also may lack comprehensiveness due to an inadequate literature review in the area. These are the limitations of the chapter. However, contributes to shedding light on the debate and hopes to stimulate further inquiries concerning the quest for democratic governance in the context of the developmental state.

Nowadays, it is common to witness a never-ending debate on democratic governance vs. development, which lucks a practical relevance. It seems a "false choice" and a sequencing fallacy form logical point view too. Hence, the author claims that future scholarship in the area should focus on practical harmony of the two than impossibility and incompatibility theorem. The chapter has also noted that Ethiopia has declared itself to be a developmental state. However, when we compare the characteristics of successful developmental states with the reality in Ethiopia, much remains to be done, especially in the areas of the autonomy and implementation capacity of the bureaucracy, and the incongruity between a shared vision (national consensus) and the quest for nations, nationalities, and people's self-determination. The hostile relationship between the government and media, political opposition, and civil societies is also a bottleneck. Furthermore, despite the overall improvement of governance indicators in Ethiopia, the index score is still lower than the African average. Therefore, one is tempted to conclude that there exists a considerable gap between form and reality concerning the key governance indicators in the Ethiopian "democratic developmental state."

The achievements Ethiopia has made in the ten years since shift toward the developmental state model are undisputed. Particularly, the improvement in human development index, infrastructural development, and expansion of higher education are promising. In addition, the explicit ideological orientation, policy, and strategic commitments and constitutional guardianship of good governance suggest it may be possible to install democratic governance without compromising development. Dealing with such a state demands appropriate innovation and a pragmatic approach in order to deepen the democratic governance agenda in the context of the developmental state.

Acknowledgements

I am indebted to the editors and the anonymous reviewers who provided critical comments and constructive suggestions that helped me in improving the chapter. I also thank the editors.

Notes

1. This paper was prepared for discussion at the national public administration conference "Administrative Resilience for Sustainable Development in Ethiopia," held from September 21 to 22, 2018 in Addis Ababa. It doesn't reference recent political developments and changes made by the current reformist government.

References

Amsden, A. (1989). *Asia's Next Giant: South Korea and Late Industrialization*. Oxford: Oxford University Press.

Asayehgn, D. (2012). The Effects of Rent-seeking in Dissipating Developmental Efforts: The Ethiopian Experience. *International Journal of Business and Management Tomorrow*, 2(1), 1-4.

Bekele, S. & Regassa, T. (2012). *Democratization in a Developmental State: The Case of Ethiopia Issues, Challenges, and Prospects*, development brief No 1.

Caldentey, E. P. (2008). The Concept and Evolution of the Developmental State. *International Journal of Political Economy*, 37(3), 27-53.

Clapham, C. (2013). Federalism and the Developmental State: Perspectives in Diversity in Ethiopia. Paper presented at Addis Ababa University, on September 23.

ECA and AUC. (2011). *Economic Report on Africa 2011: Governing Developments in Africa–The Role of the State in Economic Transformation*. Addis Ababa, Ethiopia: Economic Commission for Africa Publishing.

Edigheji, O. (2005). A Democratic Developmental State in Africa? A Concept Paper. Research Report No. 105, Centre for Policy Studies, Johannesburg. In Edigheji, O.(ed.) 2010, *Constructing a Democratic Developmental State in South Africa: Potential and Challenges*, pp. 1–36.

Edigheji, O. (2010). *Constructing a Democratic Developmental State in South Africa*. Cape Town: HSRC Press.

Evans, P. (1995). *Embedded Autonomy: States and Industrial Transformation*. Princeton: Princeton University Press.

Evans, P. (2011, October 13). *The capability enhancing developmental state: Concepts and national trajectories [Paper Presentation]*. The UNRISD-KOICA conference, Seoul, Korea.

FDRE. (1995). *Federal Negarit Gazeta of the Federal Democratic Republic of Ethiopia.* Addis Ababa, Ethiopia.

Federal Democratic Republic of Ethiopia [FDRE]. (2009). Higher Education Proclamation No. 650/2009. *Federal Negarit Gazeta* 15(64), 4976-5044.

Fritz, V., and Menocal, R. (2006). *(Re) building Developmental States: From Theory to Practice.* Working Paper 274, September 2006. Overseas Development Institute, London: UK

Gebremichael, A. (2013). Democratic State versus Developmental State: Unraveling a False Dichotomy to Promote an Adaptive Democratic Developmental State. Retrieved on May 24, 2016, from http://aigaforum.com/articles/ADDS Dynamics 013.pdf.

Hollander, B (2011). *Booms, bubbles and busts- the economic cycle.* Harlow, United Kingdom: Pearson Education Limited

IIAG, Country Insights. (2015). Ibrahim Index of African Governance: Ethiopia. www.moibrahimfoundation.org/iiag/downloads/. Retrieved on March 8, 2017.

Jalata, G. G. (2015, July 20-22). *An African Developmental State: Ethiopia's Emergent Experience* [paper presentation]. Building democratic developmental states for economic transformation in southern Africa, regional conference, Pretoria, South Africa.

Johnson, C. (1982). *MITI and the Japanese Miracle.* Stanford, CA: Stanford University Press.

Kelsall, T. (2013). *Business, Politics, and the State in Africa: Challenging the Orthodoxies on Growth and Transformation.* London: Zed Books.

Leftwich, A. (2010). Beyond Institutions: Rethinking the Role of Leaders, Elites and Coalitions in the Industrial Formation of Developmental States and Strategies. *Forum for Development Studies,* 37(1),93-111.

Mbabazi, P. and Taylor, I. (2005). Botswana and Uganda as Developmental States (?). In P. Mbabazi & Taylor, I. (eds), *The Potentiality of "Developmental States" in Africa: Botswana and Uganda Compared* (pp. 65-81). Dakar: CODESRIA.

McKinsey and Company (2010). *Lions on the Move: The Progress and Potential of African Economies.* McKinsey Global Institute.

Mebratu, D.K (2015, September 21). *Ending hiding behind development: Challenges of civil service political neutrality* [Paper presentation]. Governance for sustainable development in Ethiopia, the first national public administration conference, CCRDA, Addis Ababa, Ethiopia.

Meyns, P. and Musamba, C. (2010). *The Developmental State in Africa: Problems and Prospects.* Institute for Development and Peace (INEF Report No 101). University of Duisburg-Essen.

Mkandawire, T. (2001). Thinking about developmental states in Africa. *Cambridge Journal of Economics, 25* (3), 289-314.

MoFED (2010). Federal Democratic Republic of Ethiopia, Growth and Transformation Plan 2010/11 – 2014/15. Addis Ababa. http://mofed.gov.et/English/Resources/Documents/GTP 2.pdf, Retrieved on September 13, 2017.

Musamba, C. (2010). The developmental state concept and its relevance for Africa. In P. Meyns and C. Musamba (eds), *The developmental state in Africa: Problems and prospects* (pp. 5-42). Institute for Development and Peace. University of Duisburg.

Negash, M. (2012). The Post-Meles Ethiopian Developmental State: The Challenges Ahead. Available at http://danielberhane.com/2012/12/08/the-post-meles-ethiopiandevlo, retrieved on August 2, 2018.

Onis, Z. (1991). The Logic of the Developmental State. *Comparative Politics*,24(1), 109-126.

Pempel, T. (1999). The Developmental Regime in a Changing World Economy. In Cumings, M. W. (ed.), *The Developmental State*. Ithaca: Cornell University Press, pp. 137-181.

Routley, L. (2012). *Developmental States: A Review of the Literature*. ESID Working Paper No. 03.

Transparency International. (2001). Global Corruption report. Berlin: Transparency International.

UNDP. (2017). *Human Development Report: The Real Wealth of Nations, Pathways to Human Development*. New York: UNDP.

UNESCAP (United Nations Economic and Social Commission for Asia and the Pacific. (n.d). What is good governance? Retrieved from https://www.unescap.org Retrieved June 14, 2018.

United Nations (2007). *Public Governance Indicators: A Literature Review*. https://publicadministration.un.org/. Retrieved June 14, 2018.

Wade, R. (1990). *Governing the Market: Economic Theory and the Role of Government in East Asian Industrialization*. Princeton: Princeton University Press.

Wade, R. (2010). *After the Crisis: Industrial Policy and Developmental State*. London School of Economics.

Waldner, D. (1999). *State Building and Late Development*. Ithaca: Cornell University Press.

Wong, J.(2004). The Adaptive Developmental State in East Asia. *Journal of East Asian Studies*, 4(3), 345-362.

World Bank. (1992).*Good Governance and Development*. Washington, DC. www.documentsworldbank.org.1992/04. Retrieved on May 8, 2017.

World Bank. (2003). The World Bank Annual Report 2003: Volume 1. Year in Review. Washington, DC. https://openknowledge.worldbank.org/handle/10986/13929. Retrieved September 4, 2018.

World Bank. (2013). *Ethiopia Public Sector Reform Approach Building the Developmental State – A Review and Assessment of the Ethiopian Approach to Public Sector Reform*. Report no. ACS3695.

Zenawi, M. (2006). African Development: Dead Ends and New Beginnings, (unpublished preliminary draft). http://cgt.columbia.edu/files/conferencespdf Retrieved September 4, 2018

Zenawi, M. (2011). States and markets: Neoliberal limitations and the case for a developmental state. In A. Noman, K. Botchwey, H. Stein, and J. E. Stiglitz (eds), *Good growth and governance in Africa: Rethinking development strategies* (pp. 140–174). Oxford University Press.

Zewde, B. (1990). The concept of Japanization in the intellectual history of modern Ethiopia. *Proceeding of the fifth seminar of the department of History*. Addis Ababa University.

Zewde, B. (2002). *Pioneers of change in Ethiopia: The reformist intellectuals of the early twentieth century:* Addis Ababa: Addis Ababa University Press.

4
Assessment of Parliamentary Oversight Tools and Mechanisms Used by the Ethiopian House of Peoples' Representatives (HoPRs)

Aklilu Wubet Lema, Challa Amdissa Jiru,
Defferew Kebebe Tessema, and Frehiwot Gebrehiwot Araya

Box 1: Key points of this chapter

Major points drawn from the chapter include:

- ✓ The federal House of People's Representatives (HoPRs) of Ethiopia uses various tools and mechanisms to control the work of executive;
- ✓ HPRs mostly relies on the evaluation of performance reports and committee hearings to conduct oversight and control the work of the executive;
- ✓ Field visits, especially sudden visits, are the most effective oversight tool to oversee the work of the executive but is rarely used due to budget shortage, capacity limitation, logistics-related issues, and other problems;
- ✓ Gaps were observed in the overall effectiveness of the oversight function of the HoPR,
- ✓ There are constraints that need to be addressed to enhance and effectively undertake the oversight functions of HPRs of Ethiopia.

Box 2: Key insights of this chapter

After reading this chapter, you will be able to understand:

- ✓ Important oversight tools and mechanisms used by the Ethiopian HoPRs;
- ✓ Whether HoPRs is effective in using those oversight tools;
- ✓ The overall effectiveness of the house in achieving oversight goals.
- ✓ Challenges faced by the HPRs in undertaking its oversight functions.

Box 3: Abbreviations

EPRDF = Ethiopian People's Revolutionary Democratic Front
FDRE = Federal Democratic Republic of Ethiopia
FGD = Focus Group Discussion
HF = House of Federation
HoPR = House of People's Representatives
IFES = International Foundation for Electoral System
IPU = Inter-Parliamentary Union
KII = Key Informant Interview
MP = Member of Parliament
NDI = National Democratic Institute

1. Introduction

Parliament is the institution that represents the people's voice in government. The functions that parliaments undertake, notably law-making, oversight, and representation, are fundamental to the legitimacy of the government and the upholding of democracy. A country in a transitional stage to democracy, in particular, needs a long-term commitment to build a culture of democracy (IPU, 2015) and there can be no democratic system of government without transparency and accountability. The primary responsibility in democratizing the system directly falls on the shoulders of Parliament. Through its core oversight function, Parliament holds the government to account on behalf of the people, ensuring that government policy and action are both efficient and commensurate with the needs of the public. Parliamentary oversight is also crucial in checking any excesses of the government (Yamamoto, 2007).

However, though the Parliament remains a symbol of hope and a voice of the people, many parliaments continue to face various challenges, in the past as well as in more recent times. According to the Inter-Parliamentary Union (2015), one of the challenges is the low level of and even decrease in public confidence in parliamentary authority. Similarly, the unequal power relationship between the executive and legislative branches of government is a widely acknowledged challenge to the parliamentary oversight function. In countries having parliamentary systems of government, in particular, the executive can exercise control over the members of its political party (i.e., the majority party in Parliament), with rewards for faithful support and sanctions for dissent. In the most extreme cases, the Parliament can be reduced as a "rubber-stamp" of popular approval for the executive branches proposals. Even in long-established democracies, many questions have been raised about whether the balance of power has swung too far in favor of the executive. A similar criticism stems from the fact that the executive can in fact influence the agenda setting in the legislature (IPU, 2015).

Based on the experience of Ghana, Gyampo (2015) for instance underscores that the imbalance of power created between the executive and the legislative arms of government undermines the authority of the Parliament as an oversight body. The Parliament, inter alia, makes itself subservient the executive, thereby sacrificing parliamentary oversight responsibility as well as objectivity during legislative debates. In a large majority of countries, parliaments have the constitutional right to initiate legislation, yet most laws originate with/in the executive. Parliament's law-making role tends to focus on the scrutiny of executive proposals, which results in limited opportunities for individual parliamentarians to craft legislation.

Parliament's power to hold government to account lies at the heart of executive-legislative relations. And yet in practice, the members of a party in a government have strong incentives not to challenge that government, such that the oversight function is typically left to opposition parties. However, in most developing countries, opposition parties are either very weak or non-existence, limiting their ability to challenge the government. For instance, in Ethiopia, the opposition parties were prevented from securing seats in parliament in two election periods (2005 and 2010). Furthermore, the human and financial resources available to the executive and its access to information put the executive in a dominant position in relation to the legislative body.

In many countries, the capacity of parliamentary administration to provide effective support for the work of Parliament, such as nonpartisan research in the interests of informed decision-making as well as the ability of the parliaments to keep up with changes in society, is limited. Unless otherwise constrained, the Parliament is ready to work with important institutions like universities and other independent researchers, to help the legislative body acquire the necessary capacity to make informed decisions. The Ethiopian Parliament is by no way an exception.

According to the Constitution of the Federal Democratic Republic of Ethiopia (FDRE), the parliament has two houses, namely, the House of Peoples' Representatives (HoPRs) and the House of Federation (FDRE Constitution, 1995). The power to legislate and to oversee the workings of the executive body is vested in the HoPRs. Major constitutional responsibilities and functions of the HoPR include law making, representation, oversight, diplomatic work, and others. However, as far as Ethiopia is concerned, no adequate research has been conducted to assess the effectiveness of the oversight function and oversight tools used by the HoPRs.

In view of this gap, this study therefore, by and large aims to assess the oversight tools and mechanisms used by the HoPRs and its effectiveness in using those tools as well as challenges faced by the HoPR in overseeing the work of executive.

2. Overview of Parliamentary Oversight

2.1. Introduction

In John Locke's model of the separation of powers, the legislative and executive powers of a government are to be separated. The legislature is to prescribe rules and the executive has the power of execution and is subordinate and accountable to the legislature. As the body that represents the people, the Parliament is called upon to see to it that the administration of public policy reflects and meets the people's needs. Parliament is also called upon to ensure that agreed policy is properly implemented and delivered to target citizens.

As the IFES's Model State of Parliament Report (2005) discussed, the five internationally recognized broad and basic functions of the Parliament are policy making, oversight of the executive, constituency representation, and political recruitment. Yet, representation, law making and oversight roles are the most important and common functions of the parliaments of various countries.

Parliamentary oversight, the theme of this research, has been defined in different ways by different authors. One defines parliamentary oversight as the legislature's review and evaluation of selected activities of the executive branch of government. In other words, oversight is about keeping an eye on the activities of the executive and holding the executive to account on behalf of the country's citizens. The legislative branch conducts oversight activities because it is not only enacting new programs for the state but also has a duty to ensure that existing programs are implemented and administered efficiently, effectively, and in a manner consistent with legislative intent (Ahmed, 2011 and Yamamoto, 2007).

Furthermore, in a parliamentary system, parliamentary oversight can be said to be a tool and means of holding the executive arm of government accountable for its actions and also for ensuring that it does implement policies in an effective and efficient manner. Parliamentary oversight is "the review, monitoring and supervision of government and public agencies, including the implementation of policy and legislation" (Yamamoto, 2007). This definition focuses on the purpose and nature of the oversight activities rather than on the procedural stages in which they take place. It covers the work of parliamentary committees and plenary sessions, as well as hearings during the parliamentary stage of bills and the budgetary cycle.

The oversight function entails accountability relations between the two government bodies. By its nature, oversight and accountability functions involve three essential obligations as discussed by the Global Parliamentary report (2017). Those obligations are the obligations of the executive to provide information on their activities and decisions; the obligation of the Parliament to scrutinize the information and provide constructive and appropriate recommendation as well as the obligation of those accountable to respond to the feedback from the Parliament. The relationship and the obligation determine the effectiveness of the oversight and scrutiny functions of the Parliament.

2.2. Key Roles of Effective Parliamentary Oversight

The concept of oversight comprises many aspects, including political, administrative, financial, ethical, legal, and strategic elements. It is important to define effectiveness in relation to the oversight function. Webb and Roberts (2014) argue that effectiveness in parliamentary oversight can be approached from the goal-based model of institutional effectiveness. For them, effectiveness is all about how an institution responds to the demands and expectations of the public and the executive. In addition, effectiveness also requires legitimacy as it is stipulated in the constitution. In most cases, parliaments suffer from a lack of legitimacy and understanding of their actual purpose and power. Thus, effectiveness in parliamentary oversight can be conceived as how far the parliament exercises the legitimate power to respond to the needs of the constituencies, the public, and other stakeholders.

As indicated by Griffith (2005), the oversight function mandates Parliament to guard public interest against legislative invasion of individual rights, to serve as watchdogs over the executive, and to serve as the guardians of integrity. Yamamoto (2007) identified a couple of key functions or roles of effective parliamentary oversight. The most important function of oversight is to protect the rights of voters from abuse of arbitrary behavior, or illegal and unconstitutional conduct on the part of the government and public agencies.

That is, parliaments, as the representatives of the citizens, should uphold the rule of law and protect the right of citizens by the monitoring policies and activities of the executives. Oversight function also contributes to providing financial accountability and helps to hold the government to account in respect of how the taxpayers' money is used. It detects waste within the machinery of government and public agencies and therefore improves the efficiency, economy, and effectiveness of government operations (Global Parliamentary Report, 2017).

Equally, parliamentary oversight holds the executive branch accountable for its performance and the outcomes of implemented policies. The oversight role scrutinizes whether the policies and programs announced by the executives and authorized by the Parliament have been implemented and whether they are having the desired impact (Global Parliamentary Report, 2017). This function includes monitoring the achievement of goals set by legislation and the government's own program. Finally, parliaments ensure the transparency and openness of the executive's activities through oversight and scrutiny. Parliaments can use the oversight function to open a room for the public to debate, scrutinize, and deliver opinions on the policies and operation of the government. Such functions improve the transparency of government operations and enhance public trust in the government, which is itself a condition of effective policy delivery.

The purposes and objectives of oversight stress the significance of oversight in holding the executive to account for its actions or inactions. These facets among others stress the obligation of Parliament to uphold and defend the constitution. This is essential and underscores the significance of the existence of a democratic parliament. In performing its constitutional mandate, the relations between Parliament and the executive is fundamental as defined through the separation of powers (Malapane, 2016). The complexity of this relationship when it comes to oversight is discussed below.

2.3. Power Relationship between the Legislative and Executive in Parliamentary System and Its Influence on Oversight

Scholars of legislative studies state that over the years, the executive has endured criticism for Parliament's inability to effectively hold the executive accountable, yet also recognize the weaknesses of Parliament (Malapane, 2016). For instance, Rapoo (2004) asserts that inadequate resources and weak institutional capacity create the overdependence of the legislative branch on the executive. This takes place regardless of the clearly defined constitutional mandate of Parliament to conduct oversight over the executive. Khmelko and Beers (2011) acknowledge that effective oversight is required to maintain the balance of power between the executive and legislative branch. However, Malapane (2016) argues that the nature of the relations between the two branches influences effective oversight.

Friedberg (2011), states that in a parliamentary system, the government emerges from Parliament. Although Ahmed (2011) is of the opinion that there is a strong relation between the legislative and executive branch in the parliamentary form of government, this creates ambiguity with regard to the separation of powers as the members of the executive are also MPs. According to Hudson and Wren (2007), it is fair to point fingers at the nature of the political systems, which include among others electoral rules, constitution, and characteristics of political parties conducive to the dominance of the executive and marginalization of Parliament. MPs are elected representatives who represent the interests of the electorate and to a certain degree the mandate of their political parties. This places Parliament in a difficult situation, as Salih (2005) asserts that Parliament is faced with competing roles as it is part of the machinery that confers legitimacy on the executive and yet is constitutionally mandated to hold the executive to account for its actions to safeguard the public interests.

Party discipline is another factor that contributes to the tension between executive-legislative relationships and effective oversight. According to Mickler (2013), partisan theory supports the role of political parties in Parliament that influence oversight. Political parties per this theory are the key actors, which makes member of the parliaments accountable to their own parties. Fredriksson and Wollscheid (2014) define party discipline as "the extent to which elected legislators keep their party's campaign promises after being elected."The ruling party utilizes the whip system to maintain strong discipline and unity among its MPs who are a majority in Parliament. Of course, instilling party discipline and unity in Parliament may not be an easy job, requiring a lot of compromise.

The aforementioned complications mean that effective oversight by the parliament is lacking in an environment where in the cost of conducting oversight outweighs the benefits, due to the nature of executive-legislative relationships and party discipline. Malapane (2016) for instance argues that MPs may know what is expected to them but are hindered by the fear of losing their seats in Parliament if they become more objective in their work. This implies that MPs may know the difference between right and wrong, yet they decide to do the latter as they are perpetually caught between serving the interests of the electorate and the mandate of their political parties. Johnson (2005) however argues that while the complex nature of the environment is recognized, this should not be the motive for neglecting oversight as "modern democracies are characterized by shared decision making between the legislative and executive branch of the state."

2.4. Tools and Mechanisms of Parliamentary Oversight

In overseeing the executive, parliaments have several different oversight tools at their disposal. The most common oversight tools are committee hearings, hearings in plenary sessions of the Parliament, the creation of commissions of inquiry, questions, question time, interpellations, the ombudsman, auditors general, and public account committees (NDI, 2000).

However, the oversight potential is greatly affected by the form of government and levels of democracy. Countries with parliamentary forms of government that are more democratic have a greater number of oversight tools and greater oversight potential (Pelizzo and Stapenhurst, 2004). The tools used by the Parliament to oversee executives in the parliamentary system of government are discussed below.

Questions

In the parliamentary system of government, members of the Cabinet are accountable collectively and individually to the Parliament for the exercise of their powers and the performance of their functions. The procedure of putting questions to the executive is one of the ways in which Parliament holds the executive to account (Yamamoto, 2007).Questions can be put for oral or written reply to the chief executive and the cabinet ministers on matters for which they are responsible. Question time affords members of Parliament the opportunity to question members of the executive on service delivery, policy, and other executive action on behalf of both their political parties and the electorate.

A parliamentary question is, by definition, a request for information and asking for clarifications. Regular questioning can be used by Parliament to hold the government to account. When there is a question from an MP, the government is obliged to provide an answer in the floor of the House (Pelizzo and Stapenhurst, 2004; and Yamamoto, 2007). Answers to questions can be available not only to the person who asks them but also to all parliamentarians in the chamber. This is in the case of oral questions that demand an oral reply. Parliamentary questions are among the most commonly used oversight tool. As identified by Yamamoto (2007), if a question is not answered, the parliament may incline to take some additional measure, such as interpellation.

Motions and Plenary Debates

Motions are a mechanism available to members of all political parties that can be used to help fulfill their oversight responsibilities in Parliament by bringing issues to debate on the floor of the House. Debates are oral exchange of opinions and views with the objective of facilitating collective decision on certain issues. Such oversight mechanism can be useful to make informed decision (Yamamoto, 2007). Both motion and debates open valuable opportunity to conduct detailed oversight and publicize the issue to the general public (Global Parliamentary Report, 2017).

Debates are about subjecting the government to public scrutiny, bringing matters into the public domain, and providing MPs and peers with opportunities to give voice to public opinion. The absence or curtailment of debate reduces parliament's ability to fulfill one of its major functions. However, since what is said in debate on the floor of the House rarely affects the result of the vote at its end or induces the government to reverse a decision already taken, it is apparent that debates are not strong instruments of control. At the same time, they are essential parts of the continuous parliamentary scrutiny of government and compelling it to explain and defend its policies.

The Committees as a Tool of Parliamentary Oversight

Parliamentary committees are the most significant and frequently used tool in the oversight function. The broad objective of committees as stated in the Global Parliamentary Report (2017) is as follows: "Parliamentary oversight in committee is to enhance the quality of government through evidence gathered in inquiries from which appropriate conclusions and recommendations are drawn and presented to parliament and beyond to the government and the wider public." Moreover, committees are identified as the most effective and powerful accountability mechanism (Griffith, 2005).

Parliamentary committees have various ways of conducting oversight, including departmental briefing session, annual and departmental budget analysis, calls for submission and petition from the public, the consideration of strategic plans and annual reports, and public hearings. In many parliaments, permanent committees oversee the programs of the corresponding government departments. Committees of inquiry can be established to examine the positive and negative aspects of particular policies and to pursue the responsibility of the officials in charge.

Though parliamentary committees are considered as the most effective tool of parliamentary oversight, their effectiveness depends on different factors (Griffith, 2005; and Pelizzo and Stapenhurst, 2004). Among such factors, the most important ones are: the legal authority to compel change, the committee's relations with the executive and its official as well as the programs and policies, resources, such as the staff of the committee, the role of the individual in the committee, the party system and the composition of the committee, and the structure, prestige, and leadership of the committee.

Legislative Oversight over Delegated Power

Delegated legislation is any law that can be made by ministers, administrative agencies, and other state authorities. Delegated legislation is necessary for a number of reasons: Parliament does not have time to contemplate and debate every small detail of complex regulations, as it only has a limited amount of time to pass legislation. Delegated legislation, however, allows thoroughly debated regulations to pass through as well as saving parliamentary time. But it is necessary to have control over delegated legislation.

Budget as an Oversight Tool

Budgetary oversight is a core function of department-related permanent committees, since most government programs entail a budget for their execution (Pelizzo and Stapenhurst, 2004). Budget scrutiny is also a significant source of parliamentary power (Global Parliamentary Report, 2017). Conversely, the budget law authorized by Parliament or documents annexed to this law show how much money is allocated to each of the policy goals to be achieved by one or more government programs. Budgetary oversight is therefore the key tool with which department-related committees assess government programs. While committee scrutiny is based on the budget law and the state accounts, the scope of inquiries can go further, into the question of the appropriateness of a policy itself.

Using Oversight Institutions

There are institutions directly accountable to the legislature, such as the Office of the Auditor General Human Right Commission, the Ombudsman, the Ethics and Anti-Corruption Commission (Pelizzo and Stapenhurst, 2004 and Yamamoto, 2007). These institutions are considered as arms of the legislature because they play a significant role in overseeing the executive's performance. Their reports are basic inputs of oversight activity of the legislature. In addition to this, information that comes from the general public and public offices is also taken as input in the oversight process.

3. Research Method Employed

The study used a mixed-method research approach to describe and explain oversight tools and their effectiveness. The principal method followed is qualitative, supplemented by the quantitative method.

In order to achieve the study's objectives, data were gathered from various sources. Both primary and secondary sources were collected, analyzed, and triangulated to answer the research questions. The primary data were collected through survey methods using a questionnaire, Key Informant Interview (KII), and Focus Group Discussions (FGD). The secondary data were collected from legal documents including the Constitution, a regulation oversight checklist, and standing committee reports.

Key Informant Interview (KII): In-depth qualitative information was generated from the standing committee chairpersons of the HoPRs, who serve as key informants using open-ended, semi-structured questions. The KIIs were administered in the informants' respective offices for their convenience. Although the research team planned to conduct key informant interview with all standing committee chairpersons (there were around twenty standing committee chairpersons at the time of data collection), only eleven KIIs were conducted due to the MPs busy schedule and lack of interest.

Focus Group Discussion (FGD) is a type of conversation conducted in an informal setting that aims at gathering data on topics of interest. A small group of people (five to ten) with specialist knowledge, interest, or who share a particular characteristic, is invited to discuss specific topics in detail. Similar to KIIs, the research team had a plan to conduct several FGDs; however, the research team was able to organize and conduct only one FGD with purposely selected parliamentarians and staff of the secretariat. Despite this limitation, the team managed to generate adequate information from the discussion.

A Questionnaire was randomly distributed to 15 percent of the total number of the federal HoPRs, of which fifty-one (62 percent) questionnaires were properly filled in and returned. Since all respondents included in the survey were member of the parliament who are well-acquainted with the issues under discussion, the research team believes that the questionnaire generated representative information.

Both quantitative and qualitative methods of analysis were employed. Quantitative data were presented and analyzed using descriptive statistics managed with the support of statistical packages for social science (SPSS), while qualitative analysis was used to present the observation and understandings of the researchers on the different qualitative aspects of oversight through the use of text and narrative techniques.

Before using primary or secondary data for analysis, the research team conducted data quality assessment with respect to the trustworthiness of the instruments employed (both for qualitative and quantitative components).

4. Findings and Discussions

4.1. Introduction

This section is concerned with the analysis of data collected through document analysis, a questionnaire survey, KIIs with representatives of Parliamentary standing committees, a FGD with both parliamentarians and member of the secretariat of the HoPR, and document reviews. The data obtained through the KIIs and FGD were triangulated with data obtained from the questionnaire and desk reviews. The responses of each key informant were related to her/his experience in the committee that he/she is representing. At the time of data collection, the House of Peoples' Representative had about twenty standing committees organized to oversee a certain number of clustered executive bodies.

4.2. Legal Provisions Expressing Powers and Functions of HoPRs on Oversight in Ethiopia

The FDRE's constitution confers the HoPRs with the powers and responsibilities to effectively undertake the function of oversight on the executive branch of government. According to article 55(17) of the constitution, the House is vested with the power to approve the appointment of higher state officials, including the chief executive and vice chief executive, the president and vice president of the federal supreme court, and the auditor and vice-auditor general of the federal government. It has also the power to approve the appointments of the member of the executive council. The same article also states that the House shall also call the PM and order him to give oral answers to the question of the House. Put otherwise, as per the FDRE Constitution, the HoPRs has the power to call and question the prime minister and other federal officials and to investigate the executive's conduct as to whether they are discharging their responsibilities in accordance to the parameters and the limit the law has conferred on them. Article 76 also confirms that the Council of Ministers is responsible to the HoPR in all its decisions.

These provisions reveal that the HoPRs has the constitutional power to oversee and hold the government accountable and answerable for the consequence of their action. This means the Parliament has the responsibility to make sure that the government institutions (especially the executive of government) exercise their power in accordance with the limit of the constitution and execute the legislature's bill, programs, and proposals.

The HoPRs has also issued Supervision and Follow-up Procedures, including Regulation No.3/2006 and proclamation No.470/2005 to oversee the work of the executive. Proclamation No.470/2005 and Regulation No.3/2006 have provided for the establishment of different standing and ad hoc committees in the HoPRs that play a great role in assisting the parliament to conduct its oversight function.

According to article 19(2) of Regulation No.3/2006, these different standing committees of the HoPRs are vested with the power to engage in active supervision of the executive institutions, which are under their supervision. As such, the performances of the various organs of administrative agencies are subject to oversight by the House through these committees. In addition, executive offices are to be overseen as to the proper implementation of laws, policies, strategies, and programs, which are enacted mainly by the HoPRs. Standing committees are also endowed with the power to examine thoroughly the budget proposal of different organs of government. The HoPRs retains the power to ensure the effective implementation of the approved budget by the executive agencies, thereby preventing the public resource from possible abuse. As per article 153(3) of the same regulation, the House requires every government agency to submit regular reports to it or before the committee concerned at least once in a year. The committees must also summon a public debate on the report after their hearing. To this end, the committees invite pertinent social bodies and the mass media to attend the discussion.

Regulation No. 3/2006, under article 93, provides the House with the power to take a motion of no confidence on the executive and take measures it deems necessary in this situation. As a result, any member of parliament may move a motion of no confidence in the Council of Ministers.

What we infer from aforementioned discussions is that every federal government institution cannot escape from the scrutiny of the legislature. They are subject to questioning, investigations, and corrective measures as deemed necessary. Besides legal provisions, the actual oversight tools employed by the HoPRs and how effectively these tools are used are discussed in the subsequent section.

4.3. Oversight Tools Used by the HoPRs

The data obtained through the KIIs and FGD show that the HoPRs uses several tools and methods of oversight to scrutinize the work of the executive. The oversight tools being used by the HoPRs are described below.

Evaluation of the Annual plan of the Executive

One of the oversight tools of the House is monitoring and evaluating the annual plans of the executive bodies by the assigned standing committee of the House. The government executive bodies are required to submit their annual plans to the committee, which will check the consistency of the annual executive plan with the relevant policies of government, with the second Growth and Transformation Plan (known as GTP II) of Ethiopia, with missions given to the organization, and the strategic goals of the organization itself. The standing committees of the House have a checklist for conducting the monitoring of the annual plan. Following the evaluation of the annual plans, feedback is given both orally and in writing.

Committee Hearings

If the annual plan of an executive body deviates significantly from the expectation of the parliamentary committee, the officials of the concerned body are required to explain the plan in person. At the committee hearing, the plan is presented to the committee by an official from the executive body. Discussions are conducted on the presentation, led by the supervising committee and the implementing body to reach a consensus. Then, the feedback given is properly documented and the incorporation of feedback in the revised annual plans is strictly followed. Committee hearing is among the oversight tools widely used by the HoPRs in controlling the executive.

Evaluation of Performance Report

The Parliament uses performance reports as one of the means of exercising oversight on the activities of the executive. Following the agreement in the annual plan, the executive has the duty to present performance reports quarterly. The standing committees use the quarterly reports to undertake their oversight functions on the performance of the executives they are supervising. Standing committees use performance evaluation checklists and the annual plan as yardsticks for evaluating the performance. Reports are presented both in softcopy and hard copy to ease the sharing of materials. Just as the annual plan is discussed in person between the standing committee and the executive in hearing sessions, discussion is also held on the quarterly report to reach an agreement between the executive and the standing committee. After the evaluation of the report and discussions are held, feedback and directions may be provided by the Parliamentary standing committee to the executive. Information collected from our respondents reveals that performance reports are among the most widely used tools by Parliament even though their importance and accuracy is not reliable, according to these respondents.

Plenary Debates

In addition to the responsibility of submitting quarterly reports to the parliamentary committee, the executives has the duty of presenting annual and semi-annual performance report to the Parliament. After the report is heard, discussions and debates are conducted in the House. Data indicates that these debates and discussions are very important mechanisms of oversight, but are rarely used by the Parliament level. The informants also said that the supervising committee plays a special role in the evaluation of the reports presented to the parliamentary session, because this committee has detailed information about the organization presenting the report.

Questioning Time

The House uses questioning time as a means of parliamentary oversight over the executive. On these occasions, the prime minister/minister is required to come in person to the House to explain issues that may arise in the parliamentary session. But questioning time is not conducted regularly and frequently by the HoPRs.

Field Visit

The field visit is another parliamentary oversight tool that is used by the HoPRs. Each standing committee conducts regular field visit twice a year; sometimes it also organizes sudden visits, when a complaint from the public creates the need for the latter. Evidence indicates that the field visit is the most important and productive oversight tool, because it is used to make actual observation and also to crosscheck reports presented by the executive. Moreover, it provides the opportunity to meet service users, to observe the job process and irregularities that may not be reported. During field visits, the standing committee arranges discussions with service users, with employees, and with managers separately. Evidence also shows that sudden the field visit is more effective when compared with the regular field visit in controlling the actual performance of the executive.

Despite it's the importance, there is limitation in using the field visit exhaustively, due to budget shortage, capacity limitation, logistics-related issues, and other problems. Instead of field visits, most standing committees are forced to depend on reports to evaluate the work of the executive. In addition, in most cases, the time given and the actual work accomplished through field visits do not match. In the two regular field visits, some committees (for example, the education affairs committee) cannot cover all the organizations they are supervising. As a result, the committee plans to visit each of organization assigned to it at least once in a five-year parliamentary term. Even this plan does not seem to have materialized, as field visits have been disrupted because of security problems. Another problem reported was lack of guidelines for oversight of bodies with different characteristics. Researchers also observed that the field visit is an effective tool of oversight, but not effectively utilized by the HoPRs, because of the mismatch between the job and time schedule and budgetary constraints.

Budgetary Oversight

Standing committees are also endowed with the power to examine thoroughly the budget proposal of the executive. In all process of oversight, the standing committees take into consideration the budget being consumed in comparison with actual performance. This implies that budget control is another parliamentary oversight tool used by the Parliament. It retains the power to ensure the effective implementation of the approved budget by the executive agencies, thereby preventing the public resource from possible abuse.

Hearing on Public Forum

Another oversight tool is the arrangement of forums where the stakeholders, including the public, are invited to engage in discussion with the executive bodies. Evidences witnessed that such a forum is helpful to get public opinions in the presence of the executive officials. Forums of this kind create mutual understanding among the users of services, the service provider, and the supervising committee of the House. But the Parliament is not effective in using this tool due to lack of interest and limited participation by the public, as well as to manipulation by government and its unwillingness to consider input from the public.

Using Democratic Institutions and Resolutions of International Organizations

Discussion with the FGD and KIIs confirmed that the reports of democratic institutions like the Audit General, ombudsman, human rights commission, and media are rarely used as inputs in oversight functions. As a result, it is better to exhaustively use information obtained through those institutions to effectively oversee the works of executives. In addition to work with domestic institutions, the respondents also strongly recommend the importance of using resolutions made by international institutions, like the International Parliamentary Union, African Parliamentary Union, and human rights organizations for effective parliamentary oversight function. Similarly, some informants recommended the use of information from research reports and whistleblowers.

Oversight on Delegated Legislations
As the informants indicated, the follow-up of the process of issuing new legislation and new regulation is taken as one of the areas of focus in parliamentary oversight over the executive works. As observed from the study, the parliamentary standing committees evaluate draft laws prepared by the executives under their supervision, in line with the constitution and other existing laws, before that draft proclamation is submitted to the Parliament for voting in the parliamentary session. Where the draft legislation is proclaimed by the HoPRs, the supervising standing committee of the Parliament ensures the issuance of necessary regulation and directives by the executive, within three months after the proclamation was issued. Though the committees are active in follow-up of the promulgation of new proclamations and directives, they are not aware of the existence of the excessively large number of directives already in use. This poor control over directives issued by the executive limits the controlling capacity of the Parliament's standing committees.

To sum up, data gathered from different sources reveals that the Ethiopian HoPRs uses various tools and mechanisms to control the activities of the executive, with varying degrees of success. Of these tools, performance reports and committee hearings are the most widely used, while the field visit is the most productive oversight tool but is rarely used due to budget shortage, capacity limitation, logistical issues, and other factors.

4.4. Effectiveness of the HoPRs in Using Oversight Tools

In addition to the question regarding what oversight tools and mechanisms are used by the HoPR, respondents were also asked to rate the effectiveness of the Parliament in using those oversight tools (where 1 represents "very high," 2 represents "high," 3 stands for "not determined," 4 for "low," and 5 stands for "very low"). As the mean values of the responses depicted in table 2 below demonstrate, the Parliament was not rated as very high (mean below 1.5) in using any of the oversight tools. In relative terms, the effectiveness of Parliament is high in using reports and hearings in committee, while it was least effective in using the random field visit and the ombudsman institution as tools for the oversight function. The paradox was observed regarding field visit. While it was considered the most effective oversight tool, it was not effectively due to budget and time constraints.

In addition to assessing the effectiveness of the Parliament in using the existing oversight tools, issues related to the overall effectiveness of the oversight function of the Parliament in achieving oversight goals were also assessed based the information obtained through KIIs and FGD. Information

Table 1: Effectiveness of the Parliament in using oversight tools

	Oversight tools	N	Mean	Std. Deviation
1	Oral question	42	2.76	1.144
2	Written question	42	2.48	1.254
3	Interpellation (formal question)	35	2.23	1.087
4	Motion for debate	40	3.50	1.281
5	Hearing in committee	39	1.95	.857
6	Conducting ad-hoc committees	39	3.03	1.423
7	Planned field visit	41	3.12	1.452
8	Random field visit	41	3.78	1.294
9	Budget oversight	41	2.93	1.367
10	Audit institutions	39	2.36	1.287
11	Ombudsman institutions	40	3.52	1.261
12	Reports	42	1.86	1.181

* The higher the mean, the less effective the Parliament in using the tool
Source: Questionnaire Survey, 2018

collected from respondents of KIIs and the FGD reveals that the aims of parliamentary oversights are enhancing public satisfaction on government services; respect of the rule of law; creation of checks and balances to minimize power monopoly; promotion of public participation; ensuring accountability; increasing commitment to the implementation of reform tools; proper use of scarce resources, including the budget; and effective implementation of agreed policies and programs by the implementing bodies. When evaluated from these perspectives, most respondents of key informants' interviews and FGD agreed on the existence of gaps in the overall effectiveness of the HoPRs' oversight function. Information evidenced that though there is a positive change in the oversight function of the Parliament, much is still left to be done in achieving desired results.

Having discussed oversight tools used and the overall effectiveness of the House in its oversight function, the subsequent section discloses the main factors leading to the House's poor performance of its oversight tasks.

4.5. Challenges of Oversight Function Faced by HoPR

To discuss issues related to challenges affecting the Ethiopian parliamentary oversight functions, data gathered from various instruments and the results of the findings are briefly described in this section.

Logistics-related Challenges

As indicated in table 2 below, from the total respondents, 42.8 percent and 31 percent responded "agree" and "strongly agree" respectively with regard to poor logistical facilities for field visits. This reveals that more than 73 percent of the respondents agreed that shortages in the required logistical facilities are challenges to Ethiopian federal parliamentary oversight.

On the other hand, according to information obtained through KII and FGD, respondents took two positions. While most informants reported that shortage of facilities – like offices for members of standing committees, halls for conducting meetings, vehicles and other office supplies – hampered their oversight work, some did not consider logistical facilities to be big problems. According to the view of those who complained about the adequacy of logistics, the main problem is budget constraints. The committees do not have their own budget account, but they use pooled resources, in which they do not have adequate autonomy. For example, field visit beyond a 40km radius require permission, due to the shortage of vehicles and due to regular meetings of the HoPRs every Tuesday and Thursday. However, those key informants who have served in previous past terms of parliament report witnessing improvement in the logistic supply of the HoPRs, although the problem has not been totally solved.

Challenges Related to Lack of Capacity

Capacity limitation is another challenge that affects the well-functioning of parliamentary oversight. As shown in table 2 above, more than 70 percent of the respondents agreed that capacity limitation, caused by the lack of the human resources with the required qualifications and the inadequacy of office support, is a challenge for the parliamentary oversight function.

In addition, the data obtained through KII and FDG also reveal that capacity limitation is an acute problem. In the opinion of these respondents, gaps were observed in investigating and properly organizing performance evidences that enable the parliament to take corrective measures. Due to this capacity gap in committees, most of the time the HoPRs do not acquire the necessary and adequate evidence about executive performance and as a result, the Parliament most of the time is forced to refrain from taking proper corrective measures.

Table 2: Challenges affecting parliamentary oversight function

		Strongly agree		Agree		No opinion		Disagree		Strongly disagree	
S.N	Challenges of oversight functions	Frequency	%	Frequency	%	Frequency	%	Frequency	%	Frequency	%
1	Logistical problems for field visit.	13	31	18	42.9	10	23.8	-	-	1	2.4
2	Inadequacy of office support from supporting staff	11	27	18	45	8	20	2	5	1	2.5
3	Lack of required human resource competence	11	26.8	22	50	6	14.6	1	2.4	1	2.4
4	Lack of clarity in legal framework for oversight function	6	15	5	12.5	22	55	4	10	3	7.5
5	Lack of access to information	7	17.5	19	47.5	12	30	2	5	-	-
6	Lack of financial resource	9	22.5	14	35	15	37.5	2	5	-	-
7	Lack of autonomously establishing its own budget by the Parliament	6	15	6	15	18	45	8	20	2	5
8	Lack of respect by the executive	9	22	13	31.7	13	31.7	4	9.8	2	4.9
9	Use of ineffective oversight tools	4	9.8	16	39	17	41.5	3	7.3	1	2.4
10	Failure by the executive to implement suggestions given by the oversight report	11	26.8	22	53.7	6	14.6	1	2.4	1	2.4
11	Failure to take corrective measure by the Parliament following the oversight report	14	34.1	21	51.2	5	12.2	1	2.4	-	-

Source: Survey Questionnaire

The lack of technical knowledge about the subject matter also limits members of the committee to dig out and obtain the information necessary for oversight function. Particularly, during the first year of their electoral term, parliamentarians need continuous capacity building training; however, according to the responses of key informants and the FGD, they are not provided with the needed trainings.

Another challenge of capacity limitation is that members of the Parliament lack access to experience-sharing opportunities with other countries because of a lack of interest from management, resource limitation, and lack of consensus on the importance of experience-sharing. Some of the respondents among our key informants had a view that their technical competence is not comparable with the executive bodies they are supervising, which implies that the committee is not in a position to give proper direction for executing bodies and is not in a position to scrutinize the works of executive. In most cases, this challenge can be solved using technical assistances provided to each committee, but information obtained from key informants and discussion in the FGD highlighted that the assistance of professionals available through the parliament secretariat was not reliable.

According to evidence obtained through the KIIs and FGD, a shortage of competent professionals in assisting the work of the parliamentarians in properly conducting their oversight function is the other reason for capacity limitation. The standing committees expressed their dissatisfaction with the adequacy and competence of the HoPRs secretariat's support staff. Only three staff members (secretary, office boy, and expert) are hired for assisting each standing committee and even these assistants do not have the required competence to provide technical support. The role of the expert is to provide the necessary information to support the oversight function of the committees. Yet, in practice, the expert mostly assists the preparation of meetings and taking minutes. Some committees face employee turnover, which worsens the shortage of supporting staff.

Failure to Use Reports of Democratic Institutions and the Lack of Participating Stakeholders

Though the KII and FDG participants believe in the importance of relying on reports by democratic institutions such as the media, audit general, ombudsman, human rights commissions, the International Parliamentary Union, and the African Parliamentary Union, the study results fore grounded the limitation of using the assistance of outside institutions to oversee the performance of the executives. Similarly, respondents confirmed that there are gaps in working with research institutions and in using the findings of those institutions in monitoring and evaluating the performance of the executive.

This weakness can be linked to a lack of adequate support staff to gather information from potentially helpful institutions on behalf of the Parliament. The MPs generally have very busy schedules as they go through all the reports, attend sessions, conduct field visits, and carry out other activities. Thus, the task of compiling the information from democratic institutions rests upon the experts.

On the other hand, evidence indicates that in addition to weakness in working with democratic institutions on the side of the Parliament, the institutions themselves are not strong enough positions to provide adequate information to the Parliament.

Lack of Media Coverage

The inadequacy of media coverage is also raised as an important challenge to the oversight activities of the HoPRs. In view of respondents of KIIs and the FGD, even if the respective committees consistently conduct serious debates, these are not fully reported to the public. The print media used by the House is not widely accessible to the general public; the proclamation itself is not published in a timely fashion; and the website of the Parliament is at an infant stage and has been visited only by very few people. The data on the website is not updated regularly and it is not user friendly. As a result, citizens are unable to get information about the process of oversight.

Low Response and Failure by Executive to Implement Suggestions

The other issue highlighted as a challenge by the parliamentary committees is the inability of the executive to take corrective measures as per the directions and recommendations provided by the supervising committee. Though there is no open resistance, in actual practice the executive routinely fails to implement the directions given for different reasons, including capacity limitation, budget shortage, and lack of coordination with other departments, among others. For example, when the department concerned is asked about poor performance, they blame the lack of cooperation from different organizations, like the customs authority, banks, telecommunications, and electricity corporation and transportation companies. In addition, respondents reported experiencing delays in regular quarter reports, which they consider as a challenge. Similarly, data gathered through the questionnaire also support this view, as more than 75 percent of the respondents agreed that the failure of the executive to implement suggestions given based on the oversight report was the main challenge to Parliament's oversight function.

Party Discipline Related Challenges

Currently all the seats of the House are occupied by EPRDF and its affiliates. In this regard, respondents of the KIIs and FGD were asked whether this condition affects the Parliament's oversight function responsibility. Most respondents agreed that they see no problem in the oversight function due to the occupation of all seats by a single party. These respondents believe that party membership even motivates them to struggle for efficient implementation of the policy of their party.

In contrast to this positive aspect, a negative aspect of oversight by members of the ruling party was inferred from what these respondents believe and behave in practice. They believe that they have the responsibility to represent the interest of their party and therefore always support whatever policy issues it proposes. Most of them argue that supporting policies proposed by their own party is customary practice, which should not be violated unless the individual parliamentarians leave his/her party. What we can infer from this response is that there is always the possibility that the MPs will stand with the interests of the party at the expense of the interest of the constituency, which of course could undermine the principle of representation. If the Parliament always supports the policies proposed by the ruling party, its role is reduced to rubber stamping the executive's proposals.

There were also some respondents who argued that there is no conflict between their conscience and party direction, as they joined the party because of the absence of any conflict. These respondents also that added that, in their view, the Parliament is in fact facing a recent tendency to violate party discipline, which they see as a problem. But unconditional agreement is against the changing nature of the interest of human beings. We also found some respondents who held the view that "there is no option of opposing any policy, because we were elected for supporting the policies, but supervising the effective implementation of the party directions is not conflicting with party discipline. We are representing our party, hence supporting its policy and program is a must."Most respondents shared a consensus that on programs and policy issues, there is no way to say ''no;'' at the same time, most of them believe party discipline has no effect on the supervision of program implementation.

Though most respondents did not consider party discipline as a challenge to their responsibility of oversight, there were a few informants who consider EPRDF party discipline as one of the major challenges affecting their oversight functions. This group of informants argued that since all of them are from only one party, they do not expose each other for wrongdoing; as a result most executive heads come to parliamentary meeting without any preparation.

In EPRDF party structure, top party leaders occupy executive positions in government and hence the power balance between the legislative and the executive favors the later. In some instances, Member of Parliament may not get the chance to participate in the process of policy or program formulation but are expected to vote in favor of it, simply because it is the party decision. This obviously creates conflict between party discipline on the one hand and conscience and public accountability on the other hand. Additionally, informants express concern that failure to observe party discipline may lead to loss of immunity. Therefore, party discipline is in effect a means of exercising control over MPs' freedom of expression.

Other Challenges

Participants of the FDG reported the low-quality reports and low-quality draft legislation as another oversight challenge they face. Furthermore, members of committees confess their inability to make field visit due to security problems, for instance in 2017. One standing committee was mandated to undertake oversight on forty-eight different organizations, which is technically impossible to cover in a year. This committee planned to visit each organization at least once in the five-year parliamentary term. Respondents said that people expect as their representative or the HoPRs to give them lasting solutions to their problems, but unfortunately the reality is different. They stressed that since democracy is becoming weakened gradually, it is very difficult to transform the voice of the public. They further demonstrated that questions coming from electorate have no owner; they are screened and filtered at each step and are not given adequate response.

5. Conclusions and Area for Further Studies

5.1. Conclusions

The following conclusions were drawn from the findings of the study:

The HoPRs of Federal Democratic Republic of Ethiopia uses various oversight tools, such as questions time, plenary debate, motion, field visit, public hearings, and reports to scrutinize the work of the executive. Among these tools, reports and committee hearing are the most widely used, while the field visit is the most productive but rarely used due to budget shortage, capacity limitation, logistical issues, and other problems.

From the perspectives of public satisfaction with government services, respect for good governance, ease of existing laws for understanding, respect of the rule of law, commitment to the implementation of reform tools and proper use of budget, the effectiveness of Parliamentary oversight is far from meeting the goals of oversight.

There are different challenges influencing the oversight functions of the Ethiopian HoPRs, including the lack of qualified and professional supportive staff; lack of strong institutional framework for coordination of interdependent organizations; lack of willingness and capacity to ensure accountability and failure by the executive to take corrective measures for wrong actions; lack of strong democratic institutions such as audit general, the ombudsman institution and human rights commission in the country; a single party system that does not entertain diverse ideas; the strictness of party discipline; and lack of media coverage.

The HoPRs also has limitations in using the assistance of other institutions, such as the audit general, ombudsman, human rights commission, media, research institutions, and international organizations that produce vital inputs for undertaking the parliamentary oversight function.

Due to the existing party discipline, member of the Parliament wrongly believe that they have the responsibility to represent the interest of their party and therefore always support whatever policy issues are proposed by it unless the individual parliamentarians leave his/her party. This shows that there is always possibility that the MP will stand with interest of party at the expense of the interest of the constituency, undermining the principle of representation. If the Parliament always supports the policies proposed by the ruling party, its role is reduced to rubber-stamping of the executive's proposals.

5.2. Areas for Further Study

The conclusions of this research on oversight were drawn only from the perspectives of HoPRs. Thus, the research team believes that to have a balanced understanding of the overall oversight functions of the House, study on oversight functions of the HoPRs from the executive and public perspectives is needed.

This research was confined only to the oversight functions of the Parliament. Hence, research on the other major functions of the HoPRs, including law-making, representation functions, diplomatic functions, and parliamentary public engagement could be carried out in order to have an understanding of the overall performances of the House in undertaking its constitutional responsibilities.

The federal parliament of Ethiopia has two Houses/chambers. From these two Houses, this research considers only the lower house (HoPRs), because it is this House that is vested with the power of overseeing the executive branch of government. Regional Councils are not part of this study. Therefore, the research team recommends for more studies to be carried out in these areas to arrive at a better understanding of the overall oversight functions of the Parliament found at each levels of government.

Acknowledgements

The research team would like to thank member of the federal Parliament of Ethiopia and their secretariat staff who were involved in the research and cooperated in providing information necessary for its successful accomplishment.

We would also like to thank those professionals who invested their precious time in reviewing and editing the chapter.

References

Ahmed, A. (2011). Parliamentary Oversight and Its Role in Ensuring Constitutionalism and Accountability under the FDRE Constitution. Thesis Submitted to the School of Graduate Studies of Addis Ababa University.

Burman, A. (2013). Legal Framework for the Parliamentary Oversight of the ExecutiveSSRN: https://ssrn.com/abstract=2265797 or http://dx.doi.org/10.2139/ssrn.2265797.

FDRE (1995). The Constitution of Federal Democratic Republic of Ethiopia, Addis Ababa.

Fredriksson, P. G., & Wollscheid, J. R. (2014). Political Institutions, Political Careers and Environmental Policy. *Kyklos*, 67(1), 54-73.

Friedberg, C. (2011). From a Top-Down to a Bottom-Up Approach to Legislative Oversight. *Journal of Legislative Studies*, 17(4), 525-544.

Global Parliamentary Report (2017). Parliamentary Oversight: Parliament's Power to Hold Government to Account. Inter-Parliamentary Union.

Griffith, G. (2005). Parliament and Accountability: The Role of Parliamentary Oversight Committees. Briefing Paper No 12/05, NSW Parliamentary Library Research Service.

Gyampo, R. E. V. (2015). Dealing with Ghana's Winner-takes-all Politics: The Case for an Independent Parliament. A Publication of the Institute of Economic Affairs, 21(3).

House of People's Representatives (2005). House of Peoples' Representatives Working Procedure and Members' Code of Conduct (Amendment) Proclamation no.470/2005, *Negarit Gazeta*, Addis Ababa.

House of People's Representatives (2006). The Regulation of Working Procedures and the Member's Code of Conduct of House of Peoples Representatives, Regulation no. 3/2006, Addis Ababa.

Hudson, A.,& Wren, C. (2007). Parliamentary Strengthening in Developing Countries. Final Report for DFID.

IPU. (2015). *Women in Parliament: 20 Years in Review.* Geneva.

Johnson, K., 2005. The Role of Parliament in Government. Washington, DC: World Bank Institute.

Justice, S.-S. (2012). *Parliamentary Oversight in Ghana –A Brief Review.* Friedrich Ebert- Sifting.

Kapur, D.& Mehta, P. Bhanu. (2006). The Indian Parliament as an Institution of Accountability. Democracy, Governance and Human Rights Programme Paper Number 23, United Nations Research Institute for Social Development (UNRISD).

Khmelko, I. S., & Beers, D. J. (2011). Legislative Oversight in the Ukrainian Rada: Assessing the Effectiveness of Parliamentary Committees. *Journal of Legislative Studies*, 17(4), 501-524.

Kit, I. P. (2005). *Global Best Practices: A Model Annual State of the Parliament Report.*

Lok Sabha. (2014). *Rules of Procedure and Conduct of Business in LOK SABHA.* New Delhi: LOK SABHA Secretariat.

Makhado, R.A., Masehela, K.L.,& Mokhari, R.W. (2012). *Effectiveness and Effiency of Public Accounts Committees (PACs) in Enhancing Oversight and Accountability in the Public Sector.* Research & Evaluation Section, Limpopo Legislature, South Africa.

Malapane, A. (2016). Holding the Executive Accountable: Parliament as the Beacon of Hope to the People. *Journal of Public Administration and Development Alternatives* (JPADA), 1(1), 135-149.

Mbete, L. (2016). An Evaluation of Oversight and Accountability by the Fourth Parliament of the Republic of South Africa Doctoral dissertation, Stellenbosch: Stellenbosch University.

Mickler, T. A. (2013). Standing Committee Assignments in the German Bundestag–Who Gets What in Within-party Negotiations? *German Politics*, 22(4), 421-440.

NDI (2000). *Guidebook for Implementing Legislative Programs.* Washington, DC. http://www.ndi.org.

Nwokora, Z, & Pelizzo, R. (2004). Sartori Reconsidered: Toward a New Predominant Party System. *Political Studies*, 62, 824-842.

Pelizzo, R. & Stapenhurst, R. (2004). Tools for Legislative Oversight: An Empirical Investigation. World Bank Policy Research Working Paper 3388.

Pelizzo, R., Stapenhurst, R.,& David Olson. (2004). *Trends in Parliamentary Oversight.* Washington, DC: World Bank Institute.

Rapoo, T. (2004). Rating the Effectiveness of Legislative Oversight Methods and Techniques at Provincial Level: The Views of Senior Public Service Officials. Centre for Policy Studies.

Salih, M. (ed.) (2005). *African Parliaments: Between Governance and Government.* Cham: Springer.

Shankar, A. & Singh, S. (2014). *Parliamentary Procedures: A Primer.* New Delhi: PRS Legislative Research.

Shephard, M. (2004). Administrative Review and Oversight: The Experience of Westminster. In Pelizzo, Stapenhurst, & Olsen, *Trends in Parliamentary Oversight*, pp. 40-47.

Singh, N. K. 2010). Improving Parliamentary Oversight. *ASCI Journal of Management*, 39(2), 95-103.

Swain, P. C. (2008). Dynamics of the Indian Party System: The Emergence of Competitive Multi- Party Coalitions. *Indian Journal of Political Science*, 69(1), 59-70.

Webb, P.& Roberts, K. (2014). *Effective Parliamentary Oversight of Human Rights A Framework for Designing and Determining Effectiveness*. The Dickson Poon School of Law, King's College London.

Yamamoto, H. (2007). *Tools for Parliamentary Oversight: A Comparative Study of 88 National Parliaments*. Geneva: Inter-Parliamentary Union.

5
Public Engagement for Improving the Relationship between the People and the Parliament

Challa Amdissa Jlru, Defferew Kebebe Tessema, and Aklilu Wubet Lema

Box 1: Key Points of this chapter

- ✓ Public engagement enhances participatory democracy and public trust by improving the relationship between people and parliament.
- ✓ Engagement strategy and policy determines the effectiveness of public engagement.
- ✓ The People's Representatives of Ethiopia lacks institutional capacity and resources required for parliamentary public engagement.
- ✓ Parliament's inaccessibility, a hasty law-making process, low coverage of constituency visits, limited use of modern communication technologies, and a one-language policy has prohibited the effectiveness of parliamentary public engagement in Ethiopia.

Box 2: Lessons of this chapter

Reading this chapter will give you insights in:

- ✓ Public engagement mechanisms set in place by the House of People's Representatives to strengthen parliamentary representation and participatory democracy
- ✓ Effectiveness of public engagement mechanism in creating public trust
- ✓ Changes desired for improving public engagement so as to combine participatory democracy with representative democracy in Ethiopia

Box 3: Abbreviations

FDRE = Federal Democratic Republic of Ethiopia
FGD = Focus Group Discussion
HoPRs = House of People's Representatives
KII = Key Informant Interview

1. Introduction

As indicators of political apathy have increased and trust in politics has fallen (Dalton, 2004; Hay, 2007; Stoker, 2006), efforts to engage citizens in politics have become a standard theme of modern democracy and a central parliamentary activity. Leston-Bandeira (2016) describes the characteristics of modern Parliament as a questioning of traditional forms of representative democracy and the expansion of participatory and advocacy types of democracy. The steadily declining levels of trust in political institutions leads to the significant role of public engagement in the democratization process, as it increases the interface between the people and the Parliament, not just every election year but every day. There is a widespread belief that above and beyond the occasional opportunity to vote, citizens should be allowed to participate in decisions that affect their daily life. This belief is enshrined in article 21 of the United Nations Declaration of Human Rights (1948) and is espoused by governments of most political persuasions (Whiteley, 2009).

Despite the importance of public engagement for deepening democracy, however, governments in undemocratic system are found to be reluctant to seize the opportunities that public engagement will create. When government fails to introduce effective parliamentary public engagement, the relationship between the people and parliament is weakened and the legislature loses its role as mediator between the people and the government. Therefore, it is essential to undertake the study of parliamentary public engagement to understand the relationship between people and parliament.

Paul (2009) recognizes the importance of public engagement beyond occasional participation in voting. He noted that while public engagement is widely accepted, the practice has remained remarkably free from empirical scrutiny. It is essential to know the relationship between public engagement and trust in government and how public engagement may help strengthen inclusive government along gender and ethnic lines. Thomas (2006) believes that while engagement has received much attention in the popular press, scholarly work has lagged behind.

While research on parliamentary public engagement is generally scarce (Leston-Bandeira, 2016), the existing studies themselves are limited to the experiences of the Western countries, which are much advanced in exercising democracy, and hence cannot be generalized to the developing context of developing countries. Therefore this research presented here contributes to the literature an understanding of the context of developing countries by focusing on the experiences of Ethiopia. Leston-Bandeira (2016) explores the role that public engagement plays in the relationship between parliament and the public in the UK, reflecting in particular on its elements of symbolic representation.

Leston-Bandeira (2016) investigates the supply side of parliamentary public engagement and suggests further studies in this area. The supply side of parliamentary public engagement is essential for exploring how the public does indeed receive public engagement and whether multiple representative claims do take place, and whether this has any effect on the public's perception of the institution. Therefore, to find a balanced view on parliamentary public engagement, the research for this chapter involved both people and parliament, by taking samples from both sides.

In response to the scarcity of research on parliamentary public engagement, this research investigated the relationship between parliaments and people in Ethiopia, with the objective of identifying changes required for combining participatory democracy with the Ethiopian representative democratic system. In order to improve the public trust in parliament, it is vital to know the perception of the people toward that institution. Hence, this research tried to address the following questions: What public engagement mechanisms are set in place by the legislature of the Federal Democratic Republic of Ethiopia to strengthen parliamentary representation and participatory democracy? And how effective is the existing form of public engagement in creating public trust?

As a true democracy develops with the emergence of demand from organized people who are capable of actively engaging in public affairs and who have skills to influence their representatives, this research serves as seeds to instigate the people to participate and take actions required to strength participatory democracy. This research also contributes to our knowledge of the importance of combining public engagement with representative democracy, which is crucial for deepening democratization in Ethiopia.

The study is delimited in scope to the identification of public engagement mechanisms being employed by House of People's Representative of Ethiopia (HoPRs) and the role of parliamentary public engagement in improving public trust in the Parliament. The study assesses public engagement practiced since 2015, focusing on parliamentary practices in during the course of one electoral term

This chapter has five parts. The first is the introduction presented here; the second presents a review of related literatures with regard to parliamentary public engagement mechanisms and its importance in promoting public trust in parliament as well as in strengthening democracy. The third part deals with methods of data collection and analysis, while the fourth is concerned with findings and discussion. The last part presents some conclusions and implications for future research.

2. Related Literatures

2.1. Purposes of Parliamentary Public Engagement

Modern parliament is characterized by a questioning of traditional forms of representative democracy that reestablished the division between the rulers and the ruled, making the people simply selectors of their rulers. The weakness of representative democracy has led to a search for alternative forms of democracy and the development of the public engagement function (Maija, 2017). Public engagement plays an important role in the democratization process, as it increases the interface between the people and the parliament, not just every election year but every day.

The term "public engagement" covers a wide range of communication activities: from straightforward awareness raising, providing information, visits programs, and education initiatives; through two-way consultation activities; to increasingly empowering citizen participation and decision-making opportunities. In parliamentary terms, this can mean anything from reading a leaflet explaining how laws are made to submitting a petition to parliament or giving views to a committee inquiry, to having direct input on bills being passed (Walker, 2017).

There are a variety of reasons for parliament seeking to engage with the public, including increasing public understanding of parliament and its work, broadening the range of voices heard by parliament, and potentially enhancing its legitimacy (Kelly and Bochel, 2018). Public engagement is said to be essential to a healthy democracy, to greater participation in democratic processes, to a better understanding of the role of parliament and members of parliament and, by extension, to greater trust that the Parliament and the people's representatives will better represent the public's interest (PNSW, 2017). Strengthening citizen involvement in parliament is a desirable democratic goal in and of itself. It improves the quality of legislative decision-making, links citizens to their government, and provides legitimacy to democratic institutions (Kurtz, 1997).

According to Walker (2017), at a fundamental level, there are three reasons why parliaments are wise to develop strategies to engage effectively with their citizens between elections. Firstly: the legitimacy of any parliament depends on the support and engagement of its electorate. Secondly: the quality of legislation and policy is improved if it is informed by citizens' concerns, experiences, and views. The scrutiny role of parliaments can positively influence national policies, priorities, and development goals and ensure that they meet the needs of the people. Thirdly: a parliament that is seen by its citizens to be connected and responsive to their concerns is more likely to earn the trust of the people.

Table 1: Form of engagement

Form of engagement	Purpose	Tools
Inform Providing the public with the information required to understand the issue	To facilitate increased knowledge of the issue and the decisions concerning it	Fact sheets, web sites, open houses, pamphlets, social media
Consult Providing the public with clear and coherent information regarding the issue, welcoming the public's thoughts on the topic, and indicating how their input affected the outcome	To obtain feedback on analysis, alternatives, or decisions	Public comment, focus groups, questionnaires, public meetings, Twitter town halls, online idea forums
Deliberate Engaging with the public in two-way conversation to make certain that the public's thoughts and concerns are factored into proposed solutions/ decisions	Greater level of participation by stakeholders as they assist in idea generation	Workshops, deliberative polling, advisory committees
Collaborate/Engage Relying on relevant stakeholders' input in combination with organizational expertise to incorporate recommendations into decisions to the maximum extent possible	Shared ownership between the organization and the stakeholders as the community is involved in each aspect (and the outcomes) of the decision	Consensus-building, participatory decision-making, panels, formal partnerships, informal coalitions, alliances, networks

Source: Public Policy Forum, 2009

If citizens understand the vital role the legislature plays in representing and championing citizens' rights and concerns, they will be more likely to value the institution and its work. When policy decisions incorporate the perspectives of those affected, they can capture a wider range of inputs, and in doing so they can secure public legitimacy (Dryzek, 2010) and relatively improve trust in the performance of public institutions (Newton and Norris, 2000).

2.2. Public Participation Framework

According to Thomson-Senanayake (2012),there are a number of recognized levels of public participation, which includes: inform, consult, involve/ deliberation, and engage/collaborate. The first level of public participation is to "inform" the public (e.g., of the status of a proposed project or the relevant process). This level provides the public with balanced and objective information to assist them in understanding the problems, alternatives, and/or solutions. Individuals and stakeholders are then able to properly assess and evaluate the impacts of policies and initiatives proposed by government. The second level is to "consult," in which the people are invited to provide feedback, input, or comment on analyses, alternatives, and/or decisions. This gives the public an opportunity to provide input on policies and initiatives before they are finalized.

The third level is to "involve/deliberation," in which the people are provided with opportunity for dialogue and interaction. This could also be described as direct public participation throughout the process to ensure that issues and concerns are consistently understood and considered. However, it is with the understanding that the legislature is still the decision maker. The fourth level is to "collaborate/engage". At this level, the public is provided with the opportunity to partner or work jointly on the active development of alternatives and the identification of the preferred solution. The purposes of engagement and tools or strategies used at each level are summarized in the table 1.

2.3. Parliamentary Public Engagement Mechanisms

The push for parliaments to engage with the public is consistent with a broader participatory trend in contemporary governance (Fung & Wright, 2003; Newman, 2005). Increasingly, decision-makers, public agencies, nongovernmental organizations, and corporations are seeking novel ways to engage with their constituents in response to perceived failings in legitimacy (Bingham et al., 2005) and an observed decline in trust in the institutions of representative politics (Tormey, 2015). In the particular context of legislatures, the drive to "connect" with the public is an attempt to make parliaments more relevant and accessible to citizens at a time when there is low public trust in politics (Leston-Bandeira, 2014).

Parliaments around the world are experimenting with new forms of public communication and engagement. We can witness, for example, legislatures taking an active approach to communicating with the public through websites, blogs, YouTube, and social media platforms, such as Twitter and Facebook. Some parliaments have experimented with novel participatory mechanisms, for example e-petitions and innovative consultative forums to engage with "hard to reach" publics (Hendriks,2019). The Parliament of New South Wales employs many engagement methods, such as comprehensive publication, "House in Review,""Running the Record," education and outreach, school tours, school outreach, community workshops, providing parliament and democracy courses, conducting public sector seminars, encouraging the public to visit the Parliament, open days, public tours, comprehensive website, and social media such as Twitter, Facebook, and others (PNSW, 2017).

According to Beetham (2006), there are a number of different ways in which parliaments are working to involve citizens in the legislative process, both through contributions to work on bills in progress and through suggestions for new or amended legislation. These may involve: open invitations to citizens to make submissions on bills; invitations to specified nongovernment organizations and social movements; ongoing arrangements for collaboration between parliamentary committees and citizen groups and experts; special forums or chambers for civil society, whether meeting independently or jointly with parliamentarians; procedures for citizens' initiatives and referendums; or some combination of a number of these modes.

2.4. Public Engagement and Public Trust in the Parliament

According to Petts (2008), public engagement through deliberative processes is promoted in both academic and policy circles as a potential means to build public trust in decision-makers. Governments in general and the parliament in particular seem to optimistically take a positive relationship between public engagement and trust almost for granted. According to the American psychologist Julian Rotter (1971), trust is the expectation that the promise of an individual or group can be relied upon. Trust in government refers to one's perceptions regarding the integrity and ability of the public agency to provide the expected service (Welch, Hinnant, & Moon, 2005).

Löfstedt (2005) argues for modifying the concept of trust in favor of confidence in the outcome as well as the decision process itself, contending that the public can in some circumstances trust a regulator even if they do not agree with the decision as long as the process by which it was reached was credible. Löfstedt (2006) in his work also favors dealing with a decline in trust through a focus on perception of competency, fairness, or efficiency of government. Hence, he contends that distrust caused by a lack of fairness should be attacked through public engagement, whereas if it is caused by perceived incompetence, greater involvement of experts in the decision may be required.

O'Neill (2002) argues that a well-placed trust grows out of active inquiry rather than blind acceptance. In other words, complete openness does not guarantee trust; rather it is built when specific elements of information can be traced to particular sources whose reliability can be ascertained. This suggests that in order to enhance or build trust, it is necessary to find ways in which people can actively check parliamentary claims. A deliberative engagement process has to engender the confidence and competence that allows all participants to generate a common framing and understanding of the risks and the management options through an equal opportunity to express opinions which are open to challenge and debate.

Most theoretical discussions of trust stress its multidimensionality, with elements of Renn and Levine's (1991) five dimensions – competence, objectivity, fairness, consistency, empathy – consistently. For building and maintaining trust (Kreitner and Kinicki, 2004) suggest six guidelines, namely, communication, support, respect, fairness, predictability, and competence. Trust needs to be earned; it cannot be demanded. They also have developed a measure of trustworthiness and provided norms for a trustworthiness scale. According to this norm, the level of trust could be "high,""moderate," or "low" depending on the score obtained, and the present study measures public trust in the institution of parliament based on this scale.

3. Research Methodology

3.1. Research Approach and Data Sources

The study employed a mixed-research approach to show the role that public engagement plays in strengthening the relationship between people and parliament in Ethiopia. Qualitative and quantitative research approaches were combined to triangulate information gathered from several sources. The primary reason for choosing the mixed research approach is that either the quantitative approach or qualitative approach alone is not sufficient to generate the relevant information pertinent to the relationship between people and parliament.

Both secondary sources and primary sources of data were collected to enrich the findings with ample evidence. Data from secondary sources were collected through document review. The documents reviewed were the constitutions, the ethics and procedural code of conduct of the Parliament, public wing participation strategy, annual plans and reports, the parliamentary website, and other published materials. The primary sources of data were collected from the "people" and parliament. The "people" comprise representatives of civil society organizations, leaders of community groups, leaders of private sectors, representatives of media organizations, members of political parties, bloggers, academicians, activists and community leaders, and prominent individuals. Data were collected from this population through a questionnaire survey and Focus Group Discussion (FGD).

From 120 questionnaires distributed to people, 100 were correctly filled in and returned and used in the analysis. Respondents were categorized in three age groups, wherein60.6 percent fall in the category of eighteen to thirty, 31.3 percent fall in the age range between thirty-one and forty-three, and 8.1 percent of respondents were in the age range between forty-four and sixty. No one was found to be above the age of sixty years, but one respondent did not want to indicate his age. In terms of gender: 90 percent of respondents were male, 8 percent were female, and the other2 percent were undisclosed. Similarly, respondents of the questionnaire were asked to which ethnic group they belong. Their responses show 35 percent of respondents were Oromo, 27 percent were Amhara, 12 percent were Gedio, 3 percent were Sidama, and 23 percent were from the rest of the nations, nationalities, and peoples of Ethiopia. The highest level of education for largest group (58.8 percent) of respondents was first degree, while 17.5 had second degree or above, 10.3 percent had attained college diploma, and 13.4 had reached the high school level of education. Three individuals did not indicate their level of education. In terms of marital status, 57 percent of the respondents were single, 39 percent were married, and 4 percent were divorced. The last question asked to differentiate the bio data of respondents was affiliation with political parties. In this regard, 87.9 percent of respondents had no affiliation with any party, while members of ruling party and members of opposition parties were found to be 6.1 percent each.

The second group studied here is members of parliament, of whom eighteen were involved in Key Informant Interviews. Among these key informants, two of them were parliamentarians; eight respondents were members of different parliamentary standing committees, two respondents were high-ranking officials at status of state minister, and six were officials of the secretariat office of the House of Peoples' Representatives. Data gathering instruments are further described below.

3.2. Data Collection Instruments and Data Analysis

Document review: This involves identification of written or electronic documents containing information on the people and parliament. The research team kept track and cited the information retrieved from these documents. The trustworthiness of documents to be reviewed was carefully checked by the review team. Following full cross-checking of data to assure completeness, accuracy, and appropriateness to the research topic, it was further triangulated with other relevant data sources.

Key Informant Interview: KII were conducted on a face-to-face basis with eighteen members of the parliament. The interviews were unstructured.

Focus Group Discussions: Three FGDs were conducted with people to generate diverse information. Respondents were made to choose to take part in one of the three FGDs on the basis of their convenience.

Questionnaire: Quantitative data were collected directly through the use of a self-administered questionnaire collected by a trained data collector. The main variables were engagement strategies and trust.

Observations were made by personal visits to the parliament call center, archives, and existing facilities. Finally, a validation workshop was conducted and further inputs were incorporated in the final research report.

Quantitative data were analyzed with the support of statistical packages for social science (SPSS). Descriptive statistics, nonparametric tests (Mann-Whitney U test, Kruskal-Wallis Test), and Spearman correlation test were applied for analysis of quantitative data, while qualitative analyses were used to present the observation and understandings of the researchers on the topic through the use of text and narrative techniques. To ensure the ethical requirements of research, participants were informed of the purpose of the research and their consent was requested prior to their taking part in the study. In addition, the anonymity and confidentiality of all the participants in the research was strictly preserved. Also, the written consent of all the participants in the entire exercise was also sought.

4. Public Engagement and Participatory Democracy in Ethiopia

4.1. Introduction

This section presents analysis of data that were collected through KIIs, the questionnaire survey, FGDs, and document review. The data collected through these different methods were triangulated, analyzed, and discussed. The main themes of the findings related to institutional set-up for parliamentary public engagement, parliamentary public engagement strategies, public engagement practices in parliamentary functions, and public trust.

4.2. Institutional Set-up for Parliamentary Public Engagement

As per the constitution of the Federal Democratic Republic of Ethiopia (FDRE) article 35 (6), 43 (2), (58), 89 (6) and 92 (3), the House of People's Representatives has a constitutional responsibility to engage the public in undertaking its functions (law making, oversight, representation, and parliamentary diplomacy). Conversely, people have the constitutional right to participate in decisions made by its representatives and to know the working of the parliament (FDRE, 1995). Article 58 of the FDRE constitution requires the meeting of the House to be public, except when close meeting is required. Where meetings are made public, the people will get information about the debates in the plenary session of the Parliament and of its acts, which will improve public awareness on the legislative process.

Article 35 of the constitution deals with provisions of the rights of women, in which the subarticle 6 provides "women have the right to full consultation, in the formulation of national development policies and the designing and execution of projects." According to this provision, law making and oversight functions should ensure the participation of women. In the same way, subarticle 6 of article 89 requires that "government shall ensure the participation of women in equally with men in all economic and social development endeavors" (FDRE, 1995).

The provisions under article 43 of the constitution are concerned with the right to development. These group rights are recognized for each of the nations, nationalities, and people of Ethiopia. Accordingly, subarticle 2 of this provision states that "the nationals have the right to participate in national development and, in particular, to be consulted with respect to policies and projects affecting their community." This article safeguards the necessity of inclusive decision making in ethnically divided Ethiopia. In other words, the HoPRs has responsibility to ensure government decision is made after adequate consultation with the nations, nationalities, and peoples of Ethiopia (FDRE, 1995). Article 89 (6) provides that "government shall at all-time promote the participation of the people in the formulation of national development policies and programs; it shall also have the duty to support the initiatives of the people in their development endeavors." Article 92 of the constitution, which deals with the cultural objectives of Ethiopia, also requires the participation of people in the policy-making process. Subarticle 3 of article 92 states that people have the right to full consultation and to the right to expression to enable the people to reflect their views in the planning and implementation of environmental policies and projects that affect them directly.

Regardless of these constitutional provisions, information obtained from key informants and FGD indicates that the HoPRs by itself is not active in the policy-making process, let alone in helping people to engage in the formulation of policies. Both research participants from people and parliament have similar thoughts, that the House is only active in ensuring the implementation of policies and programs and leaves policy formulation responsibility for the party central committees. In the norm of the ruling party of Ethiopia, a party member is not allowed to argue against a centrally proposed policy or program. The failure by a parliamentarian to support the program proposed by the party leads to a loss of position both in government and in party structure. Therefore, members of the Parliament neither actively engage in policy formulation process by themselves nor encourage the people to engage in the policy-making process; rather, their focus is on oversight of how well the concerned bodies are committed to the implementation of policies.

Beside the FDRE constitution of Ethiopia, which has well recognized the importance of parliamentary public engagement, as provided in articles35 (6), 43 (2), (58), 89 (6) and 92(3), and the Code of Ethics and Procedure of the HoPR Regulation number 6/2008, which gives little attention to public engagement, no other laws exist to enforce parliamentary public engagement. Indeed, the HoPRs of Ethiopia does not have well-developed public engagement guidelines or strategy. It was only in 2018 that the HoPRs began developing a public engagement framework and strategy, which was not yet implemented at the time of data collection. The major objective of the framework is to facilitate and ensure regular parliamentary public engagement in an organized way in the wide areas of parliamentary functions such as law making, monitoring of enforcement of laws, budget ratification process, budget utilization, audit findings, preparation, implementation and monitoring of government policies and strategies, field visits during oversight and reporting of the findings, constituency questions and suggestions, planning and plan evaluation of the House, and research findings of the House.

As indicated in this engagement framework of the HoPRs, the parliament is expected to conduct regular meeting with people every three months. The responsibilities of the HoPRs according to this engagement framework are: increasing public awareness on parliamentary public engagement, facilitating participation in discussion of draft legislation, setting place, time, and agenda for discussion, announcing the agenda of the day, and conducting research on parliamentary public engagement. This activity is managed by the secretariat of the HoPRs.

The secretariat of the HoPRs has a program called the parliamentary public wing, which is a common forum for parliament and the people. The participants of the parliamentary public wings are chambers of commerce at the national level and the Addis Ababa chamber of commerce, the women association, the youth association, professional associations, political parties and their councils, religious organizations, universities, trade unions, the journalist association, policy research institutions, and others. According to our informants in both the FGD and KII, the parliamentary public wing has not been effective in promoting participatory democracy due to various factors. One of the challenges of this forum is that the parliament controls the agenda. The agenda of discussion is unilaterally determined by the parliament, so the participants of the public wing come to the forum without information and without preparation to influence the discussion. In addition, most of the groups of the public wing are not independent of the government; and some of them are not well-organized to have influence in the parliamentary decision-making process. The most active civil and political organizations are systematically excluded from participation in the forum. Beside the problem of government control over participation, a low level of public awareness on the importance of participation also hinders the effectiveness of parliamentary public engagement by the so-called public wing.

Information obtained from KIIs indicates that there is no department or unit responsible for public engagement in the Parliament; instead the work of promoting public engagement is mainstreamed in the work of standing committees and parliamentary secretariat directorates, such as the law directorate and communication directorate. The absence of an organizational unit with full responsibility for management of parliamentary public engagement in the parliamentary structure blurs the responsible body for the failure of parliamentary public engagement.

The evidence from the document review and FGD shows that the constitution provided enabling condition for public engagement, but other laws give little attention to public engagement. Furthermore, the practice of parliamentary public engagement is restricted by institutional limitations. The failure of the HoPRs to develop engagement strategies and policies and procedural directives to guide public engagement, a lack of commitment to strengthen the parliamentary public wing, the absence of a specifically responsible body assigned to manage engagement, and the lack of a budget specifically allocated for public engagement have deterred the technical and infrastructural capacity of the Parliament for effective public engagement.

4.3. Usage of Common Parliamentary Public Engagement Strategies by the HoPRs of Ethiopia

Through the questionnaire survey, the study measured several variables using a five-point Likert scales that ranges from strongly disagree to strongly agree. Four of these variables were: the usage of parliamentary public engagement strategies, that include strategies to inform, to consult, to deliberate, and to collaborate with the people. The other variable is public trust, which is presented in section 4.6 of this chapter.

Respondents were asked to indicate their level of agreement on the extent of public engagement along different engagement mechanisms and strategies. The views of the respondents show that the Ethiopian parliament's use of different tools of securing public engagement was found unsatisfactory. As shown in table 2, the rating score of engagement strategies to inform, consult, deliberate, and collaborate were below the average point in the scale ranging between 1 and 5. The value below 3 implies that the number of people who did not agree with different level of parliamentary public engagement is higher than the number of people who did agree with the employment of parliamentary public engagement mechanisms.

Table 2: Opinion on public engagement and trust

Descriptive statistics	Mean	SD	N
Public trust in HoPR	2.8034	1.00908	98
The strategies of HoPR to inform	2.9066	1.01035	98
The strategies of HoPR to consult	2.7781	1.07460	98
The strategies of HoPR to deliberate	2.6570	.98187	98
The strategies of HoPR to collaborate	2.8010	1.05212	98

Source: Computed from Questionnaire Survey, 2019

As far as parliamentary public engagement is concerned, the first thing expected from parliament is sharing information regarding its decisions, working procedures, functions, and services. From the outset, sharing information is a necessary step to ensure transparency and accountability to the electorate and to create a fertile ground for bringing the Parliament close to the people and enhancing democracy. Thus, five statements were used to assess the situation of sharing information (strategies of the HoPR to inform) regarding the parliamentary decisions and functions. These statements were: the availability of parliamentary publications in the form of posters, leaflets, guides, and research briefings to disseminate basic information; the availability and accessibility of records of committee meetings and plenary secessions; the supports of civic education in schools by the Parliament; the practice of tours to visit the Parliament; and the broadcasting of legislative sessions that can be viewed on television without edition. In the view of the majority of respondents (mean 2.9), the HoPRs did not sufficiently use the above strategies of sharing information.

The score of the engagement with people for consultation was even lower than the score of engagement to share information (mean 2.78). The strategies to consult the concerned people in decisions that affect them requires arrangement of face-to-face meetings, using traditional consultation forums, conducting workshops, conferences, or panel discussions with expert or focus groups, and aggressively seeking public inputs by means of public hearings. The data obtained from respondents through the questionnaire show that the efforts of the HoPRs to engage in consultation were not adequate to meet the demand for participation. The participants of interviews and FGD also unanimously agreed that the House did not establish any regular program for traditional consultation, for example with village councils, with tribal leaders and religious leaders, which is expected to play a crucial role in improving the relationship between people and parliament. Similarly, the House did not use common practices of consultation like citizen advisory councils and citizens cards, which are essential elements of participatory democracy.

Where the parliament fails to inform and to consult the people, it is not expected to meet the requirements to give people the chance to influence outcomes of parliamentary decisions. Our respondents confirm this fact by rating the performance of the House on deliberating the with the lowest score (mean 2.66) of all forms of engagement. The parliamentary public engagement strategies to deliberate, against which the views the respondents' were collected, include timely response to public problems, people's influence of the outcome of legislative decisions, involvement of people in designing and evaluation of programs, conducting deliberative polling, and working with advisory committee for deliberation. Data gathered from respondents in this respect show that the parliamentary public engagement in Ethiopia did not reach the level of deliberation and as a consequence, the people have insignificant influence on parliamentary decisions.

The final form of parliamentary public engagement is the parliamentary engagement strategy intended to collaborate with people in program designing, implementation, and evaluation. Engagement strategies to collaborate include, but are not limited to, invitation to specified civil society organizations and social movements for working together; ongoing arrangements for collaboration between parliament and people; setting procedures for citizens' initiatives and referendums; joint work with people in the active development of alternatives; and inviting public to actively engage in monitoring and evaluation of policies. Again, such collaboration strategies to engage with people have not applied by the HoPRs to a satisfactory level (mean 2.8) as per the view of the respondents. Comparison of data from interviews and FGD with data from the questionnaire shows the convergence of the views of the respondents in both categories on the reluctance of the HoPRs to engage with people, both to deliberate and to collaborate.

Parliament is a political institution that is expected to engage men and women as well as majority and minority ethnic groups; therefore, it indispensable to assess the inclusiveness in parliamentary public engagement along gender and ethnic aspects. Thus, by comparing the perception of respondents from different gender and ethnic groups on public engagement, the difference of opinion on engagement was assessed to measure inclusiveness. Accordingly, the Mann-Whitney U Test and Kruskal-Wallis Test were applied to examine if differences exist on perceptions on public engagement between male and female participants as well as among different ethnic groups.

A non-parametric Mann-Whitney U Test was conducted to see the differences in the perception of female and male respondents with regards to the performance of public engagement strategies of the HoPRs to inform, to consult, to deliberate, and to collaborate. The result of the test statistics indicates that the p-value or Exact. sig. (2-tailed) in all forms of public engagement strategies were above 5 percent. Thus, we could not reject the hypothesis that there is no significant difference between perceptions of female and male respondents in all levels of engagement. This result indicates that there is no significant difference in this respect between male and female at 5 percent level of significance. In other words, this test result implies gender does not influence the perception on parliamentary public engagement.

Table 3: Test of difference between the perception of female and male respondents on public engagement strategies

Test statistics[a]	Strategies of HoPR to inform	Strategies of HoPR to consult	Strategies of HoPR to deliberate	Strategies of HoPR to collaborate
Mann-Whitney U	330.000	233.000	281.000	267.500
Wilcoxon W	4425.000	4328.000	4376.000	4362.500
Z	-.390	-1.652	-1.028	-1.202
Asymp. Sig. (2-tailed)	.696	.099	.304	.229
Exact Sig. (2-tailed)	.704	.100	.312	.235
Point Probability	.002	.001	.002	.001

a. Grouping Variable: Gender

In addition to the Mann-Whitney U Test, a non-parametric Kruskal-Wallis Test was also conducted to see the difference in the perception of the respondents on the same issues among the different ethnic groups. As it is shown in table 4, the result of the test statistics indicates that the p-value or Asymptotic. sig. (2-tailed) of all variables was greater than 0.05, which again indicates that there is no significant difference among the ethnic groups on the performance of public engagement strategies of the HoPR at a 5 percent level of significance.

Table 4: Test of difference among the perception of different ethnic groups on public engagement strategies

Test statistics[a,b]	Strategies of HoPR to inform	Strategies of HoPR to consult	Strategies of HoPR to deliberate	Strategies of HoPR to collaborate
Chi-Square	3.830	.870	.968	.122
Df	1	1	1	1
Asymp. Sig.	.050	.351	.325	.727

a. Kruskal Wallis Test
b. Grouping Variable: Ethnicity

4.4. The Practice of Public Engagement in the Law-Making Process

The procedure of law making in Ethiopia customarily begins by the initiation of the idea in the executive branch of government. The initiation for producing new law or amendment to existing proclamations is then first sent to the Council of Ministers, for endorsement, before it is sent to the Parliament for final ratification. The draft legislation being sent to the Parliament is seen in plenary session and referred to the legal affairs standing committee and in some cases to other additional concerned parliamentary standing committees for detailed review.

The committees responsible for review the draft legislation in detail conduct a public hearing, in which interested individuals and concerned stakeholders are invited to participate in the debate, and make a report to the plenary section, usually with a proposal for ratification. The arrangement for a public hearing is announced through mass media, mainly radio and TV, with information regarding the issue of discussion and the time and place of the public hearing, so that interested people may have the opportunity to take part in the open discussions on draft legislation. If honestly utilized, this public hearing on draft legislation is a useful parliamentary public engagement mechanism of sharing information and consultation.

In addition to the public hearing, telephone and e-mail are alternatively used to collect inputs from those who cannot directly raise their concerns during public hearings. Recently, the Parliament has also started using the parliamentary call center, website, and social media for disseminating information and collecting opinions from the people. At the time of data collection, the Parliament has introduced other public engagement mechanisms, such as video conference, free call service (8557), and was on the way to launching a new TV channel and digitizing archives. The objective of the digitization process was to save data from loss and to make parliamentary archives easily accessible.

The existence of a forum via the public wing, public hearings, and other means of communication for public engagement, however, did not promote direct democracy in Ethiopia at a significant level, because their existence reflects more form than reality. Our discussions and interviews indicate that the mechanisms employed by the HoPRs to disseminate information on draft law legislations have limitations in terms of accessibility, time, coverage, and language. The Parliament is ineffective in soliciting public input during the crafting of legislation, let alone in creating public awareness of the promulgation of new laws.

The print media used by the House is not widely accessible to the general public; the proclamation itself is not published timely; the website of the Parliament is at an infant stage and has been visited only by very few people. The data on the website is not updated regularly and it is not user friendly. A government report (2018) on the performance of parliamentary public engagement confirms the existence of wide gaps in creating a public forum to engage with the people in the process of law making. The report also shows the existence of weakness in the dissemination of information about the ratification of proclamations and the usual delay in publishing the ratified proclamation in the official legal notice.

The FGD discussants indicate that people living in regional towns/cities are disadvantaged when it comes to taking part in the discussion, as public hearings are always conducted only in Addis Ababa. The HoPRs does not monitor whether participants in the public hearing can represent various interest groups, regions, nationalities, and gender. The key informants disclosed that since all public hearings are conducted at Addis Ababa, people outside of Addis Ababa rarely take part in the public hearings. Moreover, time constraints are found to be another challenge for public engagement in the legislation process. Information from key informants indicates that the HoPR has a tradition of endorsing new proclamations within twenty days, where possible. This tradition deters the opportunity to entertain enough engagement of the people with parliament. There is usually very limited time for the public to forward their suggestion on the draft legislation; for instance, the HoPRs ratified eighteen proclamations in its regular meeting conducted on February 6, 2018, where it is not imagined that member of the parliament themselves engage in sufficient discussion, let alone collecting inputs from the people. The informants believed that urgency in law making not only affects the public engagement but also puts constraints on the due process of law.

The language policy of the House is another challenge that hinders participation in the legislation process. All information is disclosed in one language, hearings are conducted only in one language, and information services on the website are provided only to people who can able speak this language of the Parliament. On the other hand, in Ethiopia, there is no single majority language (spoken by more than half) and as such the communication between the House and the people is visibly exclusive. If the HoPRs were able to disclose information in five languages, it could reach more than 75 percent of the people of Ethiopia, and if it were able to use ten languages, it could address about 90 percent of the population of the country (Central Statistical Agency, 2008). However, the Parliament prefers to use a single language and put a limit on its relation with people of different languages.

The other problem that challenged the effectiveness of parliamentary public engagement in Ethiopia is the fact that the incorporation of the public inputs depends only on the blessing of the ruling party, which controls all the seats of the Parliament and all its standing committees after the 2010 election and 2015 election. Participants of the KIIs and FGD spoke convincingly that the views reflected in the public hearing are not systematically organized, analyzed, and interpreted. As there is no control over the Parliament to ensure people's participation, there is also no way to ensure that views arising during public hearings are considered. In this regard, the Civil Society Law, which was promulgated at the time of data collection for this research report, can be taken as a good example of the case where the public inputs and suggestions were undermined and the participants were unable to make any influence the content of the final legislation. On the other hand, the inputs of the public in the Food and Drug Control proclamation were well acknowledged in final result. Both proclamations were passed in the same period and both attracted the highest level of public participation in public hearings; however, the Parliament approached the public's views differently in these two cases.

4.5. The Practice of Public Engagement in the Representation Function of the HoPRs

This research reveals the relationship between the parliamentarians and constituency at the current stage is not conducive to promoting either participation or parliamentary democracy. According to our respondents, the failure of the parliament to effectively answer the constituency's questions, which are particularly related to lack of good governance and the lagging of infrastructural projects, has eroded public trust in parliament.

Members of parliament have direct contact with the electorate twice each year, according to parliamentary procedure and the code of ethics. On these occasions, the MPs report the annual activities of the Parliament to their respective electorates and in return, listen to the people in the constituency to raise questions they have, to demand clarifications for various parliamentary activities, and raise problems in relation to their specific constituency. Such meetings with the constituency are expected to be reported by each MP to the Parliament, at which point related public questions reported by the parliamentarians are sorted and forwarded to the concerned executive bodies for action.

Even though this type of direct relationship between MPs and the constituency is a good option to combine participatory democracy with parliamentary democracy, in Ethiopia, the relationship between the Parliament and people is restrained by many factors. Government reports (2018/2019) shows that from all the activities of the House in the year 2017/18, the lowest performance was recorded in parliamentary constituency relations. One of the challenges is the absence of outreach services through which the people can have contact with their representative without time and space restrictions. The chance of meeting representative is restricted to only two occasions in a year, when parliament is closed in the summer and in February. It is unlikely many people will have contact with their representative, even in cases where the twice yearly schedule is respected, which it sometimes is not due to low coverage of visits. One of the informants among the MPs disclosed that his constituency has forty-two rural districts and two urban districts, out of which he usually makes it to meetings with two to three districts in one period. This implies that if he will have meeting with three districts in one period, six districts will be covered in a year and thirty districts will be covered in one term of election, while the remaining fourteen districts will be left out during his five years term of office. When direct face-to-face contact is difficult, technology-based information exchange is a good alternative for enhancing parliamentary public engagement. However, despite the importance of information technologies, the representatives are not available via Twitter, Facebook, email and other technology-based channels.

In the worst cases, MPs do not visit their respective constituency, particularly in a time of public protests. The other barrier to the relationship between people and parliament is the failure of members of parliament to make a report to the Parliament. As indicated in a government report (2018/2019), of those MPs who visited their constituency, some did not fully report the situation of their constituency to the Parliament. Therefore, public questions are suppressed due to failure of the representatives to report the concerns of the electorate.

When public questions are reported to the Parliament by a representative, they face other hurdles. The issues reported from different constituencies are combined to ease response by the executive but are also distorted in the process. Once public questions reach the Parliament, merged and forwarded to the executive for proper response, it is the end of the story. Most often, the executive bodies do not respond to issues forwarded since, the parliament does not follow-up on the actions taken by the executive; no one can give feedback to the constituency that brought the questions to the Parliament. As a result, the people lose hope in the capacity of the Parliament to solve their problems. The MPs indicate in their report to the Parliament that they are visiting their constituency year after year without any change in the agenda brought to them. Members of the Parliament are not able to answer questions repetitively asked by the communities in their constituency. Surprisingly, the executive is not made accountable for not responding to the public questions directed to it.

4.6. Public Trust in the Parliament

Respondents were asked to rank the overall public trust in the HoPRs of Ethiopia based on ten survey items. The aggregate response indicates that the public did not have such trust in their representatives (see table 2). This response is expected, because the Parliament performed poorly in engagement with the people. To test whether the low level of trust has any association with parliamentary public engagement, a non-parametric Spearman correlation coefficient test was conducted. The result of test statistics shows that there are positive and strong relationships among all variables: informing, consulting, deliberation, collaboration, and trust. Trust has a positive association with all forms of engagement (to inform 0.44, to consult 0.596, to deliberate 0.61, and to collaborate 0.66). The test result is shown in table 5. This result shows that improvement in engagement will have an association with improvement in public trust in the HoPRs of Ethiopia. Furthermore, we can infer from the test result that a higher level of engagement has a stronger association with trust than lower levels of parliamentary public engagement.

Table 5: Association of public engagement and trust

Correlations		Sharing information	Consultation	Deliberation	Collaboration
Consultation	Correlation Coefficient	.660**			
	Sig. (2-tailed)	.000			
	N	100			
Deliberation	Correlation Coefficient	.603**	.725**		
	Sig. (2-tailed)	.000	.000		
	N	100	100		
Collaboration	Correlation Coefficient	.605**	.784**	.865**	
	Sig. (2-tailed)	.000	.000	.000	.
	N	100	100	100	
Public trust in HoPR	Correlation Coefficient	.439**	.596**	.608**	.660**
	Sig. (2-tailed)	.000	.000	.000	.000
	N	98	98	98	98

**. Correlation is significant at the 0.01 level (2-tailed).

According to our interview respondents, the relationship between parliament and the public in Ethiopia needs improvement. The people have lost confidence in the Parliament by assuming that they have no capacity to address public issues. Participants of the FGD argue that most people do not know the work and responsibilities of the Parliament, due to limited efforts made by the Parliament at public engagement. According to respondents, the Parliament is perceived as a rubber-stamp to endorse all decision required by the party leaders. The people have developed a belief that suggestions do not make a difference. MPs are also criticized for having a "the party knows better than me" attitude. Informants also confirm that the Parliament fails to deliver on its promises to the people in terms of oversight of the budget utilization, mega project performance, and combating corruption. The parliament has refrained from taking measures despite various suspected malpractices by the executive. As a result, people consider the Parliament as a "lion without teeth," according to respondents.

5. Conclusions and Areas for Further Study

Although the HoPRs of Ethiopia has a constitutional responsibility to engage with people, in actual practice, the level of public engagement is low. Our findings show that the HoPRs has institutional limitations in understanding the role of public engagement and in designing the engagement strategies that enhance participatory democracy in a parliamentary system. The absence of a specifically responsible body, with a necessary staff, budget, and other infrastructure has hindered the capacity of the HoPRs to develop an engagement strategy, policy, and procedural directives that would guide public engagement. Participatory democracy is weakened by the restriction of participation to a handful people in public hearings on draft legislations and by systematic control of participation to handpicked public wing groups in the so-called public forum.

The mechanisms used by the HoPRs to inform and consult the people are challenged by a lack of accessibility to people outside of Addis Ababa, time constraints due to a hasty law-making process, low coverage of constituency visits by MPs, and the implicit one-language policy of the parliament. The Parliament's low effort at engaging with people to deliberate and to collaborate creates a situation in which there is no way for the people to influence the parliamentary decisions, while for the Parliament there is little means of ensuring its decisions are consistent with the interest of the people it represents. The discussions in this chapter show that the parliamentary public engagement strategy of the HoPR is not effective in bringing the Parliament close to the people and thereby creating public trust. On the other hand the finding of this research indicates a strong and positive linkage between all forms of parliamentary public engagement and public trust.

Finally, on the basis of the delimitation of this research, we call for more research into public engagement, to include the House of Federation of Ethiopia and the regional councils.

Acknowledgement

The authors would like to thank the Global Research Network on Parliaments and People (GRNPP) for funding the research; the Forum for Social Studies (FSS) for facilitating researches on the relationship between people and parliament in Ethiopia; Adede PLC for hosting the research; and the House of Peoples Representative of Ethiopia for facilitating data collection. Furthermore, among individuals who contributed to the realization of this research project, we are thankful to Mihret Ayenew for his guidance, advice, and encouragement; the Parliament for People (P4P) project Team for their constructive comments; Wondeson Kebede, president of Ethiopian Visual Arts Association for designing posters we have used to communicate the research findings; Member of Parliamentarians, members of the secretariat of the House of Peoples Representative and all other participants of the KII and FGD for being part of the research. Finally, we would also want to extend our thanks to Bacha Kebede Debela, President of Ethiopian Public Administration Association, and to the editors and reviewers for their contribution in improving this last version of the research report.

References

Ayenew, M. (2019). *Parliament-Public Engagement in Ethiopia: Selected Notes and Case Studies on a Politically Fragile State.* Forum for Social Studies.

Beeri, I., Uster, A., & Vigoda-Gadot, E. (2019). Does Performance Management Relate to Good Governance? A Study of Its Relationship with Citizens' Satisfaction with and Trust in Israeli Local Government. *Public Performance & Management Review*, 42(2), 241-279.

Beetham, D. (ed.). (2006). *Parliament and Democracy in the Twenty-first Century: A Guide to Good Practice.* Geneva: Inter-Parliamentary Union.

Bingham, L. B., Nabatchi, T., & O'Leary, R. (2005). The New Governance: Practices and Processes for Stakeholder and Citizen Participation in the Work of Government. *Public Administration Review*, 65(5), 547-558.

Bird, K. (2003). *The Political Representation of Women and Ethnic Minorities in Established Democracies: A Framework for Comparative Research.* Documento presentado ante la Academia de estudios de migración de Dinamarca, Universidad de Aalborg, 11.

Burton, P. (2009). Conceptual, Theoretical and Practical Issues in Measuring the Benefits of Public Participation. *Evaluation*, 15(3), 263-284.

Dalton, R. (2004). *Democratic Challenges, Democratic Choices: The Erosion of Political Support in Advanced Industrial Democracies.* Oxford: Oxford University Press.

European Network against Racism. (2010). Political Participation &Representation of Ethnic Minorities: From Wishful Thinking to Reality? www.enar-eu.org.

Fung, A., & Wright, E. O. (2003). *Deepening Democracy: Institutional Innovations in Empowered Participatory Governance*, vol. 4. London: Verso.

Hay, C. (2007). *Why We Hate Politics*. Cambridge: Polity Press.

He, B. (2010). A Deliberative Approach to the Tibet Autonomy Issue: Promoting Mutual Trust through Dialogue. *Asian Survey*, 50(4), 709-734.

Hendriks, C. M., & Kay, A. (2019). From "Opening Up" to Democratic Renewal: Deepening Public Engagement in Legislative Committees. *Government and Opposition*, 54(1), 25-51.

IDEA (2005). *Women in Parliament: Beyond Numbers, A Revised Edition*. Stockholm: IDEA.

Inter-Parliamentary Union (2011), *Gender-sensitive Parliament, towards Parliaments That Respond to the Needs and Interests of Both Men and Women in Their Structures, Operations, Methods and Work*. Interparliamentary Union.

Jungermann, H., Pfister, H. R., & Fischer, K. (1996). Credibility, Information Preferences, and Information Interests. *Risk Analysis*, 16(2), 251-261.

Kelly, R., & Bochel, C. (2018). *Parliament's Engagement with the Public*. Briefing Paper Number 8279, 6, House of Commons Library.

Kurtz, K. T. (1997). *Legislatures and Citizens: Public Participation and Confidence in the Legislature*. Denver: National Conference of State Legislatures.

Lenihan D. (2009). *Rethinking the Public Policy Process*. Framework paper: Public Policy Forum.

Leston-Bandeira, C. (2016). Why Symbolic Representation Frames Parliamentary Public Engagement. *British Journal of Politics and International Relations*, 18(2), 498-516.

Löfstedt, R. (2005). *Risk Management in Post-trust Societies*. New York: Palgrave Macmillan.

Lofstedt, R. E. (2006). How Can We Make Food Risk Communication Better: Where Are We and Where Are We Going? *Journal of Risk Research*, 9(8), 869-890.

Mattila, M. (2017). *From Representative Democracy to Democratic Representation: Lessons from the Talvivaara Controversy*. Tampere: Acta Universitatis Tamperensis

Newman, J. (2005). The New Public Management, modernization and institutional change. In K. McLaughlin, E. Ferlie & S. Osborne (eds). *New Public Management: Current Trends and Future Prospects* (p. 77). London: Routledge.

Newton, K., & Norris, P. (2000). Confidence in Public Institutions: Faith, Culture, or Performance. In S.J. Parr & R.D. Putnam (eds). *Disaffected Democracies: What's Troubling the Trilateral Countries* (pp. 52–73). Chicago: Princeton University Press.

Norris, P. (2011). *Democratic Deficit: Critical Citizens Revisited*. Cambridge, UK: Cambridge University Press.

O'Neill, O. (2002). *A Question of Trust: The BBC Reith Lectures 2002*. Cambridge, UK: Cambridge University Press.

Parliament of New South Wales. (2017). Re-engaging the Disengaged: Why Parliamentary Education and Community Engagement is Core business.

Peters, R. G., Covello, V. T., & McCallum, D. B. (1997). The Determinants of Trust and Credibility in Environmental Risk Communication: An Empirical Study. *Risk Analysis*, 17(1), 43-54.

Petts, J. (2008). Public Engagement to Build Trust: False Hopes? *Journal of Risk Research*, 11(6), 821-835.

Renn, O. (2009). White Paper on Risk Governance: Towards an Integrative Approach. International Risk Governance Council (IRGC).

Renn, O., & Levine, D. (1991). Credibility and Trust in Risk Communication. In R. Kasperson & P. Stallen (eds). *Communicating Risks to the Public* (pp. 175-217). Dordrecht: Springer.

Rosenberg, S. (ed.) (2007). *Can the People Govern?* Basingstoke: Palgrave.

Rotter, J. B. (1971). Generalized Expectancies for Interpersonal Trust. *American Psychologist*, 26(5), 443.

Ruedin, D. (2009). Ethnic Group Representation in a Cross-national Comparison. *Journal of Legislative Studies*, 15(4), 335-354.

Smith, G. (2009). *Democratic Innovations: Designing Institutions for Citizen Participation*. Cambridge, UK: Cambridge University Press.

South Africa Legislative Sector. (2013). Public Participation Framework for the South African Legislative Sector. www.sals.gov.za.

Stoker, G. (2006). *Why Politics Matters*. Basingstoke: Palgrave.

Stoker, G. (2006). Public Value Management: A New Narrative for Networked Governance? *American Review of Public Administration*, 36(1), 41-57.

The Race and Social Justice Initiative. (2009). *Inclusive Outreach and Public Engagement Guide.*

Thomas, C. H. (2006). Clarifying the Concept of Work Engagement: Construct Validation and an Empirical (Doctoral dissertation, University of Georgia).

Thomson-Senanayake J. (2012). Political Trust, Community Engagement in Public Policy and the Role of Parliamentary Committees PLPP Research Paper.

Tormey, S. (2015). *The End of Representative Politics*. John Wiley & Sons.

Walker, A. (2012). A People's Parliament? *Parliamentary Affairs*,65(1): 270-80.

Walker A. (2017). Parliaments and Public Engagement; Guide to Parliaments, paper 9. Global Partner Governance

Welch, E. W., Hinnant, C. C., & Moon, M. J. (2005). Linking Citizen Satisfaction with e-government and Trust in Government. *Journal of Public Administration Research and Theory*, 15(3), 371-391.

Whiteley, P. (2009). Government Effectiveness and Political Participation in Britain. *Representation* 45(3), 247-257.

Whiteley, P. (2011). *Political Participation in Britain: The Decline and Revival of Civic Culture*. London: Macmillan International Higher Education.

II.2

PARTNERSHIPS AND PARTICIPATION

6
Multi-Stakeholder Partnership for Health Service Delivery in the Context of Developmental State: The Ethiopian Experience

Hiwot Amare Tadesse and Trui Steen

Box 1. Key points of the chapter

- ✓ Policy direction, pressing health problems, the need for resources, in combination with the state's developmental vision, facilitates the emergence of MSPs that involve both state and nonactors in the Ethiopian health sector.
- ✓ MSPs can involve both mutuality and power differences. The manifestation of the development state (DS) impacts the organization and functioning of MSPs in both positive and negative ways. While DS contributes to enhancing the reciprocal relations between actors through shared purpose and commitment, it diminishes the opportunity for interaction and negotiation, developing more collaborative and trusting relationships, and MSPs capacity for self-regulation.

Box 2: Reading this chapter will give you insights in

- ✓ How partnerships involving diverse sets of actors are organized and operate in a Developmental State (DS) context.
- ✓ The manifestation of the DS in the Ethiopian health sector and its impact on the organization and functioning of MSPs.

Box 3: Abbreviations

CCRDA = Christian Consortium Relief Development Agency
CSO = Civil Society Organization
DS = Developmental State
EPRDF = Ethiopian People Revolutionary Democratic Front
FMOH = Federal Ministry of Health
GTP = Growth and Transformation Plan
HDA = Health Development Army
HEW = Health Extension Workers

HSDP = Health Sector Development Programs
MDGs = Millennium Development Goals
MSPs = Multi-Stakeholder Partnerships
NGO = Non-Governmental Organization
PHCU = Primary Health Care Unit
SDGs = Sustainable Development Goals

Introduction

In this day and age, societies are struggling with multidimensional problems that require bringing together resources and expertise from a diverse set of actors (Sullivan & Skelcher, 2002). Given the complexity of problems, governmental entities are increasingly challenged to horizontally coordinate their policy planning and production of services not only between each other but also with other actors (Kickert et al. 1997; Rhodes, 1997; Stoker, 1998). Although the need to engage in collaborative efforts between state and non-state actors might not be a new thing, it has taken on a particular form since the end of the 1980s and the beginning of the 1990s following the reforms in public administration. This has resulted in the evolution of our understanding the nature of policy making and implementation the monocentric to pluricentric. More specifically, the new public governance is presented as a framework recognizing

> *"the collaborative nature of modern efforts to meet human needs, the widespread use of tools of action that engage complex networks of public and private actors, and the resulting need for a different style of public management, and a different type of public sector, emphasizing collaboration and enablement rather than hierarchy and control"* (Salamon 2002, vii).

Therefore, governments in many parts of the world are becoming more collaborative by engaging citizens, nongovernmental organizations (NGOs), and private sector organizations in devising and implementing solutions to society's challenges.

In the scholarly literature, the concept of partnership has emerged as a new form of governance arrangement that changes the traditional governance structure of states (Johnston, 2015; Lowndes & Skelcher 1998; Osborne 2000; Sorensen & Torfing, 2005; Sullivan & Skelcher, 2002). Subsequently, partnerships involving diverse sets of stakeholders have developed as a practical approach with which to address complex social problems (Benner et al., 2004). These partnerships proceed from the basic need for sharing resources and information in meeting collective goals as well as the individual goals of actors involved. However, approaches to partnerships vary greatly across and within nations. Different types of partnerships exist, and their share in the overall creation and production of public services differs too (Selsky & Parker, 2005). This is especially related to the fact that partnerships exist in a certain environment. For instance, Sørensen & Torfing (2005) argue that the level of political support and dependency on partnerships as a new governance mechanism differs between countries, scales, and policy sectors because of past national political cultures, traditions, and institutions. Pattberg & Widerberg (2014) confirm that "partnerships are embedded in a political and social context that will influence their chances to thrive" (p. 30).

The state and its agencies are not only important actors in partnerships, they also provide the ideological, legal, and institutional foundation based on which partnerships will emerge, evolve, and function (Batley, 2006). Hence, the overarching political philosophy of states can determine the nature and practice of partnerships. For instance, the kind of partnership that may exist in a liberal state with a huge role for the private sector is expected to be different from the kind of partnership that prevails in a centralized state that gives little space to the private sector. An example of the latter is the Developmental State, which is depicted as an ideology that encourages state intervention. States with DS ideology usually prefer to shape the direction and pace of economic and social development by intervening in the development process to check the uncoordinated influences of market forces (Johnson, 1982).

This chapter examines the overall functioning of three Multi-Stakeholder Partnerships (MSPs) organized for health service delivery in Ethiopia. The primary focus of this chapter is derived from the observation that there is a surge of working relationships among state and non-state actors in the Ethiopian health-care sector despite the government's DS orientation. This study follows the growing body of public administration studies that stress the importance of the national and institutional context in shaping the public sectors reforms and the practice and outcome of such reform initiatives as partnerships (Christensen & Lægreid, 2007; Osborne, 2010; Røvik, 2002).

Ethiopia adopted a different politico-administrative structure following the declaration of the DS. Hence, the argument we want to make in this chapter is that studying the form and operation of partnerships should consider the national context wherein these partnerships take place. Two major perspectives, one common to public administration literature (the concept of governance) and the other concerning the DS, seem to offer promising directions from which to investigate this issue. Especially in a DS context, the relation between state and nonstate actors in collaborative settings is unclear. To increase our understanding of how partnership arrangements work and to develop knowledge on the overall nature and operation of horizontal partnerships for the coproduction of public services in Ethiopia, this chapter focuses on answering the following main research question: **What is the impact of the developmental state context on the functioning of multi-stakeholder partnerships for health service delivery in Ethiopia?**

The chapter is divided as follows: first, we discuss some of the theoretical concepts and how these are used in framing the study: "governance," "network governance," "partnerships," and "developmental state." Second, we present a brief overview on the role of partnerships for health service provision in Ethiopia. The methods and data used in the process of the study are presented next. Fourth, the case analysis and findings in accordance with the network governance and developmental state frameworks are presented. In section five, we discuss and draw conclusions from the findings of the study. We present some of the implications that such a context has for public governance in general and for state and nonstate actor relationships in particular.

1. Governance, Network Governance, Partnerships, and Developmental State

1.1. Governance

A wide-ranging use of the term governance indicates that scholars within the current public administration literature view governance from different perspectives. In his widely cited book *Understanding Governance*, Rhodes (1997) distinguished six ways in which the term governance is used in the literature: governance as the minimal state, as corporate governance, as the new public management, as good governance, as a socio-cybernetic system, and as self-organizing networks. Klijn (2008) also differentiates four main definitions that dominate the literature: governance as good governance or as corporate governance, governance as New Public Management (NPM) or as market governance, governance as multilevel governance or inter-governmental relations, and governance as network governance (self-steering or non-self-steering).

Although the above definitions represent different conceptions of governance, they have something that unites them. Many of them focus on mechanisms involved in solving societal problems rather than on what the government can do with its authority and predetermined structure. This is in line with the notion that governments are changing the way they govern society by focusing on the process that can best achieve outcomes rather than concentrating on centralized power (Klijn, 2008). As is widely acknowledged, the shift from government to governance entails the establishment of new systems that stimulate different forms of cooperation between state and nonstate actors in formulating and implementing public policy (Noor et al. 2010). Hence, governance allows us to conceptualize the different processes, structures, and arrangements needed to embrace complex interactions wherein both state and nonstate actors engage together in dealing with societal issues.

The depiction of state and other societal actors' relationship as the main emblem of the governance concept has pushed some scholars toward seeing governance from a network perspective only. This relational aspect of governance has stimulated many scholars "to use the term governance as a synonym for what others call 'network governance'" (Meuleman, 2008; p. 15). Nevertheless, one can find different understandings of governance that are equally important as the network perspective (see Osborne & Gaebler, 1992; Rhodes, 1997). In broader understanding, the concept can be used to describe a plethora of formal and informal institutions, mechanisms, and process through which public policy is being formulated and implemented (Johnston, 2015; Pierre & Peters, 2000; Sorensen & Torfing, 2005). Stoker (1998) puts forward a definition that he thinks can form a baseline agreement in understanding governance. He refers to governance as "the development of governing styles in which boundaries between and within public and private actors have become blurred" (p. 17). This chapter starts with a theoretical insight that there is a change from government to governance, namely, the increased focus on the involvement of a range of societal actors when addressing public issues. However, different governing styles can be involved in framing the relation between these actors, such as hierarchy or market, besides networks. Taking a broad perspective in understanding governance allows us to use a wide angle in capturing the interaction of state and nonstate actors. Following this broad perspective, we then use the term "governance" to describe "... [t]he totality of interactions, in which government, other public bodies, private sector and civil society participate, aiming at solving societal problems or creating societal opportunities" (Meuleman, 2008; p. 11).

1.2. Network Governance

Since the 1990s a vast amount of literature has been devoted to the development of network governance, including work by Rhodes (1997, 2000); Pierre (2000); Klijn (2008); Klijn & Koppenjan (2000); Kooiman (2003); and Sørensen & Torfing (2007). In the governance literature, network governance relates to the configuration of relatively organized relations that involves interdependent actors and their complex interaction (Klijn & Koppenjan, 2000; Klijn, 2008). The formation of these networks aims at resolving societal problems. Consequently, many scholars describe networks as the interplay of interdependent actors in society aimed at policy making and implementation (Kickert et al. 1997; Klijn, 2002; Klijn & Koppenjan, 2000). In line with this, we found Sorensen & Torfing's definition of network governance most suitable in the context of this research. First, it captures the basic ideas that are commonly ascribed to networks governance. Second, it is in line with our argument about the relation between governance and network concepts. Sorensen & Torfing (2005) define network governance as:

> *"A relatively stable horizontal articulation of interdependent, but operationally autonomous actors; Who interact through negotiations; Which take place within a regulative, normative, cognitive and imaginary framework; That to a certain extent is self-regulating; and Which contributes to the production of public purpose within or across particular policy areas."* (p. 203)

This study considers this network governance model to frame the analysis of our cases. Most network governance scholarship focuses upon developed countries where there exist positive relations between state and civil society in an open and participatory governance system (Hudson, 2004; Huxhham & Vangen, 2005; Klijn & Koppenjan, 2000; Sorensen & Torfing, 2007). In contrast, there is little knowledge as to whether network governance is possible in a developing context and to what extent the existing partnerships between state and nonstate actors resemble network governance. Since many developing countries, including Ethiopia, lack some of the features of developed countries' political-administrative structure, it may be difficult to picture network governance in these countries. Yet we do not know if it has potential for world-wide application, how it takes shape and form, and what factors influence its creation and functioning. Thus, applying the network governance framework of analysis in a developing country context has the potential to extend its theoretical relevance and application: "Certainly theorization is strengthened by confirmatory analyses. But theorization is also strengthened by reflecting upon non-confirmatory cases" (Moloney, 2013, p. 3).

1.3. Partnerships in a network governance context

In a governance environment where pluricentric relations with network-like features dominate, partnership can provide a means of developing strategic direction and coordination (Brinkerhoff, 2002; Lowndes & Skelcher, 1998;

Rees, et al., 2012). According to Lowndes & Skelcher (1998) partnerships are most affiliated with network governance in the market-hierarchy–network modes of governance as "the development of interdependent relationship based on trust, loyalty and reciprocity enables collaborative activity to be developed and maintained" (p. 319). Skelcher et al. (2005) argue that governance is well manifested through partnerships that are capable of engaging a variety of actors with their differing interests. Scholars like Rhodes (1997) and Stoker (1998) differentiate partnerships from other interorganizational relationships, such as contracts, by taking partnership as being identical with self-governing networks that exhibit high levels of trust among network member. However, the totality of interaction among a diverse set of actors may not completely rely on trust, which may give rise to different types of network forms and relationships (Davies, 2002; Thompson, 2003). Governance in general and partnerships in particular are contested by scholars who interpret the concepts differently. For instance, though Lowndes & Skelcher (1998) indicate that partnerships may resemble network governance, they denounce the idea that partnerships are identical with network as a mode of governance. Stoker (1998) determines different types of relations that may exist among actors in a network context through a classification of partnerships as principal-agent relations, interorganizational negotiation, and systematic coordination. While the first and second partnership types involve formal and less collaborative relationship, only the last one shows the characteristics of ideal network governance, which involves higher mutual understanding. In contrast, Davies (2002) views partnerships as analytically distinct from network governance and as a "... distinctive mode of governance characterized simultaneously by the diffusion and augmentation of State power" (p. 302).

Despite these differing arguments, the literature on partnerships tends to focus on elements that correspond with network governance (see Bode & Brandsen, 2014; Stewart & Gray, 2006). For instance, Brinkerhoff (2002) defines the ideal type of partnership as:

> *"A dynamic relationship among diverse actors, based on mutually agreed objectives, pursued through a shared understanding of the most rational division of labour based on the respective comparative advantages of each partner. Partnership encompasses mutual influence, with a careful balance between synergy and respective autonomy, which incorporates mutual respect, equal participation in decision making, mutual accountability and transparency."* (p. 21)

While acknowledging that there exist a number of dimensions for conceptualizing partnership, it is important to use insights from the network governance literature, which suggest factors that can sustain the relationship between state and nonstate actors. Therefore, it would be more appropriate to question governance as a theory of state and nonstate actors' relation in the delivery of public services through empirically examining MSPs in a network governance framework. In this respect, and following Sorensen & Torfing's (2005) defining characteristics of network arrangements, outlined as interdependency among various actors, interaction through negotiation, institutionalized framework, ability to self-regulate, and production of public purpose, our main and focal point of analysis is ***to what extent the relations between actors in MSPs are conducted on the basis of the above-listed characteristics of a (ideal type) network mode of governance.***

1.4. Developmental State

Usually, the concept of DS is viewed as distinct from both liberal and centrally planned economic models. The definition of DS and the elaboration of the concept followed the rapid economic growth of East Asian countries, since their growth is associated with state-led policies and intervention. Caldentey (2003) defines the DS as "a state that intervenes and guides the direction and pace of economic growth" (pp. 28). Hence, the DS is committed to bringing economic growth mainly through state guidance and interventions. According to Bolesta "[t]he introduction of developmental state theory into the state ideology means, in real terms, a departure from a neo-liberal economic ideology and a drift towards state interventionism" (2007, p. 105). However, in a DS context state intervention focuses on promoting development rather than hindering the socioeconomic development as is the case in centrally planned economies (Bolesta, 2007; Ghebremusse, 2015). In reviewing DS related literature, it becomes apparent that states have a critical role in promoting development.

Various authors use one or more features as a central organizing concept for defining the DS. Developmental structures (state capacity) and developmental roles, for example, have been identified as two fundamental aspects of the DS (Routley, 2012). Vu (2007) refers to these as "structure and ideology" (p. 28). Similarly, Ghebremusse (2015) points out that the link between ideology and structure differentiates the DS from other states. Hence, a DS has to be defined considering both its objectives and structure. Routley (2012) provides a definition that takes the above concepts into account: "a developmental state has sufficient state capacity to be effective in its targeted areas and has a developmental vision such that it chooses to use this capacity to work towards economic development." (p. 8).

The fundamental institutional features of the DS related to state capacity are "autonomy" and "embeddedness." These elements enable states to achieve their developmental goals (Routley, 2012). According to Edigheji (2005), autonomy is all about installing autonomous and competent public institutions that are capable of executing developmental goals. The literature argues that the purpose of building an autonomous bureaucracy is to free the state and its structure from being captured by forces outside the state (Edigheji, 2005; Evans, 1995). The concept of embeddedness refers to the process of building collaborative relationships with various societal actors, including private actors, civil society organizations, and citizens (Evans, 1995). Scholars such as Johnson (1982) and Evans (1995) indicate that the presence of an independent and coherent state structure that is capable to plan and lead the developmental activities is an essential element in the overall success of a DS. The literature asserts that the value of state structure or bureaucracies enhances when they function independently (Evans 1995; Kohli 2004)

2. Health Service Provision and Partnerships in Ethiopia

Ethiopia, being one of the world's least developed countries, struggles in meeting the basic health needs of its rapidly increasing population. With limited resources, severe poverty, and other pressing problems, the state remains an important actor in providing health services. Before the coming of the current regime, there was limited participation of NGOs and the private sector in public service provision (Clark, 2000; CRDA, 2006). However, following a change of government in 1991, the new regime developed a national health policy and reorganized the health services delivery system, among other things by encouraging partnerships with and participation of nongovernmental actors.

Since the 1990s there has been a governmental concern to involve private for profit and nonprofit partners and more recently community groups and citizens in health service delivery. The government has been radical in the development of its approach to public service delivery (particularly in health), with the promotion of partnerships involving new and expanded roles for Civil Society Organizations (CSOs) in almost all areas of health care and service delivery (Rahmato et al., 2008) and through decentralization of the health sector, with a devolution of rights and responsibilities from the center to the local level.

Simultaneously, Ethiopia has embraced the DS ideology. Unlike the free-market orientation of neoliberalism, the DS heavily privileges a vanguard role for the state on various economic and social development fronts (Tadesse & Steen, 2019). With the introduction of the developmental principles, the government's drive to work with different societal actors has taken on its own form. In particular, interest in entering into collaboration with a diverse set of actors has been reinforced by the drive to meet both international and local strategic development plans, made more pressing by restricted resources. The international development goals such as the Millennium Development Goals (MDGs) and, later on, the Sustainable Development Goals (SDGs), which trigger many low- and middle-income countries to develop aspiring health policies and strategies, complemented the Ethiopian government's intention on health policy and development plans. As part of the international development goals and overall national health strategies, Ethiopia has implemented several health strategies of significant scale in the past two decades. Promoting partnership across sectors to improve health sector development and thereby to tackle the health service problems was a very prominent aspect of these efforts (El-Saharty et al., 2009).

3. Research Method and Data

3.1. Research Design

The aim of this study is to examine the existence and actual application of partnerships as a new form of governance in the Ethiopian context. The study is based on a qualitative approach using observations, semi structured interviews, focus group discussions, and a review of internal and published documents. As the topic in this study is fairly unexplored and highly related to its political, social, and cultural context, the collection of in-depth data in a natural setting sensitive to the people and place under study is highly valuable. Qualitative inquiry allows the researcher to conduct extensive collection of data; typically from multiple sources of information (Flick, 2002).The study employs a multiple case study research design in which the units of analysis are three different MSPs organized for health service delivery in different parts of Ethiopia.

3.2. Federal Democratic Republic of Ethiopia's Health Sector

The choice of the Ethiopian health sector as the main study domain can be attributed to different reasons. First, following the 1991 government change in Ethiopia, the new government of Ethiopia developed the first national health policy to give a sound direction for the involvement of diverse sets of stakeholders in the health sector. In addition to the national policy document, different policy and strategy documents (Health Sector Development Programs [HSDP I, II, III & IV], and the Growth and Transformation Plan [GTP I & II]) encourage joint efforts of state and nonstate actors in the health sector.

Second, the Ethiopian health sector is characterized by the involvement of a wide variety of national and international donors, NGOs, CSOs, and other stakeholders. The participation and contribution of these diverse set of actors is well recognized: introducing new and innovative approaches working in collaboration with health offices at different levels of government; boosting health service coverage and utilization and providing complementary services to support government health policy and programs (CCRDA, 2014; FMOH, 2014). Hence, the role and involvement of a diverse set of stakeholders in the health sector provides an opportunity to examine state and nonstate actors in a partnership setting. The available information on state and nonstate actors partnerships supported by both policy documents and information provided by local practitioners encouraged us to select the health sector as a critical case (Levy, 2008; Patton, 2001) that can produce sufficient information in addressing the research questions.

3.3. Case selection

Selecting three cases from the variety of health programs seems a difficult task. Therefore, we decided to have some minimum criteria that match the cases to our MSP definition:

- MSPs that are organized for health service delivery; more specifically working on maternal and child health;
- MSPs organized with private sector, not-for-profit (CSOs), public and citizens' participation, preferably involving three types of actors – private, public and civil – with at least one public sector representative and at least one civil society representative. But we sought to select MSPs that involve a maximum of actors, as it gives a chance to see the complex interaction patterns and different perspectives on the issues that will be raised;
- MSPs that are initiated at the local, regional, or federal level, thus excluding partnerships that are initiated on a supra-national level;
- MSPs that are functioning for at least one year, before January 2016 (the starting time of the empirical research) and at least (planned to) continue until five months in the future.

On the basis of the above listed criteria and consultation with experts from FMOH, three cases were selected. Since the preliminary analysis provided the impression that partnerships are a newly emerging phenomenon in Ethiopia, it is difficult if not impossible to identify a well-developed MSP in the actual conceptual and theoretical sense of the term. Therefore, we made a careful analysis of each organization's website, contacted the organizations in person and through phone and email to select cases with a maximum number of actors and that most resemble our definition of MSPs.

An additional criteria used to select the cases was convenience. While the data collection process proceeded, the ongoing protest in Ethiopia which started in 2016 intensified. Hence, we selected cases that were more convenient for data collection. In conducting the field works, avoiding conflict places was the major obstacle to the research. Using convenience as a sampling technique can be scrutinized for credibility since the most convenient sample may not be the best sample. However, in selecting cases from different places (conflict free), we made a careful attempt not to compromise the first criteria.

In the three MSPs, the project activities include among others strengthening the functional level of health facilities, building the capacity of the health system especially at the district level, building the capacity of health workers, and mobilizing community demand and ownership over maternal and child health care interventions. Most of these activities take place at the district and sub district levels, where health centers and health posts are located. The cases involve a diverse set of actors, including international donors, NGOs, local NGOs, state actors at different levels, and stakeholders from the community.

3.4. Data collection

In total seventy semi structured interviews were conducted in person by the first author at the location of the interviewees' workplace (health offices, health centers, government offices). In addition, five shorter interviews and follow-up talks over telephone and email were added to verify or discuss specific issues and in some cases to collect additional information. Of the seventy respondents, ten interviewees were key informants who represent the government at the federal and regional levels, within academic and policy institutions, yet were not directly part of the partnership. However, they were experts and knowledgeable in the area of partnerships and political conditions of the country. Respondents were asked about the organization of the partnerships, actors' interaction, and decision-making processes. In addition, respondents were interviewed in order to gain insights on the DS orientations and its impact on the MSPs. Also, a total of seven focus group discussions were conducted. For each case, we conducted two focus group discussions on selected project sites at the local level, and one at federal level. The data from these discussions have been used to provide a depth of interpretation unavailable from the interviews (cf. Small, 2011). Moreover, they helped to further explore the different perceptions or opinions of the different actors involved in the MSPs: partners, users, and local authorities. Moreover, observations and a review of documents added to the data.

4. Case Analysis and Findings[1]

4.1. Explaining MSPs from a Network Governance Perspective

In this section, we analyze the three MSPs in accordance with Sorensen & Torfing's (2005) defining characteristics of network arrangements: interdependency, interaction through negotiation, institutionalized framework, ability to self-regulate and production of public purpose.

The interdependency of various societal actors plays a significant role in establishing and continuing the operation of MSPs in the studied cases. MSPs for health service delivery are organized articulating a diverse set of actors with different competencies and resources that help the local state actors to provide health services that otherwise would be difficult to do. Studies find that interdependency that arises from the division of resources is a key element for networked relationships of actors to arise and to continue (Kickert et al. 1997; Mandell 2001; Rhodes 1997; Scharpf 1997). The study shows that two major issues reflect the interdependency of the actors in MSPs: exchange of resources and actors' stakes in issues at hand. In all cases, the partnerships incorporate the community groups that have resources and stakes in the issues, which further reinforce the reciprocal relations of societal actors. We, therefore, argue that interdependency of various societal actors plays an important role in the establishment of the partnerships.

Negotiation lies at the heart of actors' relationships as it gives a chance for the actors to interact through discussion and deliberation. The three cases show that actors execute the project activities through engaging in discussions and negotiations. For example, actors engage in discussion to determine specific roles in executing specific activities or when faced with problems. These discussions are conducted at different levels of government, resulting in a different negotiation process and output. We found that actors' interaction at the local level is more framed by negotiation and interaction resulting in common decision-making as compared to similar interaction on the regional and federal levels. While at the federal and regional levels there is established a framework for negotiating with nonstate actors, this system involves continues interaction and communication between the FMOH, Regional Health Bureau, and nonstate actors in the decision chain. However, these frameworks involve limited space for fully realizing negotiation capacity and alternatives. The cases indicate that these negotiation processes at the federal and regional levels are constrained by strict administrative formalities and predesigned frameworks despite the recognized need for common effort towards alleviating maternal and child health problems. This is not to say that the negotiations at the local level are perfect, which is not the case, but the day-to-day interaction of the actors and the development of trust through time at local level pave the way for smooth negotiation. Besides, state and nonstate actors at the local level are well aware of their scope of engagement, resulting in a more focused and productive negotiation within a determined policy and program framework.

In all three cases, there was an explicit institutional framework that ties the interaction between state and nonstate actors. Formal agreements and action plans frame the interaction of the actors in the MSP through establishing roles and procedures. Informal agreement through dialogue, strong bonds and shared common identity and ideology were found to be as important as the formal agreement in forming the institutional framework, positively affecting the operation of MSPs. Such informal agreement helps to establish values like trust, commitment, and cooperation, which further provide a normative and imaginary framework for the interaction.

The institutional setting in all MSPs is dominated by regulatory arrangements. While in the first case the regulatory framework is relatively loosely bound by a memorandum of understanding, in the other two cases there exist formal contractual agreements. Rules are relevant as they facilitate interaction in networks, thus reducing transaction costs and influencing the performance of the networks (Koppenjan & Klijn, 2004). However, when the regulatory aspect dominates the overall institutional framework of the collaboration, it reflects on the overall nature of the collaboration as it leads the partnership into a more formal and contractual relationship. The literature indicates that networks may not possess the capacity for complete self-regulation as they operate in an environment filled with state agencies. In particular, the state, although a participant in networks, is found to play a dominant role in governance networks (Bell & Hindmoor, 2009; Johnston, 2015; Pierre & Peters, 2000). Based on this study, we add some evidence on the dominant role of the state in networks. For example, the operating environment at different levels is filled with state actors that regulate the partnership, and the state exerted effort to put into place a regulatory structure at different levels that sets strong accountability measures for collective actions.

The production of a public purpose in MSPs to some extent helps to explain the organization and function of the MSPs. The collaboration effort can help the societal actors to develop new methods and techniques that can be scaled up to various areas and be an input in policy formulation. In accordance with their scope and objectives, through their interventions, strategies, and programs all three MSPs contribute something of value that can sum up to the national goal of improving maternal and child health. However, meeting short-term objectives and supporting immediate need seems more prominent in the cases studied as compared to the production of sustainable public purposes.

4.2. Analyzing MSPs in a DS context

The following section aims to understand which aspect of DS influence the relation between state and nonstate actors in Ethiopia. Therefore it studies developmental vision and role, state autonomy, and embeddedness.

Developmental Vision and Role

The results of the cases indicate that the state uses MSPs as a tool to achieve its national health objectives and goals. At the national level, health is now one of the very critical development endeavors of the Ethiopian state and various actions in the health sector prove the state's developmentalist vision and role. First, the state reflects its developmental visions and goals through the articulation of various long-term national development plans and strategies that are aimed at bringing about social and economic development. The detailed articulation of health developmental goals and strategies both at the national and sectoral levels played a major role in stimulating the formation of MSPs as they were important in aligning a diverse set of actors into the health sector, including international and local NGOs, state agencies, and other community groups. This implies that the development of a national health plan serves as a tool in assembling and connecting a diverse set of stakeholders.

Besides stimulating the formation of MSPs, the articulation of health development plans impacts the functioning of MSPs. The analysis of the plan documents and our interviews show that some features of the health development plans contribute to the strengthening of a reciprocal relation and the production of public purpose in the studied MSPs. First, many of the development plans put forward strategies and directions that encourage reciprocal relations through resource mobilization in the health sector. Second, the plans were effective in clearly communicating national health goals and priorities, which contributed to the formation of a common agenda that is shared among many stakeholders. These national health goals and priorities were important to convey similar messages to various sections of the society and helped to increase stakeholders' stake on health issues. Interviews with community health workers and community volunteer revealed that they are committed to the current health plan and goals as these prioritize their community's major problem:

> *When the government tells us no mother should die because of pregnancy and children should not die before 28 days, I take it seriously. My job makes me happy, and my reward is when I see a pregnant woman gives birth safely and when you vaccinate a child and walks, I am very happy with my work, because it is solves our major problem. Though our work is very hard, I am happy and I am committed (Interviewee SR 5, case 1)*

With the developmental state ideology, EPRDF focuses on building the capacity of the state and asserts the need for taking ownership and leadership of the development process (Kelsall, 2013). The health sector has accordingly witnessed a massive presence and intervention of the state. Basically the health service delivery is monopolized by the state, which takes the leading role in providing health services through government structures and departments. This involves putting in place a structure that stretches to the grass root level and involves the network relations of all Primary Health Care Units (PHCUs), Health Extension Workers (HEWs), and the community network compromising women volunteers (Health Development Army: HDA). Despite the differences among the cases studied, the collaboration activities took place within this state structure, indicating that the organization of MSPs takes a similar format and design. Hence, in all cases studied, the MSPs are integrated in the wider administrative structure of the state. This includes among others applying the programs and activities at health centers and health posts which are a prominent element of the state structure and working with HEWs and HAD at grassroots level.

Regardless of the political ideology and state culture, in network literature one can find that networks are used as a means to achieve national goals (e.g., Davies, 2012). Hence, it is no surprise that these MSPs are used for the same purpose in a DS context. In particular the study indicates that to execute its developmental vision, government coexists with various societal actors while assuming the major responsibilities for shaping their orientations, coordinating their activities, and providing a structure to the fulfillment of developmental goals.

State Autonomy

The presence of a competent and autonomous bureaucracy is presented as an essential element to promote better policy decisions and effective resource allocation (Burrier, 2016; Edigheji, 2005; Evans, 1995;). However, in the Ethiopian case, scholars like Lefort (2013) argue that the construction of the Ethiopian DS misses the basic imperatives of state autonomy, which is an autonomous and competent bureaucracy. Despite having installed a government structure that stretches across different levels, it is often claimed that the Ethiopian public service has moved to neither an independent nor meritocratic bureaucracy arrangement (Di Nunzio 2014; Lefort, 2013). For instance, when reviewing the ideological book of EPRDF, which analyzes the Ethiopian DS, we find nothing about building a competent and autonomous bureaucracy. Rather, maintaining a strong social base was presented as a prerequisite for state autonomy in designing the Ethiopian DS, and this social base has been associated with the privileged and ideological links with the peasantry and their strong support in elections or other political activities (EPRDF, 2003). The controlling strategies consist of mechanisms such as monitoring and coordination: while some are intended for controlling individual nonstate actors, the others are for controlling collaborative activities of both state and nonstate actors. In creating a bureaucratic sphere, the government has mobilized significant portions of the grass-roots community toward its policies and strategies to the extent of making it an unofficial bureaucratic sphere to be confronted by private actors. These strategies bring their own effect on the organization and functioning of MSPs involving state and nonstate actors.

Monitoring and Coordination

A number of actions are used by the state to monitor the activities of nonstate actors and their interaction with state actors, comprising central registration and monitoring, legal instruments and administrative measures that include periodic evaluation and reporting the collaborative efforts involving nonstate actors. At the national level, the government focuses on regulating the civil society sector by establishing a central registration system: the charities and societies proclamations that lasted from 2009 to 2018 and the new Civil Society Proclamation (2018) imposed registration and reporting requirements on both international and local CSOs that work in Ethiopia, including in the health sector. However, we found that the registration process can sometimes bring bureaucratic delay and impede the timely establishment of health partnerships. Beside compulsory registration and periodic reporting, the 2009 proclamation laid restrictive articles on fundraising, engagement areas, and activities. Except for the Ethiopian-funded charities and societies, the proclamation prevented international and other organizations addressing political and human right issues such as democracy, gender, or religion. These categorizations were used to avoid CSOs that have the potential to affect the political sphere of the state. Many of the nonstate respondents viewed the presence of restricting regulation on fundraising and administration as state coercive measures toward civil society: due to this, some of the NGOS are not able to address pressing health issues, though these issues require combined efforts and resources. One of the respondents noted:

> *"We want to support, but they restrict us in some ways. For example, they specifically tell you which area to engage and which areas not to engage; they discourage us from working on issues related to human right. These obstacles hinder us from supporting the government and the community in our full capacity."* (Interview NSR 4: case 1)

In our study, all MSPs were subject to periodic evaluation and reporting. Public authorities conduct field visits and evaluation by going to the project sites at the local level and usually demand reports on activities performed. The monitoring strategy impacts the functioning of the MSPs through decreasing the capacity of MSPs for self-regulation and creating a line of hierarchical accountability, including performance and financial accountability. An international NGO representative illustrates:

> *"With government we define the relation as partnership, our agreement also talks about partnership. In principle, we think we are in a partnership. But somehow when the process is going, somewhere, the state emerges dominant, this is mainly because the system is designed that way. Rather than assuming the partner role, the controlling role of state weights more. Generally, the system doesn't allow us to be free."* (Interview NSR2: case 2)

In addition, the state uses coordination as a tool to direct the resources and contribution of societal actors toward the realization of state development plans. State agencies at different level are involved in coordinating health initiatives in accordance with the national health development plans and strategies. These agencies use a state-installed framework of administrative procedures to coordinate health initiatives.

Unofficial Bureaucratic Sphere

On top of these controlling mechanisms, the Ethiopian government relies on its social base at a grassroots level to maintain its autonomy. State agencies at the local level take the responsibility to mobilize the grassroots community and organize it into different structure and networks. As our discussion with different public authorities at the local level indicated, these arrangements are considered as a basic tool by the state in the development process as they are key to mobilizing the society toward development goals and strategies. However, in mobilizing society, the line that differentiates development and politics becomes blurred, as the process involves luring the social base through party ideology. While some civil servants are required to be a party member and promote the party ideology, others should at least speak the same language with the party members. The interviews and document analysis indicated that these networks are stretched up to each household level, which allows the state to control the information flow on different political and social issues. Some respondents (Interviewee SR 5 and NSR 2, NSR 6) agree that on top of community mobilization, these structures and networks are instruments for ideological promotion and safeguarding the community from penetration of other alternative ideologies and views other than those of the leading party.

The party holds an antagonistic stance toward NGOs and other possible alternative power bases. In the handbook of the EPRDF (2003), NGOs are criticized as abusing foreign fund for personal use, being unaccountable, and promoting a neoliberal agenda. This ideological assumption drives the regime to hold a very restrictive relation with the (for-profit and not-for-profit) private sector. Some interviewees were positive about the contribution of NGOs and other nonstate actors and appreciated their good intention for supporting the health sector. However, some expressed the opinion that government's trust in CSOs is influenced, among others, by the history of the organizations in misusing funds or in mixing a political agenda with their activities, and inefficient deliverables. In focus group discussions, state actors repeatedly mentioned words like "hidden agenda," "political motive," and "donor motives" that indicate their suspicion of CSOs.

Moreover, party affiliation erodes the neutrality of the public sector and forces many state actors at the local level to see nonstate actors with suspicion. This negatively impacts the trusting relationship between state and nonstate actors. For instance, in case 1, it took a long time for the participating international NGO to develop a trustful relationship with the local state actors. The local state actors developed their trust and became more cooperative once they saw the contribution of the NGO. The state can lessen control if organizations deliver what they promised and prove that they are trustworthy. For instance, a respondent from district administration (Interviewee SR8) assured us that the commitment and experience of actors in the project "brings good results in our district." Successful accomplishment of project activities creates a high level of trust, which helps CSOs to develop and sustain strong relationships with state institutions at the district level, thereby easing the controlling role of the state. Though trust is important for building and sustaining network governance, in Ethiopia the past antagonizing history and the political orientation negatively impact the trusting relationship between state and nonstate actors. The cases indicate that it take a long time to develop trusting relations, undermining the collaborative process and outcome of MSPs.

Embeddedness

A key feature of embeddedness in DS literature is the state's effort in developing and sustaining cooperative relations with societal actors. When a developmental state wants to embed its bureaucrats into society it focuses on building concrete social ties and institutionalized channels, which facilitates the interaction of state and society (Evans, 2010). EPRDF as a leading party in Ethiopia has always been fond of creating strong links with the peasants (Alemayehu, 2009; Bach, 2011). This is mainly because EPRDF maintains its ideological link with the revolutionary democracy which "favors a populist discourse claiming a direct connection between the leadership and the masses" (Gagliardone, 2014:287). Even in taking the developmental state ideology, the party dwells on the importance of creating strong social ties with the masses as one of the basic principles of the developmental state model. However, unlike with the grassroots community, the government takes precautions in creating social ties with the private sector and civil society. It mainly focuses on working with developmental elite that can support the economic development of the country (Di Nunzio, 2015).

However, the Ethiopian state is not self-sustained; it is highly funded by international donors and organizations that are even commonly known for prescribing the neoliberal ideology. Thus, the government works with many sections of civil society and private sector that can offer a more robust foundation for implementing developmental policies. Based on this, we argue that the DS orientation in Ethiopia created a less responsive government, which allowed the public to put its influence more on public policy implementation than on public policy formulation. Besides the formal collaborative arrangements in the health sector, the public sector is embedded into the society through different social ties methods, such as grassroots networking, public consultation, and institutionalized channels such as review meetings. These mechanisms have their own implication for the organization and functioning of partnerships across our three cases.

In each of the case studies' districts, there were numerous social ties among state and society through grassroots networks, including HEWs and HDAs, increasing the intensity of state society linkage. These societal networks integrated with the MSPs, with important implications for the number and type of stakeholders included in organizing the MSPs and widening horizontal state-society linkages. This in turn enhances the inclusivity of MSPs to the extent that it encompasses individual citizens.

The existence of concrete social ties not only increases the number and type of stakeholders, it impacts the functioning of MSPs in a variety ways. These social ties facilitate information exchange, the accomplishment of activities, and exchange of resources. At the very least, the link between state and citizen is important in enhancing the reciprocal relations in the MSPs through bringing together actors that possess resources. These networks facilitate and coordinate direct communication between the local people and state and nonstate actors. The communities' network arrangements complement state and nonstate actors' efforts in MSPs by providing information, local knowledge, experience, labor, and materials that could cost outsiders much time and effort to acquire.

5. Discussion and Conclusion

5.1. Mutuality and Power Asymmetry: Toward Establishing a Framework for State and Nonstate Relations in Ethiopia

The discussion above provides answers on why and how networks work in Ethiopia. The policy determination, pressing health problems, and state developmental orientations set an opportunity for increasing the need for and the practice of collaborative relations in the health sector. There is an exchange of both material and nonmaterial resources between state and nonstate actors, contributing to growing interdependent relations in the MSPs. Besides, the participation of community groups and volunteers on many of the project programs and activities served to build consensus and commitment as community stakeholders developed a sense of ownership. The MSPs reflect expanded horizontal relations with a high degree of interdependence among actors. The cases indicate that many of the program outcomes and successes are dependent on the joint participation and collective contribution of various societal actors.

It is evident from the cases that the state dominates the partnership initiatives and uses nonstate actors' resources to achieve its developmental goals. However, this process has contributed to creating a common agenda for improving maternal and child health. The partnerships offer an opportunity for both state and nonstate actors to contribute something of value and affect the policy implementation process. These interdependencies and mutual efforts were at least important in creating a common understanding and good working relationship. Though their integration can go to the extent of sharing vision and goals, however, this result should be seen carefully, as CSOs are working in a constrained environment where they are forced to align their goals without a chance to negotiate comprehensively. Despite state domination of policy space and agenda setting, there is some window of opportunity for negotiation and integration at the local level where actors engage in continues interaction, participatory planning and evaluation, shared decision making, and extensive integration of activities.

However, the interdependency and interaction of actors in the studied cases do not meet the ideal of network governance, as this would reflect more collaborative horizontal relations based on trust, autonomy, and self-regulating capacity. In contrast, the state utilizes a number of legal and institutional instruments to guide, coordinate, and control MSPs and there appears to be low autonomy in the partnership initiatives. This shows that in Ethiopia at least partnerships as a network form of governance are dominated by the state. The logical question would be what model exactly captures the relationship between state and nonstate actor's relation in the Ethiopian health sector? Based on the analysis of the cases' network governance dimensions, what concepts can be used to describe the Ethiopian state and nonstate actor relationship? As the above discussion indicates, the simple categorization of the relation between state and nonstate actors relation as an authority-based or hierarchal system doesn't add up, yet the complete categorization of MSPs into the network governance category doesn't add up either.

5.2. Implications for Public Governance Insights

One of the major goals of this chapter was to assess the value of network governance in accordance with a developmental state orientation. The most important theoretical contribution of this chapter is related to a criticism of governance theory, which posits that the theory is questionable when the state's authoritative role creates asymmetries in governance networks and debates whether there exist state-centered governance or society-centered governance in reality (see Bell & Hindmoor, 2009). Because of the Ethiopian political context, we have built on a network-governance theory which to some extent considers the dominant role of the state in networks. Considering the DS, the study supports the argument that the state, although a participant in networks, maintains a central role in governance networks. In the case studies, the key insights of the network governance theory were used as a framework to explain the formation and functioning of MSPs and we paid particular attention to the role of state actors/agencies at different levels of state structure. We believe this study contributes to the theoretical debate through addressing two major issues that are prominent in governance literature: which coordinating mechanisms dominate the governance arrangements and whether the role of state is expanding or restraining. Thus, in the following pages, the answers for these two fundamental questions are presented.

Coordinating Mechanisms in Governance Networks: The Extent of Self-Regulation

The adoption of governance schemes includes the complex interaction of a diverse set of actors within the governing process. However, the mechanisms used to coordinate the interaction of these actors in these governance arrangements are different from hierarchical and market type governance. The organization of networks on negotiated principles rather than hierarchical command and rule mainly relates to the self-regulation capacity of the networks that rests on the autonomy of the networks. However, this study revealed networks that are not fully autonomous and self-governing. Rather, the MSPs are self-regulating to some extent, as they lie inside the hierarchical and bureaucratic supervision of state structure, which coincides with Scharpf's (1994) indication that networks operate in the "shadow of hierarchy." This implies that government which is still the legitimate authority and the sole provider of health services does not lose its power in relation to the other societal actors. Government plays a prominent role by providing the legal context in which MSPs function. It also installs the mechanisms that monitor and control MSPs processes and outcomes in order to ensure proper utilization of resources and meeting the developmental goals. Nevertheless, the case studies also indicated there are opportunities for MSPs to function autonomously and not to completely lose their self-governing capacity by utilizing different mechanisms such as negotiation, trust, contract obligation, action plans, and mutual dependency. These are used for safeguarding the organizational autonomy of each actor in MSPs.

Hence, the overall operation of networks and its chance for surviving in a complex governance environment depends on ethical virtues that promote cooperative and collaborative relations (Jones et al., 1997; Thompson, 2003). This suggests that networks may lose their distinctiveness and importance or transform into an order-taking bureaucratic tools unless efforts are made to build trust-based collaborative relationships among participating actors. Despite the presence of other coordinating mechanisms, in much network literature trust is presented as the most important coordinating mechanism

(Huxham & Vangen, 2000; Thompson et al. 1991). However, trust may have received an overstated value as evidence indicates that networks may rely on other coordinating mechanisms. The MSPs in this study were subject to strict financial and administrative control by the regional and local officials. This may be related to the fact that state and nonstate actors, in particular civil society actors, had a prior antagonistic relationship characterized by low trust. In many instances they were unable to develop trust in each other, leading them to operate apart from each other.

The Role of State in Governance Context: Expanding or Retreating?

The cases in this study show that state agencies at different levels of government play an important role in coordinating and supervising the MSPs. This is against the argument that public actors do not have a distinctive role or authority vis-à-vis private actors. Indeed our discussion goes beyond this argument and focuses on whether the role of state in the administrative and political setting is expanding or retreating following the change from government to governance.

In a large body of literature the process in which government changes to governance is presented as resulting in the decline of a state-dominant role in the governance of society (Klijn & Koppenjan, 2000; Salamon, 2002; Stoker, 1998). Nevertheless, the increasing role of other societal actors in the public sphere does not necessarily mean that the state becomes less important or that its role is completely eroded. Some scholars indicate that despite the increasing use of governance mechanisms, the state remains the key political actor in society (Newman, 2005; Pierre & Peters, 2000). On top of this, Bell & Hindmoor (2009) argue that

> *"The scope and scale of governance is actually expanding, and that state-based, hierarchical or top-down forms of governance are doing likewise. States are attempting to expand their governing capacities not only by strengthening central state institutions but by forging new governance partnerships with a range of social actors."*

Our findings indicate that state agencies in the Ethiopian health sector are actively building and managing new governance partnerships and other collaborative arrangements with a diverse set of societal actors. According to the DS ideology, the state's capacity to achieve its developmental goals depends on two main institutional features: the state's ability to maintain its autonomy from outside forces and its ability to build and maintain collaborative relationships with societal actors. In this study, there are a number of indications that the Ethiopian state attempts to enhance its capacity through building collaborative relationship with nonstate actors. This indicates that the state is purposely choosing its governance strategies to meet its developmental goals, which in turn shows the expanding role of the state in determining the governance and administrative issues of society.

In the Ethiopian health sector, the government prefers to experiment with strategies and popular initiatives to engage the community and create collaborative relations with NGOs. However, the extent to which there is a fundamental change in basic forms of governing society in the country and its health sector domain is small because the state is still utilizing top-down hierarchical governance mechanisms along with other governance mechanisms. The cases indicate that public actors do not refrain themselves from using government authority in restructuring and managing the governance modes. The general finding in respect to the effect of the state's DS ideology on MSPs typically matches with Bell & Hindmoor's conclusion (2009) that

> *"States can extend their capacity to achieve their policy objectives by developing closer relations with non-state actors. But this cooperation with non-state actors will involve some loss of government flexibility, and governments will require a strong theoretical and policy compass with some strengthening of central policy control if it is to avoid capture by special interests and to retain its independence."* (p. 15)

In fact, the case studies showed that the Ethiopian government applies strategies that can provide policy freedom through restricting the societal actors from affecting the policy domain and thereby avoiding being captured by the interests of societal actors.

Notes

1. Some of the analysis in this section is reproduced from the article published by the authors: Exploring the Impact of Political Context on State–Civil Society Relations: Actors' Strategies in a Developmental State, in Voluntas, 30(6), 1256-1269.

References

Alemayehu, T. (2009). The Ethiopian Developmental State: Requirements and Perquisites. *Journal of Business & Economics Research*, 7(8), 11-18.

Bach, J. N. (2011). Abyotawi Democracy: Neither Revolutionary nor Democratic, a Critical review of EPRDF's Conception of Revolutionary Democracy in post-1991 Ethiopia. *Journal of Eastern African Studies*, 5(4), 641–663.

Batley, R. (2006). Engaged or Divorced? Cross-service Findings on Government Relations with Non-state Service-providers. *Public Administration and Development*, 26, 241-251.

Bell, S & Hindmoor, A. (2009). *Rethinking Governance: The Centrality of the State in Modern Society.* Cambridge University Press

Benner, T., Streck, C. & Witte, J.M. (2003). *Progress or Peril?: Networks and Partnerships in Global Environmental Governance; the post-Johannesburg Agenda.* Global Public Policy Institute, Berlin.

Bode, I., & Brandsen, T. (2014). State-Third Sector Partnerships: A Short Overview of Key Issues in the Debate, introduction to the special issue on state-third sector partnerships. *Public Management Review*, 16, 1055–1066.

Bolesta, A. (2007). *China as a Developmental state.* London: London School of Economics and Political Science.

Brinkerhoff, J.M. (2002). Government–Nonprofit Partnership: A Defining Framework. *Public Admin. Dev.* 22, 19–30.

Burrier, G. (2016). The Developmental State, Civil Society and Hydroelectric Politics in Brazil. *Journal of Environment & Development*, 25(3), 332–358.

Caldentey, E. P. (2008). The concept and evolution of the developmental state. *International Journal of Political Economy*, *37(3)*, 27–53.

Christian Relief and Development Association. (2006). Assessment of the Operating Environment for CSOs/NGOs in Ethiopia. Working paper, Addis Ababa: CRDA.

Consortium of Christian Relief Development Organizations. (2014).The Contribution of Civil Society Organizations towards the National Health Sector in Ethiopia in the Year 2012. Addis Ababa.

Christensen, T. & Lægreid, P. (2007).The Whole-of-Government Approach to Public Service Reform. *Public Administration Review*, 67(6), 1059-1066.

Clark, J. (2000). Civil Society, NGOs and Development in Ethiopia. A Snapshot View. World Bank Working Paper.

Davies, J. (2002).The Governance of Urban Regeneration: A Critique of the "Governing without Government" thesis, *Public Administration*, 80(2), 301-322.

Davies, J. (2012).Network Governance Theory: A Gramscian Critique. *Environment and Planning, 44*, 2687-2704.

Di Nunzio, M. (2014). Do Not Cross the Red Line: The 2010 General Election, Dissent and Political Mobilization in Urban Ethiopia. *African Affairs*, 113(452), 409–430.

Edigheji, O. (2005). A Democratic Developmental State in Africa? Centre for Policy Studies, Johannesburg: A concept paper.

El-Saharty, S., Kebede, S., Dubusho, P. O., & Siadat, B. (2009). Ethiopia: Improving Health Service Delivery. Paper prepared for the Health, Nutrition and Population Unit, Human Development Network, the World Bank.

Ethiopian People Revolutionary Democratic Front. (2010). The Renaissance Line and Ethiopian Renaissance. (2003 Ethiopian Calendar) (Translated from Amharic).

Evans, P. (1995). *Embedded Autonomy: States and Industrial Transformation.* Princeton: Princeton University Press.

Evans, P. (2010). The Challenge of 21st Century Development: Building Capability—Enhancing States. New York: United Nations Development Programme.

Flick, U. (2002). Qualitative Research – State of the Art. *Social Science Information*, 41 (1), 5-24.

FMOH. (2014). Federal Democratic Republic of Ethiopia Ministry of Health: Ethiopia's Fifth National Health Accounts, 2010/2011, April 2014, Addis Ababa.

Gagliardone, I. (2014) New Media and the Developmental State in Ethiopia. *African Affairs*, 113(451), 279–299.

Hudson, B. (2004). Analyzing Network Partnership: Benson Re-visited. *Public Management Review*, 6(1), 75-94.

Huxham, C. & Vangen, S. (2000). Ambiguity, Complexity and Dynamics in the Membership of Collaboration. *Human Relations*, 53(6), 771-806.

Huxham, C and Vangen, S. (2005). *Managing to Collaborate.* London: Routledge.

Johnson, C. (1982). *MITI and the Japanese Miracle: The Growth of Industrial Policy 1925–1975.* Stanford: Stanford University Press.

Jones, C., Hesterly, W. S., & Borgatti, S. P. (1997). A General Theory of Network Governance: Exchange Conditions and Social Mechanisms. *The Academy of Management Review*, 22(4) 911–45.

Johnston. K. (2015). Public Governance: The Government of Non-state Actors in "Partnerships." *Public Money & Management*, 35(1), 15-22.

Kelsall, T. (2013). *Business, Politics and the State in Africa. Challenging the Orthodoxies on Growth and Transformation.* London: Zed Books.

Kickert, W. J. M., Klijn, E. H., & Koppenjan, J. F. M. (eds) (1997). *Managing Complex Networks: Strategies for the Public Sector.* London: Sage.

Klijn, E.H. (2002). Governing Networks in the Hallow State: Contracting-Out, Process Management or a Combination of the Two. *Public Management Review*, 4(2), 149-66.

Klijn, E. H. (2008). Complexity Theory and Public Administration: What Is New; Key Concepts in Complexity Theory Compared to Their Counterparts in Public Administration Research. *Public Management Review*, 10 (3), 299-317.

Klijn, E.H., & Koppenjan, J. (2000). Public Management and Policy Networks: Foundations of a Network Approach to Governance. *Public Management Review*, (2)2, 135-58.

Kohli A. (2004). *State-directed Development: Political Power and Industrialization in the Global South.* Cambridge: Cambridge University Press.

Kooiman, J. (2003). *Governing as Governance.* London: SAGE.

Koppenjan, J. F. M., & Klijn, E. H. (2004). *Managing Uncertainties in Networks: A Network Approach to Problem Solving and Decision Making.* London: Routledge.

Lefort, R. (2013). The Theory and Practice of Meles Zenawi: A Response to Alex De Waal. *African Affairs,* 112(448), 460–470.

Levy, J. S. (2008). Case Studies: Types, Designs, and Logics of Inference. *Conflict Management and Peace Science,* 25(1), 1-18.

Lowndes.V. & Skelcher C. (1998). The Dynamics of Multi-organizational Partnerships: An Analysis of Changing Modes of Governance. *Public Administration,* 76(2), 313-333.

Mandell, M. P. (ed.) (2001). *Getting Results through Collaboration: Networks and Network Structures for Public Policy and Management.* Westport, CT: Quorum Books.

Meuleman, L. (2008). *Public Management and the Metagovernance of Hierarchies, Networks and Markets; The Feasibility of Designing and Managing Governance Style Communications.* Heidelberg: PhysicaVerlag.

Moloney, K. (2013). Governing without Collaboration: State and Civil Society Relations in Jamaica. *International Public Management Review,* 14(1), 2013.

Newman, J. (ed.) (2005). *Remaking Governance, Peoples, Politics and the Public Sphere.* Bristol: Policy Press.

Noor, M., Douma, N., Van der Haar, G., Hilhorst, D., Van der Molen, I., & Stel, N. (2010). Multi-Stakeholder Processes, Service Delivery and State Institutions. Theoretical Framework and Methodologies Paper for the Peace, Security and Development Network.

Osborne, D., and T. Gaebler. (1992). *Reinventing Government: How the Entrepreneurial Spirit is Transforming the Public Sector.* New York: Plume.

Osborne, S. P. (ed.) (2010). *The New Public Governance? Emerging Perspectives on the Theory and Practice of Public Governance.* London: Routledge.

Pattberg, P. & Widerberg, O. (2014). *Transnational Multi-stakeholder Partnerships for Sustainable Development; Building Blocks for success.* IVM Institute for Environmental Studies.

Patton, M. Q. (2001). *Qualitative Research and Evaluation Methods* (3rd ed.). Sage: Thousand Oaks.

Pierre, J. & Peters, G. B. (2000). *Governance, Politics, and the State.* New York: St. Martin's Press.

Pierre, J. (ed.) (2000). *Debating Governance: Authority, Steering, and Democracy.* Oxford: Oxford University Press.

Rahmato, D. (2008). The Voluntary Sector in Ethiopia: Challenges and Future Prospects. In T. Assefa & Zewde B. (eds). *Civil society at Crossroads: Challenges and Prospects in Ethiopia* (pp. 81-134). Addis Ababa: Forum for Social Studies.

Rees, J., Mullins, D. & Bovaird, T. (2012). Third Sector Partnerships for Public Service Delivery: An Evidence Review, TSRC Working Paper 60.

Rhodes, R. (1997). *Understanding Governance: Policy Networks, Governance, Reflexity and Accountability.* Bristrol, PA: Open University Press.

Rhodes, R. (2000). The Governance Narrative: Key Findings and Lessons from the ESRC's Whitehall Programme. *Public Administration*, 78(2): 345-363.

Routley, L. (2012). Developmental States: A Review of the Literature. ESID Working Paper, no. 3.

Røvik, K.A. (2002). The Secrets of the Winners: Management Ideas That Flow. In K. Sahlin-Andersson & Engwall, L. (eds). *The Expansion of Management Knowledge – Carriers, Flows and Sources*. (pp. 113-144). Stanford, CA: Stanford University Press.

Salamon, L. M. (ed.) (2002). *The Tools of Government: A Guide to the New Governance*. New York: Oxford University Press.

Scharpf, F.W. (1994). Games Real Actors Could Play: Positive and Negative Coordination in Embedded Negotiations. *Journal of Theoretical Politics, (6),* 27–53.

Scharpf, F.W. (1997). *Games Real Actors Play: Actor Centered Institutionalism in Policy Research*. Boulder: Westview Press.

Selsky, J. W., & Parker, B. (2005). Cross-Sector Partnerships to Address Social Issues: Challenges to Theory and Practice. *Journal of Management*, 31(6), 849-873.

Sketcher, C., Mathur, N., & Smith, M. (2005). The Public Governance of Collaborative Spaces: Discourse, Design and Democracy. *Public Administration*, 83(3), 573-96.

Small, M. L. (2011). How to Conduct a Mixed Methods Study: Recent Trends in a Rapidly Growing Literature. *Annual Review of Sociology*, 37(1), 57-86.

Sørensen, E., & Torfing, J. (2005). The Democratic Anchorage of Governance Networks. *Scandinavian Political Studies*, 28(3), 195-218.

Sørensen, E., & Torfing, J. (2007). *Theories of Democratic Network Governance*. London: Palgrave Macmillan.

Steward, A. and Gray, T. (2006).The Authenticity of "Type Two" Multi-stakeholder Partnerships for Water and Sanitation in Africa: When is a Stakeholder a Partner? *Environmental Politics 15(03), 362-378.*

Stoker, G. (1998a). Governance as Theory: Five propositions. *International Social Science Journal*, 155, 17-28.

Sullivan, H., & Skelcher, C. (2002). *Working across Boundaries: Collaboration in Public Services*. Basingstoke: Palgrave Macmillan.

Tadesse, H. A., & Steen, T. (2019). Exploring the Impact of Political Context on State–Civil Society Relations: Actors' Strategies in a Developmental State. *Voluntas; International Journal of Voluntary and Nonprofit Organizations*, 30(6), 1256-1269.

Thompson, G. F. (2003). *Between Hierarchies and Markets: The Logic and Limits of Network Forms of Organization*. Oxford University Press, Oxford

Thompson, G., Frances, J., Levacic, R., and Mitchell, J. (1991). *Markets, Hierarchies and Networks: The Coordination of Social Life*. London: Sage.

Vu, T. (2007). State Formation and the Origins of Developmental States in South Korea and Indonesia. *Studies in Comparative International Development*, 41(4), 27-56.

7
The Role of Participation in Development in Enhancing Local People Empowerment: The case of Bishoftu City Administration (BCA), Oromia

Bahiru Detti Heyi

Box 1: Key points of this chapter

- ✓ Participation in development relatively enhanced personal empowerment among local people.
- ✓ Participation in setting needs priorities and planning phases of the development process influences personal empowerment.
- ✓ Participation in development generated "power within," "power to," "power with" and "power over" forms of power among local people.
- ✓ Empowerment through participation was hindered by the extent of participation, a top-down approach of participation, elite domination, institutional factors, and corruption.

Box 2: After reading this chapter, you will be able to

- ✓ Understand local people participation and empowerment in Oromia/Ethiopia
- ✓ Articulate indicators of different forms of empowerment
- ✓ Explain the effect on participation in development on local people empowerment
- ✓ Grasp the gap between participation and empowerment rhetoric and practice
- ✓ Realize policy implications of empowerment through participation
- ✓ Comprehend the magnitudes of people empowerment through participation

Box 3: Abbreviations

ANOVA = Analysis of variance
BCA = Bishoftu City Administration
CPE = Community Participation Expert
FGD = Focus Group Discussion
HH = Household
ONRS = Oromia National Regional State

QUAL = Qualitative
QUAN = Quantitative
VIF = Variance Inflation Factor

Box 4: Glossary

Akayi: fried cereals, especially barely
Budena: Traditional food prepared from some sort of cereals
Ganda: administrative unit below central City Administration
Jarsuma: conciliation
Shane: an organization encompassing one to five residents.

1. Introduction

The role of participatory development in empowering people at the grass roots level has attracted the attention of development scholars, governments, and nongovernment organizations. Participation and empowerment have gained an extensive use in the policies, plans, and reports of development projects. Participatory development brings the people to the center of development and pays attention to empowerment that focused on local people, local context, and local forms of power and change (Freire, 1970). Though participation plays a crucial role in empowering local people, empowerment through participation in development has been impeded by lack of genuine participation (Cooke and Kothari, 2001; Kesby, 2005); elites domination of decision-making process (Ali Shah and Baporikar, 2012; Chambers, 1997); and lack of commitment by the state to create a space for communities (Cooke and Kothari 2001; Kesby 2005). Therefore, this study tries to contribute to the endeavors to bridge the gap in analyzing the linkages between participatory development processes and empowerment.

Participation is an ideologically contested concept that has produced a range of competing meanings and applications (Pelling, 1998). The concepts of participation differed over the goals, processes, agents, effects, and value of participation (Crocker, 2003). For the purpose of this study participation is conceptualized as per the following definition. Hentschel & Lanjouw (1996: xi) pursue the transformational approach to define participation as "a process through which stakeholders influence and share control over development initiatives and the decisions and resources which affect them." Empowerment is a very complex concept, which is not easily defined (Craig and Mayo, 1995; Rowlands, 1997). The complexity of the concept of empowerment arises from its root word "power," giving rise to different interpretations and contrasting views on the centrality of power for the development process. Despite competing views of empowerment among scholars, empowerment in this chapter is seen as a consequence of people participation in development projects and refers to improvement in social relations, personal conditions, and heightened awareness regarding political issues.

2. Theoretical Framework

The analysis of "empowerment is most effective when it draws on the full range of concepts and meanings of power…" (Pettit, 2012:5). Thus, Rowlands (1997) empowerment framework was used to evaluate the effect of participation on empowerment. Rowlands (1997) identified four types of power relations: power over, power to, power with, and power within.

Empowerment based on a view of power as "power over" emphasizes the need for participation in existing economic and political structures but does not involve changes to those structures (Luttrell et al., 2009). Conceptualization of empowerment based on "power over" suggests that empowerment is more than participation in decision- making; it must also include the processes that lead people to perceive themselves as able and entitled to make decisions (Rowlands, 1997).

"Power to" refers to the unique potential of every person to shape, direct, and control his or her life in the world, and is also referred to as an individual's generative or productive power (Chambers, 2005; Nelson & Wright, 1995). Empowerment based on "power to" refers to a power that includes the ability to make decisions, have authority, and find solutions to problems, and which can be creative and enabling. "Power with" is a collective form of power wherein people feel empowered by organizing and uniting around a common purpose or understanding. It involves a sense of the whole greater than the sum of individuals (Rowlands, 1995). "Power within" involves spiritual strength based on self-acceptance, self-respect, self-esteem, self-awareness, consciousness raising, self-confidence, and assertiveness. "Power within" is the capacity to imagine and have hope; it affirms the common human search for dignity and fulfillment (Veneklasen & Miller, 2002).

3. Legal and Policy Frameworks

Proper government policies and legal provisions facilitate effective participation that favors the local situation and creates favorable ground for local people empowerment. Hence, related government policies such as the Constitution of Oromia National Regional State (ONRS) and the Oromia Urban Local Government Proclamation were assessed.

3.1. Revised Constitution of (ONRS), Proclamation No. 46/2001

The ONRS Constitution stipulated a general provision about the rights of the people of the region to participate in development. The constitution granted the public the right to participate in developing and monitoring the environment, to improve their living standards, and to enhance and sustain development (article 43 [1]). These facts imply that the constitution recognized that participation is a means for the local people to manage their affairs. In other words, the Constitution recognized participation as a means of local people empowerment.

The ONRS Revised Constitution stipulated that "all the people of the Region have the right to participate in Regional development, and, in particular, to be consulted in respect to policies and projects affecting their community" (article 43 [2]). It endorsed participation at different levels. Public participation in grass roots or local development, which is the concern of this study, refers to the right of the public to participation at the development policy level and at the project level, which directly influences their life. However, this provision considered consultation as a form of participation, which is the lowest level of participation. Hence, the provision creates a loophole that allows power holders to manipulate the voice of the public. In fact, manipulation of public voice took place on the ground.

The constitution further stipulated that "the aim of development policies and programs shall be to enhance the capacity of residents of the Region for development and meet their basic needs" (article 43 [3]). The provision of this article advocates that public policies should create the condition that enhances empowerment. The provision emphasizes the role of public policies in fostering participation in development that boosts the empowerment of local people. The implication is that the constitution recognized participation as a means of local people empowerment that in turn prepares them for further participation in governance. Participation in governance further implicated people's participation in decision-making.

3.2. Oromia Urban Local Government, Proclamation No. 65/2003

According to the preamble of this Proclamation, one rationale for enacting the Proclamation was "to streamline the operation and organization of urban local governments on the basis of good governance and democratic principles so as to enable them create huge development capacity for the development of the Region and improvement of the living standard of the residents" (ONRS, 2003:1).

A close look at this rationale suggests that the Proclamation is intended to create a conducive urban local government structure, which facilitates participation. Moreover, this provision implies that the urban local government structure is a crucial institutional context for the empowerment of local people through participation. However, the results of document analysis and FGDs in fact suggest that the structure of the city government on the ground was not conducive to participation. This suggests that there is a gap in policy formulation and policy implementation regarding popular participation in development. Consequently, local people empowerment through participation has been hampered by the gap between policy formulation and implementation.

Proclamation No. 65/2003 enacted general provisions that directly related to participation as follows: "Residents, mass organizations and the private sector shall discuss, debate and express their views on the city annual work program, budget proposals, project ideas, performance as well as financial and audit reports" (article 32 [1]). This provision calls for public participation in all activities of government at all stages. A glance at the provision of this sub article suggests that the public has the exclusive right to participate at each stage of local development processes, from the initiation of local development project ideas to performance evaluation. However, the results of FGDs and Key Informant Interviews (KII) revealed that the public in Oromia does not in fact participate in performance evaluation. This finding implies that there is gap in implementing the provision, preventing it from fostering the public participation that enhances local popular empowerment.

4. Methodology

For the purpose of this study, a pragmatic research philosophy was adopted for guiding the overall process of the study over interpretive and positivist research paradigms. Pragmatism allows for flexibility in the research process (Morgan, 2007) and enables flexibility in investigate methods (Onwuegbuzie and Leech, 2005). Along with the selected research philosophy, a mixed methods research approach was adopted for this chapter. Mixed methods allows for the combination of quantitative and qualitative research techniques, methods, approaches, concepts, and language into a single study (Greene, 2006; Johnson and Onuegbuzie, 2004; Johnson et al., 2007). In line with the research approach followed, a parallel triangulation design (Creswell & Clark, 2007) was adopted, with equal attention to both QUAN and QUAL phases.

Both primary and secondary data sources were employed to generate data that help to address the objectives of the study. Primary data were generated through interviews, Focus Group Discussion (FGD), and a questionnaire. The questionnaire incorporated characteristics of the respondents, items regarding the practice of participation in phases of development, and empowerment in different forms. The main relevant characteristics of respondents, such as socioeconomic factors and demographic characteristics (sex, age, family size, educational status, occupational status, and employment categories and income) were incorporated in the questionnaire. The majority of the respondents were males (62.7 percent). Respondents' age distribution indicated that the majority of the respondents were younger people (64.8 percent). The distribution of family size indicated that more than half of the respondents (57.7 percent) had a family size of two and below. The occupational distribution of the respondents revealed that the highest proportion was skilled and unskilled labor (32.3 percent) followed by managerial, professional, and supervisory occupation groups (27.5 percent). The distribution of employment type revealed that higher proportions of the respondents are self-employed (31.1 percent) and civil servants (30.4 percent). The distribution of education levels indicated that a high proportion of the respondents had attained secondary school education (27.8 percent). The distribution of monthly income of the respondents indicated a relatively high rate of those earning less than 1000 Birr per month (26 percent).

The items devised to measure each form of empowerment were drawn from literature and incorporated in the questionnaire. Detailed consultation of various literatures on empowerment was conducted to identify indicators of empowerments. The items about the process of participation were binary. However, to prepare the data for parametric analysis (regression analysis in the case of this study), dummies were developed for each item regarding the phases of participation process. Personal, social, and political empowerments were measured by ten, seven, and eight items respectively. These items were structured around a Likert scale response form in the questionnaire. The value of each response for these items in the questionnaire is as follows: 1 = strongly agree; 2 = agree; 3 = undecided; 4 = disagree; 5 = strongly disagree.

A concurrent/parallel mixed method sampling strategy was utilized to draw sample respondents. These sampling procedures occurred independently. A snowball sampling technique was used to select participants for FGDs and key informants. A judgmental sampling technique was used to draw samples for interviews. A multi-stage sampling technique was employed to draw questionnaire respondents. The sample size for questionnaire respondents was drawn using the Krejcie and Morgan (1970). Accordingly, using 85 percent response rate a sample of 436 HHs were selected. This sample size was drawn from each *ganda* through proportional allocation. Hence, 173, 124, and 139 respondents were selected from sample *gandas* 01, 05, and 09 in that order. Although 436 questionnaires were distributed to respondents, only 418 complete questionnaires were returned. Thus, the analysis was conducted on returned questionnaires. Thematic analysis was applied to analyze qualitative data. Item analysis and multiple liner regression were used to analyze quantitative data. A multiple linear regression model applied to determine the effect of participation in development on empowerments was developed as follows:

$= \beta_o + \beta_1 X_1 + \beta_2 X_2 + \beta_3 X_3 + \beta_4 X_4 + \beta_5 X_5 + \beta_6 X_6 + \varepsilon$
Where: Y = Outcome variable (empowerment)
β_o = Constant terms
ε = Error term
$\beta_1 - \beta_6$ = Regression coefficients
X_1 = Participation in needs identification
X_2 = Participation in setting priority of needs
X_3 = Participation in planning
X_4 = Participation in the implementation
X_5 = Participation in monitoring
X_6 = Participation in performance evaluation

To prepare the data for multiple regression analysis, a cumulative empowerment index (CEI) for three types of empowerment was developed adding the obtained scores of ten, seven, and eight empowerment indicators for personal, social, and political empowerments respectively. Dummies were developed for categorical predictors to run multiple regressions.

5. Findings of the Study

This part of the study examined the role of participation in personal, social, political, and economic empowerment. The effect of participation on local popular empowerment was determined based on quantitative and qualitative data. However, economic empowerment was assessed based on only qualitative data. In order to determine the role of participation in empowering local people using multiple regression analysis, first the assumptions of multiple regressions were checked. As per the result of preliminary analysis all the assumptions of multiple regression analysis were satisfied.

The output of preliminary multiple regression analysis, ANOVA Table, was used to test the statistical significance of the model. The result of the analysis revealed that the model is statistically significant in explaining personal empowerment ($F [6, 353] = 4.12$, $p = 0.00$) and social empowerment ($F [6, 353] = 2.10$, $p = 0.05$) through participation in local development.

However, the model is not statistically significant in explaining political empowerment ($F [6, 353] = 1.20$, $p = 0.31$). This finding implies that participation did result in the political empowerment of local people in BCA. Therefore, the null hypothesis $\beta = 0$ (For all the independent variables Coefficient of determination is zero) was rejected, while the alternative hypothesis $\beta \neq 0$ (For all the independent variables Coefficient of determination is different from zero) was accepted in the case of personal and social empowerment. This means that at least one predictor has an influence on the outcome variable and determined variations in the dependent variable.

5.1. Personal Empowerment through Participation

Personal empowerment is the foundation of the empowerment process. That means the transformation of the individual or the group and the circumstances encourage or inhibit the process of empowerment. Personal empowerment through participation was assessed by determining skill acquired and psychological improvements as the result of participation. The result of multiple regression analysis about the combined effect of all predictors and the influence of individual predictor variables on the dependent variable are depicted in table 1.

The results in table 1 revealed that all the independent variables included in the model explained approximately 7 percent (R square (0.07) x 100%) of the variance in dependent variable (personal empowerment through participation). Among the predictor variables, participation in setting the priority of needs ($\beta = -.24$, $p = 0.00$) and planning ($\beta = .17$, $p = 0.03$) were found to have an influence on personal empowerment in BCA. Thus, the model of multiple regression analysis is found to be:

$$\hat{Y} = 25.53 - 3.28X_2 + 2.33X_3$$

The finding indicated a negative relationship between participation in setting the priority of needs and personal empowerment. In other words, when participation in setting priority of needs increase by one standard deviation, personal empowerment decrease by .24 standard deviation. The results of FGDs pointed out that the negative relationship between the variables was

Table 1: Multiple regression estimates of personal empowerment through participation

	Unstandardized coefficients		Standardized coefficients			95% confidence interval for B	
Model	B	SE	Beta	t	Sig.	LB	UB
Participation in needs identification	-.59	1.10	-.04	-.54	.59	-2.75	1.57
Participation in setting priority of needs	-3.28	1.10	-.24	-2.98	.00	-5.45	-1.11
Participation in planning	2.33	1.06	.17	2.21	.03	.25	4.41
Participation in the implementation	-1.38	1.03	-.11	-1.34	.18	-3.41	.65
Participation in monitoring	.26	1.04	.02	.25	.80	-1.78	2.30
Participation performance evaluation	.01	.96	.00	.01	1.00	1.88	1.89
(Constant)	25.53	.65	---	39.30	.00	24.26	26.81
R Square	0.07						

Source: Field survey, 2015

the result of low-level public participation in decisions regarding priority setting. There was a positive relationship between participation in the planning and personal empowerment. Accordingly, when participation in planning increased by one standard deviation, personal empowerment increased by .17 standard deviation.

Item Analysis of Personal Empowerment through Participation

Item analysis of indicators of personal empowerment was conducted to determine the effect of participation on individual indicators of personal empowerment. Then, the mean of individual indicators were compared against the overall mean of personal empowerment in order to determine the degree to which participation influences individual indicators. The results of the analysis are illustrated in table 2.

As indicated in table 2, the overall mean score of item analysis of indicators of personal empowerment through participation was 2.34. The comparison of individual means and the overall mean score of item analysis indicated that participation influences indicators of personal empowerment to various degrees. The means of strategic accumulation of practical experiences (M = 2.03); skills improvement (M = 2.19); development of self-esteem (M = 2.20); and enhancement of self-reliance to improve one's life (M = 2.27) were lower than the overall mean. These findings imply that participation influences these indicators to relatively lesser degrees. However, participation still influences personal empowerment along these indicators. This can be observed from the frequency distribution of item analysis of these indicators. A glance at table 2 reveals that participation relatively enhanced the personal confidence that I could do things (M = 2.55); capacity to control over personal decision (M = 2.43); freedom of choice (M = 2.44); creativity that improves one's life (M = 2.39); improvement of ability to analyze own situation and solve problems (M = 2.50); and creating the belief that my actions can have effects (M = 2.35) indicators of personal empowerment.

The results of Key Informant Interviews conducted with *ganda* managers and FGD at *Ganda* 05 also revealed personal empowerment along predictors other than those hypothesized in the quantitative strand. Accordingly, participation enhanced the personal empowerment of local people through providing the chance to share problems and get support. The above results further suggest that participation also creates wider opportunities for interaction. The individual has the chance to develop particular skills, both practical (such as literacy) and social (participation in meetings and discussions).

Using Rowlands (1997) framework, the above finding implies that participation generated "power within" and "power to" forms of power among

Table 2: Item analysis for personal empowerment through participation (N= 418, M = 2.34)
SA: strongly Agree; A: Agree; UD: Undecided; DA: Disagree; SDA: Strongly disagree

Items	Mean	SD	SA (%)	A (%)	UD (%)	DA (%)	SDA (%)
Boosting strategic accumulation of practical experiences	2.03	.94	29.9	48.6	12.4	7.2	1.9
Improvement in personal confidence that I could do things	2.55	1.16	12.9	50.5	15.6	10.5	10.5
Skills improvement	2.19	1.01	23.0	51.4	13.4	8.4	3.8
Improvement of ability to analyze own situation and solve problems	2.50	1.12	12.9	53.1	13.4	12.2	8.4
Creating the belief that your actions can have effects	2.35	1.06	16.5	53.6	13.6	10.5	5.7
Enhancing capacity to control over personal decisions that affect one's everyday life	2.43	1.07	14.4	52.6	14.6	12.2	6.2
Enhancing the development of self-esteem	2.20	1.03	23.4	50.5	11.5	11.5	3.1
Enhancing the development of feeling of freedom of choice	2.44	1.06	13.2	54.8	13.2	12.9	6.0
Enhancing self-reliance to improve one's life	2.27	.98	19.1	51.7	15.1	11.7	2.4
Enhancing creativity that improves one's life	2.39	1.09	15.3	55.3	12.4	9.3	7.7

Source: Field survey, 2015

the public. To recall, power within refers to the development of self-efficacy, freedom of choice, the belief that one's action can have effect. "Power to" refers to the development of a capacity to control personal decisions, creativity that improves one's life, and ability to analyze personal situations.

The above forms of empowerment developed through participation focus on the process to understand and conceptualize power. These powers are generative; the power people have of stimulating activity in others and raising their morale. More than participation in decision-making, personal empowerment through participation will have positive impact on people to perceive themselves as able and entitled to make decisions. Thus, participation in the case of our study gave scope to the full range of human abilities and potential (Rowlands, 1997). Although participation in decision-making was low, personal empowerment was developed as a result of participation. Because, "power within" needs experiential recognition and analysis of issues to do with one's own subordination and how it is maintained. Such power cannot be given; it has to be self-generative (Kabeer, 1999a).

5.2. Social Empowerment through Participation

People's collective action on common matters creates opportunities that cultivate social empowerment. Collective action engenders favorable conditions that enhance social relationships among the members of the public. It crafts a forum through which residents share their social values with each other. The interaction escalates the bond between members of the public. Based on these facts, we assessed social empowerment through participation. The results of multiple regression analysis performed to determine the effect of participation on social empowerment are portrayed in table 3.

A close look at table 3 suggests that all the independent variables included in the model explained approximately 3 percent (0.03 x 100%) of the variance in dependent variable (social empowerment). Of the six variables included in the model only participation in planning ($\beta = .19$, $p = 0.02$) significantly predicted social empowerment. Thus, the model of multiple regression analysis is found to be:

$$\hat{Y} = 16.45 + 1.92X_3$$

The result here indicates a positive relationship between participation in planning and social empowerment. In other words, when participation in planning increased by one standard deviation, social empowerment increased by .19 standard deviation. The examination of the above findings clearly indicated

Table 3: Multiple regression estimates of social empowerment through participation

Model	Unstandardized coefficients		Standardized coefficients			95% Confidence interval for B	
	B	SE	Beta	t	Sig.	LB	UB
Participation in needs identification	-.99	.82	-.09	-1.20	.23	-2.61	.64
Participation in setting priority of needs	-.85	.83	-.08	-1.03	.30	-2.48	.78
Participation in planning	1.92	.79	.19	2.42	.02	.36	3.48
Participation in implementation	-1.24	.78	-.13	-1.60	.11	-2.77	.29
Participation in monitoring	.03	.79	.00	.04	.97	-1.50	1.56
Participate in performance evaluation	-.27	.72	-.03	-.37	.71	-1.68	1.15
(Constant)	16.45	.49		33.72	.00	.00	17.41
R Square	0.03						

Source: Field survey, 2015

a very low level of social empowerment through participation in BCA. The result of FGD conducted in *Ganda* 09 attached this low degree of social empowerment to institutional problems. According to this result, the main challenge of social empowerment was the cooption of public participation by the formal top-down approach of the City Government structures, mainly involving loyal party members. The above results stress that the involuntary organizing of the public to one to five government structure fostered fear of each other among the public. This resulted in lack of trust among the public, which in turn hindered social empowerment through participation. Moreover, the result revealed that government officials' lack of interest in working with the public also exacerbated the lack of closeness among the public. These findings imply that there was no conducive institutional environment to facilitate empowerment through public participation. That means the government facilitates public participation through structures that are not suitable for enhancing social empowerment through participation.

Furthermore, an institutional assessment indicated that the absence of people's own organization through which they could participate was also a major reason of lower degrees of social empowerment. Rather than facilitating the creation of popular organizations that foster favorable ground for social empowerment, the government forced the public to participate along the government's structures. This in turn hampered social empowerment through participation.

Item Analysis of Social Empowerment through Participation

The result of multiple regression analysis indicated social empowerment through participation. Thus, it is imperative to determine the degree of social empowerment along the hypothesized indicators. The degree to which participation influences each indicator was determined through comparing the mean of individual items against the overall mean of social empowerment. The result of the analysis is illustrated in table 4.

A close look at table 4 indicates that participation influenced the formation of internal mechanisms for popular cohesion (M = 1.98); level of trust among the people (M = 2.03); group work or interaction among work groups (M = 2.17); and feeling of togetherness or closeness among people (M = 2.13) relatively to lesser degrees. Participation influenced relationship and cooperation among the people (M = 2.31); the sense of helping each other among the people (M = 2.34); and social links among the people (M = 2.33) to a relatively higher degree.

Despite low level of social empowerment indicated by the result of quantitative analysis, the results of FGDs elucidated some emerging aspects of

Table 4: Item analysis for Social empowerment through participation (N= 418, M = 2.18).
SA: Strongly agree; A: Agree; UD: Undecided; DA Disagree; SDA Strongly disagree

Items	Mean	SD	SA (%)	A (%)	UD (%)	DA (%)	SDA (%)
Enhancing formation of internal mechanisms for cohesion of the people	1.98	.93	32.3	47.1	13.4	4.8	2.4
Enhancing good relationship and cooperation among the people	2.31	1.01	16.5	55.5	13.9	9.1	5.0
Increasing the level of trust among the people	2.03	.91	27.8	52.2	12.0	6.0	2.2
Increasing the sense of helping each other among the people	2.34	1.12	16.7	54.1	12.4	8.4	8.4
Enhancing group work or interaction among work groups in the City	2.17	.95	21.3	54.8	12.0	9.8	2.2
Enhancing social links among the people	2.33	1.04	16.3	55.3	13.6	8.9	6.0
Enhancing the feeling of togetherness or closeness among people	2.13	.98	24.9	51.7	12.0	8.6	2.9

Source: Field survey, 2015

social empowerment through participation. Participation improved conflict resolution capacity or the tendency to solve conflict between members of the public by recourse to the mediation of elders. The conflict resolution was done through *Jarsuma* (conciliation). This implies that participation enhanced the optimal utilization of local resources (local knowledge of the elders). Using Rowlands (1997) empowerment framework, this refers to "power with," the capacity to solve its own problem by the public.

5.3. Political Empowerment through Participation

Participation in development can result in public awareness about the public policy process. It also improves the relationship between government and the public. It can achieve these results through improving the capacity of the public to demand their rights, to negotiate with government, and to influence public policy process. Based on these general facts, the effects of participation on local people's political empowerment were assessed in BCA. To this end both quantitative and qualitative data were corroborated. However, the result of multiple regression analysis revealed that participation had no statistically significant influence on political empowerment. The result of the analysis is presented in table 5.

The result of analysis in table 5 revealed that there is no statistically significant relationship between all predictors and political empowerment. This finding implies that participation did not bring about political empowerment in BCA. Since none of the predictors had an effect on political empowerment, item analysis was not conducted. However, the result of quantitative analysis and qualitative analysis diverge regarding the influence of participation on political empowerment. Thus, this question needs further investigation.

Despite the above result of quantitative data analysis, which indicated the absence of political empowerment through participation, the results of FGDs in *Ganda* 05 and 09 highlighted the development of some aspects of political empowerment. These include: improvement in access to government services, improvement of public capacity for demanding that the government fill the gap in public service delivery, and an attempt to petition public officials and make them accountable for failure to discharge his/her responsibilities. There was also an improvement in recognizing the right to better public service and asking for its provision. This result suggests a divergence between qualitative and quantitative results.

Despite some aspects of political empowerment exhibited, participation did not create opportunities to influence decisions in the public policy process. Per the results of FGDs and interviews with Key Informants from the public,

Table 5: Multiple regression estimates of political empowerment through participation

Model	Unstandardized coefficients		Standardized coefficients			95.0% confidence interval for B	
	B	SE	Beta	t	Sig.	Lower Bound	Upper Bound
Participation in need identification	-.71	.95	-.06	-.75	.46	-2.59	1.17
Participation in priority setting	-.68	.96	-.06	-.71	.48	-2.56	1.20
Participation in planning	1.19	.92	.11	1.29	.20	-.62	2.99
Participation in implementation	-.91	.90	-.08	-1.02	.31	-2.68	.85
Participation in monitoring	.67	.90	.06	.75	.46	-1.10	2.44
Participation in evaluation	.79	.83	.07	.95	.35	-.85	2.42
(Constant)	19.56	.56		34.66	.00	18.45	20.67
R Square	.02						

Source: Field survey, 2015

different factors hindered political empowerment through participation in BCA. The factors include: (1) the approach of participation; (2) the involuntary aspect of participation; (3) the low extent of participation in decision-making; and (4) institutional contexts.

The above results indicate that channelling public participation through top-down governmental bureaucratic structures stands in the way of empowerment through participation. According to the above results, the involuntary participation also made the public develop a negative attitude toward the city government. The results further indicated that the public attitude toward the structure of the city government was also a major factor hindering the public-government relationship.

The results of interviews with key informants from the public and FGDs highlighted that decision-making regarding participatory development was controlled by government officials and experts without any real involvement from the public. As a result, little political empowerment of local people through participation was exhibited in BCA. Using Rowlands (1997) empowerment framework, the city government exercised "power over" in its negative definition, if one thinks of power as a "zero sum" (Chambers, 2007). This implies that the government exercises "power over," the "ability to exert control and influence over others" (Friedmann, 1992) in facilitating participation in development, inevitably resulting in the loss of power by the public. As attested by the evidence from FGDs and Key informant interviews, this leads to the marginalization of the public from influencing the public policy making process. As a result, participation failed to create public access to political structures and formal decision-making processes in the economic, social, and political spheres.

Using "power over" in its positive sense (outside zero-sum commodity) (Chambers, 2007), the above problems restrict the power of the public over political decision-making. That means it failed to bring people who are outside the policy decision-making process into it. The institutional contexts failed to enable the public to maximize empowerment opportunities available to them through participation without constraints.

The results of key informant interviews with CPEs stressed that the absence of communities' own development project was also a major factor holding back political empowerment. The above results pointed out that the public was not allowed to develop their own projects that would help them to develop the capacity to exercise political issues. They were forced to participate in government projects, which were top down in nature. This approach was not empowering by its nature. Using Rowlands (1997) empowerment framework, the lack of the public's own project prohibited people from developing the "power to" influence the public policy process. These findings imply that the failure to enhance political empowerment impedes the public's opportunities to develop political capacity to influence government activities.

The results of FGDs and interviews with key informant from the public indicated that lack of access to government information hampered transparency, which in turn reduced the potential to empower the public politically. The above results further suggest that low levels of participation impeded political empowerment that could be acquired through evaluating the systems, interpreting the results of evaluation, and improving management. As a result, using Rowlands (1997) empowerment framework, the public lost "power to" influence government activities.

As stated elsewhere in this paper, the extent of participation in different phase of local development was very low. In many cases the public officials made decisions regarding participatory development and communicated them to the public through channels that did not allow much debate. As the result, the public did not get the chance to influence decision-making in a way that would help to develop the capacity to exercise political issues. This condition hampered the opportunity of the public to develop the power to influence the political process. Thus, elite dominance of decisions regarding participatory development hampered political empowerment through participation.

The structural arrangement of the city became the main actor rather than a facilitator of participation. Moreover, the base for determining the government structure was not created in a manner that enhances empowerment. For example *shane* (an organization encompassing one to five residents) were organized in ways that prohibited interaction among the large portion of the public, preventing the latter from acquiring empowering experience. Using Rowlands (1997) empowerment framework, the opportunity to develop capacity ("power to") to negotiate with the government was not developed.

The results of FGDs and interviews conducted with government officials and experts indicated divergent views among government officials and the public regarding political empowerment through participation. Public officials and experts argued that political empowerment was enhanced as the result of participation, whereas the public argued on the contrary that political empowerment was at its lowest stage. The public further argued that political empowerment was set back due to public officials' and experts' domination of decision-making regarding participatory development. This fact implies that public officials considered empowerment as something to be provided by the government. However, by its nature empowerment is bottom up. Using Rowlands (1997) empowerment framework, this finding suggested that the city government exercised "power over" in its negative sense, that is, by controlling and influencing the public.

The results of FGDs indicated that lack of accountability by public officials and lack of trust in them by the public hindered political empowerment through participation. Public officials were not made accountable for their failure to discharge their responsibility to enhance participation. They were only accountable for the failure to enforce the government's political philosophy. Although the public complained about the failure of officials to listen to their demands, and that they abused government money, the government did not take any corrective measures. .

The result of FGDs revealed that the public had no trust in government officials, since they were not elected by them. They were assigned by the government from other places unknown to the public. Hence the public hesitated to believe that these officials serve their interests. This adversely affected interaction between the local government and the public, one form of political empowerment.

5.4. Economic Empowerment through Participation

Determining actual economic gain as the result of participatory development was a difficult task. Thus, the role of participation in the economic empowerment of local people can be considered in terms of the actual economic gain or the opportunity to generate economic resources. For the purposes of this study, economic empowerment of local people through participation was assessed by determining the opportunities created as a result of participatory development. I employed qualitative data to assess potential economic empowerment created as the result of participation. Accordingly, the analysis and interpretation were based on the data generated through interviews, Key Informant Interviews, and FGDs.

The results of interview with Government officials and FGDs pointed out that the improvements of crucial urban services, road networks and electric service, as the result of participation paved the way for economic empowerment of the public in various forms. Thus, the effect of participation in empowering local people was considered along three dimensions, namely, its role in creating business activities, increasing the value of existing assets, and creating employment opportunities.

The results of interview with key informant CPEs and FGDs disclosed that participation resulted in actual and potential business activities. These business activities include: the opening of new shops, cafeterias, greenhouses, clinics, kindergarten, primary schools, butchery, and petty trades like pot coffee and selling *budena* (traditional food prepared from some sort of cereals), bread, and *akayi* (fried cereals, especially barely).

This situation has double edged benefits. In one hand, participation here improved the life of those engaged in business activities; on the other hand it created a market for those living through renting houses. Using Alsop et al.'s (2006) empowerment framework, the widening of economic activities enables the public to develop "agency," the capacity to make purposive choice. Using Rowland's (1997) empowerment framework, participation developed "power to" among the public, the capacity to improve living conditions and "power over," which is the power over the means of livelihood.

The results of FGDs and interviews with *ganda* managers and CPEs pointed out that the improvements in road conditions through participation, in turn, improved transportation services, thereby contributing to residents' potential economic empowerment. For example, cobble stone roads constructed through participation in *Ganda* 05 from Libenedingle to Millennium Schools may be mentioned. The results of FGD in *Ganda* 05 revealed that prior to the construction of cobble stone in this area, horse carts were the means of transportation on this road. As a result, there was serious transportation problem in the absence of carts. The construction of cobble stone transformed the means of transportation from cart to bajaj. This condition played two important roles: (1) the transformation of means of transportation from a traditional to modern one; and (2) reducing the distance of the road from 500 meters to 100 meters. Using Alsop et al (2006) empowerment framework, improvement in the transportation service enhanced opportunity structure, paving the way for the development of "agency." Furthermore, it saved time that could be invested on the performance of other living activities performance.

Petty economic activities like mini shops, pot coffee, and selling *budena* flourished as the result of road renewal through participation. Per the result of FGD at *Ganda* 05, the flourishing of these petty business activities at Berhan Mender and Sefere Misale in *Ganda* 05 were the best example of such activities flourishing as the result of cobble stone construction in the area.

The above findings imply that the flourishing of new shops and cafeteria services, in addition to improving the economic wellbeing of those engaged in these activities, also helped to improve the provision of service for the residents. It also created simple access to services for the public in their vicinity. Similarly, the opening of clinics on the one hand enhanced the economic empowerment of the service providers; on the other hand it improved social service and access to services in the city. As the result, it contributed to the production of a healthy work force. Using Rowland's

(1997) empowerment framework, this finding implies that participation created "power over" economic resources. Using the Alsop et al. (2006) empowerment framework, it created agency, via a potential work force that contributed to further economic development of the nation in general and the city in particular.

The results of FGDs and interviews with CPEs show that improvements in the road network contributed to the development of greeneries along the roads. The development of green areas in turn played great roles in improving the environmental conditions and beautification of the city. The improvement of environmental conditions, in turn, contributed to economic empowerment through creating a healthy work force. The FDGs and interview results further pointed out that the development of green areas along the newly opened roads enhanced economic empowerment for young people in the city through creating employment opportunities. Using the Alsop et al. (2006) empowerment framework, this finding implies that participation created an opportunity structure, which facilitated the development "agency."

The result of interviews with CPEs and FGDs conducted at Babogaya and *Ganda* 01 indicated that participation created both temporary and relatively permanent employment opportunities in cobble stone and other road constructions. Using Rowland's (1997) the creation of employment suggested the development of "power to," the capacity to improve living conditions. Based on the Alsop et al. (2006) empowerment framework, job opportunities enhance the development of "agency," the ability to make purposeful choices in one's life.

The results of FGDs and interviews with key informant from the public revealed that participation increased the value of assets through improving the quality and quantity of roads and security in the area. The security of the area was improved as the result of streetlight provision through participation. Participation increased the value of assets through increasing land values and raising demand for housing and rent prices. Moreover, the above data indicated that the increase in value of assets was indebted to improvement in environmental conditions, which played a great role in making the area attractive and livable. The results of an interview with the CPE of *Ganda* 09 highlighted Village 15 of *Ganda* 09 as a prominent example, where increases in house rent came about as a result of participation. Using Rowland's (1997) empowerment framework, these findings imply the development of "power to," the capacity to generate assets. Using the Alsop et al. (2006) empowerment framework, the above findings suggests that participation created "agency," the resource for making purposeful choices to improve living conditions.

5.5. Corruption: An Impediment to Economic Empowerment

Corruption emerged as a serious challenge to economic empowerment through participation in BCA. The results of FGDs attested that multifaceted corruption practices hampered empowerment through participation. The above results further pointed out that corruption practices impeded participation from creating employment opportunities for poor people (especially youth) and access to economic resources.

The results of FGD conducted at *Ganda* 05 exclusively indicated that the residents were not benefiting from employment opportunities created by participatory development activities. The above results revealed that government officials bring their relatives from other areas to capitalize on the opportunities created by participatory projects. As a result, the residents of the city were excluded from the job opportunities created by participatory development projects. The FGD's results conducted at different places further revealed that the residents are employed only and only if they have a relative in the city administration. Respondents stressed that this unfair employment practice is deeply rooted in the city. The FGD results further indicated that this problem is exacerbated from time to time as previous officials give behavioral lessons to incoming experts and officials. This finding implies that corruption is a systematic practice in relation to participatory development.

The results of FGDs showed that as a result of corruption, participation has failed to play its role in reducing poverty through the elimination of unemployment and creating access to economic resources. According to the above results, contributing factors included a lack of fair employment opportunities and failure to provide equitable and quality infrastructure. Hence, the corrupt practices related to participatory development hamper the spillover effects of participatory development on the achievement of other policy goals. Among these, the major one is the role of participation in development in alleviating poverty through economic empowerment. Thus, using Rowlands (1997) empowerment framework, corruption has hindered the abilities of participation to develop "power to" and "power over" resources.

The results of FGDs and interviews with key informants from the public suggest that only those who have close relationships with officials and experts have access to the benefits of participatory development. The above results further stressed that this was intentionally done to grasp the benefit derived from participatory development activities. These finding imply that there was an absence of fair distribution of benefits of development among the public in BCA. This systematic alienation of the local people from access to benefits of participatory development has hampered economic empowerment through participation.

As indicated by the results of the FDGs, major forms of corruption prevailing in relation to participatory development include: giving cobble stone construction and red ash paving contracts to relatives; and organizing pseudo MSEs and winning auctions by government officials and experts. As an example, the FDGs highlighted the assignment of inappropriate persons to responsible positions in managing the cobble stone project. The FGD results and interview with key informants from the public revealed that government official and experts played a dual role in corruption activities. On the one hand, they committed corruption themselves; on the other hand, they created favorable grounds for others to commit corruption. The result of the FGD conducted at *Ganda* 05 elaborated the corruption practices as follows: "The previous officials give lessons on the corruption to the successor and aggravated corrupt behavior in the society." This highlights the fact that corruption has become a systematic problem in BCA. Moreover, it contributes to the sustenance of corruption over time in the process of participatory development. This finding implies that government officials and experts have utilized official power for their personal interests.

It was learned from the assessment of documents that the absence of a legal framework that would guide local development benefit sharing has also created a favorable ground for corruption practices related to participation. This implies that the gap in legal and policy framework is also one of the factors contributing to the proliferation of corruption related to participatory development.

6. Conclusions

The general objective of this chapter was to explore the effect of participation in local development on empowerment. Participation and empowerment are considered as buzz words among different scholars and practitioners. Whether participation and empowerment are means or ends is the subject of an ongoing debate. Hence, this chapter tested whether participation is rhetoric or practice and sought to address the debate on participation and empowerment as end or means. This chapter concluded that participation and empowerment are, in fact, practice. Moreover, this chapter highlighted that participation is a means for empowerment. If properly handled, participation in the development process plays a fundamental role in enabling local people to manage their affairs. However, participation in local development contributed less to enable ordinary people to take charge of their lives, to make communities more responsible for their development, and to make governments listen to their people in BCA. Participation relatively enhances the personal empowerment of local people. However, participation did not significantly enhance local people's political empowerment. Thus, participation generates "power within," "power to," "power with," and "power over" forms of power among local people. Participation in different phases of development did not equally contribute to local popular empowerment. Participation in setting the priority of needs and planning phases of development played a great role in empowering local people. Context and the extent of participation highly constrain the role of participation in empowering local people. The approach of participation (whether top-down or bottom-up), elite domination, institutional factors, some aspects of participation, and corruption highly hampered empowerment through participation in development. The chapter was limited in developing and testing hypothesis regarding the effect of participation in each phase development on local people empowerment, instead dealing with a general hypothesis related to the effect of participation on empowerment.

7. Theoretical, Methodological, and Policy Implications

The findings of the chapter enhance the development of participation and empowerment theory. The findings of this study advance our understanding of the participatory approach to development in several ways. The chapter contributes to the ongoing debate regarding the empowering effect of participation by investigating their relationship at grassroots level. It contributes to bridging the gap between participation and empowerment rhetoric and practice. It also contributes to knowledge about participation and empowerment through showing how these buzz/catch-all words can be operationalized and studied in particular situations and settings. The findings contribute to the debate on whether participation is a means or an end by arguing that participation can be both instrumental and transformational. The chapter does so through relating the instrumental value of participation (as a means to enhance local development) to its transformative value (empowerment through participation in development). It contributes to the advancement of the literature of empowerment through indicating how theory and concept are integrated. To this end, the author attempted to integrate the concept of empowerment with appropriate theory in order to explain the actual situation on the ground.

The chapter has various methodological contributions to the discipline of public administration. It contributes to the advancement of public administration research through the application of mixed methods on the catch-all concepts of participation and empowerment. Hence, it emphasized the appropriateness of mixed methods in dealing with fluid public problems, helping to shift the bias of public administration research toward the qualitative approach.

The chapter has different policy contributions, enhancing the development of public capacity to influence policy process. Participatory development enhances the development of policy capacity through empowering the public to negotiate with institutions and bureaucracies, allowing the public to influence public policy and providing a check on the power of government. Furthermore, the results of this paper contribute to community capacity building. Participation in development builds community capacity through empowering the local people economically, socially, and psychologically. Empowerment increases the capacity of local people to initiate actions of their own or to negotiate with powerful actors.

Acknowledgements

I am indebted to the anonymous reviewers who provided critical comments and constructive suggestions that helped me in improving the chapter. I also sincerely thank the editors.

References

Ali Shah, I., & Baporikar, N. (2012). Participatory Approach to Development in Pakistan, *Journal of Economic and Social Studies*, 2(1), 111-141.

Chambers, R. (1997). *Whose Reality counts? Putting the First Last.* London: Intermediate Technology Publications Ltd (ITP).

Chambers, R. (2005). *Ideas for Development*, London: Earths can.

Cook, B., & Kothari, U. (2001). The Case for Participation as Tyranny. *Participation: The New Tyranny*, 1-15. London: Zed Books.

Craig, G., & Mayo, M. (1995). *Community Empowerment: A Reader in Participation and Development.* London: Zed Books.

Creswell, J. W., & Clark, V. L. P. (2007). *Designing and Conducting Mixed Methods Research.* Thousand Oaks, CA: Sage.

Crocker, D. (2003). Participatory Development: The Capabilities Approach, and Deliberative Democracy. College Park, Maryland, unpublished manuscript.

Freire, P. (1970). *Pedagogy of the Oppressed.* New York: Herder and Herder.

Greene, J. C. (2006). Toward a Methodology of Mixed Methods Social Inquiry, *Research in the Schools*, 13(1), 93-98.

Hentschel, J., & Lanjouw, P. (1996). *The World Bank Participation Sourcebook*. Washington, DC: The World Bank.

Johnson, R. B., & Onwuegbuzie, A. J. (2004). Mixed Methods Research: A Research Paradigm Whose Time Has Come. *Educational Researcher*, 33(7), 14-26.

Johnson, R. B., Onwuegbuzie, A. J., & Turner, L. A. (2007). Toward a Definition of Mixed Methods Research. *Journal of Mixed Methods Research*, 1(2), 112-133.

Kesby, M. (2005). Retheorizing Empowerment-through-participation as a Performance in Space: Beyond Tyranny to Transformation. *Signs: Journal of Women in Culture and Society*, 30(4), 2037-2065.

Krejcie, R. V., & Morgan, D. W. (1970). Determining Sample size for Research Activities. *Educational and Psychological Measurement*, 30(3), 607-610.

Luttrell, C., Quiroz, S., Scrutton, C., & Bird, K. (2009). Understanding and Operationalizing Empowerment. *Working Paper 308*, 1-16. London: Overseas Development Institute.

Morgan, D. L. (2007). Paradigms Lost and Pragmatism Regained: Methodological Implications of Combining Qualitative and Quantitative Methods. *Journal of Mixed Methods Research*, 1(1), 48-76.

Nelson, N., & Wright, S. (1995). Participation and Power. In N. Nelson & S. Wright (eds). *Power and Participatory Development: Theory and Practice* (pp. 1-18). Michigan: Intermediate Technology Publications.

ONRS. (2001). Oromia Regional State Revised Constitution. *Proclamation No. 46/2001.*

ONRS. (2003). The Urban Local Government Proclamation of the Oromia National Regional State. *Proclamation No. 65/2003.*

Onwuegbuzie, A. J., & Leech, N. L. (2005). On Becoming a Pragmatic Researcher: The Importance of Combining Quantitative and Qualitative Research Methodologies. *International Journal of Social Research Methodology*, 8(5), 375-387.

Pelling, M. (1998). Participation, Social Capital and Vulnerability to Urban Flooding in Guyana. *Journal of International Development*, 10(4), 469-486.

Pettit, J. (2012). Empowerment and Participation: Bridging the Gap between Understanding and Practice. *United Nations Headquaters. Schools*, 13(1), 93-98.

Rowlands, J. (1995). Empowerment Examined. *Development in Practice*, 5(2), 101-107.

Rowlands, (1997). *Questioning Empowerment: Working with Women in Honduras*. London: Oxfam.

VeneKlasen, L., & Miller, V. (2002). Power and Empowerment. *PLA Notes*, 43, 39-41.

8
Glass Ceiling and Glass Wall, and Women in Local Governments: Evidence from West Shoa Zone, Oromia National Regional State, Ethiopia

Bacha Kebede Debela

Box 1: Key Points of this chapter

- ✓ Many SSA are not on track to meet the aspirations of the UN and AU in political and managerial jobs.
- ✓ Increasing the number of women legislators may not increase the number of women political leaders and managers.
- ✓ A lot must be done to shatter the glass ceiling and glass walls in political and managerial jobs.

Box 2: Reading this chapter will give you insights in

- ✓ Gender inequality is caused by multiple national, institutional, and political contexts.
- ✓ Gender inequality on political and managerial jobs varies across countries, by sectors and by leadership and managerial levels.
- ✓ Feminist theorists provide different solutions for gender inequality.
- ✓ The deep-seated sociocultural and politico-administrative occupational segregation has significant implications for the UN's Sustainable Development Goal (SDGs) and African Union (AU) Agenda 2063.

Box 3: Abbreviations

AU = African Union
DS = Developmental State
SDGs = Sustainable Development Goals
SSA = Sub-Saharan Africa
UN = United Nation
UN-ECA = United Nation Economic Commission for Africa

1. Introduction

The UN in Sustainable Development Goals, Goal 5, has made a bold commitment to "ensure women's full and effective participation and equal opportunities for leadership and managerial positions at all levels of decision-making in political, economic and public life" (UN, 2015: 22). Similarly, the African Union (AU) aspires to ensure "gender parity at all levels of decision-making positions, women to hold at least 30% of all elected officials at national, regional, and local levels and in judicial institutions, and end all forms of political, legal or administrative discrimination against women and girls by 2023" (AU et al., 2017: 67-68). Ethiopia has also emphasized gender equality and equity in legal and policy frameworks and development programs. For example, since the appointment of Prime Minister Abiy Ahmed, the Ethiopian government has ensured gender parity in ministerial positions and has appointed women to key ministerial positions (for example to the Ministry of Revenue) and seen the rise of a female national president and president of the Federal Supreme Court (Ayenew, 2019).

At the global level, the proportion of national women parliamentarians has increased from 12 percent (1997) to 24 percent (2017) (see https://datacatalog.worldbank.org/dataset/gender-statistics). However, there are cross country variations. In 2017, Rwanda and Bolivia were the only countries with more than 50 percent of women in the national parliament, while the national parliament of countries such as Qatar and the Yemen Republic was constituted only by men. Wirth (2001) claims the progress is attributed to a change in perception of men and women due to institutional and legal reforms. A World Bank (2016) study shows over 40 percent of countries have reserved quotas for women parliamentarians in national and local governments.

The number of women ministers and presidents, and the proportion of women managers, however, remains very low; women constituted only 18 percent of ministerial positions (out of 149 countries), 34 percent of global managerial positions, and only 17 countries had a female president (World Economic Forum, 2018). In 2001, Wirth found that women managers held less than 20 percent of managerial positions, meaning a nearly 14 percent increase by 2018.

Wirth (2001) distinguishes two barriers that preventing women from holding managerial and political positions: a glass ceiling (vertical) and a glass wall (horizontal). Wirth defines the glass ceiling as the invisible artificial barriers created by attitudinal and organizational prejudices that block women from holding senior organizational positions. The glass wall denotes occupational segregation patterns that concentrate women managers and politicians in less strategic areas (Wirth, 2001).

Despite the encouraging progress, much remains to be done to shatter the glass ceiling and glass walls, all over the world (World Economic Forum, 2018; Wirth, 2001). The World Bank (2016) notes that many economies (155 out of 173 countries) have at least one law that differentiates between women and men in public and private spheres. The Bank also observes gender-based job restrictions in 100 economies out of 173 countries. The literature on Sub-Saharan Africa (SSA) illustrates the magnitude of gender inequality, as levels of job segregation remains high, despite significant cross-country variation (see for example Odusola et al., 2017; AU et al., 2017), reflecting the fact that gender inequality is shaped by multiple national, institutional, and political contexts (Wirth, 2001).

Global data on women politicians and managers at the local government level are seldom available (World Economic Forum, 2018). Research on the effect of politico-administrative reform on the share of female political leadership and managerial positions are scarce, particularly in the context of developing countries (Ethiopia). This chapter contributes to the literature and to the debate on gender inequality in political and managerial jobs. To reach a broader perspective, the chapter examines the proportion of women in the national parliaments in SSA. The research aims to answer: what is the trend of women parliamentarians in the national parliament in SSA countries? To what extent do the quota system, government effectiveness, the rule of law, and the female harmonized human capital index explain the variations in the proportion of women parliamentarians at the national parliament in the SSA countries? What is the percentage of women parliamentarians in the Ethiopian National and Oromia National Regional state parliaments and what is the proportion of women in political and managerial jobs in the West Shoa local governments, in Oromia National Reginal State?

The chapter is structured as follows. The next section presents feminist theories. Following this section, the research method will be presented. The fourth section focuses on the study's results. The last section will offer some concluding remarks.

2. Feminist Theories: Literature Review

Feminist theories primarily focus on exploring the role of expectations, status, power relations, and subordination of women due to social, political, and economic structures (Turner & Maschi, 2015; Hayes & Franklin, 2017). The most common feminists theories are Liberal Feminism, Radical Feminism, Marxist and Socialist Feminism, Black Feminism, and Post-structural Feminism (Saulnier, 2000).

2.1. Liberal Feminism

The liberal feminists emphasize equal access to basic services, such as education and health, equal opportunity and recognition in the workplace, and individual female power and rights (Turner & Maschi, 2015). The proponents maintain the division between public and private domains (Saulnier, 2000).

Therefore, liberal feminists are closely related to organizational sociologists, as both argue organization and personal responsibilities should not converge at work (Bandarage, 1984). They also adhere to the ideas of human capital theorists, who focus on building individual knowledge and skills (Judiesch & Lyness, 1992) and emphasize equal opportunity and the rule of law and effective enforcement (Kantola, 2006; Saulnier, 2000). The proponents are less interested in sociopolitical transformation (Dominelli, 2002). The World Bank reports on gender equality appear to be driven by the liberal feminism perspective (see for example World Bank 2016).

2.2. Radical Feminism

Radical feminism focuses on problematizing patriarchy. Proponents argue patriarchy allows men to dominate the social organization to subordinate women, including using violence (Dominelli, 2002; Kantola, 2006). To correct gender power imbalances, unlike the liberal feminists, they draw much attention to the interaction between private and public issues and seek fundamental sociopolitical structural transformation (Turner & Maschi, 2015). Scholars have found that some radical feminists do not have confidence in legal reforms (Saulnier, 2000). As such, some radical feminists claim women should exclude themselves from male circles (Dominelli, 2002).

2.3. Marxist and Socialist Feminists

Both Marxist and socialist feminists focus on economic forms of power, the capitalist mode of social relations, and the resulting inequalities (Turner & Maschi, 2015). They argue that simply putting women in occupations held by men will not necessarily liberate women from oppression; they seek fundamental change in society (Dominelli, 2002). However, while socialist feminists focus on problematizing masculinity, Marxist feminists problematize the capitalist mode of production (Dominelli, 2002). To correct historical injustice, the Marxist feminists urge women to struggle against capitalism as part of the female proletariat (not just as women), while the socialist feminists focus on unpaid domestic labor and seek economic justice for women (Kantola, 2006).

2.4. Black Feminism (Womanism)

The black feminists focus on race and contend that race plays a decisive role in people's lives (Turner & Maschi, 2015, Saulnier, 2000). They critique studies that focus on white middle-class women and have broadened the span of analysis by concentrating on the oppression of women due to the intersection of race, gender, and class in time and space (Dominelli, 2002). Dominelli observes that, unlike radical feminists, black feminists do not accept that all men have benefited from patriarchy. Instead, they accentuate the importance of family and other relationships to survive in the women-unfriendly world and overcome the exploitation of black women by white women, without ignoring the patriarchal culture of black men.

2.5. Cultural Feminism

The cultural feminists acknowledge the difference between women and men and value the unique behavior of women and focus on women-centered personal values, such as close a connection with natural forces and spirituality (Saulnier, 2000). Unlike black feminists, they do not accept difference among women on any criteria, including race, and concentrate on strengthening women-to-women bonds (Saulnier, 2000). The cultural feminists appear to echo the egalitarian way; they maintain the importance of self-management, mutual control, and maximum connectivity and accountability (Hood, 2000; Verge et al., 2018).

2.6. Post-Structural Feminism

The post-structural feminists (also called postmodernist feminists) focus on the micro-state; they argue that the oppression of women differs among and within the state: "the states are not inherently patriarchal, but the patriarchal state is historically constructed through the political process, languages, and discourses" (Kantola, 2006:125; Saulnier, 2000). They acknowledge the dynamic and multidimensional interaction between the state and female oppression and regard institutions as the effects of the process (Kantola, 2006). Unlike socialist feminists, advocates focus on individuals and the role of individual actors in agenda-setting and related discourse; they pay little attention to the role of individuals in social relations and collective identity (Dominelli, 2002). Feminist post-structuralist does not accept the dichotomy between micro and macro practice and seeks change in social, political, and economic structures (Turner & Maschi, 2015).

3. Research Methods

To analyse gender-based inequality at the global and SSA level, an extensive body of literature and reports were reviewed. Data were collected from various sources, including the World Bank Database (women in national parliaments), World Governance Indicators, and the Human Capital Index (female human capital index). Data on the quotas for women in national parliament were collected from the World Bank report on Women Business and the Law (2016). In addition, the UN's agenda 2030, the AU's agenda 2063, the UNDP's reports on gender inequalities, and feminist theories were reviewed.

To examine the position of women in management and political jobs on the level of local government, data were obtained from West Shoa Zone Districts, with the support of the West Shoa Zone's Public Service and Human Resource Development Office and Zonal Oromo Democratic Party (ODP) office. The Zonal Public Service and Human Resource Development Office requested each district line office to submit staff data from all sectors (thirty-two sectors)[1], following new job placement, in soft copy, within two weeks. Data on the number of appointed political leaders (top executives) in the twenty-two zonal districts in public organization was obtained from the Zonal ODP office. The data set excluded top political leaders in the local government ODP offices and local government councils.

Concerning the human resources placement in the twenty-two districts' public sector, despite the personal follow-up to obtain data in time, only three districts were able to submit complete data after more than four weeks. The data sets obtained from the three districts were used to analyze the proportion of women managers in lower-level management. The data, among others, include the name of the employee, gender, field and level of education, employee performance result, and employee job position (placement). Following the official classification, the organizations were stratified into the administrative sector, economic sector, and social sector.

To parallel the analysis, data on the number of district councillors (thirteen districts), by gender, were obtained from the Zonal Gender, Children, and Youth Office. It was not possible to obtain data from nine districts.

To provide easily understandable information, the collected data were analysed descriptively, using percentages and graphs.

4. Results

4.1. Women in National Parliament in SSA

Table 1 reports the proportion and trend of women parliamentarians in the national parliaments in forty-eight SSA countries, in 2017. The table also presents countries that adopt a gender quota system. The results reveal that the proportion of female seats substantially varies across countries. Women parliamentarians held less than 10 percent of seats in nine countries,[2] (the lowest in Nigeria [5.6 percent]), between 10 percent and 20 percent of seats in seventeen countries,[3] between 20 percent and 30 percent seats in nine countries,[4] and between 30 percent and 40 percent of seats in nine economies.[5] Only four countries had more than 40 percent of women parliamentarians: Rwanda (61 percent), Namibia (41.3 percent), Senegal (41.8 percent), and South Africa (42 percent).

There are also cross-country differences in the trend of women parliamentarians. The numbers of female legislators showed an upward trend in twelve economies. Botswana, Mali, and Sierra Leone had dwindling trends. Mauritius, Angola, Equatorial Guinea, Gabon, The Gambia, Guinea-Bissau, and Zambia had a fluctuating "N"-shaped trend. Seychelles had an "M"-shaped trend. Despite small differences, seven countries had a stable trend.

The trend of women parliamentarians does not depend on national income. The proportion of women parliamentarians in nine low-income nations[6] was more than 30 percent. Only in Cameroon, Namibia, South Africa, and Sudan (upper income and lower-middle-income countries) women held over 30 percent of seats. Strikingly, the percentage of women parliamentarians is low in better-off countries, such as Seychelles (HI-21.2 percent), Botswana (UI-9.5 percent), and Mauritius (UI-11.6 percent).

The pattern also depends less than one would think on quotas system. While ten countries have adopted a quota system, the percentage of women in the national parliament is better in many countries that do not have a quota system. Rwanda is an exception. Kenya provides an interesting example demonstrating that the quota system is not sufficient on its own to increase the number of women parliamentarians.

However, the importance of the quota system cannot be dismissed; all countries with quotas (except Kenya) have achieved their target. Wirth

(2004:26) notes that without the quota system "the number of women party candidates would be much lower."

Table 1: Income, quotas and women parliamentarians in national parliaments (% 2017)

Country (income)	Quotas?	(Women 2017%)	Trend (2000-2017)
1. Angola (LI)	No	38.2	+-+
2. Benin (LI)	No	7.2	+ Stable
3. Botswana (UMI)	No	9.5	-
4. Burkina Faso (LI)	No	11	+-?
5. Burundi (LI)	30	36.4	+
6. Cabo Verde (LI)	N/A	23.6	+
7. Cameroon (LMI)	No	31.1	+
8. Central African Republic (LI)	N/A	8.6	N/A
9. Chad (LI)		No	12.8
10. Comoros (LI)	N/A	6.1	+?
11. Congo, Dem.(LI)	No	8.9	Stable +
12. Congo, Rep (LMI)	No	11.3	+?
13. Cote d'Ivoire (LMI)	No	10.6	Stable +
14. Equatorial Guinea (LI)	No	24	+-+
15. Eritrea (LI)	N/A	22	+ stable
16. Ethiopia (LI)	No	38.8	+
17. Gabon (UMI)	No	17.1	+-+
18. Gambia, The (LI)	N/A	10.3	+-+
19. Ghana (LMI)	No	12.7	+-?+
20. Guinea (LI)	No	21.9	N/A
21. Guinea-Bissau (LI)	N/A	13.7	+-+
22. Kenya (LMI)	33	21.8	+
23. Lesotho (LMI)	No	22.9	+-
24. Liberia (LI)	No	12.3	+-
25. Madagascar (LI)	No	19.2	+?
26. Malawi (LI)	No	16.7	+-
27. Mauritania (LMI)	>0	25.2	+?
28. Mauritius (UMI)	No	11.6	+-

Country (income)	Quotas?	(Women 2017%)	Trend (2000-2017)
29. Mozambique (LI)	No	39.6	+
30. Namibia (UMI)	No	41.3	Stable?
31. Niger (LI)	15	17	+?
32. Nigeria (LMI)	No	5.6	Stable
33. Rwanda (LI)	30	61.3	+
34. Sao Tome and Principe (LI)	No	18.2	-+
35. Senegal (LI)	No	41.8	+
36. Seychelles (HI)	No	21.2	+-+-
37. Mali (LI)	No	8.8	-
38. Sierra Leone (LI)	No	12.4	-
39. Somalia (LI)	N/A	24.4	+
40. South Africa (UMI)	No	42	+ stable
41. South Sudan (LI)	25	28.5	+
42. Sudan (LMI)	30	30.5	+
43. Swaziland (LMI)	No	6.2	+-
44. Tanzania (LI)	30	36.4	+
45. Togo (LI)	No	17.6	+
46. Uganda (LI)	29	34.3	+
47. Zambia (LMI)	No	18	+-+
48. Zimbabwe (LI)	22	32.6	+

Source: Quota compiled from World Bank report on Women, Business and the Law (2016); Seats extracted from https://datacatalog.worldbank.org/dataset/gender-statistics; Trend computed from https://datacatalog.worldbank.org/dataset/gender-statistics.

4.2. Female Harmonized Test Score and Women in National Parliament in SSA

Figure 1 compares women in the national parliaments and the female harmonized test score in SSA, in 2017. The results show that increasing females' harmonized test score is necessary but inadequate to increase the share of women in the national parliament. For instance, while the female harmonized test score is relatively better in Gabon, Botswana, Burkina Faso, and Guinea, women do not hold a comparable number of seats in the national parliament. Senegal was an exception. Conversely, women held higher numbers of seats in

Figure 1: Female harmonized score and women parliamentarians in SSA

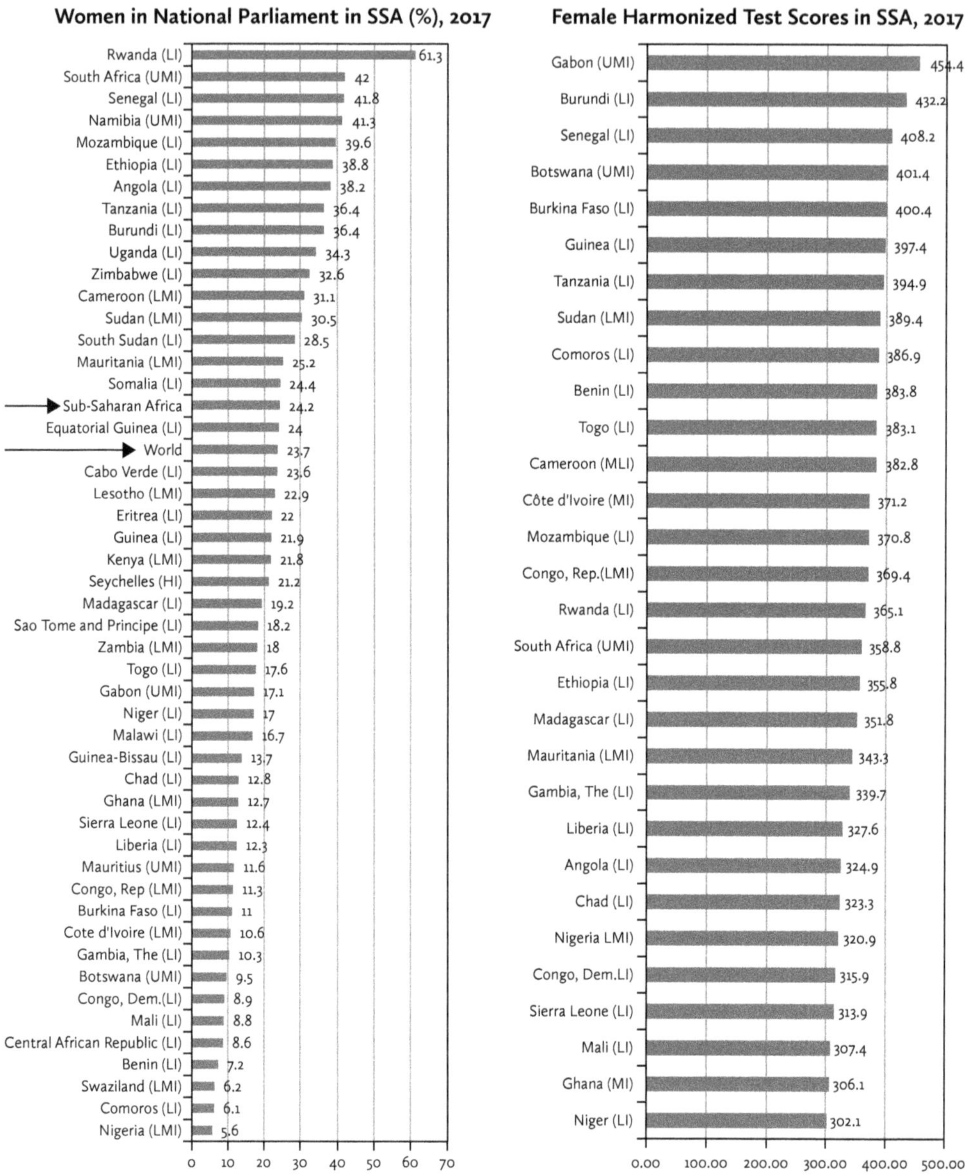

Source: Compiled from World Bank Database (Gender and Human Capital), 2017

Rwanda, South Africa, and Ethiopia. Indeed, caution is important here. The female harmonized test score and the percentage of women in the national parliament are not directly related. However, all things remaining constant, closing the human capital gap is important (World Economic Forum, 2018; Wirth, 2001).

4.3. Government Effectiveness and Women in National Parliament in SSA

Government effectiveness is one of the six[7] broad worldwide dimensions (indicators) of governance and it measures the perceptions of the quality of public services, the quality of the civil service, the degree of its independence from political pressures, and the quality of policy on a scale between -2.5 (weak) to 2.5 (strong) performances. One might expect government effectiveness and the percentage of women parliamentarians to be related. This assumption, however, is not confirmed (see figure 2). Mauritius, Botswana, Seychelles, South Africa, Rwanda, Namibia, and Cabo Verde had a positive score on government effectiveness. However, while there was a higher percentage of women parliamentarians in Rwanda, South Africa, and Namibia, the percentage of women parliamentarian were much lower in Botswana (9.5%), Mauritius (11.6%) and Cabo Verde (23.6%). Many countries with negative government effectiveness scores, such as South Sudan and Somalia (with nearly -2.5 score), had higher percentages of women parliamentarian than Botswana, and Mauritius; the African developmental states (DS) often used as an example to resist the neoliberal ideology in Africa (Seshamani & Ndhlovu, 2016). The pro-DS scholars and practitioners emphasize the relevance of DS to address socio-economic inequalities (Joshi, 2012; Edigheji; 2010). The UN-ECA also promotes the DS doctrine (UN ECA, 2011).

4.4. Rule of Law and Women in National Parliament in SSA

Out of seven countries in SSA that had a positive score on the rule of law, women parliamentarians hold better seats only in Rwanda and Namibia (See figure 3). In many countries, the percentage of women parliamentarians and the score on the rule of law are negatively correlated. For example, Somalia and South Sudan scored worse on the rule of law, respectively -2.31 and -1.94, but had much higher percentage of women parliamentarians than Mauritius, Botswana, Cabo Verde, Ghana, and Seychelles (all having a positive score). Namibia and Zimbabwe, the only two SSA countries that have adopted all six gender-egalitarian laws (AU et al., 2017), had more than 30 percent of of women politicians in the national parliament. Zimbabwe is an interesting case; it scored negative (-1.38) on the rule of law.

Figure 2: Government effectiveness and women parliamentarian in SSA

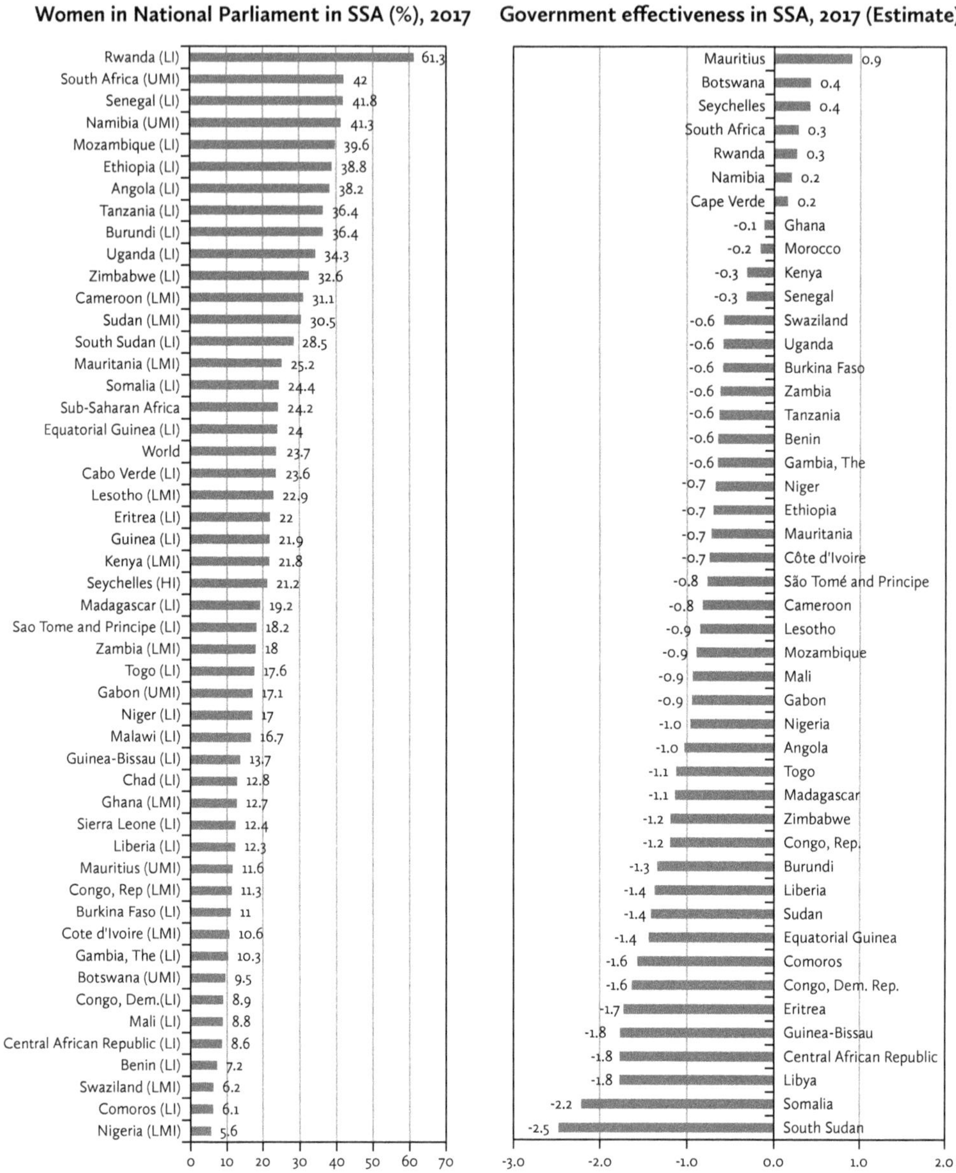

Source: Compiled from World Bank Database (2017) and Worldwide Governance indicators (www.govindicators.org)

Figure 3: Rule of law and women parliamentarians in SSA

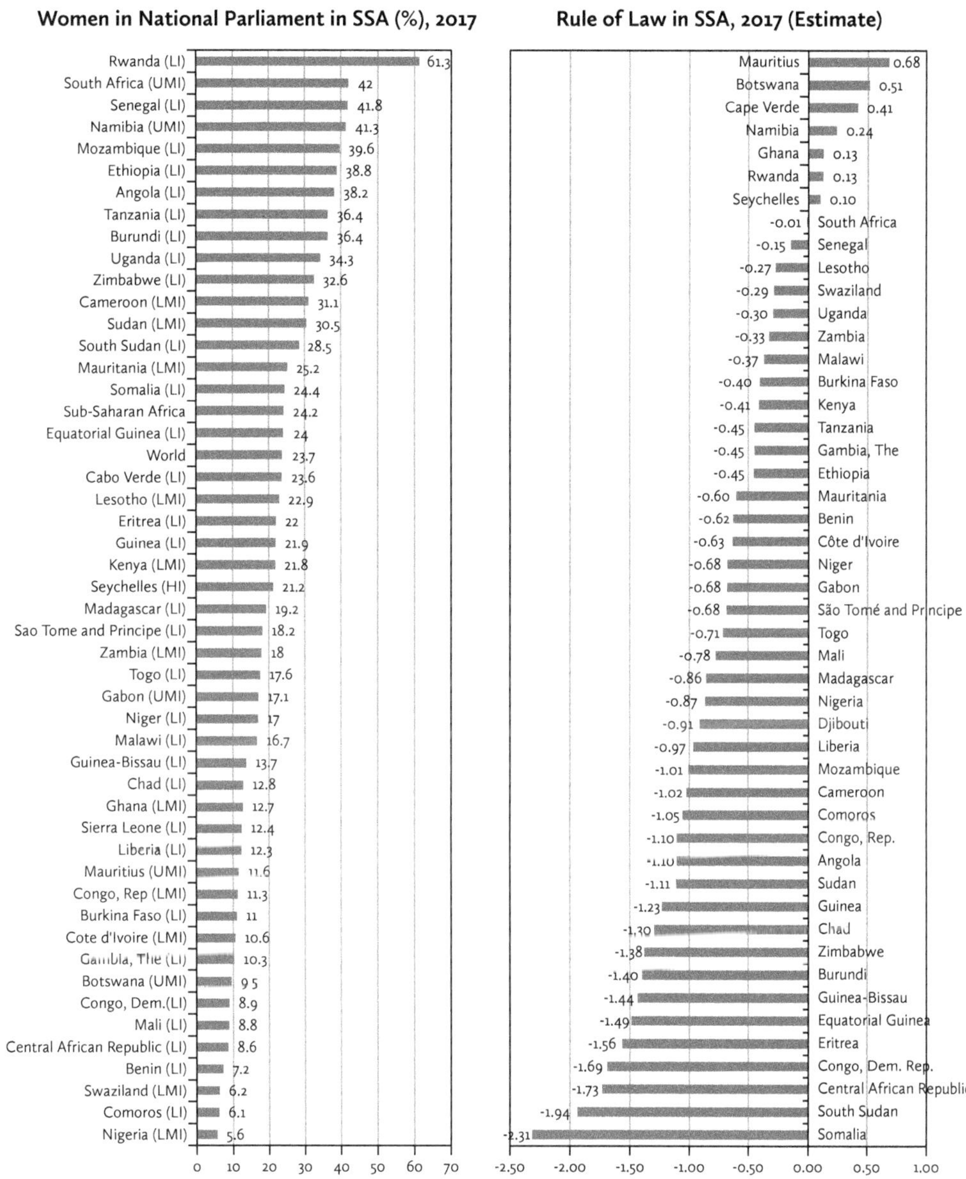

Source: Compiled from World Bank Database (2017) and Worldwide Governance indicators (www.govindicators.org)

4.5. Women in Federal and Oromia National Regional State Parliament, Ethiopia

The proportion of seats held by women in the National and the Oromia National Regional State parliament has drastically increased (see figure 4). While there were only 3.4 percent (Oromia) and 2 percent (national) of women parliamentarians in the first election, the percentage of women quadrupled respectively in the second election. In the relatively competitive but contested 2005 election, the share of women parliamentarians was 36.5 perent (Oromia) and 21.9 percent (national). In the fourth election, in which the opposition parties held only two seats in the national parliament, women held 27.8 percent of seats (Oromia) and 28.8 percent of seats (national). Compared

Figure 4: Proportion of women parliamentarians (1997-2017)

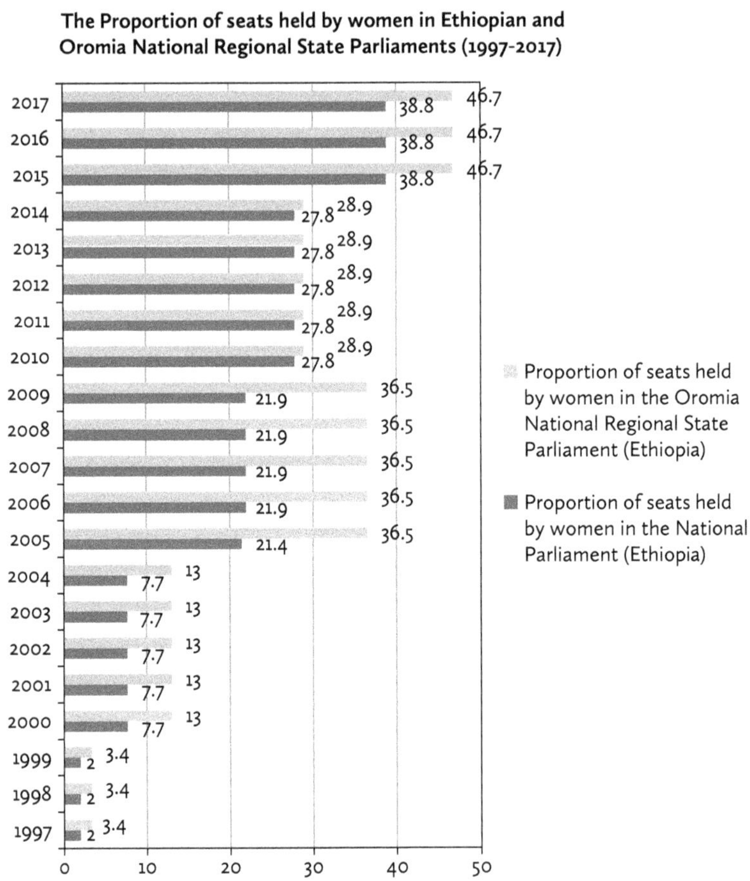

Source: National (World Bank Database) and Oromia (Cafee Oromia Report)

to the third election, Oromia had a nearly 8 percent drop in female legislators in the fourth election. In the fifth election, in which the national parliament is filled only by the ruling party, women hold 38.8 percent of seats (national) and 46.7 percent of seats (Oromia).

4.6. Women in Local Government Politics in West Shoa Zone, Oromia National Regional State

Notwithstanding the existence of a one-party state (including at the local governments) since the first election, and the variations in the number of local government councils, women hold relatively high numbers of seats in the West Shoa Zone local governments (see figure 5). Gender parity is maintained in the councils of the Meta Wolkite, Chobi, and Ginda Beret districts. The difference between female and male councilors is insignificant in the Dano, Iluu Gelan, and Ilfeta districts. In other districts, the local government councils

Figure 5: The number of women and men in local government councils (2019)

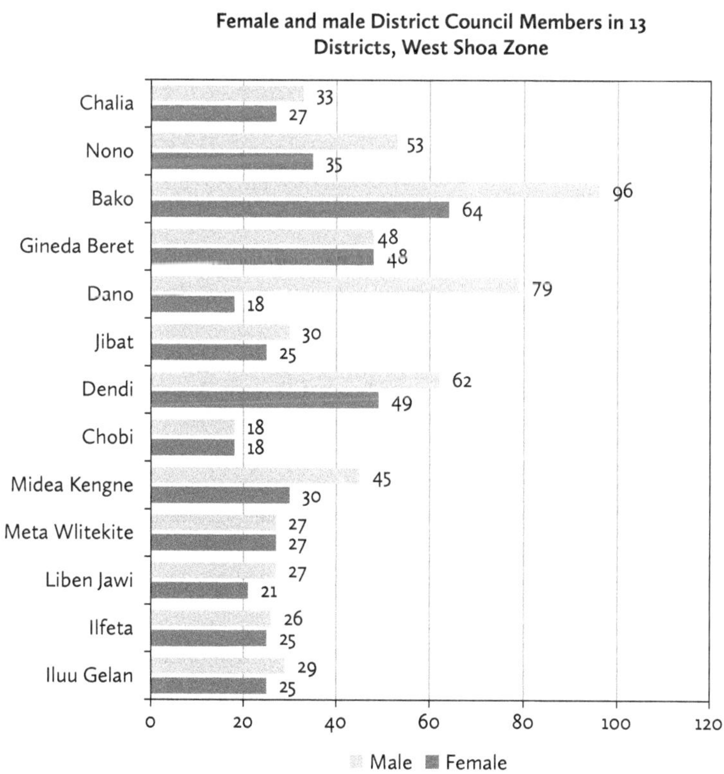

Source: Compiled from West Shoa Zone Women, Children and Youth Office Dataset

Table 2: The number of top women and men managers in West Shoa Zone local governments (2019)

District Name	Head and vice head		Which sectors are led/ managed by women?
	Men	Women	
Abuna G/ Beret	28	4	Women, Children and Youth Affairs (***soc***), Workers and Social Affairs (***soc***), TEVT, and Culture and Tourism (***soc***)
Adea Berega	28	4	Women, Children and Youth Affairs (***soc***), Workers and Social Affairs (***soc***), TEVT, and Culture and Tourism (***soc***)
Ambo	27	5	Women, Children and Youth Affairs (***soc***), Workers and Social Affairs (***soc***), TEVT (***soc***), Investment (***eco***), and Market Development (***eco***)
Bako Tibe	28	4	Women, Children and Youth Affairs (***soc***), Workers and Social affairs (***soc***), Agriculture & Natural Resource Protection (***eco***), and Culture and Tourism (***soc***)
Chaliya	28	4	Women, Children and Youth Affairs (***soc***), Sport (***soc***), City Administration (***adm***) and Culture and Tourism (***soc***)
Dano	29	3	Women, Children and Youth Affairs (***soc***), Environment, Forest & Climate Change Authority (***eco***), and Culture and Tourism (***soc***)
Dendi	31	1	Women, Children and Youth Affairs (***soc***)
Dire Inchin	30	2	Women, Children and Youth Affairs (***soc***), and Market Development Office (***eco***)
Egree	27	5	Women, Children and Youth Affairs (***soc***), Workers and Social affairs (***soc***), Sport (***soc***), Government Communication (***soc***), and Investment(***eco***)
Gende Beret	28	4	Women, Children and Youth Affairs (***soc***), Workers and Social Affairs (***soc***), Public Service and Human Resource Development (***adm***), and Vital Event Registration (***adm***)
Iifata	29	3	Women, Children and Youth Affairs (***soc***), Disaster Prevention (***adm***), and Education (***soc***)
Iluu Gelan	30	2	Women, Children and Youth Affairs (***soc***), and Water, Energy and Mineral(***eco***)
Jelduu	30	2	Women, Children and Youth Affairs (***soc***), and Water, Energy and Mineral(***eco***)
Jibat	31	1	Women, Children and Youth Affairs (***soc***)

Meta Robi	30	2	Women, Children and Youth Affairs (***soc***), and Livestock and Fishery Agency (***eco***)
Meda Kegne	31	1	Women, Children and Youth Affairs (***soc***)
Nanoo	30	2	Women, Children and Youth Affairs (***soc***), and Workers and Social affairs (***soc***)
Toke Kutaye	30	2	Women, Children and Youth Affairs (***soc***), and Workers and Social affairs (***soc***)
Liban Jawi	29	3	Women, Children and Youth Affairs (***soc***), TEVT (***soc***), Culture and Tourism (***soc***)
Cobi	30	2	Women, Children and Youth Affairs (***soc***), and Urban Development (***eco***)
Meta Wolkite	29	3	Women, Children and Youth Affairs (***soc***), Workers and Social Affairs (***soc***), and Government Communication (***adm***)
Egersa Lefo	26	6	Women, Children and Youth Affairs (***soc***), Workers and Social Affairs (***soc***), Revenue (***adm***), Sport (***soc***), Environment, Forest & Climate Change Authority (***eco***), and Culture and Tourism (***soc***)
Total (22)	639	65	

Source: West Shoa Zone ODP Office Report (2019)

were dominated by men. Bako Tibe, Dendi, and Midea Kengne are outliers in this cluster. Furthermore, due to family responsibilities and other factors, women councilors' participation in council meetings may be low, suggesting that in practice women councilors may be subordinate to men in all districts. Even if their participation is higher, due to power relations and other factors, popular womens' issues may not be systematically on the agenda. Yet, strong politicians can impact change in time and space (Wirth, 2004).

4.7. Top Women Political Leaders in West Shoa Zone Local Governments: The Glass Ceiling and Glass Wall

Table 2 reveals top executive women political leaders (office heads and deputy office heads) in twenty-two local governments' the public sectors, in the (West Shoa Zone), were critically underrepresented. This holds true including in those districts which ensured gender parity in the district council: Meta Wolkite, Chobi, and Ginda Beret. In addition, almost the top women political leaders were leading/managing predominantly nonstrategic sectors – the administration and social sectors – sectors that are perceived to be suitable for women, confirming that both the glass ceiling and glass wall are significantly strong. The results also show that increasing the number of district women councilors and female education cannot guarantee gender parity in top leadership and managerial positions. Yet, article 79 of the Oromia National Regional State Constitution sets out that top local political leaders (heads and vice heads) are appointed by the district council (ONRS, 2001).

4.8. Lower Managers in West Shoa Zone Local Governments and the Glass Wall

The new employee placement directive, issued by the Oromia Public Service and Human Resource Development Bureau (2019), emphasizes the merit principle in appointments to the lower-level managerial positions. The directive gives due attention to qualification and fields of study, employee performance appraisal results, direct work experiences in managerial jobs, and gender in the assessment of applications for lower-level managerial positions. It sets out that women applicants and physically challenged persons should get three and four additional points, respectively. Figure 6 presents the proportion of women and men by level of education (top left figure), by sector (top right figure), and women and men managers by sectors (the bottom figure) in three rural local governments in West Shoa Zone, Oromia National Regional State.

The left figure shows the majority of male and female civil servants, in the three districts at least, have BA/ BSc degrees. Yet, the proportion of men is higher than of women. While females with BA/BSc comprise of civil servants in Chalia 59 (56 percent), Toke Kutaye 91 (60 percent), Adea Berga 83 (56 percent), men respectively account for 209 (69 percent), 232 (66 percent) and 223 (71 percent).

The top right figure shows that female civil servants were underrepresented in all districts and in all sectors. The other important observation is that the majority of male civil servants were working in the economic sector in Chalia and Toke Kutaye districts, followed by the administration sector. For the Adea Berga district the opposite is the case. The number of female and male civil servants is proportionally low in the social sector in all districts.

The bottom figure reveals an interesting perspective. First, women lower-level managers were underrepresented in all sectors. Second, when all districts are combined, the proportion of women managers in the administration and economic sectors is equivalent, but there are variations between districts. The majority of women mangers in Adea Berga District were in the administration sector. Men lower-level managers constitute the majority in the administration sector in Chalia district. In contrast, the proportion of men managers in economic sector (a strategic sector) was higher than in the administration

Figure 6: Staff profile by education level, gender, sector, and managerial position

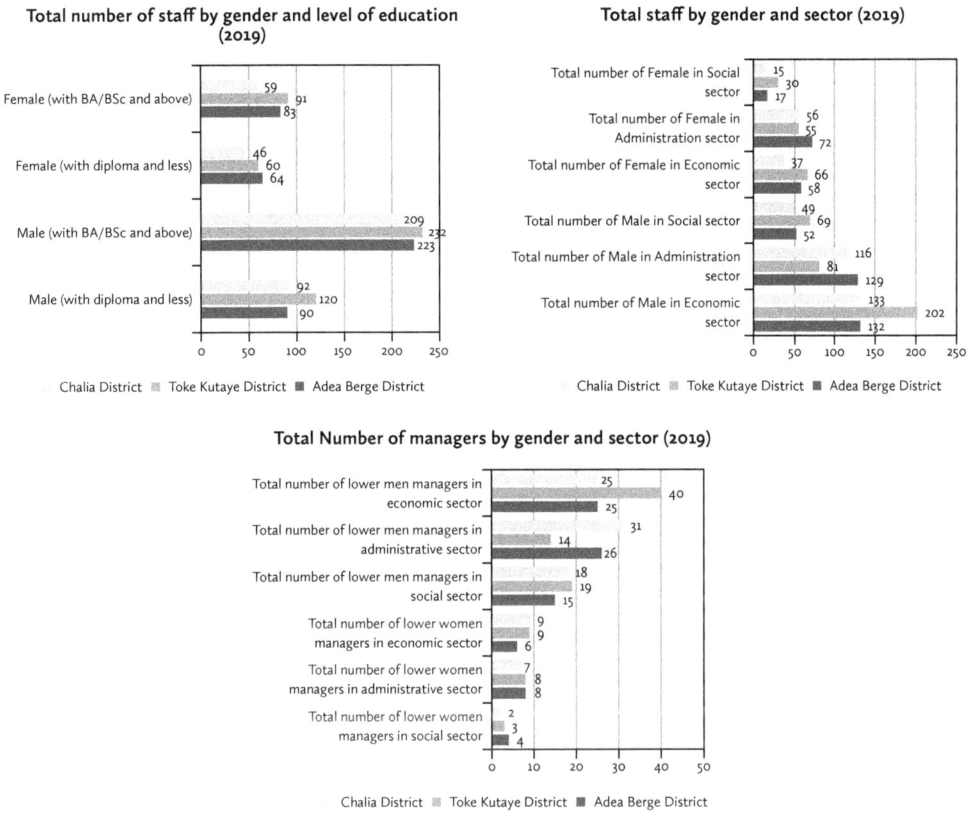

Source: Compiled from employee job placement database

sector in Toke Kutay district. Interestingly, when the three districts are combined, men managers comprise a higher majority in the economic sector than in the administration sector.

How can we explain the glass ceiling and glass wall? The first important factor could be the field of study, the academic qualifications. Female applicant may lack the appropriate educational profile outlined by the job specifications. The second important factor could be the difference in managerial jobs experience. The placement directive pays attention to direct work experience, which female applicant more likely to lack, thus despite the additional points they could not compete with men. Third, the effect of "think manager think men perception" could be very significant, restricting female civil servants from applying for managerial jobs. If they do apply, women may prefer managerial jobs in the administrative and social sectors. The proportion of women managers in the administration sector in the Adea Begra district is a good example of this. The underrepresentation of female civil servants in public administration could have also played a role. The combination of these factors provides a fairly clear explanation for the glass ceiling and the glass wall.

5. Discussion, Conclusions, and Implications

This chapter reviews the feminist theories and provides an empirical account of women in politics in SSA countries and women in top political leadership and lower-level managerial positions in West Shoa Zone local governments. It is apparent that each feminist theory frames the problem of gender inequality from a different perspective and offers different solution thereof. Liberal feminists claim that the problem resides in the lack of legal rights and prescribes legal reforms and equal opportunities. Radical feminists have no confidence in legal reforms and focus on dismantling patriarchy. The Marxist and socialist feminists promote changing the capitalist mode of production (Marxist) and challenging masculinity (socialist). Black feminists focus on changing gender inequality due to race and class. Cultural feminists emphasize women-to-women networks, collective action, and accountability. Post-structural feminists concentrate on state-women interactions at the micro level and the role of individuals in framing ideas (agenda) and discourse.

Empirical results show that many SSA countries are not on track to meet the aspirations of the UN, which has set out to end gender-based discrimination in political and managerial jobs; neither are they on track to meet AU goals of ensuring that women to hold least 30 percent of political and managerial positions at all levels. Equally, the evidence from West Shoa Zone local governments shows that increasing the number of women politicians may not increase the number of top women political leaders and lower managers. Women were extremely underrepresented in both top political leadership and lower managerial positions, including in districts where women hold 50 percent of local government council seats. The results also reveal that the proportion of women politicians and managers did not correlate with the democratic developmental state doctrine promoted by UN-ECA and AU to decrease socio-economic structural inequality.

The findings disclose that policy and legal reforms, which are promoted by liberal feminists, are important but insufficient on their own. Strikingly, women's share of seats in the national parliament, in many SSA countries, did not correlate with the score on rule of law and government effectiveness, or with the female harmonized test score, which is the core measure according to liberal feminists. This paradox clarifies the gap in enforcing the legal frameworks and policies (Wirth, 2001) on the one hand and the importance of the radical feminist perspective in time and space on the other. The World Bank (2016:5) asserts that gender law "on paper not necessarily reflect gender legal realities." Going further, the UNDP (2017) claims that legal equality is not enough in its self to ensure gender equality. In extreme cases gender reforms can reinforce the deep-seated norms and practice; alternatively, due to resistance from privileged actors, the reforms may not be implemented at all (Verge et al., 2018).

The results highlight the need to understand the political economy of the nation. It is apparent that increased economic growth is insufficient to explaining women's share of parliamentarian seats in SSA. Neither is the quota system sufficient. Understanding the politics of the day and state-society interaction in time and space is therefore crucial. Here the Marxist and socialist feminists' perspectives have relevance, although the prescription of Marxist feminism is questionable particularly in the context of Africa, where class formation is unconsolidated and indigenous institutions remain powerful.

Evidence supports the relevance of cultural feminists to address gender inequality in political and managerial jobs. Despite the variation, it appears that "think politics and management think men mentality" remains strong in many SSA countries. The underrepresentation of top women political leaders and lower managers in West Shoa Zone local government also confirms the existence of this phenomenon.

One may ask why the local government councils, in West Shoa Zone, could not nominate and appoint many women political leaders? This draws our attention to concerns about how policies and legal frameworks are formulated. It also draws our attention to issues of numerical majority and power majority. This in turn leads to a number of key questions: Who were/are the actors and who are the gatekeepers? What were/are the nature of power relations among actors and whose interest/s prevailed? and What were/are the rules of the game? The gatekeepers control access to power and resources. As Dominelli (2002) observes, globally, critical legal frameworks, including gender policies, are usually formulated by men. Akanle et al. (2018) maintain the problem could be worse in Africa due to the results of colonial legacy and the ruthless authoritarianism of post-independence African leaders, which institutionalized the male as breadwinners and women's complementary role. This raises the importance of women-to-women networks and collective action to deflect the ingrained institutional culture. Buranajaroenkij et al. (2018) find the women's social movement in Thailand has increased their political competence and engagement in politics and hence acceptance by different actors.

The underrepresentation of top women political leaders and managers in the executive offices of the West Shoa Zone's local governments discloses the importance of post-structural feminists' perspective. The proportion of women political leaders and managers does not correspond with the decision of PM Abiy Ahemed to maintain gender parity in ministerial positions, which clarifies the role of individuals in agenda setting and the enforcement thereof.

Finally, ethnicity rather than race may be also a relevant factor in some SSA countries. In general, women's participation in political and managerial jobs appears to depend on multiple national, structural-institutional, socio-cultural, and political contexts, reflecting "more is more" only when there are more model women political leaders and managers, which in turn depends on enabling politico-administrative contexts. That is to say, although important, a high number of women parliamentarians does not necessarily reflect a strong democratic system, nor does it produce strong gender laws and policies, particularly in single-party authoritarian regimes such as Ethiopia, where the executive and legislative power are considerably fused and the executive is dominant, and where there is strong party discipline (Ayenew, 2019). This suggests the relevance of pragmatism to shattering the glass ceiling and the glass wall. Yet the limitation of the research presented here should be noted. The study relied on secondary data: the perception and actual situation of women politicians, political leaders (top), and lower managers was not investigated. This could be the focus area for future research.

Acknowledgments

This study was carried out in the framework of the academic cooperation in the development project "Professionalizing Ethiopian Public Administration to Support Development Practitioners" between KU Leuven, Ambo University, and Addis Ababa University, financed by VLIR-UOS (Belgium). I earnestly thank these institutions. I also thank others who have provided necessary data and information.

Notes

1. Staff data of all sectors are organized into pools: the civil service pool, and the administration pool.
2. Benin, Botswana, Central African Republic, Comoros, Congo, Dem, Nigeria, Mali, and Swaziland

3. Burkina Faso, Chad, Congo, Rep, Cote d'Ivoire, Gabon, Gambia, The, Ghana, Guinea-Bissau, Liberia, Madagascar, Malawi, Mauritius, Niger, Sao Tome and Principe, Sierra Leone, Togo, and Zambia.
4. Cabo Verde, Equatorial Guinea, Eritrea, Kenya, Lesotho, Mauritania, Seychelles, Somalia, South Sudan
5. Angola, Burundi, Cameroon, Ethiopia, Mozambique, Sudan, Tanzania, Uganda, Zimbabwe
6. Angola, Burundi, Ethiopia, Mozambique, Rwanda, Senegal, Tanzania, Uganda, and Zimbabwe
7. The indicators are Voice and Accountability, Political Stability and Absence of Violence/Terrorism, Government Effectiveness, Regulatory Quality, Rule of Law and Control of Corruption.

References

African Union (AU), Economic Commission for Africa (ECA); African Development Bank (ADB) and United Nations Development Programme (UNPD) (2017). Africa Sustainable Development Report: Tracking Progress on Agenda 2063 and the Sustainable Development Goals. Economic Commission for Africa.

Akanle, O., Adesina, J. O., & Nwaobiala, U. R. (2018). Turbulent but I Must Endure in Silence: Female Breadwinners and Survival in Southwestern Nigeria. *Journal of Asian and African Studies*, 53(1), 98-114.

Ayenew, M. (2019). Parliament–Public Engagement in Ethiopia: Selected Notes and Case Studies on a Political Fragile State. Addis Ababa: Forum for Social Studies.

Bandarage, A. (1984). Women in Development: Liberalism Marxism and Marxist Feminism. *Enzymologia*, 15(4), 495-515.

Buranajaroenkij, D., Doneys, P., Kusakabe, K., & Doane, D. (2018). Expansion of Women's Political Participation through Social Movements: The Case of the Red and Yellow Shirts in Thailand. *Journal of Asian and African Studies*, 53(1): 34-48.

Dominelli, L. (2002). *Feminist Social Work Theory and Practice*. London: Macmillan International Higher Education.

Edigheji, O. (2010) Constructing a Democratic Developmental State in South Africa: Potentials and Challenges. In O. Edigheji (ed.). *Constructing a Democratic Developmental State in South Africa: Potentials and Challenges* (pp.1-33). Cape Town South Africa: HSRC Press.

Hayes, B. E., & Franklin, C. A. (2017). Community Effects on Women's Help-seeking Behaviour for Intimate Partner Violence in India: Gender Disparity, Feminist Theory, and Empowerment. *International Journal of Comparative and Applied Criminal Justice*, 41(1-2), 79-94.

Hood, C. (2000). *The Art of the State: Culture, Rhetoric, and Public Management*. Oxford: Oxford University Press.

https://datacatalog.worldbank.org/dataset/gender-statistics

Joshi, DK. (2012). Varieties of Developmental States: Three Non-Western Pathways to the Millennium Development Goals. *Journal of Developing Societies*, 28(3): 355-78.

Judiesch, M. K., & Lyness, K. S. (1999). Left Behind? The Impact of Leaves of Absence on Managers' Career Success. *Academy of Management Journal*, 42(6), 641-651.

Kantola, J. (2006). Feminism. In C. Hay, Lister, M. & Marsh D. (eds). *The State: Theories and Issues* (pp. 118-134). London: Palgrave Macmillan.

Mukherjee, S., Lusigi, A., Kamwendo, E., & Bonini, A. (2017). *Income Inequality Trends in sub-Saharan Africa: Divergence, Determinants and Consequences: Inequality, Gender and Human Development in Africa*. United Nations Development Programme, Regional Bureau for Africa.

Odusola, A. F., Cornia, G. A., Bhorat, H., & Conceição, P. (eds.). (2017). *Income Inequality Trends in sub-Saharan Africa: Divergence, Determinants and Consequences*. United Nations Development Programme, Regional Bureau for Africa.

Oromia National Regional State (ONRS). (2001). Revised Constitution of Oromia National Regional Government (Proc. No. 46/2001). Megeleta Oromia, Finfine.

Saulnier, C. F. (2000). Incorporating Feminist Theory into Social Work Practice: Group Work Examples. *Social Work with Groups*, 23(1), 5-29.

Seshamani, V. and Ndhlovu, O. (2016). Prospects for the Formation of Developmental States in Africa: The Case of Zambia. *An Online International Research Journal*, 2(1), 757-73.

Turner, S. G., & Maschi, T. M. (2015). Feminist and Empowerment Theory and Social Work Practice. *Journal of Social Work Practice*, 29(2), 151-162.

UNDP (2018). Localizing the 2030 Agenda and the SDGs: Strengthening Local Government Action in Central Africa, United Nations Development Programme – Regional Service Centre for Africa.

United Nations (UN). (2015). Transforming Our World: The 2030 Agenda for Sustainable Development. General Assembly (A/RES/70/1).

United Nations Development Programme (UNDP). (2017). Closing Gender Gaps in Labour and Productive Resources in Africa Analytical Report, Regional Bureau for Africa.

United Nations Economic Commission for Africa (UN-ECA). (2011). Economic Report on Governing Development in Africa – The Role of the State in Economic Transformation, UN-ECA, Addis Ababa, Ethiopia.

Verge, T., Ferrer-Fons, M. and González, M. J., (2018). Resistance to Mainstreaming Gender into the Higher Education Curriculum. *European Journal of Women's Studies*, 25(1), pp. 86-101.

Wirth, L. (2001). *Breaking through the Glass Ceiling. Women in Management*. Geneva: International Labor Office.

Wirth, L. (2004). *Breaking through the Glass Ceiling. Women in Management*. Update.Geneva: International Labor Office.

World Bank (2016). *Women, Business and the Law, Getting to Equal*. Washingotn, DC: World Bank; http://pubdocs.worldbank.org/en/810421519921949813/Women-Business-and-the-Law-2016.pdf.

II.3

MANAGING INSTITUTIONS

9

Institutional Change and Reform in Oromia's Public Sector: *Challenges and Prospects*

Hirko Wakgari Amanta

Box 1: Key messages of this chapter

- ✓ Ethiopia's civil service system has never been politically neutral, professional, and stable.
- ✓ NPM-inspired public sector reforms in Oromia have largely failed, mainly because of incompatibility with historical and politico-administrative contexts.
- ✓ Historically, NPM presumes the existence of a longstanding, professional, and rule-bound bureaucratic system, which has never been the case in Oromia.
- ✓ Lack of political settlements has been a major challenge to institutional reforms in Oromia.
- ✓ Inclusive political settlements, customized (re)-bureaucratization, and meritocracy will provide good prospects for future reform efforts in the region/country.

Box 2: Key lessons of this chapter

Reading this chapter will give you insights in:

- ✓ The concepts of institutions and contemporary institutional change theories;
- ✓ The key precepts of NPM and its role as a paradigm of public sector reform in Ethiopia;
- ✓ The institutional evolution of Ethiopia's/Oromia's civil service and reform waves since the 1990s and
- ✓ The politico-administrative contexts of (and challenges to) reforms in Oromia since the 1990s.

Box 3: Abbreviations

BPR = Business Process Reengineering

BSC = Balanced Score Card

CSRP = Civil Service Reform Program

EPLF = Eritrean People's Liberation Front

EPRDF = Ethiopian People's Revolutionary Democratic Front
FDRE = Federal Democratic Republic of Ethiopia
GoE = Government of Ethiopia
MCB = Ministry of Capacity Building
MoCS = Ministry of Civil Service
NPM = New Public Management
OLF = Oromo Liberation Front
OPDO = Oromo People's Democratic Organization
PEA = Political Economy Analysis
PSCAP = Public Sector Capacity Building Program
PSR = Public Sector Reform
TPLF = Tigray People's Liberation Front

1. Introduction

The view that the contemporary varying level of countries' development has been heavily influenced by their institutional histories has become a well-established line of argument in both the administrative and development literatures (Acemoglu & Robinson, 2012; Evans, 2004; Shand, 2015; Todaro & Smith, 2015). As a corollary to this basic argument, Acemoglu & Robinson (2012) further emphasize that the prospect of a country to embark upon a path to sustainable development depends highly on its ability to seize opportunities provided during critical junctures to reform its governance institutions.

Seen from the above perspective, and as has been suggested by several scholars (Asefa, 2001; Bedasso, 2017; Moges, 2013; Zawude, 2000), the present-day general underdevelopment and poverty in Ethiopia has primarily been a problem of institutional failure. In relation to this, Zawude (2000) categorizes the turbulent institutional evolution of the Ethiopian state into three historically distinct periods: 1941-1974 (the period of institutional building), 1974-1991 (the period of distress), and the years since 1991 (the period of restructuring). He, like several other scholarly observers (Hassen, 2009; Lata, 1999), also notes that the beginning of each period was marked by critical junctures and missed historic opportunities for effecting desirable institutional changes.

Particularly, the 1991 change of government was widely expected to serve as a critical turning point for addressing a mass of both old and new institutional challenges in the country (Hassen, 2009; Miruts & Daba, 2016; Terefe, 2016). Supposedly consistent with those expectations, the EPRDF-led GoE soon embarked upon a series of public sector institutional reforms that broadly fall under three major phases (1992-1996, 1996-2000, and 2001-onwards)[1] (Mengesha & Common, 2007). The last reform phase, in particular, involved the adoption of a plethora of NPM-inspired reform initiatives, including district level decentralization, BPR, BSC, and the Citizens' Charter, all of which have since been under implementation (Fida, 2016; Araya et al., 2017).

However, implementation of those reforms was seriously hindered by several problems and challenges that rendered their practical contributions very much questionable. For example, the results of numerous past studies and official assessments (Beyene, 2009; Fida, 2016; Kacho et al., 2016; World Bank, 2013; PSCO, 2015; Wakgari, 2016) identified competency and attitudinal gaps among civil servants and their organizational managers, lack of sustained leadership commitment, and inadequate incentives as major challenges to the successful implementation of reforms in the country in general and in Oromia National Regional State in particular. Some of the studies (Kacho et al., 2016; Wakgari, 2016) also reported lack of meritocracy and professionalism and prevalence of political partisanship in the civil service as being among the critical challenges that constrained effective implementation of PSRs in Oromia's public sector.

Nevertheless, most of the existing studies on the public sector institutional reform in Ethiopia/Oromia have focused mainly on the operational challenges and immediate causes of ineffectiveness in reform implementations rather than looking into the contextual root causes of those challenges. In particular, this author is unaware of any study that has explicitly treated challenges posed by historical and broader political contexts to effective implementation of public sector institutional reforms in Oromia National Regional State. On the other hand, the currently unfolding political and socioeconomic conditions (beginning with the coming into power of a new administration in April 2018) in the aftermath of several years of popular protests has heralded the arrival of yet another critical juncture in the country's institutional history. This further necessitates a proper understanding of the forces that shape implementation of institutional reforms within specific local/regional historical and political contexts, which are currently lacking in the institutional change literature in general (Batley et al., 2011; Shand, 2015) and in the Ethiopian context in particular (as highlighted above). It is thus against this background that the author set out to explore the topic with the general objective of analyzing past challenges and future prospects for undertaking effective reforms for sustainable institutional change in Oromia's public sector.

In view of its stated objective, the study attempts to critically examine a series of research questions that have not yet been addressed, to the best of my knowledge. The key questions to be addressed are: how compatible was the institutional heritage in Oromia's public sector with the main assumptions behind the PSRs in general and the NPM-inspired reforms in particular? Were the political economy contexts in the country/region favorable for introducing those reform measures? If they were not, what repercussions have they had in the process of reform implementations? The ultimate goal in trying to answer these questions is to explore possible mechanisms for getting around similar problems in future reform efforts in general and during the currently unfolding critical juncture in particular.

Attempts shall be made to provide answers to the basic research questions through analysis of theoretical and empirical evidence drawn from diverse sources. The main sources of evidence include: reform-related country policy documents, reviews of the institutional change and reform literature, past scholarly researches, official government agency reports, independent evaluation reports by international (donor) agencies, and empirical data from a 2016 survey of over five hundred civil servants and managers across Oromia's public sector as part of my past research work on a related topic. This shall further be supplemented by insights drawn from my firsthand experience as a practitioner in providing technical support for implementation of reforms in the region's public sector for close to a decade and several rounds of in-depth discussions with over a dozen senior public sector experts and past and present members of the political leadership in the region.

Nonetheless, one possible methodological limitation that needs to be admitted from the outset is that the discussions here shall focus on macro-level analysis of the issue at hand without delving into sectoral and micro-level investigations. This is so mainly because of the lack of relevant empirical data at those levels, which in turn has been dictated by constraints related to lack of research funds.

The rest of this chapter is divided into five main sections. The first section begins with a conceptualization of institutions, institutional change, and reforms followed by a brief account of institutional change and reform theories and paradigms. The second section examines the evolution and practice of public sector reforms and institutional change in Oromia/Ethiopia's public sector. The third section examines the historical and political contexts of those reforms and the challenges posed thereby to reform implementation. This is followed by empirical discussions to demonstrate how over-politicization of the civil service sector deprived it of the human resource capacity necessary for effective execution of reforms. The fourth section highlights the need for inclusive political settlements, which it argues would open the door for positive and sustainable institutional change. The final section provides brief conclusions and implications.

2. Institutions and Institutional Changes: Concepts and Theories

2.1. Conceptualizations

Institutions

There is a considerable literature dealing with the question of how best to define institutions (Hodgson, 2006; Leftwich, 2009; Kingston & Caballero, 2008; North, 1990). However, there has not yet appeared a universally accepted definition across the literature. Instead, the different theories (which shall be briefly discussed below) define institutions variously and authors use different definitions,[2] which vary depending on the theoretical perspectives they adopt.

Among others, one relatively common definition of institutions considers them as the rules of the game in a society (Herrera et al., 2005; Lindegaard, 2013). However, according to Leftwich (2009), institutions are best understood in broadly Northian terms (North, 1991), which define institutions as the humanly devised constraints and/or enabling mechanisms that structure political, economic, and social interactions. The constraints and enabling mechanisms as stated in the latter definition can further take the form of either formal or informal institutions. Formal institutions exist in the form of laws, acts, regulations, constitutions etc., which are enacted and (usually) written. Informal institutions, on the other hand, are the unwritten but socially shared norms and codes of behavior enforced outside official channels (Leftwich, 2009; Lindegaard, 2013; Shand, 2015).

Institutional Change

Since institutions are humanly devised, they exist only as far as a sufficiently high number of individuals believe they exist and act accordingly (Olsen, 2009). In other words, dissent can lead to collective actions that may result in changing existing institutions or the establishment of new ones. Institutional change thus refers to changes in formal and informal rules of behavior both between agents and between agents and organizations (Wegerich, 2001). The changes so defined may further take the form of either a de-institutionalization, where existing institutions become discontinued, or a re-institutionalization, which implies either a retrogression or a transformation from one set to another (new) set of institutions (Olsen, 2009; Peters, 2000).

In short, every institution is vulnerable to influences and hence to change, which means that formally organized public sector institutions that maintain a certain kind of order are nonetheless liable to change under certain conditions. These conditions for change can arise from deliberate reforms embarked upon by governments or from collective dissent and revolutionary movements against incumbent governments that may contribute as much as peaceful reform to the change of existing institutions or the establishment of new ones (Olsen, 2009; Wegerich, 2001).

Public Sector Institutional Reforms

Reform implies a deliberate action taken toward a change for the better as a way of correcting wrongdoing or defects in a system (Omoyefa, 2008). The change so implied may range from minor adjustments to management arrangements to fundamental changes in governance and management arrangements (EU, 2009). Given the diverse scope of the concept of reform itself, it is no wonder that there also exist numerous definitions of public sector reforms, depending on the scope and context of the reform one is dealing with.

One of the definitions that goes with the theme of this study is the one provided by Ayee (2008), which describes public sector administrative reform as deliberately designed efforts to induce fundamental changes in a public administrative system through system-wide change (of institutional arrangements) or at least through measures for improvement of one or more of its key elements in terms of their scope, modus operandi, and implications. Another related definition, suggested by Omoyefa (2008), also considers public sector reform as deliberate policy measures and administrative actions taken by a government (or a government agency) to change existing institutional arrangements (organizational structures, processes, and people's behavior) in an attempt to improve its administrative machinery for performance at optimal level.

Recent PSR measures, in particular, have focused on the need for reforms toward a private-style management for achieving better results (especially in terms of efficiency) in the public sector (Olsen, 2008; Peters 2003). The presupposition is that things are not properly managed in the public sector, that unnecessary wastage has crept into the ways the public sector is being run, and that too many people are doing poorly what fewer people can do efficiently (Omoyefa, 2008). These kinds of approaches towards PSR have generally come to be labeled under the umbrella term of the "New Public Management," which is the subject of the discussion in the next section.

The New Public Management (NPM) as a Paradigm of Public Sector Reform

NPM is a model of public administration that has developed in opposition to the bureaucratic model (Charbonneau, 2012). It assumes that bureaucracy inhibits adaptation and thus advocates for the replacement of the traditional model of public administration based on the principles of bureaucracy by market-based public service management (ECA, 2004; Olsen, 2008). Moreover, proponents of NPM claim that the kind of governments that developed during the industrial era, with sluggish centralized bureaucracies, preoccupation with rules, and hierarchical chains of command simply no longer work very well (Peters, 2003).

The fundamental logic of proponents of NPM is that management in the public sector is not in any meaningful way different from management in the private sector, and that the public sector has not paid sufficient attention to management and to the role of the manager. They further maintain that if managers and their organizations are released from the constraints that politics places on them, then the system will perform better (Charbonneau, 2012; Peters, 2003).

With the aforementioned theoretical assumptions, the NPM perspective also developed positive, action-oriented phrases, such as: reinventing government, re-engineering, transformation, downsizing and "rightsizing," and the likes (Ayee, 2008). In regard to the historical evolution of such NPM thinking, Peters (2003) suggests that, like many changes in the political and social life, it is difficult to assign it an exact date. Rather, according to Peters (2003), there was the growing sense during the 1970s and into the 1980s that something was wrong with the way in which government worked and that change was necessary. For some authors (Charbonneau, 2012; ECA, 2004), however, the event consecrating the emergence of NPM was the reform of Britain's administration, launched in the wake of nascent neoliberalism and coinciding with the coming to power of Margaret Thatcher in 1979. What is evident, in either case, is that the percepts of NPM have dominated the public administration reform agenda of most OECD countries from the late 1970s (Charbonneau, 2012; Peters 2003; ECA, 2004).

Moreover, NPM has since served as an umbrella term for a variety of approaches going under different names. One common typology of approaches seen in the evolution of NPM practices has been provided by Ferlie et al. (1996). According to these authors, the first NPM model is characterized by an efficiency drive in public administration, wherein improvements are sought through tight hierarchical control of work processes. The second model seeks to introduce flexibility into organizational structures through downsizing and decentralization. The third model seeks to develop a culture of excellence within public administration through an emphasis on innovation. The fourth model accords customers/service users a greater role and voice in decision-making (Ferlie et al., 1996). The NPM models thus developed have become the source of the principal impetus for reform across many countries in Africa (ECA, 2004), including Ethiopia, as shall further be demonstrated in a later section.

2.2. Institutional Change Theories: Towards a Theoretical Framework

The New Institutionalism

Analyses of institutional change in recent decades have been set within what has been collectively termed as "New Institutionalism," which embraces rational choice institutionalism, historical institutionalism, and sociological institutionalism (Lindegaard, 2013; Peters, 2005).

Rational choice institutionalism draws heavily on neoclassical microeconomics and political economy and emphasizes the function of institutions through systems of rules and incentives as individuals maximize self-interest (Lindegaard, 2013; Shand, 2015). Its underlying logic is that institutions are arrangements of rules and incentives and that the members of the institutions behave in response to those basic components of institutional structure (Peters, 2000). Rational choice institutionalism also presumes that individuals (or groups) are rational and calculating in making choices within constraints to obtain their desired ends and that their decisions rest on an assessment of the probable actions of others (Leftwich, 2007). Given its emphasis on actors' rational, strategic behavior to fulfill their preferences, rational choice institutionalism explains the creation of (and changes in) certain institutional structures in terms of their benefit to pertinent actors and thus generally relies on exogenous bases for change (Lindegaard, 2013; Shand, 2015).

On the other hand, **sociological institutionalism** considers institutions in the context of more informal, cultural practices (Lindegaard, 2013). It argues that culture, not just efficiency, shapes institutions, and considers institutional forms and practices in light of the cognitive scripts and moral templates that provide the "frames of meaning" guiding human action (ibid). Central to this perspective is also the view that institutional conditions are malleable and, while there may be strong forces that work to preserve particular arrangements where these favor elite interests, institutions can change as a result of the "friction" between rules and the effects of their application on social actors. It thus emphasizes the importance of social interaction in forming and changing institutions (Mahoney & Thelen 2010; Shand, 2015).

In contrast, **historical institutionalism** defines institutions largely as the formal or informal procedures, routines, norms, and conventions embedded in the organizational structure of a polity or political economy (Lindegaard, 2013). Nonetheless, this perspective often focuses on formal aspects of institutions and the asymmetric power relations they propagate (ibid). With regard to change, historical institutionalism holds that institutional function is governed by precedents and emphasizes the persistence of rules along a "path" until affected by exogenous shocks (Shand, 2015). Thus, while maintaining an implicit focus on the role of power in explaining institutional change, the historical institutionalism perspective generally considers institutional trajectories as being "path dependent," or prone to continuing along an established trajectory. It presumes that change occurs sporadically when institutional trajectories are punctuated by points of sudden and substantial changes leading to a new trajectory, referred to as "critical junctures" (Lindegaard, 2013). The overall implication of this perspective is that the policy and structural choices made at the inception of institutions will have a persistent influence over their behavior for the remainder of their existence (Peters, 2000).

Incidentally, it is to be stressed here that the central theme of this paper is to analyze challenges to past institutional change and reform efforts in Oromia's public sector from historical and political perspectives and to map out future prospects for such changes. The foregoing descriptions of institutional change theories has thus been made in search of the most relevant theoretical framework that best accommodates the underlying objectives of this study. In relation to this, despite some advances in historical institutionalism in terms of engaging the role of power relations in explaining institutional change, the new institutionalisms in general have not yet grappled seriously with the critical role of political factors in explaining how domestically legitimate and appropriate institutions might be set up, reformed, or maintained (Combarnous & Rougier, 2010; Hudson & Leftwich, 2014;). On the other hand, over the last two decades, the variety of scholarly works analyzing the role of political factors in explaining such changes have together come to be loosely labeled as political economy analysis (PEA) (DFID, 2009; Hudson & Leftwich, 2014), which shall be briefly discussed below.

The Political Economy Approach to Institutional Change

The political economy approach to institutional change focuses on how political power and resources are distributed and contested in different contexts. It also emphasizes the role of political settlement for facilitating effective PSRs (DFID, 2009; Jones, 2015; Khemani, 2017).

According to DFID (2009), political economy analysis is concerned with the interaction of political and economic processes in a society: the distribution of power and wealth between different groups and individuals and the processes that create, sustain, and transform these relationships. DFID (2009)'s definition draws particular attention to politics, understood in terms of contestation and bargaining between interest groups with competing claims over rights and resources.

Similarly, a framework for assessing the political economy of reform suggested by the World Bank (2008) stresses the need to look particularly at the reform context in terms of political contexts and the related social and ethnic cleavages affecting the reform under consideration. With regard to conceptualization, the standard definition of an institution used in most PEA studies considers institutions as the rules of the game that determine the limits of choice and structure incentives, wherein incentives determine whether or not players follow the rules of the game (Hudson & Leftwich, 2014; North 1990).

Finally, in light of the foregoing discussions, this study shall draw on the historical institutionalism theory (a strand of the new institutionalism) along with a political economy analysis approach to understand the challenges posed by the historical and political contexts of reforms in Ethiopia in general and in Oromia National Regional State in particular to the effective implementation of PSR since the 1990s. In view of this, the study adopts an operational definition of institutions that considers them as the formal and informal structural properties of social groups within an organization, which are constituted by the rules and procedures that constrain some forms of behavior while enabling other forms of behavior between people and groups across public sector organizational domains.

3. Public Sector Reforms and Institutional Change in Oromia/Ethiopia

3.1. Overview of Reform Waves since the 1990s (PSRs under the EPRDF Regime)

The EPRDF-led Ethiopian government embarked on multiple administrative reforms that have generally evolved over three phases beginning from early 1990s (1992-1996, 1996-2000, and 2001 onwards) (Mengesha & Common, 2007). In the first reform phase (1991 to 1996) the focus was essentially on structural adjustment, with economic liberalization and structural reforms in the public sector. Accordingly, among the main objectives of this phase of reforms was to reassign the civil service employees hitherto organized under the unitary state to the newly emerging regional states and to improve the efficiency of public service delivery (Debela & Hagos, 2012).

However, public sector services did not improve much; consequently, the government attempted to systematically articulate the problems of the civil service by establishing a task force (TF) that was supposed to produce a new reform program suited to the needs of the country. The TF made assessment of the existing system and made reform recommendations, based on which the Civil Service Reform Program (CSRP) was prepared (Araya et al., 2017; Mengesha & Common, 2007).

The CSRP was thus designed in 1996 as the second reform phase consisting of five sub-programs: top management system, human resource management, service delivery, expenditure management and control, and ethics (FDRE, 2001; Mesfin, 2008). Moreover, the CSRP also involved the introduction of new policy and legal frameworks as well as operating systems and procedures into the civil service. Among others, institutional reform initiatives such as amending civil service laws and codes of ethics, setting up complaints-handling procedures, and the adoption of a new service delivery policy in 2001 were undertaken as part of the reform measure packaged under the CSRP (Beyene, 2009; Fida, 2016).

In the meantime, the occurrence of internal dissent within the EPRDF in 2001 and the resulting renewal scheme undertaken by the front provided yet another milestone in setting the government's subsequent reform direction. Among other initiatives, the front ventured into a new ideological terrain in favor of the "developmental state" in the aftermath of concluding its renewal process in 2001 (Araya et al., 2017). Following the decision to adopt a developmental state model and by drawing on the success factors of earlier developmental states in East Asia, the government also apparently felt the need for further reforms to build a professional and capable civil service system (World Bank, 2013). Consequently, the EPRDF-led GoE commenced the third phase of its reform agenda in 2003 in the form of a five year Public Service Capacity Building Program (PSCAP) by establishing a Ministry of Capacity Building as a new super ministry in charge of coordinating all civil service reform initiatives (Araya et al., 2017).

Subsequently, the PSCAP arranged its intervention by repackaging the CSRP into seven areas: strengthening the capacity of the civil service reform coordinating structures at the federal, regional, and local levels, improving expenditure management and control activities, improving governance of human resource management, improving public service delivery, improving accountability and transparency, strengthening top-management systems, and building the capacity of emerging regions (Mesfin, 2008).

Moreover, following the adoption the developmental state as an important ideological model in 2001 and as part of the third reform wave, the EPRDF-led GoE also moved on to a second phase of decentralization, which was ostensibly meant to devolve service delivery to districts (*woredas*) (Araya et al., 2017). Theoretically, Ethiopia's system of decentralization had multiple dimensions that included political, administrative, and fiscal decentralization (World Bank, 2013). However, despite the outward commitment to such decentralization initiatives, the actual practice has been severely constrained. For example, it has been reported by several studies that parallel to the professed processes of decentralization, the EPEDF government in practice developed structures of top-down rule, particularly through its party apparatus that was used to dwarf local initiatives and autonomy (Harald, et al., 2018; Kena, 2016; Pausewang et al., 2002).

Besides, and in particular, the Ethiopian government also launched a range of other reform initiatives that broadly fall under the umbrella of the "New Public Management" paradigm as part of its third reform wave (Araya et al., 2017). Such NPM-inspired reforms implemented in Ethiopia as part of the third reform wave under EPRDF included Business Process Re-engineering (BPR), Balanced Score Card (BSC), and the Citizens Charter (Fida, 2016), which shall be described in the next section.

3.2. The New Public Management as a Paradigm for Reform in Ethiopia/Oromia: *Selected Cases of NPM Inspired Reform Initiatives*

It has been widely attested that the initiation of many reforms in Africa since the 1990s have been inspired by the concept of NPM (ECA, 2004; UNDP, 2009). Likewise, conceptual descriptions of the NPM and the range of reforms inspired by the paradigm (as described earlier under section 2.1.4 of this chapter) also capture well most of the structural, organizational, and managerial changes taking place in the public services of Ethiopia.

For example, beginning from 2003 (and with the rather flawed assumption, as shall be argued in the next section, that the Ethiopian civil service had grown into an overly hierarchical bureaucratic system), the GoE made a sweeping decision to initiate BPR across all government agencies (Araya et al., 2017). According to Hammer & Champy (1993), BPR focuses on changing four components of an organization, namely; business processes, job and structure (which involves changing a hierarchical organizational structure to a flat one), management and measurement, and values and beliefs.

In relation to NPM, the focus on work processes and flexibility in organizational structures through downsizing as described in the first two models provided by Ferlie et al. (1996) (discussed under section 2.1.4) have been well taken up through the adoption of the BPR reform initiative in Ethiopia.

Moreover, BPR also shares with the NPM reform paradigm such core issues as restructuring to reduce cost, de-bureaucratizing hierarchical organizational structures for greater efficiency, enhancing outcome measurement for better performance management, and increasing customer satisfaction by placing customers at the center of business decision-making. Furthermore, Pollit and Bouckaert (2011) describe BPR as being at the more "radical" end of NPM initiatives, pursued by countries especially interested in importing private sector practices into the civil service and in reducing the distinctions between the two, such as New Zealand, Australia, and the UK (cited in Araya et al., 2017).

Similarly, the emphasis on innovation and a culture of excellence within public administration in the third model and the centrality of customers in decision-making emphasized in the fourth model following Ferlie et al. (1996) perfectly aligns with the BSC and Citizen Charter reform initiatives that have been under implementation in Ethiopia as components of the third reform wave under the EPRDF regime. For example, BSC is commonly described as a management, communication, and measurement system for translating an organization's strategic objectives into a set of performance indicators distributed among four perspectives: Financial, Customer, Internal Business Process, and Learning and Growth (Kaplan & Norton, 1996). BSC is thus an essentially NPM-inspired reform tool with a customer focus as one of its four pillars and an emphasis on innovation through its learning and growth perspective. Moreover, its emphasis on performance management based on clear and explicit managerial targets combined with managerial autonomy and incentives to perform is also at the core of the NPM (ECA, 2004). In the same way, the Citizen Charter, which has been under implementation in Ethiopia since 2012, incorporates the concept of perceiving the citizen as a "customer" of public services, which is a key feature of the NPM as well (Ayee, 2008).

Overall, the discussion in this section has attempted to provide a quick overview of the three broad waves of reform initiatives undertaken in EPRDF-led Ethiopia since the early 1990s. The final parts of this section in particular described how reform tools such as BPR, BSC, and Citizen Charter implemented in Ethiopia over the last decades relate to the NPM paradigm of de-bureaucratized and private-style management. The following section examines particular challenges encountered in the implementation of reforms in Oromia National Regional State since the 1990s in general and the third wave NPM-inspired reform measures in particular from the historical and political points of view.

4. Challenges to Institutional Change and Reform in Oromia/Ethiopia

4.1. Historical Challenges: De-bureaucratization before Bureaucratization

As discussed earlier (see section 2.1.4), the NPM paradigm is based on a number of fundamental assumptions about the existing civil service systems that determine the viability of its reform recommendations. The most important of these assumptions is that there is already a well-established system of public administration in place to be reformed and that this system is generally infused with the values of the traditional hierarchical and rule-bound bureaucratic system of state administration (Olsen, 2008; Peters, 2003). With this note of caution in mind, the following paragraphs highlight the historical evolution of Ethiopia's civil service system in general, and the genesis of Oromia's public administration system in particular, to discern whether it meets the stated fundamental assumptions of the NPM.

To begin with, the establishment of modern civil service in Ethiopia dates back to 1907, when Emperor Menelik II initiated the formation of a few ministries (Kacho et al., 2016). Later, Emperor Haileselassie introduced some measures to modernize public administration by appointing salaried and educated personnel in the civil service (Beyene, 2009). However, given the high regard to political loyalty and the level of political interference affecting standard operating procedures, the civil service repeatedly failed to deliver the intended service to the public. This contributed to public discontent that finally resulted in overthrow of the imperial regime by the Dergue military junta in 1974 (Kacho et al., 2016; Mengesha & Common, 2007).

The Dergue regime, in its move to establish a socialist state, took extensive nationalization measures accompanied by the proliferation of new government institutions, parallel party structures, and the appointment of party functionaries to key decision-making civil service positions. Such measures resulted in a tremendous expansion along with the overlapping of roles in the public sector, which created a mix of military-bureaucratic dictatorship (Ayenew, 1997, Clapham, 2002). The subsequent years were characterized by the centralization of administration, duplication and fragmentation of public functions, utter downplaying of merit and professionalism, and inefficiency in service delivery until the Dergue too was finally ousted in 1991 by a coalition of several rebel groups, including the EPRDF/TPLF, EPLF, and OLF (Gebresslase & Berhutesfa, 2016; Mengesha & Common, 2007; Pausewang, 2009).

The Post Dergue Period: Genesis of the Existing Oromia's Public Sector Institutions

It has been argued in the literature of institutional change that periods of institutional genesis correspond to critical junctures that place institutional arrangements on trajectories that are difficult to alter (Hogan, 2006; Pierson, 2004). This is mainly because of the fact that institutions express the ideas, interests, purpose, and power of those who designed and supervise them (Leftwich, 2007). Understanding the origins of institutions thus requires knowledge of the "all-important matter of the material and ideological conditions on which they are founded and of the political leadership and their ideas" (Grindle, 2001; Leftwich, 2007). Taking this fact into consideration, the subsequent discussions examine the ideological conditions on which Oromia National Regional State public institutions were founded, starting from the period of their genesis, which also corresponds with the critical juncture marked by Ethiopia's political transition in the early 1990s.

From the outset, several rebel groups were involved in actively fighting the Dergue regime before its final demise in 1991 (Smith, 2007). However, toward the end of the military dictatorship, around 1989, when TPLF together with EPRDF and several other liberation movements (among them the OLF) was on the verge of winning the resistance war, TPLF organized Oromo prisoners of war into the OPDO with the intent of preparing it in its image for controlling the political arena in the future Oromia regional state. On the eve of the final ousting of the Dergue in May 1991, OLF was invited together with TPLF and EPLF to a conference in London, where the future structure for Ethiopia was discussed and a Transitional Charter was proposed in lieu of a constitution for a transitional period. And OLF leaders were reported to be the key players in the subsequent drafting of the proposed Transitional Charter (Hassen, 2009; Lata, 1999; Pausewang, 2009).

As a follow-up to the London Conference, the Addis Ababa Conference of July 1999 was organized in which a total of thirty-one parties (including the OLF, OPDO and three other Oromo political parties) met to discuss the future of Ethiopia and agreed upon a Transitional Charter (Hassen, 2009). The conference established these representatives as a transitional parliament, adopted the Transitional Charter, and called on TPLF and their leader, Meles Zenawi, to form a central transitional government (Pausewang, 2009). The transitional government thus assumed power in 1991 and subsequently passed several proclamations in accordance with the spirit of the Transitional Charter. This included Proclamation No 7/1992, which provided for the setting up of regional state governments (TGE; 1992; Terefe, 2016).

Accordingly, the Oromia National Regional State was set up with its own organs of government (with legislative councils, executive committees, and judicial bodies) adapted to its own newly adopted regional constitution. The government of the Oromia National Regional State, now under the exclusive leadership of the OPDO[3] (a member of the TPLF-led EPRDF coalition which was leading the central transitional government) also created regional public sector agencies (bureaus) and built up administrative structures at zonal, district, and village levels to replace the structures of the now defunct military regime (Harald, et al., 2018; Pausewang, 2009). In short, the genesis of the existing Oromia National Regional State public sector institutions, which were exclusively managed by the OPDO, traces its origins back to this period of the transitional government of Ethiopia (early 1990s).

The overall implication of the foregoing description of the evolution of the public administration system in Ethiopia in general and that of the Oromia National Regional State in particular is that the country has never had a politically neutral, professional, and stable bureaucracy throughout its history of modern public administration. In other words, the country has never had a well-bureaucratized and longstanding system of public administration whose ills needed to be cured through the de-bureaucratization remedy prescribed by the NPM-inspired reforms. Given this, it needed to be clear from the outset that the proposals for institutional change through de-bureaucratization inherent in the NPM reform measures were poorly suited to the actual problems and reform needs of the Ethiopian civil service systems in general and to the even much younger administrative system of Oromia's public sector in particular. Even worse, some scholars (Olsen, 2008; Peters, 2003) have long warned that if there is not such a system in place, the loosening of hierarchical controls inherent in NPM can become a recipe for mismanagement, as has been the case in Oromia/Ethiopia.[4]

4.2. Political Challenges: Institutional Reforms without Political Settlement

Existing political accounts of the transitional period (Hassen, 2009; Lata, 1999; Pausewang, 2009) during which the Oromia National Regional State's public sector institutions were founded indicate that the period (1991-1995) was characterized by political polarization between EPRDF/TPLF/OPDO and the other Oromo political parties. Among the five political parties that represented the interests of Oromia in the TGE, OLF was given four ministerial posts in the central government, against three for OPDO. On the other hand, the OPDO, under the direct leadership and guidance of the TPLF/

EPRDF, was put in charge of singlehandedly building up the region's system of public administration. It thus controlled organization and recruitment into all of the region's public sector agencies across the regional, zonal, district, and village levels (Pausewang, 2009).

Moreover, by forcing out key political groups such as the OLF from the TGE, the EPRDF later came to control and monopolize the political process (Smith, 2007). After the OLF and all other Oromo political parties were forced to withdraw from the TGE in 1992, the OPDO continued to administer in Oromia on behalf of the EPRDF (Pausewang, 2009). Nonetheless, because of its origin and ideological dependence on the TPLF/EPRDF, the OPDO did not have any meaningful support or legitimacy among the Oromo people (Harald et al., 2018; Vaughan 2011). As a result, it turned out that OPDO found it difficult to find qualified people locally. It thus went on recruiting school dropouts and a few other unemployed and merely literate opportunist individuals who, having seen their chance for secure jobs and positions in being recruited for the party, acted swiftly to take advantage of the opportunity. Among these elements, OPDO recruited a corps of unconditionally loyal administrators who knew that their positions, their newly won social roles, and their power were owed to and depended on their loyalty to the party (Lata 1999; Pausewang, 2009).

Consequently, what emerged in subsequent years was the domination of the region's public administrative sector by one political party (the OPDO), which itself was a member of a larger governing coalition of political parties (EPRDF) dominated by another party/front (TPLF), thereby leading to two layers of domination in the region's public sector institutions. One clear testimony to this phenomena is a remark made by Lemma Megersa, the president of the Oromia National Regional State from 2016-2019, in a televised speech during the massive protests in the region in 2017, in which he noted that the region's administrative institutions were designed and run for the purpose of serving "God fathers," a situation that he stressed must come to an end. Similarly, in the words of Hassen Ali, the first President of Oromia (from 1992-1995): "The government of Oromia is autonomous according to the Ethiopian Constitution, [but] the Federal Government and [the EPRDF] soldiers interfere in all matters of the Oromia regional state" (cited in Hassen, 2009).

Such practices arising from lack of political settlements have particularly hampered the effectiveness of decentralization reform initiatives. According to the World Bank (2013), the predominance of a single party has been the principal factor constraining decentralization in Ethiopia. As a result of the centralization of power in the dominant party, hierarchical party discipline and top-down management have substituted upward accountability for the desired downward accountability of sub-national officials and civil servants to the citizens (World Bank, 2013).

Similarly, a study report by Kena (2016) notes that, despite the rhetoric of decentralization, regional and local level government units and their institutions of public administration remained instruments of political control by the central government throughout the EPRDF's rule. This and other related institutional violations of human, political, and socioeconomic rights generated a chain of unrelenting public protests over the course of several years (Kena, 2016). Other commentators have gone even further to suggest that the federal state under the EPRDF rule – which at the formal level may appear highly decentralized – has had a stronger administrative and political presence in the periphery compared to any other previous regime (Lie & Mesfin, 2018; Pausewang et al. 2002).

In conclusion, the lack of inclusive political settlements resulted in a weak base of human resource capacity and a lack of ideological diversity and inclusiveness that were important for effective execution of reforms for a meaningful institutional change that would maintain professionalism and impartiality in the region's civil service. Likewise, as shall be empirically demonstrated in the following section, it paved the way for over-politicization of the civil service, which resulted in fomenting a complex set of clintelism and political patronage across the regions public sector that curtailed any meaningful reform efforts.

4.3. Civil Service Politicization and Capacity Challenges

As already indicated, the lack of amicable political settlement in the formation and maintenance of the regional state's public sector institutions undermined public sector neutrality and professionalism. For example, in my own 2016 survey of over five hundred civil servants across Oromia's public sector, more than half said they did not perceive the region's civil service system to be politically neutral; meanwhile, around three quarter of respondents believed that the public sector in Oromia does not provide equal opportunity for staff members for promotion to management positions. Moreover, empirical evidence from the survey also showed that close to two thirds of respondents believed that individuals come to public sector leadership positions in Oromia mainly through their client-patron relationships with individuals holding political leadership positions. Similarly, the majority of the surveyed civil servants also believed that political loyalty and support from external political power networks are the major routes to public sector leadership positions in the regional state (Wakgari, 2016).

Overall, the results of my 2016 survey indicated that there is little distinction between the bureaucratic and political arena in the region's public sector and that the practice of applying the merit principle has been overridden by political patronage. These obstacles to meritocracy and the consequent predominance of patronage over merit-based selection, promotion, and appointment practices were considered to have weakened the region's public sector human resource capacity, which in turn constrained effective implementation of reform measures for institutional change in Oromia's public sector over the past two decades (ibid).

In relation to this, a study by World Bank (2013) also reported that capacity for critical tasks such as management, planning, administration, and service delivery is constrained by low levels of professional competence and preparedness among many staff and officials at the sub-national level. Likewise, several other studies and official assessments (Fida, 2016; Kacho et al., 2016; ONRS, 2011; PSCO, 2015) have reported that competency gaps among civil servants and public sector managers as well as the prevalence of political partisanship in the civil service have been major challenges to the successful implementation of reforms in Oromia National Regional State.

5. Prospects for Institutional Change: The Ongoing Critical Juncture as a New Window of Opportunity for Political Settlement

Critical junctures are major events that disrupt the existing political and economic balance in one or many societies (Acemoglu & Robinson, 2012). The concept of the "critical juncture" is thus used to identify moments when institutional innovation or change may be initiated or, at least, which create the opportunity for it to occur. It is marked by the occurrence of contingent events that call into question existing institutional arrangements or allow the chance for them to be changed, for good or for bad (Leftwich, 2009).

In this regard, the occurrence of a new inter-coalition settlement among EPRDF member parties in late March 2018 could certainly be considered as yet another critical juncture in the history of Ethiopia's political evolution. Although many complex and worrisome roadblocks remain, it has opened a new window of opportunity for a long overdue inclusive political settlement, which is much needed for the realization of effective reforms towards positive and sustainable institutional change that is necessary for the country's sustainable development. It is, hence, highly imperative for all stakeholders to seize the opportunity, first to forge inclusive political settlements, and then to initiate contextually relevant reform measures toward building inclusive and sustainable institutions in the region's public sector.

6. Conclusions and Implications

This chapter examined the challenges to institutional change through PSR in general and the NPM-inspired reform measure in particular in Oromia's public sector by drawing on historical institutionalism theory and the political economy analysis approach to institutional change as a theoretical framework. In view of this, first, NPM assumes that civil service systems to which its reform initiatives are applied are overly bureaucratized and hence prescribes de-bureaucratization as a desirable reform measure for bringing about positive institutional change. This chapter argued that Ethiopia's civil service in general and Oromia's public administration in particular has never been adequately bureaucratized and as such did not need the de-bureaucratization prescriptions of NPM reforms for realizing positive institutional change in the first palace. Second and even then, NPM reforms also assume the adequate autonomy of managers from political interference. On the contrary, this chapter has demonstrated that Oromia's public sector has remained highly politicized and civil service neutrality has been an almost alien concept to the region's administrative system.

In a nutshell, historical, political, and capacity constraints have posed strong challenges to any meaningful institutional change through NPM reforms in the region's public sector over the past two decades. The chapter also highlighted the ongoing critical juncture as a new window of opportunity for realizing the long overdue political settlements which it argued shall provide a new opportunity for institutional change in the region's public sector.

The main implications that can be distilled from the analysis and conclusions provided in this chapter for future reform efforts in the region's public sector include the need for:

- ***Political settlement:*** Depoliticizing the civil service by forging political consensus through inclusive political settlements to establish a merit-based career civil service as part of the ongoing transitional reform measures.
- ***(Re)bureaucratization:*** Designing and implementing a customized civil service reform package that reinvigorates desirable principles of the traditional bureaucratic model, such as impartiality, meritocracy, rule of law and professionalism, while at the same time espousing relevant NPM reform elements, such as innovations and efficiency improvements.

- ***Meritocracy:*** Strengthening merit-based public sector employment, promotion, and appointment through legislative amendments.
- **Further research:** Undertaking further comprehensive and micro-level research to identify the likely lingering cultural effects of past malpractices in the region's/country's civil service system, particularly by using sociological institutionalism as a key theoretical framework. Future reform efforts should also be informed and shaped by inputs from the result of such research.

Acknowledgements

I am indebted to the anonymous reviewers who provided critical comments and constructive suggestions that helped me in improving the chapter. I also thank the editors.

Notes

1. Detailed treatment of each reform phase shall follow in a later section.
2. Operational definition of institutions used in this study shall be provided in a later section.
3. The OLF and the other Oromo political parties were later forced out of the TGE.
4. This has been highlighted in the introduction section and shall be discussed further in the next sections.

References

Aalen, L. (2009). Ethiopia since the Derg: Democratic Pretension and Performance. In S. Pausewang (ed.). *Exploring New Political Alternatives for the Oromo in Ethiopia, Report from Oromo Workshop and Its After-effects*. Christian Michelsen Institute Bergen, Norway. Available at: http//www.cmi.no/publications.

Acemoglu, D., & Robinson, J. (2012). *Why Nations Fail: The Origins of Power, Prosperity, and Poverty*. New York. Crown Publishers.

Araya, E., Fritz, V, Kay, K., Rogger, D., Somani, R, Digie, T & Abay, A. (2017). *Moving Further on Civil Service Reforms in Ethiopia: Findings and Implications from a Civil Service Survey and Qualitative Analysis*. Washington, DC: World Bank Synthesis Report.

Asefa, S. (2001). Perspectives on Institutional Reform and Development in Ethiopia: The Critical Role of Building Enabling Institutions for Economic Growth and Development. Paper presented at the International Conference on African Development. Available at http://scholarworks.wmich.edu/africancenter_icad_archive/11.

Ayee, J.R.A. (2008). *Reforming the African Public Sector: Retrospect and Prospects*. Dakar: Council for the Development of Social Science Research in Africa.

Ayenew, M. (1997). Public Administration in Ethiopia 1974-1992: Administrative and Policy Response to Turbulence, PhD Thesis, State University of New York.

Batley, R., McCourt, W., Mcloughlin, C. (2012). The Politics and Governance of Public Services in Developing Countries. *Public Management Review*, 14(2), 131-44.

Bedasso, B. E. (2017). Measuring Political and Economic Institutions in Ethiopia: c.1888–2016. ERSA working paper 716 Economic Research Southern Africa (ERSA), South Africa.

Beyene, B. G. (2009). Ethiopia – Civil Service Reform Programme, Addis Ababa.

Broesamle, K. (2012). Civil Service Reform in Developing Countries: We Do Not Really Know What We Are Doing?' Available at https://www.hertie-school.org/fileadmin/pdf.

Charbonneau, M. (2012). New Public Management. In L. Côté & Savard, J. F. (eds). *Encyclopedic Dictionary of Public Administration*, Available at http://www.dictionnaire.enap.ca.

Clapham, C. (2002). Controlling Space in Ethiopia. In W. James, Donham, D.L., Kurimoto, E., & Triulzi, A. (eds). *Remapping Ethiopia. Socialism & After* (pp. 9-32). Oxford: James Curry / Athens, OH: Ohio University Press/ Addis Ababa: Addis Ababa University Press.

Combarnous, F. & Rougier, E. (2010). Institutions, Socio-Economic Models and Development: An Overview of the Literature and a Methodology. Available at http://www.cesifo.de.

Debela, T. & Hagos, A. (2012). Towards a Results-based Performance Management: Practices and Challenges in the Ethiopian Public Sector. Available at http://www.opendocs.ids.ac.uk/opendocs/.

DFID (2009). Political Economy Analysis: How to Note. A Practice Paper, Department for International Development, London. Available at http://www.gsdrc.org/docs/open/PO58.pdf.

ECA (2004). Public Sector Management Reforms in Africa: Lessons Learned. Addis Ababa: Economic Commission for Africa.

EU (2009). Public Sector Reform: An Introduction. Concept Paper N°1. Luxembourg: Office for Official Publications of the European Communities.

Evans, P. (2004). Development as Institutional Change: The Pitfalls of Monocropping and the Potentials of Deliberation. *Studies in Comparative International Development*, 38(4), 30-52.

Farazmand, A. (2009). Bureaucracy, Administration, and Politics: An Introduction. In A. Farazmand (ed.). *Bureaucracy and Administration*. Florida: LLC CRC Press.

FDRE (2001). The Federal Democratic Republic of Ethiopia 2001. *Service Delivery Policy in the Civil Service*. Addis Ababa: Artistic Printing Enterprise.

Ferlie, E., Ashburner, L. Fitzgerald, L. & Pettigrew, A.M. (1996). *The New Public Management in Action*, Oxford University Press, Oxford.

Fida, S. (2016). Practices and Problems of the Implementation of Civil Service Reform Tools in Sebeta City Administration of ONRS. In T. Tafesse & Zigiju, S. (eds). *Public Sector Transformation and Development, Proceedings of the 2nd National Conference*, June 27-28, 2016, volume 1, number 1, 2016. Ethiopian Civil Service University.

Gebresslase, T. & Berhutesfa, C. (2016). State Building and Resilience Strategies against the contemporary public crises of Ethiopia: A Critical Analysis. *International Journal of Science and Research (IJSR)*, 5(11), 622-630.

Grindle, M. (2001). In Quest of the Political: The Political Economy of Development Policy Making. In G. Meier & Stiglitz, J. (eds). *Frontiers of Development Economics* (pp. 345-380). New York, NY: Oxford University Press.

Hammer, M. & Champy, J. (1993). *Reengineering the Corporation: A Manifesto for Business Revolution*. London: Nicholas Brealey Publishing.

Harald J., Lie S. & Mesfin B. (2018). Ethiopia: A Political Economy Analysis. Report commissioned by the Norwegian Ministry of Foreign Affairs, Norwegian Institute of International Affairs. Oslo, Norway.

Hassen, M. (2009). Oromo Nationalism and the Continuous Multifaceted Attack on the Oromo Cultural, Civic and Political Organizations. In S. Pausewang (ed.). *Exploring New Political Alternatives for the Oromo in Ethiopia, Report from Oromo Workshop and Its After-effects*. Bergen, Norway: Chr. Michelsen Institute. Available at: http://www.cmi.no/publications.

Herrera, P., Van-Huylenbroeck, G. & Espinel, R. (2005). A Generic Four-Step Methodology for Institutional Analysis of Governance Structures. Paper prepared for presentation at the 99th seminar of the EAAE (European Association of Agricultural Economists), Copenhagen, Denmark: August 24-27, 2005.

Hodgson, G. (2006). What are Institutions? *Journal of Economic Issues*, 40(1), 1-25.

Hogan, J. (2006). Re-molding the Critical Junctures Approach. *Canadian Journal of Political Science*, 39(3), 657-679.

Hudson, D. & Leftwich, A. (2014). From Political Economy to Political Analysis. Policy and Practice for Developmental Leaders, Elites and Coalitions. Research Paper 25. Developmental Leadership Program (DLP). Available at http://www.dlprog.org.

Jean-Claude, T. (2003). Institutional Theories and Public Institutions: Traditions and Appropriateness. In B. Guy Peeters & Pierre, J. (eds). *Handbook of Public Administration* (p. 23). New York: Sage.

Jones, S. D. (2015). Bridging Political Economy Analysis and Critical Institutionalism: An Approach to Help Analyze Institutional Change for Rural Water Services. *International Journal of the Commons*, 9(1), 65-86.

Jreisat, J. E. (2009). Bureaucracy and Reform in the Arab World. In A. Farazmand (ed.). *Bureaucracy and Administration*. Florida: LLC CRC Press.

Kacho, B., Zeleke, T., & Gebremedhin, G. (2016). The Implementation of Human Resource Management Reform Program and Practices of Professionalism in Selected Cities in Ethiopia. In T. Tafesse (ed.). *Public Sector Transformation and Development*. Proceedings of the 2nd National Conference June 27-28, 2016.

Kaplan, R.& Norton, D. (1996). The Balanced Score Card: Translating Strategy into Action. Boston: Harvard Business School Press.

Kena, D. J. (2016). Decentralization of Power and Local Autonomy in Ethiopian Federal System: A Look at Two Decades Experiment. *Urban and Regional Planning,* 1(3),45-58.

Khemani, S. (2017). Political Economy of Reform. World Bank Policy Research Working Paper 8224 WPS8224. Available at: http://www.econ.worldbank.org.

Kingston, C. & Caballero, G. (2008). Comparing Theories of Institutional Change. *Journal of Institutional Economics,* 5 (2):151-180. Available at http://dx.doi.org/10.1017/s1744137409001283.

Lata, L. (1999). *The Ethiopian State at the Crossroads: Decolonization & Democratization or Disintegration.* Lawrenceville, NJ: The Red Sea Press.

Leftwich, A. (2007). The Political Approach to Institutional Formation, Maintenance and Change. IPPG Discussion Paper 14. Available at: http://www.ippg.org.uk/papers/dp14.pdf.

Leftwich, A. (2009). Analyzing the Politics of State Business Relations. A Methodological Concept Note on the Historical Institutionalist Approach. Discussion Paper Series, no. 23.

Lindegaard, L. S. (2013). Power and Change: Locating Institutional Change Theories in a Power Context. DIIS Working Paper 20.

Mahoney, J., and Thelen, K. (2010). A Theory of Gradual Institutional Change. In J. Mahoney & Thelen, K. (eds). *Explaining Institutional Change: Ambiguity, Agency and Power* (pp. 1-37). Cambridge, UK: Cambridge University Press.

Mengesha, G. H. & Common, R.K. (2007). Public Sector Capacity Reform in Ethiopia: A Tale of Success in Two Ministries? *Public Administration and Development,* Wiley InterScience, www.interscience.wiley.com/DOI: 10.1002/pad.456.

Mesfin T. (2008). The Ethiopian Civil Service Reform Program. In T. Assefa (ed.). *Digest of Ethiopia's National Policies, Strategies and Programs* (pp. 373-418). Addis Ababa: Forum for Social Studies.

Miruts, G. & Daba, N. (2016). Change Army: The New Face of Modernizing Civil Service in Ethiopia (The Case of Addis Ababa). In T. Tafesse (ed.). *Public Sector Transformation and Development.* Proceedings of the 2nd National Conference June 27-28, 2016.

MoCS. (2011). The Direction of Reform Army Building in the Civil Service. Unpublished document of the Ministry of Civil Service (Prepared in Amharic).

Moges, A. G. (2013). Political Economy of Poverty Reduction. *International Journal of African Development,*1(1), 19-39. Available at http://scholarworks.wmich.edu/ijad

North, D. (1990). *Institutions, Institutional Change and Economic Performance.* Cambridge University Press, Cambridge.

North, C. D. (1991). Institutions. *The Journal of Economic Perspectives,* 5(1), 97-112.

Olsen, J. P. (2008). The Ups and Downs of Bureaucratic Organization. *Annual Review of Political Science,* 11: 13-37. Available at http://annualreviews.org.

Omoyefa, P.S. (2008). Public Sector Reforms in Africa: A Philosophical Re-Thinking. *Africa Development,* 33(4), 15-30.

Pausewang, S. (2009). The Oromo between Past and Future. In Exploring New Political Alternatives for the Oromo in Ethiopia. CMI Report from Oromo workshop and its after-effedts.

Pausewang, S., Kjetil, T. & Aalen, L. (eds) (2002). *Ethiopia Since the Derg. A Decade of Democratic Pretension and Performance.* London: Zed Books.

Peters, B.G. (2003). The Changing Nature of Public Administration: From Easy Answers to Hard Questions. *Viešoji Politika Ir Administravimas* 5: 7-20.

Peters, B.G. (2001). The Politics of Policy Instruments. In L.M. Salamon (ed.). *Handbook of Policy Instruments.* New York: Oxford University Press, 2001.

Peters, B.G. (2005). *Institutional Theory in Political Science: The "New institutionalism".* London: Continuum.

Peters, G. (2000).Institutional Theory: Problems and Prospects. Stumpergasse, Vienna: Institute for Advanced Studies (IHS). Available at http://www.ihs.ac.at.

Pierson, P. (2004). *Politics in Time: History, Institutions, and Social Analysis.* Princeton, NJ: Princeton University Press.

Pollitt, C. and Bouckaert, G. (2011) *Public Management Reform – A Comparative Analysis. New Public Management, Governance, and the Neo-Weberian State.* Oxford: Oxford University Press.

Proclamation to Provide for the Establishment of National/ Regional Self-Governments, Addis Ababa: *Negarit Gazeta* Proclamation no. 7/1992.

PSCO. (2015). Implementation of Reform Tools and Good Governance in Oromia National Regional State. A paper presented on the 4th Annual Research Symposium on Ensuring Institutional Transformation to Advance Ethiopian Renaissance: Public Service College of Oromia.

Shand, W. (2015). Exploring Institutional Change: The Contribution of Co-production to Shaping Institutions. IIED Working Paper. IIED, London. Available at http://pubs.iied.org/10763IIED.

Smith, L. (2007). *Political Violence and Democratic Uncertainty in Ethiopia.* New York: State University of New York.

Terefe, D. (2016). Assessment of Policy Implementation Capacity: Opportunities and Challenges, (The case of Selected Wereda Administrations in Yeka Sub-City, Addis Ababa). In T. Tafesse (ed.). *Public Sector Transformation and Development.* Proceedings of the 2nd National Conference June 27-28, 2016.

Tilaye K. (2007). Civil Service Reform in Ethiopia: Achievements, Problems and Possible Solutions. Proceedings of the First National Conference on the Achievements, Challenges and Prospects of the Civil Service Reform Program Implementation in Ethiopia, Addis Ababa, May 31-June 1, 2007.

Todaro, M.P. & Smith, S.C. (2015). *Economic Development.* Twelfth edition. New York University & The George Washington University. Available at http: www.pearsonhighered.com.

United Nations Development Program (2009). Users' Guide for Measuring Public Administration Performance. United Nations Development Programme, Oslo, Norway.

Vaughan, S. (2011). Revolutionary Democratic State-building: Party, State and People in the EPRDF's Ethiopia. *Journal of Eastern African Studies*, 5(4), 619-640.

Wakgari, H. (2016). The Politics-Bureaucracy Interface in Oromia's Public Sector: Impacts on Human Capacity and Reform. In Proceedings of the 5th Annual Research Symposium at Adama, Public Service College of Oromia.

Wegerich, K. (2001). Institutional Change: A Theoretical Approach. Occasional Paper no. 30, Water Issues Study Group School of Oriental and African Studies (SOAS), University of London.

World Bank (2008). The Political Economy of Policy Reform: Issues and Implications for Policy Dialogue and Development Operations, Report No. – 44288-GLB, Social Development Department. Available at http://siteresources.worldbank.org.

World Bank (2013). *Ethiopia Public Sector Reform Approach: Building the Developmental State – A Review and Assessment of the Ethiopian Approach to Public Sector Reform*. Addis Ababa: World Bank Report No: ACS3695.

Zawude, B. (2000). The Problems of Institutionalization in Modern Ethiopia: A Historical Perspective. In A. Mekonnen & Aredo, D. (eds), *Proceedings of the Ninth Annual Conference on the Ethiopian Economy* (pp. 13-22). Addis Ababa: Friedrich Ebert Stiftung.

10

New Public Management and Path Dependence in Public Organizations in Ethiopia: A Multiple Case Study

Tewelde Mezgobo Ghrmay

Box 1: Key Points of this chapter

Key findings of the study show that in Ethiopia:

✓ NPM reforms have been introduced following a system-wide approach for all government organizations, obstructing their clear articulation and communication thereof.

✓ The levels of performance in design, implementation, output in terms of service delivery, and social outcomes vary among enterprises.

✓ Leadership commitment, persistence, necessary work in the reward system, and human resource policies (soft S's), institutional development, autonomy and accountability, and benchmarking and contextualization are some of the factors for effective adoption of NPM reforms.

Box 2: Learning objectives

Reading this chapter will give you insights in:

✓ The effect of path dependency in reform implementation in Ethiopia.

✓ How do managers in public organizations in Ethiopia describe path-breaking interventions for the effective adoption of new public management (NPM) in order to improve public services for low-income populations?

✓ How do managers in public organizations in Ethiopia describe how path-breaking interventions for the effective adoption of NPM can be implemented in order to improve social outcomes for low-income populations?

Box 3: Abbreviations

AWWCE = Afar Water Works and Construction Enterprise

BA = Bachelor of Arts

BSc = Bachelor of Science

FDRE = Federal Democratic Republic of Ethiopia

GG = Good Governance
LLM = Master of Laws
MBA = Master of Business Administration
MCom = Master of Commerce
NPM = New Public Management
PEM = Public Enterprise Manager
PSR = Public Sector Reform
SME = Subject Matter Expert

1. Introduction

The problem this study addressed is that while considerable resources and attention have been allocated to recent good governance (GG) public administration reform in low-income and fragile states, there is little evidence as to what degree this agenda has been implemented, or if it has led to improved services and social outcomes for low-income populations (Goldfinch, DeRouen, & Pospieszna, 2013; Yanguas & Bukenya, 2016). Understanding how NPM reforms can be effectively implemented in public organizations requires broad knowledge of the path dependencies that create barriers in implementing the reforms (Stuteville & Jumara, 2010). Although the views of different writers are in support of the path dependency theory on why reform in the public sector is hampered, it is realistic to expect that organizations should not be stuck in the past if they are to respond to the realities prevailing in the world today (Yanguas & Bukenya, 2016). Hence, to effectively implement NPM programs, public managers must know the social and political contexts and develop new paradigms that direct their strategic thinking and actions (Stuteville & Jumara, 2010). In this regard, extending organizational path dependence research into the public sector is helpful.

The purpose of this qualitative multiple case study was to document how managers in public organizations in Ethiopia describe the nature and implementation of path-breaking interventions for the effective adoption of NPM in order to improve services and social outcomes for low-income populations. Therefore, the unit of analysis in this study was the manager in a public organization in Ethiopia. Data collection was achieved with a purposeful sample using a snowball and chain sampling strategy (Yin, 2014). A structured but open-ended interview process was used in order to elicit the ten identified participants' perceptions regarding the issues raised in the study (Yin, 2014). The method, scope, and number of interviews for this descriptive case study were similar to other studies relying upon in-depth interviews

(Griffin, Maloney, Price, Sim, & Vojak, 2009; Stanko, Molina-Castillo, & Bohlmann, 2011). Data was also collected through observational field notes (Katz, 2014) and a quality audit through SME examination and reflection on the data (Yin, 2014).

2. Background

NPM embraces a wide range of approaches. Each approach draws on various tools used by the private sector and later adopted by public sector (Hope, 2012). The first criticism of NPM has to do with the paradox of centralization through decentralization (Mongkol, 2011). This situation may arise when more authority is given to public managers in order to appropriately discharge their projects, which may lead to a concentration of power, contrary to the initial claim of decentralization in decision-making. The second criticism is concerned with applying private sector management techniques to the public sector. As the public and private sectors exist in different contexts, it is difficult to directly transplant the management techniques that have proven to be successful in the private sector into the different contexts in the public sector. The third criticism is that although NPM enhances transparency in the public sector, it can lead to the prevalence of corruption. Finally, NPM has become controversial in terms its results, as seen in Western countries. Applying this reform strategy in the contexts of developing countries is certain to create additional levels of complexities.

Hence, Pollitt (2003), looking at the transferability of NPM, argued for the importance of context by raising serious concerns and questions about existing knowledge in the transferability of NPM and other reform initiatives between countries and contexts. In this regard, Pollitt (2003) contended that the success or failure in transferring management techniques is heavily context dependent. The fact that is there is no general management innovation that can work throughout the world and at every time means we have to look carefully at contexts and at the "terms of trade each time we are thinking of borrowing a good management idea from somewhere else" (Pollitt, 2003:122). The author contended that the transfer of management technologies should not be considered as simple transactional relations, as in the purchase of a car. In this regard he claimed that "in short, the analogy of acquiring a car or other mainly mechanical technology does not fit" (p. 126). He further said: "It is not just a question of the complexity of the import, but also one of the complexities of the task and context into which the new management technology is being introduced" (p. 126).

Additionally, the belief that the implementation of management techniques is straightforward and can be undertaken quickly is erroneous. Rather, implementation is a process that demands significant time. In other words, there are debates about the management techniques, but little action. In this regard, the same author maintained that "there can be a formal decision to adopt, but implementation may be unenthusiastic or incompetent" (Pollitt, 2003:127-128).

In explaining the paradox of managerialism, Hood (2000) maintained that although public sector management movements were aimed at making public sector management more businesslike and less politicized, in practice the result has been the opposite. This was supported by Maor's (1999, cited in Hood, 2000) argument that the images of depoliticized public service management conjured up by advocates of managerial reform in fact produce the opposite result. On the basis of observation of changes in six parliamentary regimes between 1980 and 1996, he argued that politicians fear loss of control over policy implementation following managerial reforms and that senior public service positions thus become more, not less, "political" (and insecure) as a result. (Hood, 2000:6).

The same findings have also been seen in the application of specific elements of NPM packages, like decentralization. For example, Smoke (2015), looking at empirical findings on the issue at hand, maintains that while many researchers have been conducting studies on different aspects of decentralization reforms, their findings are not conclusive and generalizable. He notes that the reasons for the failure of robust generalizations may, first of all, be attributed to variations "on political, institutional, and socioeconomic context and how reform is approached, but in rather idiosyncratic ways" (Smoke, 2015:106). He goes on to say that those seeking success or failure will both be able to find evidence to support their view, and those with no preconceived expectations may be left confused. Second, instances of relatively good performance exist, but many empirical studies reveal more problems than achievements. (Smoke, 2015:106).

Discussing the concept of path dependence, Pierson (2000) maintained that there is no clear understanding of the concept. According to the author, "in the broader version, path dependence refers to the causal relevance of proceeding stages in a temporal sequence" (Pierson, 2000:252). This definition generally means that "history matters." This is a loose definition of the concept. In this regard, Sydow, Schreyogg, and Koch (2009) contended that

> if we base path dependence explanations on the "history matters" argument only, the notion is likely to become indistinct. All human activity and organizational processes are imprinted by their history in a way, so we would end up by concluding that all organizational decisions and actions are path dependent. (Sydow et al., 2009:690).

Accordingly, in order to get the advantage of greater clarity, Pierson (2000) proposed a more narrow definition, noting that the concept of path dependence, in which preceding steps in a particular direction induce further movement in the same direction, is well captured by the idea of the increasing returns process, in which the probability of further steps along the same path increases with each move down that path. (Pierson, 2000:252).

Based on the economists' application of increasing returns, North's (1990) research on institutional emergence enabled him to provide a prominent argument on the divergence of economic performance and increasing returns. More recent research has highlighted that "up to now, studies of path dependence (in this specified sense) neither addressed the persistence of organizations nor explored the logic and dynamics of internal organizational processes leading to a lock-in" (Sydow et al., 2009:690). Beyond that, Notteboom, De Langen, and Jacobs (2013) have applied the concept of path dependence and lock-in in seaports through the research lens of institutional economics, evolutional economics, and the role of geography and place.

Institutions are the humanly devised and/or socially constructed sets of rules that constrain and enable human interaction (North, 1990), or "formal and informal rules guiding actors' perceptions and activities" (Strambach, 2010: 408). Scott (2001) distinguishes three pillars of institutions: the regulative, the normative, and the cultural-cognitive, each with their own unique sets of logic, mechanisms of enforcement, and bases of compliance and legitimacy. Common to all three pillars is that institutions both constrain and enable human behavior. While economic historians have focused on regulative institutions at the macro level in the form of constitutions and rule of law governing capitalist societies, transaction cost economists look at firm-level structures, or what is referred to as governance systems (Notteboom et al., 2013). A critical source of regional path dependence as distinguished by Martin and Sunley (2006) is region-specific institutions or regulatory frameworks, social conventions, and cultural traditions, which can make firms and organizations located in a region become "socially embedded" (Granovetter, 1985).

3. Statement of the Problem

The problem is that while considerable resources and attention have been allocated to recent "good governance" (GG) public administration reform in low-income and fragile states, there is little evidence regarding to what degree path-breaking interventions have been implemented or if they have led to improved services and social outcomes for low-income populations

(Goldfinch, DeRouen, & Pospieszna, 2013; Yanguas & Bukenya, 2016). Previous research indicates mixed results regarding NPM performance in developing countries (e.g., Larbi, 2003; Smoke, 2015).

Although there are instances of relatively good performances in some countries, there are many failure stories. This implies that it is imperative to fill the research gap on how to effectively implement reform initiatives of NPM in the public sector and the reasons for the mixed performance. Additionally, many important aspects of path dependence and lock-in and how to implement NPM are identified in the extant literature as place-dependent processes, and as such require geographical explanation (Boschma, 2014; Martin & Sunley, 2006). Although many sub-Saharan African countries introduced NPM in reforming their public sector, evidence shows that there is a mismatch between the reform initiatives and their intended outcome of enhancing service delivery and poverty alleviation (Goldfinch et al., 2013).

Public sector reform (PSR) initiatives as currently designed in sub-Saharan countries consistently fall short of their intended targets, with much less significant outcomes than expected in terms of service delivery or poverty reduction (Goldfinch et al., 2013; Yanguas & Bukenya, 2016). The different lines of research undertaken to explain these phenomena includes research by dependence theorists. However, most of the theorists in this vein follow a retrospective approach and emphasize the constraints of NPM resulting from past decisions on present actions. Kelman and Hong (2013) have indicated the need for a new approach to path dependence in public administration that strives to look beyond the identification of constraints as advocated by most research on path dependence, which takes a retrospective approach. In this regard, they "propose a different theoretical stance as a path forward for public administration research to make a contribution to path dependence literature" (Kelman & Hong, 2013: 14). Accordingly, this study seeks to make an original contribution to path dependence theory, by taking a prospective approach on how to break the path in the effective implementation of NPM.

After the fall of the Dergue through military defeat by the EPRDF in 1991, the new government undertook numerous different reform endeavors in order to solve the socio-political and economic problems of Ethiopia. The process of bureaucratic reform in Ethiopia is a chain effect of whatbegan in 1991. These reforms can be categorized in to the following phases: The *first phase of the reform was from 1991 to 1995*, and took place in three interrelated areas, namely, economic, political and constitutional reforms. In terms of economic reform, the old form of central planning was replaced by a market economy. The adoption of federalism and power and fiscal decentralization was also one of the breakthroughs in political reforms. In terms of constitutional reform, a new constitutionwas enacted to accommodate the new state structure. The question was, however, whether Ethiopia had a bureaucracy capable of carrying out these reforms. The Ethiopian bureaucracy of the time was quite hierarchical, and characterized by many non-value adding works/positions/staffs, nepotism and lack of transparency and accountability, corruption, lack of leadership capacity, and an input-based (as opposed to output-based) orientation (Berihu, 2000).

As this the system was not prepared to implement change, the government established a new institution called The "Ministry of Capacity Building" with the mandate of undertaking reforms in all public institutions (Proclamation No. 256/2001: 1630-1632). This ministry was the leading institution to implement the civil service reform programs throughout the country, with the objective of creating a modern civil service staffed with high human resource capacity. Simultaneously, the government established an "Anti-corruption Commission" with the mandate of eradicating unaccountable and nontransparent procedures in public institutions.

Subsequently, the second phase of public sector management reform was initiated with the launch of the Civil Service Reform Program (CSRP) in 1996. The CSRP was designed to improve the efficiency, effectiveness, and transparency of public institutions, while seeking to build on the bureaucracy's reputation for discipline and compliance. It included as the following components: (i) expenditure management and control (ii) human resource management, (iii) top management systems, (iv) ethics, and (v) service delivery.

This reform effort tried to address issues like improving governance of human resource management and control, improving performance and service delivery in the entire civil service, improving transparency and accountability in civil service, and strengthening the top management system of the federal civil service. Yet, even with all the above efforts, the bureaucratic system was still too archaic and nonresponsive to the technological and social changes that had already been taking place for a number of years.

Following the prescriptions of International Monetary Fund and World Bank, the Ethiopian government implemented reform tools in order to improve the performance of government institutions in their service delivery in the beginning of 1990s. The reform tools (based on NPM) included BPR, BSC, Change Army, Citizens Charter, and deliverology. These change tools were implemented across all government organizations in the country.The problems in effective implementation of NPM in the Ethiopian context have been identified in the process, contents, contexts, and outcomes of the reform initiatives implemented in the country (Assefa, 1996; Assefa & Gebre-Egziabher, 2007; Getachew & Common, 2006; Merera, 2007; Paulos, 2001). However, there is no single study that specifically addresses path dependence as an impediment in implementing NPM in public organizations in Ethiopia and what interventions are needed to break the barriers of effective implementation of NPM.

4. Research Questions

In line with the proposed research problem and purpose of the study, the research questions are as follows:
RQ1: How do managers in public organizations in Ethiopia describe path-breaking interventions for the effective adoption of NPM in order to improve public services for low-income populations?
RQ2: How do managers in public organizations in Ethiopia describe how path-breaking interventions for the effective adoption of NPM can be implemented in order to improve social outcomes for low-income populations?

5. Theoretical Framework

From the literature review there are many research studies on NPM reforms that either consider specific elements like decentralization or that follow a holistic approach. In both cases, although there are many findings regarding the success or failures in implementing NPM programs in different parts of the world, there are no robust findings. Regarding path dependence theory in public organizations, there are many findings that explain how path dependence can be a constraint for effective implementation of NPM reforms. Looking at areas of future research on path dependence, Kasabov (2010) contended that there is a lack of research on demand-side determinants like informal institutions in explaining path dependence in the public sector. Beyond that, there are few attempts that follow a prescriptive approach to the study of public organizations.

Accordingly, rather than attributing contextual factors as reasons for failures in NPM implementatio, this study sought to identify path dependence in public organizations in Ethiopia and what can be done to break the path. As such, this study sought out the opinions of different managers in different public organizations and researchers on the issue to gain insights as to what makes these organizations path dependent and what interventions are needed to change their trajectories.

The concept of path dependency is broadly defined as "history matters" (Pierson, 2000). For analytical purposes, he recommended even more narrow definitions, suggesting that path dependence can be characterized as an increasing returns, positive feedback, or self-reinforcing process. The concept of increasing returns points to two important features of path dependence: "First, they pinpoint how the costs of switching from one alternative to another will, in certain social contexts, increases markedly over time. Second, and related, they draw attention to issues of timing and, distinguishing formative events" (Pierson, 2000, p. 251). Stuteville and Jumara (2010) have also cited Pierson (2000), noting: "Early events matter more than later ones in an 'increasing returns,' path-dependent process" (Stuteville & Jumara, 2010: 5).

Path dependence theory is significant in comprehending the challenges of formal and intentional reform programs emanating from institutional inertia (Torfing, 2009, cited in Stuteville & Jumara, 2010). Beyond that, the present study employed Sydow et al.'s (2009) framework of path dependence, which offers insights into the possibilities and limitations of breaking out of organizational path dependence. In particular, path breaking requires a thorough understanding of the social mechanisms driving the path process. Understanding these mechanisms in turn provides a platform for developing path-breaking interventions. (Sydow et al., 2009: 704)

Thus, this research aimed at providing an original contribution to path dependence theory.

6. Literature Review

The transfer of NPM has engendered mixed results, and elicited both praise and criticism from outside observers. While some have concluded that such transfers are futile (Hood & Jackson, 1991; Metcalfe & Richards, 1991; Osborne, 2006, citing Farnham & Horton, 1996), others enthusiastically advocate NPM initiatives (Flynn, 2002; Hughes 2002). Similarly, research findings in developing countries show mixed results on the application of NPM (Bhatta, 2003; Samaratunge, Alam, & Teicher, 2009). In developing nations, an attempt to transfer NPM can create further complications due to variations in levels of development, capacity, culture, and other related context differences. This view is supported by different institutional theories (Thoenig, 2011) that propose context variation as a challenge. Other institutional theories consider how successful institutional change may be accomplished (Kingston & Caballero, 2009).

The implication is that contextualization and adaptation to institutional variation is crucial. On the other hand, context variations are identified as reasons for failures in reform. Therefore, it was deemed imperative to conduct case studies on how NPM is adopted in developing countries and to develop theories and a hypothesis to explore the reason why NPM philosophies cannot work in the specific cases (Smoke, 2015).

From the different lines of research on path dependency, this study selected Kelman and Hong's (2013) approach to path dependence in public administration, which strives to look beyond the identification of constraints as advocated by most research on path dependence that takes a retrospective approach. In this regard, they "propose a different theoretical stance as a path forward for public administration research to make a contribution to path dependence literature" (Kelman & Hong, 2013:14). On top of that, "governments need to accompany their reform proposals with a strategy to manage change" (Melchor, 2008: 4). As many PSR initiatives are related to the politics of the public sector, the literature review discussed the role of the state in development. In this connection, Dang and Pheng (2015) maintained that the early views concerning the role of the state were characterized by extreme debates of communism (Smith, 1976) and capitalism (Marx, 1933). This ideological debate was explained by the historical developments surrounding PSR in developing countries (Ayee, 2015; Bukenya & Yanguas, 2013). Despite the differences in the focus of the PSR in developing countries, there has been a general agreement as to the role of the state in development.

However, there is less clarity on the concept of state. Despite continuing disagreements about the issue at hand, the developmental role of state capacity is well recognized.

According to Barkey and Sunita (1991), generally state capacity means the capability to implement policy, enforce legislation, and deliver services. "State capacity provides a powerful tool for the study of development" (vom Hau, 2012:4). Approaching state capacity from bureaucratic or administrative capacity is appropriate to address the capability of government organizations to effectively manage and implement public policies (Barkey & Sunita, 1991; Evans & Rauch, 1999; Fukuyama, 2013). This is also supported by policy researchers emphasizing institutional deterrents in the effective implementation of NPM designs and policies (Andrews, 2013; Booth, 2012b; Grindle, 2007). However, according to Yanguas and Bukenya (2016), the major challenge in PSR is related to incorrect assumptions about the state capacity in developing countries. Looking at the prevailing realities in developing countries, these authors maintain that the political and moral economy of PSR is challenged by administrative patrimonialism, public corruption, and political capture. From these bold analytical critiques of the underlying assumptions of public service reform new PSR agendas have emerged, advocated by development communities: leadership, social accountability, and policy adaptation.

7. Research Method

This study employed a multiple-case study approach (Yin, 2014) to address the topic "New Public Management and Path Dependence in Public Organizations in Ethiopia." The study's research problem was that while considerable resources and attention have been allocated to recent GG public administration reform in low-income and fragile states, there is little evidence as to what degree this agenda has been implemented, or if it has led to improved services and social outcomes for low-income populations (Goldfinch et al., 2013; Yanguas & Bukenya, 2016). In order to answer this question, data for the study was gathered from interviews withten managers of public enterprises in Ethiopia (the following table provides a brief summary of the ten cases).

Table 1: Summary of the ten cases

Participant	Sex	Age	Education (highest degree)	Management experience in years	Organization
1	F	55	LLM	21	Ethiopian Airlines
2	M	40	MBA	20	Commercial Bank of Ethiopia
3	M	34	MSc	8	AWWCE
4	M	36	MBA	8	Adamitulu Pesticides Development Co
5	M	42	MCom	6	Ethiopian Insurance Company
6	M	51	MSc	17	Ethiopian Shipping and Logistics Enterprise
7	M	39	MBA	8	Bahir Dar Textile Factory
8	M	32	BSc Electrical Engineering	7	Ethiotelecom
9	M	35	BA	5	Tendaho Sugar Factory
10	M	56	Post Graduate Diploma in Hydropower	23	Ethiopian Electric Power Corporation/EEP

In selecting the sample respondents, both purposeful and network/snowball sampling (Hatch, 2002) was used. Specifically, the sampling procedure began with random sampling to minimize the total population into a manageable size that guaranteed an equal chance for all public enterprises to be included in the sample (Zikmund, Babin, & Carr, 2012). After that, and in line with the selection criteria, the typical cases of the sample were chosen (Seawright & Gerring, 2008).

To fulfill the purpose of this descriptive case study, a multiple-case study research design (Yin, 2014) was employed. The data sources and evidence included ten in-depth, face-to-face, semistructured interviews with PEMs, field notes (Katz 2014), and SME review and reflection on the data collected (Patton, 2002). The recorded interviews were transcribed. For coding and analysis, NVivo for Microsoft was employed. To reinforce data security, the data has been stored and coded anonymously and confidentially (Patton, 2002; Yin, 2014).

As the research topic was complex, the researcher had (almost) no control over the observed phenomenon, and the issue at hand was dynamic and could not be isolated in a laboratory experiment, a multiple-case study research design was selected as the best fit (Baxter & Jack, 2008). The design was further justified because PEMs' (unit of analysis) perceptions and opinions were inseparable from the context of the study, and NPM in the public sector is a contemporary issue (Yin, 2014). To analyze the content of the qualitative interview data, a thematic analysis was applied, using the cross-case synthesis analytical technique.. Accordingly, each individual case was treated as a separate case, but synthesis of the data of each case strengthened the overall case study data. In other words, research data was collected on individual cases and compared to determine consistency and variance between cases (Yin, 2014). To ensure validity and reliability, data triangulation was applied. The use of multiple sources of evidence and different data collection strategies enhanced construct validity (Gibbert, Ruigrok, & Wicki, 2008). Additionally, the careful sampling of the ten cases enhanced the validity and reliability of this multiple-case study research.

8. Findings

Based on the key insights emerging from the in-depth interviews, an overarching theme was that there is no one criteria or variable that makes one public enterprise effective in adopting the NPM reforms and enhances the services and outcomes for the low-income population. PEMs suggested that the factors for success in NPM reforms were different for every public enterprise and depended on that organization's specific situation and external influences. However, a number of themes were identified that relate to effective adoption of the NPM reforms in public enterprises in Ethiopia.

The first research question revealed twelve themes. These include the types of NPM tools introduced, the rationale or intentions of the NPM tools, the initiator of the reform tools, the appropriateness of the NPM tools, the pressure for the NPM tools, the rhetoric on NPM, by whom the rhetoric was communicated or announced, the way it was communicated, the design process, level of contextualization, responsibility for the design process, challenges in the design process, and extent of success from rhetoric to actual design.

The second research question revealed twenty-one themes. These include the process, contextualization, challenges, level of success, the level of customer service, specific changes for the level of performance, challenges faced, system of evaluation, the impact of the reform, employment, social responsibility, local business development, accessibility of the services to low-income populations, capacity building, leadership commitment, persistence, soft S's, institutional development, about the NPM reform tools, autonomy and accountability, and benchmarking and contextualization.

The evaluation of findings based on the literature used for this multiple-case study research indicates that there is no single answer on how NPM reforms can be effectively implemented in public organizations in Ethiopia and lead to service improvements and impact the socioeconomic outcomes of the population in general and the low-income society in particular. This is because understanding how NPM reforms can be effectively implemented in public organizations requires broad knowledge of the path dependencies that create barriers in implementing the reforms (Stuteville & Jumara, 2010). Hence, to effectively implement NPM programs, public managers must know the social and political contexts and develop new paradigms that direct their strategic thinking and actions (Stuteville & Jumara, 2010; Yanguas & Bukenya, 2016).

In this regard, NPM reform initiatives should begin with proper analysis of the existing situation and the rationale of the reform should be well articulated and clearly defined (Goldfinch et al., 2013). As the different NPM technologies have their own particular emphasis and application (Goldfinch et al., 2013), it is imperative for reformers to clearly define the rationale that the NPM technologies are going to address (EuropAid, 2009; Goldfinch et al., 2013).

For the NPM reform to be successful, the management of the organizations should have a clear understanding of the pressures and intentions in introducing the different NPM tools (EuropAid, 2009; Goldfinch et al., 2013). Then, they should clearly communicate the rhetoric of the NPM reform both internally and externally (Goldfinch et al., 2013). Scholars have underscored the importance of context on how reforms should be designed (Mongkol, 2011; Pollitt, 2003; Smoke, 2015). Regarding the level of success in the actual design of the NPM tools in comparison with the rhetoric, there were mixed findings (Larbi, 2003; Smoke, 2015).

Related to the extent to which NPM reforms moved from design to actual action, the first conclusion concerns the care that must be exercised in the process (Andrews, 2013; Pollitt, 2003; Pollitt & Bouckaert, 2011; Yanguas & Bukenya, 2016). The need for contextualization is the second (Pollitt, 2003; Smoke, 2015). The third concerns the challenges in implementing the NPM designs into actual action, identified by almost all of the interview participants (EuropAid, 2009; Kelman & Hong, 2013; Pollitt & Bouckaert, 2011). The fourth concerns the extent of success in the actual implementation, which was described by the PEMs as mixed (Larbi, 2003; Smoke, 2015).

When it comes to the factors identified by PEMs as necessary for effective adoption of NPM reform, the first is leadership commitment (Bhatta, 2003; Samaratunge et al., 2009; Yanguas & Bukenya, 2016). The second factor is persistence (Pollitt, 2003). The third is related to soft S's (EuropAid, 2009; Galbraith, 2002; Goldfinch et al., 2013; Paulos, 2001; Yanguas & Bukenya, 2016). The fourth factor is institutional development (Bhatta, 2003; Stuteville & Jumara, 2010; Thoenig, 2011; Yanguas & Bukenya, 2016). The fifth concerns the suitability of NPM tools (Pollitt & Bouckaert, 2011; Yanguas & Bukenya, 2016). The sixth is related to the availability of autonomy and accountability (Smoke, 2015; Yanguas & Bukenya, 2016). The seventh and final factor is the need for benchmarking and contextualization (Booth, 2012; Mongkol, 2011; Smoke, 2015).

9. Conclusions, Implications, Limitations, and Recommendations

9.1. Conclusions

To achieve the purpose of the study a multiple case study was applied to compare and contrast the divergent opinions of mangers working in different government organizations. In this regard, Yin (2014) contended that multiple case studies are selected to follow a replication logic: each case study should be selected to establish either similar results (literal prediction) or contrasting results (theoretical replication). Accordingly, this study used a multiple-case study design in order to compare and contrast results. This was also helpful in achieving the goals of objectivity and rigor in the research design (Yin 2014).

The unit of analysis in this study was the manager in a public organization in Ethiopia. Qualitative data was based on insights derived from in-depth interviews from the identified participants. Data collection was achieved with a purposeful sample using a snowball and chain sampling strategy (Yin, 2011). A structured but open-ended interview process was used in order to elicit the ten identified participants' perceptions regarding the issues raised by the study (Yin, 2011). The method, scope, and number of interviews for this descriptive case study were similar to other studies relying upon in-depth interviews (Griffin et al., 2009; Stanko et al., 2011). Data was also collected through observational field notes (Katz, 2014), and a quality audit was conducted through SME examination and reflection on the data (Yin, 2011).

The section on findings presented the implications from the research findings and compared these to the literature review. Discoveries and implications were analyzed in response to the study's statement of the problem and alignment with the research purpose and its significance. Recommendations for future research conducive to path-breaking interventions on the effective adoption of NPM reforms in order to enhance services and outcomes for the population in general and low-income populations in particular were also discussed. Additionally, findings and implications that were identified during the research phase that relate to the effective adoption of NPM reforms were presented. PEMs, SMEs, and policymakers will be able to reference this study as they attempt to understand the key criteria for the successful adoptation of NPM reform tools aimed at enhancing service delivery and outcomes related to the socioeconomic development of the population in general and low-income populations in particular.

Additional opportunities for research include expanding the scope of this research through qualitative analysis of PEMs living and working in different global regions as well as quantitative analysis of PEMs. The research can also be expanded to SMEs of public enterprises and other government organizations to determine the extent to which there is convergence or divergence on the findings between these groups. There is also an opportunity to find and develop case studies that support each of the main research questions as a way to highlight successful organizations that have implemented the suggested findings. Finally, qualitative and quantitative research can be completed on current and historic NPM reform trends to test assumptions stated by PEMs as essential for the effective adoption and performance of NPM reform technologies.

9.2. Implications of the Study

The implications of the study findings are discussed in this section and are organized by research question. In relation to the first research question, the first implication is that there is a gap in clearly articulating the rationale for the reform at national level (EuropAid, 2009; Goldfinch et al., 2013). This is because the Ethiopian government announced the NPM reforms for all government organizations without a clear specification of which tool should be used for which public enterprise, which is a serious deficiency given that there is variation in emphasis and application across enterprises (Goldfinch et al., 2013).

According to EuropAid (2009), NPM reforms can follow either a system-wide approach or reforms targeted to specific public organizations. To decide on the level of the reform, it is imperative to decide on the level of change required. If there is a need for cultural change in the whole public sector, it is logical to do something at a system-wide level. On the other hand, as different government organizations have different socio-technical systems, each organization should select from the bundles of NPM tools for its own purposes. However, the NPM reform in Ethiopia followed a system-wide prescription of bundles of NPM technologies for all government organizations despite variations in the socio-technical systems. Hence, there is no clear decision on the level of change intended by the NPM reforms (EuropAid, 2009; Goldfinch et al., 2013).

Another implication is that whatever the specific targets of the NPM tools, the general move in introducing private sector technologies into the public sector has created some positive changes. Having a clear understanding of the pressure that forced governments to introduce NPM reform is a fundamental prerequisite before prescribing the specific reform designs (EuropAid, 2009). This implies that the PEMs are trying to employ the NPM tools to address the specific organizational pressure, even though the national pressure for the reform is not clearly articulated.

In relation to the national rhetoric, the fact that interviewed PEMs had divergent opinions on the latter suggests it is not clearly articulated and communicated to the specific PEMs. Evidently, the PEMs were not clear about the intended outcome of the NPM reforms in relation to the general public. This clearly shows a gap in cascading the national rhetoric down to each enterprise.

Concerning the way the rhetoric was transferred to actual design, the implication is that as each enterprise follows its own process, there is no clear guidance by the higher government agencies in charge of the reform. In relation to contextualization, the implication is that there is a gap in how the reform designs should be applied in the specific circumstances and contexts of the different enterprises.

A further finding concerns responsibility in the design process. In this regard, the implication is that the gap in NPM transfer and implementation could be filled by combining technical and functional knowledge and taking into account the local context. Hence, to address the knowledge gap, both practitioners and experts in the NPM tools have been involved in the design process.

Furthermore, our study revealed challenges in the design process. The implication in this connection is that necessary preconditions in breaking the learning curve, attitudinal problem, and awareness creation about the NPM tools have not been realized. The second implication is that the level of knowledge of the PEMs about the NPM tools was not enhanced, required resources for the NPM technologies were not in place, and necessary work in breaking the past bureaucratic procedures was not accomplished.

We further found that there were mixed results regarding the level of success in the actual design of the NPM tools in line with the rhetoric. Hence, PEMs need to study the specific factors necessary for effective performance in the adoption of NPM tools.

In relation to research question two, analysis of the data from the semi-structured PEM interviews revealed twenty-one themes. Of these, one subset is related to the extent to which NPM reforms moved from design to actual action, and addressed the thematic areas of: process, contextualization, challenges, and level of success. In this connection, the implication is that the way the design was implemented into actual action varies from enterprise to enterprise, to the extent that in some enterprises there was no persistence and full follow-up of the implementation process. The other implication is that there was a general tendency to accept what the higher officials said without considering the objective realities on the ground.

Regarding contextualization, in six out of the PEMs, there was a tendency not to consider contextual situations of the enterprises in turning design into actual action. In relation to the reform technologies, the implication is that there was confusion on how the intentions of the reform tools should be reconciled with the objectives of the enterprises, contradictions in the different NPM tools, a lack of awareness of the objectives of the NPM tools, diverse interpretations of the NPM tools, and lack of persistence or full follow-up and support in full-scale implementations of the NPM tools. These problems clearly show that the reform process lacked a proper strategic change management process (Melchor, 2008). Similarly, strategic leadership in the NPM reform process was lacking (Melchor, 2008).

Concerning the extent of success in the actual implementation of the NPM reform designs, the implication is that there is a need for detailed investigation by PEMs on the factors contributing to the successful implementation of NPM tools.

After the implementation of the NPM tools, even though in most cases there was an increase in the level of customer service, there were also negative evaluations of the issue at hand. Hence, detailed investigation of the issue at hand is imperative in order to understand the factors for effective performance in customer service improvements.

In relation to the specific changes necessary to reach a satisfactory level of performance, the first implication is that whatever the level of performance in enhancing the level of customer service, the introduction of the NPM tools made PEMs think about the customer service orientation and they devised some mechanisms to measure the level of performance in that regard. Moreover, there is a lot that needs to be done for the NPM tools to deliver positive performance in enhancing customer service.

A further finding is related to the challenges inherent in the actual implementation of the NPM tools. In this regard, according to North (1990, cited in Pierson, 2000), "Established institutions generate powerful inducements that reinforce their own stability and further development" (Pierson, 2000: 225). Hence, without changing these institutional frameworks into a type that would favor the requirements of the NPM tools, the effective implementation of the reform tools will be a futile endeavor. This implies that the NPM reform process was implemented without the required preconditions of institutional change.

Regarding the system of evaluation, the implication is that the level of success of the reform initiatives was not linked with the outcome in socio-economic aspects of the population in general and the low-income society in particular.

Another subset of themes from data related to question two concerns the outcome of the reform. Here the thematic areas are: impact of the reform, employment, social responsibility, local business development, accessibility of the services to low-income populations, and capacity building.

In regard to the impact of the reform, the implication is that although it is very difficult to specifically measure the outcome of the NPM reforms, it is clear that after the introduction of these tools there are positive changes in outcomes to the population. In the same way, the impacts in terms of employment and social responsibility are positive. Similarly, when it comes to business development for the MSEs and local businesses the implication is that there is a positive impact in local business development.

In relation to the accessibility of services to low-income populations and capacity building there were positive impacts. In other words, the implication is that there is a positive impact in terms of accessibility of services and capacity building to low-income populations.

Finally, a subset of themes in data from question two dealt with the effective adoption of NPM reform. The themes are: leadership commitment, persistence, soft S's, institutional development, about the NPM reform tools, autonomy and accountability, and benchmarking and contextualization.

Looking at NPM in Asia, Samaratunge et al. (2009) concluded that "countries like Bangladesh and Sri Lanka, where strong leadership and appropriate accountability systems are not in place, could not expect successful outcomes from their NPM reform agenda" (Samaratunge et al., 2009:42). On the other hand, countries with strong leadership and effective accountability mechanisms experience success in their efforts. In other words, Bhatta (2003) concluded that "while different countries will focus on different aspects of NPM, the key to any success in public sector governance will remain the level of political will" (Bhatta, 2003:13). Likewise, strengthening the capability of top-level executives to spearhead the nucleus of PSR initiatives comes out as a new reform agenda (Yanguas & Bukenya, 2016). This implies that for NPM reforms to be effectively implemented leadership commitment is a very crucial factor.

A further finding here is that the crucial factor for effective adoption of the NPM technologies is persistence. This implies that on top of leadership commitment to the issue at hand, the existence of persistence and follow-up from start to finish is critical for effective adoption of NPM reform tools.

In introducing new management technologies like NPM, many organizations emphasize the changes to their structures and operational procedures. However, it is equally important is to change the soft S's related to human resources (Galbraith, 2002; Yanguas & Bukenya, 2016). Similarly, according to Paulos (2001), the absence of a well-developed bureaucratic structure with competent personnel was identified as a major challenge in Ethiopian PSR.

Regarding the soft S's, the implication is that if the NPM reform initiatives are to be successfully implemented there is a need to work on the soft S's.

In connection to the preconditions of effective NPM reform the implication is that there should be a proper governance environment and institutional development (Yanguas & Bukenya, 2016). In the same way, for effective adoption of NPM reforms, proper governance structure and institutional development is a critical factor.

Yet another finding is related to the NPM tools introduced by the Federal Government of Ethiopia for all government organizations. This implies that in relation to the NPM tools prescribed by the government for all government organizations, there is no clear understanding about the philosophy behind these new technologies and the difference and similarities behind the different bundles prescribed by the general name NPM reform; moreover, there is no credible governmental agency at national level with a capacity to alleviate these confusions and concerns.

Another finding concerned autonomy and accountability. In this regard, the implication is that rather than ordering PEMs to follow this or that tool, it is better to give them autonomy to select which NPM tool is appropriate for their enterprise's context and, in fact, make them accountable for their independent decisions.

The final finding is related to benchmarking and contextualization. In this connection, the implication is that the NPM reform tools should be internally motivated and be applied based on the given context of the different government organizations; additionally, there is a need for the benchmarking of successful adopters in the effective implementation of the NPM technologies.

9.3. Limitations of the Study

This research has several limitations. The first limitation is the broadness of the concept of NPM. Second, because empirical studies on path dependence in the adoption of NPM in public enterprises in Ethiopia are rare, the current study will significantly depend on the primary sources and office documents. Third, this multiple case study research is based on a sample of ten PE managers, which represents a case study of public organizations that have both public and enterprise objectives. A sample of other category of public organizations like ministries, and various types of specialized or executive agencies (Ayee, 2015) might come up with different findings. Fourth, geography and location are important considerations in path dependence and lock-in (Martin & Sunley 2006; Notteboom, DeLangen, & Jabobs, 2013).

In this study only PEs in Ethiopia are considered. Accordingly, the findings of this study are mainly relevant for PEs in Ethiopia. Consequently, further research is required in order to judge the generalizability and transferability of this research to PEs in other countries and places (Hancock, Ockleford, & Windridge, 2009). The final limitation of this study is related to the source of evidence. This study mainly uses semi-structured personal interviews rather than actual observation in the workplace. In this regard, Yin (2014) maintained that the major problem of the interview as a source of evidence is the problem of question and answer bias. Thus this problem is also a limitation of this study.

9.4. Recommendations

Recommendations for Management Practice

The first recommendation is that rather than prescribing the same NPM tools for all public enterprises, the specific NPM tools prescribed should take into account the specific context and problem of each enterprise (EuropAid,

2009). This is because of the fact that each NPM tool has its own emphasis and application (Goldfinch et al., 2013).

The second recommendation is that before introducing these NPM tools the government should clearly define and articulate the rationale of the reform at the national level (EuropAid, 2009). Then, to address the rationale at the national level the government should make strategic decisions on the logical link between the specific NPM tools and the rationale. This is because of the fact that the emphasis and application of the NPM tools differ from one tool to another (Goldfinch et al., 2013).

The third recommendation is that instead of introducing the NPM reform at the national level as a campaign, the government should first become clear on the level of change required (EuropAid, 2009). Then, among the different reform tools, the government should first make a policy decision in connection with the NPM tools that should be system-wide and the NPM tools that should be internally motivated and selected by the different public enterprises, given context variations and the specific problems they face.

The fourth recommendation is that although the general NPM reform as applied in the government enterprises in Ethiopia has created positive changes, further achievements and positive changes could be realized if the government clearly specifies which NPM tools are to be used for which enterprise and decides on the specific target of each NPM tool given contextual difference and variations in the problems faced by each enterprise.

The fifth recommendation is that for effective adoption of the NPM tools in the context of public enterprises, the government should make concerted efforts in effectively communicating the national pressure for introducing the NPM reforms at the national level, and allow the PEMs to make a logical link with their respective enterprises.

The sixth recommendation is that the national rhetoric should be clearly communicated to the specific PEMs for the effective adoption of the NPM reforms.

The seventh recommendation is that to justify the investment in the introduction of NPM tools, PEMs should develop their strategic plan by incorporating specific and measurable targets regarding the level of change in the outcome to the society and measure the level of change after the introduction of the NPM reform tools.

Concerning the way the rhetoric was transferred to actual design, the first recommendation is that rather than leave each enterprise to design and implement the NPM reforms prescribed by the government based on their own interpretations, which results in variation in the process, the government should establish an agency at the national level with the capacity, knowledge, resources, and the mandate of providing effective guidance in the specific reform processes for each enterprise. The other alternative is to give each enterprise's managers the autonomy and resources to select specific reform tools that are appropriate in their specific context and to follow their own reform process by employing international consultants who are well-versed and experienced in guiding the effective adoption of reform processes.

A corollary recommendation is that rather than giving the reform design and implementation process solely to the PEMs or consultant experts, involving both practitioners and experts is appropriate for an effective reform process as each participant has complementary knowledge of the issue at hand.

We further recommend that for effective design and implementation of the NPM reforms, required interventions should be devised in breaking the learning curve, past bureaucratic procedures, and attitudinal problems. On top of that, enhancing the knowledge and understanding about the reform tools and providing required resources for the NPM technologies are necessary preconditions for success. Additionally, for effective adoption and performance of the NPM tools, the PEMs should undertake detailed investigation into the factors most conducive to effective performance and adoption.

Regarding the extent to which NPM reforms moved from design to actual action, the first recommendation is that rather than simply accepting what higher officials said, in turning the NPM reform designs into actual action, there should be some flexibility in relation to the objective realities on the ground. On top of that, there should be persistent follow-up in the implementation process. Concerning the level of contextualization on actual implementation of the NPM reform tools, four out of the ten participants emphasized the need for contextualization (PEM 4, PEM 5, PEM 8, and PEM 10). On the other hand, the remaining PEMs did not mention the need for contextualization, which is advocated by writers like Smoke (2015) and Pollitt (2003). In this connection, a second recommendation is that, for the effective adoption of NPM tools, PEMs should take into account the contextual situations of their enterprises. The third recommendation is that, for effective implementation of the NPM reforms, PEMs should accompany their reform initiatives with a proper strategic change management process (Melchor, 2008).

Related to the level of performance in customer service improvements, the recommendation is that had the NPM reform tools been prescribed based on the specific conditions of the enterprises and implemented accordingly, its output in enhancing service delivery could have been more than the current level of performance. A second corrolary is that there should be concerted efforts to develop the preconditions for institutional development. A third recommendation here is that the level of success of the reform initiatives should be linked with the outcome in socioeconomic aspects of the population in general and the low-income society in particular.

Regarding the outcome of the reform, it is recommended that the PEMs should develop mechanisms on how the specific impact of the reform should be measured if the investments related to the introduction of the NPM reforms are to be justified.

In relation to the effective adoption of NPM reforms, the final recommendation is that leadership commitment, persistence, required work on a reward system and human resource policies (soft S's) (Galbraith, 2002), and institutional development be recognized as the crucial path-breaking interventions required for the effective adoption of NPM reforms. Additionally, in relation to the NPM tools prescribed by the government for all government organizations, there should be clear understanding about the philosophy behind these new technologies and the difference and similarities behind the different bundles prescribed under the general name NPM reform. Furthermore, there should be a credible governmental agency at the national level with the capacity to alleviate these confusions and concerns. Beyond that, rather than ordering PEMs to follow this or that tool, it is better to give them autonomy to select which NPM tool is appropriate for their enterprise's context and, in fact, make them accountable for their independent decisions. Finally, the NPM reform tools should be internally motivated and be applied based on the given context of the different government organizations, and there should be a benchmarking of successful adopters in the effective implementation of NPM technologies.

Recommendations for Further Research

This qualitative multiple-case study research has several limitations that can offer new ideas for future research. Additional opportunities for research include expanding the scope of this research through qualitative analysis of PEMs living and working in different global regions as well as quantitative analysis of PEMs. The research can also be expanded to SMEs of public enterprises and other government organizations to determine the extent to which there is convergence or divergence on the findings between these groups. There is also an opportunity to find and develop case studies that support each of the main research questions as a way to highlight successful organizations that have implemented the suggested findings. Finally, qualitative and quantitative research can be completed on current and historic NPM reform trends to test assumptions stated by PEMs about the factors necessary for the effective adoption and performance of NPM reform technologies.

Acknowledgements

I especially thank my dissertation chair Professor Daphne Halkias for her systematic and scholarly guidance and superb mentorship. Her professional guidance and direction of my PhD dissertation (New Public Management and Path Dependence in Public Organizations in Ethiopia: A Multiple Case Study), and the feedbacks and support during the entire PhD process gave me the real opportunity to acquire new insights and develop my research skills and confidence. I also owe special thanks to the reviewers for their constructive feedback and commitment in bringing this book chapter to its completion. Finally, I thank my colleagues from foreign language and literature in MU (Mekone Amare, Endeshaw Letera, and the late Dr. Mekonnen Alemu) who thoroughly proofread every chapter and provided invaluable feedback in the whole process.

References

Andrews, M. (2013). *The Limits of Institutional Reform in Development: Changing Rules for Realistic Solutions*. Cambridge: Cambridge University Press.

Assefa, A. (1996). *Civil Service Reform and Administrative Modernization*. Addis Ababa, Ethiopia: Ethiopian Civil Service Commission.

Assefa, T., & Gebre-Egziabher, T. (eds) (2007). *Decentralization in Ethiopia*. Addis Ababa, Ethiopia: Forum for Social Studies.

Ayee, J. R. (2015). Public Sector Reform in Africa: A-state-of-the art. *Commonwealth Innovations Review*, 21(3), 14-28.

Barkey, K., & Sunita, P. (1991). Comparative Perspectives on the State. *Annual Review of Sociology*, 17, 523-549.

Baxter, P., & Jack, S. (2008). Qualitative Case Study Methodology: Study Design and Implementation for Novice Researchers. *The Qualitative Report*, 13(4), 544-559.

Bhatta, G. (2003). Post-NPM Themes in Public Sector Governance. Working paper no. 17. Wellington, New Zealand: State Services Commission. Retrieved from http://www.ssc.govt.nz/search/google_cse_adv/bhatta.

Booth, D. (2012). *Development as a Collective Action Problem: Addressing the Real Challenges of African Governance*. Synthesis report of the Africa Power and Politics Programme. London: Overseas Development Institute.

Boschma, R. (2014). Towards an Evolutionary Perspective on Regional Resilience. *Regional Studies*, 49(5), 733-751.

Berihu, A. G. (2010). *Comparative Analysis of Some Western versus Japanese Management Techniques in the Context of Ethiopia. https://www.grips.ac.jp/forum/af-growth/support_ethiopia/document/Berihu_Kaizen&BPR.pdf*

Bukenya, B., & Yanguas, P. (2013). Building State Capacity for Inclusive Development: The Politics of Public Sector Reform. ESID Working Paper No. 25. Manchester, UK: Effective States and Inclusive Development Research Centre (ESID). Retrieved from http://www.effective-states.org/working-paper-25/.

Dang, G., & Pheng, L. S. (2015). *Infrastructure Investments in Developing Economies.* Singapore: Springer Science+Business Media.

EuropAid. (2009). Public Sector Reform – An Introduction. Tools and Methods Series, Concept Paper no. 1. Luxemburg: European Communities.

Evans, P., & Rauch, J. E. (1999). Bureaucracy and Growth: A Cross-national Analysis of the Effects of "Weberian" State Structures on Economic Growth. *American Sociological Review,* 64(5), 748-765.

Flynn, N. (2002). *Public Sector Management.* London: Prentice Hall.

Fukuyama, F. (2013). *What is Governance?* Washington, DC: Center for Global Development.

Galbraith, J. R. (2002). Organizing to Deliver Solutions. *Organizational Dynamics,* 31(2), 194-207.

Getachew, M. H., & Common, R. (2006). *Civil Service Reform in Ethiopia: Success in Two Ministries. Research Memorandum 59.* Hull, UK: University of Hull, Business School.

Gibbert, M., Ruigrok, W., & Wicki, B. (2008). What Passes as a Rigorous Case Study? *Strategic Management Journal,* 29(13), 1465-1474.

Goldfinch, S., DeRouen, K., & Pospieszna, P. (2013). Flying Blind? Evidence for Good Governance Public Management Reform Agendas, Implementation and Outcomes in Low Income Countries. *Public Administration and Development,* 33(1), 50-61.

Granovetter, M. (1985). Economic Action and Social Structure; The Problem of Embeddedness. *American Journal of Sociology,* 91(3), 481-510.

Griffin, A., Maloney, B. A., Price, R. L. Sim, E. W., & Vojak, M. M. (2009). Voices from the Field: How Exceptional Electronic Industrial Innovators Innovate. *Journal of Product Innovation Management,* 26(2), 222-240.

Grindle, M. S. (2007). Good Enough Governance Revisited. *Development Policy Review,* 25(5), 533-574.

Hancock, B., Ockleford, E., & Windridge, K. (2009). *An Introduction to Qualitative Research.* Leicester, UK: The NIHR RDS EM / YH.

Hatch, J. A. (2002). *Doing Qualitative Research in Education Dettings.* Albany, NY: SUNY Press.

Hope, R. K. (2012). Managing the Public Sector in Kenya: Reform and Transformation for Improved Performance. *Journal of Public Administration and Governance,* 2(4), 128-143.

Hood, C. (2000). Paradoxes of Public-sector Managerialism, Old Public Management and Public Service Bargains. *International Public Management Journal,* 3(1), 1-22.

Hughes, O. (2002). *Public Management and Administration.* Basingstoke, UK: Palgrave Macmillan.

Kasabov, E. (2010). Success of Path Dependence through Perpetuation of Failure during Reform. *Economic Issues*, 15(1), 55-81.

Katz, J. (2014). Situational Evidence – Strategies for Causal Reasoning from Observational Field Notes. *Sociological Methods & Research*, 44(1), 108-144.

Kelman, S., & Hong, S. (2013). This Could be the Start of Something Big: Linking Early Managerial Choices with Subsequent Organizational Performance. HKS Faculty Research Working Paper Series RWP13-042, October 2013. Retrieved from https://research.hks.harvard.edu/publications/workingpapers/citation.aspx?PubId=9151&type=FN&PersonId=69.

Kingston, C., & Caballero, G. (2009). Comparing Theories of Institutional Change. *Journal of Institutional Economics*, 5(2), 1-27.

Larbi, G. A. (2003). Overview of Public Sector Management Reform. Discussion paper no. 112 (pp. 1-9). Geneva: United Nations Research Institute for Social Development.

Martin, R., & Sunley, P. (2006). Path Dependence and Regional Economic Evolution. *Journal of Economic Geography*, 6(4), 395-437.

Marx, K. (1933). *Capital*. London: J. M. Dent.

Melchor, O. H. (2008). Managing Change in OECD Governments – An Introductory Framework. OECD Working Papers on Public Governance, no. 12. Paris: OECD Publishing.

Merera, G. (2007). Ethnicity, Democratisation and Decentralization in Ethiopia: The Case of Oromia. *Eastern Africa Social Science Research Review*, 23(1), 81-106.

Mongkol, K. (2011). The Critical Review of New Public Management Model and Its Criticisms. *Research Journal of Business Management*, 5(1), 35-43.

North, D. C. (1990). *Institutions, Institutional Change and Economic Performance*. Cambridge: Cambridge University Press.

Notteboom, T., De Langen, P., & Jacobs, W. (2013). Institutional Plasticity and Path Dependence in Seaports: Interactions between Institutions, Port Governance Reforms and Port Authority Routines. *Journal of Transport Geography*, 27(2013), 26-35.

Osborne, S. P. (2006). The New Public Governance? *Public Management Review*, 8(3), 377-387.

Patton, M. Q. (2002). *Qualitative Research and Evaluation Methods*. Thousand Oaks, CA: Sage Publications.

Paulos, C. (2001). The Challenges of the Civil Service Reform in Ethiopia: Initial Observation. *Eastern Africa Social Science Research Review*, 17(1), 79-102.

Pierson, P. (2000). Increasing Returns, Path Dependence, and the Study of Politics. *The American Political Science Review*, 94(2), 251-267.

Pollitt, C. (2003). Public Management Reform: Reliable Knowledge and International Experience. *OECD Journal on Budgeting*, 3(3), 121-136.

Pollitt, C., & Bouckaert, G. (2011). *Public Management Reform: A Comparative Analysis – New Public Management, Governance, and the neo-Weberian State* (3rd ed.). Oxford: Oxford University Press.

Proclamation on Reorganization of the Executive Organs of the FDRE. (2001). Negarit Gazette, Proclamation no. 256/2001, Addis Ababa, Ethiopia.

Samaratunge, R., Alam, Q., & Teicher, J. (2009). The New Public Management Reforms in Asia: A Comparison of South and Southeast Asian Countries. *International Review of Administrative Sciences*, 74(1), 25-46.

Scott, W. R. (2001). *Institutions and Organizations* (2nd ed). Thousand Oaks, CA: Sage Publications Inc.

Seawright, J., & Gerring, J. (2008). Case Selection Techniques in Case Study Research: A Menu of Qualitative and Quantitative Options. *Political Research Quarterly*, 61(2), 294-308.

Smith, A. (1976). *An Inquiry into the Nature and Causes of the Wealth of Nations.* Oxford: Clarendon Press.

Smoke, P. (2015). Rethinking Decentralization: Assessing Challenges to a Popular Public Sector Reform. *Public Administration and Development*, 35(2), 97-112.

Stanko, M.A., Molina-Castillo F.-J., & Bohlmann, J. D., (2011). Thinking Inside the Box: Incumbent Firms' Innovativeness and Demand-side Inertia. *AMA Summer Educators Conference 2011*, 22(4), 569-570.

Strambach, S. (2010). Path Dependency, Path Plasticity – The Co-evolution of Institutions and Innovation. The German business software industry. In R. A. Boschma & Martin, R. (eds.), *Handbook for Evolutionary Economic Geography*Cheltenham (pp. 406-431). UK: Edward Elgar Publishing Ltd.

Stuteville, R., & Jumara, J. (2010). *The Role of Path-dependency in Public Administration and Economics and Implications for the Future.* Retrieved from https://ecpr.eu/Events/PaperDetails.aspx?PaperID=9295&EventID=1.

Sydow, J., Schreyogg, G., & Koch, J. (2009). Organizational Path Dependence: Opening the Black Box. *Academy of Management Review*, 34(4), 689-709.

Thoenig, J.-C. (2011). Institutional Theories and Public Institutions. In Pierre, P. B. J. (ed.), *The Handbook of Public Administration* (pp. 185-101). Thousand Oaks, CA: Sage Publications.

Yanguas, P., & Bukenya, B. (2016). "New" Approaches Confront "old" Challenges in African Public Sector Reform. *Third World Quarterly*, 37(1), 136-152.

Yin, R. K. (2011). *Qualitative Research from Start to Finish.* New York, NY: Guilford Press.

Yin, R. K. (2014). *Case Study Research: Design and Methods* (5th ed). Thousand Oaks, CA: Sage Publications Inc.

Zikmund, W. J., Babin, B. J., & Carr, J. C. (2012). *Business Research Methods* (9th ed.). Hampshire, UK: Cengage Learning (EMEA).

11
The Analysis of the Gadaa System in Comparison to Western Democracy

Moti Mosisa Gutema

Box 1: Key points of the chapter

- ✓ Apart from the Western model of democracy, there are other indigenous models of democracy in different communities with their own unique qualities and achievements, one of which is the Gadaa system.
- ✓ The Gadaa system is more egalitarian than the Western model of democracy in terms of the quality of the decision-making process, accountability, inclusiveness, participation, political game, and the leadership development process.
- ✓ The government should support the development of indigenous governance systems through the provision of policy and other structural adjustments.

Box 2: Key Insights of this chapter

Reading this chapter will give you insight in

- ✓ Indigenous governance system and its dynamics
- ✓ Convergence and divergence between the Gadaa system and Western democracy
- ✓ Basic qualities of the Gadaa system and its comparison with the Western model of democracy.

Box 3: Abbreviations

MPs = Member of Parliaments

CCEFD = Conclusions of the Council of Europe Forum for the Future of Democracy

1. Introduction

Since 1980s several scholars and international institutions such as the World Bank have recognized indigenous knowledge as a significant resource for sustainable development (Zelalem, 2015). Particularly, indigenous knowledge of governance is defined as using indigenous institutions and practices for the exercising of economic, political, and administrative authorities to manage a country's affairs at all levels (Sithole & Mbele, 2008; Warren, 1991). In Africa, many ethnic groups have thier own (indigenous) forms of governance characterized by remarkable qualities (Ayittey, 1991). Even though in contemporary Africa, the mode of governance is undoubtedly influenced by Western values and ideals, the majority of African citizens value their indigenous system as it influences their daily life, including the food they eat, the languages they speak, the way they dress, etc. (Kojo, 2017).

Similarly, the Oromos are one of the indigneous peoples living in Ethiopia having their own indigenous governance system. Prior to their colonization by the alliance of European imperialism and Ethiopian colonialism the Oromos were independently organized both culturally and politically using their own governance system, called "Sirna Gadaa," or the Gadaa sytem (Aseffa, 2012; 2005; Holcomb and Sisai, 1990;). The term "Gadaa" has no single and unanimously accepted definition and has been defined differently in different disciplines by different scholars (Zelalem, 2012). This reveals that the Gadaa system is a comprehensive and multidimensional indigenous system that can be conceptualized from diverse but complementary perspectives (Debela, 2017).

The system has been defined from political, philosophical, sociological, anthropological, legal, theological, astronomical, and other point of views (Asmarom, 1973). For instance, etymologically, Tsegaye Gebremedihn conceptualized *Gadaa* as coined from the combination of two terms *ka* (God or Creator) and *aada* (norms), which taken together mean the *norms of God* (Tsegaye, 1964). Further, Asmarom (1973) defined the Gadaa system as an age grade system, wherein a class of people assumes politico-ritual leadership for a period of eight years, via an electoral mechanism. According to Asmarom, the system enabled the Oromos to unite their people both militarily and organizationally so that they were able to expand or to recover their territories and accommodate their increased population and stock.

Vis-à-vis its emergence, Aseffa (2012) has stated that nobody knows when and how the Gadaa system emerged as a system of governance. Nontheless, Aseffa has argued that, irrespective of the absence of adequate knowledge of Oromo history before the sixteenth century, it is reasonable to think that the Oromo people did not invent the system only at the moment they consolidated as a group through the defensive and offensive wars that took place during the sixteenth century. Additionally, Baissa (2004) confirms that the Oromos were already under the governance of the Gadaa system by the sixteenth century; at the same time, a special publication of Guji Culture and Tourism Bureau (2016) contends that the system was already in existence in the fifteenth century. Thus, regardless of the varying conceptions of what the Gadaa system is and when it emerged, the system has been organizing the Oromo people around political, economic, social, cultural, and religious institutions for at least the last five hundred years (Asmarom, 1973; Baissa 2004).

2. The Context of the Problem

The Gadaa system has been investigated by both domestic and expatriate scholars from different perspectives. For instance, in a series of publications, the prominent scholar Asmarom (1973, 1980, 2006) has mainly focused on the nature of the system and how it operates among the Oromos. Similarly, scholars like Zelalem (2012, 2015, 2018), Baissa (1994), Aseffa (2011), and Dirribi (2011) have conducted different studies of the system. Their analysis has focused on the characterization of the system and on the question of its suitability to different contexts, in particular that of present-day Ethiopia.

Other scholars have also studied the system from the point of view of its contribution to conflict resolution and its grand philosophies regarding women's empowerment. For instance, Kuwe (1997) stressed the role of the Siiqqee (women's organization) institution in promoting women into the decision-making process under the Gadaa system. Meanwhile, Debela (2017) analyzed system's suitability and feasibility to be used as an alternative system to the one presently in place in Ethiopia and argued that it should be considered as one of the recognized means of Afsol (the so-called Africa Solution), focusing in particular on the role of the system in resolving local conflicts and empowering women. But all the above studies mainly focused on describing the nature and structural setup of the system, while considering its values from different perspectives. Only a very few of them have conducted a critical analysis of the system in comparison with the Western model of democracy. To address this gap, this chapter means to identify the values of the Gadaa system and to compare it with the values of the Western model of democracy.

3. Indigenous Governance System and Western Democracy

In parallel to the old and indigenous system of governance, the so-called modern governance system (Western democracy) is often defined as "the rule of the people where rules are determined by the people who are to obey those rules." Thus, as the system (Western democracy) has a positive connotations, many governments of the world connect themselves with it and claim to belong to it even if their society is characterized by little or no communal participation.[1]

For instance, among the 193 countries of the world that are recognized by the United Nations, 123 are said to have modern system of governance with the connotation of Western democracy (www.freedomhouse.org). More than half of those states claim that they have already set up the form of government that is characterized by communal participation, no matter what forms (legal or illegal) they are in fact operating under (Paula & Jean-Aime, 2008).

Despite its popularity, the modern model of governance is never perfect and never complete, and it was with this mind that Karl Popper said, "Democracy is the word for something that does not exist."[2] Moreover, it should be understood that democratic society is more than a democratically elected government. There is even a universal concern about the status of Western democracy, and political discontents and skepticisms toward the system are becoming widespread. Due to this, citizens often feel powerless and are discouraged from taking a more active role in their society (ibid).

Consequently, given this need for an alternative governance system, particularly an indigenous governance system that would meet the needs of non-Western societies[3] has led to advocates of indigenous governance celebrating it as the single largest knowledge resource not yet mobilized in the development enterprise (Paul, cited in Warren et al. 1996). Accordingly, policy makers have recognized the importance of indigenous knowledge systems and developed funding mechanisms, legislations, and policy frameworks to identify and protect them (Tshwane University, 2013).

Particularly in Africa, the indigenous governance system plays a significant role in the thinking, behavior, and welfare of the community. For instance, in Ethiopia, the Oromo[4] people have their own indigenous governance system called the Gadaa system, which has been described as an autonomous, egalitarian, and inclusive system of governance covering all sections of the society. Thus, it is the main objective of this chapter to analyze the fundamental principles of the "Gadaa system" and compare it with the fundamental principles of Western democracy in terms of its governance and power transferring procedures/practices.

4. Methodology

In answering the research questions and achieving the objectives set, the study utilized both primary and secondary data sources, while taking a fully qualitative approach. Primary data was gathered through an observation check lists by visiting all the ceremonies and events involved in the power transferring process under the Gadaa system at a place called Mi'ee

Boku, a place where this process is undertaken every eight years. In addition observation, Abbaa Gadaas, Hayyuus, elders, and key informants from local communities were selected using snowball sampling, and in-depth interviews were intensively employed. Finally, secondary data sources were collected from books, journals, bulletins, newspapers, and official publications.

5. Oromo's Governance System before the Gadaa System

In order to analyze the governance system of the Oromo people before the development of the Gadaa system, the study used both primary and secondary sources, in which the kings (Abbaa Gadaas) and senior law makers (Hayyuus) were interviewed intensively and publications perused thoroughly. Accordingly, the study found that the Oromos experienced two phases of governance systems before the establishment of the Gadaa system. Firstly, there was a period of multiple kingships, wherein each family tree and clan used to govern themselves by appointing their own kings. However, there is no concrete data for how many years this multiple kingships system functione, although the oral tradition of the Abba Gadaas and Hayyuus asserts that it persisted for many centuries (Jiloo Mandhoo, March, 2015; Guyo, March, 2015)

The second stage was a period of single kingship and queenship, in which men and women ruled as a king and a queen one after another respectively. This period was marked by many social problems, which forced the then-rulers governors to consider a different system of governance. As a result of these deliberations, which evolved over a period of time during which they considered the concept of dual administration, they came to consider a system of team leadership.[5] Then, they devised a system of governance for their own social, cultural, political, economic problems and named it the Gadaa system (Guji Zone Culture and Tourism Bureau, 2016). Although some scholars argue that the system emerged fully-fledged rather than evolved, the Guji Zone's Culture and Tourism Bureau confirms that the system has reached its present status through evolution.

6. The Leading Laws under the Gadaa System

Like any other society, the Oromos have been conscious of their cultural identity, their relationship with nature, and the existence of a powerful force that regulates the connection between nature and society. Accordingly, their knowledge of society and the world is classified into two categories: a) cultural and customary knowledge known as *Beekumsa Aadaa*, and b) knowledge of laws, known as *Beekumsa Seera*. The knowledge of laws is further subdivided into the laws of God (*Seera Waaqa*), and the laws of human beings (*Seera nama*). While the laws of God are immutable, the laws of human beings may be changed through consensus and democratic means. Oromo customary knowledge is a public and common knowledge that guides and regulates the activities of members of society; some elements of this customary knowledge could be developed into rules or laws, depending on the interest of society (Gemetchu, 1993).

The Oromos' political, social, economic, and cultural traits are highly determined by the values of the Gadaa system. There cannot be development (*finna*), peace, social justice, freedom (*kao*), prosperity, success, happiness, and moral values (*safu*) without the Gadaa system (Assefa, 2012).In an interview, Abbaa Gadaa Waqo Duubee affirmed that "Gadaa is our system of governance with age; grade and party descriptions and we use it for all of our spiritual, cultural, political, economic and social matters" (Waaqoo Duubee, 2015). Abbaa Gadaa Jiloo Mandhoo strengthened the argument by saying, "Gadaa system is all in all for us, and it is a means of governing each other, preserving our culture, and protecting our boundary, our peace and security" (Jiloo Mandhoo, 2015).

7. Structural Set Up of the Gadaa Sytem

As will become clear below, the Gadaa system has its own governance structure that depicts the relationship between different actors. Under the system, out of the two fundamental laws (the laws of God and the laws of human beings), the law of God is the guiding principle of the overall governance system. Thus, the Gadaa and its officials are more accountable to the guiding laws of God than to the people. This means the fear of God and His values are the guiding and leading rules. Likewise, under God/next to God, the general public is the most respected and the most influential stakeholder in any kind of decision-making. Then, the assembly (*gumi gayo*) occuppies the decision-making sphere, and the Abbaa Gadaa and his team are highly accountable to the general public. Most importantly, the assembly acts and works in the interest of the people. The seven cabinets are: Abbaa Torbiis (monitors of the implementation of any decisions and laws delivered during sessions of the gumi gayo), Hayyuus (formulators of rules, regulations, and laws), Fagaa (spiritual counselors/advisors and supporters of Luba /Abba Gadaa), Jalkeenya (the protocol officers of Abba Gadaa, and facilitators of the cases), Jaldhaaba (protectors of the laws of the land), and the Waamuras (facilitators of the meetings/assemblies and supporters of Abbaa Gadaa).

Diagram 1: Governance Structure of Gadaa System

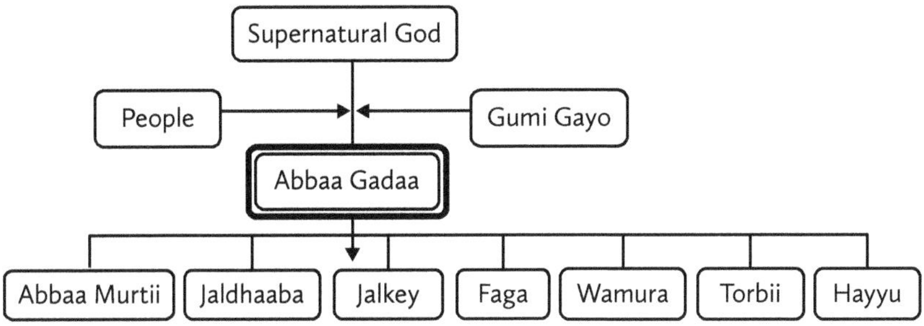

8. Gadaa System's Party Structure

Under the Gadaa system (particularly Guji's Gadaa system) there are five parties (Harmuufa, Roobalee, Muudana, Haalchisa, and Dhallana) that govern/rule as a government one after the other. One party rules for eight years and waits the other four parties to rule and come back to power after forty years. For instance, the party governing up to November 2015 was *Dhallana*, and the *Harmuufa* party came to powerin January 2016. Hence, the *Harmufaa* will govern for the coming eight years, and then will pass power on to *Roobale* in January 2024. The last year's outgoing Gadaa will come back after forty years. Despite their peacefull power transfer and peaceful preparation of candidates, there is tough competition among them. The parties compete with each other, and want their period of governance to be more powerful and fruitful than that of the outgoing and the incoming party.

Diagram 2: Gadaa System's Party Structure

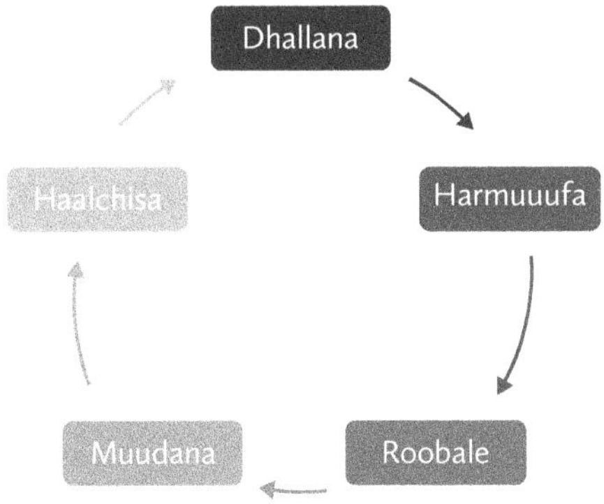

Source: Author

9. Comparative Analysis of the Modern Approach with Gadaa System

Based on the data gathered through a review of literatures on both the Gadaa system and the modern/Western model/approach of democracy, field visits (observation), and the key informant interviews, the researcher identified the basic elements and features of the Gadaa system and compared it with the Western approach/model of democracy. Accordingly, the below table shows the comparison made, and the argument arising out of it.

Table 1: Gadaa system Vs Modern/Western democracy

	Areas of comparison	Gadaa system	Modern/Western democracy
1	Leadership values	God's Value approach	Law's value approach
2	Base of decision-making	Truth-based	Evidence-based
3	Sovereignty	God's Sovereignty and then popular	Popular sovereignty and then elites
4	Center of leadership	In the community	Out of the community
5	Result of political game	Win-win approach	Win-lose approach
6	Inclusiveness/ participation	Inclusive	Exclusion-Limited inclusive
7	Leadership development	Mentorship /continous development	Reactive /chance/ opportunistic
8	Competition	Socially and spiritually guided	Personally or group interests based
10	Means and ends correlation	Communal grand philosophy (means justify ends)	Majority (end justify means)
11	Tests of leadership	Based on excellence	Based on laws

- **Leadership values:** Leadership values are the governing morals and beliefs guiding the practices and procedures of a leadership system. Under the Western model of democracy, the guiding values and principles are the laws formulated by higher decision-makers/MPs. In contrast, under the Gadaa system priority is given to the values and principles of God (*Waaqa*), and these Godly values serve as the general frameworks for all laws and principles. Thus, the fear of God and His values comes first, and respecting the laws of the land takes the second priority. This does not mean that the system resembles a theocratic system, where the divinely appointed officials and priests claiming to know the will of God rule the people or where the state's legal system is based on religious law. It is a system with two foundations. The first foundation is that Oromo's philosophy, culture, governance, and politics build themselves on the fear of a supernatural God and do not engage in any evil acts. The Oromos believe that doing evil is moving against the will of the supernatural God, and they do have fixed norms defining evil. Secondly, under the Gadaa system, a *Qaallu* (spiritual father and counsellor) is very much autonomous and powerful in overseeing the performance, excellence, and the decisions of leaders (Abbaa Gadaa and his councils). Therefore, in contrast to the Western model of democracy, where the fear of God and His powerful laws are overridden and separated from politics and governance in the name of secularism, the Gadaa system prioritizes the fear of the supernatural God in every action and decision and –delegates to *Qalluu* great power in overseeing the leadership and leading some ritual and ceremonial activities. That is why any blessings and proclamations under the Gadaa system starts with *"Waaqa hin Wayyu,"*which means "God shall not be better?"

- **Bases of DecisionMaking:** It is apparent that any decision-making process needs a base for its validity. For instance, under the Western liberal approach to democracy, any decision-making process bases itself on the existence of evidence, and the evidence at hand determines the result of the decision. In the absence of evidence either there is no decision or an incorrect decision. In contrast, under the Gadaa system, as the governance system is highly attached to spiritual values and principles, priority is given to searching for the truth, rather than the evidence. For instance, under the Western model, if someone is accused of sexual harassment and there is no evidence for it, a person would be free, even if he had committed the crime. Under the Gadaa system, the spiritual values are the most respected elements and there is a belief that the result of lying is very harmful. Thus, even in the absence of evidence, the accused person would speak the truth to the court.

- **Sovereignty:** In the Western model of democracy, the principle of popular sovereignty is prioritized and praised publically. But in practice, elites' sovereignty is highly appreciated. However, under the Gadaa System, God's values are the sovereign and highly valued principles and receive the highest consideration, while popular sovereignty is valued as the second most important priority.

- **Center of Leadership:** By its very nature, the Western model of leadership spotlights the headquarters leadership model, where the higher decision-makers live and work at the capital city of the nation or the country so that leadership is by distance, and laws and procedures are propogated down to the people. This system is called *off-the community leadership,* wherein leadership is located far from the populace. But under the Gadaa system, the leadership takes power and immediately starts its journey within the community. For their eight years of leadership, the officials move within the community so that they can treat all local community problems in person. This leadership is called *in the community leadership,* in which the life and living of leadership bases itself in and with the community.

- **The Result of Political Game:** Politics is a game where the outcome of competing actors results in either lose-lose or win-win or win-lose scenarios. Hence, in a democracy of the Western model, political games mostly result in a win-lose outcome, in which the incoming party would win the game of politics and the outgoing one is always the loser, and election is the instrument of the game. Under the Gadaa system, as a rule of politics there are five political parties, and age set generations with different stages. Both the incoming and the outgoing Abba Gadaas are winners in the game. This is because when the incoming Abba Gadaa holds the position, his team moves one step forward with in Gadaa class; likewise, the outgoing Abba Gadaa also joins the Baatu class, or one step forward within the class. Then, with his team, the outgoing Abba Gadaa becomes a senior advisor and part of the highest decision-making class. Thus, the power transferring system always results in a win-win outcome where both the incoming and outgoing Abbaa Gadaas wait for the day of power transfer with a lovely gift in kind for each other. Finally, they discuss and consult each other on how to go forward together in the future.

- **Inclusiveness/Participation:** Basically in a Western model of democracy, politics is dominated by those who can and are capable of running the affairs of the state. It implicitly excludes children, the young, and the elderly from the stadium of political affairs. But as the political participation under Gadaa system is based on age set, anyone joins the age set structure based on the age class, and the system is inclusive of all the age sets. On the other hand, the system is partly criticized by its lower concern to women's representation, particularly in the age-set of the Gadaa class. The research conducted for this chapter confirmed the concerns of critics in two ways. Firstly, the system excludes women from the age-set leadership development process. Secondly, the system also puts zero probability for women to compete with men and hold leadership positions, particularly the Abba Gadaaship.

Nevertheless the system includes the following two main ground rules to validate women's participation in various arenas. Firstly, under the Gadaa system there is an assumption that there are two types of power: positional power and influencing power. The men have positional power and the women have influencing power in the decision-making process. In other words, the women do influence the system of decision-making either through direct or indirect consultation. Secondly, the system provides an indirect mechanism for engaging women into political and leadership positions. For instance, to protect their rights and to ensure that their interests are included in any spheres of decision-making, the women have their own institution, called *Siiqqee*. This institution is a means through which women influence the processes and the structures of decision-making under the Gadaa system. Debela (2017) and Aseffa (2011) also confirm that the Gadaa system promotes women's participation in all cases and that the women are the pillars of the Gadaa system.

– **Leadership Development:** The Western model of democracy is well-known for its competitive nature. The one who is the fittest will gain of all the chances, and the *survival of the fittest approach* is the guiding principle of leadership. With this value, an opportunistic approach to leadership is the most widely visible one, and chances and opportunities play an important role in helping people to engage in a leadership and political environment. In contrast, under the Gadaa system, mentorship of leadership starts from early childhood, and leadership development is progressive by its very nature. Thus, leadership development is the main value of the system, wherein all people attach themselves to their respective leadership development categories and a junior-senior hierarchy and mentorship process is arranged within the system.

– **System of Political Competition:** Under both systems there is competition for different reasons, especially for power and political representations. Under the Western model of democracy, the culture of political competition is based on hate, personal decisions, and determinations, which exacerbates conflicts, hates, and hatred. In contrast, under the Gadaa system, the competition is very peaceful where it is based on performance and excellence; keeping social and spiritual values as it is.

Any competition which runs out of the social values would be condemned publically.

- **Accountability:** Regarding the level of accountability, in the so-called Western democracy, elected and appointed officials are responsible for their actions and are accountable to the people. Officials must make decisions and perform their duties according to the wishes of the people they represent. Thus, irrespective of the interests and claims (good or bad) of the people, officials' leadership is supposed to be guided by the values of the people they represent, which is why homosexuality, racism, and immorality are re-emerging globally. But, as we have already mentioned, currently the system is criticized in many ways, and citizens often feel powerless and discouraged from taking active role in their society (CEFFD, 2007). As a result, the reality shows the reverse of the proclaimed vision, where a party's accountability is the dominating concern over popular accountability. But, under the Gadaa system, the first and foremost accountability is the supernatural God (*Waaqa*), where all leaders believe that God is the master of everything, and the provider of any authority. Thus, not only elitits' and party superiority but even popular accountability comes aftera God's accountability.

- **Means – Ends Correlation:** In the Western model of governance, the fundamental principle guiding any actions and efforts is the fact that ends justify the means. In contrast, the reverse works under the Gadaa system. For instance, under the Western model of governance, despite the intentions and the reasons behind a given act, if the majority agrees with the act, it will be valid. But, under the Gadaa system, it is not the majority which matters but that which t doesn't contradict God's and social values, tbenefits the people, and does not contradict cultural laws and the philosophies of the community.

- **Tests of Leadership:** Under the Western model of democracy there is no specific term of leadership for all countries: different countries use different periods (terms) of leadership. Leaders stay in power for the term of leadership given to them either by periodic election or by constitutional provision. In contrast, under the Gadaa system, firstly, the term of leadership is fixed, always eight years by its very nature. Secondly, the term of leadership is not a guarantee of remaining in power. Though the term is eight years, if the leading Gadaa class is not functioning well, evaluation will be carried out in the middle of the term (four years) and the leadership will continue leading based on the result of mid-term evaluation.

10. Conclusion

In Africa, many ethnic groups have their own (indigenous) forms of governance characterized by remarkable qualities. In Ethiopia, the Oromos are one of the indigenous peoples with their own indigenous governance system, called the Gadaa System. The main objective of the study was to assess the basic qualities of the Gadaa system and to compare it with the Western model of democracy. The comparison was made based on eleven identified values, like leadership values, base of decision-making, sovereignty, center of leadership, result of political game, inclusiveness/participation, leadership development, competition means and ends correlation, and tests of leadership. Finally the study found that the Gadaa system is imbedded in the heart and soul of the people and is superior to the Western model of democracy in terms of the above values. Finally, the study suggests that the government should support indigenous knowledge, particularly the indigenous governance system in terms of policy provision and structural setup.

Acknowledgements

This chapter is based on fieldwork research financed by the Institute of Indigenous Studies, Dilla University. So, I would like to thank the Institute, and Mr. Zelalem Tesfaye Sirna for their cooperation during fieldwork. I also thank anonymous reviewers for their very constructive comments.

Notes

1. www.google.nl/search?q Org iities of Abya Yala: of Citizens (ATTAC): Iipftaa. Org/ the Principles of Democracy.
2. www.google.nl/search?q Org iities of Abya Yala: of Citizens (ATTAC): Iipftaa. Org/ the Principles of Democracy.
3. is defined as the cumulative body of strategies, practices, techniques, tools, intellectual resources, explanations, beliefs, and values accumulated over time in a particular locality, without the interference and impositions of external hegemonic forces (Gloria and George 2004).
4. Ethiopia's largest ethnic group living in central and southern Ethiopia.
5. The Gadaa system took its present-day structure only during the fifteenth century; previously, the system was very complex and not as strong as of today's.

References

Asebe, R. (2007): Ethnicity and Inter-ethnic Relations: The "Ethiopian Experiment" and the Case of the Guji and Gedeo. MPhil Thesis, University of Tromsø Norway.

Aseffa, J. (2005): *Oromia & Ethiopia: State Formation and Ethno-national Conflict*, 1868-2004. Lawrenceville, NJ: The Red Sea Press.

Aseffa, J. (2012): Gadaa (Oromo Democracy): An Example of Classical African Civilization. *The Journal of Pan African Studies*, 5(1): 126-152.

Aseffa, J. (2011): The Oromo in Exile: Creating Knowledge and Promoting Social Justice. *Societies without Borders* 6(1):33-72.A

Asmarom, J. (1973): Gada: Three Approaches to the Study of African Society, The Free Press, A division of Macmillan Publishing Co., Inc., New York.

Asmarom, L. (1980): Human Rights in African Political Culture. In K. W. Thompson (ed.). *The Moral Imperatives of Human Rights: a World Survey*. Washington, DC: University Press of America.pp, 123-138.

Asmarom, L. (2006). *Oromo Democracy; An Indigenous African Political System*. Lawrenceville, NJ: Red Sea Press.

Ayittey, G. (1991). *Indigenous African Institutions*. New York: Transnational Publishers Inc.

Baissa, L. (2004). The Oromo Gadaa System of Government: An Indigenous African Democracy. In Jalata, A. (ed.). *State Crises, Globalisation and National Movements in Democratic Pretension and Performance* (pp. 101-121). London: Zed Books.

Baissa, L. (1994). Gada Values: The Building Blocks of Democratic Oromo Polity. *Journal of Oromo Studies*, 1(2): 53-58.

CEFFD. (2007). Conclusions of the Council of Europe Forum for the Future of Democracy, June 2007.

Debela, F. (2017). Indegneous Mechanism as a Foundation for AfSol Comprehension: Lessons from Gadaa Sytem of the Oromo Nation in Ethiopia. *Sociology and Anthropology*, 5(5): 279.

Demissie, D. (2011). Oromo Wisdom in Black Civilization. *Addis Ababa: Finfinne Printing and Publishing SC.*

Forbrig, J. (2005). *Revisiting Youth Political Participation, Challenges for Research and Democratic Practise in Europe*. Council of Europe Publishing.

Gemetchu, M. (1993). Knowledge, Identity, and the Colonizing Structure: The Case of the Oromo in East and Northeast Africa. PhD dissertation: University of London.

Gloria.E and George, D. (2004). *African Indigenous Knowledge and the Disciplines*. Rotterdam: Sense Publishers.

Guji Zone Culture and Tourism Bureau. (2016). Power Transfering Sytem of Oromo Guji, Bulletin, Finfinne.

Hassen, M. (1990). *The Oromo of Ethiopia: A History 1570-1860*. Cambridge: Cambridge University Press.

Holcomb, B. and Sisai, I. (1990). *The Invention of Ethiopia: The Making of a Dependent Colonial State in North Africa*. Trenton, NJ: The Red Sea Press, Inc.

Jan, Z. (2011). *The Oromo Secessionism in a Broader Context of the Horn of Africa. The Horn of Africa at the Brink of the 21st Century – Coping with Fragmentation, Isolation and Marginalization in a Globalizing Environment*. Uppsala: ECAS 4.

Kojo, D. (2017). Rethinking the Role of Indigenous Governance Practices in Contemporary Governance in Africa: The Case of Ghana. MA Thesis, Royal Roads University Victoria, British Columbia.

Kuwee, K. (1997). The Siiqqee Institution of Oromo Women. *Journal of Oromo Studies*, 4(1): 115-152.

Paula and Jean-Aime (2008). *What is Democracy*: Realized by KMF-CNOE & NOVA STELLA with the assistance of the Friedrich-Ebert-Stiftung (FES) and with the Collaboration of Friedel Daiber (University of Trier), Antananarivo.

Sithole, P., and Thamsanqa, M. (2008). Fifteen Years Review on Traditional Leadership. Research Paper, Human Science Research Council.

Terry, D. (2006). Introductory Speech at the Summer University for Democracy, organized by the Council of Europe.

Tsegaye, G. (1964). http://www.youtube.com/watch?v=8b0VWiEyN7I (January 08, 2015) (Madha Galama Abba Gada; a poem).

Tshwane University. (2013). Second International Arts Conference Poster Document, Hhosted by the Faculty of the Arts, Tshwane University of Technology, South Africa.

Warren, D. (1991). Using Indigenous Knowledge in Agricultural Development. World Bank Discussion Paper.

Zelalem, T. (2012). Ethiopia: When the Gadaa Democracy Rules in a Federal State Bridging Indigenous Institutions of Governance to Modern Democracy. MA Thesis, University of Tromso.

Zelalem, T. (2015): Old Wine in New Bottles: Bridging the Peripheral Gadaa Rule to the Mainstream Constitutional Order of the 21st C Ethiopia. *Oromia Law Journal*.

Zelalem, T. (2018): A Future Gaze: Gadaa Oriented Constitutional Structure for Oromia. *Journal of Institute of Oromoo Studies* 1 (1): 9-25.

III

PEOPLE AS HUMAN RESOURCES

Introduction

Among existing managerial functions and resources, human resources are a key leverage function for a performing public sector. This part consists of four complementary chapters. The first chapter (chapter 12) discusses meritocracy, career development, and promotion in the Ethiopian civil service. One of the prime messages of the chapter is that, despite the human resource management legal frameworks and directives, the recruitment, promotion, and career development in the federal civil service combines elements of meritocracy and patronage. The latter appears to be more significant, particularly for top and strategic positions. The next chapter (chapter 13) explores the continuities and changes in human resource management in the Oromia National Regional State, the largest region in Ethiopia. It reveals that, notwithstanding the changes, the politico-administrative reforms were predominantly used to enhance the loyalty of the civil servants to the political executives at the expense of improving their well-being and serving the citizens. Chapter 14 focuses on identifying the role of middle-level managers in Ethiopian civil service organizations. One of the key findings of the chapter is that middle-level managers are systematically balancing competing roles, but the balance shifts. They do tend to give higher priorities to certain roles over others. Chapter 15 explores the Ethiopian civil service system and its implications for leadership roles. All authors have presented key conclusions and insights demonstrating the essential and dynamic nature of HRM in the context of a developing state.

12

Meritocracy, Career Development, and Promotion in Ethiopian Civil Service

Henok Seyoum Assefa

Box 1: Key Points of this chapter

- ✓ A system that guides the process of recruitment and selection in civil service institutions does exist.
- ✓ There is a gap with regard to its proper implementation.
- ✓ The Ethiopian civil service is basically a position-based civil service system.
- ✓ In practice, Ethiopian civil service is characterized by "mixed" recruitment patterns: competitive written examinations and comparison of the paper qualifications already possessed by the candidate.
- ✓ Personal connections and nepotism are prevalent in recruitment processes.
- ✓ Recruitment and appointment of senior civil servants is loosely regulated.

Box 2: Key Insights of this chapter

This chapter intends to discuss meritocracy within the Ethiopian bureaucracy based on empirical data so as to answer the questions to what extent is the Ethiopian civil service characterized by meritocratic recruitment; does it predictable, rewarding long-term careers; and what factors influence meritocratic recruitments and career development.

Box 3: Abbreviations

DS = Developmental State
FDRE = Federal Democratic Republic of Ethiopia
HR = Human Resource
NGOs = Non-Governmental Organizations

1. Introduction

Ethiopia is a federal state with civil service systems at the central, state, and local government levels. Therefore, the Ethiopian bureaucracy comprises many local governments' "civil services," nine regional state civil services, two city administrations, a federal civil service and several federal and state government agencies, parastatals, and corporations. An examination of bureaucracy in this study shall primarily focuses on the federal civil service. It is, however, pertinent to point out that the character of bureaucracy at the central level to some extent gives a general picture of at the situation in the different states of the federation.

Ethiopia has officially been branding itself as a developmental state since the early 2000s. In the context of the developmental state, the basic framework of the public administration might be expected to incorporate a highly competitive, extensive, relatively efficient, and effective public bureaucracy.

In this light, it is pertinent to argue that Ethiopia needs to have a public service that is competent, professional, autonomous, and strong, among other qualities,; if it desires to use the state as a crucial vehicle to realize its developmental objectives. However, Ethiopian public service is said, by the government and others, to be weak, and daily government reports (i.e., many parliamentary reports and higher government officials' press releases) indicate that implementation failure is the major problem of the government. By the same token, studies of the Ethiopian developmental state (Desta Asayehgn, 2012; Fantini, 2013; UNDP, 2012) criticize the current public service as dysfunctional and unable to implement policies and carry out the ideals of the developmental state (DS).

Thus, the creation of a meritocratic bureaucracy and extensive state capacity is imperative

Meritocratic bureaucracy depends, among other things, on the organization and management of career development. Civil servants should have opportunities to realize their full potential. They should be able to attain higher positions commensurate with their capabilities and demonstrated achievements. In other words, apart from the meritocratic recruitment into the public service, it is essential to consider merit in the promotion of personnel. This is accepted universally as a general principle. By the same token, since civil servants at top management positions have major impact on government policy implementation, they need to be selected and/or promoted carefully.

In order to address these issues the chapter is organized into five sections. The first section is an introduction that gives an overview of the chapter, including the objective, statement of the problem, and the main question.

This study questions whether Ethiopian civil service is meritocratic or not. To this end, meritocracy in the Ethiopian civil service is evaluated in terms of the legal environment, recruitment, promotion, performance appraisal, and transfer. In section 2, the relevant literature (books, journals, and research proceedings) related to the topic under discussion is reviewed. The third section presents the methodology by which the research was guided and data were collected and analyzed. Data presentation and discussions are entertained in the fourth section. Section five presents conclusions and possible recommendations.

2. Literature Review

2.1. The Concept of Meritocracy

Meritocracy, or government by those with talent, seems self-evidently a good idea. The most able people will produce the best possible results and therefore the public welfare of the whole population will be optimized. Meritocracy, therefore, offers a fair system that result in better outcomes for both the individual and society. Meritocracy provides talented and hard-working people from all walks of life with a means of advancement and the opportunity to contribute to the well-being of the larger society. It can be a powerful vehicle for social mobility and incentivize people to do their best and reach their fullest potential (UNDP, 2015:4).

Meritocratic recruitment and career progression is one of the key features of Weber's ideal type bureaucracy. Meritocratic civil service emphasizes talent and education. It is a system of governance based on ability rather than on wealth, race, or other determinants of induction. The literature tells us that bureaucracies in successful developmental states are characterized by meritocratic recruitment, provision of promotion incentives, rationality, and guarantees of high levels of prestige and legitimacy to bureaucratic officials (Johnson, 1982).

An important study by Evans and Rauch (1999) considered whether state bureaucracies characterized by meritocratic recruitment and predictable, rewarding career ladders are associated with higher growth rates (Evans and Rauch, 1999:760).

Furthermore, the highly influential 1997 World Development Report asserted that "making a meritocracy of the civil service helps bring in high-quality staff, confers prestige on civil service positions, and can do a great deal to motivate good performance" (World Bank, 1997: 92). Where instead promotions are personalized or politicized, civil servants worry more about pleasing their superiors among influential politicians, and efforts to build prestige through tough recruitment standards are undercut (World Bank, 1997:93).

Meritocratic bureaucracies typically attract the best graduates in a country, who upon entering public administration are able to follow long-term career paths and work according to the rules and established norms within the bureaucracy (Dasandi, 2014).The absence of meritocracy in the bureaucracy, on the other hand, is generally seen to produce public administrations that are inflated, inefficient, dishonest, and lacking in autonomy from political leaders (Fritzen and Menocal, 2007).

In the context of the civil service, meritocracy is commonly discussed in connection with recruitment and promotion practices. Evans and Rauch underline that the importance of meritocratic recruitment, which ideally is based on some combination of education and examination, needs to be considered with a second characteristic: a predictable career ladder, which provides long-term tangible and intangible rewards for those recruited into the bureaucracy (Evans and Rauch, 1999:751).

As far as promotion is concerned, two systems are popular in many countries: career-based and position-based. Countries with a career-based system tend to have a relatively high degree of mobility and sophisticated promotion mechanisms. As a result, they also usually have a definition of senior civil servants which includes a large number and goes relatively low in the hierarchy. However, one of the main drawbacks of such systems lies in the difficulty of maintaining a good degree of competition between candidates to senior positions over time, resulting, to various degrees, in weaker performance criteria for promotion (OECD, 2003:15).

Therefore, meritocracy, basically, includes: meritocratic recruitment, an objective performance evaluation system accompanied by incentives and punishments, and merit based promotion.

2.2. Bureaucracies in Developmental States

The civil service is the major facilitator for implementing the will of the state as expressed through public policy; and it is a professional body of officials, permanent, paid, and skilled (Finer, cited in Briggs, 2007). It is a system that offers equal opportunities to all citizens to enter the government service, equal pay to all employees doing work requiring the same degree of intelligence and capacity, equal opportunities for advancement, equal favorable conditions, and equal participation in retirement allowances, and equal demands upon the employees (Willoughby cited in Briggs, 2007). It is indispensable to the functioning of the modern state, which is why the fate of a society is largely determined by the performance of the public service (Basu, cited in Briggs, 2007).

The major requirements of meritocratic civil service are that it should be impartially selected, administratively competent, politically neutral, and imbued with the spirit of service to the community (Gladden, 1948). Hence, human resource management and development processes in effective bureaucracies are required to abide by competence-based recruitment, promotion, appraisal, remuneration, etc. based on merit principles.

The literature tells us that bureaucracies in successful developmental states are characterized by meritocratic recruitment, provision of promotion incentives, rationality, and guarantees of high levels of prestige and legitimacy to bureaucratic officials (Johnson, 1982). This has also been identified as a key factor distinguishing developmental states from the neo-patrimonial: while in the former recruitment and promotions in the bureaucracy are meritocratic, they are more personalized in the latter (Leftwich, 1995). Meritocratic bureaucracies, in successful developmental states, typically attract the best graduates in a country, who upon entering public administration are able to follow long-term career paths and work according to the rules and established norms within the bureaucracy (Dasandi, 2014).

In Korea, for example, a major reform took place within the bureaucracy in the 1960s. The government reintroduced a highly competitive and open exam system for the higher and lower echelons of the civil service,which attracted the best Korean students from the country's two universities due to the social prestige usually associated with administrative positions. What is more, a strong policy of internal promotion and reducing the share of appointees also contributed to bureaucratic competence in the Korean developmental state (Mah, 2011). Similarly, the public administration in Singapore is probably the most educated professional body among public servants in the world and constitutes a major explanatory factor in the meteoric rise of that country (Adei, 2008). The absence of meritocratic bureaucracy, on the other hand, is generally seen to produce public administrations that are inflated, inefficient, dishonest, and lacking autonomy from political leaders (Smith, 2009).

In the early 2000s, the developmental state rhetoric surfaced in Ethiopian politics. A policy discussion document titled "Democratic Developmental State" was produced in 2003 by the government. A series of seminars and conferences were organized around this issue. Hence, taking the claim made by Ethiopian government to be developmental state into consideration, it is imperative to evaluate the civil service and ask whether it is in alignment with the requirements of the developmental state, inter alia, with meritocratic bureaucracy.

2.3. Historical Overview of Ethiopian Civil Service

Early Stage

The Ethiopian civil service is a century old. Yet, the establishment of modern state organizations in Ethiopia took place very late relative to Europe and other parts of the world. The early years of the twentieth century witnessed the beginning of modern public administration and the emergence of civil servants in Ethiopia (Adebabay, 2011). In 1907 nine ministries were established, with the aim of ensuring an orderly and efficient arrangement for the workings of government (MoCSGG, 2012). The ministries were: Ministry of Justice, Ministry of Interior, Ministry of Commerce and Foreign Affairs, Ministry of Finance, Ministry of Agriculture and Industry, Ministry of Public Works, Ministry of War, Ministry of Pen, and Ministry of Palace (Bahiru, 1991; MoCSGG, 2012; Pankhurst, 1997).

Initially, the ministries were organized in the crude form of the 20th-century European civil service model. As Perham, cited in Paulos (2001:83) states, in 1907-1908 the ministries of justice, war, the interior, commerce and foreign affairs, finance and agriculture, and public works were created and in 1911 a ministry for posts and telegraphs were added while foreign affairs became a separate ministry. The ministries were housed in buildings set up within the palace enclosure (Ibid., 2001:84). The same source states that the ministers were not salaried and appointment was based on loyalty and the number of followers that they could mobilize during wartime. The civil servants were also small in number and were primarily engaged in maintaining law and order.

This formal framework of government under "a Western-inspired" administrative system brought Ethiopia into the twentieth century (Adebabay, 2011:7). Prior to this period, the country was under traditional administration and the different Ethiopian monarchs had failed to build any kind of administrative framework through which they could exercise their absolute power (Paulos, 2001:83).

The attempt to establish modern government organizations was made before the introduction of any formal education, in a sense, putting the horse before the cart. As a result, these ministries were run by feudal lords and priests, with a slight of knowledge reading and writing obtained from church education. Hence, the establishment of the modern administration was not accompanied by the promulgation of personnel rules and regulations. Indeed, the initial years were characterized by inadequate structures, inefficient services, corruption, and the interference of the nobility in the due process of law in public matters (MoCSGG, 2012). The government officials' prime objective was to promote the personal interest of the clergy and the nobility. This situation prevailed for about half a century, leading to mass dissatisfaction and frustration (Getachew and Richard, 2006).

Civil Service during Emperor Hailesellassie I

Emperor Hailesellassie I had the best claim of instituting modern public administration. It was during his reign that the process of centralizing and modernizing the state reached a relatively advanced stage.

The emperor, during his early days in power, created further ministries for industry, education and fine arts, justice, and public works and Communications (Perham cited in Paulos, 2001:84). From 1930-1935 many important attempts at reform were taken, including: new measures for training the army, the inauguration of a parliament, the development of education, judicial reform, the engagement of foreign advisors, and measures for the abolition of slavery (Ibid).

The implementation of reforms was discontinued as a result of the Italian occupation of 1935-1941. But, after its end and the emperor's return to power, many reforms were carried out and the whole ministerial system was completely reorganized and greatly extended (Bahru, 1991). Later on in his reign, Emperor Hailesellassie undertook a series of institutionalization and restructuring measures in the hope of bringing about an effective and efficient civil service governed by specified rules and procedures of a uniform nature. These included:

a) **The Administrative Regulation Decree No. 1 of 1942:** Among other things, the decree instituted the appointment by the center of governors general, directors, governors, principal secretaries, *meslanes*,[1] and police to each province.
b) **An Order to Define the Powers and Duties of the Ministries, No. 1 of 1943 and An Order to Amend the Ministers (Definition of Powers) Order, 1943, No. 2 of 1943:** Through these two orders, the Council of Ministers was created. Twelve ministers were listed, their powers and relations were defined, and the Office of the Prime Minister was established. The Office of the Prime Minster was made head of all ministries and was responsible for the good administration of all the work in the ministries, harmonizing their duties and transmitting the emperor's orders (Perham, cited inPaulos, 2001:84). The ministers, among other duties and responsibilities, were charged with the duty of preparing draft

laws – except those reserved for the emperor. They were also empowered to appoint their staff and prepare budget estimates.

c) **The revised constitution of 1955**: This constitution made a clear distinction between posts of confidence and career posts. In Article 66, it states that the emperor has the right to select, appoint, and dismiss the prime minister and all other ministers and vice-ministers. The appointment, promotion, transfer, suspension, retirement, dismissal, and discipline of all other government officials and employees was to be governed by regulations made by the Council of Ministers, to be approved and proclaimed by the emperor.
d) **The establishment of the Imperial Institute of Public Administration in 1952:** this was a significant development for the administration of the country. Its objectives included the training of civil servants, consultation, and research.

The 1960s were a remarkable period in Ethiopian civil service history. During this time modern personnel orders, policies, and directives were introduced. The Central Personnel Agency was established in the same period. The purpose of all these reforms was to establish uniform and rule-driven civil service across Ethiopia. Almost all orders and directives were adopted from the Western personnel management systems, mainly from the United States. The reforms had the following effects: a uniform personnel management system was established throughout the nation; Western-type merit principles were introduced for the first time in the nation's history; the principle of equal pay for equal value of work was introduced with the position classification job evaluation method; and the Central Personnel Agency was established (Adebabay, 2011:7).

As a result, some very important tasks were attached to the agency. First, it was entrusted with the responsibility of establishing a homogeneous public service governed by uniform rules and principles. Second, it was assigned the responsibility to recruit for both classified and unclassified positions, based on open competitive examination. In other words, merit as a criterion for appointment was introduced, replacing the old method, which was based on favoritism or ascription. Likewise, the agency had the power and responsibility of all appointments exceptto ministerial ranks. The grading and the salary structure were to be based on the position classification system. Finally, a pension scheme for public servants was instituted (Asmelash, cited in Paulos, 2001:86).

However, despite these administrative and institutional arrangements, the high regard given to political loyalty in assigning civil service posts and the level of political interference negatively affected standard operating procedures

(Getachew and Richard, 2006). For example, people were employed through personal acquaintance and relationships withthe nobility. Anyone who did not have some kind of relationships, no matter how intelligent, was refused any kind of service or employment. It was, therefore, a widely established culture among the people to pay tribute and bribes to the nobility in order to get any kind of service from the public office. Judges and local officials were under the influence of the nobility (MoCSGG, 2012). As a result, the Ethiopian civil service repeatedly failed to deliver intended services to the public.

Paulos (2001:86) also discussed some other problems of the then civil service as:

> ... *the absence of strict adherence to the civil service rules and regulations, and political interference in administrative affairs were seen as chronic problems of the time. However, generally speaking, during the period, the foundation of the modern bureaucracy was laid down and the importance of an efficient administrative system was recognized. Consequently, the civil service seemed to be accepted as the chief instrument available to governments for promoting economic and social development.*

Civil Service during Dergue

The political economy system of this regime favored central economic planning and banned private ownership. As a result, the nationalization measures, along with the proliferation of new government institutions and corporations, led to a tremendous expansion of the public sector (Getachew and Richard, 2006). At the same time, the government converted the civil service into an instrument for promoting its communist ideology and ruling the people.

There were two confusing structures at this time (Paulos, cited in Adebabay, 2011): the political and the functional. All the decisions in the civil service institutions were made through the political structures by political cadres. There was virtually no place for apolitical professionals. In other words, under the military regime, the civil service was highly politicized and most top- and middle-ranking civil servants were members of the military regime's party, known as the Ethiopian Workers Party.

Therefore, as described by Hiwet, (cited in Getachew and Richard, 2006) the regime was a combined "military/bureaucratic dictatorship." In connection with this, the military administration issued many instructions, rules, and regulations to control the civil service institutions within the boundary of its ideology (Debela, nd).

During this period there were no fundamental reform measures promulgated to alter or modify the functioning and management of the civil service. Except for the introduction of a few reform measures, the civil service operated under the different orders and decrees issued during the reign of Hailesellassie (Paulos, 2001:86). Of course, some new ministries, commissions, agencies, and authorities were created, while others were merged or dissolved. Many were also renamed. A case in point is the Central Personnel Agency, which was renamed the Public Service Commission. The Dergue also took some reform measures with regard to the salary scale of the civil service. The major ones were: the increase in the starting salary of the civil service from Br. 25 to Br. 50 (in 1975) and a shift in the ceiling from Br. 285 to Br. 636 for eligibility of periodic salary increment (in 1982) (Paulos, 2001:86).

However, despite such attempts of organizational and administrative reforms, the civil service remained problematic. According to Meheret (cited in Getachew and Richard, 2006), the Dergue regime was put in disarray by the fusion of the institutions of party, state, and government. It also encouraged the proliferation of parallel structures by appointing party functionaries to key decision-making civil service positions (Paulos, 2001:87) Hence duplication and fragmentation of public functions and the downplaying of merit and professionalism became the order of the day. The subsequent years were characterized by the centralization of administration in addition to increases in corruption, inefficient service delivery, and the routine neglect of the due process of law in matters of public concern (Getachew and Richard, 2006). As a result, the civil service inherited by the succeeding government was seriously weak in its capacity to implement government policies and to deliver public services.

2.4. The Legal Framework Governing the Ethiopian Civil Service

The currently effective rule under implementation for the Ethiopian civil service is the Federal Civil Servants Proclamation No. 1064/2017, which was issued to address the problems identified during the implementation of proclamation No. 515/2007. Every aspect of the Ethiopian civil service is supposed to function in accordance with this proclamation and the then-FDRE public service commission follows up if every civil service institution implements the proclamation accordingly.

In the context of Ethiopia, the public service is broadly defined as those employees of the state who are covered by national and civil service laws. Accordingly, civil servants are government employees governed by the Federal Civil Servants' Proclamation number 1064/2017. According to Proclamation No 1064/2017, article 1: A civil servant means a person employed permanently by a federal government institution; provided, however, it shall not include the following:

a) Government officials with the rank of state minister, deputy director general, and their equivalent and above;
b) Members of the House of Peoples' Representatives and the House of Federation;
c) Federal judges and prosecutors;
d) Members of the armed forces and the federal police, including other employees governed by the regulations of the armed forces and the federal police; and
e) Employees who are excluded from the coverage of this proclamation by other appropriate laws.

Thus the proclamation excludes from the civil service elected officials, legislators, the judiciary, the armed forces, and the federal police. The civil service therefore denotes the nonpolitical or permanent executives recruited to serve the government in the implementation of policies through the management and conduct of governmental affairs.

The Ethiopian civil service applies a "career-based system" of employment for civil servants in several sectors, like teachers and health professionals, and a "position-based" system for others. Many of the merit principles in setting up career structures from recruitment to promotion are adapted to the Proclamation. Typically, civil servants are recruited at various services and grades within the public service. Entry grades may be at junior level or at senior level. "A vacant position shall be filled only by a person who meets a qualification required for the position and scores higher than any other candidates" (Federal Civil Servants Proclamation No. 1064/2017, article 13). This shows that civil service institutions make an effort to match the competencies of new recruits to specific classified positions. Thus, in general, staffs are expected to successfully meet the position requirements and there are no specialist career paths. Basically, therefore, it is more of a position-based civil service system.

The Federal Civil Service Proclamation lays down requirements for entry into the public service. Concerning selection and recruitment of new staff, the human resource planning of each civil service organization is expected to enable a government institution to take measure to meet the objective specified in the strategic plan and to forecast its human resource demand. The Proclamation declares that while filling vacancies in the civil service, there shall be no discrimination among job seekers or civil servants because of their ethnic origin, sex, religion, political outlook, disability, HIV/AIDS status, or any other ground. Similarly, the HRM reform program has recognized that greater use of open recruitment and improved competitive promotions are fundamental to the development of a "modern" civil service (MoCSGG, 2012). Thus, at least legally public service positions are supposed to be filled on the basis of merit.

As stipulated in the FDRE constitution article 74/2 the prime minister appoints ministers for ministerial posts (FDRE, 1995). Similarly regional governments appoint the heads of various institutions under their jurisdiction. It is, therefore, both at national and regional levels that ministers and bureau heads are expected to lead their respective offices, including HR activities. In many government institutions HR activity is located within a specific HR unit within the ministry or bureau. Responsibility for examining and recommending a candidate for a post lies with the human resource/personnel department of the respective institution. Accordingly, civil service can recruit at the department and service head levels. In the higher service the successful candidate is appointed to office by the concerned minister. The middle and lower staff are appointed to office by the director of the service concerned or the head of the personnel department of the ministry. Hence, despite the fact that the civil service is centrally controlled, staff management in the Ethiopian civil service is still relatively decentralized.

According to the federal civil servants' Proclamation (No. 1064/2017) promotion shall be given for the purpose of enhancing the performance of government institutions with an intention of motivating the employees. Similarly, transfer in the civil service system, whenever necessary, is based on a transparent procedure. A government institution may transfer a civil servant to another similar position of an equal grade and salary or to another place of work within the government institution. This can happen among other government institutions also, whenever necessary and when the recipient and sender government institutions as well as the civil servant agree. Once the consent of the aforementioned parties isgained, transferring a civil servant to a similar position of equal grade and salary from other government institution can be done by notifying the ministry (ibid). According to this proclamation, the purpose of promotion and transfer is to enable civil servants to discharge their duties effectively in accordance with the expected level, quality standards, time, and expense.

Concerning remunerations, the Ethiopian civil service proclamation states that any newly appointed civil servant shall be paid the base salary as fixed by the civil service salary scale for the position to which he/she is appointed. According to the proclamation, the civil service minister prepares a salary scale to be applicable to the civil service in general, submits the same to the Council of Ministers, and supervises its proper implementation upon approval. The ministry, also upon permission of the Council of Ministers and based on the specific nature of thegovernment institution concerned, shall study salary scales and submit the same to the council. Upon approval, it supervises their proper implementation and when necessary, shall undertake periodical revisions of salary scales based on economic changes and other relevant conditions and submit these revisions to for approval by the Council of Ministers.

The proclamation also states that all positions of equal value shall have equal base salary and that periodical salary increases to civil servants shall be based on their performance evaluation results. That is, if a civil servant obtains an evaluation result of satisfactory or above satisfactory, he/she shall be entitled to a salary increase to be made every two years (FDRE Proclamation No. 1064/2017).

Generally speaking, the country has good policy frameworks that promote meritocratic recruitment practices. However, empirical evidence in this study reveals that guidelines for recruitment and other human resource functions mostly do not adhere to the legal frameworks. Thus, it can be argued that the problem is not the absence of legislative framework, but rather the implementation of the legislation.

3. Theoretical Framework and Methodology

The theoretical framework used to analyze the meritocracy in the Ethiopian civil service is institutional theory. Generally speaking, institutional theory is a theoretical framework for analyzing social phenomena that views the social world as significantly comprised of institutions – enduring rules, practices, and structures that set conditions for action. Institutions are fundamental in explaining the social world because they are built into the social order and direct the flow of social life.

Thus, the main argument of institutional theory is that institutional factors play a major role in defining and underpinning state capacity. The key to state/bureaucratic capacity is, therefore, "finding the right institutional framework" or rules of the game (Andrews, 2013:4).The theory also tries to explain how and why this is so. As a result, institutions become the key explanatory variables for state capacity, including bureaucratic capacity. Hence, institutional theory becomes relevant to the study of public administration and its institutions because government organizations are institutional in many ways.

The research approach is basically a qualitative case study. The actual data collection covered three institutions: The Public Service Commission, the Ministry of Finance and Economic Development, and Ministry of Trade and Industry, which are purposely, selected for their strong relevance vis-à-vis the issue under study. The instruments used for collecting data wherein-depth interview with key informants; focus group discussions; and document analysis. A total of sixty-three personnel, including all levels of officers, participated in interviews and focus group discussions.

4. Discussions

4.1. Assessment of Recruitment Practices in the Ethiopian Civil Service

Recruitment and selection are important components of the human resource management reform of Ethiopia. It was introduced to bring about a merit-based system in civil service institutions throughout the country. The reform is meant to solve the problems that were identified in the process of recruitment and selection that hindered the achievement of a merit-based system in the civil service. Hence, issues related to recruitment and selection procedures, definition of job requirements, and human resource planning were given due emphasis to properly consider the process of recruitment and selection in a way that supports the achievement of a merit-based system in the civil service.

However, the findings of various studies show that the intended result of such programs has not been achieved. For example, a study by Tesfaye and Atakilt (2012) reveals the human resource capacity gap as a critical challenge adversely affecting organizational efficiency, effectiveness, and good governance in Ethiopian public organizations. Their assertion resonates with frequent reports of federal institutions as well as other concerned government officials. In their consecutive annual implementation reports, almost all the ministries have admitted their inability to attract qualified personnel from the market. The shortage of skilled human resource across the civil service is further aggravated by insufficient recruitment practices. The public sector recruits employees from universities, colleges, technical and vocational schools, as well as from other sectors. In most cases, the usual difficulty is that of attracting adequate numbers of civil servants with sufficient specialized training to enable them to carry out developmental state ideals.

The literature on the East Asian developmental states stipulates that though the bureaucracy in those countries was challenged by geographical affiliation, school connections, and kinship networks, it usually introduced a meritocracy, united and coherent. For example, in Korea, "the bureaucracy was indeed selected according to a highly competitive entrance examination that has usually attracted the countries' best students" (ibid: 7). What is more, public servants were recruited through a closed-career merit system. In other words, appointments were made on the basis of university qualifications and a selection examination.

In the case of Ethiopia, article 13, and sub-article 2 of the FDRE Civil Servants Proclamation states that a vacant position shall be filled only by a person who meets the qualification required for the position and who scores higher than other candidates (FDRE, Civil Servants Proclamation, 2007). There is also an implementation manual that indicates the procedure of recruitment and selection to be followed uniformly by all civil service institutions. The manual covers the issues of merit principles, like qualifications, work experience, knowledge, and skills as well as other capabilities and the overall procedure to achieve fair and open competition. Thus, it can be argued that at the policy level, except for being a position-based system, the recruitment procedures and considerations are similar to those of other developmental states. However, in practice various reasons account for the non-meritocratic recruitment into the Ethiopian public services.

The first issue examined by this study was how merit is considered; and whether non-meritocratic parameters influence the recruitment process in selecting candidates at the entry level. The purpose was to know civil servants' perceptions regarding the criteria for recruitment at the entry level.

Results show that, primarily at the entry level, employees are recruited based on their qualification, experience, and performance. Similarly, the implementation of job specifications seems encouraging, with some limitations. However, job descriptions are not utilized at the expected level to support the implementation of recruitment and selection. It seems also that even entry level recruitment does not exclude the possibility of political affiliation in recruiting and promoting employees in the civil service. In fact managerial positions, especially middle and higher ones, are reported to be exclusively reserved for politically loyal personnel with ethnic background as a supplementary qualification.

Empirical data also disclosed that there are violations of merit principles, exacerbated by poor attention to human resource planning and definitions of job requirements in the recruitment and selection process. The guidelines are violated to the extent that individuals are selected and assigned without competition and on the basis of personal connections and sometimes with political interference. The overall sentiment appears to indicate that the guidelines are not strictly considered as required in a way that convinces and satisfies most of the civil servants.

The related issue is written examination in the recruitment process. In this regard, the federal civil servants' recruitment manual states that civil service institutions shall set examinations to screen the most eligible candidates depending on the nature of respective organizations. In practice, however, recruitment under this provision has been negligible. Instead, Ethiopian civil service is characterized by "mixed" recruitment patterns that fall into two categories: those which recruit personnel by competitive written examinations and those which recruit them by comparison of the paper qualifications already possessed by the candidate.

The most common recruitment practice in the institutions under study does not apply formal examinations in screening the most eligible candidates. The most common practice is that of screening candidates based on educational credentials and relevant work experience produced by the candidates. In such institutions, the procedure for entry to the civil service requires the candidate to apply to an individual government institution in writing, stating his/her qualifications. Because the civil service may recruit at department and service head levels most of the time, it is highly prone to nepotism.

Therefore, the abandonment of the guidelines for recruitment into public service inadvertently opens the gate of entry into the service for incompetent persons. As a result of de facto recruitment procedures and conditions, merit is compromised. This, to a large extent, affects the performance of the Ethiopian bureaucracy in the area of policy articulation, implementation, and evaluation. It is worthy of note that the inadequacy of personnel, particularly as it relates to expertise and skilled manpower, results in part from the personnel recruitment practices, which are essentially based on non-meritocratic criteria that contrast with objectively measurable criteria like qualification and professional competence.

In addition to malpractices regarding recruitment, lack of proper and attractive incentives is also mentioned as a factor affecting the competence and effectiveness of the civil service.

4.2. Practice of Promotion in Ethiopian Civil Service

The Ethiopian civil service system, in terms of recruitment and promotion, resembles the position-based system. However, such a system is less favorable to civil services in other developmental states (DS). Civil services in DS require, among other things, that the political and permanent executives in the civil service share common culture and goals. Such a civil service also needs to be merit-based. Alas, as discussed in the literature review and also in the above section, while a position-based civil service system facilitates high mobility among civil servants, it results in the lack of a common culture among top executives. What is more, such a system tends to undermine merit-based promotion. Because of this, unlike Ethiopia, many developmental states prefer a career-based civil service system to one that is position-based.

Empirical data from the institutes researched for this study show that the promotion of civil servants is determined more by the interests of political officials and personnel officers than by their merit. In an interview with a state minister for the Ministry of Public service and Human Resources, he explained how promotions are made and the role of party affiliation regarding promotion as follows:

> De jure, Ethiopian Civil Service is apolitical and professional. However, in practice there may be some deviations from the rule. Civil Service promotes professional achievements and merit as requirements for entry into and promotion within the Service. But political backing may be an important factor for promotion to senior ranks. Of course, senior civil servants (directors) must first meet professional requirements, but support for the government's ideologies and policies may also be important for an appointment.

As reflected in different documents, procedures for assessing the suitability of candidates for internal promotion vary somewhat across ministries. In recent years, there have been attempts to make the promotion process relatively competitive. In this regard, the tradition of promotion, which used to be based on consistory approach (based only upon seniority and suitability), has been supplemented by competitive processes, though the practice varies among ministries and also among departments within a ministry. In general, a combination of interview performance, manager assessment, and success in meeting the requirements of the candidate's current job are all taken into consideration to varying degrees.

There is no or little hope for the civil servants to be promoted to the next position. So, they are co-opted to remain hopeless in terms of civil service career progression. As a result, they are obliged to search for other options outside the civil service or join some networks within the service which may help them rise up the ladder.

For those who are outside the given ministry, political party officials have the power to make and unmake higher officials. They may recommend persons for holding higher posts in a given ministry and also can recall personnel they are not comfortable with. As a result, in these ministries the promotion of civil servants without the necessary political affiliation is slow or absent.

Therefore, in addition to the malpractices and abuses of the existing system, the civil service system which Ethiopian civil service prefers to practice does match the requirements of a developmental state's bureaucracy. This lack of fit, as discussed here, causes problems in the Ethiopian civil service in relation to promotion. Another area of challenge in the civil service is the transfer and mobility of civil servants within and outside the civil service. Related to this, respondents identified as problematic the subjective transfer and posting of civil servants.

4.3. Transfer and Mobility

A feature of a wide range of developmental contexts concerns the movement of high-level bureaucrats into political office, and vice-versa. This can be seen by the high number of important cabinet ministers who are former senior civil servants in many developmental governments (Leftwich, 1995).In many developmental states, a significant proportion of the country'shigh-level politicians are former civil servants. For example, in Botswana, the ruling Botswana Democratic Party (BDP) actively encourages civil servants identified as being politically smart to enter politics at both the local and national level (Charlton, 1991).

For such movement between civil servants and political executives to be realized, however, there is a need to establish a system of promotion, transfer, and appointment that allows it. The Ethiopian civil service, because its system resembles a position- based system, does potentially allow mobility.

At the very least, a significant majority of civil servants doubt or do not expect that positions are filled by civil servants within their own institution. It seems that transferees are more privileged when it comes to positions at higher levels. This practice obviously demoralizes senior civil servants who have served their respective ministries for long years but are ignored when it comes to assuming higher positions.

Here, it is important to note that transfer is useful if managed properly and used for matching skills with the relevant positions. The Ministry of Public Service and Human Resources has prepared a manual that should, in principle, be abided by all federal civil service organizations in Ethiopia. However, existing malpractices related to transfer combine to undermine the manual. The net result of abusing the transfer scheme is a prevalence of transferees within the civil service whose competence is put in doubt, not to mention its instrumentality for politicians' will. When the senior management of the civil service is dominated by transferee politicians instead of by the brightest and the best in its system, ministries and other government institutions cannot function at their best as the capacity of higher civil servants to support them in carrying out their functions is largely impaired.

As a result, the civil service does not give due attention to internal mobility. This, in turn, leads to neglecting the processes of proper staff appraisal, which, of course, should be used properly, as it is a useful tool for proper promotion decisions. Indeed there is a gap in this regard.

Generally speaking, there are two other consequences of the uncertainty that arises from tenure that is not mandated or merit based. The incumbent is not sure of how long he/she will stay on the job, as political winds change. This has an adverse effect on his/her attention to detail, his/her capacity to master the situation, and his/her confidence that his/her judgment will be respected. Unsure or unwilling to make difficult but necessary decisions, he/she opts for the tried and tested, or to second guess the preferences of his/her political masters. He/she may ignore, neglect, or discard worthwhile changes made by his/her predecessor. His/her staff may assume that reforms will not stick and avoid the commitment necessary to effect long term change.

Hence, it is in this context that it is crucial and critical to remove uncertainty and imbue the officers with a certain security of tenure in every post, assuming it is merited by proven competence. Stable tenures will motivate senior officers to provide credible leadership and improve organizational performance. A healthy personnel tenure policy should reduce the overall incidence of transfers, and eliminate the emergence of a "transfer industry" or politicized transfers.

4.4. Performance Appraisal to Promotion

Among other things, meritocratic bureaucracy needs merit-based reward, i.e., rewarding civil servants based on their real performance. Career development based on the principle of rewarding merit constitutes the central element for professionalizing the civil service and motivating its officials. In order to reward merit, it is first necessary to put in place an evaluation system that makes possible decisions related to career development. The evaluation system needs to be based on a fair assessment of qualifications and performance, thereby ensuring the promotion of those officials whose competencies can be objectively recognized.

In this regard, the experience of East Asian developmental states is that bureaucrats were given the assurance that if they achieve the performance goals set at the top, they would be promoted to a more prestigious positions, "all the way up that of minister"(Mah, 2011:17).Similarly, merit-based appointments and promotion of technocrats and bureaucrats, their training, and the reward system have remained crucial in achieving techno-bureaucratic governance in the developmental state of Botswana (Adamolekun, 1999). The other important point is that in many developmental states, the trend regarding ministerial position has been the selection of domestic-oriented ministers with patronage appointments while guarantying the professionalism of the economic ministers, such as for finance, trade, industry, agriculture, etc. (Mah, 2011:17).

In the FDRE civil service, career development is based on two factors taken into account simultaneously: seniority on the one hand and assessment of professional skills on the other. However, while seniority does not pose any question, setting objective criteria for performance appraisals poses problems, despite the provisions in legislative texts, which in some cases lay down precise procedures. In practice, in the Ethiopian civil service, non-parametric standards are dominant in evaluating civil servants and thereby promotion related to performance. Hence, a lack of proper evaluation criteria is one of the challenges of the civil service in practicing performance-based promotion. In order to reward merit, therefore, it is first necessary to put in place an evaluation system that makes it possible for decisions relating to career development to be based on a fair assessment of qualifications and performance.

Cognizant of this, Ethiopia has undertaken a civil service reform program with the objective of implementing "result based performance evaluation" throughout the service. A results-based performance evaluation needs a transparent system, accountable management, and measurable performance standards. The intention was that promotion based on merit would to a large degree increase the level of commitment of the bureaucrats and also ensures that competent people are promoted to relevant positions. Any movements within the career space must be based on merits: that is, a demonstrated contribution to the furthering of the organization's goals, possession of competencies, or potential for development.

In this regard, the civil servants who participated in the research complained that though promotion in principle is by merit, there is no objective and functioning standard of performance appraisal:"Rules for promotion fail to differentiate between productive and non-productive workers."This diminishes the value of the evaluation.

Thus, the promotion scheme prevents senior civil service positions from being held by competent career civil servants. In the absence of strict implementation of results-based evaluation systems, rewards have been seen as being less objective and unable to discriminate hard-working and effective people from those who are. Many respondents complaint of cases where less hard-working and corrupt people are rewarded and promoted based on some other unethical yardsticks, such as loyalty to the supervisor, favoritism, nepotism and so on. This implies thatfor the vast majority of civil servants there is no hope of promotion to the highest levels, and therefore no motivation to properly execute one's duty, let alone work overtime. By implication, it seems that in practice, performance appraisal has nothing to do with rewarding civil servants in Ethiopia.

5. Findings and Implications

Given the findings of this study, one of the key challenges in the development of Ethiopian federal civil service capacities is to establish and safeguard the merit principle of recruitment and promotion.

To achieve short- or long-term organizational goals, there is a need for an efficient workforce, which can only be attained by recruiting people with appropriate skills, qualifications, and experiences. Strengthening appointments based on merit requires that the human resources employed by government to execute its policies become efficient and effective. The findings in this research indicate that there indeed exists a system that guides the process of recruitment and selection in Ethiopian civil service institutions, but there is a gap in terms of its proper implementation. In this regard, various reasons account for the non-meritocratic recruitment into the Ethiopian public services.

First, the Ethiopian civil service basically follows a position-based system. In practice, civil servants are recruited at various services and grades within the public service. In general, staffs are expected to successfully meet the position requirements and there are no specialist career paths. In most cases, the usual difficulty is that of attracting adequate numbers of civil servants with sufficient specialized training to enable them to carry out the developmental objectives of the state.

Second, in practice, the Ethiopian civil service is characterized by "mixed" recruitment patterns that fall into two categories: those which recruit personnel by competitive written examinations and those which recruit them by comparison of the paper qualifications already possessed by the candidate. The most common recruitment practice in the institutions under study does not apply formal examinations in screening the most eligible candidates.

Third, the ministries, primarily at the entry level, recruit employees based on their qualification, experience, and performance. Though the role of political interference, at least at entry level, is insignificant, personal connections and by implication nepotism are prevalent in recruitment processes. Of course, this does not exclude the possibility of political affiliation in recruiting and promoting employees in the civil service.

Fourth, practice demonstrates that that basis for recruitment into the Ethiopian public sector has largely shifted from the principles of meritocracy (educational qualification and experience) toward factors such as nepotism, political patronage, (God-fatherism), and ethnicity.

Fifth, the study finds that recruitment and appointment of senior civil servants is loosely regulated. Loose recruitment practices make senior civil service positions a subject of inter-party bargaining. This suggests that there are informal party quotas for distribution of top posts in state administration. In fact, managerial positions, especially middle and higher ones, are found to be exclusively reserved for politically loyal personnel with ethnic background as a supplementary characteristic. Many senior civil servants are at the same time members of the main bodies of the ruling parties, signifying that lines between state and politics are still blurred. Hence, this lack of a system of publicly known and acknowledged political appointment at all levels of the civil service has been undermining the career structure. It prevents senior civil service positions from being held by competent career civil servants. Furthermore, there is no awareness of the need for the appointments of senior civil servants to be merit-driven. This is clearly against the principle of merit-based recruitment in state administration.

Generally, the abandonment of the guidelines for recruitment into public service inadvertently opens the gate for entry into the service for incompetent persons. Therefore, merit is compromised, and as a result, real recruitment procedures and conditions represent major problem in the ministries studied. This, to a large extent, affects the performance of the Ethiopian bureaucracy in the area of policy articulation, implementation, and evaluation. It is worthy of note that the inadequacy of personnel, particularly as it relates to expertise and skilled manpower, results in part from the personnel recruitment practices essentially based on non-meritocratic criteria that stand in contrast to objectively measurable criteria like qualification and professional competence.

A proper and reasonable incentive package is a crucial factor in attracting and retaining competent and effective civil servants. However, in this regard, the studied institutions have been facing critical challenges. In relation to this, the study reveals that:

First, the Ethiopian civil service faces critical shortage of skills resulting from lack of the civil service competitiveness in recruiting and retaining competent employees compared to other sectors like the private sector, government enterprises, and NGOs. While the challenge to recruit and retain employees with competent skills is apparent, it is a more daunting task to acquire professionals, like IT specialists, research and training staff, and officials in finance.

Second, the lack of a connection between rewards and civil servants' performance is another challenge. Unlike other developmental states' civil services, rewards to encourage good performance are not common in the Ethiopian civil service. There is no recognition and punishment attached to discipline and –working hard. This means outstanding performance is not recognized and rewarded. Instead, remuneration in the civil service is based on job grade and length of service. This is partly related to an inflexible pay structure, which hinders rewarding performance. Similarly, resolving the critical skills shortage also remains a serious problem in the public sector.

Generally, due to the government's limited competence to create a decent and attractive work environment, the civil service faces a major challenge in attracting and retaining quality staff. This is attributed mainly to low incentive schemes, with large erosion in real salary income having a crucial bearing on low morale, low levels of productivity, and efficiency.

6. Recommendations

Reduce scope for nepotism: To prevent nepotism, it is necessary to select managers based on merit, using transparent criteria communicated across and even outside the administration. The decision-making must be shared in such a way that the immediate superior should not be the only one to take the final decision on selection. There should either be collective decision-making, e.g., through commissions of some kind, or the "grandfather principle" should be introduced. This principle for balancing powers means that decision on selection or recruitment is formally taken at the level above the immediate superior. Subsequently, the highest civil servants or managers should formally be appointed by a decision of the Council of Ministers or the prime minister.

Establish an assessment centre: In order to improve the recruitment and selection system, establishing an assessment centre is critically important. The centre would enable the combination of more selective methods, which would be very useful. Thus, it would enhance the competitiveness of the public employer and enable it to cope with the critical skills shortage. Such a system has been proven successful in many countries, not only for the selection of personnel to be employed in public administration but also for the career progression of employees who are already part of it.

Improving professional continuity and development within public institutions: Selecting the right staff in the first place is an absolute precondition for subsequent performance. Recruitment situations should also give employers the opportunity to explain career prospects. To make career path opportunities clearer, strategic actions are needed at several stages. In this regard, issues needing to be considered include: how to incorporate career planning in regular performance and career discussions; and how to create pay and other HRM systems that promote both kind of careers: one leading to leadership positions and one leading to expert positions.

Increasing mobility is closely related to this issue. However, since there is no established design regarding mobility, both horizontal and vertical, mobility is a random action. In this sense, the federal civil service faces difficulty in maximally utilizing the mobility of civil servants across departments and in keeping senior civil servants over time. Therefore, in order to make the mobility of civil servants more effective, there is a need to establish central databases of civil servants and potential future senior civil servants with full information on their careers. Of course, the database needs to be public. By doing this, potential appropriate candidates for every position can be easily identified. Such a system would give special attention to civil servants' career development, while at the same time allowing them to remain in competition with potential future staff coming from outside their group.

Design and establish rational and functional appraisal system: All state administration authorities should consistently implement the performance appraisal of senior managerial staff, as it is already envisaged by the existing appraisal manual.

Acknowledgements

I am indebted to the anonymous reviewers who provided critical comments and constructive suggestions that helped me in improving the chapter. I also thank the editors.

Notes

1. *Mesläné* refers to a sub district governor during the feudal regimes (till the coming to power of the Dergue in 1974).

References

Adamolekun, L. (1999).*Public Administration in Africa: Main Issues and Selected Country Studies.* Colorado: Westview Press.

Abay, A. (2011). Promoting and Strengthening Professionalism in the Civil Service: The Ethiopian Case. Paper presented atcapacity building workshop on promoting professionalism in thepublic service, Strengthening the Role of Human Resource Managers in the Public Sector for the Effective Implementation of the Charter for Public Service in Africa, March 14-18, in Addis Ababa, Ethiopia.

Adei, S.(2008). The Role of Public Service in a Developmental State: Lessons from the Newly Industrialized Countries (NICS) for Africa. Paper presented at African Association for Public Administration and Management 30th AAPAM Annual Roundtable Conference, Accra, Ghana,October 6 to 8.

Andrews, M. (2013). *The Limits of Institutional Reform in Development.* Cambridge: Cambridge University Press.

Armstrong, M. (2006). *Armstrong's Handbook of Management and Leadership for Human Resource: Developing Effective People Skills for Better Leadership and Management,* 10th ed. London: Kogan Page.

Briggs, R. B. (2007). Problems of Recruitment in Civil Service: Case of the Nigerian Civil Service. *African Journal of Business Management,* 1(6), 142-153.

Charlton, R. (1991). Bureaucrats and Politicians in Botswana's Policy-Making Process: A Reinterpretation. *Journal of Commonwealth and Comparative Politics,* 29(3), 265-282.

Dasandi, N.(2014).The Politics – Bureaucracy Interface : Impact on Development Reform. *State of the Art* 2, www.dlprog.org

Debela, T. (n.d). *Civil Service in Ethiopia: The Marriage Between Profession and Politics.*

Debela, T.&Hagos, A. (2012). Towards a Results-Based Performance Management: Practices and Challenges in the Ethiopian Public Sector.*JBAS*,4(1),79-129.

Desta, A. (2012). The Effects of Rent seeking in Dissipating Developmental Efforts: the Ethiopian Experience. *International Journal of Business and Management Tomorrow*,2(1), 1-4.

Evans, P. B.,&Raunch, J. E. (1999).Bureaucracy and Growth: A Cross-National Analysis of the Effects of "Weberian" State Structures on Economic Growth.*American Sociological Review,* 64(5),748-765.

Fantini, E.(2013).Developmental State, Economic Transformation and Social Diversification in Ethiopia. *ISPI,* no. 163.

FDRE. (1995).The Constitution of the Federal Democratic Republic of Ethiopia (FDRE).

Federal Democratic Republic of Ethiopia.(2007). Ethiopian Federal Civil Servants' Proclamation no. 515/2007. Addis Ababa, Ethiopia.

Fritz, V., &Rocha Menocal, A. (2007). Developmental States in the New Millennium: Concepts and Challenges for a New Aid Agenda. *Development Policy Review.* 25(5), 531-532.

Gladden, E.N.(1948). The Future of the Public Corporation. *Australian Journal of Public Administration*, 7(2):60-67.
Getachew, H. and Common, R. (2006). Civil Service Reform in Ethiopia: Success in Two Ministries. Research Memorandum, no. 59.
Johnson, C. (1982).*MITI and the Japanese Miracle*.Stanford, CA: Stanford University Press.
Leftwich, Adria. (1995).Bringing Politics Back In: Towards a Model of the Developmental State. *Journal of Development Studies*, 31(3), 400-427.
Mah, Luis. (2011). Lessons from Korea to Africa: Leaders, Politics and Developmental States. Originally presented at the 4th European Conferenceon African Studies in Uppsalaon June 17.
MoCSGG. (2012). Civil Service Reform Program in Ethiopia: General Overview with Special Emphasis on Civil Service Reform Program.Federal Democratic Republic of Ethiopia Civil Service Transformation Research Centre Ministry of Civil Service, Article 001.
O'Riordan, J.&Humphreys, P. C. (2002). Career Progression in the Irish Civil Service. www.ipa.ie.
OECD (2003). Managing Senior Management: Senior Civil Reform in OECD Member Countries. Presentation at 28th Session of the Public Management Committee, November 13-14, Chateau de la Muette, Paris.
Pankhrust, R.(1997). A History of Early 20th Century Ethiopia, *Addis Tribune*, n.d.
Paulos, C. (2001). *The Challenges of Civil Service Reform in Ethiopia: Initial Observation*. Addis Ababa: Addis Ababa University
UNDP Global Centre for Public Sector Excellence. (2011).*Meritocracy for Public Service Excellence*.
UNDP. (2012).Democratization in a Developmental State: The Case of Ethiopia Issues, Challenges, and Prospects. UNDP Ethiopia, no. 1/2012.
World Bank. (1997).*The State in a Changing World (World Development Report)*. Washington, DC: The World Bank.
Zewdie, B. (1991). *A History of Modern Ethiopia: 1855-1974*. Addis Ababa: Addis Ababa University Press.

13
Continuities and Changes in Human Resource Management in Oromia National Regional State: The Post 1991

Bacha Kebede Debela, Geert Bouckaert, and Steve Troupin

Box 1: Key Points of this chapter

- ✓ The responsibilities of the institution mandated for civil service and HRM has increased.
- ✓ There is an insufficient link between NPM-inspired result-oriented performance management and pay in HRM.
- ✓ The reforms/tools were used to strengthen vertical and horizontal coordination and control and to enhance the allegiance of civil servants to political executives.
- ✓ The influence of historical factors on HRM is significant.

Box 2: Reading this chapter will give you insights in

- ✓ The Ethiopian politico-administrative reforms and its effect on HRM.
- ✓ The key features of HRM organizational structure, legal frameworks, and directives in Oromia National Regional State.
- ✓ The effect of administrative reform tools and legal frameworks and directives on HRM.
- ✓ The potential negative consequences of the HRM-related challenges on the UN's Sustainable Development Goal (SDGs) and African Union (AU) Agenda 2063.

Box 3: Abbreviations

AU = African Union
BPR = Business Process Reengineering
BSC = Balanced Score Card
CSRP = Civil Service Reform Program
DDS = Democratic Developmental State
ETB = Ethiopian Birr
HRM = Human Resources Management
NPM = New Public Management

PSCAP = Public Sector Capacity-Building Program
SDGs = Sustainable Development Goals
UN = United Nations

1. Introduction

From the 1980s to the 1990s, the neoliberal ideal known as the New Public Management (NPM) was used as a received model to reform the public sector, including human resource management (HRM), all over the world (Ongaro & Ferlie, 2019; Pollitt & Bouckaert, 2017). Advocates argue the public sector should adopt the market principle and a decentralized, customer- and result-oriented approach (Lægreid et al., 2008; Pollitt & Bouckaert, 2017). In consequence, much attention was given to performance management and improving public servant quality through training and development and quality circles (Pollitt, Bouckaert, & Löffler, 2004; Steen et al., 2017), and staff tenure was conceived as depending on performance (Brans, 1997).

However, in the early 1990s the private sector approach to the public sector was attacked, among other reasons, for reducing trust in government (Bovaird & Löffler, 2001) and for privileging the short-term perspective (Lampropoulou & Oikonomou, 2018). To deal with unintended consequences, the West has shifted attention to the new public governance, new public service, and the neo-Weberian models, yet without dismissing the elements of neoliberal ideals (Pollitt & Bouckaert, 2017). The trajectory of politico-administrative reforms, however, varies, which is partly explained by the differences in politico-administrative culture (Pollitt & Bouckaert, 2017; Schwab et al., 2017).

Since the 1990s, Ethiopia has introduced a series of reforms. The Civil Service Reform Program (CSRP), which has an NPM element and five sub-programs,[1] was introduced in 1996 (Mengesha & Common, 2006). The country has also introduced five reform tools: Business Process Reengineering (BPR), Balanced Score Card (BSC), Change Army, Citizen Charter, and Kaizen, at all government levels and in all public institutions. Moreover, the executive agencies were restructured many times, with consequences for HRM. The trajectories of the reforms and their consequences, however, have not been well studied. A few Ethiopian studies exist but have limitations. Using an institutional perspective, Mitiku (2018) studied the Ethiopian public sector leadership profile in the federal civil service organizations. However, he did not analyze the effect of executive agency restructuring and HRM-related instruments on HRM in time and space. The World Bank

(2019) studied the implementation of reform tools; Daba (2016) studied the trends and challenges of HR dynamics in Oromia Regional State; Assefa (2017) examined professionalism in the federal institutions; and Kacho et al. (2016) investigated the implementation of HRM reform in five Ethiopian cities. However, these researches have not explored the effect of politico-administrative reform on HRM. A study by Tadesse (2019) generically focuses on public service reform.

Drawing on the historical neo-institutionalist perspective and relying on a secondary dataset, this chapter explores ***the continuities and changes in human resource management (HRM) in the Oromia National Regional State and the consequences of the HRM reforms***.

The chapter unfolds as follows. The next section establishes the theoretical framework and research design. The third section systematically discusses the results. The last section provides conclusions and implications.

2. Historical Neo-Institutionalism and Research Design

The chapter draws on the historical neo-institutionalist perspective, for three major reasons. First, the advocates of historical neo-institutionalism focus on the structures and power relations among actors (Hall & Taylor, 1996; Schmidt, 2006). The structural-instrumentalist perspective allows exploring continuity and change, over long periods, due to administrative reforms (Christensen et al., 2019; Pollitt & Bouckaert, 2017). Second, the historical neo-institutionalist perspective contends that institutions are path-dependent; that administrative structures, historical factors, and memories inform the present politico-administrative contexts, including historical injustice (Pollitt & Bouckaert, 2009; Schmidt, 2006). Third, the historical neo-institutionalist framework maintains that institutions provide a frame of reference for interpretation and action (Hall & Taylor, 1996; Pollitt & Bouckaert, 2009), allowing for the explanation of the influence of administrative reforms on HRM, civil servants' well-being, and their decision-making behavior (Christensen et al., 2019; Pollitt, 2005).

The study is primarily empirical and descriptive in nature. We relied extensively on a secondary dataset, including relevant legal frameworks, directives, guidelines, executive agencies' establishing proclamations, and the Federal Civil Service Commission (HR database). We also reviewed published academic resources and conference proceedings. The data were obtained through web searches and personal contact with relevant people in the Federal Civil Service Commission. Furthermore, to track the effect of structural reforms, we analyzed the career path of a civil servant working in local government in the Oromia National Regional State. We closely looked at his placement letters, and the first author conducted an exploratory unstructured interview for clarifications. The first author also conducted an exploratory semi-structured interview with a senior staff member at Oromia State University, previously called the Public Service College of Oromia. The interviewee participated greatly in regional reform programs since 2008. The thirty-five-minute interview focused on exploring major challenges encountered by the regional technical reform team and was conducted by phone.

3. The Scope of the Civil Service and HRM

Civil servants include all employees (permanent and temporary) except bureau/office heads and deputy heads (regions, zones, and districts), members of regional, district, and *Kebele* council, judges and public prosecutors, members of the prison administration, the police commission, and other employees excluded by law (Oromia Regional State [ORS], 2002). The bureau and office heads and vice heads are appointed by the regional and local government administrative council. All newly hired civil servants are subjected to a six-month probation period to become a permanent civil servant, and permanent appointment depends on performance evaluation results (a minimum of a satisfactory performance).

A removed political executive, who was a civil servant before the appointment, can be assigned as a civil servant, allowing such individuals the privilege of wearing a double coat with the potential to be reappointed to a political executive position at another time. The other paradox is that appointed officials who were not civil servants may also be directly placed as a civil servant, to relevant positions, when they are removed from office (ORS, 2010). Surprisingly, the salary of a removed political leader who served for at least one year (2006-2016) and at least two years (since 2016) remains unaffected (CSC, 2006). Appointees who were civil servants and are removed before serving for one year, will be placed in their position or an equivalent position. Moreover, while they were running the office, all the removed heads were extremely privileged; they were entitled to special allowance and benefits, and per diem, which is significantly different from the civil servants (World Bank, 2019). The Oromia Civil Servant Proclamation and directives specify open vacancies, competitive selection, and performance-based placement.

4. Federal and Regional Structural Reforms

Three major types of structural reforms that affect HRM could be distinguished: The first decentralisation wave, the second decentralization wave, and executive agency restructuring.

The first decentralization wave occurred during the Transitional Government (TG) of Ethiopia (1991-1995) and continued until 2001. After outing the Dergue in 1991, the EPRDF implemented a regionalization policy, which was largely driven by political interest (Mengesha & Common, 2006). The TG of Ethiopia established fourteen ethno-linguistic regional governments (TG, 1992). The 1993 Act of the TG, among others, transferred the responsibility for personal administration to the regional governments (TG, 1993). In consequence, regional public servants administration bureaus were established.

In 1995 the Federal Democratic Republic of Ethiopia was established, comprising nine ethnolinguistic regional states and two city administrations, implying that civil servants are expected to be proficient in the regional official language. The 1995 constitution grants regions the right to self-administration, including the right to secession.

After the 2000 national election and the devastating Ethio-Eritrean war (1989-2000) and the resulting internal EPRDF party crises, the second decentralization wave occurred, in 2001, leading to extensive public sector restructuring (Mengesha & Common, 2006). In 2001, the Ministry of Capacity Building (MOC) was established and mandated to supervise, coordinate, and guide the implementation of national capacity building and reform initiatives. There were also regional level equivalents, since 2002. Next, in 2003, the government developed the Public Sector Capacity-Building Program (PSCAP) consisting of five interrelated reform programs,[2] all focusing on result-oriented performance management, decentralized service delivery, capacity building, and increased local fiscal capacity (World Bank, 2013). The federal government also forced regions to transfer 65percent of the resources obtained from the federal government to local governments (Peterson, 2015), allowing the federal government to systematically disperse the threat from regional governments by transferring the responsibility for service to local governments.

In 2005 another big official change occurred. In the aftermath of the relatively fair but contested 2005 election (Abbink, 2006), the government officially adopted the Democratic Developmental State (DDS) doctrine (World Bank, 2013) and committed to strengthening vertical and horizontal coordination, including controlling the society at the grass-root level (Debela & Troupin, 2016; Peterson, 2015).

Another noticeable change is the continuous restructuring of executive agencies. Since 1995 the institution responsible for HR administration management in Oromia saw seven structural changes. Table 1 summarizes the responsibilities of the institutions mandated with HR administration/management.

Table 1: Executive agency restructuring and personnel/HRM key responsibilities

Proclamation No.	No. of executive agency	Who is responsible for personnel/HR?	What are the key responsibilities?
7/1995	19	Public Servants Administration Bureau (1995-2001)	- Personnel administration and legal and technical - Policy design and implementation
50/2002	36	Oromia Capacity Building Supreme Office (CBSO) (2002-2003) and the Civil Service Commission (CSC)	- CBSO – Policy design and implementation, coordination, and capacity building - CSC – all responsibilities specified by Proclamation No. 7/1195, create enabling environment for women employment and supervise the implementation of performance appraisal
87/2004	25	Education and Capacity building Bureau (ECBB) (2004-2004) and the Civil Service Commission (CSC)	- ECBB – Policy design and implementation, coordination, education, and capacity building - CSC – all responsibilities specified by Proclamation No. 50/2002 and develop and implement HR training and development programs and take corrective measures on personnel matters attributed to illegal documents
105/2005	30	Capacity Building Bureau (CBB) (2005-2010) and the Civil Service Commission (CSC)	- CBB – Policy design and implementation, coordination, and capacity building - CSC – all responsibilities specified by CS Proclamations
132/2007	30	CBB (2005-2010) and the Civil Service Commission (CSC)	- CBB – Policy design and implementation, coordination, and capacity building - CSC – all responsibilities specified by CS Proclamations, and conduct study on government offices with special works that deserve special salary scale, prepare domestic and foreign training policy, and issue directives on how the public sector organizations are organized and determine their HR needs

Procla-mation No.	No. of executive agency	Who is responsible for personnel/HR?	What are the key responsibilities?
163/2011	34	Civil service and Good Governance Bureau (CSGGB) (2011-2015)	- Policy design and implementation, and coordination - All responsibilities specified by CS Proclamations and three major functions - (A) Institutional capacity functions - (B) HR functions - (C) Civil service and good governance functions
199/2016	42	Public Service and Human Resource Devel-opment Bureau (OPSHRDB) (2016....)	- All responsibilities entrusted to the CSGGB and undertake studies on reform programs, strengthen leadership capacity and improve public service, ensure correct placement, and study the organizations of government institutions and recommend (merge, dissolve, or establish new)

Source: Authors Compilation (2020)

There are three crucial issues worth discussing. First, the number of regional executive agencies has frequently changed. For instance, there were nineteen (in 1995) and forty-two (in 2016) regional level executive agencies (see table 1). The changes were due to the establishment of new agencies and the merger and separation of existing institutions, with implications for HRM. For example, the regional government established the Oromia Capacity Building Supreme Office and the Civil Service Commission (CSC) in 2002. In 2004 the Education Bureau and the Capacity Building Supreme Office were merged and constituted the Education and Capacity Building Bureau, which a year later (2005) was divided into two independent agencies, the Education Bureau and the Capacity Building Bureau. The 2007 Act did not change the number of regional executive agencies but redefined their responsibilities (ORS, 2007). The 2011 and the 2016 regional executive agency Acts, among others, respectively created the Oromia Civil Service and Good Governance Bureau and the Oromia Public Service and Human Resource Development Bureau. Interestingly, except 1995, 2004, and 2007 all Acts establishing regional executive agencies were issued after national elections.

Second, the power relationships between the institution responsible for civil service and HRM and the regional administrative council have changed over time. The Public Servants Administration Bureau was a member of the regional administrative council (1995-2002).The Civil Service Commission

(CSC) was accountable to the Capacity Building Supreme Office,[3] to the Education and Capacity Building Bureau,[4] and to the Capacity Building Bureau.[5] Between 2011 and 2015 and since 2016, at the time of the writing this chapter, the CSGGB and the OPSHRDB were responsible for HRM and both bureaus were members of the regional administrative council.

Third, the responsibilities of the institution responsible for HRM have increased over time, particularly since 2011. As revealed in table 1, three noticeable and interrelated functions were entrusted to CSGGB. The institutional capacity dimension consists, among others, of initiating and coordinating institutional capacity-building programs and preparing special capacity-building programs for disadvantaged districts. HR functions among others comprise ensuring competency-based HRM, preparing and implementing HR policies and directives, and studying different types of benefits and special salary scale government offices, ensuring uniform HRM (ORS, 2011). The civil service and good governance dimension focus on ensuring the efficiency and effectiveness of civil services, preparing and implementing a good governance package, sustaining and ensuring effective reform programs implementation, benchmarking and organizing a public forum to achieve good governance, and institutionalizing the implementation of service delivery standards and a complaint handling system. Table 1 reveals that responsibilities of OPSHRDB have increased over time.

5. Instrumental-Managerial Reform

5.1. The Reform Approach

A systematic but top-down approach to administrative and civil service reform was started in the mid-1990s. In 1994, a special task force established in Prime Minister's Office distinguished several weaknesses and bottlenecks in the civil service (World Bank, 2013; 2019). In response, in 1996, the country rolled out the CSRP, which is inspired by NPM doctrine, at all government levels. HRM is one component of the CSRP. The objective of the CSRP was to create an effective and efficient, fair, ethical, transparent, accountable, and performance-oriented civil service, accompanied by client-oriented service delivery (World Bank, 2019).

The full-scale implementation of the CSRP rolled out in 2002. To facilitate the implementation and follow-up and institutionalize the reform, special civil reform offices were established at the federal and regional government levels and a reform unit was created in each public institution.

5.2. The Reform Tools

To institutionalize the ongoing reform programs, and to promote the DS model, the ruling party introduced five reform tools: BPR, BSC, Change Army, Citizen Charter, and Kaizen, at all government levels and in all public sectors (World Bank, 2019), each affecting HRM-related activities. Table 2 presents the reform tools, their focus and key purpose, and key supporting institution.

The implementation of reform tools differs by type of reform tools, by government levels and by sectors, with apparent greater success at the federal level institutions (OPSHRDB, 2016; OPSHRDB, 2017; World Bank, 2019). This could be due to a relatively better administrative and coordination capacity at the federal level. While Change Army is widely implemented at all levels and in all sectors, Citizen Charter was unsuccessful at all levels of governments (OPSHRDB, 2016; World Bank, 2019). The implementation of Kaizen in the public sector has not been well studied.

The inter-sectorial variation in reform tools implementation could be explained by the nature of the task (Pollitt, 2005). The unsuccessful implementation of Citizen Charter is most likely explained by a deep-seated top-down politico-administrative and upward accountability tradition reinforced by socioeconomic and structural inequalities in public service delivery (Debela, 2017). In addition, the interviewee distinguished nine challenges in implementing reform:

- Inadequate understanding of reforms/tools by implementing organizations;
- One-size-fits-all reform across all sectors and functions (lack of contextualization);
- Lack of continuous evaluation and documentation;
- Lack of continuous engagement (considering reform as a one-time activity);
- Externalization of reforms, including by political leadership;
- High leadership turnover;
- Absence of performance-based reward and incentive;
- Misuse of reforms, including overly advancing political interests; and
- Inadequate resources and infrastructure for implementation.

Table 2: Reform tools, focus, key purpose, and supporting institution

Reform tools and other supports	When introduced?	What are the focus and key purpose/s?
BPR	2005-2006 In many organizations in 2007 (Peterson, 2015)	- Radically change the job and structure, public service delivery process, measurement and management, and values and beliefs of public sector.
BSC	2008	- Institutionalize strategic planning, performance measurement, management, and reporting (Markos, 2013; Tadesse, 2019).
Change Army	Rural areas in 2011 (World Bank, 2019) and all public sectors in 2014 (Miruts & Daba, 2016)	- Learning, performance, and strengthening vertical and horizontal coordination and control
Citizen Charter	2011 (World Bank, 2019)	- Improve accountability to citizens and reinforce the standards set by BPR
Kaizen	Pilot project (2010) and full-scale implementation since 2011 (Kitaw, 2011)	- Incremental reform tool - Reduce waste and improve work environment
Public Service College of Oromia/Oromia State University (support)	College/university Regional reform support center (2008), University branch since 2009 (Finfine/ Addis Ababa)	- Support reforms implementation - Research, training, and consultancy services

Source: Author's compilation (2020)

5.3. Civil Service Legal Frameworks and Directives

The Oromia regional government issued a Civil Servant Proclamation in 2002 (ORS, 2002) and amended the proclamation three times: in 2004, 2005, and 2006. In addition, four directives and one guideline were issued. Table 3 reports the civil servant legal frameworks/directives and their key features.

Table 3: Civil servant legal frameworks/Directives and key features

Legal frameworks/directives	What are the key features?
Civil Servant Proclamation (ORS, 2002)	- CSC is responsible for HR and related functions - Defines the responsibility of public organizations[6]
Civil Servants Revised Proclamation (ORS, 2004).	- Focuses on CSRP implementation and individual performance evaluation criteria[7]
Civil Servants Revised Proclamation (ORS, 2005).	- Focuses on external transfer and distinguishes four causes[8]
Civil Servants Revised Proclamation (ORS, 2006).	- Focuses on incentive schemes for district employees and specifies the responsibility of CSC[9]
Civil servants directive (CSO, 2006)	- Recruitment (open vacancies) and competitive selection, promotion and placement, and transfer - Focus on merit rather than seniority - Inclusiveness[10] - Internal transfer[11]
Performance evaluation and reward system directive (OPSHRD, 2012)	- Focuses on the implementation of results-oriented performance management - Distinguishes sources of information for individual and organizational performance evaluation[12]
Reform Tools Implementation Guideline (OPSHRD, 2016)	- Focuses on BPR, BSC, Change and Citizen Charter implementation - Five implementation rating scales and modified scale set by performance evaluation and reward system directive[13]
Job evaluation, standardization, and reward implementation directive (OPSHRDB, 2017).	- Distinguished sources organizational[14] and individual information performance[15]
Employee Placement directive (OPSHRDB, 2017)	- Performance, academic relevance and competency, experience, and inclusiveness - Individual performance criteria[16] - External and internal transfer (placement)
Employee Placement directive (OPSHRDB, 2019)	- Implement the point rating job classification - Performance, academic relevance and competency, experience, and inclusiveness - More attention to direct work experience - Restriction on promotion level - Modified the placement assessment criteria[17] - External and internal transfer (placement)

Source: Author's compilation (2020)

The legal frameworks, directives, and guidelines have implications for HRM. For example, the Civil Servants Proclamations could open windows for political executives to arbitrarily transfer (2004) and dismiss civil servants (2005). The continuous modification of the source of performance information and performance evaluation scale may increase performance gaming and affect employee decision-making behavior.

The 2017 Job Evaluation and Grading assessment by OPSHRD Bureau brought to light some realities and brought about a change in HRM. The assessment, among others, showed massive pay discrepancies for similar jobs and misplacement of civil servants. Consequently, the long-lived position-based job classification (in existence since the 1960s) was changed into a point-rating classification method, ranging from level one to level twenty. The aim was to calibrate civil servants' salaries and ensure competency-based correct placement. The placement of civil servants was completed in 2018.

Nevertheless, due to huge financial implications, the government was unable to implement the salary adjustment, at a time of writing this chapter. A new civil servants' placement was made, based on the 2019 directive that set a limit on promotion levels. While an employee with a sub-professional science occupational standard and its equivalent and less can be promoted to a maximum of three higher levels, an employee with a professional sciences occupational standard can be only promoted to two higher levels. Employees who are working in special salary organizations can be promoted to only one higher level. This means that performance results and competency have limited effect; promotion based on remarkable performance is impossible.

Both in 2018 and 2019 those civil servants who did not have the required competencies and were thereby suspended, and those who were out-competed, were assigned by the placement committee or the higher political executives to the same (internal transfer) or other public organizations (external transfer).

6. The Effects of Structural-Instrumental Reforms

The structural changes had four major consequences for HRM. First, based on ethno-linguistic criteria, the civil servants under the Dergue regime were transferred to the regional states, resulting in profound civil servants' mobility. Surprisingly, despite significant staffing shortages and challenges in each region, the unwanted civil servants were removed (Mitiku, 2018; World Bank, 2019). The regional parties appeared to play a significant role in facilitating the civil servants' mobility. Second, following the second wave of decentralization, the size of HR at the local level changed drastically and was converted into a pyramid structure, with more number at the local than regional levels. Third, the continuous restructuring of the executive agencies has not only significantly increased the responsibilities of the institutions responsible for HRM but also the mobility of civil servants. Fourth, the creation of special public organizations having a special salary pay scale, since 2013, allowed civil servants who were working in special organizations to earn a relatively better salary than others.

The managerial-instrumental reforms (reform tools) have also affected HRM. The BPR organized HRM into a support function – not as a core function – and dismissed the seniority principle, shifted attention to merit and qualification and abandoned the behavioral elements in employee performance evaluation. As a result, qualified young civil servants were assigned to higher positions previously held by experienced but academically less qualified or unqualified civil servants (Peterson, 2015). At the levels of zonal administration and local government, the civil service pool and administration pool are responsible for HR functions.

The government also used BPR as an instrument to systematically remove senior civil servants. The 2004 Public Servants' Pension Amendment Act was also used to remove senior civil servants. The Act reduced the retirement age from fifty-five years to forty-five years; and civil servants aged forty-five who had served for at least twenty years were entitled to receive a retirement pension for life (FDRE, 2004).

The BSC has linked strategic planning, performance measurement, and performance evaluation and reporting. Individual and team targets were linked to organizational targets since 2012 (World Bank, 2019). Individual performance accounted for two dimensions: performance (60 performance) and behavioral aspects (40 percent) (World Bank, 2019), implying the behavioral dimension has come back. However, the civil servants have a profound concern about the lack of meritocracy and objectivity in employee performance evaluation and performance-based rewards and incentives (ibid).

Change Army has a peer learning and performance improvement perspective comparable to the so-called quality circle, which according to a World Bank (2019) study of civil servants, is perceived as the most effective tool to discussing and finding solutions to corrupt practices in the civil services. Here, civil servants were organized into one to five arrangements (one group leader [model civil servant, preferably ruling party member] and other followers) and were responsible for evaluating team performance on daily/weekly bases and reporting to the lower level leadership, which in turn reports to middle-level leadership (directors) and ultimately to the top political leadership to be discussed at least once a month (Tadesse, 2019; World Bank, 2019).

Figure 1: HRM organizational structure and reform tools timeline

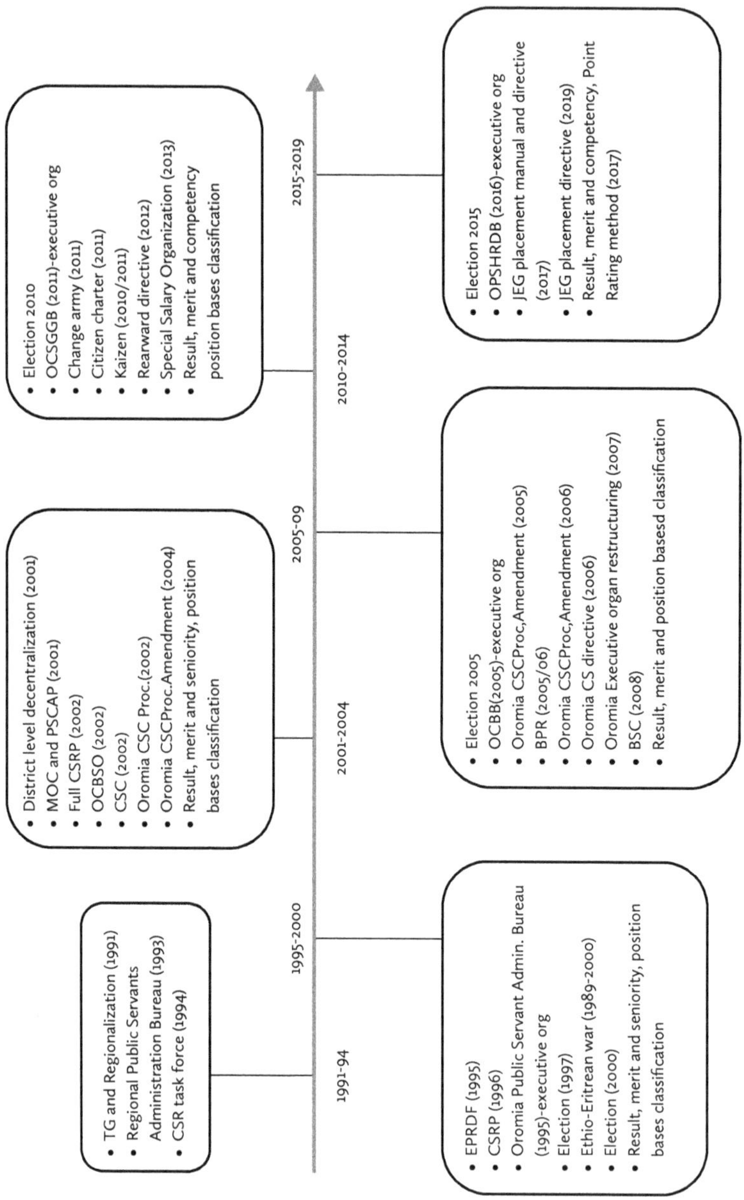

Source: Authors (2020)

However, the Change Army allowed a one-party regime to considerably fuse the party and the state (the civil service) and ultimately increased the allegiance of civil servants to political executives, allowing them to become an instrument of the arbitrary power center. Therefore, one could argue that the election result of 2015, to some extent, may be attributed to the influence of the Change Army, because all national parliamentarian seats were held by EPRDF (Abbink; 2017), leading to increased political centralism and authoritarianism (Gudina, 2007). This is in sharp contrast to the goals of NPM-inspired reform, which aims to split politics and public administration. The effect of Citizen Charter and Kaizen is not explored. Figure 1 summarizes HRM organizational structure and reform tools.

7. Combined Effects of Structural-Instrumental Reforms.

7.1. The Number of Civil Servants and Education Profile

Table 4 reports the change in the number and educational profile of civil servants.

The results in table 4 show that the number of civil servants, in Oromia, has increased drastically from 108,410 in 2001 to 515,624 in 2018. This is contrary to the trend in OECD countries (see Pollitt & Bouckaert, 2017:89). Moreover, female civil servants are underrepresented in the regional public administration. Of the total civil servants, females constituted only 27.4 percent in 2001 and increased to 34.2 percent in 2018, suggesting the feminization of public administration has shown an upsurge of 7 percent.

The educational profile of civil servants has also changed. In 2001 most men (79.62 percent) and women (91.26 percent) were certificate holders had completed less than twelve grades. Conversely, in 2018, 68.2 percent of male and 58.7 percent of female civil servants held college diplomas and undergraduate degrees, suggesting remarkable progress in female civil servants' academic qualification. As mentioned above, the reforms emphasized academic qualification, which in turn triggered the civil servants to invest in better academic certificates. Increased access to higher education also appears to play a role. On the downside, the push for better academic qualification has allegedly increased the number of civil servants and political executives having false academic and work experience credentials. This problem seems to have triggered the OPSHRDB to issue the False Academic and Professional Competency Certificate Investigation Directive in 2017 (OPSHRDB, 2017). The directive imposes serious penalties, including dismissal, if civil servants and

Table 4: Civil servants number and education

Educaion level	2001				2018			
	Male		Female		Male		Female	
	No.	%	No.	%	No.	%	No.	%
Less and eqaul to 12 grade	22737	28,91	11939	40,13	45414	13,4	26411	15
Certifcate	39884	50,71	15211	51,13	2116	0,6	1393	0,8
Diploma(Voc/Tech)	2679	3,41	1028	3,46	0	0	0	0
Level 1-5					46847	13,8	40872	23,2
1st-4th year (University)	689	0,88	75	0,25	5751	1,7	3186	1,8
College Diploma (college (10+3)	9028	11,48	1292	4,34	103490	30,5	60724	34,4
B.A./B.Sc./L.L.B	2874	3,65	136	0,46	127936	37,7	42930	24,3
M.D/D.V.M	323	0,41	35	0,12	1959	0,6	278	0,2
M.A./M.Sc./L.L.M	466	0,59	35	0,12	5642	1,7	621	0,4
Ph,D.	10	0,01	0	0	53	0	1	0
Not Statd	8	0,01	1	0	0	0	0	0
Total (%)	78658 (72.6%)	100	29752 (27.4%)	100	339208 (65.8%)	100	176416 (34.2%)	100
Total	108410				515624			

Source: Compiled from Federal Civil Service Commission Database

officials are found to have false credentials. However, against the civil service ethos, guilty civil servants and officials who officially declare themselves within one month of the directive's issuance (mid-July 2017 to mid-August 2017) were excused from dismissal. Such individuals were reassigned to relevant posts. This is reportedly the case in Oromia; however, full data were unavailable.

7.2. Civil Servants Age Structure

Table 5 reveals that the majority of civil servants in the Oromia National Regional State public administration are young; female civil servants are relatively younger. The change in the age structure for male and female civil servants was also significant. In 2018, the proportion of male civil servants aged less than thirty-three changed from 67.67 percent to 57.85 percent, a drop in 12 percent. The percentage of female civil servants, in the same age group, dwindled from 80.75 percent to 66.07 percent, a decrease of 26 percent. The decreasing rate of the civil servants' recruitments explains the change in age structure.

Table 5: Civil Servants Age

Age	2008				2018			
	Male		Female		Male		Female	
	No.	%	No.	%	No.	%	No.	%
18-22	52917	36,03	26471	46,22	27230	8,03	22142	12,55
23-27	27933	19,02	11279	19,7	82335	24,27	52174	29,57
28-32	21473	14,62	8490	14,83	86663	25,55	42260	23,95
33-37	15004	10,22	4342	7,58	55786	16,45	25863	14,66
38-42	12746	8,68	3454	6,03	34578	10,19	15892	9,01
43-47	9429	6,42	2252	3,93	23712	6,99	9135	5,18
48-52	5249	3,57	790	1,38	15589	4,6	4831	2,74
53-57	211	1,44	189	0,33	7745	2,28	2452	1,39
58-60	0	0	0	0	5412	1,6	1643	0,93
Above 60	0	0	0	0	158	0,05	24	0,01
Male	146862 (71.9%)		100		339208 (65.8%)		100	
Female	57267 (28.1%)		100		176416 (34.2%)		100	
Total	204129				515624			

Source: Compiled from Federal Civil Service Commission Database

The age structures have implications for the civil service. The minimum official employment age, in Ethiopia, is eighteen years and the official retirement age, since 2011, is sixty years. However, a civil servant can request an extended retirement, currently, for a maximum of six years, that has to be approved by the mandated institution, presently the OPSHRDB. In 2018 there were 158 male and 24 female civil servants aged over sixty years (table 5). Given the low life expectancy, a sixty-year retirement age suggests many civil servants could die while working, and that only the survivors will receive a pension benefit payment.

On the other hand, there is a huge unemployment problem in Ethiopia, which has both economic and political implications. Freezing employment opportunities in the public sector and increasing the retirement age to control the number of civil servants, with a consequent increasing expenditure in civil service, may not be feasible. In Oromia, the public sector is the biggest sector providing employment opportunity.

7.3. Civil Servants and Job Structure

Table 6 reports civil servants by occupation in Oromia (2012-2018).

Table 6: Civil Servants by occupation (2012-2018)

	2012	2013	2014	2015	2016	2017	2018
Professional Science (PS) (M)	14.1%	18.1%	18.1%	17%	16.0%	17.0%	8.0%
Professional Science (PS) (F)	8.7%	11.7%	11.7%	12%	11.0%	12.0%	6.0%
Administrative (AD) (M)	2.8%	3.2%	3.3%	3%	3.0%	3.0%	2.0%
Administrative (AD) (F)	3.6%	4.3%	3.9%	-	4.0%	4.0%	2.0%
Sub Professional (SP) (M)	8.9%	9.2%	8.2%	7.0%	6.0%	6.0%	4.0%
Sub Professional (SP) (F)	6.0%	7.0%	6.5%	7.0%	5.0%	6.0%	4.0%
Clerical and Fiscal (CF) (M)	1.5%	2.6%	3.0%	3.0%	3.0%	3.0%	2.0%
Clerical and Fiscal (CF) (F)	6.9%	7.6%	8.4%	8.0%	7.0%	7.0%	4.0%
Trades and Crafts (TC) (M)	1.3%	1.1%	1.1%	1.0%	1.1%	1.0%	1.0%
Trades and Crafts (TC) (F)	0.7%	0.3%	0.5%	1.0%	0.4%	1.0%	1.0%
Custodial & Manual (CM) (M)	3.2%	3.2%	5.0%	5.0%	5.0%	5.0%	3.0%
Custodial & Manual (CM) (F)	4.0%	4.4%	7.6%	8.0%	7.0%	6.0%	5.0%
Teachers (M)	38.7%	39.4%	39.5%	38%	37.0%	36.0%	37.0%

	2012	2013	2014	2015	2016	2017	2018
Teachers (F)	36.9%	37.5%	35.7%	37%	35.0%	33.0%	36.0%
Health Professionals (M)	8.2	6.4%	6.5%	11%	8.0%	6.0%	6.0%
Health Professionals (F)	21%	17.2	17.4%	20%	18.0%	14.0%	13.0%
Appointment (M)	4.9%	5.3%	4.8%	5.0%	5.0%	5.0%	5.0%
Appointment (F)	2.8%	2.4%	2.3%	2.0%	2.0%	2.0%	2.0%
Special Classification (SC) (M)	3.9%	0.7%	7.0%	9.0%	11.0%	14.0%	31.0%
Special Classification (SC) (F)	3.7%	0.2%	4.5%	6.0%	8.0%	12.0%	27.0%
Not Stated (NS) (M)	11.7%	10.9%	2.7%	0	0	0	0
Not Stated (NS) (F)	5.8%	7.4%	1.2%	0	0	0	0
Agricultural professionals (M)	0	0	0.9%	0.4%	5.0%	5.0%	0.4%
Agricultural professionals (F)	0	0	0.3%	0.01%	2.0%	3.0%	0.2%
Total (M)	**229522 (68.12%)**	**242841 (69.22%)**	**263505 (68.4%)**	**282933 (68.4%)**	**301267 (66.6%)**	**323547 (66.4%)**	**339208 (65.8%)**
Total (F)	**107412 (31.88%)**	**107962 (30.78%)**	**121591 (31.6%)**	**130555 (31.6%)**	**150851 (33.4%)**	**163910 (33.6%)**	**176416 (34.2%)**
Total (M+F)	**336934**	**350803**	**385096**	**413488**	**452118**	**487457**	**515624**

Source: Compiled from Federal Civil Service Commission Database

Until 2018, excluding teachers, health professionals, and special classification jobs, in Oromia, civil servants jobs are structured into five horizontal grades each having different levels (vertical grades): Custodial and Manual (five levels), Trade and Crafts (ten levels), Clerical and Fiscal (12 levels), Administration (9 levels), Sub Professionals (12 levels) and Professional Sciences (9 levels).

Table 6 clarifies three important issues. First, the proportion of civil servants' occupation substantially differs by gender. Female civil servants encounter both vertical (glass ceiling) and horizontal (glass wall) occupational segregation. In terms of the glass ceiling, female civil servants are underrepresented in professional sciences and sub-professional jobs, though there is an upward trend. Concerning the glass wall, the majority of females are working in the custodial and manual, clerical and fiscal, and health sectors jobs that are stereotypically and socially defined as suitable for females. The proportion of female civil servants that were appointed is also low. The general implication is that the influence of administrative reforms to reduce gender-based occupational inequality is modest.

Second, a substantial majority of civil servants (female and male) are working in the health and education sector. Teachers show an increasing trend, but female teachers comprise less than half their male counterparts. The third crucial observation is that the proportion of civil servants (male and female) in special classification jobs is increasing.

7.4. Civil Servants Pay Scale

Since 1996, civil servants in Oromia have seen several job placement and salary adjustments. For example, a civil servant whose document was reviewed during this study, was serving as a socioeconomic expert (with a monthly salary of 420 Ethiopian Birr [ETB]), in 1996. In 2005, the civil servant was serving as a head of personnel administration earning 895 ETB monthly. Next, in the year 2006, he had changed his position to record and documentation expert (salary 1040 ETB).

As a result of the BSC initiative, the civil servant became a mining license and documentation expert; his salary was 1617 ETB. The 2012 job restructuring changed the civil servant's position to a planning, monitoring, and evaluation expert earning 2249 (ETB), which was increased to 2934 ETB in 2013, due to a civil servants' salary adjustment initiative. In 2016, the civil servant under consideration was earning 3909 (ETB) working as a socio-economic expert. The 2017 salary adjustment initiative increased his salary to 7346 ETB. In Ethiopia/ Oromia, the government is using salary adjustment to respond to an inflation problem; it has stopped issuing biannual civil servant's salary increment specified as a right in the civil service proclamation of 2003 (World Bank, 2019). Table 7 presents the pay scale and the proportion of civil servants in each pay structure for selected years.

The results in table 7 reveal that civil servants saw three salary adjustments between 2008 and 2018. While the lower pay scale in 2008 was 235 ETB, it was nearly 1000 ETB in 2017. A significant majority of male civil servants (79 percent in 2008 and 72 percent in 2010) and female civil servants (88 percent in 2008 and 83% in 2010) were earning a monthly salary between 400 ETB to 1500 ETB. In 2013, gender-based pay inequality remained

Table 7: Civil servants' pay scale

Pay scale	2008		2010		Pay scale	2013		2010	
	M %	F%	M %	F%		M %	F%	M %	F%
235-399	6,5	8,1	4	5,4	400-499	5,6	7,2	0,3	0,3
400-999	**55,3**	**71,8**	**47,2**	**61,7**	500-999	**49,3**	**64,9**	7,4	10,5
1000-1499	**24,1**	**16,4**	**25,5**	**21**	1000-1499	**27,4**	**22,6**	8,4	11,2
1500-1999	9,5	2,6	10,2	3,5	1500-1999	10,9	3,7	**18,1**	**27,6**
2000-2499	3,6	0,9	4,9	1,2	2000-2499	5,3	1,3	**18,9**	**17**
2500-2999	0,7	0,1	0,7	0,1	2500-2999	0,8	0,1	**12,7**	**12,6**
>3000	0,3	0,1	0,6	0,1	>3000	0,7	0,1	**34,3**	**20,7**
Not Stated			6,8	7	Not Stated				

Pay scale	2016		Pay scale	2017		2018	
	M %	F%		M %	F%	M %	F%
500-599	0,5	1,7	<1000	0,8	0,9	0,7	1,1
600-999	7,4	8,9	1000-1999	**11,5**	**15,1**	**11,2**	**14,3**
1000-1499	**5,4**	**7,6**	2000-2999	**18,9**	**27,8**	**19,6**	**28,3**
1500-1999	**16,8**	**26,7**	3000-3999	**20,2**	**22,3**	**18,8**	**20,6**
2000-2499	**16,6**	**16,1**	4000-4999	**18**	**15,6**	**17,1**	**16,6**
2500-2999	**13,2**	**14**	5000-5999	13,1	9,2	12,7	8,9
3000-3499	12,9	10,5	6000-6999	11,6	6,7	12,3	7,1
3500-3999	12	7,4	7000-7999	3,1	1,5	3,8	1,7
> 4000	15,1	7,2	8000-8999	1,4	0,5	1,6	0,6
			9000-9999	0,7	0,3	1	0,3
			>10000	0,9	0,2	1,2	0,4

Source: Complied from Federal Civil Service Commission Database

significant; 77 of men percent and 88 percent of women earned between 400 ETB to 1500 ETB. However, in 2015 the pay gap between male and female civil servants was relatively reduced. Contrarily, in 2016, gender-based pay inequality relatively increased; 52 percent of male and 64.4 percent of female civil servants were receiving monthly salary between 1000 to 3000 ETB. In

2017 and 2018 the pay gap between males and females earning a monthly salary between 1000 to 3000 ETB was relatively reduced.

But pay inequality is not necessarily due solely to performance results and academic qualification and gender. As already discussed, it may also be due to the presence privileged and removed political executives who were assigned as civil servants, and due to the creation of a special organization. Overall this contradicts the Civil Servant Proclamation, which mandates equal pay for equal work and competitive promotion (a minimum of satisfactory performance, all things remaining constant) (ORS, 2002).

7.5. Civil Servants Separation

According to the Federal Civil Service Commission database, between 2008 and 2018, in Oromia National Regional State, a total of 87,997 (male) and 35,760 (female) civil servants were separated from their positions. Table 8 reports the cause of civil servants' separation for selected years.

The table reveals a great number of civil servants were separated due to transfer and voluntary departure, followed by separations due to appointments, retirement, and structural change (see table 8). Separation due to performance (inefficiency) and disciplinary cases was scant, suggesting these factors have limited effect on civil servants' tenure. Concerning gender, the vast majority of female civil servants were separated due to transfer and voluntary resignation, while a relatively higher percentage of male civil servants were detached due to retirement and appointment.

8. Conclusions and Implications

Empirical analysis reveals that the changing politico-administrative contexts, the structural-instrumental reforms by a single-party state since the 1990s, increased the responsibilities of the institution mandated for civil service and HRM. There were also other official changes. Among others, we observed a shift from centralized HRM to a decentralized system, a shift from seniority to merit and qualification, and a shift from position-based job classification to a points-rating job classification method.

We found that the reforms reinforce the NPM-inspired customer- and result-oriented performance management rhetoric. However, we have not found a linkage between meritocracy, result-oriented performance, and competence and the separation of civil servants due to incompetence (performance). Excellent performance results and competency do not warranty

Table 8: Civil Servants Separation

Item	2012		2014		2016		2018	
	M(%)	F(%)	M(%)	F(%)	M(%)	F(%)	M(%)	F(%)
Retirement	**5,4**	**1,2**	**6**	**3**	**8,5**	**6,9**	**8,3**	**5,6**
Illness	2,4	1,2	0,4	0,6	2,2	1,6	0,8	1,4
Death	3,8	3,3	2,3	2,2	3	3,4	3	3,7
Discipline Case	1,3	0,3	1	0,2	1,1	0,9	1	0,6
Inefficiency (performance)	0,5	0,9	0,5	0,5	1,1	0,9	0,4	0,5
Personal Case (Voluntarily)	**24,7**	**19,2**	**34,9**	**37,8**	**26,8**	**30**	**18,6**	**18,9**
Transfer	**31,4**	**24,5**	**37,6**	**43,9**	**39,6**	**44,9**	**39,3**	**44,9**
Appointment	**9,6**	**4,3**	**7,2**	**3,3**	**10,7**	**6,7**	**13,9**	**9,4**
Order	1,4	7,7	2,5	1,7	0	0	0	0
Other (Due to Structural Change)	16,9	17,5	4,8	3,6	4,6	4	0	0
Not Stated	2,7	19,8	2,9	3,2	2,4	0,6	14,7	15,2
Total	8194	4623	12552	5322	11390	4628	10036	4000
Total(M+F)	12817		17874		16018		14036	

Source: Compiled from Federal Civil Service Commission Database

spectacular promotion and increased pay. Periodic nominal salary adjustment apply to all civil servants and pay is inadequate for civil servants' well-being. In 2018, the vast majority of civil servants were earning monthly less than or equal to 3000 ETB. There are also high rates of gender-based occupational segregation, contributing to pay inequality. Moreover, the reform privileged ex-political executives and civil servants working in special salary organizations. And also, unlike the trend in OECD countries, the number of civil servants has spectacularly increased.

We also observed four major continuities. First, a government institution responsible for civil service is also responsible for HRM. Second, the reforms/tools were used to strengthen vertical and horizontal coordination and control (see also Gudina, 2007). Third, they were also used to increasingly politicize the civil service, particularly top civil servants – a feature common to all Ethiopian regimes – and to remove unwanted civil servants (Mitiku, 2018).

Political interference in HRM also appears to be significant (Kacho et al., 2016). Fourth, fundamentally, rather than primarily serving the public and improving public sector performance, the reforms were used as an instrument to enhance the allegiance of civil servants to political executives, particularly in the aftermath of the 2005 national election. This appears to be partly due to the deep-seated, top-down and discriminatory neo-patrimonialism and authoritarian administrative tradition (Abbink, 2006; Gudina, 2007), as well as to the lessons learned from the self- and group-evaluation and compliance culturecharacteristic of the EPRDF party (Abbink, 2006; Mitiku, 2018). Similarly, during Emperor Hailesellassie's regime, public servants held extraordinary loyalty to the emperor (Emperor Hailesellassie, 1961). Overall, the HRM and civil service trajectories are explained by path dependency and the diffusions of NPM ideas.

Two major implications could be made. First, notwithstanding positive gains, frequent, excessive, and improper HRM reform has a significant negative effect on the sustainability of public administration and civil service. Improper work-related relationships and actions can increasingly affect the behavior of civil servants (Perry & Van de Walle, 2008) and imperil their public service motivation (Paarlberg et al., 2008). They may also disrupt the institutional memory of the public sector. Second, the inadequate salary and increasing pay gap in general, and the underrepresentation of female civil servants and gender-based occupational segregation, in particular, have a negative consequence on Ethiopia's to meet the UN's Sustainable Development Goals (SDGs) and African Union (AU) Agenda 2063, which put citizens at the center in public administration and aim to ensure inclusiveness, gender parity in public administration, and justice for all at all levels (AU, 2014; UN, 2015).

Finally, given the deep-seated top-down public policymaking approach, wherein regions and local governments are responsible for public policy implementation (Debela, 2017), we assume the results of this study can be fairly generalized to other Ethiopian regions and city administrations. However, since there is inter-regional politico-administrative cultural variation (Peterson, 2015), we suggest comparative research for the future. In addition, future research should use secondary and primary data and investigate the overall impacts of HRM instruments combining theory and practice.

Acknowledgements

This study has been carried out in the framework of the academic cooperation for development project "Professionalizing Ethiopian Public Administration to Support Development Practitioners" between KU Leuven, Ambo University, and Addis Ababa University, financed by VLIR-UOS (Belgium). We earnestly thank these institutions. We also thank the Ethiopian Federal Civil Service Commission for providing the civil servants database. We are also indebted to a civil servant for sharing his placement letters and clarifying the context. We also sincerely thank our interviewee at Oromia State University.

Notes

1. HRM, Expenditure Management and Control, Top Management Systems, Service Delivery and Quality service, and Civil Service Ethics.
2. Civil Service Reform, District Level Decentralized Service Delivery, Information and Communications Technology, Justice System Reform, Tax System Reform and Urban Management.
3. member of the regional administrative council (2002-04)
4. member of the regional administrative council (2004)
5. member of the regional administrative council (2005-10)
6. The public organizations were responsible for preparing their organizational structure, with detailed duties and responsibilities for each position, and the CSC was mandated to approve it.
7. (a) Preparedness to implement government policies and development plans, (b) performance results, (c) free from corruption, (d) free from participation in anti-peace and affiliation to unlawful political parties, and (5) readiness to accept structural change and practice. A civil servant can be dismissed on the grounds of failing to meet of one of the criteria or combination thereof.
8. (a) when mutual agreement is maintained between the office with which the civil servants is working and to which the civil servant is to be transferred, (b) when the civil servant agrees to transfer, (c) when the CSC approves the transfer, and (d) when the regional government causes the transfer on the grounds of the necessity of work.
9. The CSC is responsible for undertaking studies on the incentive schemes for district employees working in harsh conditions and implementing it upon approval by the regional administrative council.
10. The directive gives three and four additional points for female and physically challenged applicants in job competition.
11. A civil servant who has a personal problem, on good faith and based on mutual consent, can be internally transferred to a horizontal position (without reducing his/her salary) or lower position (reduced salary).

12. Organizational BCS based-performance results (50 percent), supervisor's evaluation (30 percent), customers' and stakeholders' evaluation (10 percent), and immediate leaders' group evaluation (10 percent); and individual performance evaluation: Supervisor evaluation (30 percent), peer evaluation (20 percent), customers' and stakeholders' evaluation (40 percent), and self-evaluation (10%). Both are rated on four performance levels (≥90 percent [excellent], 75 percent-89 percent [very good], 60 percent-74 percent [satisfactory], and ≤59% [low]).
13. ≥90 percent (excellent), 80 percent-89 percent (very good), 65 percent-79 percent (good), 50 percent-64 percent (satisfactory), <50 percent (low).
14. BSC-based performance results (70 percent), supervisor evaluation (10 percent), customers' and stakeholders' evaluation (10 percent), and immediate leader group evaluation (10 percent).
15. BSC-based performance results (50 percent), peer evaluation (20 percent), customers' and stakeholders' evaluation (20 percent), and self-evaluation (10 percent).
16. Performance results (70 percent), willingness and commitment to implement government policies and plans (10 percent), personal record (file) quality related to disciplinary cases (10 percent), and service at higher position (10 percent).
17. Individual performance result (35 percent), competence in discharging duties and responsibilities (30 percent, assessed by employee's head/processor), professionalism in service delivery (30 percent, assessed by employee's head/processor), and personal file quality related to disciplinary case (5 percent).

References

Abbink, J. (2017). Paradoxes of Electoral Authoritarianism: The 2015 Ethiopian Elections as Hegemonic Performance. *Journal of Contemporary African Studies*, 35(3), 03-323.

Abbink, J. (2006). Discomfiture of Democracy? The 2005 Election Crisis in Ethiopia and Its Aftermath. *African Affairs*, 105(419), 173-199.

African Union (AU). (2014). Agenda 2063. The Africa We Want. https://au.int/agenda2063

Assefa, H. (2017). The Quest for Professional Civil Service in Ethiopia: Practices and Challenges. *International Journal of Advance Research and Development*, 2(7), 100-107. www.IJARND.com.

Bovaird, T., & Loffler, E. (2001). Emerging Trends in Public Management and Governance. *BBS Teaching and Research Review*, 5, 1-10.

Brans, M. (1997). Challenges to the Practice and Theory of Public Administration in Europe. *Journal of Theoretical Politics*, 9(3), 389-415.

Christensen, T., Lægreid, O. M., & Lægreid, P. (2019). Administrative Coordination Capacity; Does the Wickedness of Policy Areas Matter?. *Policy and Society*, *38*(2), 237-254.

Daba, N. (2016). Human Resource Dynamics in Oromia Regional State, Ethiopia: Trends and Challenges. *European Journal of Business and Management*, 8(25), 74-81.

Debela, B. & Troupin S. (2016). Transforming Ethiopian Public Administration for Sustainable Development: The Impact of Organizational Proliferation and Policy Coordination on Access to Drinking Water. 37th AAPAM Roundtable Conference, Zambia, Lusaka, February 29 to March 4, 2016.

Debela, B. (2017). Managing Performance in Ethiopian Municipalities: A Benchlearning Approach of Urban Water Services in Oromia National Regional State. PhD thesis, KU Leuven.

Emperor Haile Sellassie. (1961). An Order to Provide for the Creation and Function of the Imperial *Ethiopian Central Personnel Agency*. Order no. 23, 1961.

Gudina, M. (2007). Ethnicity, Democratisation and Decentralization in Ethiopia: The Case of Oromia. *Eastern Africa Social Science Research Review*, 23(1), 81-106.

Federal Democratic Republic of Ethiopia (FDRE). (2004). A Proclamation to Amend the Public Servants Pension, Proclamation no. 424/2004, *Federal Negarit Gazeta*, Addis Ababa.

Hall, P., & Taylor, R. (1996). Political Science and the Three New Institutionalisms. *Political Studies*, 44(5), 936-57.

Kacho, B., Zeleke, T. & Gebremedhin, G. (2016). The Implementation of Human Resource Management Reform Program and Practices of Professionalism in Selected Cities in Ethiopia. In *Public Sector Transformation and Development Proceedings of the 2nd National Conference*, Vol. 1 (18-33).

Kitaw, D. (2011). Experience of Kaizen in Ethiopia and the Way Forward. October 17. Tokyo, Japan. www.grips.ac.jp.

Lægreid, P., Roness, P. G., & Rubecksen, K. (2008). Performance Information and Performance Steering: Integrated System or Loose Coupling? In Van Dooren, W and Van de Walle, S. (ed) *Performance Information in the Public Sector: How it is used*. London: Palgrave Macmillan, pp. 42-57.

Lampropoulou, M., & Oikonomou, G. (2018). Theoretical Models of Public Administration and Patterns of State Reform in Greece. *International Review of Administrative Sciences*, 84(1), 101-121.

Markos, S. (2013). Civil Service Reform in Ethiopia: Issues, Lessons, and Future Directions. *International Journal of Public Administration*, 36(4), 235-247.

Miruts, G. & Daba, N. (2016). Change Army: The New Face of Modernizing Civil Service in Ethiopia (The Case of Addis Ababa). In *Public Sector Transformation and Development Proceedings of the 2nd National Conference*, vol. 1, 93-102.

Mitiku A. (2018). The Ethiopian Public Sector Leadership Profile Unveiled; Determining the Leadership Profile of the Ethiopian Federal Civil Service Organizations. Adapted PhD thesis (book), KU Leuven, Public Governance Institute, Belgium.

Ongaro, E., & Ferlie, E. (2019). Exploring Strategy-Making in "Non-New Public Management" Public Services Settings: The Case of European Union Agencies. *Administrative Sciences*, 9(1), 23.

Oromia Civil Service Commission. (OCSC) (2006). Oromia Regional State Human Resource Management Directive, vol. 1, Finfine.

Oromia Public Service and Human Resource Development Bureau (OPSHRDB) (2012). Oromia Regional State Human Resource Performance Based Reward Directive. Finfine.

— (2016). Reform tools implementation guideline. Finfine.

— (2017). Oromia Regional State Human Resource Placement Directive. Finfine.

— (2017). Oromia Regional State Performance evaluation, Standardization and Reward implementation directive. Finfine.

— (2017).Oromia Regional State false academic and professional competency certificate investigation directive. Finfine.

— (2018). Oromia Regional State Human Resource Placement Directive. Finfine.

Oromia Regional State (1995). The Establishment of the Executive Organs of the Oromia Regional State. Proclamation No. 7/1995. Megeleta Oromia, Finfine.

— (2002). Oromia Regional State Civil Servants Proclamation. Proclamation No. 61/2002. Megeleta Oromia, Finfine.

— (2002). A proclamation to Provide for the Reorganization and Redefinition of Powers and Duties of the Executive Organs of the Regional State of Oromia. Proclamation No. 50/2002. Megeleta Oromia, Finfine.

— (2004). A proclamation to Provide for the Reorganization and Redefinition of Powers and Duties of the Executive Organs of the Oromia Regional State. Proclamation No. 87/2004. Megeleta Oromia, Finfine.

— (2004). Oromia Regional State Civil Servants Amendment Proclamation. Proclamation No. 79/2004. Megeleta Oromia, Finfine.

— (2005). A Proclamation Issued to Amend Oromia National Regional State Civil Servants Proclamation, Pro. No. 61/2002. Proclamation No. 104/2005. Megeleta Oromia, Finfine.

— (2005). A proclamation Issued to Amend the Reorganization and Redefinition of Powers and Duties of the Executive Organs of the Oromia Regional State. Pro. No. 87/2004. Proclamation No. 105/2005 Megeleta Oromia, Finfine.

— (2006). A Proclamation Issued to Amend Oromia Regional State Civil Servants Proclamation, Pro. No. 61/2002. Proclamation No. 123/2006. Megeleta Oromia, Finfine.

— (2007). A proclamation Issued to Amend the Reorganization and Redefinition of Powers and Duties of the Executive Organs of the Oromia Regional State. Proc. No. 87/2004 and its amending Proc. 105/2005. Proclamation No. 132/2007 Megeleta Oromia, Finfine.

— (2011). A proclamation to Provide for the Reorganization and Redefinition of Powers and Duties of the Executive Organs of the Oromia National Regional State. Proclamation No. 163/2011. Megeleta Oromia, Finfine.

— (2016). A proclamation to Provide for the Reorganization and Redefinition of Powers and Duties of the Executive Organs of the Oromia National Regional State. Proclamation No. 199/2016. Megeleta Oromia, Finfine.

Paarlberg, L., Perry, J., & Hondeghem, A. (2008). Editor's Introduction. In J. Perry & A. Hondeghem (eds). *Motivation in Public Management: the Call of Public Service* (pp. 268-293). Oxford: Oxford University Press.

Perry, J. & Van de Walle S. (2008). Behavioral Dynamics: Institutions, Identities, and Self-Regulation. In J. Perry & A. Hondeghem (eds). *Motivation in Public Management: the Call of Public Service* (pp. 56-79). Oxford: Oxford University Press.

Peterson, S. B. (2015). *Public Finance and Economic Growth in Developing Countries: Lessons from Ethiopia's Reforms.* London: Routledge.

Pollitt, C. & Bouckaert, G. (2009). *Continuity and Change in Public Policy Management.* Edward Elgar Publishing Limited.

Pollitt, C. (2005). Performance Management in Practice: A Comparative Study of Executive Agencies. *Journal of Public Administration Research and Theory,* 16(1), 25-44.

Pollitt, C., & Bouckaert, G. (2017). Public Management Reform: A Comparative Analysis – into the Age of Austerity, 4th ed. New York: Oxford University Press.

Pollitt, C., Bouckaert, G. & Löffler, E. (2004). Quality Journeys in the European Public Sector: From There, to Here, to Where? In *3rd Quality Conference for Public Administrations in the EU, Rotterdam,* http://www. 3qconference. org.

Schmidt, V. (2006). Institutionalism. In Hay C., Lister, M. & Marsh D. (ed.), *The State: Theories and Issues* (pp. 98-117). London: Palgrave Macmillan.

Schwab, C., Bouckaert, G., & Kuhlmann, S. (eds). (2017). *The Future of Local Government in Europe, Lessons from Research and Practice in 31 Countries.* Nomos Verlagsgesellschaft mbH & Co.KG.

Steen, T., Teles, F., & Torsteinsen, H. (2017). Improving Local Service Delivery: Increasing Performance through Reforms. In C. Schwab, G. Bouckaert & S. Kuhlmann (eds). *The Future of Local Government in Europe* (pp. 53-78). Nomos Verlagsgesellschaft mbH & Co. KG.

Tadesse, W. M. (2019). Public Service Reform in Ethiopia: Challenges and Gaps Post-implementation. *Africa's Public Service Delivery and Performance Review,* 7(1), 1-9.

Transitional Government of Ethiopia (1992). Proclamation to Provide for the Establishment of National Regional Self-Governments. Proclamation No. 7/1992. *Negarit Gazeta,* Addis Ababa.

Transitional Government of Ethiopia (1993). Proclamation Defining the Powers and Duties of the Central and Regional Governments. Proclamation No. 41/1993. *Negarit Gazeta,* Addis Ababa.

United Nations. (2015). Transforming Our World: The 2030 Agenda for Sustainable Development. General Assembly (70/1).

World Bank. (2013). Federal Democratic Republic of Ethiopia Public Sector Reform Approach Building the Developmental State–A Review and Assessment of the Ethiopian Approach to Public Sector Reform, Report No: ACS3695, The World, USA, Washington, DC. http://documents.worldbank.org. Accessed August 20, 2014.

World Bank. (2019). Moving Further on Civil Service Reforms in Ethiopia: Findings and Implications from a Civil Survey and Qualitative Analysis, Synthesis Report, the World Bank. **http://documents.worldbank.org/curated/en/981311547566282423/pdf/133754-WP** November 19.

14
Strategic Contribution of Middle Managers in the Ethiopian Civil Service Organization

Alebachew Asfaw Yimer

Box 1: Key conclusions

- ✓ Middle managers in the Ethiopian civil service context are managers who are placed between the top layers of executives (heads and deputies) and the operating staff (supervisory level managers and frontline workers) in the organization.
- ✓ Middle managers presently contribute a great deal in the overall strategic management of civil service organizations.
- ✓ The key role middle managers play in the Ethiopian civil service falls in the fourth quadrant of the competing value framework (CVF), where an emphasis is given to facilitation and mentoring activities.
- ✓ Middle managers serve as an information hub in the organization due their unique place in the organizational hierarchy.
- ✓ Middle managers manage both human and physical resources to achieve organizational objectives.

Box 2: Middle managers' contribution in organizations

Reading this chapter will give insights in:

- ✓ defining middle managers in civil service organizations;
- ✓ articulating the strategic contributions of middle managers in the Ethiopian civil service at present;
- ✓ understanding the competing roles middle managers play in Ethiopian politic-administrative contexts.

Box 3: Abbreviations used in this chapter

CSOs = Civil Service Organizations
CHANFOC = Change Focused
CVF = Competing Value Framework

HRFOC = Human Relation Focused
MM/s = Middle Manager/s
PRODFOC = Production/result Focused
RULFOC = Rule Focused

1. Introduction

Middle managers (MMs) occupy a unique position that enables them to mediate between an organization's top-level executives and lower-level employees. They are responsible for planning, coordinating, leading, and controlling staff and other resources in the execution of tasks. Recent literature in the field (Balogun, 2003; Balogun & Johnson, 2004; Huy, 2001; Kaiser, Craig, Overfield, & Yarborough, 2011; Mintzberg, 2009; Wooldridge, Schmid, & Floyd, 2008) asserts that middle managers are active in the entire strategy process of organizations, from formulation to implementation and evaluation. Yet, there are also scholars like Kealy (2013) who consider middle managers as order recipients from the organization's leadership. This topic is an uncharted area in the Ethiopian public sector case. Consequently, this chapter aims at contributing to the understanding of middle managers' strategic contributions in civil service organizations in Ethiopia. A document review on how the civil service works toward strategy development and execution was conducted. The theoretical foundation used in analyzing the strategic roles middle managers play in the Ethiopian civil service was the competing value framework (CVF) initially developed by Quinn, Faerman, Thompson, and McGrath (2003) in the 1980s. 368 middle managers and 12 senior officials participated in this research project. This study contributes toward the scant literature regarding middle managers in the Ethiopian context.

2. The Problem

Significant work in the area of public managers has been made across the globe; yet, there is a paucity of literature concerning middle managers in relation to the Ethiopian context (Mitiku, Hondeghem, & Troupin, 2017). In addition to this, researches of public management are more focused on senior public managers engaged in political decision-making than those working to interface decisions with actions in the public sector (Kellerman & Webster, 2001).

The government of Ethiopia has introduced various change initiatives to ensure efficient and effective service delivery. The BPR, BSC, Kaizen, Citizen's

Charter, Change Army, and similar other outside-tested tools have been introduced in this respect (Araya, 2019; Ethiopian Civil Service University, 2016). BPR was used to reorganize government institutions in early 2000, while the introduction of BSC was an immediate follow-up to the BPR. Kaizen was also introduced in many of the state-owned enterprises to reduce waste and improve efficiency. The application of the Change Army concept was a recent effort by the government in building teams at the organizational level to streamline efforts by the different actors, including the public (Araya, 2019). Although middle managers are the center in all these initiatives, no special attention was given to them. Little was done to learn about their influence in the change process.

Examining the Ethiopian civil service, this study highlights the strategic engagement of middle managers in general and their inclination at present in executing their tasks in particular. The study utilizes the competing value framework (CVF) to conceptualize the current experiences of organizations' middle managers.

Professional middle managers play a vital role in connecting the entire workforce with the top executives of the civil service. That is why it is important to deal with the definition, roles, and responsibilities of middle-level public managers in civil service organizations at present. We rely on a literature review, observations of practical situations, and findings from interviews to arrive at a clear framework describing middle managers in the Ethiopian civil service. This research set out to explore who middle managers are in civil service organizations and identify the most dominant roles they are playing at present. Through the use of cross-sectional data, this chapter examines the following two research questions:

1. Who are the middle managers in the Ethiopian civil service?
2. What managerial roles are most emphasized by middle managers in Ethiopian civil services at present?

3. Review of Literature

3.1. Managerial Jobs in the Public Sector

Managers are individuals responsible for the work of other people (Drucker, 2008; McIntosh & Luecke, 2010) to achieve an organization's objectives. Managers are expected to be rational (Clegg, Kornberger, & Pitsis, 2015) and predictable by making sense of things around them. They are expected to demonstrate a steady focus in times of confusion, ambiguity, and puzzle by making sense of their environment (Clegg et al., 2015; Weick, 1995). Being the representative of their organization, managers interact with different stakeholders from within and outside the organization. Stakeholders' need for information, assistance, direction, and authorization requires the attention organization managers (Yukl, 2010). The degree of managerial activities, skills required, and roles played are different at different hierarchal levels (Hales & Mustapha, 2000). Managers influence systems, conditions, and environments as they strive for success in their unit or organization. Consequently, the functions of management carried out by managers depend on the hierarchical level, functional specialization, and jobs given to them at a given time (Hales & Mustapha, 2000).

Managers engage in a variety of activities that are brief in duration, fragmented, and varied in nature (Mintzberg, 1971, 2009). They encounter frequent interruptions (Daft, 2008; Mintzberg, 2009; Yukl, 2010). Due to the voluminous and fragmented nature of activities and an overload of trivial activities, managers devote little time to reflective planning (Daft, 2008; Mintzberg, 2009; Yukl, 2010). Public managers differentiate among issues to be resolved based on pressure from subordinates, superiors, peers, staff, and people from government agencies (HBR, 2011; Yukl, 2010).

Managerial work is defined by the functions of management, such as planning, staffing, coordinating, supervising, negotiating, representing, and evaluating (Mahoney, Jerdee & Carroll, as cited in Allan, 1981). For Mintzberg (1990), managerial work involves performing regular duties that link the organization with its external environment. Exploring managerial work carried out by public managers in city governments, Allan (1981) found that they are highly engaged in task dimensions that include supervision of employees, harmonizing or integrating work activities, information handling, analyzing and evaluating, change-initiating, and monitoring regardless of title or agency.

Managers play different roles in organizations, from showing how to operate a machine to making decisions about where to invest scarce company resources. Clegg et al. (2015) concludes that managers' jobs:

> ... *involve interpreting, understanding, directing, cajoling, communicating, leading, empowering, training, politicking, negotiating, enthusing, encouraging, focusing, explaining, excusing, obfuscating, communicating – a job full of action words that are all to do with the manager as a speaking subject, a person who manages to shape and express directions, in writing and in speech.* (Clegg et al., 2015:9)

Using an importance rating, Kraut, Pedigo, McKenna, and Dunnette (1989) conducted research to find out the difference in managerial roles and activities across different levels and functions in organizations. Based on their research, they identified seven major factors or groups of management tasks, including: managing individual performance, instructing subordinates, planning and allocating resources, coordinating interdependent groups, managing group performance, monitoring the business environment, and representing one's staff. Therefore, managerial work in an organization is full of activities that are not as limited to specific engagement as one would think.

3.2. Strategy Process and Public Managers

Public managers formulate and execute strategies with many actors, including elected officials, legislative bodies, the courts, interest groups, the media, and the general public (Feldman, 1980; Nutt & Backoff, 1995). Consequently, public managers have constrained capacity over different issues in formulating and executing government strategies. Though constrained by internal and external factors, public managers are expected to work and deliver results for their organization. Public managers execute a plan with scarce resources, pressures from within and outside the organization, and poorly coordinated teams. Weak cross-functional cooperation, time pressures, the poorly defined nature of tasks, and lack of incentive and support from above add to the challenge they face in their journey (Noble, 1999a).

Strategy development in the public sector must consider government policies, direction and objectives based on its place in the governance structure. The institutional mission or purpose and basic goals of public organizations are determined externally by the legislature and hence, the freedom of public managers in setting goals, amending missions, or adjusting the methods is far less than that of their private sector counterparts (Tompkins, 2005). The growing complexity of societal demand for better goods and services (in education, health, transportation, ecology, and other social services) is leading governments to the introduction of various measures, including privatizing firms, issuing laws on consultations to workers and citizens, and adding a business flavor to publicly owned enterprises (Ansoff, 1990). In this regard, public managers are contributing significantly to the strategy-making process of organizations by linking endorsed policies with the daily operations of the organization. Cascading goals, allocating resources among the different units, formulating and implementing strategies that span individual work units and providing leadership are the duties of public managers.

Execution is the other stage of the strategy process that is crucial in the public sector. Many observers agree on the problem of executions rather than planning in public organizations (Kaplan & Norton, 2001; Rajasekar, 2014; Zagotta & Robinson, 2002). Execution is a disciplined process with a logical set of connected activities that create a conducive platform for an organization to realize its strategy (Hrebiniak, 2005). It is a process of selecting the most appropriate organizational structure for the chosen strategy, support systems for resource allocation, suitable leadership, and control mechanisms for a smooth flow of operations (Alkhafaji, 2003). Implementing strategies requires going beyond rational decisions by public managers and incorporating calibration to the existing situations, which leads to what Mintzberg and Waters (1985) described as emergent strategies. It also requires focusing on business priority, cascading accountabilities, high-quality interactions, and ensured sustainability (Coon & Wolf, 2005).

Strategy execution takes place through the fabrics of the organizational architecture, including structure, policies, procedures, systems, incentives, and governance (Lussier & Achua, 2015). The ability to execute strategy flawlessly contributes to the success of organizations. However, there are formidable roadblocks or hurdles that get in the way of executing strategies (Hrebiniak, 2005). According to Hrebiniak (2005) and Noble (1999b) the major problems or hurdles affecting strategy implementation include the longer time frames needed for execution; the need for the involvement of many actors in the execution process; poor or vague strategy; conflicts with the organizational power structure; problems in cross-functional coordination; poor structure, including information sharing and coordination methods; unclear responsibility and accountability in the execution process; and capacity problems in managing change, including cultural change.

3.3. Understanding Managerial Roles at the Middle

Defining Middle Managers in Organizations

Middle management is a broad term (Carlson, as cited in Mintzberg, 2009) and so the subject of much confusion in organizations (Hassard, McCann, & Morris, 2009). Authors like Huy (2001) and Mintzberg (2009) define middle managers as any managers who are positioned two levels below the senior executives and one level above the frontline workers, including professionals. According to some scholars (Hassard et al., 2009), MMs are individuals currying favor from above and communicating top management's orders down to the bottom ranks. For Kaplan and Norton (2001), middle managers implement programs based on orders from the senior managers. Middle managers (MMs) are managers who are found between the senior management that formulates strategy and the frontline supervisors and employees who implement it (Livian & Burgoyne, 1997; Mintzberg, 2009). Kay (as cited in Livian & Burgoyne, 1997) defined MMs as managers and technical people found below the senior executives (presidents and vice presidents) who run businesses without a profit/loss responsibilities. Similarly, Breen (as cited in Livian & Burgoyne, 1997) also defined MMs as people who keep the wheel of business running through a multitude of small and continuous decisions. Dopson, Neumann, and Newell (as cited in Livian & Burgoyne, 1997) defined MMs as individuals who are placed below a few top strategic managers and above first-line supervisors in organizations.

In the case of public sectors, middle managers occupy the place between first-line supervisors and department heads in local government (Morgan, Bacon, Bunch, Cameron, & Deis, 1996), bureau heads in regional governments, and ministers and their deputies at the federal level. They receive directions and milestones from the top, communicate these to employees, and critically follow up progress in implementation. It is the duty of this level of management to observe signs and symptoms of deviation and to take measures accordingly (Livian & Burgoyne, 1997).

Middle managers need to interpret corporate goals and strategic objectives into daily actionable plans so that frontline employees engage in operation effectively (Balogun & Johnson, 2004). Similarly, they secure senior management attention through "issue-selling," which creates an opportunity for them to exert influence upward in the organization hierarchy (Dutton & Ashford, as cited in Dutton, O'Neill, Hayes and Wierba, 1997). They serve as resource persons in strategy formulation and as key drivers in strategy implementation (Kuyvenhoven & Buss, 2011). They are important in connecting diverse work areas, serving as an interface between disconnected actors and an agent of change (Wooldridge et al., 2008).

Organizational performance is heavily influenced by what happens in the middle of the organization, rather than at the top (Currie & Procter, 2005). As most organizations are organized in multi tier hierarchies, MMs who are found between the top executives and the frontline supervisors and employees play a critical role in realizing organizational objectives. Middle managers carry out a variety of tasks, serving as nodal officers who help coordinate different units. They have tacit knowledge about their organization, which can help in addressing issues of high importance in executing strategies. They coordinate, mediate, negotiate, interpret, and connect organizational objectives at the strategic level with operational units at the lower levels (Floyd & Wooldridge, 1997). They serve as the providers of information to the upper-level management and as the people who are responsible for exerting pressure on the frontline workers and supervisors.

Middle managers occupy a strategic position in an organization, which enables them to observe daily routines with challenges and opportunities.

They are always involved in reading the general environment for any opportunities or threats relevant to the organization (White, 2004). Due to this unique position, they easily recognize the need for change and influence perceptions around the organization –up, down and across the hierarchy – regarding the required change (Huy, 2001). Therefore, they are management groups that translate strategies into detailed plans and enable employees to make sense of the plan to achieve the business's end result (Caye et al., 2010)

Having a better opportunity than others to understand the inner and outer environment of the organization, MMs are capable of detecting new ideas essential to the strategy (Dutton, Ashford, O'neill, Hayes, & Wierba, 1997). This task requires industry knowledge, working with others, and searching for current information. Implementation is more of the middle managers' job in an organization, and with this task they take the lion's share in completing the feedback loop in the system. During the implementation of a strategy, MMs are required to help others through the process, meeting the continuing operational demands of the business, and implementing required change in the system (Kuyvenhoven & Buss, 2011). Although strategy implementation brings many actors together, the middle managers have a strong influence on the way the lower-level actors interpret, adapt, and implement the designed strategy (Balogun, as cited in Kuyvenhoven & Buss; Hantang, 2005).

In general middle managers are indispensable in organizations, for three main reasons (Livian & Burgoyne, 1997). First, they serve as a lynchpin between the upper and the lower level, easing downward and upward communication in the strategy formulation and implementation process. Secondly, they help organizations in the articulation and transformation of organizational culture by aligning institutional and personal goals. The final reason for their importance lies in their role in matching jobs and individual action through experiential learning and their responsibility in dealing with a broad range of human resource issues within the organization. Hence, their managerial tasks are mainly integrative, focusing on cultural flexibility, experiential learning, and human resource management responsibility.

Managerial Roles at the Middle – The CVF Perspective

Named one of the forty most important frameworks in the history of business, the competing values framework (CVF) has been used in studying organization's effectiveness, managerial leadership, culture, development need, and other features for more than thirty years (Cameron, Quinn, DeGraff, & Thakor, 2006; Have, Have, Stevens, Elst, & Pol-Coyne, 2003; Lindquist & Marcy, 2014). According to Cameron et al. (2006, p. 6), the CVF serves as "a map, an organizing mechanism, a sense-making device, a source of new ideas, and a learning system." The framework shows the relationship, contradictions, and complementary nature of organizational features that coexist in a system. In analyzing the role of managers in an organization, eight roles of managers were identified through this framework. These roles are identified as innovating, brokering, producing, directing, coordinating, monitoring, facilitating, and mentoring. According to Denison, Hooijberg, and Quinn (1995, p. 526), effective managers are "those who have the cognitive and behavioral complexity to respond appropriately to a wide range of situations that may, in fact, require contrary or opposing behaviors." These roles are also designed in alignment with the four quadrants of organizational effectiveness models (Lindquist & Marcy, 2014; Quinn et al., 2003): the rational goal, internal process, human relations, and open system models.

The competing value framework (CVF) explains what makes managers effective in a paradoxical environment. Divided by two axes, each continuum between internal-external and flexibility-stability highlights an opposite value at the end of their range. The two axes form two-by-two tables (four quadrants). The four quadrants are labeled based on the orientation and relationships among the competing values that can arise in organizations. The first quadrant is called the "human relation model," which results from internal orientation and flexibility in the framework. The human relation model emphasizes people who are working in organizations. Core values in this model include participation, conflict resolution, and consensus building in the workplace. The "open system" model is focused on leading change, which requires adaptability and external focus in an organization. In the "rational goal" model, executing results is important and maintaining a stable structure is considered as a significant factor in achieving results. The "internal process" model associates itself with the strength of the organization, which includes the quality of internal communications, rules, and procedures. This model is related to formal organizational structure and bureaucratic arrangement of work processes, including documentation, measurement, and management of information.

The competing value framework (CVF) is an appropriate framework in public organizations, as "there are certainly multiple values, different leadership and managerial styles, and considerable change and evolving challenges at play" (Lindquist & Marcy, 2014:7). It is an integrative approach to contradictory and paradoxical elements within organizations. The imperatives to be efficient, effective, and responsive on the one hand and being legal, ethical, and impartial on the other often contradict each other, while both are needed equally from managers in public institutions. The CVF is helpful in integrating important managerial leadership values and behaviors that seem

Table 1: Summary of managerial roles and their descriptions in the competing value framework

No.	Managerial Roles	Defining descriptions of the managerial roles
1	**Mentoring role** (human relation quadrant)	- Relates to being considerate, helpful, sensitive, approachable, and open to followers - It is about empathy, credibility, and recognizing emotions in others (Clutterbuck & Megginson, 1999)
2	**Facilitating role** (human relation quadrant)	- Emphasis on managerial intention and action that foster collective effort, team spirits and morale in overcoming interpersonal conflicts (Quinn et al., 2003). - Enable managers to develop teams, ensure participative decision making, and apply conflict management skills in order to carry out the role effectively
3	**Monitoring role** (internal process quadrant)	- Controlling internal issues to ensure consistency and consolidate continuity - Seeking information to make a sound judgment regarding the organization
4	**Coordinating role** (internal process quadrant)	- Oversee routine work performances of subordinates and give due attention to tasks and projects, results, and people (DiPadova & Faerman, 1993) - Responsible for connecting the different individuals and work units - Emphasizes structures, including rules, policies, and procedures
5	**Directing role** (rational goal quadrant)	- Relates to setting goals which reflect the vision and mission of the organization - Emphasis on providing direction and clarifying expectations to subordinates to achieve predetermined goals (DiPadova & Faerman, 1993)
6	**Producing role** (rational goal quadrant)	- Reflected in the manager's personal productivity, commitment, and empowerment - Relates to the motivation and encouragement of employees (DiPadova & Faerman, 1993)
7	**Brokering role** (open system quadrant)	- Networking with the external environment to create a strategic alliance (Belasen, 1998) - Influencing subordinates through trust, expertise, social capital, and opportunity to command resources (Quinn et al., 2003).
8	**Innovating role** (open system quadrant)	- Focusing on adaptability and responsiveness as important features in organization - Creatively deal with risk and uncertainty, envision needed changes, and help others adapt to the turbulent environment (Belasen, 1998)

Figure 1: Managerial roles in the competing value framework (Source: Quinn et al., 2003:16)

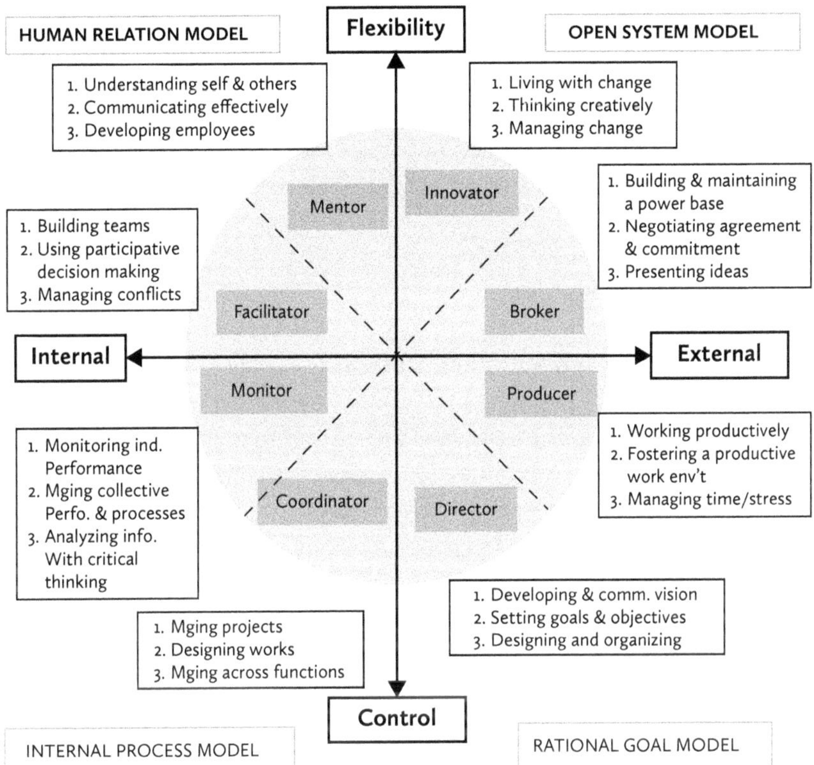

opposed to each other. Managers as leaders are required to carry out different roles in achieving organizational goals while they are working with others. These responsibilities are not always compatible with one another and may put managers in paradoxical tensions. Consequently, such responsibilities demand that they wear different hats on different occasions. The CVF considers this tension and helps managers to reach their goal by creating a balance among the conflicting demands for managerial leadership in organizations. Accordingly, the eight managerial leadership roles incorporated in the CVF were used in this study, to help find out where Ethiopian MMs focus at work. A brief explanation of these roles is presented below in table 1.

The four quadrants forming the overall model in the CVF are essential, as they are simultaneous and complementary opposites (Quinn & Rohrbaugh, 1983). Therefore, overusing any of the managerial leadership traits is catastrophic, as focusing on some leads to marginalizing the others. Overusing the internal process model (monitor and coordinator roles of managers) will result in maintaining the status quo. Too much focus on the human relation model (mentor and facilitator roles of managers) will lead to insufficient concern for productivity and goal accomplishment. Unchecked emphasis to change (focusing on innovator and broker roles) can lead to chaos. Therefore, managers are required to assess the dynamic environment regularly and play managerial roles in a balanced manner to accommodate conflicting demands in their organization. The four quadrants with the eight distinct managerial roles are presented in figure 1.

4. Methodology

4.1. Population and Sampling Design

This study focuses on the assessment of middle managers' strategic contribution in civil service organizations. The research approach was nonexperimental, mixed, and descriptive. For the purpose of this study, middle managers (MMs) are defined as people working under the heads or deputy heads of organizations and managing other managers and/or employees in that same organization. Based on this definition, the study required a national representative sample to generalize finding related to MMs in the country. Collecting data from a widely dispersed population of MMs in the entire public sector in the country was not possible due to cost as well as time constraints. Therefore, sample data were collected from representative offices identified randomly.

To represent offices at various levels, civil service organizations were categorized based on the government's mode of sectoral arrangements during the first half of 2018. 121 institutions were found at the federal level (Ministry of Public Service & Human Resource Development, 2015) and 21 were taken as a sample frame for the study. Educational institutions (like universities and colleges) and those engaged in medical care (like hospitals and health centers) were excluded from the sample due to the nature of their operations and administration. One regional state (Amhara), federal institutions (ministries and agencies), and a chartered city administration (Addis Ababa) were considered as appropriate for taking samples for this study. Though institutions at different levels follow one framework designed at the federal level, each level is mandated to craft their own procedures, manuals, and regulation based on their unique situation. Accordingly, proportional numbers of samples were included in the study to represent the clusters identified for this research.

4.2. Sample Size and Sampling Techniques

The sample size of quantitative data was calculated based on the total number of mid-level public sector managers in the federal, regional, and chartered city administration levels. For the purpose of this study, the Yemane sampling formula (as cited in Israel, 1992) was used to determine the appropriate sample size. Based on data acquired from the Ministry of Public Service & Human Resource Development (2015), the number of directorate and process owners (considered as middle managers in this study) was found to be around 4626. At a 95 percent confidence interval and with 0.05 margin of error, the sample size to be used was calculated as 368 MMs.

The population and sample size for the study were 4636 and 368 respectively. Proportional stratified sampling (Leedy & Ormrod, 2015) was used to apportion the total sample to each category in this study. Accordingly, the sample distribution for federal, regional, and city administrations were 125, 195, and 48 respectively. All 368 responses from middle managers were collected through strict follow-up and replacing missed participants in the process.

4.3. Characteristics of the Research Participants

Based on reviewed literature and existing practice in the civil service, middle managers in the Ethiopian civil service organizations are managers who are placed next to the politically appointed officials. As they assume their post through the merit system, middle managers are professionals in their work unit. Participants for the research were nominated using this definition, even though a variety of names and job titles are used in the civil service currently. With regard to individual middle manager characteristics, the majority of the study participants were young and adults below forty-five (65 percent), predominantly male (87 percent), and mostly from line departments (70 percent). According to the data, the gender gap at the middle management level was found to be significant. In terms of education, 50 percent of MMs held a BA degree, 48 percent held master's degrees, and 2 percent were PhDs. In addition, participants were taken from various sectors to represent the civil service in the country, namely, the economic (34 percent), administrative and governance (29.3 percent), and social sectors (27 percent).

Interviewees were senior public officials who were supervising middle managers in civil service organizations. A total of twelve participants (one female) were included from the three locations for this study. Five officials were taken from Amhara region, four were from the federal institutions, and three were from Addis Ababa city administration. All senior managers interviewed had attained the MA degree and worked as professionals in the civil service prior to their assignment in their current position.

4.4. Research Procedures and Measurement of Variables

The purpose of the study mainly was to explore the dominant role MMs play, in an effort describe their strategic engagement in the civil service organization. In the meantime, "who MMs are" in the civil service was assessed. Self-administered survey questions were used to collect information about managerial behaviors. Senior executives were interviewed on critical roles MMs play in organizations to triangulate the result from the survey. In addition to this, documents related to MMs' engagement in the strategy process were reviewed in sampled institutions.

Semi-structured interviews were conducted and interview questions were directly linked to middle managers' strategic engagement in organizations. The questions also include elements helpful for discerning the way senior officials defined MMs in the actual work setting. Accordingly, efforts were made to solicit the perceptions of senior managers on who middle managers are and how much they contribute to the overall strategic management of a civil service organization. Documents reviewed for this research include BPR and BSC documents from the Bureau of Civil service and the Bureau of Finance and Economic Development in the Amhara region.

As use of standardized and widely used measures would help a researcher to save time and effort (Blankenship, 2010), avoid mistakes (Tharenou, Donohue, & Cooper, 2007), and enable findings to compare with earlier work in the field (Price & Mueller as cited in Hinkin, 1995), tested measures with amendment were used for this study. Consequently, indicators developed by Quinn et al. (2003) were used to assess the basic research question in this study.

As data collected for this study were mainly ordinal data in nature, special attention was given to the design and coding to fulfill the requirement of equidistance. Consequently, a 7-point Likert scale having a mid-point in the center and using linguistic qualifiers for each category was utilized to assess the responses from the research participants.

The eight managerial roles identified by Quinn et al. (2003) are considered for the purpose of this study. The four quadrants in the CVF are made up of two major dimensions in organizations. The first dimension is the vertical axis, which demonstrates the flexibility-control continuum indicating how much an organization emphasizes centralization and control over flexibility and change. The second dimension indicates the internal-external continuum demonstrating the degree to which the organization is oriented toward its own internal issues as opposed to the external environment. Based on these premises, the CVF employs the human relation model, the open system model, the rational goal model, and the internal process model in the four major quadrants indicating the inclination of managers in organization. Considering the required behavioral needs of managers with respect to these four quadrants, the managerial roles in each quadrant were coined as change focused (CHANFOC), rule focused (RULFOC), production focused (PRODFOC), and human relation focused (HRFOC) in this study.

4.5. Data Analysis

The theoretical perspective of the competing value framework requires data analysis methods that would facilitate exploration of the most emphasized roles middle managers play in the civil service at present. This involved summarizing the quantitative data into categories to identify the roles middle managers play and the interviews with senior level officials about who middle managers are in their organizations. Quantitative data was analyzed using simple descriptive statistics, while qualitative data from the interviews was analyzed by aligning responses to predetermined themes. Analysis of qualitative data starts with transcribing the recorded documents. Transcripts were verified separately by the researcher to ensure accuracy and fill gaps that were found to be difficult by the stenographer during transcription.

Data obtained from the survey questionnaire on the demographic profile of participants was analyzed using descriptive statistics, including measures of mean, median, and standard deviation. Similar statistical analysis was used to identify dominant managerial roles played by MMs. Mean was calculated to understand what MMs on average think about their role in the civil service. The results from the quantitative data are also presented in a radar chart. Content analysis was used to analyze the data found through interviews. This was done using Microsoft Word and printed output from the interview transcripts.

5. Results

5.1. Who Are the Middle Managers in the Ethiopian Civil Service?

Based on the confirmation of all the research participants, an agreed upon definition of middle managers in the civil service is nonexistent. Consequently, senior officials' perspective about who middle managers are and what they do in the civil service is reviewed in this research, mainly using interviews. In the process, senior officials were asked to describe the various names given to middle managers in their organizations. They were also asked to give details on the various tasks (repetitive and occasional) middle managers perform in organization.

Senior officials mainly identified middle managers as directorate directors, process owners, and in some cases team leaders mostly working immediately under them. Research participants agree on the general pictures of middle managers, with very few differences between organizations. All those managers below the politically appointed officials are considered as middle managers in general. However, some officials in the civil service also consider professionals participating in the management committee as middle managers, even though these individuals do not have any managerial responsibilities in their work unit. For this reason, some described them as post holders below politically appointed officials, while others see middle managers as all individuals who belong to the management committee in their organization.

Participants broadly explained the lack of consistent and standard definitions of middle managers in civil service organizations (CSOs). Some also questioned the need for defining it, as they are civil servants who are not different from the others in any form, including skills, knowledge, and remuneration in general. In sum, participants reflected on the complexity and lack of clarity in the definition of middle management in CSOs, which often provoked personal consideration to the issue. Concerning the issue, one respondent said

> *I never come across a clear and standard definition to middle management. The only criterion we consider is the place of the manager in the organizational hierarchy. When managers are placed just below the politically appointed heads, we consider them as middle managers.* (Participant 12)

Participants explained that MMs are managers who take care of the day-to-day operation in the organization. The majority of the participants expressed their belief that MMs are the pillars of organization, placed next to the senior appointed officials. In praising middle managers' role and expressing their influence on the overall successes of CSOs, one participant said,

> *We, the politically appointed officials, are not experts in many respects. We spend much of our time in carrying out political assignments which made middle managers very crucial in running the organization. They have the expertise and the knowledge of the internal and external environment. They understand employees' and citizens' demand in respect to the given organization. Middle*

managers are the ones who take care of the detail in the overall mission of the organization. (Participant 4)

Documents were reviewed based on the information received from head and deputy heads of organizations about middle managers. Accordingly, MMs were found to be active in many respects covering the planning, execution, and evaluation of various tasks in CSOs. Jobs at the middle management level vary widely; however, some basic roles of MMs are fairly common. Based on job descriptions from various offices at the federal, regional, and Addis Ababa level, MMs are given tasks related to understanding and interpretation of organizational strategy, management of daily operations, and the management of resources in organizations.

Table 2: Middle managers' strategic involvement
(Sample tasks taken from middle managers' job descriptions)

Job title	Issues included in job descriptions
Operations Head	- Ensures possible synergy among work units - Advises the head and deputy head on policy matters - Sets goal and objectives to guide the overall operation of the organization - Monitors work unit performance and takes actions for improvements - Monitors department materials and supplies, ordering as needed and verifying the accuracy of supplies received
Human Resource Management (HRM) Director	- Prepares strategic HR Plan consistent with the overall organizational strategies - Designs and recommends administrative policies by adapting national and regional policies to ensure consistent standards with others in the civil service - Develops HRM-related strategies and operational plan to execute later - Ensures efficient and effective handling of HRM tasks, such as human resource planning, recruitment, placement, development, promotion, and transfer - Coordinates the human resource tasks across the organization

Source: Job descriptions from the civil service offices

Job description documents found in the Amhara civil service commission were reviewed in order to check similarities and differences in task assignment for middle managers. Accordingly, it was observed that some MMs were found to enjoy a narrower span of control while the others have many subordinates under their supervision. Managers in the staff departments have more subordinates than technical (line) managers in organizations where they use pool administrative services. Line department heads have a wider span of control, especially in bureaus like Finance and Economic Cooperation at the regional level. But, as data for such comparison were not collected, it would be misleading to conclude such observation as final for the entire civil service. Therefore, this area can be considered as a limitation in this research.

According to the findings, MMs were found to be responsible for detailed planning and execution. Conclusions drawn from the interviews and document review on the definition of middle managers revealed that

- middle managers (MMs) are not defined well in CSOs, though they serve as a bridge between the top-level officials and the employees to achieve objectives;
- middle managers (MMs) are assigned by merit fulfilling the minimum requirement, even though there is a point (up to 15 percent) to be given by the head of the organization during the competition;
- middle managers in CSOs are found to be professionals who can guide and coordinate complex tasks in the area they are assigned to lead.

5.2. Emphasized Roles Middle Managers Play in the Ethiopian Civil Service

The roles of middle managers in the civil service were assessed using the CVF. These roles include broker, facilitator, mentor, director, innovator, producer, coordinator, and monitor. The CVF defines each of the roles by four distinct variables or statements. The managerial roles again are divided into four major groups following the quadrants that are formed on the basis of two axes: stability/flexibility on the vertical and internal/external on the horizontal line. Accordingly, MMs were asked to evaluate their actions in organizations based on these four categories: inclinations to change (CHANFOC), orientation toward production/result (PRODFOC), focus on rules (RULFOC), and their tendency to emphasize human relation (HRFOC).

Table 3 shows descriptive statistics for roles played by middle managers as perceived by themselves in CSOs. As the data was skewed slightly, central tendency measures like mean, median, and standard deviation with the coefficient of variation were taken to assess the result. By calculating the average focus of MMs based on the four quadrants of the CVF, efforts were made to identify which inclination was prevalent during their tenure. The median measure of the data was also taken to assess the tendency to check whether there exist significant discrepancies with the mean. The standard

Table 3: Middle managers' role emphasis in organizations

		Average MMs' change focused attitude		Average MMs' rule & std focused attitude		Average MMs' production and result focused		Average MMs' HR focused attitude	
		Statistic	Std. Error	Statistic	Std. Error	Statistic	Std. Error	Statistic	Std. Error
Mean		4.52	0.045	4.97	0.05	5.14	0.046	5.18	0.05
95% CI for Mean	Lower Bound	4.44		4.88		5.05		5.08	
	Upper Bound	4.61		5.05		5.23		5.28	
5% Trimmed Mean		4.54		4.99		5.17		5.22	
Median		4.5		5		5.13		5.25.	
Variance		0.761		0.762		0.791		0.938	
Std. Deviation		0.872		0.873		0.889		0.968	
Skewness		-0.224	0.127	0.554	0.13	-0.529	0.127	-0.629	0.127
Kurtosis		0.373	0.254	1.003	0.25	0.747	0.254	0.519	0.254
Coefficient of variation		0.19		0.18		0.17		0.19	

deviation and the coefficient of variation were also considered to see variability in the data.

As observed in table 3, MMs were found to be more engaged in human relation activities (HRFOC) compared to other models in the competing value framework (m=5.18, med= 5.25, STD = 0.97, and CV=.19). Managers focusing on the fourth quadrant of the CVF (human relation model) are active in communicating effectively with their subordinates, mentoring and coaching employees, engaging followers in decision-making, and building strong teams to tap talents and ideas from their employees. This show the human resource concern MMs have in CSOs, indicating their effort in handling subordinates during task performance. Based on this study, therefore, the most emphasized role of MMs in civil service organizations was their human relation focus, which involves realizing potential and commitment of staff, encouraging a supportive workplace, developing teams, and serving as facilitators and mentors in work settings.

Figure 2: Radar chart for the emphasized role of MMs in CSOs (Research result)

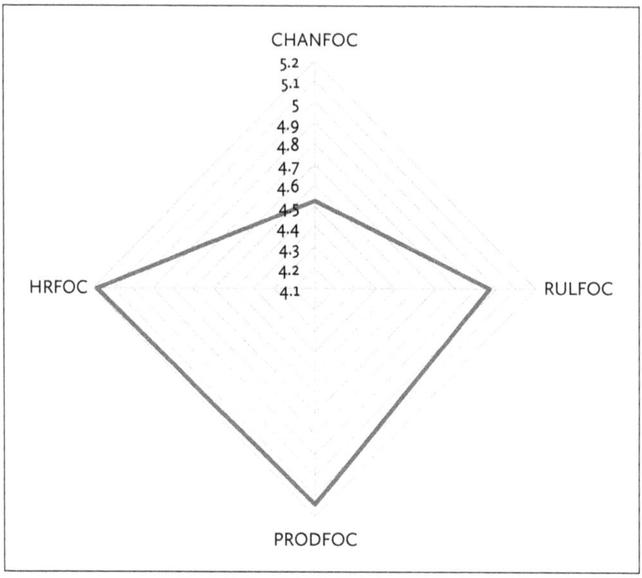

Focusing on results (PRODFOC) was found to be the second priority for middle managers in this research (m=5.14, med= 5.13, STD = 0.90, and CV=.17). Goal attainment is a feature found in the second quadrant of the CVF with competing values that directly oppose the first orientation middle managers possess in the study. Managerial actions considered in this quadrant (rational goal model) include structure and direction in an organization. The key roles middle managers play in this quadrant are those of producer and director, which are characterized by focusing on tasks and clarifying expectations and objectives in the work unit. Developing meaningful goals and communicating them clearly to subordinates are the main task of middle managers in this quadrant.

Maintaining stability and managing through strict control was found to be the third orientation (RULFOC) middle managers have in CSOs (m=4.97, med= 5.00, STD dev. = 0.87, and CV=.18). According to the CVF, this quadrant (internal process model) focuses on giving attention to internal work processes, such as record keeping, documentation, and measurement. It focuses also on keeping order as a means for effective workflow in an organization. Key managerial roles in this model are those of monitor and coordinator, which focus on detailed task analysis, coordinating staff efforts, monitoring facts, and applying of rules and regulations during task accomplishments.

Figure 3: Managerial focus based on middle managers' place of work (Research result)

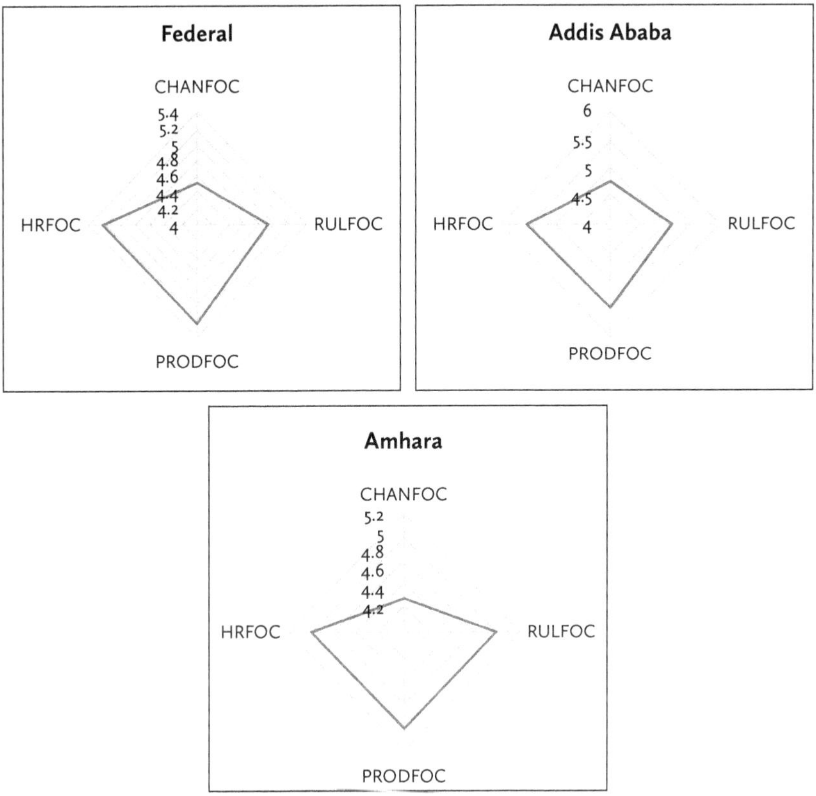

Compared to the previous three orientations, the least focused model by middle managers in CSOs is the open system model (CHANFOC), where change is the central purpose of their work (m=4.52, med= 4.50, STD dev. = 0.87, and CV=.19). Change-related activities are the central area in this model, whereby middle managers are required to exhibit entrepreneurial and innovative characteristics. The key managerial roles in this model are broker and innovator. Managers in this category represent their subordinates in the external world effectively and are expected to be creative, skillful, and take risks to achieve organizational objectives.

As the descriptive statistics indicated in table 3 and the radar diagram presented in figure 2, MMs play all roles that can influence the overall strategic management processes in CSOs in the country. However, two roles (HRFOC and PRODFOC) are more dominant than the other two (RULFOC and

CHANFOC). Successful managerial leadership requires the ability to navigate across the various managerial roles to balance contradictory demands from diverse environmental conditions. Effective public managers are required to demonstrate all eight managerial roles, with a frequency depending on situational demands that exist in CSOs. As indicated in figure 2, middle managers in this study exhibit all managerial roles (though with varying magnitude), which can be related to the actual work environment they are assigned to at present.

Analysis was done to compare differences in managerial emphasis based on respondents' places of work. However, we did not conduct such a comparison based on sectoral categorization in the civil service, which can be taken as limitation in this research. As to the former, a significant difference was not observed for the different category of MMs who work at federal, Amhara region, and Addis Ababa levels, as indicated in the separate radar diagram in figure 3.

As indicated in the diagrams, MMs at all locations exhibited similar inclinations; i.e., privileging human relations and result-orientation as compared to change and rules. The conventional judgment in theory and practices regarding MMs assumes their preference for strict adherence to rules and regulations. However, the finding clearly demonstrated their engagement in all the four categories of managerial activities, integrating all roles indicated in the competing value framework (CVF).

According to senior officials, although there is a great deal of similarity in tasks carried out by MMs, their roles are varied. Detailed planning, human resource management, record keeping, operation follow-up, and representing the work unit are jobs performed by middle managers. Depending on their position (line or staff), networks (internal and external), skills, and experience, their tasks may differ from one to the other. Some MMs quite mature, with long years of experience, education, and professional training while others are fresh graduates without any managerial experience and training. As most of the participants stated, middle managers are professional who have access to information from both the lower level employees and their supervisors. Due to the long tenure they have in the environment, they are well-informed about the opportunities and challenges of their organization compared to the top-level managers assigned by the government.

Middle managers have complex and demanding roles (Balogun, 2003) to play. They carry out mediation, buffering, and negotiation tasks during the generation of new ideas, the preparation of detailed plans for implementation, and an active involvement in the final execution. They also engage in counseling staff, mentoring, coaching, communicating, and team building.

The following excerpt from the interviews (senior managers) indicates the strategic engagement middle managers have in their respective organizations.

> *We are more of politicians than professionals. And sometimes we are assigned in offices that we don't have any clue about its past, current operations, and future directions. Yet, the government expects us to run the organization effectively, including by leading specific projects and programs as head of the organization. We are also expected to engage in entrepreneurial activities to transform our institution into a more citizen-oriented domain through an effective and efficient service delivery. We, the senior officials heavily rely on middle managers skills, knowledge, and efforts for all these responsibilities. Therefore, it is possible to say that CSOs are as strong and effective as the middle managers working in that given organization.* (Participant 9)

In practice, middle managers set goals with top managers in organizations. As interviewed officials confirmed, the job of a middle manager has never been limited to execution as described in the literature. They actively participate in the design of strategies, communicate goals to front-line managers, and engage in operational activities with their subordinates. According to interviewees, strategic plans, including the Growth and Transformation Plan (GTP 1 & 2) were prepared mainly by MMs and senior experts within the organizations.

Similarly, research participants confirmed that most of the MMs in their organization care for their staffs, listen to their problems, and try to solve problems within their jurisdictions. They try to mediate between the need of the employees and the organization's requirements when these are incompatible. Aligned with this, most participants mentioned the need of empowering MMs and encouraging teamwork as a venue for performance excellence. This is how one senior level manager described their contribution:

> *When allowed to exercise power, MMs perform a great deal in organizations. Most of the failures in the civil service are the results of not including the MMs in both planning and decision making as well. Senior managers should give open space for MMs to exercise their managerial and expertise power to achieve organizational objectives. They should listen to their comments, suggestions and in some cases give the whole power to them. You can't lead alone, you know … on your own. This is challenging, especially for us who are politically appointed. We need the support of the people around us, mainly the MMs.* (Participant 6)

6. Discussion

Defining a concept is a basis for scholarly discourse, yet the concept of middle manger still requires definition on a contextual basis (Huy, 2002). Until recently, middle managers were considered as operational people in organizations, mainly focusing on coordination and control. Though variability is common, middle managers these days enjoy the liberty of presiding over budgets, making personnel decisions, and engaging in strategy development. However, there are institutions that are so centralized and controlled that middle managers are still passive receivers of orders from the top. These managers are denied appropriate power to make their own decisions. Consequently, the influences of these middle managers in such organizations is very low.

Despite the fact that the term "middle manager" is used widely both in the private and the public sectors (Van Rensburg, Davis, & Venter, 2014), it is not possible to find individuals with such a title in an organization. Rather the position of middle manager indicates the placement of a position within the organizational hierarchy. The term refers to managers having equal positions in the organizational hierarchy but with different responsibilities. Different authors attempted to conceptualize the term in the past. It has been described as managers managing managers (Osterman, as cited in Van Rensburg, Davis, & Venter, 2014), as mediators between strategy and operation (Nonakaas, cited in Van Rensburg, Davis, & Venter, 2014), as positions between the top executives and supervisors above employees (Huy, 2001), and managers operating at the middle of the organization (Floyd & Wooldridge, 1992). Similarly, Ikavalko (as cited in Van Rensburg, Davis, & Venter, 2014) considered them as individuals who have both superiors and subordinates within the organization. Authors like Kaiser et al. (2011) took access to senior executives and knowledge of operations as the bases for being considered a middle manager. Similar to what has been narrated by various scholars in the field, respondents in the present study described middle managers as individuals who are placed at the middle of an organizational hierarchy. They associated them with titles like director, process owners, and department heads, whose positions are next to the politically appointed officials in that organization. This was further checked by observing individuals who are appointed politically and termed as senior executives, though they have an equal hierarchical position in the organization.

In the Ethiopian civil service, those considered as MMs are individuals located between the strategic apex and the operating core of the organization. They manage human and physical resources in an effort to achieve organizational objectives. They easily access both the senior managers at the top and operating staff on the frontline, influencing information flow between the two groups. They have a unique place in the organization as they have access to each and every move made by either the senior manager or the operating staff.

Based on the survey, there was a high level of agreement among study participants on who middle managers are and what they do within the civil service. According to participants, middle managers in CSOs were found to be mangers two levels below the senior officials assigned on the basis of civil service regulations. Research participants agreed that middle managers in most cases are knowledgeable individuals in relation to their work unit.

Middle managers engage in a variety of assignments in the organization, either in teams or individually. According to research participants, middle managers carry out tasks that are related to both the present and the future. According to the data from the interviews and survey questions, MMs were found to be active in all strategic and operational activities. Based on the study finding, therefore, the researcher defined MMs in CSOs as those managers who have a responsibility of running and representing their work unit and who have the privilege of accessing organizational officials directly to sell their ideas by assuming responsibility on a meritorious basis.

The findings in this study also revealed the positioning of middle managers in terms of the competing value framework (CVF). Middle managers participating in this study were confirmed to have been balancing the different competing roles that are expected of managers particularly in CSOs. As results from both quantitative and qualitative data analyses indicated, middle managers in the civil service were engaged in carrying out the eight managerial roles identified by Quinn et al. (2003). Based on empirical data from the field and knowledge from the scholarly community, middle managers in Ethiopian civil service are mangers who report directly to appointed officials in their organization. Though it was found from the interviews that senior level officials manipulate the process, generally middle managers are assigned through a competitive process. This research identified middle managers' managerial priorities to include implementing strategies, interpreting and communicating information, and exerting both upward and downward influence.

7. Conclusion

This study examined the most emphasized roles of middle managers in the Ethiopian civil service using the competing value framework (CVF). Though the magnitudes are different, the findings from this study confirmed that

MMs in the Ethiopian civil service play pivotal roles in their organization. Based on the research findings, the most emphasized roles MMs play in CSOs fall in the fourth quadrant of the CVF, where an emphasis is given to facilitation and mentoring roles at the internal-flexible junction. Production, rule, and change orientations were found to be the other areas of concern for MMs in this study. Similarly the research showed the need to define MMs in the civil service, as an agreed-upon definition for the concept is lacking. A definition is proposed in this chapter to help CSOs in recruiting, selecting, developing, and retaining talented managers.

In general, the conclusions of this study indicate that MMs have a contribution to the strategic management of a civil service organization. However, contrary to declarations in the literature, the findings indicate that middle managers focus more on human relation than rules in executing their organizational task. Although the conclusions were drawn based on responses of managers on a given day whose views might change at another time/place, the findings revealed different managerial roles played by MMs that require specific sets of skill. Hence, this study clearly unveils the critical need by institutions in capacitating this group of managers to deliver the best possible goods and services to citizens by the government.

Failure or unsatisfactory results in delivering government goods and services are a common problem in Ethiopia. Though many factors may contribute to such inefficiency and ineffectiveness, different studies have indicated managerial problems as fundamental challenges in the Ethiopian civil service. The attention given to MMs, in this regard, requires due consideration as they are very crucial in the overall management of an organization. Thus, rather than expecting MMs to be effective and efficient by simply following the conventional career path in the civil service, executives above them should design contextual mechanisms that enable them to do a better job in their organization. After all, experience show that these groups of managers are the successors in the bureaucratic hierarchy of the government structure.

8. Limitations and Suggestions for Further Research

Like any study in social science, this research has limitations that must be acknowledged. First, strategic involvement in CSOs is a relative issue, as most strategies emanate from the ruling political parties. This research considers the wide room middle managers have in design, implementation, and evaluation at the civil service. Thus, similar studies in such an environment may result in different findings and conclusions. Second, as discussed earlier, the study excludes health and educational institutions. The reason for such exclusion was the different structural and managerial arrangement of educational and medical institutions in the country. Third, comparison to prior findings was not done as getting prior research on Ethiopia was difficult. This may be considered as another limitation for this study.

Future research is necessary for areas where this research lack depth or coverage. Among others, assessing the situation in specific areas like health and education is recommended. Future research could also explore the strategic contributions of middle managers in relation to formulation, implementation, or evaluation separately.

Acknowledgements

I am indebted to Dr. Worku Negash, Professor G. Ramakrishna, and Professor Melesse Asfaw for their patience and constructive critique during the course of this study. I also want to thank the anonymous reviewers who provided critical comments and constructive suggestions that helped me in improving the entire chapter.

References

Alkhafaji, Abbass F. (2003). *Strategic Management: Formulation, Implementation, and Control in A Dynamic Environment*, The Haworth Press, Inc.

Allan, P. (1981). Managers at Work: A Large-scale Study of the Managerial Job in New York City Government. *Academy of Management Journal*, 24(3), 613-619.

Ansoff, H. I. (1990). *Strategic Management*. London: Macmillan Academic and Professional ltd.

Araya, E. (2019). Moving Further on Civil Service Reforms in Ethiopia: Findings and Implications from a Civil Service Survey and Qualitative Analysis, Synthesis Report (pp. 1-149).

Balogun, J. (2003). From Blaming the Middle to Harnessing Its Potential: Creating Change Intermediaries. *British Journal of Management*, 14(1), 69-83.

Balogun, J., & Johnson, G. (2004). Organizational Restructuring and Middle Manager Sensemaking. *Academy of Management Journal*, 47(4), 523-549.

Belasen, A. T. (1998). Paradoxes and Leadership Roles. *Management*, 1(2), 98.

Blankenship, D. C. (2010). *Applied Research and Evaluation Methods in Recreation*. Champaign: Sheridan Books.

Cameron, K. S., Quinn, R. E., DeGraff, J., & Thakor, A. V. (2006). *Competing Values Leadership: Creating Value in Organizations*. Cheltenham: Edward Elgar Publishing Limited.

Caye, J.-M., Strack, R., Orlander, P., Kilmann, J., Espinosa, E. G., Francoeur, F., & Haen, P., White Paper. (2010). Creating a New Deal for Middle Managers. Empowering a Neglected but Critical Group. In T. B. C. Group (Ed.). Frankfurt: The Boston Consulting Group and World Federation of People Management Associations.

Clegg, S. R., Kornberger, M., & Pitsis, T. (2015). *Managing and Organizations: An Introduction to Theory and Practice*. London: Sage.

Clutterbuck, D., & Megginson, D. (1999). *Mentoring Executives and Directors*. Oxford: Butterworth-Heinemann.

Coon, B., & Wolf, S. (2005). The Alchemy of Strategy Execution. *Employment Relations Today*, 32(3), 19-30.

Currie, G., & Procter, S. J. (2005). The Antecedents of Middle Managers' Strategic Contribution: The Case of a Professional Bureaucracy. *Journal of Management Studies*, 42(7), 1325-1356.

Daft, R. L. (2008). *Management*. Cengage Learning.

Denison, D. R., Hooijberg, R., & Quinn, R. E. (1995). Paradox and Performance: Toward a Theory of Behavioral Complexity in Managerial Leadership. *Organization Science*, 6(5), 524-540.

DiPadova, L. N., & Faerman, S. R. (1993). Using the Competing Values Framework to Facilitate Managerial Understanding across Levels of Organizational Hierarchy. *Human Resource Management*, 32(1), 143-174.

Drucker, P. F. (2008). *Management Rev Ed*. Zondervan.

Dutton, J. E., Ashford, S. J., O'Neill, R. M., Hayes, E., & Wierba, E. E. (1997). Reading the Wind: How Middle Managers Assess the Context for Selling Issues to Top Managers. *Strategic Management Journal*, 18(5), 407-423.

Gebre, M. and Nigussie, D.(2016). *Change Army: The New Face of Modernizing Civil Service in Ethiopia: The Case of Addis Ababa* in Teshome T. (Ed.), Public Sector Transformation and Development Proceedings of the 2nd National Conference, 1(1), 86-102.

Feldman, S. (1980). The Middle Management Muddle. *Administration in Mental Health*, 8(1), 3-11.

Floyd, S. W., & Wooldridge, B. (1992). Middle Management Involvement in Strategy and Its Association with Strategic Type: A Research Note. *Strategic Management Journal*, 13, 153-167.

Floyd, S. W., & Wooldridge, B. (1997). Middle Management's Strategic Influence and Organizational Performance. *Journal of Management Studies*, 34(3), 465-485.

Hales, C., & Mustapha, N. a. (2000). Commonalities and Variations in Managerial Work: A Study of Middle Managers in Malaysia. *Asia Pacific Journal of Human Resources*, 38(1), 1-25.

Hassard, J., McCann, L., & Morris, J. (2009). *Managing in the Modern Corporation: The Intensification of Managerial Work in the USA, UK and Japan*. Cambridge: Cambridge University Press.

Have, S. T., Have, W. T., Stevens, F., Elst, M. v. d., & Pol-Coyne, F. (2003). *Key Management Models: The Management Tools and Practices That Will Improve Your Business*. London: Financial Times Prentice Hall.

HBR. (2011). *HBR's 10 Must Reads on Leadership*. Boston, MA: Harvard Business Review Press.

Hrebiniak, L. G. (2005). *Making Strategy Work: Leading Effective Execution and Change*. New Jersey: Wharton School Publishing.

Huy, Q. N. (2001). In Praise of Middle Managers. *Harvard Business Review*, 79(8), 72-79, 160.

Huy, Q. N. (2002). Emotional Balancing of Organizational Continuity and Radical Change: The Contribution of Middle Managers. *Administrative Science Quarterly*, 47(1), 31-69.

Israel, G. D. (1992). Determining Sample Size Fact Sheet PEOD-6. In *Institute of Food and Agricultural Sciences* (Ed.). University of Florida.

Kaiser, R. B., Craig, S. B., Overfield, D. V., & Yarborough, P. (2011). Differences in Managerial Jobs at the Bottom, Middle, and Top: A Review of Empirical Research. *The Psychologist-Manager Journal*, 14(2), 76-91.

Kaplan, R. S., & Norton, D. P. (2001). The Strategy-focused Organization. *Strategy and Leadership*, 29(3), 41-42.

Kealy, T. (2013). Do Middle Managers Contribute to Their Organisation's Strategy? *International Journal of Humanities and Social Science*, 5(1), 108-116.

Kellerman, B., & Webster, S. W. (2001). The Recent Literature on Public Leadership Reviewed and Considered. *The Leadership Quarterly*, *12*, 485-514.

Kraut, A. I., Pedigo, P. R., McKenna, D. D., & Dunnette, M. D. (1989). The Role of the Manager: What's Really Important in Different Management Jobs. *The Academy of Management Executive*, 3(4), 286-293.

Kuyvenhoven, R., & Buss, W. C. (2011). A Normative View of the Role of Middle Management in the Implementation of Strategic Change. *Journal of Management and Marketing Research*, 8, 1.

Leedy, P. D., & Ormrod, J. E. (2015). *Practical Research: Planning and Design* (11th ed.). Essex: Pearson Education Limited.

Lindquist, E. A., & Marcy, R. T. (2014). *The Competing Values Framework: Strategic Implications for Leadership, Conflict and Change in Public Organizations*. Paper presented at the 3rd Research Conference of the Canadian Association of Programs in Public Administration Queen's University, Kingston, Ontario.

Livian, Y.-F., & Burgoyne, J. G. (1997). *Middle Managers in Europe*. London: Routledge.

Lussier, R. N., & Achua, C. F. (2015). *Leadership: Theory, Application, & Skill Development*: Nelson Education.

McIntosh, P., & Luecke, R. A. (2010). *Becoming a Manager*. AMACOM Div American Mgmt Assn.

Ministry of Public Service & Human Resource Development. (2015). *National Public Service Human Resource Statistics*, Addis Ababa.

Mintzberg, H. (1971). Managerial Work: Analysis from Observation. *Management Science*, 18(2), B-97-B-110.

Mintzberg, H. (1990). The Manager's Job: Folklore and Fact. *Harvard Business Review, HBR Classic*.

Mintzberg, H. (2009). *Managing*. Berrett-Koehler Publishers.

Mintzberg, H., & Waters, J. A. (1985). Of Strategies, Deliberate and Emergent. *Strategic Management Journal*, 6(3), 257-272.

Mitiku, A. A., Hondeghem, A., & Troupin, S. (2017). Administrative Leadership: Understanding the Preferred Leadership Roles of the Ethiopian Civil Service Managers. *African Journal of Economic and Management Studies*, 8(3), 366-394.

Morgan, D., Bacon, K. G., Bunch, R., Cameron, C. D., & Deis, R. (1996). What Middle Managers Do in Local Government: Stewardship of the Public Trust and the Limits of Reinventing Government. *Public Administration Review*, 56(4), 359-366.

Noble, C. H. (1999a). Building the Strategy Implementation Network. *Business Horizons*, 42(6), 19-28.

Noble, C. H. (1999b). The Eclectic Roots of Strategy Implementation Research. *Journal of business research*, 45(2), 119-134.

Nutt, P. C., & Backoff, R. W. (1995). Strategy for Public and Third-sector Organizations. *Journal of Public Administration Research and Theory: J-PART*, 5(2), 189-211.

Quinn, R. E., Faerman, S. R., Thompson, M. P., & McGrath, M. R. (2003). *Becoming a Master Manager: A Competency Framework* (third ed.). New Jersy: John Wiley & Sons Inc.

Quinn, R. E., & Rohrbaugh, J. (1983). A Spatial Model of Effectiveness Criteria: Towards a Competing Values Approach to Organizational Analysis. *Management Science*, 29(3), 363-377.

Rajasekar, J. (2014). Factors Affecting Effective Strategy Implementation in a Service Industry: A Study of Electricity Distribution Companies in the Sultanate of Oman. *International Journal of Business and Social Science*, 5(9), 169-183

Tharenou, P., Donohue, R., & Cooper, B. (2007). *Management Research Methods*. Cambridge University Press: Cambridge.

Tompkins, J. (2005). *Organization Theory and Public Management*: Wadsworth Publishing Company.

Van Rensburg, M. J., Davis, A., & Venter, P. (2014). Making Strategy Work: The Role of the Middle Manager. *Journal of Management & Organization*, 20(02), 165-186.

Weick, K. E. (1995). *Sensemaking in Organizations*, vol. 3.London: Sage.

White, C. (2004). *Strategic Management*. New York: Palgrave Macmillan.

Wooldridge, B., Schmid, T., & Floyd, S. W. (2008). The Middle Management Perspective on Strategy Process: Contributions, Synthesis, and Future Research. *Journal of Management*, 34(6), 1190-1221.

Yukl, G. A. (2010). *Leadership in Organizations*. New Jersey: Prentice Hall.

Zagotta, R., & Robinson, D. (2002). Keys to Successful Strategy Execution. *Journal of Business Strategy*, 23(1), 30-34.

15
The Ethiopian Civil Service System in Perspective: Implications for Leadership Roles

Adare Assefa Mitiku and Annie Hondeghem

Box 1: Key points in this chapter

- ✓ The leadership contexts are myriad of multifaceted overlapping realities, inextricably intertwined, and are subject to change
- ✓ The leadership contexts influence how leaders are likely to act
- ✓ The leadership contexts may call for distinct but interrelated roles, but as some roles may be more appropriate in some organizations than in others, leaders are expected to make choices that fit well with their work context.

Box 2: Reading this work will give you insights in

- ✓ the evolution and current features of the Ethiopian civil service – the context
- ✓ the ramifications of leadership contexts for the role of leaders

Box 3: Abbreviations

CSS = civil service system
SSA = Sub-Saharan Africa
T&D = Training and Development
TCCs = top civil servants

Introduction

The present work studies the leadership context and its ramifications for leadership roles. The overarching context of public sector leaders, as defined by Van Wart et al. (2015) and Jackson (2004), is the cultural settings and political backgrounds at the "macro level" and the function and structure of administrative systems at the "meso level."

Van Wart et al (2015) have further specified that the antecedents—cultural-, political-, and organizational-administrative level—factors are a myriad of multifaceted overlapping realities, inextricably intertwined, and are subject to change. Cultural setting influences and is influenced by the political system, which influences and is influenced by the administrative systems. The cultural context also influences and is influenced by the administrative system.

The foregoing antecedents determine beliefs as to how the leaders are ideally expected to act. For instance, explaining the cultural context, Jackson (2004) discusses Hofstede's "power distance" dimension. According to Jackson, leaders in high-power distance countries are expected to "act autocratically." In the low-power distance countries, leaders are considered as "loyal democrats." And in those with the medium score on the said cultural dimension, leaders are expected to "act mainly as a benevolent autocrat." Similar deductions can be made based on the political setting and organization-administrative level factors.

The broader context influences and is influenced by the content of the leaders. According to Jackson (2004:98), "The content of leadership assumes particular orientations towards acting in certain ways." Indeed, this may not necessarily say anything about their actual conduct, but it does articulate the way they perceive their own conduct as a leader. To be sure, perception is a powerful phenomenon dictating individuals' actions, and as such it "eventually transforms into reality" (Saha, 2008:29). Conduct of leadership refers to what people actually do. It influences and is influenced by the content of leadership and the context (Jackson, 2004). Assessment of leaders' role conception and conduct is beyond the scope of the present work (for assessments of the former refer to Adare et al., 2018).

In assessing the leadership context, the civil service is defined as a "system." This, according to Van der Meer (2011:4), suggests the use of an "institutional approach." Thus, relying on the two theoretical traditions – "historical new institutionalism" and "sociological new institutionalism" (see section 1 below) – the study deals with the subject by asking a straightforward question: *What are the ramifications of the Ethiopian public leadership context for leadership roles?*

The study has strong pragmatic relevance because understanding public leadership in the Ethiopian context – a topic that is unaccountably missing from systematic academic inquiries – informs recruitment, promotion, and T&D practices in the civil service. It also contributes to theory by adding specificity and nuances to the existing conceptualization of leadership and civil service in the context of Africa in general.

The balance of this work is organized into five sections. It begins by elucidating the theoretical approaches and the methodology and methods applied in the study. Next, the historical progression of the Ethiopian CSS is discussed. Afterwards, the basic features of the current civil service are presented. Finally, analysis is made along the lines of the antecedents of public leadership and their ramifications for leadership roles. The study ends with some concluding remarks.

1. Theoretical Approaches and Methodology and Methods

1.1. Theoretical Approaches

Scholars (see Lynn, 2006; Pollitt, 2008) have suggested the need to follow an institutional approach in the study of public management. The question though is which strand among institutional approaches should be used? Old or new institutionalism? As each strand has sub-strands, which particular sub-strand or combination thereof is appropriate? And why?

The full answer to the aforementioned questions requires an extensive study of each strand and its sub-strands. Yet, the objective here is not to contribute to the institutional debate but to use it as a framework to understand and explain the leadership context. The study therefore captures the main characteristics of each of the main strands and then switches to the selection of a sub-strand or combinations thereof.

Briefly, the difference between old and new institutionalism is both epistemological and ideological (Aspinwall & Schneider, 2000). Although old institutionalism predominantly places a great deal of attention on the study of formal structures, new institutionalism goes further to consider informal structures and their role in molding the behavior of the participants (Peters, 1999). To reap the benefit of these new developments, the present study is informed by the "new institutionalism" analytic strand. Such a claim, however, is not enough. It requires answering a question concerning which specific type of new institutionalism is applied. Then again, the number of types means that, despite their similarities, there are heavy disagreements between them and that they paint different pictures about institutional phenomena. The differences among them further imply that often there may be a need to apply combinations of two or more of these types (Ibid).

Under the banner of new institutionalism, different approaches exist for studying institutional phenomena. For the purpose of the present study, only three of them are presented: historical new institutionalism, rational choice new institutionalism, and sociological new institutionalism (see Hall & Taylor, 1996; Peters, 1999).

Before selecting one or a combination of these analytic sub-strands, we first scanned their defining features. Our criteria for selection were based on the research design in terms of the time span privileged by each sub-strand and the underlying ways of knowing. The result of our inquiry uncovered the limited utility of rational choice institutionalism for the present study. This is because while both historical new institutionalism and sociological new institutionalism emphasize long-term institutional effects, rational choice institutionalism emphasizes short-term outcomes (Hall & Taylor, 1996). Although the first two approaches demand an inductive logic of inquiry, the latter requires a deductive logic of inquiry (Aspinwall & Schneider, 2000). The present work therefore excluded rational choice institutionalism from further discussions because the study examines the CSS of Ethiopia from the beginning of modern public administration to the present. Moreover, although the study applied a mixed approach, it predominantly relies on the interpretive logic of inquiry.

In sum, in this study, the assessment of the leadership context is informed by two theoretical traditions: the historical new institutionalism and its central explanatory notion of path dependency, and the sociological new institutionalism and its central explanatory idea of cognitive and cultural links.

1.2. Methodology and Methods

Haverland and Yanow (2012:401) noted that the terms methods and methodology are not synonyms. The former refers to the "tools and techniques that are used to carry out research: surveys, questionnaires"; the latter concerns "ways of knowing or logics of inquiry"—the 'positivist' and the 'interpretative' approaches. The 'choices of methods and their underlying ways of knowing should depend on and reflect the goal or purpose of the research—the research question' (Ibid: 402). In this study a mix of inductive and deductive logics of inquiries is applied. That is, it focuses on contextual meaning making. And in deducing the ramifications of the context for leadership roles, it is also informed by theories and concepts in the field.

As to the methods of accessing and generating data, analysis in this study mainly relies on the documentary data. The sources comprise relevant current and retrospective public documents, such as the constitution, legislation, proclamations, directives, and circulars. Moreover, policy documents, reports, and various statistics (e.g., the civil service human resource statistics, population census data) are used.

The study also relies on various informative sources, such as IndexMundi, Global Integrity–African Integrity Indicators, the Mo Ibrahim Index, the

Transparency International corruption perception index, and so forth. The bulk of extant literature, both published and unpublished, related to the subject of investigation was also reviewed.

Moreover, in undertaking a context-specific study, "restricting the documentary evidence to written materials alone can also be limiting" (Yanow & Schwartz-Shea, 2006:122). This is because the "political, social, organizational, and cultural identities and values are embedded also in films ... in folk songs ... military (marching), revolutionary, and women's songs" (Ibid:122). The present work, therefore, uses indigenous aphorisms or proverbs to extend the scope of the written documents, as needed.

Finally, sections 3.3 to 3.7 of this chapter are also informed by from the results of a recent PhD survey on Ethiopian public sector leadership (see Adare et al. 2018).

The documentary sources were analyzed using the "content analysis" recommended by Bowen (2009:32), involving "a first-pass document review, in which meaningful and relevant passages of text or other data are identified." In analyzing the results of the survey, a univariate analysis approach, particularly frequency distribution, was applied.

2. The Historical Progression of the Ethiopian Civil Service System

In Ethiopia, the commencement of modern civil service goes back to the early periods of the twentieth century (Paulos, 2001). No doubt, in the last hundred plus years, it has been transformed several times over. Over these periods, the country was governed as a unitary feudal state during the imperial regime (-1974); as a unitary socialist state during the Dergue government (1974-1991); and currently, as a federal parliamentary republic by the EPRDF government (1991-). Below, we analyze the changes, consolidations, and stasis in the CSS under each of these administrations.

2.1. The Era of Menelik II (1889-1913)

In Ethiopia, this era is known for state formation and establishment of a modern public administration (see Paulos, 2001). The former is said to have come about through the northerners' (aka Amhara) influence (Marcus, 1994). In the process the regime privileged the Orthodox Christian religion. It endorsed a Christian conceptualization of the state and Amharic became "a lingua franca" (Adejumobi, 2007).

In modernizing the public administration, the "European line" was followed. The first step was creating various ministries in 1907. Likewise, for the first time, the state was "divided into smaller administrative units" (Paulos, 2001:83). Gradually, many other initiatives were implemented (see Clapham, 2006; Marcus, 1994; Paulos, 2001).

Moreover, the emperor, seeing his health deteriorating (in 1904), took measures meant to ensure the continuity of his administration (see Marcus, 1994). Among these were the following:

- 1907: Established Ethiopia's first cabinet
- 1907: Established an independent appellate court system in the provinces
- 1908: Decreed a new inheritance law
- 1908: Established the office of prime minister
- 1908: Instituted a crown council.

It is important to note that during this era individuals' political loyalty and their ability to mobilize an army were the basis for them to assume a ministerial position. Ministers were not salaried and were all housed in a building set up within the palace compound. The civil service, in general, was small in size and principally "engaged in maintaining law and order" (Paulos, 2001:84).

2.2. The Period between Emperor Menelik II and Emperor Haile Selassie

This period was marked by confusion and significantly eroded central government authority. The progress of the CSS was briefly stalled by the coming to power of Lij Iyasu (1911-1916); and after his dethronement, of Empress Zawditu, Menelik's daughter (1916-1930). Even Zewditu hardly made any attempt to improve the CSS founded during her father's reign (see Marcus, 1994; Solomon, 2013).

2.3. The Era of Emperor Haile Selassie (1930-1974)

This era mainly tried to uphold the legacies of Emperor Menelik II. As such, Christianity remained important, and Ethiopia was identified as a Christian state. Amharic continued as the sole official language of the empire (see Adejumobi, 2007; Marcus, 1994).

Likewise, Haile Selassie advanced the administrative modernism begun during the era of Menelik II. He adopted Ethiopia's first Japanese-style constitution in 1931 (see Clapham, 2006). Moreover, before the Italian occupation (1930-1935), he embarked on many reform initiatives. Progress, however, was interrupted during the period the county was under Italian occupation (1936-1941), a colonization attempt that forced the emperor into exile (see Marcus, 1994).

Upon his return from exile (1941), Haile Selassie continued with his ambitious reforms. The following are among the prominent administrative reform measures during his reign (see Paulos, 2001).

- 1943: Defined powers and duties of ministries
- 1952: Established the Imperial Institute of Public Administration
- 1955: Revised the constitution of 1931
- 1961: Established the central personnel agency (CPA) and entrusted it with maintaining a standardized public service governed by uniform rules and principles.

Note that almost all of Haile Selassie's attempts at modernization, like the reign of Menelik II, were based on emulation of foreign development models (see Clapham, 2006). As such, the revised constitution of 1955 reflected the adoption of "a British model of constitutional monarchy" (Ibid:112). Similarly, the CPA was mainly adopted from the personnel management system of the USA (Adebabay, 2011). These developments imply that the attempts to modernize the country's public administration did not have a strong indigenous basis.

Moreover, the successes of the regime's civil service reform were undermined by the shortage of a competent workforce, limited stakeholder participation, and defiance of the civil service principles (see Paulos, 2001; Solomon, 2013).

2.4. The Derg Government (1974-1991)

The Dergue government adopted the Marxist Leninist ideology and declared socialism to be at the core of its economic policies. In view of this, the regime "embraced the maximalist view of the state" (Adejumobi, 2007:120).

Although the regime pledged separation of state and religion, a Christian demarcation of the state remained. And, as was the case under the previous regimes, Amharic remained the only "working language of the state" (see the Constitution of PDRE, 1987).

The Dergue regime was also known for expanding "the state apparatus," "restructuring the cabinet," and amending "the salary scale of the civil service" (Paulos, 2001:86). Associated with these expansion actions, the number of civil servants increased from 101,147 under the preceding reign to 216,058 when the regime left office (see National Civil Service Human Resource Statistics 2013-2014).

Despite the abovementioned changes, there were no major amendments to the legal framework of the nation's civil service. The civil service was mainly run by "different orders and decrees issued during the reign of Haile Selassie" (Paulos, 2001:86; see also MoCS, 2013).

Furthermore, the Dergue regime is remembered for politicians' distrust of career civil servants. This distrust led to the replacement of the latter, at almost all levels, by political patrons, thereby downplaying professionalism in personnel management. Likewise, a parallel political structure was introduced and was used to pass decisions in the civil service. Such measures, however, deteriorated its performance encouraging administrative misconduct (Paulos, 2001; Solomon, 2013).

2.5. The Ethiopian People's Democratic Front (EPRDF) (1991–)

The EPRDF government, although overwhelmed by concern for politics (Assefa, 2015), has implemented "multiple reform interventions." In doing this, a top-down, "big-push" approach to reform was followed (Ibid.). Thus far, the transformation measures have been implemented in three phases (see Solomon, 2013).

Phase I: From 1991-1996

Transformation in this phase emphasized political and economic reforms (Solomon, 2013; World Bank, 2013). Related to the former is the constitutional reform of 1995. The new constitution recognizes the state as "the federal parliamentary republic." It also declared a "separation of state and religion" (see art. 11).

During this period, Ethiopia selectively implemented a structural adjustment program (SAP) and the free market economic policy (Henze, 2003; Stiglitz, 2002). However, international institutions such as IMF not only objected to the Ethiopian choice but also suspended its loan to the country (De Waal, 2012; Stiglitz, 2002).

Associated with SAP, a "retrenchment policy" meant to reduce "redundant employees" was implemented. This policy, according to the government, was based on new structures and position reviews (Paulos, 2001). In reality, the total number of civil servants increased from 216,058 in 1991 to 287,716 in 1996 (see table 1). Critics also claim that, at the time, the ratio of civil servants to the total population was low. Equally, the reduction was based on predetermined percentages (by 10 percent), not based on a call for new structures. The policy's hidden mission was replacing the civil servants who appeared to be associated with the previous regime. Such action further eroded the existing limited administrative capacity of the civil service. The policy also created an environment of uncertainty and distrust (Ibid).

Phase II: From 1996-2003

Reform during this phase is known as the "comprehensive civil service reform programme (CSRP)." CSRP was meant to address "the deep institutional constraints on basic functions such as policymaking, service delivery, and regulation"(MoCB, 2004:2). It was also encouraged by the influence of the NPM reform wave (see Peterson, 2001).

The outcome of the CSRP is mixed. On the positive side, there was the development of new legislations (e.g. a civil service law); the emergence of an "operating system for budget, procurement, and some aspects of personnel management (e.g. salary survey and record management)," and the implementation of a "prototype for expenditure management" (MoCB, 2004:2). On the minus side, the constraints that the reform purported to address continued to exist.

Phase III: from 2003-

Reform during this period has been labelled the "Public Sector Capacity Building Support Programme (PSCAP)." Its implementation was technically supported by leading institutions (see MoCB, 2004).

Putting the PSCAP into action encouraged the use of reform tools such as BPR, management by objectives (MBOs), the integrated performance management system (IPMS), the balanced scorecard (BSC), and the *yelawut serawit* (Amharic for "the civil service change army") (MoCS, 2013).

Moreover, the PSCAP is backed by *gemgema,* a peer evaluation through both self-criticism and criticism tactics. Such an evaluation approach, among others, has been used to maintain political control up to the Kebele (Amharic for "neighborhoods") level (Aalen, 2002); to shape the behavior of officials; and to give input for performance evaluation (Hagmann, 2005; World Bank, 1998). In sum, gemgema is a "politico-administrative evaluation" (Hagmann, 2005:16).

A notable success reported as a result of the PSCAP is a relative improvement of public service delivery. More importantly, BPR has brought an attitudinal change in the civil service, imbuing their operations with a client-oriented approach. It has also been praised for simplifying the work process cycle (Getachew & Common, 2006; World Bank, 2010).

3. The current Civil Service

3.1. The Internal Labour Market (ILM)

Until the collapse of the imperial regime, the nobility enjoyed the best of every opportunity in the nation. Indeed, education, historically and in modern times, was mainly made available to the progeny of nobility, who ultimately joined the civil service. As the Dergue government came to power, however, some of the individuals in this class were executed; some were exiled; and those remaining were systematically distanced from the civil service. Such actions opened the door for the middle and lower classes to enter into administration (*see* Adejumobi, 2007; Andargachew, 1993).

3.2. Public Sector Employment

The human resource statistics over the last fifty years shows a remarkable increase in the number of people employed by the public sector. Table 1 depicts the number of civil servants at each moment of major political change since 1962.

Table 1: Permanent Employees from 1962–63 to 2013–14

Year	Male	Female	Total	Major Events/Descriptions
1962-63	—	—	46,701	No. of civil servants at the time the Central Personnel Agency was established
1974-75	82,941	18,206	101, 147	No. of civil servants as the Dergue government came to power
1990-91	163,090	52,968	216,058	No. of civil servants as the EPRDF government came to power, beginning of the implementation of the Retrenchment policy
1995-96	207,358	80,358	287,716	The end of Retrenchment policy
2013-14	816,686	440,263	1,256,946	Total no. of civil servants as of 2013-2014
	75,558	**49,775**	**125,333**	No. of civil servants working in the federal administration (about 10 percent of the total civil servants)
			1.43	Ratio of civil servants to the population, calculated on a total population of 88,144,515

Source: National Civil Service Human Resource Statistics 2013-2014.

Of equal importance, over time, the qualifications of civil servants have been improving. For instance, of the total civil servants inherited by the Dergue government, six thousand were university graduates and twenty thousand had completed secondary school; the balance had no more than knowledge of reading and writing Amharic (Andargachew, 1993). At present, over 70 percent of civil servants hold qualifications of a "Diploma"[1] and higher (see National Civil Service Human Resource Statistics, 2013-2014).

Of the total 1,256,946 civil servants, about 10 percent (125,333) work in the federal administration. Of these employees, 43 percent hold a qualification less than a college Diploma. The balance has a qualification of a college Diploma and above. Figure 1 shows the educational levels of the civil servants working in the federal administration.

Figure 1: Educational levels of civil servants working in the federal administration.

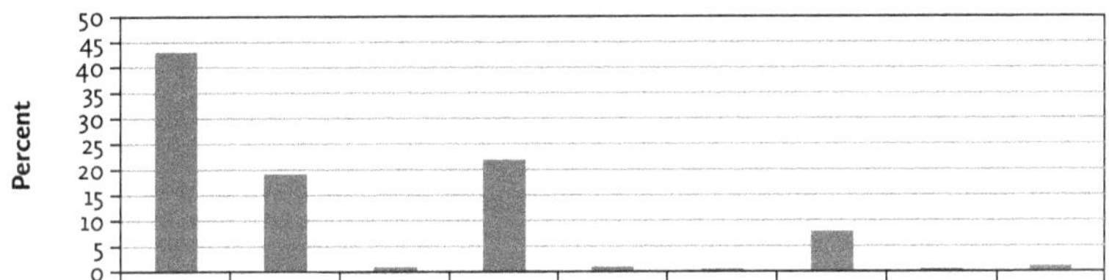

	< College Diploma *	Diploma **	LLB	BA/BSC	MD	DVM	MA/MSc	LLM	PhD
■ Percentages***	43.1	19.3	0.8	21.8	1	0.2	7.9	0.2	0.8

*Includes illiterate, read and write, grades 1-4, 5-8, 9-12, certificate, Voc/tech. levels 1-3.
** Includes a college diploma (10+3), Voc/tech. levels 4 & 5, 1st-4th year college study.
*** Percentage of employees whose level of qualification is not stated is 4.9 percent.
LLB = a first professional degree in law; BA/BSc = Bachelor of Art/Science; MD = Medical Doctor; DVM=Doctor of Veterinary Medicine; MA/MSc= Masters of Art/Science; LLM = Master of Law; PhD = Doctor of Philosophy.
Source: National Civil Service Human Resource Statistics 2013-2014.

What is the distribution of civil servants by field of academic specialization? Thus far, there are no organized data about the civil servants' educational backgrounds. Yet the information displayed in figure 1 seems to indicate that employees in most organizations are predominantly generalists rather than specialists.

In what forms of federal organizations are the civil servants working? The organizations under the federal administration are hierarchically arranged. On the top of the hierarchy are ministries, offices, and applicable commissions.

These are disaggregated into diverse forms of organizations: offices, boards, centers, projects, authorities, institutes, universities, administrations, commissions, funds, and agencies. Some of these diverse forms of organizations have no executive boards while the others do and are relatively more autonomous.

3.3. Recruitment Approaches

The question here concerns efforts to fill vacancies for the top positions and the criteria most often used in selecting the candidates. The responses of survey participants related to this issue are summarized in table 2 and table 3, respectively.

In recruiting top civil servants (TCS), the vacancies in most cases are either internally or publicly advertised. Circulating a vacancy notice across the public sector and relying on recruitment consultants is seldom practised. Undeniably, recruiting the TCSs through public advertisement symbolizes an important influence of the scantily implemented NPM reform, if at all intended.

Table 2: Approaches to Fill the Vacancies for the TCSs

	Never	Sometimes	In about half of the cases	In most cases	Always
How often are the vacancies for the recruitment of top civil servants ... (percentage)*					
... internally advertised? (n=213)	7.9	29.4	16.4	33.8	12.2
... circulated to another part of the public sector to seek applicants? (n=208)	55.1	25.2	5.6	8.4	2.8
... publicly advertised? (n=212)	9.8	21.0	11.2	30.4	26.6
... filled by using executive search consultants? (n = 203)	62.6	21.5	3.3	5.6	1.9

* n = Difference from 214, indicating there was a missing value to the extent of the difference.

In Ethiopian civil service, the criteria for the recruitment of civil servants, after the establishment of the CPA, was expected to be meritocratic. However, actual practices have juxtaposed the "merit and patronage approaches" (Assefa, 2015). Often, the former is practised in hiring individuals for lower positions. The higher the position, the greater the possibility for individuals to be recruited at best on a "quasi-merit" basis and at worst on a pure patronage basis. This is confirmed by a survey we conducted on matters considered in recruiting candidates for top positions (see table 3).

Moreover, table 3 presents TCSs claim about the influence of politicians on their recruitment. The influence of politicians on their selection is quite high (44.9 percent). This figure, if added to the category of "somewhat significant" responses, climbs to over 70 percent. Such results speak to how politicized the Ethiopian civil service is (for details see section 3.7).

Table 3: Factors considered when recruiting TCSs, and the influence of politicians

	Never	Sometimes	In about half of the cases	In most cases	Always
In recruiting TCSs, to what extent is consideration given to candidates' ... (percentage)*					
... political sensitivity? (n = 212)	13.6	24.3	18.7	25.2	17.3
... seniority (n = 212)	3.7	17.3	16.8	39.3	22.0
.... professional expertise (n = 214)	0.5	12.6	11.2	34.6	41.1
	Very significantly	Somewhat significantly	Not significantly	Somewhat insignificantly	Very insignificantly
To what extent do politicians influence the selection of top civil servants? (n = 214, percentage)	44.9	26.6	15	5.1	8.4

*n = Difference from 214, indicating there was a missing value to the extent of the difference.

3.4. Tenure Security

The Ethiopian civil service is a system with strong tenure security offering lifelong tenure of employment. Commonly, new recruits enter the civil service with a probation period of six months and, based on their performance, progress to the status of permanent employee (Federal Civil Servants Proclamation, 2007). The same holds true for the tenure of the TCSs. The majority of TCSs (over 80 percent) replied that their employment in the civil service is permanent. Despite this, TCSs face the highest possibility of removal by their political masters (see table 4).

Table 4: The tenure security of TCSs

	Frequency	Percent
The tenure of the TCSs is ... (n = 214)		
... temporary-contractual basis – renewable based on performance (frequency, %)	43	20.1
... permanent – lifetime (frequency, %)	171	79.9
In general, can politicians remove top civil servants from their positions as they deem necessary? (n = 214) (frequency, %yes)	128	59.8

3.5. The Pay System

In the Ethiopian civil service, the pay system is guided by grades and cadres. The former denotes occupational groupings, and the latter refers to the SKA requirements of jobs in a specific cadre. The amount of pay is determined based on a civil servant's grade. As such, a particular grade correlates to a specific salary scale, which defines the base salary, the horizontal increments, and the maximum pay for that specific grade. The pay system is summarised in table 5.

Periodic pay increases reward seniority. To date, "performance evaluation is more subjective and not yet aligned to an incentive system" (World Bank, 2013:ix). Although a pay reform has been implemented, it is stalled, partial, and ineffective. Similarly, a performance-based arrangement, although proposed, has not yet been implemented (Evans, 2008). Civil servants, including the TCSs, mainly receive a standard salary based on the pay scale (see table 6).

Although measured, there is not much linkage between the performance of civil servants and their remuneration (see table 7). The civil service, in general, does not pay much (see MoCB, 2004).

Table 5: Ethiopian Civil Service Cadres and Grades

→ Horizontal salary increase

Salary scale/ level	Cadres						Step Salary in a Grade *									
	Custodian and manual	Trade and crafts	Clerical and financial	Sub-professional	Administrative	Professional and scientific	Base salary	1	2	3	4	5	6	7	8	9
I	Grade 1															
II	Grade 2	Grade 1	Grade 1													
III	Grade 3	Grade 2	Grade 2	Grade 1												
IV	Grade 4	Grade 3	Grade 3	Grade 2												
V	Grade 5	Grade 4	Grade 4	Grade 3												
VI		Grade 5	Grade 5	Grade 4												
VII		Grade 6	Grade 6	Grade 5												
VIII		Grade 7	Grade 7	Grade 6	Grade 1											
IX		Grade 8	Grade 8	Grade 7	Grade 2											
X		Grade 9	Grade 9	Grade 8	Grade 3	Grade 1										
XI		Grade 10	Grade 10	Grade 9	Grade 4	Grade 2										
XII			Grade 11	Grade 10	Grade 5	Grade 3										
XIII			Grade 12	Grade 11	Grade 6	Grade 4										
XIV				Grade 12	Grade 7	Grade 5										
XV					Grade 8	Grade 6										
XVI					Grade 9	Grade 7										
XVII						Grade 8										
XVIII						Grade 9										

→ Promotion

*Although proclaimed, a step increment in a grade has been paused since 2007/08 awaiting the approval of the performance-based increment approach.
Source: National Civil Service Human Resource Statistics 2013/14

Table 6: The pay system for TCS (n = 214)

	Frequency	Percentage
Standardised – based on pay scale	196	91.6
Flexible – based on bargain between civil servant and organisation	16	7.5
Other*	2	0.9

* Both fixed and flexible scales coexist in the CS

Table 7: Performance-Pay Link (n = 214)

	Frequency	Percentage
Performance is not measured.	28	13.1
Performance is measured but has no effect on pay.	149	69.6
Performance is measured and has an effect on pay.	37	17.3

Although promotion should be carried out according to the Federal Civil Servants Promotion Guideline (2008), in practice it is often based on seniority. The practice encourages fast advancement to the next scale within or across the cadres at the beginning. The progress, however, stagnates as individuals get closer to the highest grade and scale, because there remain only a few higher posts to which individuals could be promoted.

However, in Ethiopia, the stagnation at the top has often been disrupted upon regime change. At the juncture of each disruption, the new administration has distanced itself from the higher officials associated with the preceding regime (see Andargachew, 1993; Paulos, 2001; Mengistu & Vogel, 2006). Such practices, according to Mengistu and Vogel (2006:212), have fashioned a "spoils system," which has "led to a unique brand of rent-seeking among government officials."

3.6. Motivational Factors for Working in the Civil Service

The other question is what motivates civil servants to work in the civil service? To understand their motivations, the TCSs were asked to give their position on the matters presented in the first column of table 8. The questions begin with whether the TCSs would recommend their own children to work in the civil service. The remaining half of the table is devoted to issues related to "public sector motivation" (items 1, 2, 3 and 5) and "public service motivation" (items 4, 6, 7, 8, 9 and 10). These factors comprise extrinsic and intrinsic considerations, respectively, for working for and in the public sector (see Perry & Hondeghem, 2008).

Table 8: Motivational reasons for working in the civil service

	Frequency		Percentage		
Whether the TCSs would recommend their own children to work in the civil service (frequency, % yes)	85.0		39.7		
Motivational factor for working in the civil service (percentage)	1*	2	3	4	5
1. Security of tenure (1)**	9.8	6.1	19.6	25.2	38.8
2. Career opportunities (0)	7.9	12.1	19.6	37.9	22.4
3. Pension benefit plans (0)	11.7	10.7	25.2	24.3	28.0
4. Altruistic motivation–living for more than one-self, serving citizens or others (0)	10.3	9.3	29.0	29.4	22.0
5. Income level or monetary incentive	36.9	15.9	18.7	12.6	15.9
6. Attraction to public policymaking (1)	11.2	9.3	26.6	32.2	20.1
7. Commitment to public interest and civic duty (1)	5.6	7.0	15.4	33.2	38.3
8. Compassion (1)	7.5	7.9	26.6	30.8	26.6
9. Self-sacrifice (1)	10.7	8.9	22.4	30.4	27.1
10. The opportunity to take on responsibility to promote the welfare of the service users (4)	7.5	5.1	20.6	36.9	28.5

*1 = Not important at all; 2 = Rather not important; 3 =More or less important; 4 = Important; and 5 = Very important
** Numbers in the brackets indicate the number of missing responses

The result reveals surprising and even contradictory claims. A large percentage of TCSs (60.3 percent) testified that they would not recommend their own children to work in the civil service. Yet, of the ten items about factors motivating the TCSs for working in the civil service, only income level is reported as an unimportant motivating factor. The question is, if all items except income level are motivating factors, why did the TCSs repudiate the idea of recommending their children to work in the civil service? This is contradictory because a higher motivation for public service should imply a higher likelihood of association with that sector (Perry & Wise, 1990).

Then again, according to Bright (2005:149), high public service motivation denotes less attraction to monetary incentives. It has a positive corollary with individuals' performance as well (Perry & Wise, 1990). Yet the need for higher pay is cited as causing a migration of talent from the civil service to nongovernmental organizations or even to employment abroad (see MoCB, 2004). Equally, the Ethiopian civil service has been blamed for inefficiency (Ibid). Briefly, except for items measuring public sector motivation (items 1, 2, 3, and 5), the TCSs' position on items related to public service motivation seems to manifest the buzzwords and politically correct propaganda of the present Ethiopian civil service.

3.7. Politicisation

In Ethiopia, politicization has been an issue ever since the establishment of the modern civil service. More specifically, prior to the 1970s, clientelism (personal links to the emperor or his political executives) ran rampant, and after the military government came to power, "the Derg … mattered much more than technical competence" (Assefa, 2015:110). Currently, notwithstanding the outward appearance of a "depoliticised civil service" (see Federal Civil Servants Proclamation, 2007; Corruption and Crime Proclamation, No. 881/2015), politicization continues to be common. As such, the boundary between politics and administration is extremely fluid (Assefa, 2015). The patronage arrangement in public appointments is a usual practice (see Evans, 2008). Such arrangements are not only limited to the top positions but also apply to lower-level posts (World Bank, 1998).

Moreover, during the EPRDF government, a small number of spin doctors, known as "special advisors," have joined the federal administration, numbering one or two per civil service institution. They are appointed by the minister/commissioner/ director general, as applicable, of those organizations. Their appointment is based on both merit and political criteria. They are usually members of the ruling party, and their tenure probably depends on the existence of their political masters. Based on the path-dependent experience of purging those who are associated with the outgoing government, their tenure unquestionably ends upon change of the regime.

Asked about the functions of the "special advisors," the TCSs indicate that they predominantly provide strategic advice on policy design and reform proposals; coordinate relations with the stakeholders; offer political/partisan advice; and assist in policy implementation. They also to some degree function as media/relation and communication assistants and partake in the management of civil servants (see table 9).

Table 9: How TCSs describe the function of advisors

	Not at al	Somewhat	Very much
Functions	%	%	%
Provide strategic advice on policy design and reform proposals (n = 214)	7.0	38.8	54.2
Coordinate relations with stakeholder (n = 213)	5.6	41.1	52.8
Offer political/partisan advice	21.0	38.3	40.2
Provide media or relation and communication assistance (n = 214)	6.5	50.5	43.0
Participate in policy implementation (n = 214)	9.3	34.6	56.1
Manage public servants (n = 214)	35.0	36.9	28.0

3.8. Representativeness

The Ethiopian civil service, in general, has a higher percentage of men than women in the workforce. Looking back to 1974, the period when maintaining employee data in terms of gender began around 82 percent of public employees were male. The expansion of the government apparatus during the Dergue government brought about only marginal changes (see table 1).

With the intention of remedying this prevailing gender imbalance, Ethiopia formulated a national policy on women in 1993. Since then, the issues of gender equity and equality have remained on top of the government agenda. In addition, the Constitution has incorporated equality in that "all persons are equal before the law" (art. 25). Similarly, the Labour Proclamation (2003: art. 14 [1][f]) and the Federal Civil Servants' Proclamation (2007; art. 13 [1]) assert discrimination based on sex, among other bases, as unlawful acts. Furthermore, the Constitution goes beyond the prohibition of discrimination to proclaim "affirmative actions for women" (art. 35 [3]). Going even further, the Constitution (art. 42 [1][d]), the Labour Proclamation (art. 87 [1]), and the Federal Civil Servants Proclamation (art. 7) proclaimed the right of "equal pay for equal work" for men and women alike.

In enacting and enforcing the above-mentioned laws and policy that promote gender equality, Ethiopia scored 59.9 (which was above the continental average [53.8]) in the 2013 Mo Ibrahim Index. Doing so also enabled the EPRDF government to increase the proportion of female TCSs to 35 percent (in the federal administration, to 39.7 percent) in 2014 (see the National Civil Service Human Resource Statistics, 2013-2014).

Despite representational improvements, gender disproportion in terms of hierarchical power persists. Briefly, in Ethiopia "women are barely represented in decision-making positions" (UN Women, 2014:39). For instance, in the federal administration, in 2013-2014 the number of women in professional science, administrative, and clerical and financial cadres was 28, 37.3, and 66.2 percent, respectively. Such figures imply uneven distributions of gender at the higher-level posts.

Similarly, if we break down job categories to grades and salary scales, a gender disparity is observable in the salary groups and level of education. That is, women largely receive a minimum wage salary, and most of them also fall into the lower level education categories (see the National Civil Service Human Resource statistics, 2013-2014).

In multi-ethnic Ethiopia, in addition to gender representation, the representativeness of various ethnic groups in the civil service has been a concern. In this regard, the three regimes discussed in the present work have demonstrated two approaches toward dealing with diversity: the assimilationist and the accomodationist policy. The former has been relegated to the past, while the latter, "despite its serious flaws" (Abbay, 2004:593), has been implemented since 1991.

The Constitution (art. 25; art. 88 [2]) underlines the equality of nations, nationalities, and people. Likewise, the Labour Proclamation (art. 14 [1] [f]) and the Federal Civil Servants Proclamation (art. 13 [1]) denounce discrimination on ethnic grounds. Furthermore, the Federal Civil Servants Proclamation proclaimed affirmative action for members of minorities (see art. 13 [3][c]). Despite these legal provisions, the federal civil service is dominated by ethnic Amhara (43 percent), followed by Oromo (17.2 percent) and Tigre (6.6 percent)[2] (see the National Civil Service Human Resource statistics for the year 2013-2014). The balance is made up of other diverse ethnic groups. This indicates that ethnic balance in the federal civil service is an unresolved issue.

3.9. Public Opinion

A comprehensive survey about public opinion toward the Ethiopian civil service is lacking. According to the Global Integrity–African Integrity Indicators, Ethiopian confidence in the civil service for the years 2013 to 2016 was, on average, "somewhat weak."

One of the arguments for the decrease of public trust in the civil service is corruption. In Ethiopia, a diagnostic study by the World Bank (2012) revealed the prevalence of wide-ranging corruption. Indeed, Ethiopia has often ranked on the low end of the corruption perception index (see Transparency International, 2016).

Related to corruption, some old aphorisms exist about holding a position in the government. Among others, these include "sishome *yalbela sishar yikochewal*," which literally means "unbenefitted when appointed, regrets when ousted;" "*shumetena mot ande new*," meaning "appointment and death come once in life," and so on. Such sayings have at least two influences. First, they entitle officials to seek illegal benefits of all forms, including corruption and rent-seeking. They also tease out society's tolerance for corruption. Finally, they inflame negative attitudes toward public officials and institutions, damaging public trust and support for them.

The other reason for the fall of confidence in the country's civil service might be the autocratic (ruling) party system, which is in evidence at every turn (see Merera, 2001). In each regime considered in this chapter, the ruling party's hegemonic aim has been to obstruct the kind of reform required to mitigate corruption. Connected to this, Ethiopia exhibits the stasis of patrimonialism (see World Bank, 2013) which inflames negative public attitudes toward government institutions.

Finally, in Ethiopia, the other reason for the drop in the support may go to what some call a "reform neurosis, "that is, public fatigue with recurring public sector reforms, which are often justified by their deficiency (see MoCB, 2004).

4. Analysis: Implications for Leadership Roles

In this section, the foregoing evidence is analysed based on the overarching antecedents of public leadership: the cultural, political, and organisational-administrative level settings. Subsequently, an attempt is made to deduce the ramifications of these antecedents for leadership roles.

4.1. Cultural Setting

It should be noted that Ethiopia, although home to many religions, was founded on conservative Orthodox Christianity. This hegemonic legacy existed from the era of Menelik II to that of Haile Selassie I. Yet its supremacy, in general, has been weakened since the downfall of imperialism. Its path dependence was visibly disruptedwhen the EPRDF government came to power. Under this regime, individuals are free to exercise the faith and beliefs of their choice. No matter what, "Ethiopians consider religion most important to who they are" (World Economic Forum, 2016).

Furthermore, Ethiopia is a multi-ethnic and multicultural state, an issue that has been handled differently by different regimes (see Abbay, 2004). Likewise, gender balance and, of course, the issue of the age cohort of civil servants have contributed to heterogeneity. Such diversities unquestionably challenge cohesion in the workplace (see Visagie & Linde, 2010).

The implication of the foregoing contexts for the leadership roles, therefore, is the importance of recognizing workforce diversity and their culture. Leaders need to entrench diversity and value heterogeneity in their organizations and welcome it through diversified leadership styles. Briefly, managing diversity requires leaders to adopt diversity leadership approaches (Fernandez et al., 2010; Jackson, 2004; Visagie & Linde, 2010), focus on collaborative leadership (Haruna, 2009), and develop a cross-cultural competency (Jackson, 2004). In SSA, upholding the concept of Ubuntu (see Sigger et al., 2010) is also important.

Additional insight into the Ethiopian culture could be obtained from Hofstede's cultural dimensions (see Hofstede et al., 2010): power distance, individualism versus collectivism, masculinity versus femininity, uncertainty avoidance, long-term versus short-term orientation, and indulgence versus restraint. For Ethiopia, only the scores for the first four dimensions are available. Ethiopia scored high on power distance (70), low on individualism (20), high on masculinity (65), and about average on uncertainty avoidance (55). These respectively denote that Ethiopians are hierarchical, collectivistic, and a largely masculine society.

With reference to the implications for leadership roles, a higher power distance implies that leaders are expected to be directive; subordinates expect to be told what to do; and the ideal boss is a benevolent autocrat. Furthermore, a hierarchical culture endorses a paternalistic leadership (Aycan et al., 2013; Jackson, 2016). A lower score on the individualism dimension or a high score on collectivism denotes that management is about the management of groups; that is, it calls for cooperative teamwork (Nzelibe, 1986) and Ubuntu. The masculinity dimension implies that "managers are expected to be decisive and assertive, the emphasis is on equity, competition and performance and conflicts are resolved by fighting them out." In short, it demands a result-oriented leadership (see Fernandez et al., 2010).

Finally, Ethiopia falls into the category of a "synchronic culture" (Trompenaars & Hampden-Turner, 1997). The issue here is about reviving the past. The past is important because, in synchronic culture, time is considered inter-connected. As such, "the past informs the present, and both inform the future." In terms of work operation, scheduling has less importance. Individuals in such a culture perform several tasks at a time. The emphasis is on "doing things right" more than "doing right things." Punctuality is not stressed to a great extent. Furthermore, Ethiopians are aa kind of "we-oriented (communitarian)" community (Ibid:131). The implication of such a culture for the role of leaders is that they need to assume, among others, the role of storyteller (see Ready, 2002).

4.2. Political Setting

All the regimes that have ruled Ethiopia, irrespective of differences in their ideologies and corollary policies, have endorsed a maximalist view of the state. Until now, except may be during the imperial rule, which in itself has violently ended in 1974, there has never been a peaceful transition of political power.

Likewise, the politicization of the civil service has been the hallmark of all the regimes considered here. In appointing civil servants, the patronage arrangement coexists with the merit approach. Similarly, Ethiopia exhibits the stasis of patrimonial authority. In fact, patrimonialism, although found in almost all polities, has often been described particularly as the core feature of SSA politics and bureaucracy (see Therkildsen, 2014).

The question is what are the influences of the aforementioned factors on how leaders are likely to act? To begin with, while leaders in a minimalist state hold a "marketizing trajectory" and are likely to opt for a performance-oriented style (see Pollitt & Bouckaert, 2011), leaders in the maximalist-type Ethiopian civil service may tend to exhibit a more mandate-driven style, being bound by and performing prescribed roles rather than approaching tasks unconventionally.

Similarly, in the Ethiopian civil service, as politicization pushes both civil servants and politicians toward a close alliance (see Peters & Pierre, 2004), it can be assumed that TCSs in such settings will focus more on ideological consistency and salience of accomplishments with their party rather than on accountability for performance. In other words, the situation calls for "political loyalty leadership" (Tummers & Knies, 2015).

4.3. Organisational-Administrative Level Factors

In Ethiopia, as just explained, the modernism of administration had external origins. Nevertheless, over the past hundred plus years, many civil service reform initiatives have been tried and the system has been progressing. Even so, critics claim that the implementation of reform is overwhelmed by a concern for politics rather than a wish to improve the operational efficiency of the civil service.

Until now, the Ethiopian civil service has not focused much on the meritocratic appointment of civil servants. Equally, the civil service allows permanency of tenure. It does not yet inject market-type mechanisms such as contract arrangements, even in recruiting TCSs. The cvil servants receive a standardised salary. There is hardly a strong performance-pay link, and promotion mainly rewards seniority. Finally, yet importantly, NPM reform-guided "agencification" measures have only been implemented to a limited extent.

The question, though is, what are the implication of the foregoing factors for the role of leaders? Despite widespread talk of reform, as just mentioned, their actual execution and resulting outcomes have been quite limited. The situation on the ground may not motivate leaders, for instance, to focus on performance excellence. Yet, the reform measures might have broadened leaders' role preferences. Currently, for instance, change-oriented leadership (*lawut tekor amerar*) and result-oriented leadership (*wutet tekor amerar*) and so forth are fashionable catchphrases in the Ethiopian civil service.

Lastly, civil servants in Ethiopia function in a work environment with low public support. Such a situation does have an impact on staff motivation. The pressures on civil servants may call for affective leadership that underscores compassion in public service (see Newman et al., 2007). Likewise, the decline of public support for the civil service, among other factors, demands ethical leadership (Sutcliffe, 2005) and emphasis on trust and integrity, such as process "fairness and equity" (Van Ryzin, 2011). It is also important to uphold following rules, accountability, and network governance leadership (Tummers & Knies, 2015). Leaders need to be stewards of the public interest (see Selden et al., 1999) as well.

5. Conclusions

Relying on historical and sociological new institutionalism, we initially studied the evolution and current features of the Ethiopian CSS. In doing so, we mainly relied on documentary analysis. Thus, as the limitation of this method (see Bowen, 2009) could have effects on the findings of the present work, the results of this study should be understood within this limit.

The results, in general, revealed that the civil service evolved in gradual fashion both during imperial and post-revolution Ethiopia. Ever since the beginning of modern public administration, the appointment of civil servants, at all levels, has mixed merit and patronage criteria. The civil service offers lifelong tenure of employment. Likewise, civil servants obtain a standard pay based on the salary scale. The current NPM motivated a movement toward "a contract regime" for employment, and the performance-based pay system has not yet reached Ethiopia.

Undeniably, there are remarkably underappreciated influences of the old institutions. The strong dominance of a single religion and culture, and discrimination on such grounds, among others, is no longer prevalent. Despite this, issues of gender and, especially, ethnic representativeness appear to cause serious concerns for the present and the future legitimacy of the Ethiopian civil service. The legitimacy of those institutions may further be questioned because Ethiopian support for them is low.

Finally, the analysis is framed based on the contextual antecedents and their ramifications for the role of leaders. Based on what is known as a cross-walk approach, the Ethiopian setting approximately calls for the following distinct but inter-related leadership roles: (a) diversity-oriented leadership, (b) collaborative leadership (c) Ubuntu (d) benevolent autocrat, (e) paternalistic leadership, (f) result-oriented leadership, (g) storytelling, (h) political loyalty leadership, (i) change-oriented leadership, (j) compassionate leadership, and (k) ethical leadership.

It should, however, be noted that the presumed ideals of the abovementioned roles might contradict each other. Yet, this is not a problem because of a recent shift from "either ... or" to "both ... and" philosophies of leading organizations (see Quinn et al., 2011). In the present case, it means that leaders may at times be expected to play contradictory roles or make "both ... and" decisions. Moreover, those roles are not "one-size-fits-all" types. As some roles may be more appropriate in some organizations than in others, leaders are expected to make choices compatible with their work context.

Equally, we leave it to the future research to deal with the question of what does and does not work best in this setting. Future works may go further and examine the content of the syllabuses of the public administration and related programs to understand if leaders and potential leaders are trained in context-specific leadership and how the gaps, if any, need to be addressed.

Acknowledgements

We thank the anonymous reviewers who provided critical comments and constructive suggestions that helped us in improving the chapter. We also thank the editors.

Notes

1. In Ethiopia, this qualification refers to one to two years of higher professional education, not a bachelor or post-graduate degree.
2. Oromo is the largest ethnic group (33,117,787); Amhara is the second largest (19, 467,829); Somali is the third largest (5,240,226); and ethnic Tigray is the fourth largest (5,162,242) (National Civil Service Human Resource statistics, 2013-2014:1.10).

References

Aalen, L. (2002). Ethnic Federalism in a Dominant Party State: The Ethiopian Experience 1991-2000. Report. Bergen: Chr. Michelsen Institute: Development and Human Rights.

Abbay, A. (2004). Diversity and State-building in Ethiopia. *African Affairs*, 103(413): 593-614.

Adare, A.M, Hondeghem, A., and Troupin, T. (2018). The Ethiopian Public Sector Leadership Profile Unveiled: Determining the Leadership Profile of the Ethiopian Federal Civil Service Organizations. ISBN 9789075376609.

Adebabay, A. G. (2011). Promoting and Strengthening Professionalism in the Civil Service: The Ethiopian Case. Paper presented at Capacity Building Workshop on Promoting Professionalism in the Public Service: Strengthening the Role of Human Resource Managers for the Effective Implementation of the Charter for Public Service in Africa, March 14-18, Addis Ababa, Ethiopia.

Adejumobi, S. A. (2007). *The History of Ethiopia*. Westport, London: Greenwood Press.

Andargachew, T. (1993). *The Ethiopian Revolution 1974–1987: A Transformation from an Aristocratic to a Totalitarian Autocracy*. Cambridge, England: Cambridge University Press.

Aspinwall, M. D., & Schneider, G. (2000). Same Menu, Separate Tables: The Institutionalist Turn in Political Science and the Study of European Integration. *European Journal of Political Research*, 38(1), 1-36.

Assefa F. Y. (2015). Ethiopia: Development with or without Freedom? In E. Brems, C. Van der Beken, & A. Y. Solomon (eds). *Human Rights and Development: Legal Perspectives from and for Ethiopia* (pp. 101–138). Leiden: Brill Nijhoff.

Aycan, Z., Schyns, B., Sun, J., Felfe, J., & Saher, N. (2013). Convergence and Divergence of Paternalistic Leadership: A Cross-cultural Investigation of Prototypes. *Journal of International Business Studies*, 44, 962969.

Bowen, G. A. (2009). Document Analysis as a Qualitative Research Method. *Qualitative Research Journal*, 9(2), 27-40. Retrieved from https://doi.org/10.3316/qrj0902027.

Bright, L. (2005). Public Employees with High Levels of Public Service Motivation: Who Are They, Where Are They, and What Do They Want? *Review of Public Personnel Administration*, 25(2), 138-154.

Clapham, C. (2006). Ethiopian Development: The Politics of Emulation. *Commonwealth & Comparative Politics*, 44(1), 108–118.

Constitution of the Federal Democratic Republic of Ethiopia (FDRE) Proclamation no. 1/1995. *Federal Negarit Gazeta of the Federal Democratic Republic of Ethiopia*. Addis Ababa, Ethiopia.

Constitution of the People's Democratic Republic of Ethiopia (PDRE), Proclamation no. 1 of 1987. *Negarit Gazetta*, 47(1).

Corruptions and Crimes Proclamation no. 881/2015. *Federal Negarit Gazeta of the Federal Democratic Republic of Ethiopia*. Addis Ababa, Ethiopia.

De Waal, A. (2012). Review Article: The Theory and Practice of Meles Zenawi. *African Affairs*, 112 (446), 148-155.

Evans, A. (2008). Civil Service and Administrative Reform: Thematic paper. Background paper to Public Sector Reform: What Works and Why? An IEG Evaluation of World Bank Support. Independent Evaluation Group, World Bank, Washington, DC.

Federal Civil Servants Proclamation. (2007). *Federal Negarit Gazeta of the Federal Democratic Republic of Ethiopia*. Addis Ababa, Ethiopia.

Federal Civil Servants Promotion Guideline (Amharic). (2008). Addis Ababa, Ethiopia.

Fernandez, S., Yoon, J. C., & James, L. P. (2010). Exploring the Link between Integrated Leadership and Public Sector Performance. *Leadership Quarterly*, 21(2), 308-323.

Getachew, H. M., & Common, R. (2007). Public Sector Capacity Reform in Ethiopia: A tale of Success in Two Ministries. *Public Administration Development*, 27, 367-380.

Hagmann, T. (2005). Beyond Clannishness and Colonialism: Understanding Political Disorder in Ethiopia's Somali Region, 1991–2004. *The Journal of Modern African Studies*, 43(4): 509-536.

Hall, P. A., & Taylor, R. C. R. (1996). Political Science and the Three New Institutionalisms, 1-32. MPIFG Discussion Paper 96/6, Max-Planck-Institut für Gesellschaftsforschung, Germany.

Haruna, P. (2009). Revising the Leadership Paradigm in Sub-Saharan Africa: A Study of Community-based Leadership. *Public Administration Review*, 69(5), 941-950.

Haverland, M., & Yanow, D. (2012). A Hitchhiker's Guide to the Public Administration Research Universe: Surviving Conversations on Methodologies and Methods. *Public Administration Review*, 72(3), 401-408.

Henze, P. B. (2003). Reflections on Development in Ethiopia. *Northeast African Studies,* 10(2), 189-201.

Hofstede, G., Hofstede, G. J., & Minkov, M. (2010). *Cultures and Organizations: Software of the Mind,* 3rd edn. New York: McGraw Hill.

IndexMundi. (2016). Ethiopia. Retrieved from http://www.indexmundi.com/ethiopia/.

Jackson, T. (2004). *Management and Change in Africa: A Cross-cultural Perspective.* London: Routledge.

Jackson, T. (2016). Paternalistic Leadership. *International Journal of Cross Cultural Management,* 16(1), 3-7.

Labour Proclamation (2003). *Federal Negarit Gazeta of the Federal Democratic Republic of Ethiopia,* No. 12. Addis Ababa, Ethiopia.

Lynn, L. E. (2006). *Public management : Old and new.* New York: Routledge.

Marcus, H. G. (1994). *A History of Ethiopia.* Berkeley, CA: University of California Press.

Mengistu, B., & Vogel, E. (2006). Bureaucratic Neutrality among Competing Bureaucratic Values in an Ethnic Federalism: The Case of Ethiopia. *Public Administration Review,* 66(2), 205-216.

Merera, G. (2003). The Elite and the Quest for Peace, Democracy, and Development in Ethiopia: Lessons to be Learnt. *Northeast African Studies,* 10(2), 141-164.

Ministry of Capacity Building (MoCB). (2004). Public Sector Capacity Building Program Support Project. A Report to World Bank, Report no. AB 616, Addis Ababa, Ethiopia.

Ministry of Civil Service (MoCS). (2013). History of Ethiopian Civil Service over the Last 100 Years, review, *Monthly Bulletin,* 003. Addis Ababa, Ethiopia.

Mo Ibrahim Index. (2013). African Governance: Summary. Retrieved from http://www.afcgn.org/wp-content/uploads/2013/11/Ibrahim-Index-of-African-Governance-2013.pdf.

National Civil Service Human Resource Statistics. (2013-2014). Ministry of Public Service and Human Resource Development. Addis Ababa, Ethiopia.

Newman, M. A., Guy, M. E., & Mastracci, S. H. (2007). *Beyond Cognition: Affective Leadership and Emotional Labor. Leading the Future of the Public Sector: The Third Transatlantic Dialogue.* Newark, DE: University of Delaware.

Nzelibe, C. O. (1986). The Evolution of African Management Thought. *International Studies of Management and Organization,* 16(2), 6-16.

Paulos, C. (2001). The Challenges of the Civil Service Reform in Ethiopia: Initial Observation. *Eastern Africa Social Service Research Review (EASSRR),* 17(1), 79-102.

Quinn, R., Faerman, S., Thompson, M. and Clair, L. (2011). *Becoming a Master Manager: A Competing Value Approaches,* 5th ed. San Francisco: Jossey-Bass.

Perry, J. L., & Hondeghem, A. (2008). Editors' introduction. In J. L. Perry & A. Hondeghem (eds). *Motivation in Public Management: The Call of Public Service* (pp. 1-16). Oxford, England: Oxford University Press.

Perry, J. L., & Wise, L. R. (1990). The Motivational Bases of Public Service. *Public Administration Review,* 50(3), 367-373.

Peters, B. G., & Pierre, J. (2004). *The Quest for Control. The Politicization of the Civil Service in Comparative Perspective.* London: Routledge.

Peters, G. (1999). *Institutional Theory in Political Science: The "New Institutionalism.".* London, Pinter.

Peterson, S. (2001). Financial Reform in a Devolved African Country: Lessons from Ethiopia. *Public Administration and Development*, 21, 131-148.

Pollitt, C. (2008). *Time, Policy, Management: Governing with the Past.* Oxford: Oxford University Press.

Pollitt, C., & Bouckaert, G. (2011). *Public Management Reform: A Comparative Analysis*, 3rd edn. Oxford: Oxford University Press.

Ready, D. A. (2002). How Storytelling Builds Next-generation Leaders. MIT *Sloan Management Review*, 45(24), 63-69.

Saha, A. (2008). Role Perception – The Role It Plays. *Icfai University Press, HRM Review* (February), 29-33. Retrieved from http://ssrn.com/abstract=1106548.

Selden, S. C., Brewer, G. A., & Brudney, J. L. (1999). Reconciling Competing Values in Public Administration: Understanding the Administrative Role Concept. *Administration and Society*, 31, 171-204.

Sigger, D. S., Polak, B. M. and Pennink, B. J. W. (2010). "Ubuntu" or "Humanness" as a Management Concept: Based on Empirical Results from Tanzania. CDS Research Report no. 29. ISSN 1385-9218.

Solomon, M. (2013) Civil Service Reform in Ethiopia: Issues, Lessons, and Future Directions. *International Journal of Public Administration*, 36(4), 235-247.

Stiglitz, J. E. (2002). *Globalization, and Its Discontents.* New York: W. W. Norton.

Sutcliffe, K. (2005). Ethics, the Heart of Leadership by Joanne B. Ciulla. Reviewed in *The Academy of Management Review*, 30(4): 869-871.

Therkildsen, O. (2014). Working in Neo Patrimonial Setting: Public Sector Staff Perceptions, in Tanzania and Uganda. In T. Bierschenk & De Sardan, J. (eds). *States at Work: Dynamics of African Bureaucracies.* London: BRILL.

Transparency International. (2016). Corruption Perception Index 2016 Results. Retrieved from https://www.transparency.org/country/.

Trompenaars, F., & Hampden-Turner, C. (1997). *Riding the Waves of Culture: Understanding Cultural Diversity Business*, 2nd edn. London: Nicholas Brealey.

Tummers, L., & Knies, E. (2015). Measuring Public Leadership: Developing Scales for Four Key Public Leadership Roles. *Public Administration*, 2015, 1-35.

UN Women. (2014). *Preliminary Gender Profile of Ethiopia*. Addis Ababa, Ethiopia.

Van der Meer, F., (2011). *Civil Service System in Western Europe*, 2nd edn. Cheltenham, UK: Edward Elgar Publishing.

Van Ryzin, G. G. (2011). Outcomes, Process, and Trust of Civil Servants. *Journal of Public Administration Research and Theory*, 21(4),745-60.

Van Wart, M., Hondeghem, A., & Schwella, E. (2015). *Leadership and Culture. Comparative Models of Top Civil Servant Training.* London: Palgrave.

Visagie, J. C., & Linde, H. (2010). Evolving Role and Nature of Workplace Leaders and Diversity: A Theoretical and Empirical Approach. *Managing Global Transitions*, 8(4), 381-403.

World Bank. (1998). Ethiopia Anti-corruption Report. (December). Washington, DC: Author. Retrieved from http://www1.worldbank.org/publicsector/anticorrupt/EthiopiaGCA.pdf.

World Bank. (2010). Ethiopia Public Sector Capacity Building Program Support Project. Report no. 51611-ET. Washington, DC.

World Bank. (2012). Diagnosing Corruption in Ethiopia: Perceptions, Realities, and the Way Forward for Key Sectors. Directions in Development – Public Sector Governance. Washington, DC: Author.

World Bank. (2013). Federal Democratic Republic of Ethiopia. Ethiopia Public Sector Reform Approach: Building the Developmental State – A Review and Assessment of the Ethiopian Approach to Public Sector Reform. Report no. ACS3695, AFTP2, AFRICA.

World Economic Forum. (2016). How Strongly Do Different Nationalities Feel about Religion? 1March 17. Retrieved from https://www.weforum.org/agenda/2016/03/how-strongly-do-different-nationalities-feel-about-religion/.

Yanow, D., & Schwartz-Shea, P. (2006). Introduction. In D. Yanow & P. Schwartz-Shea (eds). *Interpretation and Method: Empirical Research Methods and the Interpretive Turn* (pp. xi-xxviii) New York: M.E. Sharpe.

IV

PERFORMANCE AND QUALITY

Introduction

Governments, their governance and policies, and their service deliveries, need to be effective, performing, and perceived as qualitative. This section is situated within the broader performance management models and discusses distinct and interrelated issues. Applying non-parametric reference technology, the first chapter (chapter 16) examines the relative efficiency of twenty-nine municipalities in drinking water supply in Ethiopia. The chapter reveals many municipalities were inefficient and unable to balance performance on the Triple Bottom Line (TBL) elements. Chapter 17 applies a descriptive research method and analyzes the performance of sugar construction projects. It finds the performance of the projects is inadequate and identifies the factors that account for poor performance. Chapter 18 investigates the trend of good governance in Ethiopia and shows that progress is needed. Chapter 19 applies inferential statistics and concerns itself with identifying factors that determine the performance of public servants in the federal public sector. The key conclusions and insights of authors have implications for public administration and public policy.

16
Managing Performance in Ethiopian Municipalities: Analysis of Technical Efficiency of Urban Water Services in Oromia National Regional State

Bacha Kebede Debela, Geert Bouckaert, and Steve Troupin

Box 1: Key Points of this chapter

- ✓ Most municipalities had inefficient water supplies.
- ✓ Most municipalities were not able to balance economic, social, and ecological goals in the urban drinking water supply.
- ✓ The efficiency of the municipalities' drinking water supply depends on model specifications.

Box 2: Reading this chapter will give you insights in

- ✓ The application of Data Envelopment Analysis (DEA) in drinking water supply efficiency analysis.
- ✓ The effect of DEA model specifications on efficiency score.
- ✓ The challenges of calibrating economic, social, and ecological goals in urban drinking water supply.

Box 3: Abbreviations

DDS = Democratic Developmental State
DEA = Data Envelopment Analysis
DMU = Decision Making Unit
GTP = Growth and Transformation Plan
MoFED = Ministry of Finance and Economic Development
MoWR = Ministry of Water Resources
MSSD = Most Similar System Design
SDGs = Sustainable Development Goals
TBL = Triple Bottom Line
UN = United Nations
UNDP = United Nations Development Program

1. Introduction

Ensuring access to drinking water remains a global problem. In 2000, the seventh United Nations (UN) Millennium Development Goal (MDG) aimed at halving the proportion of people without access to drinking water by 2015 (UN, 2000). The UN Sustainable Development Goals (SDGs) in Goal 6 seeks to "achieve universal and equitable access to safe and affordable drinking water for all by 2030" (UN, 2015).

Ensuring access to drinking water remains challenging due to the increasing pressure from population growth, urbanization, agriculture, industry, and other sectors all competing for water (Axworthy & Sandford, 2012; Neto; 2016; Pangare & Idris, 2012;); to historically significant structural social inequalities (Castro & Heller, 2009); and to the increasing need to ensure sustainable use of water resources (Akhmouch & Correia, 2016; Neto, 2016).

In its policy frameworks and development plans, Ethiopia, like many other countries, has recognised the importance of ensuring access to drinking water to improve the well-being of society and enhance socioeconomic development (MoWR, 1999). It has also subscribed to the MDGs and SDG. In its Growth and Transformation Plan (GTP I), the country aimed at 100 percent urban drinking water coverage, with twenty liters per day person within 0.5 km by 2014-2015 (MoFED, 2010). In GTP II, the target was revised downward to 75 percent urban access (National Planning Commission, 2016).

In Ethiopia, management of the drinking water supply has been decentralized in two waves: from central to regional governments in 1991-1995 in the framework of a Structural Adjustment Program, and further down to local governments, under the motto of New Public Management since the early 2000s (Transitional Government of Ethiopia, 1993; Peterson, 2015). Since 2005 the government has strengthened vertical and horizontal coordination, in line with the "Democratic Developmental State" (DDS) doctrine (Lefort, 2012; Peterson, 2015).

The Ethiopian policy on drinking water supply emphasizes efficiency (MoWR, 1999). Yet research on the efficiency of urban local governments in drinking water supply remains scarce. Arsano et al. (2010) covered only two municipalities in Ethiopia, while Banerjee et al. (2008) performed a generic study. Furthermore, these studies have not used Data Envelopment Analysis (DEA), the contemporary approach used in other countries to analyze performance of the public sector. Remarkably, micro-level studies assessing tensions which could surface when local governments attempt to achieve the economic, social, and ecological performance goals codified in the Triple Bottom Line (TBL) are scarce, if not absent. The TBL emphasizes concurrently auditing economic, social, and ecological performance (Wiedmann & Lenzen 2008).

This chapter fills the gaps in the literature by comparing the technical efficiency of twenty-nine Grade 2B towns in Oromia National Regional State, Ethiopia,[1] using DEA reference technology. The study seeks to answer the question: What is the relative technical efficiency of Grade 2B towns of the Oromia National Regional State, Ethiopia, in supplying urban drinking water?

To answer the research question, longitudinal data on two inputs and five outputs from the twenty-nine cases were collected. Furthermore, to allow the comparability of cases, a population is used as non-discretionary input. Moreover, to check the robustness of efficiency scores, forty-two DEA model specifications were performed. The study finds many municipalities need to improve their technical efficiency on the TBL dimensions. It also finds trade-offs between and among TBL elements. Thus, the chapter contributes to the SDGs agenda by stimulating dialogue among drinking water supply actors. It also adds to the evolving literature on local government performance management.

The chapter unfolds as follows. The next section offers analytical frameworks. A section on research methodology follows. In the fourth section, collected data are analyzed and results are presented. Lastly, concluding remarks are given.

2. Analytical Frameworks

2.1. The TBL as Analytical Framework

TBL provides a strategic framework to measure and report organizational performance against social, economic, and ecological dimensions (Glavas & Mish, 2015). The necessity of integrating the three dimensions in performance management is underscored by several international legal frameworks, protocols, and reports on water and environment (Akhmouch & Correia, 2016; Aureli & Brelet, 2004; Dublin Statement and Report of the Conference, 1992; European Commission, 2014; Munkonge & Harvey, 2008; Neto, 2016; Solanes & Gonzalez-Villarreal, 1999; UN, 1992; UN, 2000, 2012, 2015; WHO & UNICEF, 2012; WHO & UNICEF, 2013). The concept of TBL is crucial for urban water services, particularly from the viewpoint of "strong sustainability," as cities mainly contribute to socioeconomic development rather than to ecological benefits (Mori & Christodoulou, 2012). The TBL, however, is generic (Pope et al., 2004). Nevertheless, the production model further operationalizes the TBL elements for assessing the drinking water supply. Figure 1 shows the relationship between TBL elements. The economy-equity corner focuses on efficiency (cost recovery and financial sustainability) and fairness and effectiveness (affordability) in drinking water supply. In the ecology-equity corner, environmental justice (sustainable withdrawals) comes into view, while equity is still at the forefront. The economy-ecology dimension seeks profitability (efficiency) while ensuring ecological justice (Flint, 2013).

Figure1: TBL model

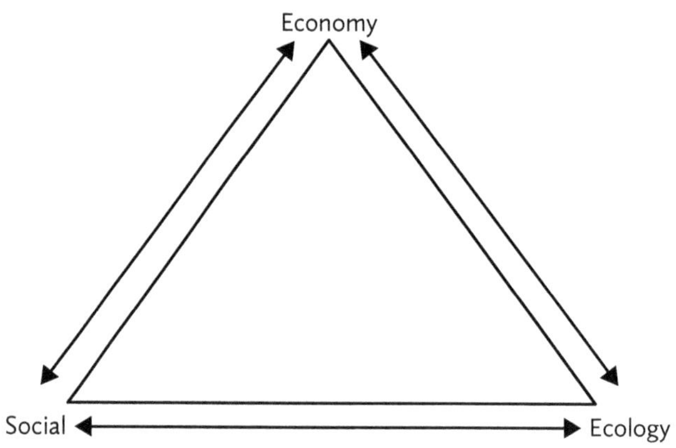

Source: Adopted from Flint (2013:82).

However, trade-offs are expected, as it is difficult for decision-makers to achieve two or three interests concurrently without having "less of the other," and the attempt to address the unachieved goals leads to a vicious cycle (Lieberherr, 2016; Pollitt & Bouckaert, 2011). The trade-offs are expected to be higher in developing countries (UNDP, 2006). For instance, the increased competition for water among various actors for economic gains (economic) may not be easily balanced with the need to supply drinking water to an increased population at an affordable price (social) and reduce the overexploitation of water resources (ecology) (UN, 2006; 2014; UNDP, 2006). Table 1 shows the trade-offs and the hypothetical relationship between TBL elements. As the table shows, in the worst case an organization fails to address all three elements of TBL.

Table 1: The TBL matrix

Criteria			
Social	Economy	Ecology	System result
Low	Low	Low	Low (bad shape)
Low	Low	High	Ecological
Low	High	Low	Economy
Low	High	High	Economy-ecology
High	Low	Low	Social
High	Low	High	Socio-ecology
High	High	Low	Socio-economy
High	High	High	TBL

Source: Authors

2.2. The Production Process Model as an Analytical Framework

Many studies of performance management in the public sector rely on Pollitt and Bouckaert's (2011) production process model. Figure 2 presents the three elements of the production process model and one generic criterion of performance assessment derived from the model.

Figure 2: The Production Process Model

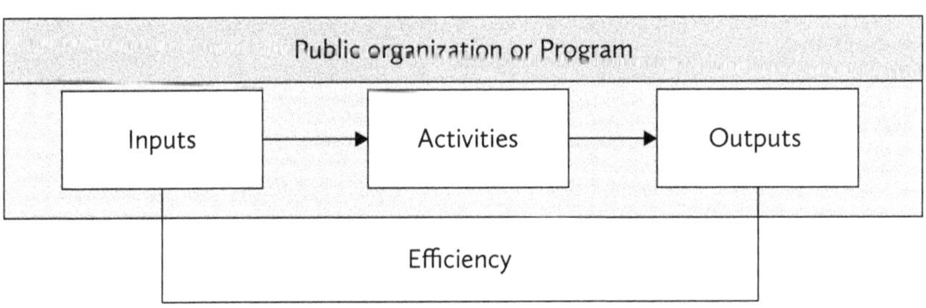

Source: Adapted from Pollitt & Bouckaert (2011)

Inputs refer to resources (human and nonhuman) that are deployed by organizations to produce output (Pollitt & Dan, 2013) through activities. Activities are of an operational and management nature and include organizational structure and arrangements, allocation of authority, and working procedures (Pollitt & Dan, 2013). Outputs refer to what an organization or program delivers or produces (Pollitt & Bouckaert, 2011)

Efficiency refers to the ratio of inputs to outputs (Woodybury & Dollery, 2004). In general, an organization/policy is performing well if it maximizes the outputs produced with a given set of inputs, or if it minimizes inputs used to produce a given set of outputs (Woodybury & Dollery, 2004). Table 2 present a description of the inputs and outputs used in this study.

Table 2: Description of input and output variables

Variables	Description
Inputs Variables	
Permanent staff	Total number of full time equivalent staff of the urban water supply and sewerage service enterprise
Expenditure	Amount of total financial resource committed to produce drinking water in100k
Outputs Variables	
Water produced	Total amount of water produced by the enterprise in km^3
Water sold	Total volume of water sold in km^3
Water loss (transformed into water loss control capacity)	Volume of water loss in m^3 because of illegal connection, authorized but not billed water, leakages, and institutional uses. Since it is unintended negative output, the amount was transformed into water loss control capacity.
Number of private connections	The total number of number of households and institutions (public, business and non-for-profit organizations) that have private connection in hundreds
Water revenue	Sum of water revenue collected from sale of water to private connections and public stand tap users in Ethiopian Birr(100k)
Non-water revenue	Revenue from water related-services and other sources such as technical service, water meter rental, permission and estimation fee, sale of enterprise properties, fines and others(100k)
Non-discretionary variable (input)	
Urban population	Refers to urban (town) population(k)

Source: Authors

These inputs and outputs were selected for four reasons. Firstly, to avoid inflated results because of too many variables (Woodbury & Dollery, 2004), to account for critical variables (Lijphart, 1975), and to comply with the rule of the thumb as to the number of variables in the DEA (Mukokoma & Dijk, 2013). Secondly, because data on these variables were available, consistent, and appeared to be reliable. Thirdly, these variables are identified by a single case study (Ambo, one of the municipalities in this study) (Debela & Troupin, 2015). Fourthly, most water sector analysis that has applied Data Envelopment Analysis (DEA) has used some of these variables. Examples include Carballo and Marques (2011) and De Witte and Marques (2012). Figure 3 shows the distribution of output variables and models on the TBL dimensions.

Figure 3: DEA Output variables and model distribution on TBL Dimensions

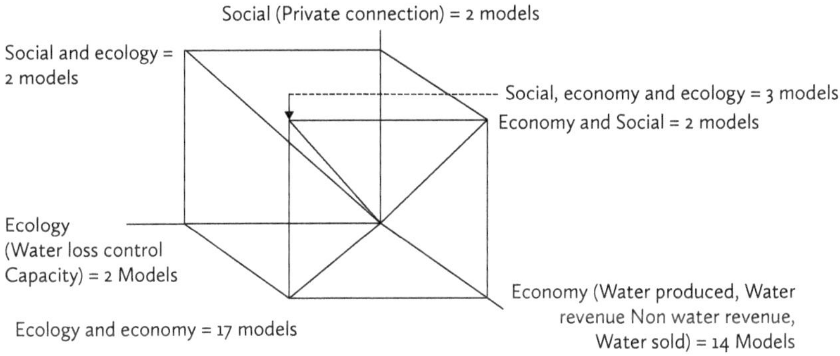

Source: Authors

3. Methodology: Data Envelopment Analysis (DEA)

This study applied the non-parametric approach to performance analysis referred to as Data Envelopment Analysis (DEA). DEA may be used to compare the efficiency of organizations or organizational units – referred to as decision-making units (DMU) – that use similar inputs and produce similar outputs (Cooper et al., 2006; Zhu, 2009). It evaluates the efficiency of each DMU relative to the efficient frontier (best practice). It produces efficiency scores between 0 (0 percent) and 1 (100 percent): a DMU is efficient if its efficiency score is 1 (100 percent); otherwise it is classified as inefficient (Cooper et al., 2006). Inefficient DMUs are enveloped by fully efficient DMUs of comparable size. Examples of authors who used DEA to analyse the efficiency of water utilities include Corton and Berg (2009), De Witte and Marques (2012), Abbott et al. (2012), Picazo-Tadeo et al. (2008), and Tupper and Resende (2004).

DEA can be either input-oriented or output-oriented. In input-oriented models, inefficient DMUs need to focus on input reduction, while in output-oriented models they should emphasize output augmentation (Jacobs et al., 2006). The target for inefficient DMUs is measured by the horizontal distance (input-oriented) or vertical distance (output-oriented) from the frontier (Cooper et al., 2006).

The most common typologies of the DEA model are the Charnes, Cooper, and Rhodes (CCR) and the Banker, Charens, and Copper (BCC) (Cooper et al., 2006; Zhu, 2009;). Both are also called the "radial efficiency" or "weak efficiency" or "technical efficiency" model and apply proportional decrease of inputs or the proportional increase of outputs.

Figure 4 shows the one input-one output BCC DEA. To become efficient under an input-oriented DEA, DMU 10 should move horizontally, reducing the input it uses (reduce expenditure to 322,499 Ethiopian Birr) while keeping its output (water produced) constant (192,968 m3). Conversely, in an output-oriented DEA, it should vertically increase the output it produces (increase water produced to 547,423 m3) while keeping current total expenditure (1,081,141 Ethiopian Birr). Note that the graph is convex and that the DMUs on the graph enveloped inefficient DMUs.

Figure 4: Input- and output-oriented DEA

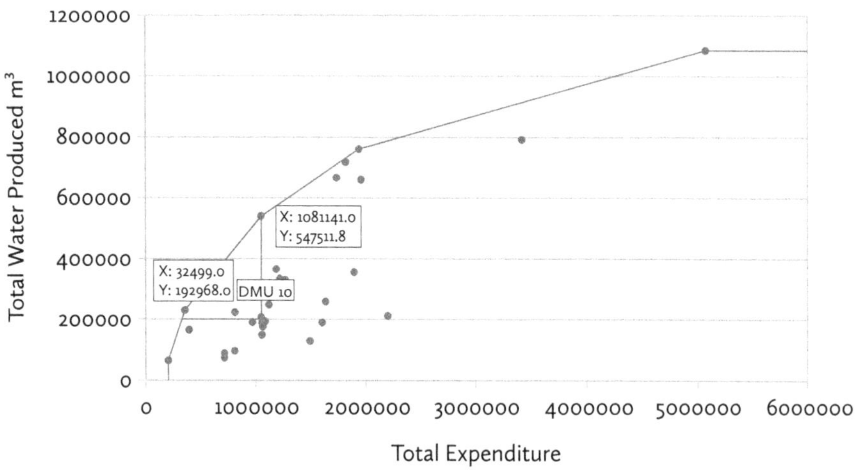

Source: Authors

This study applied the BCC DEA, for four major reasons. Frist, the BCC is more appropriate for managerial use, particularly in cases involving complexity and uncertainty, than CCR (Cherchye & Van Puyenbroeck, 1999). This is because the BCC is flexible and postulates variable return to scale (VRS) – increasing or decreasing returns – on the assumption that the scale of operation matters. The CCR applies a constant return to scale assumption and is relevant from a societal perspective, as society is more interested in efficiency than the scale of operation in drinking water supply (Jacobs et al., 2006; Stroobants & Bouckaert, 2014).

Second, the BCC can handle institutional constraints that could narrow the space for dialogue between policy makers, managers, and other stakeholders on drinking water supply. Thus, it is more suitable, particularly when the market is imperfect and distorted by subsidies and when there is a difference among DMUs in terms of managerial experience and access to resources, which is particularly common in Africa (Banerjee & Morella, 2011). Specifically, the BCC output-oriented DEA is suitable when it appears that proportional augmentation of outputs is more acceptable both politically and administratively (for reasons such as the politics of the day and employee association pressure) than the proportional decrease of inputs (Bouckaert, 2013; Cooper et al., 2006; Zhu, 2009). Fourth, more specifically, the BCC output-oriented VRS DEA is more relevant in the context of Ethiopia, where managers, among others, are more likely to be constrained by many factors such as the top-down political culture and DDS doctrine (Lefort, 2012; Peterson, 2015).

3.1. Case Selection

This study used the Most Similar System Design (MSSD) case study strategy. The MSSD helps control factors that are common to cases and explains differences in terms of any variables that differentiate the cases (Lijphart, 1975; Meckstroth, 1975). To enhance the validity and reliability of research in MSSD, Lijphart suggests:

> [...] *increase[ing] the number of cases as much as possible by extending the analysis both geographically and historically; reduce[ing] the property-space of the analysis by combining variables and/or categories; focus[ing] the analysis on comparable cases and restrict[ing] the analysis to the key variables and omit[ting] those of only marginal importance* (Lijphart 1975: 159).

The features of selected Grade 2B municipalities fit with the requirements of MSSD and DEA. First, these towns were constituted as urban local

Table 3 Features of Selected Grade 2B Cities, Oromia National Reginal State, Ethiopia (June 2013)

Source of raw water	Population size			
	Small (18,000-30,000)	Medium (30,000-50,000)	Large (50,000-90,000)	Total
Surface	DMU7 (28,711)	DMU4 (45,572), DMU19 (42,343), DMU24 (36,228)	DMU25 (64,203)	5
Groundwater	DMU3 (26,744), DMU8 (22,406), DMU10 (25,155), DMU11 (26,101), DMU12 (27,943), DMU27 (19,064), DMU29 (22,053)	DMU2 (43,479), DMU6(45,195), DMU16 (40,467), DMU17 (33,740), DMU20 (49,502), DMU21 (30,629), DMU23 (37,447), DMU26 (40,913), DMU28 (43,312)	DMU5 (69,580), DMU22 (65,284)	18
Surface and groundwater	DMU9 (25,725),	DMU14 (47,135), DMU18 (34,276)	DMU1 (51,860), DMU13 (70,853), DMU15 (55,726)	6
Total DMUs	9	14	6	29

DMU1=Negele Borena, DMU2= Modjo, DMU3= Bedessa, DMU4= Gimbi, DMU5= Arsi Negele, DMU6= Haromaya, DMU7= Bedele, DMU8= Sendafa Beke, DMU9= Yabello, DMU10= Ghinir, DMU11= Bekoji, DMU12= Nedjo, DMU13= Ambo, DMU14= Goba, DMU15= Weliso, DMU16= Fiche, DMU17= Adola, DMU18= Holeta, DMU19=Metu, DMU20= Chiro, DMU21= Dodola, DMU22= Bale Robe, DMU23=Agaro, DMU24= Metahara, DMU25= Batu, DMU26= Bule Hora, DMU27= Deder, DMU28= Dembi Dolo, DMU29= Shambu
N.B. population CSA (2014)

governments (Oromia National Regional Government, 2003) and have Urban Water Supply and Sewerage Service Enterprises that are mandated, among other things, to provide drinking water service efficiently (Ibid.:art. 7 &9). Second, they were sufficient in number (twenty-nine) to make reasonable performance comparisons using DEA. Third, these towns have a similar organizational structure, are located in the same region, and function in accordance with the same proclamation (Ibid.): they are thus suitable for benchmarking and bench-learning. Furthermore, according to CSA (2014), about 1.17 million inhabitants were living in these towns, and the annual urban population growth rate was 4 percent, suggesting the necessity to improve performance in drinking water supply on the TBL dimensions (Akhmouch & Correia, 2016).

The similarity of cases is important in DEA (Stroobants & Bouckaert, 2014). Thus, to ensure comparability of cases, the urban population was used as a non-discretionary input. This is because data from CSA (2014) shows only ten out of twenty-nine grade 2B municipalities had a population from 45,000 to 89, 999 (official range of second-gradecities). Table 3 shows the basic features of the selected cases. This approach follows one of the propositions made by Jacobs et al. (2006) to deal with environmental variables (for other propositions readers may look at Jacobs et al., 2006).

3.2. Data Collection

Data collection went through four major stages. First, a data collection format seeking fifteen years data (1995-2014/15) was developed in consultation with drinking water experts working with the Oromia Water and Energy Bureau. Second, support was obtained from the Oromia Water and Energy Bureau, and the bureau officially requested that the Urban Water Supply and Sewerage Services Enterprises of the selected municipalities submit data. Third, to ensure timely submission, telephone calls were made to the enterprises. Fourth, submitted data were checked and to ensure completeness and consistency some enterprises were asked to resubmit their data. In general, data collection took about three months. Collected data were filtered, and it was found that data from 2010 to 2014/15 were consistent and deemed reliable.

3.3. Data Processing and Model Specifications

Contrary to some proposition such as Zhu (2009), who suggested multiplying negative variable with "-1" or the direct inversion of the variable, water loss (negative output) was transformed into water loss control capacity using a formula:

$$\text{Water loss control capacity} = 1 - \frac{\textbf{Water loss in cubic meter}}{\textbf{Total water produced in cubic meter}}$$

Although relevant according to Jacobs et al. (2006), due to the small number of DMUs (twenty-nine) and the number of inputs and outputs used, dividing and undertaking independent DEA based on the source of raw water was found to be unfeasible.

To look at the impact of the number and different combinations of input and output variables on the frontier and targets, forty-two DEA model specifications[2] were performed (Cooper et al., 2006; Zhu, 2009). The rule of thumb in DEA model formulation stating that the number of DMUs should be at least three times greater than the sum of input and output variables (Jacobs et al., 2006; Mukokoma & Dijk, 2013) was applied. Sensitivity analysis has been suggested in the DEA literature (see for example Cooper et al. 2006; Zhu, 2009), but it should be emphasized that DEA studies that have used several model specifications and longitudinal data are scarce in general. However, recently there has been a trend in this direction. For example, Stroobants and Bouckaert (2014) applied longitudinal data and the one input–one output and two input–two output approach in their study on benchmarking local libraries in Flanders (Belgium). They have shown possible expansion of results in time and space and the potential of such an approach for efficiency improvement.

The principle of exclusiveness and exhaustiveness was applied in the DEA model formulation (Jacobs et al., 2006). To maintain the principle of exclusiveness, a Pearson correlation (2-tailed) was performed over five years, assuming a two-way influence. Table 4 gives the results on output variables. The number in parentheses shows there is a strong correlation between variables. For example, WP and WR are significantly correlated at a 0.01 level of significance, as are WP and PC. Thus, the combination of these variables was avoided in DEA specifications. In general, the exercises allowed for excluding variables that have significant correlation and overcome the problem of multicollinearity on one hand and complying with the rule of thumb in DEA model formulation on the other.

In four DEA model specifications, however, the principle of exclusiveness was not maintained for input variables (staff and total expenditure), although the Pearson's correlation (2-tailed) test shows a strong correlation between the variables (see models 39 to 42). This allowed for assessing the effect of a combination of the two inputs on the efficiency of DMUs and on the TBL dimensions. It is also noteworthy that, unlike Stochastic Frontier Analysis, DEA does not make assumptions about the relationships between variables (Jacobs et al., 2006); furthermore, DEA is relevant when the nature of the relationship between multiple inputs and outputs is complex (Cooper et al., 2006), although this cannot be the best argument as the results are sensitive to model specifications, thus its limitation (Cooper et al., 2006; Jacobs et al., 2006). In addition, several authors who analyzed water utility efficiency using DEA applied used labor (staff) and operating expenses, which are expected to have a strong correlation, as input variables. Examples include Berga and Lin (2008), Corton and Berg (2009), Picazo-Tadeo et al. (2008), and Picazo-Tadeo et al.(2009).

Finally, since DEA applies linear programming methods, Performance Improvement Management (PIM) Software, PIM-DEAsoft-V3.0, and DEA Frontier software was used. It should be noted that no weight restrictions are applied in the analysis.

Table 4: DEA variable correlation matrix over five years in sequential order

	Output variables						Decision
	WP	WR	NWR	PC	WLC	WS	
WP	-	**(0.01**), (-@), (0.01), (0.01), (0.01)**	(0.05*), (-), (-), (-), (-),	**0.01), (-), (0.01), (0.01), (0.01)**	(-), (0.01), (-), (-), (-)	**(0.01), (-), (0.01), (0.01), (0.01)**	Avoid any combination with **High correlation** in DEA model specifications
WR	-	-	(0.05*), (-), (-), (-), (-),	**(0.01), (0.01), (0.01), (0.01), (0.01)**	(-), (-), (-), (-), (-)	**(0.01), (0.01), (0.01), (0.01), (0.01)**	
NWR	-	-	-	(0.01), (-), (-), (-), (-)	(-), (-), (-), (-), (-)	(0.05), (-), (-), (-), (-),	
PC	-	-	-	-	(0.01), (-), (-), (-), (-)	**(0.01), (0.01), (0.01), (0.01), (0.01)**	
WLC	-	-	-	-	-	(-), (-), (-), (-), (-)	
WS	-	-	-	-	-	-	

**. Correlation is significant at the 0.01 level (Pearson, 2-tailed).
*. Correlation is significant at the 0.05 level (Pearson, 2-tailed).
(-). No significant correlation (Pearson, 2-tailed).
WP=Total Water Produced m^3, NWR=Total Non-water Revenue, WS= Water Sold m^3, PC= Total Private Connections, WLC= Water Loss Control Capacity, WR= Total Water revenue
Source: Authors

4. Results and Discussion

4.1. Descriptive statistics

The results from descriptive statistics (figure 5) indicate variations among the DMUs over five periods. Substantial variations were observed on all variables except on water loss control capacity. Second, the standard deviation of total water revenue was much higher than the standard deviation of nonwater revenue except in periods three and five. Third, the figure shows that these municipalities have much potential to improve their technical efficiency. In particular, municipalities that rely on groundwater might have better potential to improve their technical efficiency, because keeping other things constant groundwater is physically and biologically purer than surface water (Byrnes et al., 2010). However, although this is plausible from the economic and social dimensions of TBL, over-extracting groundwater may threaten ecological sustainability, which would threaten the other dimension. Thus, caution is needed.

Figure 5: Descriptive Statistics (Std Dev)

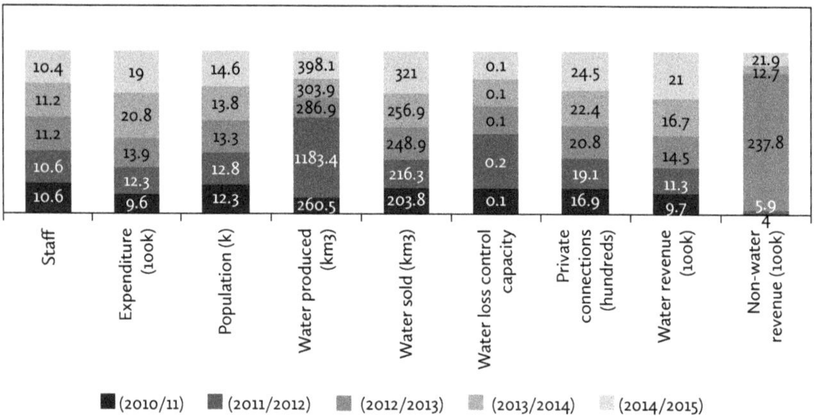

Source: Authors

4.2. Technical Efficiency Distribution

A summary of the results of forty-two DEA model specifications is reported in Debela (2017). As inputs and outputs changed, as more variables were progressively added and as model specifications changed, several things happened.

In general, as expected, as the number of inputs and outputs increased, more DMUs were classified as efficient (Cooper et al., 2006). For example, the results of DEA Models 31 to 37, each with two inputs and three outputs, yielded more best practice DMUs as compared to DEA models from 1 to 5.

The discriminatory power of DEA also depends on the combination of inputs and outputs, although on the surface the number of efficient DMUs with a similar number of inputs and outputs may be in close agreement. For example, in period one there were as many efficient DMUs in DEA Model 25 as in DEA Model 28. However, in the same period, in Model 28 there were nine DMUs with less than 60 percent efficiency scores, meaning that DMUs operating with 40 percent or more waste ought to exert more effort to be efficient. This is particularly necessary when total staff is kept constant compared to total expenditure.

The inclusion of the "non-water revenue" and "water loss control capacity" output variables appeared to have a different impact on the target for inefficient DMUs. In general, when "non-water revenue" is included, many DMUs were found to operate with less than 40 percent efficiency, particularly in periods three and five. In contrast, the inclusion of the "water loss control capacity" output variable has much impact, as many DMUs were able to improve their efficiency scores, although those on the frontier were less or equal to the effect of "non-water revenue." Figure 6 shows instances where a DMU score 100 percent efficiency was achieved in all models over five years (max 210). The distribution of the DMUs efficiency score over five years is reported in Debela (2017).

Figure 6: Instances where a 100% efficiency score was reached-max 210

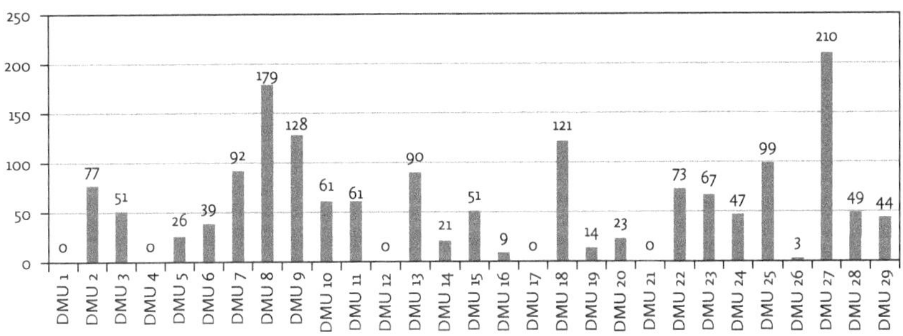

Source: Authors

From figure 6 it is noticeable that the number of fully efficient and inefficient DMUs varies. There were 11, 10, 15, 10, and 14 inefficient DMUs over five years (see Debela, 2017). The results show that size and source of raw water appear to have weak explanatory power for the inefficiency of the DMUs. Figure 6, in particular, shows that DMU1, DMU4, DMU12, DMU17, and DMU21 were inefficient over five periods in all model specifications. While DMU12, DMU17, and DMU21 were relying on groundwater, DMU1 and DUM 4 were respectively using surface and groundwater, and surface water. The performance of inefficient DMUs could be explained by hazard and geo-environmental conditions, but this should be verified by further research.

Second, figure 6 reveals that only DMU27 was classified as fully efficient in all model specifications. DMU8, DMU9, and DMU18 were relatively better and ranked second, third, and fourth respectively (see annex for rank of DMUs). The rank and efficiency scores of DMUs, in general, may be misleading, as some DMUs became efficient by default. The next section clarifies this phenomenon. Third, the difference in the efficiency score indicates that the efficiency of DMUs varies over five years. For instance, in DEA model 10 there were 3, 2, 5, 4, and 4 fully efficient DMUs over five years, respectively, meaning that the efficiency scores of some DMUs were unstable.

5. Distribution of DMUs on TBL Output Dimensions

The results in figure 6 clearly show DMU1, DMU4, DMU12, DMU17, and DMU21 were in bad shape on the TBL dimensions. It appears also that only DMU 27 was able to balance the TBL output dimensions. Such a conclusion, however, cannot be held when efficiency by default phenomena (due to lack of comparable cases) is considered. Figure 7 shows the performance of the DMUs on TBL dimensions. The efficiency by dominance and default phenomena is found by mapping peers from each model over five years. However, due to limited space we did not report, peers for inefficient DMUs (for peers see Debela, 2017).

The distribution of DMUs on the TBL dimensions brings several interesting insights into the foreground. First, many DMUs were weak on ecological performance, but relatively better on the economy, followed by social performance. Second, the pattern of distribution is unstable and the performance of DMUs on TBL does not correlate with the rank of DMUs (see annex 3 for rank). For example, DMU15, ranked 12th, was more efficient by dominance than DMU22, which was ranked 9th. This means DMU22 exhibits the efficiency by default phenomenon. Interestingly, even DMU27, ranked 1st, has some features of efficiency by default, and it was not classified as following best practices on social dimension when compared with DMU9 and DMU15.

Third, there were trade-offs between the economic, social, and ecological output dimensions. For instance, DMU15, which was efficient by dominance on the social dimension, was classified as inefficient on the economy dimension. DMU9 was best only on the ecological dimension. All DMUs that have good efficiency scores on the economy and social dimensions sacrificed the ecological dimension.

An interesting insight also emerges when the combination of TBL dimensions is considered. It is observed that the increase in the number of variables has not completely eliminated the trade-offs between TBL dimensions. Secondly, even with the maximum number of variable combinations, only five DMUs were classified as best on TBL dimensions.

In general, the results show that balancing the TBL dimensions in urban drinking water supply is difficult (Jamali, 2006; UNDP, 2006) but not impossible.

Figure 7: Distribution of DMUs on TBL dimensions in 42 DEA model specifications (average five years)

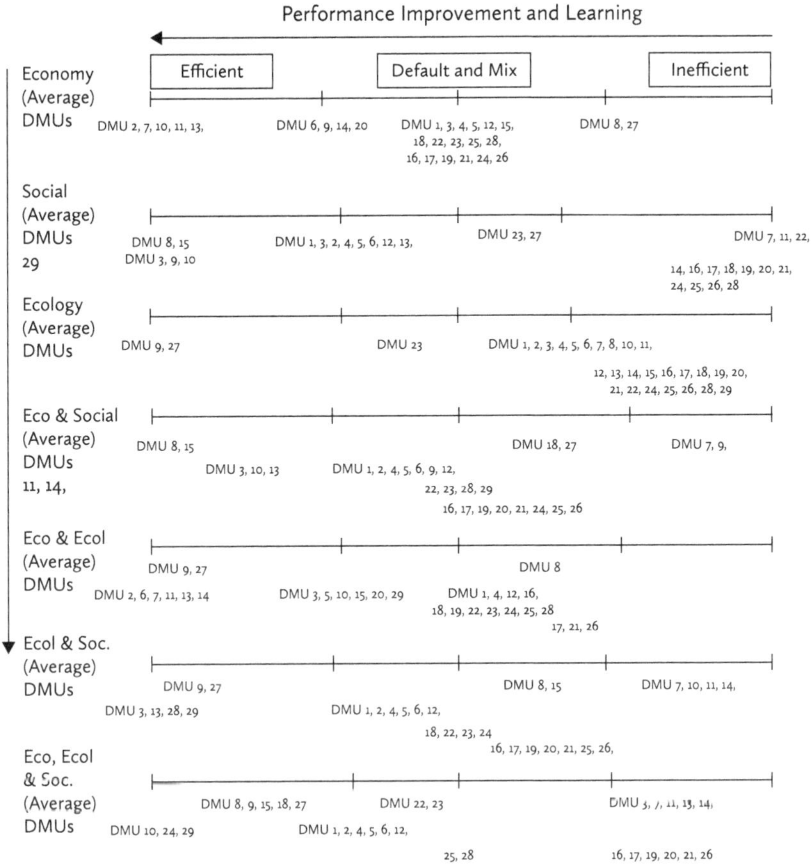

Source: Authors

6. The TBL and Efficiency Improvement Strategies: The Trade-Offs

The difference in the efficiency score of DMUs and the target thereof due to the combination of variables leads to different efficiency improvement strategies, which are often conflicting. For example, when we consider the economy dimension of the TBL in the case of "nonwater revenue," the inefficient DMUs among others need to focus on increasing technical service charges. Clearly, such a strategy contradicts the social dimensions of TBL, particularly as an increase in technical service charge and connection fees which go beyond threshold negatively affects the poor and the disadvantaged (UNDP, 2006).

The inefficient DMUs can also increase efficiency gains by proportionally augmenting private connection, water produced, and increasing water revenue and water sold. The Pearson correlation results already clarified that there was a significant correlation between these variables (see table 2). But each of these outputs invites different strategies, which are often conflicting.

Beyond the threshold, over-extraction of raw water to augment water production jeopardizes the ecological dimension, which itself affects the other dimensions. Increasing water revenue by increasing private connection appears to be a plausible strategy to improve social and economic goals. However, all things being equal, it remains uncertain whether the inefficient DMUs can increase distribution networks to augment private connections, among other factors due to challenging urban topography.

Weak DMUs can also improve their economy by increasing water tariff rates, which could contradict the social dimensions, without jeopardizing the ecological dimension. As such this strategy depends on political decisions and is out of the authority of water enterprise managers.

Augmenting water sold and water loss control capacity generates preferential advantage to balance TBL dimensions. Increasing water sold by minimizing unbilled authorized consumption and apparent loss (due to illegal connections and water meter inaccuracy) is a relevant strategy. By the same token, augmenting water loss control capacity has greater potential to improve the economic, social, and ecological output performance. Keeping existing inputs constant, increasing water loss control capacity helps to avoid the real loss related to leaks in the distribution system, service connection leaks, and reservoir overflows, if any, and thus minimizes over-extraction of raw water while also improving economic and social dimensions.

So what can be said about the learning effect of the story? Notwithstanding the potential tensions and conflicts discussed above, the best practice DMUs (see figure 4) provide interesting insights. First, the source of raw water for these DMUs came from two categories: groundwater (DMU27 and DMU8) groundwater, and ground and surface water (DMU9, DMU15, and DMU18). Thus, these relatively well-performing DMUs provide lessons for the totally inefficient and relatively weakest DMUs. All things being equal, totally inefficient and weak DMUs that are relying on surface and groundwater sources can switch to one source to balance the TBL dimensions if possible, thereby achieving at least some progress. In practice the choice necessities a clear understanding of the associated risks, as a simple switching of the raw water source may lead to a worse situation if not done correctly.

Finally, the unstable pattern of distribution of relatively better DMUs underlines the importance of continuous learning from their own experience and that of others as a group to balance the TBL dimensions as much as possible. It also benefits those DMUs that are classified as best practice by default. Importantly, DMUs that are classified as best practice on one or two dimensions of TBL need to improve their performance on the remaining dimensions and learn from best practice and from their own experience.

7. Conclusions and Implications

Based on empirical work, the following concluding remarks may be made. First, the empirical results show that many DMUs need to improve their technical efficiency by augmenting short failed outputs, particularly when the numbers of variables are modest. But caution is needed. This is because the initiative to proportionally increase one output area could contradict positive results on the other TBL dimensions.

Second, the efficiency of DMUs was impacted by model specifications and therefore unstable over time. It means that DEA applications that focus on a single period and only a few model specifications are insufficient. From a methodological perspective, therefore, the use of longitudinal data and different combinations of variables in DEA is useful to check the robustness of DMUs efficiency scores in time and space (Stroobants & Bouckaert, 2014). This approach is useful because a best-practice DMU in one model specification may not be so in another model specification on TBL dimensions. The targets of weak DMUs also change over time and space.

Third, from the policy and managerial perspectives, differences in the efficiency scores of DMUs over time allow decision makers to identify the most efficient DMUs over time and to initiate a dialogue among stakeholders to distinguish reasons for declining performance (Stroobants & Bouckaert, 2014).

Fourth, related to the third, this study has demonstrated the importance of analyzing the performance of water utilities on TBL dimensions, and its implications on the agenda of sustainable urban water supply and environmental management. The results show that many DMUs are better on economic performance than on ecological performance, suggesting the prevalence of trade-offs. It should be noted that the study argues that except in the cases of water loss control capacity and water sold, proportionally increasing other outputs leads to trade-offs. Similar studies on urban water service can also be undertaken in any country, particularly in those central to the SDG agenda.

Lastly, in the context of this study, future work may focus on examining factors that could explain the relative technical efficiency of the studied municipalities.

Acknowledgements

The authors gratefully acknowledge Oromia Water Resources and Energy Bureau for providing support and useful documents.

This study has been carried out in the framework of the academic cooperation in the development project "Strengthening Institutional Capacity to Support Public Administration and/or Development Management Programmes at Ambo University" between KU Leuven University and Ambo University, financed by VLIR-UOS (Belgium). Thus, the authors are grateful for the support of these institutions. We also thank the participants of the open call group at the IIAS Congress, May 29 to June 2, 2017, Aix-en-Provence-France, in particular Christian Schwab from University of Postdam (Germany) and Dominique Köppen, German University of Administrative Sciences Speyer, for their constructive comments and suggestions. We also thank Prof. Nils Soguel, University of Lausanne, Switzerland, for his useful comments at the IDHEAP/IMPGT/KU Leuven Doctoral Seminar, June 22 to 23, 2017.

Notes

1. Oromia is the largest and most populous National Regional State in Ethiopia. It occupies 363.136 km2. In 2011/12 the population of the region was estimated at 28 million, accounting for about 35 percent of the Ethiopian population. In 2012, about 4 million people (15 percent) lived in urban centers (CSA, 2012).

   In 2013, there were 546 urban centers in Oromia National Regional State (Industry and Urban Development Bureau of Oromia, 2013), 6 of which were 1st Grade towns, 38 were 2nd grade towns (6 Grade 2A and 32 Grade 2B), 55 were 3rd grade towns ranging from 3A to 3D, and the remaining (466) were 4th grade towns ranging from 4A to 4C (IUDBO, 2013). Grade 1 towns/cities have more than 90,000 residents, Grade2o towns/cities have 45,000 to 89,999, Grade 3 towns have between 10,000 to 44,999 while Grade 4 towns have populations ranging from 2,000 to 9,999 (Oromia National Regional Government, 2003).
2. The forty-two DEA model specifications are reported in Debela (2017)

References

Abbott, M., Cohen, B., & Wang, W. C. (2012). The Performance of the Urban Water and Wastewater Sectors in Australia. *Utilities Policy*, 20(1), 52–63.

Afonso, A., & Fernandes, S. (2008). Assessing and Explaining the Relative Efficiency of Local Government. *The Journal of Socioeconomics*, 37(5), 1946-1979.

Akhmouch, A., & Correia, F. N. (2016). The 12 OECD Principles on Water Governance–When Science Meets Policy. *Utilities Policy*, 43, 14-20.

Arsano, Y., Mekonnen, E., Gudisa D, Achiso. D., O'Meally S., Calow R., & Eva L. (2010). Governance and Drivers of Change in Ethiopia's Water Supply Sector. Organisation for Social Science Research in Eastern and Southern Africa (OSSREA), Addis Ababa, in collaboration with the Overseas Development Institute (ODI). https://www.odi.org. Accessed March 22, 2017.

Axworthy, T., & Sandford, B. (2012). The Global Water Crisis: Framing the Issue. In H. Bigas, T. Morris, B. Sandford, & Adeel, D. (eds). *The Global Water Crisis: Addressing an Urgent Security Issue* (pp. 2–7). Papers for the InterAction Council 2011-2012, Hamilton, Canada: UNU-INWEH.

Banerjee, S., & Morella, E. (2011). *Africa's Water and Sanitation Infrastructure: Access, Affordability, and Alternatives*. Washington, DC: World Bank Publications.

Banerjee, S., Skilling, H., Foster, V., Briceño-Garmendia, C., Morella, E., & Chfadi, T. (2008). Ebbing Water, Surging Deficits: Urban Water Supply in Sub-Saharan Africa. Background Paper No. 12. Washington, DC: World Bank Publications.

Berga, S., & Lin, C. (2008). Consistency in Performance Rankings: The Peru Water Sector. *Applied Economics*, 40(6), 793-805.

Bouckaert, G. (2013). Numbers in Context: Applying Frege's Principles to Public Administration. In C. Pollitt (ed.). *Context in Public Policy and Management: The Missing Link?* (pp. 74-87). Cheltenham, UK, and Northampton, MA: Edward Elgar.

Byrnes, J., Crase, L., Dollery, B., & Villano, R. (2010). The Relative Economic Efficiency of Urban Water Utilities in Regional New South Wales and Victoria. *Resource and Energy Economics*, 32(3), 439-455.

Carvalho, P., & Marques, R. C. (2011). The Influence of the Operational Environment on the Efficiency of Water Utilities. *Journal of Environmental Management*, 92(10), 2698-2707.

Castro, J., & Heller, L. (2009). Introduction. In J. Castro & Heller, L. (eds). *Water and Sanitation Services, Public Policy and Management* (pp. 1-16). London: Earthscan.

Central Statistical Authority of Ethiopia (CSA) (2014). Statistical Abstract (Projected Population), Addis Ababa. http://www.populationcommunication.com, accessed on March 22, 2017.

Cherchye, L., & Van Puyenbroeck, T. (1999). Learning from Input–Output Mixes in DEA: A Proportional Measure for Slack-based Efficient Projections. *Managerial and Decision Economics*, 20(3), 151-161.

Cooper, W. W., Seiford, L. M., & Tone, K. (2006). *Introduction to Data Envelopment Analysis and Its Uses: With DEA-solver Software and References*. Berlin/Heidelberg: Springer Science & Business Media.

Corton, M. L., & Berg, S. V. (2009). Benchmarking Central American Water Utilities. *Utilities Policy*, 17(3), 267-175.

De Witte, K., & Marques, R. C. (2012). Gaming in a Benchmarking Environment. A Non-parametric Analysis of Benchmarking in the Water Sector. *Water Policy*, 14(1), 45-66.

Debela, B. (2017). Managing Performance in Ethiopian Municipalities: A Benchlearning Approach of Urban Water Services in Oromia National Regional State. PhD thesis, KU Leuven.

Debela, B., & Troupin, S. (2015). Towards an Analytical Framework to Benchmark the Performance of Urban Drinking Water Supply: Preliminary Findings from Ambo, Ethiopia, 36th AAPAM Roundtable Conference, Morocco, Rabat March 2-6, 2015.

European Commission. (2014). Communication from the Commission: On the European Citizens' Initiative "Water and Sanitation Are a Human Right! Water Is a Public Good, Not a Commodity!"

Flint, R. W. (2013). Practice of Sustainable Community Development, a Participatory Framework for Change. Springer.

Glavas, A., & Mish, J. (2015). Resources and Capabilities of Triple Bottom Line Firms: Going Over Old or Breaking New Ground?. *Journal of Business Ethics*, 127(3), 623-664.

Industry and Urban Development Bureau of Oromia (IUDBO). (2013). List of Urban/ Cities and Urban Grade in Oromia National Regional State, Report. Finfine.

Jacobs, R., Smith, P. C., & Street, A. (2006). *Measuring Efficiency in Health Care: Analytic Techniques and Health Policy*. Cambridge: Cambridge University Press.

Jamali, D. (2006). Insights into Triple Bottom Line Integration from a Learning Organization Perspective. *Business Process Management Journal*, 12(6), 809-821.

Lefort, R. (2012). Free Market Economy, "Developmental State" and Party-state Hegemony in Ethiopia: The Case of the "Model Farmers." *The Journal of Modern African Studies*, 50(04), 681-706.

Lieberherr, E. (2016). Trade-offs and Synergies: Horizontalization and Legitimacy in the Swiss Wastewater Sector. *Public Management Review*, 18(3), 456-478.

Lijphart, A. (1975). The Comparable-cases Strategy in Comparative Research. *Comparative Political Studies*, 8(2), 158-177.

Meckstroth, T. W. (1975). "Most Different Systems" and "Most Similar Systems": A Study in the Logic of Comparative Inquiry. *Comparative Political Studies*, 8(2), 132-157.

MoFED. (2010). Growth and Transformation Plan (GTP), 2010/11-2014/15, Volume I: Main text, Addis Ababa. http://www.ethiopians.com/Ethiopia, accessed March 22, 2017.

Mori, K., & Christodoulou, A. (2012). Review of Sustainability Indices and Indicators: Towards a New City Sustainability Index (CSI). *Environmental Impact Assessment Review*, 32(1), 94-106.

MoWR (1999). Ethiopian Water Resources Management Policy. http://www.ethiopiaembassy.ru, accessed March 22, 2017.

Mukokoma, M. M. N., & van Dijk, M. P. (2013). New Public Management Reforms and Efficiency in Urban Water Service Delivery in Developing Countries: Blessing or Fad?. *Public Works Management & Policy*, 18(1), 23-40.

Munkonge, M. A., & Harvey, P. A. (2008). Access to Sanitation and Safe Water: Reflection of Dublin Principles in Rural Water Supply Approaches in Zambia. 33rd WEDC International Conference, Accra, Ghana, 2008.

National Planning Commission. (2016). Growth and Transformation Plan II (GTP II) (2015/16-2019/20) of the Federal Democratic Republic of Ethiopia, Volume I: Main Text. http://www.dagethiopia.org, accessed March 22, 2017.

Neto, S. (2016). Water Governance in an Urban Age. *Utilities Policy*, 43, 32-41.

Oromia National Regional Government (2003). Urban Local Government Proclamation (Proc. No. 65/2003), Megeleta Oromia, Finfine. http://www.extwprlegs1.fao.org, accessed on 22 March 2017.

Pangare, G., & Idris, L. (2012). Water and Health Security. In H. Bigas, T. Morris, B. Sandford & Adeel, D. (eds). *The Global Water Crisis: Addressing an Urgent Security Issue* (pp. 77–83). Papers for the InterAction Council 2011–2012, Hamilton, Canada: UNU-INWEH.

Peterson, S. B. (2015). *Public Finance and Economic Growth in Developing Countries: Lessons from Ethiopia's Reforms*. London: Routledge.

Picazo-Tadeo, A. J., Sáez-Fernández, F. J., & González-Gómez, F. (2008). Does service quality matter in measuring the performance of water utilities? *Utilities Policy*, *16*(1), 30–38.

Picazo-Tadeo, A. J., González-Gómez, F. J., & Sáez-Fernández, F. (2009). Accounting for Operating Environments in Measuring Water Utilities' Managerial Efficiency. *The Service Industries Journal*, 29(6), 761-773.

Pollitt, C., & Bouckaert, G. (2011). *Public Management Reform: A Comparative Analysis – New Public Management, Governance, and the Neo-Weberian State*, 3rd ed. New York: Oxford University Press.

Pollitt, C., & Dan, S. (2013). Searching for Impacts in Performance-oriented Management Reform: A Review of the European Literature. *Public Performance & Management Review*, 37(1), 7-32.

Pope, J., Annandale, D., & Morrison-Saunders, A. (2004). Conceptualising Sustainability Assessment. *Environmental Impact Assessment Review*, 24(6), 595-616.

Solanes, M., & Gonzalez-Villarreal, F. (1999). *The Dublin Principles for Water as Reflected in a Comparative Assessment of Institutional and Legal Arrangements for Integrated Water Resources Management*. Global Water Partnership. http://citeseerx.ist.psu.edu/index, accessed on June 9, 2016.

Stroobants, J., & Bouckaert, G. (2014). Benchmarking Local Public Libraries Using Non-parametric Frontier Methods: A Case Study of Flanders. *Library & Information Science Research*, 36(3), 211-224.

The Dublin Statement and Report of the Conference (1992). The Dublin International Conference on Water and the Environment (ICWE) in Dublin, Ireland. www.ircwash.org, accessed 31 January,2016

Transitional Government of Ethiopia (1993). Proclamation Defining the Powers and Duties of the Central and Regional Governments. Proclamation no. 41/1993. *Negarit Gazeta*, Addis Ababa.

Tupper, H. C., & Resende, M. (2004). Efficiency and Regulatory Issues in the Brazilian Water and Sewage Sector: An Empirical Study. *Utilities Policy*, 12(1), 29-40.

UN Water. (2006). Water, a Shared Responsibility, the United Nations World Water Development Report 2.

United Nations. (UN) (2000). The Millennium Development Goals Declaration. General Assembly (55/2).

United Nations (UN). (1992) United Nations Conference on Environment and Development Rio de Janerio, Brazil, 3-14 June 1992, AGENDA 21.

United Nations (UN). (2012). The Future We Want. General Assembly Resolution, *66*, 288.

United Nations (UN). (2015). Transforming Our World: The 2030 Agenda for Sustainable Development. General Assembly (70/1). http://www.unctad.org, accessed March 22, 2017.

United Nations Development Programme (UNDP). (2006) Human Development Report 2006: Beyond Scarcity: Power, Poverty and the Global Water Crisis.

WHO & UNICEF. (2012). Report of the Second Consultation on Post-2015 Monitoring of Drinking-water, Sanitation and Hygiene, Organized by WHO and UNICEF, Hosted by the Royal Government of the Netherlands in the Hague, 3-5 December 2012. www.unosd.org, accessed July 9, 2016.

WHO & UNICEF. (2013). Joint Water Supply, Sanitation Monitoring Programme (2013). Progress on Drinking Water and Sanitation.

Wiedmann, T., & Lenzen, M. (2008). Unravelling the Impacts of Supply Chains—a New Triple-bottom-line Accounting Approach and Software Tool. In *Environmental Management Accounting for Cleaner Production*. Springer Netherlands, 65-90.

Woodbury, K., & Dollery, B. (2004). Efficiency Measurement in Australian Local Government: The Case of New South Wales Municipal Water Services. *Review of Policy Research*, 21(5), 615-636.

Zhu, J. (2009). *Quantitative Models for Performance Evaluation and Benchmarking: Data Envelopment Analysis with Spreadsheets*. New York: Springer.

17
Performance Evaluation of Governance and Political System of Ethiopia: Post 1991

Gutata Goshu Amante

Box 1: Key messages of this chapter

- ✓ Insignificant attention to the voice of the people and low accountability
- ✓ Weak adherence to the rule of law
- ✓ Declining government effectiveness
- ✓ Inadequate efforts to control corruption
- ✓ Regulations promulgated without considering the interests of all actors
- ✓ Very little political exchange between and among different actors in society
- ✓ Rampant maladministration, which has held back the poor in a vicious circle of poverty

Box 2: After reading this chapter you will have insight in

- ✓ Dimensions of governance
- ✓ The six measures/indicators of governance and their interdependence
- ✓ Measures of governance and the political system in Ethiopia
- ✓ The nature of government and the practice of governance in Ethiopia
- ✓ The level of engagement and coordination among governance actors
- ✓ The level of trust and respect for the contribution of each actor
- ✓ Whether public interest precedes actors' personal interests

Box 3: Abbreviations

CC = Control of Corruption
CED = Committee for Economic Development
EPRDF = Ethiopian People's Revolutionary Democratic Front
FAO = Food and Agricultural Organization
GDP = Gross Domestic Product
GE = Government Effectiveness
NGO = None Governmental Organization

OECD = Organization for Economic Co-operation and Development
PS = Political Stability
RL = Rule of Law
RQ = Regulatory Quality
UN = United Nation
VA = Voice and Accountability
WB = World Bank
WGI = Worldwide Governance Indicators

1. Introduction

This chapter presents a concise evaluation of the performance of the governing system of Ethiopia, primarily focusing on the period after 1991. The evaluation measures the deviations evident in the implementation of proposed plans (Calidoni-Lundberg, 2006). Generally, there are ten indicators used to evaluate the performance of governance and political systems: rule of law, government effectiveness, control of corruption, regulatory quality, voice and accountability, political stability, corruption perceptions, political rights, civil liberties, and women in parliament. Yet, this present study has used only the first six, which are considered by many scholars as critical, as the presence or absence of each provides a good measure for the performance of the system overall (Kaufmann, Kraay, & Mastruzzi, 2011).

Governance as a concept and as a practice is not new, even though it has been understood and defined differently by different scholars over time. The roots of governance can be found in the Greek word "kybernan," which means to steer or to pilot a ship, but the concept was also used during the Roman Empire under the Latin word "gubernare," meaning to direct, rule, and guide (Ysa et al., 2014). Nowadays, different definitions have been given by different scholars and organizations.

Despite the difficulties in understanding "governance," it is of great importance for governments and government leaders to keep looking for more innovative and genuine mechanisms for making government work better in terms of serving the public interest (Katsamunska, 2016). In other word, the term may be understood as the traditions, institutions, and processes that determine how power is exercised, how citizens are given a voice, and how decisions are made and implemented on issues of public concern (www.iog.ca/about_us.asp).

On the other hand, Högström, (2011, citing Almond et al. 1996:28-29) defines political system as:

> a set of institutions concerned with formulating and implementing the collective goals of a society or of groups within it. That is, it has institutions, agencies, or *structures*, such as political parties, parliaments, bureaucracies, and courts, which carry on specific activities, or perform *functions*, which in turn enable the political system to formulate and enforce its politics.

For Troupin (2016, citing Linz 2000: 51), political systems are "ways of organizing political life and the relationship between citizens and government."

The idea of unifying modern Ethiopia was first put forward by Tewodros around 1850 and materialized at the end of the 1880s by Menelik, in a fashion whereby the domination of Orthodox Christianity and the Amharic language and culture undermined the multi-ethnic character of the country (Gudina, 2007). Since then, the struggle for freedom continued, until the Ethiopian People's Revolutionary Democratic Front (EPRDF) overthrew the Dergue regime through armed struggle and took the responsibility of governing in 1991. This government has adopted a multiparty parliamentary system, devolved power to regional state and local governments, and established norms and policies and institutional frameworks aimed at promoting and protecting human rights (Lives & Nations, 2015). They further embarked on a process of reforming the civil service and the justice sector and improving the processes and mechanisms for ensuring effective and efficient public service delivery. Yet, EPRDF has failed in consolidating its regime and achieving nationwide acceptance, leading to a lack of public trust (Abbink, 2006).

Moreover, de facto Ethiopia lives under a "monolithic party-state system" (Lefort, 2013 citing Clapham, 2009), governed by a so called Revolutionary Democracy (Lefort, 2013) without real participation, despite the claimed "multi-party system." Lefort further asserts that "the federal state, despite nominally decentralized power to regional and local authorities, is stronger than any previous Ethiopian state and has developed structures of central control and top-down rule that preclude local initiative and autonomy." This could best be described as "centralized, authoritarian state that had monopolized access to resources and decision-making" (Lie & Mesfin, 2018). Abbink (2006) has described the system as "centralist authoritarianism" that does not guarantee even the "professional autonomy" of the technocracy (Lefort, 2013). Thus, it may be said that, as in most developing countries, governance in Ethiopia is still a century behind where it ought to be.

In addition, leaders of the so-called Revolutionary Democracy ignore societal forces, which itself has a pernicious: because the government labels them as "backward," "uneducated," and "unorganized," they have a tendency to "to fall into the nets of rent seekers" and may have "little capacity to fight anti-democracy"(Lie & Mesfin, 2018). Therefore, it requires a "vanguard" that should maintain a "strong revolutionary democratic leadership" (Lefort, 2013).

In reality, community organizations, for example, can contribute to bridging the gap between people and government, by highlighting key societal problems and thereby improving the effectiveness of policies and development strategies (Lives & Nations, 2015).

While periodic evaluation of political performance to determine whether a state is doing well or badly is a must (Högström, 2011 citing Eckstein, 1971), it is not so common in most developing countries, including Ethiopia. Yet, periodic performance evaluation of governance and political system should be mandatory at the end of each budget year, as it would allow the government to consciously navigate in the desired direction by making corrective actions whenever policies deviate from the route of progress before it is too late. This is all the more important as former UN secretary-general Kofi Annan (1998) has stated that "alleviation of poverty would only be possible through enhancing good governance." However, research on evaluation of governance and political systems is scarce.

Therefore, using the Kaufmann et al. (2011) governance indicators to assesses the performance of the government and political system of Ethiopia post 1991, the chapter answers the following questions:

- What does the governance and political system look like under the current regime in Ethiopia?
- Has there been progress or regress on the scores of governance and political system over time?
- Are poor scores in terms of the governance and political system related to poverty?

This chapter has four sections. The first section gives a brief introduction, statement of the problem, and the research question. The second section presents the theoretical framework and reviews the previous literature, highlighting key relevant concepts. The third section presents the methodology while the fourth section presents result and discussion. Finally, the fifth section presents the practical implications and some concluding remarks.

2. Literature Review

2.1. Governance

Different scholars define the term governance differently, depending on their experience and educational background. For Lee (2003, citing Newman, 2001) governance can be broadly defined as a wide variety of ways to solve common problems, including organizational, social, national, and international. Defined in this way, governance generally refers to questions about forms of power and authority, patterns of relationships, and rights and obligations among the people facing common problems. This definition anticipates that all affected shall contribute their fair share in solving common issues, as they cannot be solved without a joint effort.

Again, Lee (2003, citing Rhodes, 2000) explains governance in seven different ways:

> *(i)* ***corporate governance*** *and (ii)* ***good governance*** *which emphasize formal processes of both private companies and governments for auditing, ensuring transparency, and information disclosure; (iii)* ***New Public Management*** *which refers to improving efficiencies of government bureaucracies by introducing private sector management methods; (iv)* ***new political economy*** *which emphasizes the changed relationship among the government, civil society and the market; (v)* ***international interdependence****, (vi)* ***socio-cybernetic system****, and (vii)* ***network*** *which deny the existence of mono-centric power.*

Encyclopedia Britannica defines the political system as the set of formal legal institutions that constitute a "government" or a "state" (https://www.britannica.com/topic/political-system).

In broad terms, FAO defines governance as "the process of governing." It is the way in which society is managed and how the competing priorities and interests of different groups are reconciled. It includes the formal institutions of government but also informal arrangements. Governance is concerned with the processes by which citizens participate in decision-making, how government is accountable to its citizens, and how society obliges its members to observe its rules and laws (FAO, 2007). In addition, Lee (2003, citing Lynn et al. [2001:7] defines governance as "regimes of laws, rules, judicial decisions, and administrative practices that constrain, prescribe, and enable the provision of publicly supported good and services. "In general, he refers to governance as changes in the role, structure, and operation process of the government, or the way social problems are resolved (ibid).

For Toikka (2011, citing Pierre 2000), "governance" could be described as "inclusions of private actors in deciding over policy and by the replacement of old, monolithic governments by something more dynamic and flexible." That is, an integrative relationship must be established between all stakeholders of governance, including state actors, the private sector, civil society organizations, NGOs, the media, and others on all matters of governance, particularly on power sharing, which shrinks the role of the state (Khan, n.d). That is, in governance, all activities should be orchestrated and managed in a manner where every stakeholder plays their own role and trusts that the other members will play theirs as well, including the leadership (Carino, 2003).

In other words, governance is a process in which there is no one independent actor able to achieve the whole task (Carino, 2003); rather all actors deliver their own slice (Stoker 1998a:18; Toikka, 2011 citing Rhodes 1996:660) without discrediting the contribution of others within society (Adshead, & Quinn, 1998, citing Rhodes, 1996a:666).

The main reason why the state must rely on other actors and share its power is the growing complexity of our current societies and the emergence of "wicked problems" (Forberger [2014] citing Rittel and Webber, 1973; Ysa et al.), which create high levels of conflict among stakeholders, where there is neither an agreement about the problem itself nor its solution (citing Roberts, 2000). Hence, more complex and sophisticated policies are necessary, in which public agencies engage with private sector entities and citizens in the decision-making and implementation process. Wicked problems require the establishment of collaborative processes between public agencies and other public, civil, society, and business organizations (citing Mendoza and Vernis, 2008:392). Furthermore, Ysa, Albareda, & Forberger (2014, citing Lozano et al. 2006:392) note that "the governance of our complex and interdependent societies will not be possible unless we turn the sense of responsibility among their many social actors into one of co-responsibility."

In this contemporary world, the classical mode of leadership, wherein command presumes compliance, has lost acceptance within a knowledgeable, interwoven, and decentralized society (Matheson, 2002). It has been replaced by a more flexible and vibrant mode of governance (Toikka, 2011). That is, power has lost its importance and no longer elicits compliance; because of this, the skill to secure compliance from followers takes on great importance (Matheson, 2002).

In addition, governance has different dimensions that must be borne in mind, which makes measuring it more difficult. That is, according to Ysa, Albareda, & Forberger (2014, citing Levi-Faur, 2011), governance can adopt the following forms: governance as a structure referring to the formal and informal set of institutions involved; governance as a process referring to the dynamics and leading functions that take place in the process of policy making; governance as a mechanism referring to the institutional procedures of decision-making, as well as compliance and control; and governance as a strategy referring to the manipulation of the institutional and mechanical design with the aim of influencing choices and preferences. These different forms makes it more challenging to evaluate governance and the political system in precise terms. In other words, measuring governance in precise terms like distance and weight is difficult for three reasons: first, most of the goods and services being delivered by governments are primarily public goods, which are not easily divisible or easily measured, like peace and order, national defense, public health, roads, etc.; second, it involves the contributions of a number of (state and nonstate) actors; and third, the instruments used to measure these performance are subjective, as mentioned in the introductory section.

2.2. Political Systems

On the other hand, Scott and Mcloughlin (2014) defined political systems as the formal and informal political processes by which decisions are made concerning the use, production, and distribution of resources in any given society. Formal political institutions can determine the process for electing leaders; the roles and responsibilities of the executive and legislature; the organization of political representation (through political parties); and the accountability and oversight of the state. Informal and customary political systems, norms, and rules can operate within or alongside these formal political institutions. That is, while formal political systems are generally publicly announced, for example in laws, regulations, and codes, informal systems are embedded in socio-cultural institutions, norms, and standards. The development of democratic political systems that provide opportunities for all, including the poor, to influence decision-making is a critical concern for this century.

Working Definition

The working definition of governance and political adopted by this study is the one provided by FAO as "the process of governing," namely, the way in which society is managed and how the competing priorities and interests of different groups are reconciled. It includes the formal institutions of government but also informal arrangements. Governance is concerned with the processes by which citizens participate in decision-making, how government is accountable to its citizens, and how society obliges its members to observe its rules and laws (FAO, 2007). This definition was taken for its inclusiveness, in the sense that it indicates the responsibilities of all actors, how they share responsibilities, how decisions are made, how different interests are reconciled, how government is accountable, and how citizens observe rules and laws.

2.3. Measuring Governance

The Worldwide Governance Indicators (WGI) specify six composite indicators of broad dimensions of governance (Kaufmann, Kraay, & Mastruzzi, 2011), which are described below. It should also be noted that these six dimensions of governance should not be thought of as being somehow independent of one another.

Rule of Law (RL): expresses "the extent to which agents have confidence in and abide by the rules of society, and in particular the quality of contract enforcement, property rights, the police, and the courts, as well as the likelihood of crime and violence."

Government Effectiveness (GE): represents "the quality of public services, the quality of civil service and the degree of its independence from political pressures, the quality of policy formulation and implementation, and the credibility of the government's commitment to such policies."

Control of Corruption (CC): "captures perceptions of the extent to which public power is exercised for private gain, including both petty and grand forms of corruption, as well as 'capture' of the state by elites and private interests."

Regulatory Quality (RQ): captures "the ability of the government to formulate and implement sound policies and regulations that permit and promote private sector development."

Voice and Accountability (VA): expresses the extent to which a country's citizens are able to participate in selecting their government, as well as freedom of expression, freedom of association, and free media.

Political Stability and Absence of Violence/Terrorism (PS): captures "the likelihood that the government will be destabilized or overthrown by unconstitutional or violent means, including politically-motivated violence and terrorism."

Rule of law

> *No free man is to be arrested, or imprisoned, or deceased diseased or outlawed, or exiled, or in any other way ruined, nor will we go against him or send against him, except by the lawful judgment of his peers or by the law of the land (The 1215 Magna Carta:Clause 39).*

Langbein & Knack (2010) define rule of law as implying an open, "not under the table" transparent market, where contracts are enforced by a "rule" that is publicly known to parties outside the contract and applied equitably no matter who the enforcer or the contracting parties are. The variable is intended to measure the probability that contracts and laws or rules are enforced collectively and accountably, rather than privately. Corrupt activities are typically illegal, and their proliferation would indicate weakness in the rule of law. Corrupt deals are enforced "under table/in darkness," where contracts are enforced not by public law but by private bandits.

Constitutional democracy is fundamentally based upon the principle of rule of law. Thus, Rosenfeld (1994) has described three essential characteristics of modern constitutionalism as: limiting the powers of government, adherence to the rule of law, and protection of fundamental rights. In the absence of the rule of law, contemporary constitutional democracy would be impossible.

According to the World Justice Project Rule of Law Index (2016), where the rule of law is weak, medicines fail to reach health facilities, criminal violence goes unchecked, laws are applied unequally, and foreign investments are held back. On the contrary, the creators of the index argue that effective rule of law reduces corruption, improves public health, enhances education, alleviates poverty, and protects people from injustices and dangers.

Government effectiveness

An effective government is one that has honest and competent bureaucrats who are capable of defending the population against any violence and enabling the provision and maintenance of infrastructure that makes possible the exchange of goods and delivery of services (Levi 2006 cited in Sacks & Levi [2010]. The more effective government is, the higher the level of social welfare, ceteris paribus.

Government effectiveness measures:

> the quality of public services, the quality of civil service and the degree of its independence from political pressures, the quality of policy formulation and implementation, and the credibility of the government's commitment to such policies (Lahouij, 2016).

The key concepts measured here are the (i) quality of civil service, (ii) quality and quantity of public infrastructure (like education, health, roads, transportation, etc.), (iii) the level of red tape, and (iv) the organizational structure of public offices, which is reflected in the ability of the bureaucracy to efficiently (a) manage public expenditures, (b) manage the budget, and (c) mobilize revenues.

Triesman (2002) argued that the behavior of public officials could be bad in two ways: a) they "might do things they are not supposed to do", which is measured by the corruption index and b) they "may fail to do things they are supposed to do," which is captured by the government effectiveness index (as measured by the quantity and quality of infrastructure like education, healthcare, etc.).

On the other hand, democracy and effective governance do not overlap conceptually or empirically: "Governability is a challenge for all regimes, not just democratic ones" (Magalhães, 2014 citing Schmitter & Karl 2008:85-86). Furthermore, Holmberg, Rothstein, & Nasiritousi(2009) have concluded that "empirically, there is no clear-cut correlation between establishing electoral representative democracy and quality of government in the exercise of public power."

On the other hand, Langbein & Knack (2010) argue that effective governments make transfers but they are not hidden (keeping with the principle of Voice &Accountability). Also, effective governments use public resources, often for public gain, so that the spending is not a deadweight loss. Effective governments charge for services that citizens want, implying again no or minimal deadweight loss. In general, for the whole-of-government, evidence-based decision-making can lead to greater effectiveness and efficiencies in achieving strategic outcomes (OECD, 2013). Evidence-based policy analysis clearly positively informs important policy decisions being taken by the government.

The GE index is intended to measure the ability of governments to deliver these public services, the quality of the civil service (the "agents" of delivery), and the independence of the bureaucracy from political influence, including the credibility of bureaucratic commitment to its policies ("unbribe-ability," implying Control of Corruption) (Langbein & Knack, 2010). There is thus a causal or definitional overlap among the three concepts of GE, RQ and CC.

Control of Corruption

According to Langbein & Knack (2010), controlling corruption implies a reduction in the use of public resources for private gain. Corruption is a costly, hidden (absence of Voice and Accountability), and usually illegal (absence of Rule of Law) transfer of revenues. Government officials often collect bribes as an ex-officio tax, fee, or "gift" in exchange for a license or service (for example, utility connection) or for exemptions to rules or taxes (implicating Regulatory Quality and Government Effectiveness).

Corruption erodes good governance and the rule of law; it adversely affects service quality and efficiency, poses threats to the principles of democracy and justice, and undermines the economy (Graycar & Sidebottom, 2012). Corruption does not only increase the price of public and private sector goods and services, it also has serious consequences for efficiency (Bertrand et al., 2006; Olken, 2009 citing Krueger [1974]; Shleifer & Vishny, 1993).That is, it has also a significant financial crime element, estimated by the World Economic Forum (2009) to cost about $2.6 trillion per year, about 5 percent of global GDP, with about $1 trillion is paid annually in bribes. In developing countries, corruption, bribery, theft, and tax evasion cost some US $1.26 trillion per year; this amount of money could be used to lift those who are living on less than $1.25 a day to above $1.25 for at least six years (UN Goal 16, facts and figures; https://www.un.org/sustainabledevelopment/peace-justice/).

Dion (2010, cited in Waldman, 1974) defined corruption as including the following components:

> a public official, who misuses his authority, position, or power, and as a result, violates some existing, legal norm in his or her particular country. The corrupt act is usually done in secret and is for personal gain in wealth or status or in preferment of family, friends, ethnic or religious groups.

Furthermore, Dion (2010, citing Okogbule, 2004:74)found that "poverty, unemployment, greed, institutional weakness, inefficient and ineffective law enforcement, disrespect for the rule of law, lack of moral standards and codes are correlated to corruption." These are primarily indicators of corruption rather than their source. The real causes of corruption are rooted in sociocultural practices as well as in political and economic systems. In addition, the most important cause of corruption is the lack of political will to deal with the problem (Ibid: 84). Dion further describes corruption as being a basic threat to the stability of societies and to the maintenance of the rule of law. Furthermore, said he asserts that corruption actually impedes economic development in the long run.

Regulatory Quality

Regulation is a major way in which governments imposes its influence on society. According to the Merriam-Webster dictionary; regulation is any statement promulgated by an executive authority or regulatory agency of a government possessing the power of compliance as a rule or order.

The Committee for Economic Development (CED) (2017, citing Dudley-and Brito 2012) defined regulations as administrative laws or rules by which the government implements laws and agency objectives which dictate what individuals, businesses, and other organizations can or cannot do from dawn to dusk. Evidently, regulations do not work well when the majority of society is ignorant about their existence. Market economies need clear "rules of the game" to function efficiently, for example.

According to Beales et al. (2017), the federal government has two main vehicles for diverting private resources to achieve policy goals. The first is through spending programs. Customs agencies collect compulsory taxes and the revenue is spent on desired public functions such as parks, roads and other infrastructure, schools, law enforcement, homeland security, and scientific research, as well as on welfare and social insurance programs such as Social Security, Medicare, Medicaid, food stamps, and unemployment assistance. The second is through regulation. Federal agencies issue and enforce standards ranging from environmental quality to consumer protection, business and banking practices, nondiscrimination in employment, internet privacy, labels and "disclosure," safe food, drugs, products, and workplaces.

When governments establish numerous barriers to conducting business, it creates opportunities for public officials to collect bribes before delivering a service. By definition, corrupt governments set up entry barriers so that public officials can act as gatekeepers and collect (hidden) bribes before opening the gate to the briber-client (Langbein & Knack, 2010). The RQ index is intended to measure the extent to which the formal (and informal) regulations that govern the relations between the public and the private sector foster growth rather than costly transfers (from the private client to the public regulator, or the other way). Thus, RQ implicates (by definition or cause) CC, RL, and VA.

While better regulation can enhance economic growth when it creates a convenient working environment, poorly designed regulation can decrease economic performance by restraining productivity and increasing wastage (Beales et al., 2017). Moreover, good regulatory policies help the poor generally via redistributive tools like creating employment opportunities or entrepreneurship, reducing opportunities for corruption, increasing the quality of public services, and improving the functioning of the housing, service, and labor markets on which they rely.

How Do We Construct and Maintain Better Regulations?

Do we have the capacity to design a better regulatory policy which would embrace a wide array of diversified interests in Ethiopia? As stated by CED (2017), researchers have designed the following guidelines for countries to design and execute rational regulations policies and avoid cronyism:

(i) **Better information**, that is, the data and economic analysis, the "tools" in the regulatory toolbox, that are used in the planning and evaluation of regulations;

(ii) **Better oversight and monitoring** of the regulatory policy process and the institutions and people involved—the regulators, or "the carpenters" who build and maintain the regulations; and
(iii) **Better collaboration** between input from regulators and all stakeholders (including businesses and the general public).

Voice and Accountability

According to Sharma (2008) voice and accountability involves a process of bargaining between those who hold power and those who seek to influence it. Thus, voice and accountability (V&A) is an important dimensions of governance: it is widely acknowledged that citizens as well as state institutions have a role to play in delivering governance that works for the poor and enhances democracy through interaction between formal and informal institutions. However, citizens need an effective "voice" in order to convey their views; and governments or states that can be held accountable for their actions are more likely to respond to the needs and demands thus articulated by their population.

Citizens' voice and government accountability ("CV&A") are important dimensions of governance. Citizens' capacity to express and exercise their views effectively has the potential to influence government priorities and processes, including a stronger demand for responsiveness, transparency, and accountability (O'Neill, Foresti, & Hudson, 2007).

According to O'Neill, Foresti, and Hudson (2007), accountability exists when those who set and implement the rules (politicians and public officials) are answerable to those whose lives are shaped by those rules and can be sanctioned if their performance is unsatisfactory. Voice and accountability are therefore important indicators of the nature of the relationship between a state and its citizens.

Corruption is usually hidden, which is part of its usual definition. Hidden transactions imply weaknesses in transparency and accountability. The Voice & Accountability index is intended to measure the ability of citizens to hold politicians accountable, including freedom of press, association, and media (Langbein & Knack, 2010). Thus, conceptually, VA and CC are either causally related or are related by definition.

Thus, voice and accountability measures "the extent to which a country's citizens are able to participate in selecting their government, as well as freedom of expression, freedom of association, and free media" (Brewer, Choi, & Walker, 2007).

Voice

Voice refers to a variety of mechanisms – formal and informal – through which people express their preferences, opinions, and views. It can include complaint, organized protest, lobbying, and participation in decision making, product delivery, or policy implementation (Sharma, 2008 citing Goetz & Gaventa 2001).

Accountability

Accountability is for the process of holding individual actors or organizations to account for their actions. Accountability requires transparency, answerability, and enforceability between decision makers and citizens (Menocal & Sharma, 2008, cited in Combaz & Mcloughlin, 2014).

Responsiveness to Citizens = f (Voice + Accountability)

The degree and quality of responsiveness to citizens achieved will depend upon context (f). In terms of responsiveness to the voice of poor people, this could include factors such as: the political and organizational culture (whether the interests of poor and marginalized groups are acknowledged as legitimate and just); the salience of the pro-poor mandate and the relative prominence of poverty concerns on the agenda of decision makers; the weight of the poor relative to other interest groups and the state's incentives to address their concerns; and the ability of decision-making agencies to comprehend the concerns of poor and marginalized men and women and to plan and implement policy in response to them (Gloppen, Rakner, & Tostensen, 2003).

How Are Voice and Accountability Inter-related?

Voice and accountability come together at the point where those exercising voice seek accountability. It is also important to note that voice can strengthen accountability, including by pushing for greater transparency, while accountability can encourage voice by demonstrating that exercising voice can make a difference. In this respect, there is a two-way relationship between voice and accountability (O'Neill, Foresti, & Hudson, 2007).

Political Stability

Political stability is the regularity of the flow of political exchanges (Ake, 1975). That is, the more regular the flow of political exchanges, the more stability. Alternatively, we might say that there is political stability to the extent that members of society restrict themselves to behavioral patterns that fall within the limits imposed by political role expectations. Any act that deviates from these limits is an instance of political instability. To determine the extent of political stability within a polity, we must be able systematically identify both regularities and irregularities in the flow of political exchanges. Political behavior is regular if it does not violate the system (or pattern) of political exchanges; it is irregular if it violates that pattern.

Radu (2015, citing Alesina, Ozler, Roubini, & Swagel, 1996) define political stability as the measure of the perceptions regarding the probability that the government will be destabilized or overthrown by unconstitutional or violent means, including domestic violence and terrorism. Therefore an unstable political environment will reduce investment and the speed of economic development and will increase the probability of a government's collapse and political unrest.

For Javed and Mamoon (2017) and Michael (1971), political stability is a pre-condition for nation building, such as political development and national integration. In most of developing countries a new government comes into the power overnight; either through a coup or army takeover. The new government introduces a new system of rules for the operation of business by totally dismantling the previous, which results in significant sunk costs holding back the development of the country. This in turn creates frustration and anger among the people, leading to state illegitimacy. For Langbein & Knack (2010), economic growth is the friend of regime longevity. Therefore, political stability is important not only for economic development, social integration, and supremacy of law but also for nation building.

On the other hand, Margolis (2010) criticizes scholars for defining political stability focusing on the state, because the state is only one example of a political object. International institutions, religious organizations, mass movements, businesses, criminal organizations, and terrorist groups, for example, all struggle with the stability of power relationships. Political stability is more than state stability.

Margolis proposes a new understanding of political stability:

> Political stability is the degree to which the formal and informal coincide. When the formal roles and structures set by authority match those constructed by informal social interaction, an object is stable. When either set of roles or structures change so they conflict, an object is unstable to some degree. That is, the closer the correspondence between formal and informal within a political object, the greater its regularity and fewer its disruptions. Perfect stability is total correlation; perfect instability, the total absence of correlation (2010).

Redefined operationally, Margolis's postulate may be rendered thus:

> Political stability is the health of authority, resilience, legitimacy, and replacement in a political object (ibid).When an authority enforces its rule

and adapts to change, and a body confers legitimacy upon it and retains the ability to replace it, an object will be stable. That is, it will have a lower potential for disruption.

On the other hand, government instability, inefficiency of political parties, and a weak political culture create a condition for a politically unstable state, which is a serious problem, especially for developing and underdeveloped countries (Memon et al., 2011). Political instability can be defined at least three ways. The first approach is to see it as the propensity for regime or government change; the second is to focus on the incidence of political disorder or violence in a society, such as killings; and the third is to focus on economic growth affected by instability. This problem is more serious for a multiethnic, underdeveloped society. In a politically stable state all sections of society get their due shares and are satisfied being a part of a multiethnic society in which they exert their energies for the development of nation, which ultimately leads toward nation-building. In cases of instability the situation is reversed, people feel unsatisfied and powerless, lose their trust in institutions, preferring their own interests to those of the state, ultimately leading to the splintering of society.

When government transitions are decided by well-defined and long-lived rules, rather than by violent overthrow or perennial coups, government officials are more likely to have a longer time horizon and to seek investment for growth (and political survival) rather than corrupt transfers (Laura & Stephen, 2010). The PS index is intended to measure the expected orderliness of political transitions according to established rules. Thus, PS is related to CC, RL, and GE, either causally or by definition.

3. Methodology

This research used mainly secondary data from different databases, including the World Bank, Transparency International, World Justice Project, the Worldwide Governance Indicators (WGI) projects, and the Central Statistical Authority. The databases of these institutions were prepared from the aggregate indicators to combine the views of a large number of enterprise, citizen, and expert survey respondents in industrial and developing countries. They are based on over thirty individual data sources produced by a variety of survey institutes, think tanks, nongovernmental organizations, international organizations, and private sector firms. In addition, articles, journals, and reports from different multinational and local NGOs were used as a source of data.

The six dimensions of governance are measured both by a governance score that gives a country a score on the aggregate indicator that ranges approximately from -2.5 to 2.5 (where2.5 is the weakest and 2.5 the strongest form of governance) and a percentile rank, which indicates the country's rank among all countries covered by the aggregate indicator, with 0 corresponding to the lowest rank and 100 to the highest rank. On the other hand, the World Justice Project (WJP) uses a scale which ranges between 0 and 1 to measure the same (with 0 being weakest and 1 being strongest form of governance).

Accordingly, the data acquired from these sources were organized in bar graphs for easy revelation of trend/patterns, after which descriptive and content analyses coupled with inferential statistics were employed.

4. Result and Discussion

This section presents data from secondary sources followed by an analysis of each respective indicator used in the evaluation of the governance and political system of Ethiopia post 1991. Based on the information available in various publications, the various dimensions of governance and political system of Ethiopia are presented subsequently. Yet, for some variables there were no data during the period 1991-1995, and 2017-2019. On the other hand, there are data outside the rage of this study which was left for comparison.

4.1. Rule of Law

Figure 1 depicts the trend of rule of law as measured by the World Bank on a scale ranging between -2.5 (weakest) and 2.5 (strongest.)

Figure 1: Ethiopia-Rule of Law

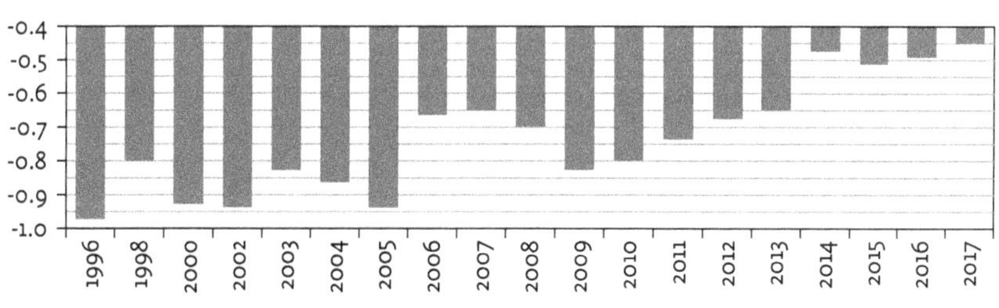

Source: The World Bank

The data on the Rule of Law given in figure 1 above covers the period 1996 to 2017. The average value for Ethiopia during this period was -0.73, revealing that the fundamental principle of rule of law has been consistently violated across this period. Ethiopia scored a minimum of -0.97 points in 1996 and a maximum of -0.45 points in 2017 and ranked 124th. In addition, the data from WJP Rule of Law Index (2016-2019), whose scale ranges from 0 to 1, shows 0.38 for the years from 2016-2018 and 0.39 for the year 2019, where 1 signifies the highest possible score (strong adherence to rule of law) and 0 signifies the lowest possible score (weak adherence to rule of law) confirming the data from the World Bank. Yet the trend shows some improvement on rule of law.

Thus, it could be concluded that: either the state subjects the citizenry to law not publicly promulgated (loosely defined, like the "anti-terrorist" law); or that the state's legislative function is not separated from the adjudicative function, and that there might be some group which is above the law; or there is no law or the existing laws are not obeyed by all; or law may not exist in publication and retrospectively executed; or, the existing laws were vague leading to unfair enforcement; or the existing law may contradict as well as command the impossible; or the law constantly changes and is not consistent with the stated rules.

Generally, figure 1 and the data from WJP Rule of Law Index (2016-2019) above show that there is weak adherence to rule of law over these extended time periods, which implies that governance functions were not being properly delivered.

4.2. Government Effectiveness

The following figure 2 reveals the trend of effectiveness of Ethiopian government on the scale ranging between -2.5 being weakest and 2.5 being strongest, according to the World Bank database.

Figure 2: Ethiopia-Government Effectiveness

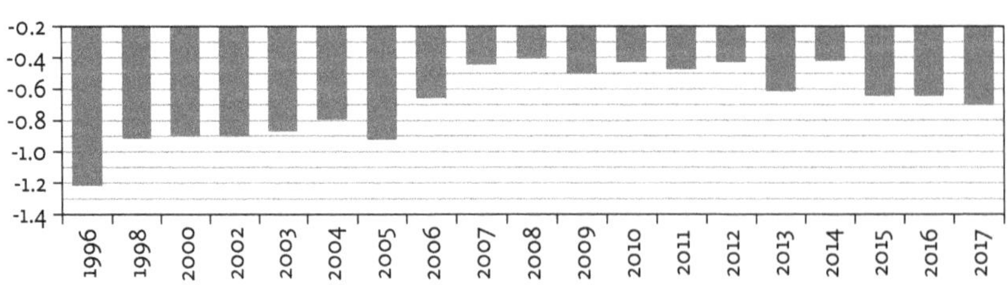

Source: The World Bank

The data presented in figure 2 above show the measure of the effectiveness level of the government for the period 1996 to 2017.The average value for Ethiopia during this period was -0.68 points, with a minimum of -1.21 points in 1996 and a maximum of -0.4 points in 2008. This negative score across these years shows that the government of Ethiopia was ineffective. In a nut shell, the graph clearly shows that the effectiveness of government improved for some time and then declined, which could be described as a move from worst [-1.21] in 1996 to bad [-0.4] in 2008, a period of stagnation from 2009-2014, and a slight improvement during the last three subsequent years.

That is, it can be concluded that there was poor quality and quantity of service delivery, including quality of civil service, quality and quantity of public infrastructure, excessive red tape, and the organizational structure of public offices, which is reflected in the inability of the bureaucracy to effectively manage public expenditures, manage the budget, and mobilize revenues.

On the other hand, the study also makes clear that conducting periodic election does not necessarily guarantee an effective use of public power. During this study period, four elections took place, while the average government effectiveness remained at -0.68, which is way below mid-point. In this era of information and knowledge, where citizens are in a better position of rating the efficiency and effectiveness of their government, it is more difficult to hide their corresponding inefficiency and ineffectiveness.

4.3. Control of Corruption

Figure 3 presented below shows the pattern of control of corruption in Ethiopia on a scale ranging between ranging between -2.5 (weakest) and 2.5 (strongest), during 1996-2017.

Figure 3: Ethiopia – Control of Corruption

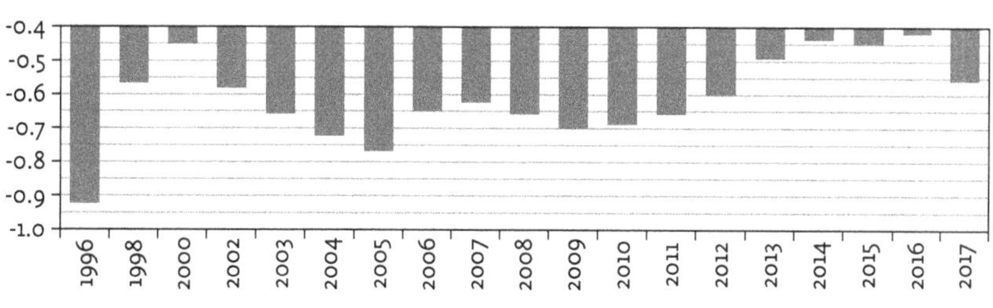

Source: The World Bank

During the period 1996 to 2017, the average value for Ethiopia during this period was -0.61 points, with a minimum of -0.93 points in 1996 and a maximum of -0.42 points in 2016, leading to Ethiopia being rated being 127th in the world (https://www.theglobaleconomy.com/rankings/wb_corruption/). The money embezzled each year ($1.26 trillion) would enable all those earning under $1.25 a day to live a better life for six years (UN Goal 16, facts and figures https://www.un.org/sustainabledevelopment/peace-justice/). If corruption were avoided totally say for five years (one Ethiopian electoral period), we can guarantee that there would not be anyone earning below $1.25 for a period of thirty years. In other words, if the country had the political will and commitment to stop corruption instead of merely establishing an "anti-corruption commission," Ethiopia would be able to use the resulting income to seriously invest long-term in alleviating extreme poverty.

In addition, socio-cultural beliefs regarding corruption should be formatted and rewritten in a manner that makes it clear that bribery is bad and categorized as socially unethical and unacceptable. Unless society ostracizes corrupted persons (and cooperating families), it will remain deep-rooted and may become unstoppable. Therefore, educating the whole of society is important as well. Otherwise, Ethiopia will keep committing a significant proportion of her scarce resources to embezzlement and increasing the burden upon the poor, keeping them poorer and poorer.

4.4. Regulatory Quality

Figure 4 reveals data on the trend of Regulatory Quality in Ethiopia as presented by the World Bank database. It was measured on a scale ranging between -2.5 (weakest) and 2.5 (strongest).

Figure 4: Ethiopia – Regulatory Quality

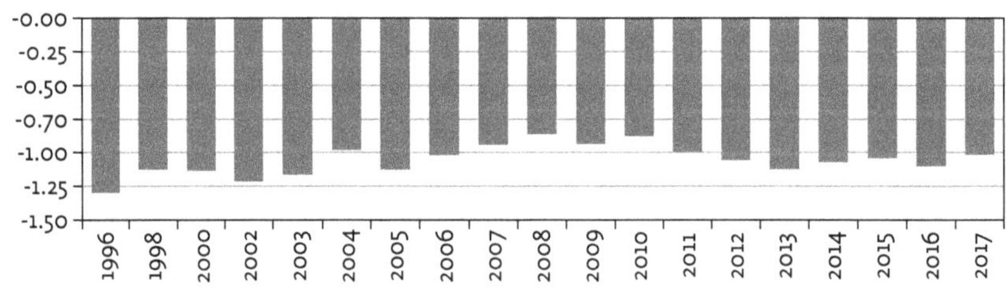

Source: The World Bank

The average value of regulatory quality during the period 1996 to 2017 for Ethiopia was -1.05, which shows that whatever regulations the country has promulgated during the aforementioned period was extremely poor. During this period, Ethiopia scored a minimum of -1.3 points in 1996 and a maximum of -0.86 points in 2008 and ranked 167th. When we look for a pattern in figure 4 above, Ethiopia's score remained almost constant, with very little deviation from the average, revealing that there were no improvements in the laws and rules promulgated to serve public interest by regulatory agencies.

This consistent poor score may be the result of the following factors: regulatory policies were not based on adequate information/data; there were no oversight and monitoring of the regulatory policy process and the institutions and people involved (the regulators); or there was no collaboration where input from stakeholders could have been collected and handed over to policy designers; or the sum of all these.

4.5. Voice and Accountability

Figure 5 below shows data on voice and accountability measures in Ethiopia as per the World Bank on a scale rated between -2.5 (weakest) and 2.5 (strongest).

Figure 5: Ethiopia – Voice and Accountability

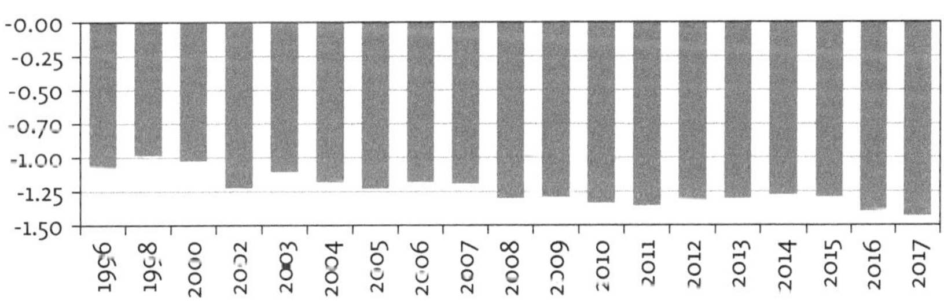

Source: The World Bank

The data presented in figure 5 covers the period from 1996 to 2017. The average value for Ethiopia during this period was -1.24 points, suggesting either that the people's voices were not heard or that the authorities were not answerable to their citizens. During this period, Ethiopia scored a minimum of -1.44 points in 2017 and a maximum of -0.99 points in 1998. When we take a closer look at figure 5, it shows a steady decline from bad ([-0.99]) in 1998 to ([-1.44]) worst in 2017. This means either that the government has either passed regressive laws to silence critics and to shutter opposition political parties and human rights organizations (Novogrodsky, et al., 2018), or the government has ignored criticism and dismissed it as political propaganda.

Thus, we can conclude that Ethiopians were not privileged to speak their mind against their government and had no power to hold all government officials accountable for all their deeds. That is, the loudness of the voice of the people turned to a whisper across this time, and they were unable to hold the government accountable for its deeds (whether good or bad). The space provided to the citizenry to express its preferences was consistently reduced throughout the specified period and their constitutionally granted right to call government officials accountable (as per article 12 [2] of the constitution) was also denied.

4.6. Political Stability

Figure 6 depicts data measuring political stability in Ethiopia from 1996-2017 on a scale rated between -2.5 (weakest) and 2.5 (strongest) as per the World Bank.

Figure 6: Ethiopia – Political stability index

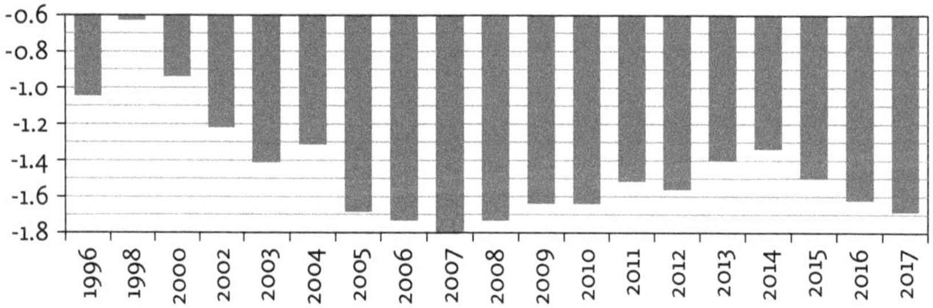

Source: The World Bank

The figure shows that the political stability of the country was consistently declining from 1998-2007, showed a little improvement until 2014, and then consistently declined till 2017. Furthermore, the graph reveals that the country scored a minimum of -1.8 in 2007 and a maximum of -0.63 score in 1998, and secured 180th rank from among 195 countries.

The average value for Ethiopia during this period was -1.44 points, revealing that either there was almost no political exchange or that the members of the society did not restrict their behavior patterns within the limits imposed by the political role expectations. In other words, there exists a mismatch between the formal roles and structures set by the authority and those constructed by the informal social interactions, causing almost perfect instability, as this result is nearer to -2.5 (weakest on the scale).

On the other hand, this negative result (-1.44) could be explained as instability of government, lower legitimacy of the state, and weak political culture, in which there is no flow of political exchange. Furthermore, this score reveals that there is high probability that the government will be destabilized or overthrown by unconstitutional or violent means, including domestic violence, resulting in a low investment rate which leads to low level of economic development leading to hunger and starvation.

Thus, it could be concluded that the history of the last century in Ethiopia demonstrates that there was no one time where there was a constitutional replacement of government, reaffirming that Ethiopia as a state has been unstable since its unification.

At the end of the day, this instability is anti-nation building and anti-development, reflecting a situation in which people feel unsatisfied and powerless; lose their trust in institutions and privilege their own interests over those of the state, which ultimately leads to societal disintegration, which is our current reality. Furthermore, the consequence of political instability is worse where the society is multiethnic like Ethiopia.

5. Conclusions

This chapter has dealt with the evaluation of the effectiveness of the governance and political system of Ethiopia primarily from 1996-2019. The indicators used for this evaluation included: Rule of Law, Government Effectiveness, Control of Corruption, Regulatory Quality, Voice and Accountability, and Political Stability. The results revealed that the effectiveness of the governance and political system of Ethiopia were far below the median on the scale throughout the specified period.

In addition, the failure in regulatory policy negatively affects not just those who design policy but actors across the entire country. That is, if we have failed to create a conducive environment for actors including the private sector, NGOs, CBOs, government agencies, authorities, and citizens at large, we cannot expect "angels" to perform the actors' work for them; nor could we expect all actors perform their best without a regulatory framework. Proper regulatory policy is a minimal government responsibility.

Our results show that the Ethiopian governance and political system has not delivered on its obligations. That is, either all stakeholders in the process of governance were not conscious of their corresponding role and thereby failed to deliver their own fair share; or the state actors were not rendering what is expected from them as the dominant actor under "revolutionary democracy;" or the state actors were impeding other actors or failing to create a conducive environment by deliberately designing constrictive rules and regulations.

Thus, we can say that there is maladministration/misgovernance; that is, the ancient old monolithic government demanding compliance from its subjects is still alive in Ethiopia. That is why we say that "we had a government," without "governance." The 21st century mode of governance only seeks commitment from its followers, not compliance to authority. Thus, this situation can be summarized as follows in general terms:

Figure 7: The Ultimate effect of failure in governance/maladministration

Stakeholders/State & Non-State Actors [Government, Political Parties CBOs, NGOs, Private Sector, and Citizens in general]

↓

Poor Performance score [Rule of Law, Government Effectiveness, Control of Corruption, Regulatory Quality, Voice and Accountability]

↓

Misgovernance/Maladministration

↓

Instability

↓

Poverty

↓

Hunger & Displacement/Migration

Source: Authors

The above diagram reveals the interdependence between governing (state and non-state) actors and poverty. That is, the higher the deviations from good governance, the higher the probability that there would be poor performance in the overall measure of governance. Poor performance in governance functions as measured by the six indicators and leads to maladministration, which in turn leads to instability. Instability by its very nature is a situation where it is difficult if not impossible to do a regular job. If your do not do your regular job, it is high likely that you are on the way to poverty. Poverty, in turn, leads to hunger, which forces population displacement in search of food and stability.

Hence, there is a need for major intervention in light of the six indicators mentioned above for the government to shift the score from negative to positive, wherein people would be in a better position relative to the government. That is, there should be a transformation from the old monolithic government to a governance mode of leadership wherein all stakeholders, civil societies, political parties, NGOs, the private sector, and citizens, own governance and where everyone wins.

Therefore, the following conclusions were drawn for each indicator used:

1. There exists weak adherence to rule of law despite an insignificant level of improvement over time. All law enforcement institutions should implement law impersonally without any discrimination, regardless of the background of the individual, for everyone is equal before law.
2. The effectiveness of government has shown "forth and back" motion without ever reaching a satisfactory level. Thus, we can say that there is a very poor quality and quantity of service delivery, including quality of civil service, quality and quantity of public infrastructure, and excessive red tape. In addition, the organizational structure of public offices is poor, which is reflected in the inability of the bureaucracy to effectively manage public expenditures, manage the budget, and mobilize revenues.
3. Even though there were some fluctuations, we can say that there was significant level of corruption throughout the study period. Thus, public resources should only be used for public purposes, to ensure that corruption is controlled.
4. Regulatory quality remained almost constant, with very little deviation from the average, revealing that there were no improvements in the laws and rules promulgated by regulatory agencies to serve public interests.
5. Throughout the study period, the people's voices were not heard and the authorities were not answerable to the citizens, with this indicator demonstrating a steady decline. The government should be aware that suppression of the voice of the people will not last long in this era of information and knowledge, and should adjust its policy accordingly in order to survive.
6. Political stability went from bad to worse during the study period, despite little deviation.

6. Implications

- If Ethiopia is to continue as a nation, the rule of law must prevail. Otherwise, contemporary constitutional democracy will be impossible, leading to lawlessness and ultimately statelessness.
- Prolonged government ineffectiveness will reduce the productivity of the population, leading to poverty and then hunger. Widespread hunger may ignite civil unrest, leading to a violent replacement of government in a manner consistent with Ethiopian political tradition.
- Reduction of corruption could mean generating extra money to be invested on those who are forced to earn below $1.25/day. Therefore, reduction of corruption may also mean uplifting the living standards of society as a whole.
- Regulation is an instrument that prescribes "the do and don'ts" of every actor in society, including state and nonstate actors. Therefore, it not only affects the people but the land, the water body, the air we breathe, and the relations we ought to have with others. Thus, it either allows or restrains any activity, be it governance or development.
- Continued suppression of the voice of the people coupled with the failure of government accountability will definitely lead to protests and violence.
- Political stability is the cornerstone upon which all other pillars of the nation, like peace and order, economic development, integration, etc. could be built. Therefore, political stability is not an option – it is a matter of Ethiopia's survival.
- Thus, for Ethiopia to continue as a country, all nations, nationalities and peoples (all sections) of society should receive proportional benefits and burdens; only then will we build a consolidated nation where all stakeholders are empowered and exert their energies only for development.

7. Recommendation

1. "Rules" should be publicly known to every member of society and equitably applied, no matter who the enforcer is, thereby ensuring rule of law.
2. Public officials should clearly know and "do things they are supposed to do" in order to enhance government effectiveness. That is, transforming the quality of civil service, quality and quantity of public infrastructure, and omission of red tape shall be enforced immediately. In addition, building the organizational structure of public offices, which is reflected in the

ability of the bureaucracy to be effective in managing public expenditures, manage the budget, and mobilize revenues is also important.

3. The government shall commit itself to the reduction of corruption, not merely establishing an "anti-corruption commission." Then, the country will have room in its budget to change the lives of the needy without allocating additional funds.
4. Any rule or regulation should consider the interest of all actors and how it either allows or restrain their acts; it should also be thoroughly negotiated before it is promulgated. In addition, regulations should be designed in a manner that creates a conducive environment for all (state and nonstate) actors, which ensures regulatory quality.
5. The ability of citizens to hold politicians accountable, including freedom of press, association, and media, should be granted in order to ensure voice and accountability. In addition, our government should recognize media as the fourth branch of government, as it is in the Western world.
6. There should be regular flow of political exchanges. The more regular the flow of political exchanges among all stakeholders, including state and nonstate actors, the more opportunity for bargaining for give-and-take (understanding), the greater the stability of the government.

8. Further Investigative Direction

To unfold the current situation, one could further study "why as instability in Ethiopia continued despite the occurring changes?"

Acknowledgements

I am indebted to the anonymous reviewers and editors who provided critical comments and constructive suggestions that helped me in improving the chapter.

References

Abbink, J.(2006). Discomfiture of Democracy? The 2005 Election Crisis in Ethiopia and Its Aftermath. African Affairs, 105(419), 173-199.

Abebe, D. (2017). *Ethnic Federalism in Ethiopia: A Means to an End*. University of Chicago law School, Conference Proceeding

Adshead, M., & Quinn, B. (1998). The Move from Government to Governance: Irish Development Policy's Paradigm Shift. Policy & Politics, 26(2), 209-225.

Ake, C. (1975). A Definition of Political Stability. *Comparative Politics*, 7(2), 271-283.

Annan, K. (1998).Report of the Secretary-General on the Work of the Organization. *Chapter II.ONU*, 174.

Beales, H., Brito, J., Davis, K. DeMuth, K., Devine, D., Dudley, S., Mannix, B. & McGinnis J. (2017). Government Regulation: The Good, The Bad, & The Ugly, released by the Regulatory Transparency Project of the Federalist Society. (https://regproject.org/wp-content/uploads/RTP-Regulatory-Process-Working-Group-Paper.pdf).

Brewer, G. A., Choi, Y., & Walker, R. M. (2007). Accountability, Corruption and Government Effectiveness in Asia: An Exploration of World Bank Governance Indicators. *International Public Management Review*, 8(2), 204-225.

Calidoni-Lundberg, F. (2006).*Evaluation: Definitions, Methods and Models–An ITPS Framework.* Östersund Swedish Institute for Growth Policy Studies.

Carino, L.V. (2000). *The Concept of Governance -From Government to Governance: reflection on the 1999 World Conference on Governance. Eastern Regional Organization for Public Administration.*

Committee for Economic Development. (2017). REGULATION & the Economy; The Relationship & How to Improve It. https://www.ced.org/reports/regulation-and-the-economy#section4, accessed on November 8, 2018.

Dion, M. (2010). What Is Corruption Corrupting? A Philosophical Viewpoint. *Journal of Money Laundering Control.* https://doi.org/10.1108/13685201011010209.

Evaluating Political Systems: Focus on the Political Performance and the Quality of Democracy. Paper presented at 6th ECPR General Conference, University of Iceland, Reykjavik, August 25 to 27, 2011.

FAO. (2007). Good Governance in Land Tenure and Administration, FAO Electronic Publishing, http://www.fao.org/sd/LTdirect/ltstudies_en.htm.

FDRo, E. (2017). *The 2017 Voluntary National Reviews on SDGs of Ethiopia: Government Commitments, National Ownership and Performance Trends.*

Gemtessa, D. (2014). Abbysinia/Ethiopia: State Formation and National State-Building Project Comparative Approach (Master's thesis, University of Oslo).

Gloppen, S., Rakner, L., & Tostensen, A. (2003). *Responsiveness to the Concerns of the Poor and Accountability to the Commitment to Poverty Reduction.* Norway: Chr. Michelsen Institute.

Graycar, A., & Sidebottom, A. (2012). *Corruption and Control: a Corruption Reduction Approach. Journal of Financial Crime*, 19(4), 384-399.

Gudina, M. (2007). Ethnicity, Democratisation and Decentralization in Ethiopia: The Case of Oromia. *Eastern Africa Social Science Research Review*, 23(1), 81-106.

Högström, J. (2011). Evaluating Political Systems: Focus on the Political Performance and the Quality of Democracy. In *6th ECPR General Conference University of Iceland Reykjavik, 25th-27th Aug 2011.*

Holmberg, S., Rothstein, B., & Nasiritousi, N. (2009).Quality of Government: What You Get. *Annual Review of Political Science*, 12, 135-161.

Javed, R., & Mamoon, D. (2017). Political Instability and Lessons for Pakistan: Case Study of 2014 PTI Sit in Protests. Munich Personal RePEc Archive, University of Management and Technology

Katsamunska, P. (2016). The Concept of Governance and Public Governance Theories. *Economic Alternatives*, 2, 133-141.

Kaufmann, D., Kraay, A., & Mastruzzi, M. (2011). The Worldwide Governance Indicators: Methodology and Analytical issues. *Hague Journal on the Rule of Law*, 3(2), 220-246.

Khan, M. (n.d) *From Government to Governance: Experience and Future Perspectives in the Asia Pacific Region.* Tejgaon, Dhaka 1215, Bangladesh Public Service Commission. *http://www.iam.or.jp/asia-pacific_panel/pdfdownloads/athens01-paper3.pdf*, accessed December 12, 2018.

Langbein, L., & Knack, S. (2010). The Worldwide Governance Indicators: Six, One, or None? *Journal of Development Studies*, 46(2), 350-370.

Lee, M. (2003).Conceptualizing the New Governance: A New Institution of Social Coordination. In *Institutional Analysis and Development Mini-Conference* (Vol. 3). Indiana University, Bloomington, USA

Lefort, R. (2013). The Theory and Practice of MelesZenawi: A Response to Alex de Waal. *African Affairs, 112*(448), 460-470.

Levi, M. (2006).Why We Need a New Theory of Government. *Perspectives on Politics*, 4(1), 5-19.

Lie, J. H. S., & Mesfin, B. (2018). Ethiopia: A Political Economy Analysis. Norwegian Institute of International Affairs, Norway.

Lives, E., & Nations, R. (2015). Accelerating Inclusive Growth for Sustainable Human Development in Ethiopia. United Nations Development Program, Addis Ababa, Ethiopia.

Magalhães, P. C. (2014). Government Effectiveness and Support for Democracy. *European Journal of Political Research*, 53(1), 77-97.

Margolis, J. E. (2010). Understanding Political Stability and Instability. *Civil Wars*, 12(3), 326-345.

Matheson, A. (2002). *Developing Public Sector Leadership in OECD Member Countries.* In 한국 행정학회 *Conference* 자료 (pp. 21-40).

Memon, A. P., Memon, K. S., Shaikh, S., & Memon, F. (2011). Political Instability: A Case Study of Pakistan. *Journal of Political Studies*, 18(1), 31.

Menocal, A. R., & Sharma, B. (2008). *Joint Evaluation of Citizens' Voice and Accountability: Synthesis Report.* DFID.

Michael, S. (1971). Federal Political System in Federal Societies. *Peter Meckison Canadian Federation (Toronto)* (pp. 119-120). Cambridge University Press.

Nunzio, M. D. (2014). "Do Not Cross the Red Line": The 2010 General Elections, Dissent, and Political Mobilization in Urban Ethiopia. *African Affairs*, 113(452), 409-430.

Novogrodsky, N., Williams, C. M., Severson, S., and Golten, R. J. (2018). *Divide, Develop, AND Rule: Human Rights Violations in Ethiopia*, Center for International Human Rights Law & Advocacy, University of Wyoming College of Law.

O'Neill, T., Foresti, M. & Hudson, A. (2007) *Evaluation of Citizens' Voice and Accountability: Review of the Literature and Donor Approaches*. London: DFID.

OECD. (2013). Colombia: Implementing Good Governance, OECD Public Governance Reviews, OECD Publishing.

Olken, B. A. (2009). Corruption Perceptions vs. Corruption Reality. *Journal of Public Economics*, 93(7-8), 950-964.

Radu, M. (2015). Political Stability –A Condition for Sustainable Growth in Romania? *Procedia Economics and Finance*, 30, 751-757.

Rosenfeld, M. (1994). Introduction: Modern Constitutionalism as Interplay Between Identity and Diversity. *Constitutionalism, Identity, Difference, and Legitimacy: Theoretical Perspectives*. Rosenfeld, ed. 434. Duke University Press

Scott, Z., & Mcloughlin, C. (2014). *Political Systems: Topic Guide*. Birmingham: GSDRC, University of Birmingham.

Sharma, B. (2008). Voice, Accountability and Civic engagement: A Conceptual Overview. Commissioned by Oslo Governance Centre, pp. 1-33.

The 1215 Magna Carta: Clause 39. *The Magna Carta Project*, trans. H. Summerson et al. http://magnacarta.cmp.uea.ac.uk/read/magna_carta_1215/Clause_39, accessed January 1, 2020].

Toikka, A. (2011). Governance Theory as a Framework for Empirical Research. A Case Study on Local Environmental Policy-Making in Helsinki, Finland. Helsinki: Department of Social Research University of Helsinki.

Treisman, D. 2002. Decentralization and the Quality of Government. Working Paper, Dept. of Political Science, UCLA.

Troupin, S. (2016). On the Political Regime of Post-1991 Ethiopia: Evidence from the Literature. Paper presented at the IIAS-IASIA Joint Congress, September 19 to 23, 2016, Chengdu, China.

UN Goal 16, Facts and Figures, https://www.un.org/sustainabledevelopment/peace-justice/, accessed May 27, 2018.

World Justice Project, Rule of Law Index (2016), *Rule of Law Around the World: Scores and Rankings*, Washington, DC.

www.govindicators.org, accessed on 02/09/2019

www.iog.ca/about_us.asp, accessed on 02/09/2019

Ysa, T., Albareda, A., & Forberger, S. (2014). *What is Governance. Reforming Addictions: Policies, Processes and Pressure, ALICE RAP Project, www.alicerap.eu*

18

Key Factors Contributing to Time and Cost Overrun in Mega Sugar Construction Projects in Ethiopia

Temesgen Genie Chekol and Denamo Addissie Nuramo

Box 1: Key contributions of this chapter

- ✓ The performance of sugar industry construction projects in Ethiopia is poor.
- ✓ There are many factors contributing to time and cost overrun of mega sugar construction projects in Ethiopia: improper planning and scheduling, unrealistic contract duration, improper and poor project feasibility study; capacity limitation, etc.

Box 2: Reading this chapter will give you insights in

- ✓ The status of sugar projects in terms of time and cost performance
- ✓ Factors contributing to delay and cost overrun in mega sugar construction projects in Ethiopia

Box 3: Abbreviations

ADSWE = Amhara Design and Supervision Works Enterprise
AWWCE – Amhara Water Works Construction Enterprise
COM PLANT – China National Complete Plant Import and export Co. Ltd.
ESC = Ethiopian Sugar Corporation
ECDSWC = Ethiopian Construction Design and Supervision Works Corporation
GDP = Growth Domestic Product
GIECD = Guangxi Gonglian Industrial Engineering Consulting & Design Ltd
GTP = Growth and Transformation Plan
ha = Hectare
METEC = Metal and Engineering Technology Corporation
MoUDC = Ministry of Urban Development and Construction
NPC = National Planning and Commission
PMBOK = Project Management Body of Knowledge
TCD = Ton Cane per Day

USA = United State of America
USDA = United State Development Association

1. Introduction

The construction industry is a vital element of the economy and has a significant effect on the efficiency and productivity of various industry sectors (Jemal, 2015). In Ethiopia, the sector has registered remarkable growth over the past eleven years. There has been increased investment in the development and expansion of various infrastructure projects (MoUDC, 2012). During the first Growth and Transportation Plan (2010/11-2014/15), the construction industry on average grew at 28.7 percent per annum, raising its share of GDP to from 4 percent in 2009/10 to 8.5 percent by 2014/15 (NPC, 2016). There was significant investment in housing, transportation, dam construction, accompanied by industry development, such as the construction of Industry Park, sugar factory construction, etc., in different parts of the country.

Sugar factory development in Ethiopia began in 1954. But the number of factories in the country was limited to three, namely Wonji/Shoa, Metahara, and Fincha Sugar factories. These three factories had a total production capacity of 316,000 tons of sugar annually. Recently the Ethiopian Sugar Corporation (ESC) made heavy investments into the country's sugar sector, among which are the construction of new sugar processing factories; the revitalization of older factories; and the expansion of land under sugar cultivation. Therefore, ESC entered into the construction of different mega projects in different parts of the country at the beginning of the first Growth and Transportation Plan (GTP-I). The projects include Tana Beles (three factories) in the Amhara Regional State; Welkayt, in the Tigray Regional State, Kessem and Tendaho in the Afar Regional State, and the Kuraz project for six factories in the South Omro Zone of the Southern Nations Nationalities and Peoples' Regional State. Through these investments, the government of Ethiopia envisions the country becoming one of the world's ten largest sugar producers by 2023 (USDA, 2015). Figure 1 below briefly summarizes the history of the Ethiopian sugar industry's development.

1.1. Purpose of the Study

According to a report by (MoUDC, 2012), the performance of the Ethiopian construction industry is low. Construction projects in Ethiopia have not been completed within the time schedule and allocated budget in the majority of the

Figure 1: Background history of Ethiopian sugar factory construction and ESC

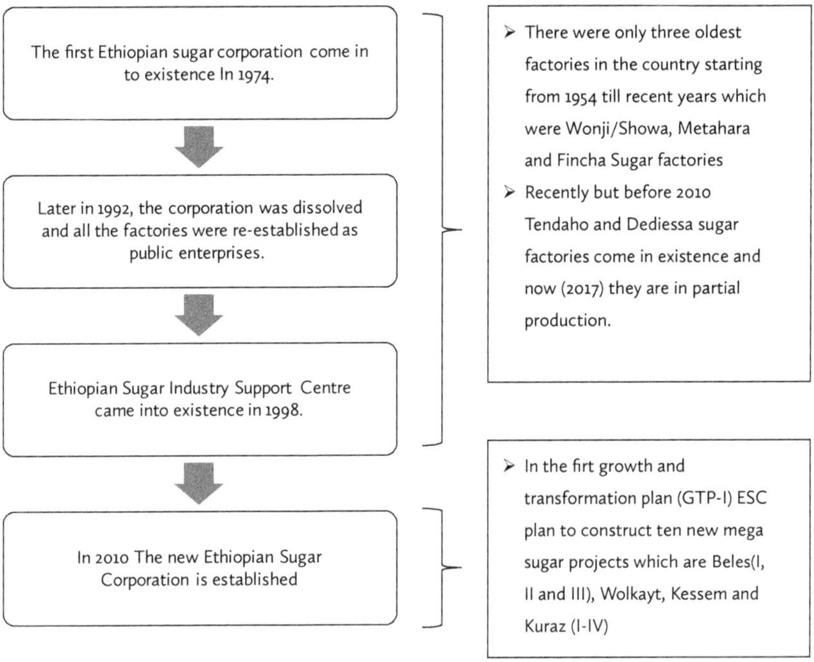

Source: USDA, 2015; ESC, January 2017

cases. Mega projects especially suffer greatly from such problems. As a result, the country has lost much revenue, job opportunities, and other economic and social benefits. The ten new mega sugar factory construction projects in Ethiopia are among those highly exposed to such problems as time delay and cost overrun. All ten mega projects were scheduled to be completed within GTP-I and begin operation at the end of the period (2014/2015). As of the time of this research study (2017), these projects were yet not completed. As a result, the country is facing a shortage of sugar and remains dependent on importing from abroad rather than implementing its plan to become a sugar exporter. It is thus important to identify the key factors that have led to the underperformance of these projects in order to come up with a nationwide mechanism to minimize time and cost overruns related to such mega projects and to the construction industry in general.

1.2. Research Questions

The following questions will be answered in this research:

- How have the sugar projects in Ethiopia performed in terms of time and cost, in respect to the original plan?
- What are the factors affecting the time and cost performance of sugar projects in Ethiopia?

2. Theory and Literature

2.1. Construction Project Management

It is obvious that project management is not new. Noah managed one of the earliest recorded projects in the Bible in building the ark. He may not have completed it within budget, but he certainly had to finish it by a specified time before the flood and it must have met his performance criteria, as it successfully accommodated pairs of all existing animals (Lester, 2006). But project management seems to have achieved the status of a science during World War II, attaining great importance due to various nuclear aerospace and other US defense programs in the 1950s and 1960s. In simple terms, a "project" is a collection of activities that are interrelated with a specific overall purpose (Mishra & Soota, 2005). Management here refers to the planning, monitoring, and control of all aspects of a project and the motivation of all those involved in it to achieve the project objectives within agreed criteria of time, cost, and performance (Lester, 2006). A project is also defined as a temporary endeavor undertaken to create a unique product, service, or result (PMBOK, 2013). The temporary nature of projects indicates that a project has a definite beginning and end. The end is reached when the project's objectives have been achieved or when the project is terminated because its objectives will not or cannot be met, or when the need for the project no longer exists. A project may also be terminated if the client (customer, or sponsor) wishes to terminate the project.

According to (PMBOK, 2013) project management typically includes, but is not limited to:

- Identifying requirements;
- Addressing the various needs, concerns, and expectations of the stakeholders in planning and executing the project;
- Setting up, maintaining, and carrying out communications among stakeholders that are active, effective, and collaborative in nature;

- Managing stakeholders towards meeting project requirements and creating project deliverables;
- Balancing the competing project constraints, which include, but are not limited to: scope, quality, schedule, budget, resources, and risks.

2.2. Project Success

Since projects are temporary in nature, the success of the project should be measured in terms of completing the project within the constraints of scope, time, cost, quality, resources, and risk as approved between the project managers and senior management (PMBOK, 2013). Many good projects as well as project management structures have failed because of the inability of the system to facilitate them (Mishra & Soota, 2005). The simplest way of defining a project as successful is to show that three primary objectives have been met. These might possibly be called the three graces of project management and are: time, cost, and specification (Lock, 2004). According to Mishra & Soota (2005), time and cost overrun are a project's main performance indicators.

Time over run or delay: is defined as the lateness in actual completion of works in relation to the baseline construction schedule or contract schedule the parties agreed upon for delivery of a project (Shete, 2016; Jemal, 2015; Ropel, 2011; Sabariah, 2009).

Cost overrun: is treated in this study as the amount by which the final cost or expenditure of the project exceeds the original estimation, which means the client has to spend more money for the completion of project than originally estimated (Shete, 2016; Ali & Kamaruzzaman, 2010; Nega, 2008). Cost overrun can also be defined as a measure of a percentage of actual costs over the estimated costs of the project (Memon, 2013).

2.3. Factors Influencing Construction Project Management

Projects and project management take place in an environment that is broader than that of the project itself. Understanding this broader context helps ensure that work is carried out in alignment with the organization's goals and managed in accordance with the organization's established practices. Organizational influences, project stakeholders and governance, project team and project life cycle are the main factors influencing project management (PMBOK, 2013).

Construction project management practice in Africa is poor as compared to Europe and North America, and Ethiopia lags far behind even poorly performing developing countries in Africa (Ayalew, Dakhli, & Lafhaj, 2016). One notable reason for this poor performance is the sluggishness of construction project management practice in terms of adapting general project management procedures, project management functions, tools, and techniques. Particularly, the level of practice in terms of safety, risk, and time management has been found to be very low. A study by Ayalew, Dakhli & Lafhaj (2016) showed that the amount of schedule slippage ranges between 61 to 80 percent and that of planned costs and other variables such as risk, quality, resources utilization, and safety deviates in the range 21 to 40 percent from requirements or predetermined or anticipated at the beginning of the project.

2.4. Causes of Time and Cost Overrun

The main causes of delay and cost overruns in construction of groundwater projects in Ghana were: monthly payment difficulties from agencies, poor contractor management, material procurement, poor technical performances, and escalation of material prices (Frimpong, Oluwoye, & Crawford, 2003). Delays in furnishing and delivering the site, financial problems, and improper planning were the common causes of time overrun and delay in construction. Inadequate supply of raw materials and equipment by contractors, design changes, and incomplete design at the time of tender were considered as the most important causes of cost overrun by (Jemal, 2015).

3. Methodology

3.1. Introduction

A research methodology is a way to systematically solve the research problem; alternatively, it may be understood as a science studying how research is done scientifically. For their part, research methods are all those methods/techniques that are used for conducting research (Kothari, 2004). Research methods are the tools one uses to gather data, such as questionnaires or interviews (Dawson, 2002). This section describes all the procedures that were undertaken to achieve the objectives set in this study. The procedures that were adopted, including how and from where relevant data for the research were gathered, are discussed. In addition, the research instruments employed and the method of analyzing collected data are presented.

3.2. Scope of the Study

The research involved the ten new mega sugar construction projects that were supposed to be constructed within the first Growth and Transformation Plan (GTP-I) by the Ethiopian Sugar Corporation (ESC) in Ethiopia. As case studies, we focused on the Tana Beles and Kessem projects located in the western part of Amhara Reginal State and in Afar Regional State respectively. The study focuses on identifying the main causes that led to time and cost overrun.

Figure 2: Location of sugar factories in Ethiopia

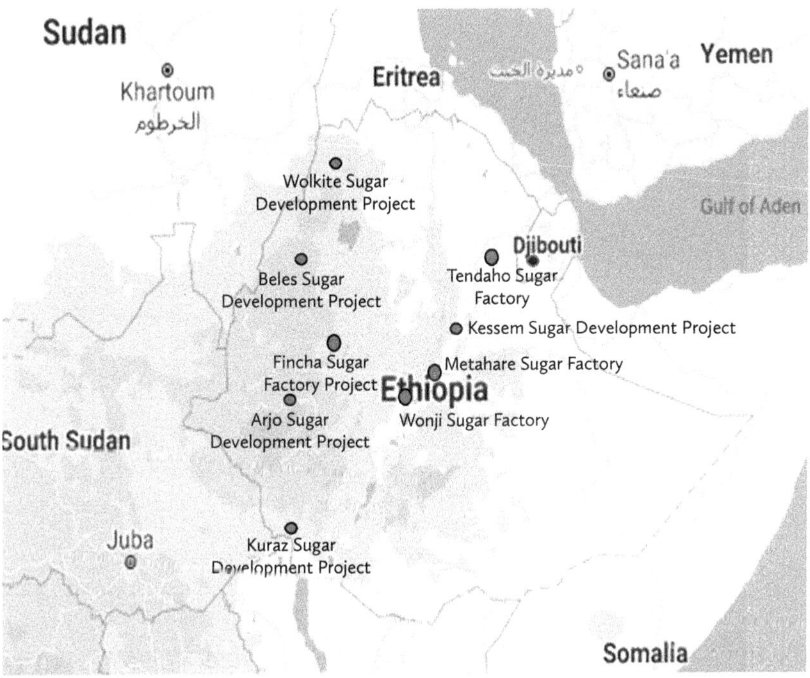

Source: ESC

3.3. Sample Project Selection for Case Study

The two projects, namely Kessem and Beles, were selected due to their relative time performance involvement of national and international contractors involved and their relative distance.

Table 1: Sample project selection criteria for case study

Projects in which the research focused on (population)	Selection criteria		
	Up to date time performance(time overrun) of the projects	Contractors involved	Distance
Kessem	102.4%	COMPLANT (international contractor)	In Afar, 250km from Addis
Kuraz-I	310%	METEC (domestic contractor)	In SNN, 900km from Addis
Kuraz-II	306%	COMPLANT (international contractor)	In SNN, 900km from Addis
Kuraz-III	268%	COMPLANT (international contractor)	In SNN, 900km from Addis
Kuraz-1V	Postponed	-	-
Kuraz-V	167.7%	JJIEC (international contractor)	In SNN, 900km from Addis
Beles-I	448%	METEC (domestic contractor)	In Amhara region, 576km from Addis.
Beles-II	1588%	METEC (domestic contractor)	
Beles-III	Postponed	-	-
Welkayt	142%	CAMC (international contractor)	In Tigray, 1,300km from Addis
Total (population) = 10	Two projects (Kessem and Belles) were selected for case study		

Based on table 1 Kessem exhibited a relatively low time overrun, was constructed by international contractor, is located a short distance from Addis Ababa. On the other hand, Beles has a relatively low time performance (demonstrating the highest time overrun) compared to other projects, was constructed by a domestic contractor, and is located an even shorter distance from Addis Ababa.

3.4. Data Sources and Collection Method

Data were collected based on the problems identified and the objectives of the research. The data collection approach adopted includes both primary and secondary sources. Primary data can be obtained either through observation or through direct communication with respondnts in one form or another and through personal interviews. The primary data collection method includes the on-site observation method, interviews, questionnaires, and mechanical devices. Secondary data refers to data that are already available, collected and/or organized by someone else. Secondary data may include either published or unpublished data, among them journals; books, magazines and newspapers, reports, and internet sources (Kothari, 2004).

Sugar projects are one of the largest governmental projects in the country, meaning they have been given serious attention by higher governmental officials. As such, gathering data from the projects was a very challenging and delicate proposition. To minimize this and other data collection problems, the researcher used different data collection mechanisms, such as desk study, interviews, and questionnaires in parallely.

In the desk study approach, several documents, such as contract documents and reports, were studied to look into the current status of the project in terms of time schedule and budgeted cost in respect to the contract agreement.

Interviews were conducted with managers and professionals who were involved in the construction projects. As projects may not have been fully recording data on the problems they have faced, it was anticipated that the desk study should be complemented by an interview. In total seven professionals from among different stakeholders were interviewed, namely, two from the client side, two from the contractor side, and two from the consultant side.

In addition to desk study and interviews, questionnaires were developed and distributed to the main parties involved in the construction projects, specifically on the Beles and Kessem projects. A total of seventy-five questionnaires were distributed. Forty client representatives, ten consultant representatives and twenty-five contractor representatives were considered in the questionnaire survey.

3.4. Data Analysis Method

To determine the time and cost performance of the projects, the amount of time and cost overrun were calculated using the following two formulas:

$$\text{Time Overrun}\left(\%\right) = \frac{\text{Actual time spent} - \text{Estimated planed time}}{\text{Estimated planed time}} * 100 \quad \text{Eq.1}$$

$$\text{Cost Overrun} = \frac{\text{Actual Cost} - \text{Estimated Cost}}{\text{Estimated Cost}} * 100 \quad \text{Eq.2}$$

The collected data from interview and desk study were recorded in a prepared format to facilitate the analysis. The list of factors was ranked based on their repetition and importance. If a factor is listed repeatedly or explicitly stated as important by the interviewees or documents, the factor was considered as "very high contributing;" if the opposite was the case, it was considered "very low contributing." The data collected through the questionnaires were analyzed via descriptive statistics using SPSS and Excel software and ranked based on mean score method which is determined based on the following formula:

$$Ms = \frac{\Sigma wixi}{\Sigma xi} \qquad \text{eq.3 (Ibironke, Oladinrin, \& Eboreine, 2013)}$$

Where:

Ms = mean score;

Wi = the weight assigned to the ith response = 1, 2, 3, 4, 5;

Xi = the frequency of the ith response given as a percentage of the total responses for each factor.

4. Results and Discussion

4.1. Introduction

This section presents and discusses the results of the desk study, interview, and questionnaire survey in regards to the extent of time and cost overruns in mega sugar projects and their causative factors from the point of view of clients, consultants, and contractors.

4.2. Questionnaire

This section provides background information about the respondents in the questionnaire survey in terms of affiliation, position, and experience.

Questionnaire Respondents

Out of the total seventy-five questionnaires produced, forty were distributed to employers' representatives, ten to consultants' representatives, and twenty-five to contractors' representatives. Of these questionnaires, sixty-three (84 percent) of them were returned, which is a valid response rate and a high percentage from the total distributed questionnaire; that is thirty-six (90 percent), six (60 percent), and twenty-one (84 percent) from employers, consultants, and contractors respectively (table 2).

Table 2: Questionnaire response rate

Respondents category	Number of questioners distributed	Number of questioners returned	Percentage of response rate (%)
Client	40	36	90
Contractor	25	21	84
Consultant	10	6	60
Total	**75**	**63**	**84**

Respondents Position in the Organization/company

Table 3 shows that fourteen (22.2 percent) of the respondents were project managers, ten (15.9 percent) were site engineers, eight (12.7 percent) were designers/engineers, four (6.3 percent) were office engineers, twenty (31.7 percent) listed "other" on the questionnaire and seven (11.1 percent) did not indicate their position in their company.

Table 3: Respondents' position in the company

Position	Number	Percent
Project manager	14	22.2
Site engineer	10	15.9
Designer/engineer	8	12.7
Office engineer	4	6.3
Other	20	31.7
Did not respond	7	11.1
Total	**63**	**100**

Experience of Respondents

The professionals involved in this questionnaire survey had different level of experience. 34.9 percent had zero to five years of experience and another 34.9 percent had six to ten years of experience. Therefore, the maximum number of respondents (69.8 percent) are in the range of zero to ten years of experience. The other 7.9 percent, 1.6 percent, and 11.1 percent of the respondents have ten to fifteen years, fifteen to twenty years, and above twenty years of experience respectively. The remaining professionals participating in the survey did not indicate their years of experience.

Table 4: Experience of the respondents

Experience (yrs.)	Employer		Consultant		Contractor		Total	
	No	%	No	%	No	%	No	%
0-5 years	13	36.1	2	33.3	7	33.3	22	34.9
6-10 years	11	30.6	2	33.3	9	42.9	22	34.9
10-15 years	3	8.3	0		2	9.5	5	7.9
15-20 years		-	1	16.7	0		1	1.6
More than 20	4	11.1	1	16.7	2	9.5	7	11.1
Did not respond	5	13.9			1	4.8	6	9.5
Total	36		6	100	21		63	100

4.3. Interviews

Initially it was planned to interview at least seven professionals; three from among client representatives, two contractors' representatives, and two from consultants' representatives from the selected projects. However, a formal interview was done only with five key professionals (one from the ESC head office, three from Kessem, and one from Beles project), complemented by several informal interviews with other professionals.

4.4. Case Study

Case Study-I: Tana Beles Development Project

In Tana Beles, the corporation proposed the construction of three factories, each with a capacity of twelve thousand tons of cane per day and farms encompassing seventy-five thousand hectares of sugar cane. However, later the plan changed to two factories and developing fifty thousand hectares. To date, only Beles-I is active. The total investment cost of the project was estimated at Birr 42.54 billion or USD 2.12 billion. From the total investment cost, the highest amount (ETB 14.85 billion) was allocated for Tana – Beles-III, followed by ETB 13.93 billion for Tana – Beles-I, and ETB 13.75 billion for and Tana – Beles-II.

The project has the following four major components:

a) Housing and infrastructure development
b) Land development and cane plantation
c) Irrigation infrastructure
d) Sugar factory

Time and Cost Overrun in Tana Beles Project

As shown in table 5, the maximum delay has occurred in the area of factory construction, which has been delayed by a factor of about 448 percent, meaning it is delayed by more than four times from the base schedule. The schedule called for the factory to be completed within eighteen months, starting from March 2011. As of 2017, the contractor METEC had completed 77 percent of the work, within seven years duration. The next delayed item of work from the given list is the irrigation infrastructure construction, which has a time overrun of 174.5 percent. Meanwhile, land development and cane plantation has a time overrun of 166.2 percent and housing and infrastructure clocked in a time overrun of 112 percent.

Table 5 below shows that land development and cane plantation have the highest cost overrun on the list, at 332 percent. While irrigation and infrastructure have a cost overrun of 182.8 percent, factory construction has a cost overrun of 113.4 percent based on the preliminary investment budget. In the case of housing and infrastructure construction, the result shows it as coming in under budget (-36.9 percent). But the researcher would argue that there is no reason to decrease the actual cost from the plan budget without changing the scope; alternatively, workers may have been paid less than originally provided for the same amount of work.

Case study-II: Kessem Development Project

Originally, the Kessem project was part of the expansion project of the Metahara sugar factory. After the establishment of the Sugar Corporation, it was decided the project should proceed as an independent entity.

This project has the following components:

a) Housing and infrastructure development
b) Land development and cane plantation
c) Irrigation infrastructure
d) Factory construction

Table 5: Time and cost overrun in Tana Beles

List of activities	Plan		Execution			Time overrun (%)	Cost overrun (%)
	Planed duration (yrs) (1)	Planned budget x 1000 (ETB) (2)	Actual to date time spent (yrs) (3)	Executed amount x 1000 (ETB) (4)	Physical execution (%) (5)	$= \frac{[3 - (1*5)]}{(1*5)}$	$= \frac{[4 - (2*5)]}{(2*5)}$
Land development and cane plantation	5yrs	229,490	7yrs	521,489	52.6%	166.2%	332%
Housing and infrastructure	5yrs	2,007,490	7yrs	836,296	66%	112%	-36.9%
Irrigation & infrastructure	5yrs	3,386,319	7yrs	4,884,384	51%	174.5%	182.8%
Factory construction	1.5yrs	4,495,533,000.00	6yrs & 4month	7,388,056	77.0%	448%	113.4%
					Average	**225.2%**	**147.8%**

Table 6: Time and cost overrun of Kessem

List of activities	Plan		Execution			Time overrun (%)	Cost overrun (%)
	Planed duration (yrs) (1)	Planned budget x 1000 (ETB) (2)	Actual to date time spent (yrs) (3)	Executed amount x 1000 (ETB) (4)	Physical execution (%) (5)	$\frac{[3-(1*5)]}{(1*5)}$	$=\frac{[4-(2*5)]}{(2*5)}$
Land development and cane plantation	5yrs	1,332,947	7yrs	171,546.7	13.5%	937%	-4.7%
Housing and infrastructure	5yrs	681,959	7yrs	231,277	26%	438.4%	-30.4%
Irrigation & infrastructure	5yrs	838,597.	12yrs	2,169,477.	81.15%	639.4%	218.8%
Factory construction	1.5yrs	4,391,168.	3yrs	5,852,721	98.8%	102.4%	34.9%
					Average	**529.3%**	**69.8%**

Time and Cost Overrun of Kessem Project

Table 6 shows that the land development and cane plantation component of the project has a considerable delay, of 937 percent. In other words it is delayed by more than nine times compared to the original plan. The second highest delayed work item on the list is irrigation and infrastructure work, which is delayed by 639.4 percent. The housing and infrastructure construction component exhibited a 438.4 percent time overrun. The factory construction (102.4 percent) was the least delayed work item on the list.

In the Kessem project, the greatest cost increase from the base contract was seen in irrigation and infrastructure, with a 218.8 percent cost overrun. This is because the sector faces so many change orders from the original contract. The second highest cost overrun was seen in factory construction (34.9 percent), while housing and infrastructure had a cost overrun of 30.4%; Although the results of land development and cane plantation (-4.7 percent) are under budget, the researcher recognizes that there was no reason to decrease the actual cost from the plan budget without changing its scope; alternatively, contractors may have been paid less than originally provided for the same amount of work.

4.5. Key Factors Contributing to Time and Cost Overrun

Factors Contributing to Time Overrun

A literature review was conducted, as a result of which fifty-three factors contributing to delay were identified. This study asked respondents (including clients, contractors, and consultants) to rank the factors based on their opinion on the relative significance of the factor's contribution to the delays in the sugar construction projects under consideration. Based on result of the survey, the top fifteen contributing factors are indicated in table 7, of which the top three are discussed afterwards.

Improper planning and scheduling, a contract-related factor, is ranked 1st, with a weighted average mean score of 3.92. Without proper planning, it is difficult to measure and control the progress of the project during construction. This may be attributed to preparing an overambitious plan with respect to the capacity of the country as well as improper time planning and scheduling. For instance, planning to execute construction of ten new mega sugar projects, including the expansion of old factories in parallel with design activities which in total costs around 200 billion birr within five years, in areas of the country where adequate experience and knowledge are limited, seems unrealistic. In addition, all ten factories were allotted to one inexperienced domestic contractor (METEC) with a mandate to complete them within 18 months, which shows poor procurement and time planning. No evidence was found in terms of a compensation plan. This is one of the reasons for the shortage of land for cane plantation in the Kessem project.

Unrealistic contract duration (MS=3.7). This is a client related factor, which ranked 2nd according to the survey result. According to respondents' responses during interviews and to the document review, the contract duration given for all ten factory projects was eighteen months; however, none of the projects were completed within the planned contract time. This shows that the planned time did not consider the ground situation and didn't take into account various risk factors in estimating the duration. It appears that the decision by the political leaders to venture into such mega projects and finish them within eighteen months was not adequately backed by scientific or technical analysis and justification.

Improper and poor project feasibility study (MS=3.66) ranked third among factors contributing to delays. While clients rank this factor as 2nd and contractors as 5th, consultants rank it in 41st place, which is a significant difference. However, information gathered through interviews and desk study shows that the construction of sugar projects started without a proper feasibility study and detailed site investigation. It is vital to note that the projects were begun based on the directions given from the government in relation to the first Growth and Transformation Plan (GTP-I). The government pushed each stakeholder to go into implementation with a slogan of "we can do the study/investigation in parallel with the execution" without first conducting a detailed socio-economic, environmental, and technical assessment of the project. Initially, the only major consideration was the availability of land and water source. For instance, problems identified in Kessem dam project included the presence of 60°C hot spring water and percolation of water through mountains, which may be attributed to poor site investigation before commencement of the project. The projects also lacked adequate participation of the community and other stakeholders. (Lewis, 2007) argues that "projects often fail at the beginning, not the end," meaning that if a project fails to conduct a proper feasibility study and project plan, it is obvious that it will fail in achieving its intended objectives, especially in terms of time and cost. According to information gathered in the conducted interviews, the project implementation was started without aquiring adequate information.

Table 7: Factors affecting time delay

Groups	Factors	Client		Contract or		Consultant		Weighted avg	
		MIS	Rank	MIS	Rank	MIS	Rank	MIS	Rank
Contract R. factors	Improper planning and scheduling	4.15	1	3.38	8	4.5	2	3.92	1
Client R. factors	Unrealistic contract duration	3.65	8	3.48	4	4.83	1	3.70	2
Client R. factors	Improper and poor project feasibility study	3.94	2	3.43	5	2.6	41	3.66	3
Consultant R. factors	Incomplete drawing, design details, and documents	3.53	11	3.9	1	3	28	3.62	4
Consultant R. factors	Slow response (late instruction, inspection, delay in approval)	3.76	5	3.57	2	2.8	36	3.62	5
Equipment R. factors	Late equipment delivery and mobilization	3.6	9	3.38	9	4	6	3.58	6
Consultant R. factors	Poor contract manage-ment	3.94	3	3.1	21	2.6	42	3.55	7
Contract R. factor	Inadequate contractor experience	3.91	4	2.86	31	3.83	8	3.55	8

Groups	Factors	Client		Contract or		Consultant		Weighted avg	
		MIS	Rank	MIS	Rank	MIS	Rank	MIS	Rank
Contract R. factors	Poor site management/coordination on site	3.69	7	3.05	27	3.2	18	3.43	9
Materials R. factors	Late delivery of ordered materials	3.21	30	3.57	3	4.4	3	3.43	10
Client R. factors	Poor procurement method for contractor selection	3.59	10	3.05	26	3.8	9	3.42	11
Client R. factors	Slow decision-making	3.74	6	3.05	25	2.6	40	3.41	12
Contract R. factors	Delay in site mobilization	3.51	13	3.1	20	3.2	19	3.34	13
Materials R. factors	Material procurement problem	3.34	21	3.14	18	4	7	3.34	14
Consultant R. factors	Lack of standardization and impractical design	3.52	12	3.14	16	3	29	3.33	15

Factors Contributing to Cost Overrun

Table 8 shows all a list of all twenty factors contributed to cost overrun identified from the literature review and their ranks based on responses from clients', contractors', and consultants' representatives. The top three factors contributing to cost overrun are found to be poor project (site) management, wastage, and construction cost underestimation

Table 8: Factors contributing to cost overrun

Factors	Client		Contractor		Consultant		Weighted avg	
	MIS	Rank	MIS	Rank	MIS	Rank	MIS	Rank
Poor project (site) management / poor cost control	3.89	1	3.38	4	4	3	3.73	1
Wastage	3.75	4	3.2	7	3.6	8	3.56	2
Construction cost underestimation	3.54	6	3.33	5	4.4	1	3.54	3
Poor site investigation and feasibility study	3.75	2	3.1	8	3.6	7	3.52	4
Lack of experience	3.67	5	2.85	14	4.4	2	3.46	5
Quantity underestimation	3.19	13	3.71	2	3.4	11	3.39	6
Design change	3.33	10	3.52	3	3.2	12	3.39	7
High cost of machineries	3.41	7	3.24	6	3.6	9	3.37	8
Additional work/variation order	3.03	15	3.81	1	3.4	10	3.33	9
Poor procurement policy	3.38	9	3.05	9	3.83	4	3.31	10
Corruption	3.75	3	2.62	16	3	14	3.31	11
Fluctuation in prices of raw materials	3.2.	12	3	11	3.8	5	3.18	12
Delays caused by the owner and his agent	3.4	8	2.95	12	2.5	18	3.16	13
Unforeseen site conditions	3.26	11	2.95	13	3	15	3.13	14
Lowest bidding procurement method	3.14	14	3.05	10	3.2	13	3.11	15
Material price escalation	2.85	17	2.57	17	3.67	6	2.84	16

Factors	Client		Contractor		Consultant		Weighted avg	
	MIS	Rank	MIS	Rank	MIS	Rank	MIS	Rank
Increasing of foreign currency exchange rate	2.91	16	2.48	19	3	17	2.77	17
Acceleration	2.52	19	2.75	15	2.4	19	2.59	18
Inappropriate government policy	2.63	18	2.14	20	3	16	2.48	19
Change in legislation	2.21	20	2.48	18	2.4	20	2.32	20

Poor project (site) management is ranked as the first factor causing cost overruns, based on questionnaire responses, with a weighted average mean score of (MS=3.73). This is the major factor for increasing the cost of project, as poor project management may lead to inefficient resource usage and in project cost increase.

Wastage (Ms=3.56) was ranked as the second significant factor as described in table 8. During interviews and site observation, it was observed that there are many equipment and resources not properly utilized for their intended purpose. For example, in the Tana Beles project, 13,148.5ha of cane was wasted, incurring an additional cost to remove aged cane. In contrast, in the Kessem project, the factory was ready to process 6000TCD, however, the available cane with which to feed the factory was not more than 4000TCD.

Construction cost underestimation, with a mean score of 3.54, is considered as the third contributing factor. The projects considered in this research entered into implementation without proper investigation and detailed cost estimation. It was apparent that the budgeted cost was not enough to execute the projects, which resulted in cost overrun after a while. The revised study done in 2016 shows there is a huge difference between the original estimate and real cost.

Capacity limitation: The other key factor affecting time and cost overrun in these projects raised by the interview participants was capacity limitation. This includes limitation on financial capacity, lack of client experience, contractors' capacity limitation, designer and consultant capacity limitation, shortage of capable man power, limitation in machinery and equipment, and limitation in using the current technology, etc. More than 80 percent of the funding sources for the project comes from a long-term loan, which highlights financial constraints. In addition, the contractors' capacity and experience is limited and not specialized in the sector; they also did not have prior experience. The Ethiopian Sugar Corporation (client) was a newly established organization which had never previously managed such sugar projects. As a result, the capacity in terms of experience managing mega projects on both the company/client levels is poor, which also contributed to time and cost overrun.

Poor coordination and communication among stakeholders: According to the data from the interviews and desk study there is poor coordination among different stakeholders in the project, which greatly contributed to time and cost overrun. Lack of coordination between two or more internal stakeholders, between internal and external stakeholders, and two and more external stakeholders were some of the major problems observed in the projects.

Professionals involved in the Tana Beles project informed that the contractor was not willing to accept instruction and direction from ESC representatives. Furthermore, a lack of coordination in resettling, compensation payments, and awareness creation in the community between the local government and ESC contributed to the shortage of land for cane plantation in the Kessem project. Another example of poor internal stakeholder coordination was seen between different tasks in the project. Wastage of matured cane due to the factory delay in the Tana Beles project, shortage of cane to feed the factory in Kessem project, the delay in infrastructure such as access roads, electric power, and telecommunication are other factors.

The existence of a railway construction project across the irrigable area of the Kessem project created an obstacle whereby the designed underpass height of the railway project didn't consider the height of cane-loaded trucks that would need to cross the road from the other side. The design only considered the height of a camel. As a result, there is a problem in transporting cane from the plantation to the factory. The type and interest of a stakeholder are of great influence on the project's success and failure (Lester, 2006). This underlines the importance of classifying and assessing the influence of each stakeholder on the project.

Poor procurement system: As it is the practice in the procurement of goods, procurement of works and services for the contractor and consultant should be properly done. However, this study revealed gaps in this area. For example, purchasing low-standard materials and machinery at high cost relative to the market was listed as a problem in the project. The other problem in relation to procurement was contractor and consultant selection. Most tasks were directly awarded to governmental organizations without considering their capacity or selecting competent bidders. Both the construction and consulting tasks for irrigation and housing projects was also given to governmental construction companies in the region. According to responses from respondents, signing both the construction and supervison contracts with firms from the same country is found to be one of the challenges they faced as it might open doors for dishonest practices.

Contract management problem: According to different respondents' point of view, the contract had problems beginning with contract document preparation all the way to contract formulation and contract administration.

In addition to the above, other factors identified through the interviews and desk study included resource management problems, poor organizational structure, lack of infrastructure in the area, compensation problems, delays in transportation, and weather conditions, Despite the long list of contributing factors, the majority of interview respondents argued that the presence of political influence and capacity limitation may be considered as the underlying factors behind other factors contributing to time and cost overruns.

5. Conclusion

This study was conducted to investigate the extent of time and cost overrun and identify the key factors leading to the latter in mega sugar industry construction projects in Ethiopia. The results of study showed such overruns are indeed severe problems. In Tana Belles, an average of 225.2 percent and 147.8 percent time overrun and cost overrun respectively were recorded based on the current status of the project (as of 2017). Similarly, in Kessem, the amount of average time and cost overrun were 529.3 percent and 69.8 percent respectively.

The research identified key factors leading to these poor results by using desk study, interviews, and questionnaires. The respondents were professionals from key stakeholders participating on the projects, including clients (ESC), contractors and consultants. Improper planning and scheduling, unrealistic contract duration, improper and poor project feasibility study, capacity limitation, poor coordination and communication among stakeholders, poor procurement and contract management, poor project (site) management, wastage and construction cost underestimation were all found to be the main contributing factors of time and cost overrun in the projects analyzed in this study.

6. Recommendation and Limitations

6.1. Recommendations

Based on the literature review and responses from participants of this study, the following recommendations for minimizing cost and time overrun in the Ethiopian mega sugar industry construction projects:

- Adequate attention has to be given to feasibility study and site investigation
- Designing, planning, and scheduling has to be given serious attention.
- Facilitate discussion, communication, and coordination between different internal and external stakeholders
- Implement proper procurement system and contract administration
- Provide projects to domestic contractors as sub-contracts from foreign experienced contractors or form a joint venture with them.
- Proceed step-by-step rather than starting several mega projects in one GTP period with a limited capacity.
- Provide the required service and infrastructure before entering into the actual construction work.
- Ensuring the availability of resources like land, water, finance, and machinery before and during construction works is crucial.
- Capacity building by the project implementer (owner), consultants, and contractors has paramount importance.

6.2. Limitation

The following were the major limitations of the research:

- Among the ten new mega sugar industry development projects in Ethiopia begun in GTP-I, the research focused only on two projects (Tana Beles and Kessem) as a case study due to the complex nature of the projects as well as time and financial limitations.
- Due to the politically sensitive nature of the project and the anticorruption campaign of the government during data collecting time, getting access to contract documents, letters, reports, etc. (especially data related to finances) was extremely challenging.
- Identification of the responsible parties for the problems of time and cost overrun was not included as part of this study.

Acknowledgements

The authors would like to acknowledge the contributions of the following organizations for their direct and indirect contributions in the preparation of this book chapter:

- Dire Dawa Institute of Technology sponsored the research.
- KU Leuven University, Ambo University, and Addis Ababa University initiated and supported the conference where the output of this research was presented.

The authors would also like to express their appreciation to Ethiopian Sugar Corporation (Head office, Beles project office and Kessem project office), Metal and Engineering Technology Corporation (METEC), China National Complete Plant Import and Export Co. Ltd. (COMPLANT), Ethiopian Construction, Design and Supervision Works Corporation (ECDSWC), Amhara Design and Supervision Works Enterprise (ADSWE), and Amhara Water Works Construction Enterprise (AWWCE), who immensely contributed to the realization of this research output and to all individuals who contributed in providing data and information. We would also like to extend our gratitude to all reviewers and editors for their valuable comments and suggestions.

References

Ali, A. S., & Kamaruzzaman, S. N. (2010). Cost Performance for Building Construction Projects in Klang Valley. *Journal of Building Performance*, *1*(1), 110-118

Ayalew, T., Dakhli, Z., & Lafhaj, Z. (2016). Assessment on Performance and Challenges of Ethiopian Construction Industry. *Journal of Architecture and Civil Engineering*, *2*(11), 01-11.

Dawson, D. C. (2002). A Practical Guide to Research Methods: A User-Friendly Manual for Mastering Research Techniques and Projects. How To Books Ltd.

Frimpong, Y., Oluwoye, J., & Crawford, L. (2003). Causes of Delay and Cost Overruns In Construction Of Groundwater Projects in A Developing Countries; Ghana as A Case Study. *International Journal of Project Management*, *21*(5), 321-326.

Ibironke, O. T., Oladinrin, T. O., Adeniyi, O., & Eboreime, I. V. (2013). Analysis of Non-Excusable Delay Factors Influencing Contractors' Performance in Lagos State, Nigeria. *Journal Of Construction In Developing Countries*, *18*(1), 53-72

Jemal, A. (2015). Factors Affecting Time and Cost Overrun in Road Construction Projects in Addis Ababa (Masters thesis, Addis Ababa Unversity).

Kothari, C. R. (2004). Research Methodology Methods and Techniques. New Age International (P) Ltd.

Lester, A. (2006). *Project Management, Planning and Control: Managing Engineering, Construction and Manufacturing Projects To PMI, APM And BSI Standards*. Elsevier.

Lewis, J. P. (2007). Fundamentals of Project Management, 3rd (ed.) American Management Association.

Lock, D. (2004). Project Management in Construction Gower Publishing Limite.

Memon, A. H. (2013). *Structural Modelling of Cost Overrun Factors in Construction Industry* (Doctoral dissertation, Universiti Tun Hussein On Malaysia).

Mishra, R. C., & Soota, T. (2005). Modern Project Management. New Age International (P) Ltd.

Ministry of Urban Development and Construction (MoUDC). (2012). Construction Industry Policy. Addis Ababa: Ministry of Urban Development and Construction. Addis Ababa

Nega, F. (2008). Causes and Effects of Cost Overrun on Public Building Construction Projects in Ethiopia (Masters thesis, Addis Ababa University).

National Planning Commission (NPC). (2016). Growth and Transformation Plan II (GTP II). Addis Ababa: National Planning Commission.

PMBOK. (2013). A Guide to The Project Management Body of Knowledge. Project Management Institute, Inc.

Ropel, M. (2011). Risk Management Practices in a Construction Project – a Case Study (Master's thesis). Masters Thesis, Chalmers University of Technology, Goteborg Sweden.

Sabariah, D. (2009). A Comparative Study of Construction Project Delays in Johor and Sabrah Region (Doctoral dissertation, Universiti Teknologi Malaysia).

Shete, A. N. (2016). An Analysis of Cost Overruns and Time Overruns of Construction Projects in India. *International Journal of Engineering Trends and Technology* 18(1), 53-72

USDA. (2015). *Assessments of Commodity and Trade Issues*. Addis Ababa: United State Development Association.

19
Determinants of Public Servants' Performance in Federal Public Service Sectors in Ethiopia

Kassa Teshager and Zekarias Minota

Box 1: Key conclusions

- ✓ Public servants are a most significant and precious asset essential for healthy operation of all other resources of the public sector. It is the only resource that is never depleted as its increased use increases human intelligence
- ✓ Organizational factors (human relations dimension, rational goals dimension, open systems dimension, and internal process dimensions) and individual factors (job selection, employee competence, employee incentives [rewards], employee's commitment and turnover intention) determine the attitude and performance of public servants in federal public sectors in Ethiopia.
- ✓ Public servants' attitude toward public service reform tools significantly mediates the relationship between individual factors and employee performance. However, attitude does not mediate the relationship between organizational factors and employee performance in the federal public sectors.
- ✓ Accordingly, public servants need to be motivated in such a way that it will bring about attitudinal change and higher satisfaction, thereby enhancing their performance.

Box 2: Key insights

Reading this chapter will give you insights in

- ✓ The nature and performance of the public sector and public servants in Ethiopia
- ✓ Factors (organizational and individual) affecting public servants in Ethiopia
- ✓ The mediating effect of attitudes on the relationship between factors (organizational and individual) and the performance of employees in the public sector.

Box 3: Abbreviations

CSRP = Civil Service Reform Program
FDRE = Federal Democratic Republic of Ethiopia
MoCS = Ministry of Civil Service
SPSS = Statistical Package for Social Sciences

1. Introduction

This chapter examines the factors determining the performance of public servants in the federal public service sector in Ethiopia. In the early 1990s the current government of Ethiopia came to power and established a task force to investigate the deep institutional constraints on basic functions, such as policy-making, service delivery, and regulation (MoCS, 2013).The task force reported that core public management systems at the federal and regional levels were hampered by outdated civil service legislation and working systems; the absence of a medium-term planning and budgeting framework; ineffective financial and personnel management controls; inadequate civil service wages and inappropriate grading systems; poor capacity for strategic and cabinet-level decision-making; and an insufficient focus on modern managerial approaches to service delivery. To address these constraints, the government undertook phased-based reform measures, the first of which (1991-1996) focused on the restructuring of government institutions and a retrenchment program. The second phase of the Civil Service Reform Program (CSRP) was launched in 1996, and included five subprograms, namely, in the areas of the top management system, expenditure management and control, human resource management, service delivery, and ethics. The subprograms were further split into various projects. The overall aim was to enhance the capacity of the public service so that it will be effective, efficient, transparent, accountable, ethical, performance oriented; promote good governance, provide client-oriented service delivery; and support the government's social and economic development policies, with the Ethiopian public being the most important beneficiary of the programs.

Since then, various efforts were undertaken, such as the development of new legislation (for example, a financial management proclamation, a civil service law, a code of ethics, complaints-handling procedures, and a service delivery policy) as well as reforms of the operating systems for budgeting, procurement, and some aspects of personnel management such as salary surveys and records management, among others. However, due to various problems, including a lack of capacity, only limited success was achieved in bringing about improvements in performance and service delivery, effective policy formulation, and program and project execution, as well as in tackling other problems of the public service in general.

As some scholars argue, public service reform is a means to an end, which involves deliberate changes to the structures and processes of public sector organizations with the purpose of getting them to run better (Pollitt & Bouckaert, 2011). The public service is the life blood of any government, given that the implementation of government policies and strategies is highly dependent on the courage and passion of the public service. The major responsibility of the public service sector is implementing government policy in accordance with on-going economic development. In line with this thought, the government of Ethiopia has been striving to replace the traditional rule-driven and highly bureaucratic public administration by an effective and responsive public service capable of facilitating and implementing developmental programs. So far, various tools have been introduced to make the necessary adjustments to the way in which public services are organized and operated, in order to sustainably respond to changing needs and the demands of the public at large.

According to the former Ministry of Civil Service (2013), three key factors are affecting the performance of the current public service sector in Ethiopia. First, the attitude of the public servants is awful. Widespread public distrust of public institutions has deep historical roots, and the removal of such distrust demands great commitment and effort from public servants. The second problem lies in the skill and knowledge gaps among public servants. Although the country has achieved remarkable socioeconomic development, its current status does not meet the demands of the situation. The public service, therefore, is under greater pressure to upgrade the knowledge and skills of public servants. The third challenge is resource constraints in discharging the monumental task of building the nation on a new foundation. Although these gaps have been identified, there is no comprehensive study dealing with the individual and organizational factors as well as with the attitude of public servants in relation to the performance of the public sector in Ethiopia. Existing studies on organizational and individual factors determining the performance of public servants are not comprehensive, up to date, or relevant to the current competitive situation. This study, therefore, fills this gap by investigating the determinants of public servants' performance in the federal public sector in Ethiopia. It does so by addressing the following questions:

1. How does bureaucratic heritage determine the reform programs and public servants' performance in Ethiopia?
2. What are the factors determining the performance of public servants in the federal public service sector?

3. Does public servants' attitude matter in improving their performance?
4. What is the policy implication of assessing the determinant factors affecting public servants' performance?

Despite the fact that positive results have been attained, encouraging the government to intensify implementation of the reform programs aimed at attaining sustainable growth and poverty reduction, the public service has not yet achieved the desired outcomes because of a combination of internal and external factors. The effective delivery of an organization's objectives depends on the harnessing of qualified and competent employees. However, the performance of employees in the public sector is not only a function of individuals factor but also depends on organizational factors. This chapter, therefore, investigates the determinant factors affecting the performance of public servants (both employees and managers) in the federal public service sector. The researchers believe that change can come only if the public servants perform well in their day-to-day activities. To achieve this goal, a clear understanding of the organizational and individual factors affecting employees' performance is important, because it provides the top management with an understanding of how to improve the performance of public servants for better organizational functionality. Moreover, the findings of this study will assist academics in broadening of the prospectus with respect to this study, hence providing a deeper understanding of the determinant factors that affect employees' performance. The study will enrich the existing literature and may be used as a cornerstone for further research in this area. The findings of this study will also help the human resource management of the organizations concerned (as well as others), by providing insight into the benefits of using different factors highlighted by this research to predict the factors that affect the performance of employees and design remedial actions to enhance their performance. Finally, the data produced as a result of this study is expected to be of some value for decision- and policy-makers with respect to determinants of employees' performance.

Following the introductory section, this chapter is organized into four sections. In section 2 the relevant theoretical and empirical literatures are reviewed. Section 3 discusses the conceptual framework, research design, and methods used in the study. The fourth section presents data analysis and the main findings of the study. The last section concludes with the policy implication of the study based on its major findings.

2. Theoretical and Empirical Literature

2.1. Institutional Factors

The literature on economic development shows that the three most determinant factors driving development are geography, trade integration, and institutions. According to Rodrik, Subramanian, and Trebbi (2004), institutional factors explain the bulk of the cross-country variation in development. It is therefore logical to assume that institutions matter for economic development, and that a good bureaucracy is an important ingredient of institutional quality.

Rauch and Evans (2000) carried out research on the bureaucratic structures of the public service institutions of thirty-five countries along three dimensions: meritocratic recruitment to the public service, internal promotion and long-term careers, and competitive salaries compared to the private sector. They found a significant correlation between meritocratic recruitment and good scores on several bureaucratic quality indices capturing bureaucratic delays, red tape, and corruption. Recanatini, Prati, & Tabellini (2005) conducted research on why some public agencies are less corrupt than others. They found that regular internal and external auditing, transparent procedures, merit-based assignments and promotions, and a nonpolitical appointment process of organization heads are all associated with lower levels of corruption.

The other relevant study was carried out by the World Bank (2003), where data from surveys among officials, households, and firms in three countries was used to investigate the links between a government performance measure (capturing bribery and service quality) and four "dimensions" of public administration, namely personnel management, administrative procedures, performance management, and financial management, while controlling for organizational culture. The main finding of this study is that (perceived) meritocratic personnel management is associated with perceived quality in all three countries. Still, although the above-mentioned studies discussed the institutional factors, they didn't address the factors determining the performance of public servants.

2.2. Public Servants' Performance

Public servants' performance has always been an important concern for managers of organizations (Kelidbari, Dizgah, & Yusefi, 2011). Because employee performance is an important building block of an organization, the factors that lay the foundation for high performance must be analyzed critically by the organizations for them to succeed (Abbas & Yaqoob, 2009).

Along these lines Wu &Lee (2011), defined job performance as employees' overall performance in meeting the expected quality and achievement of tasks under the policy and time requirements of the organization. Similarly, Liao, Lu, Huang & Chiang (2012) define job performance as the benchmark for promotions, redundancy, rewards, punishments, reviews, and salary adjustments. Ahmad & Shahzad (2011) also argue that employee performance represents the general belief of the employees about their behavior and contributions toward the success of the organization.

Anitha (2013) defines employee performance as an indicator of financial or nonfinancial outcomes of the employee that have a direct relationship with the performance of the organization and its success; he further mentioned working environment, leadership, team and coworker relationships, training and career development, compensation program, policies and procedures, workplace well-being, and as major factors that determine employee performance. However, a study conducted by Alagaraja & Shuck (2015), which aimed to explore existing perspectives of organizational alignment and employee engagement in order to understand factors associated with enhancing individual performance, argues that employee performance can be enhanced through training and development.

Based on the above definitions, employee performance can be referred to as the extent to which an employee carries out assigned duties and responsibilities. It encompasses the level of efficiency and effectiveness of an employee in accomplishing assigned tasks. Moreover, optimal employee performance leads to innovative and enhanced firm performance as a whole, in that the successful efforts of satisfied, motivated, and committed human resources generate innovative ideas for new products or services and improve quality performance, operating performance, and customer satisfaction (Sadikoglu & Zehi, 2010).

Employee performance is, therefore, paramount to the achievement of organizational objectives. The employee needs to be motivated accordingly in such a way that it brings about higher job satisfaction, thereby enhancing employee and organizational productivity.

2.3. Factors Determining Public Servants Performance

Among all the assets of an organization, employees are the most significant and precious, essential for the healthy operation of all the other resources of the organization. Furthermore, this resource, which relies on human intelligence, is never depleted. Due to these very important reasons, employees are the spinal cord of any organization. By taking this premise into account, a well-managed organization normally considers the average employee as the primary source of productivity gains (Qasim, Cheema, & Syed, 2012). These organizations consider employees rather than capital as the core foundation of the business and as contributors to firm development. Mulatu Takele (2013:122) noted that:

> *Without people organizations are simply empty buildings and unused equipment. It is people who give them life, purpose, and meaning. Healthy and vibrant organizations are those with healthy and vibrant workers. Happy and vibrant workers are productive workers; and productive organizations are those with satisfied workers and conducive environment.*

Satisfied employees develop loyalty or commitment to the organization, which results in greater productivity and lower turnover rates (Mahamuda, 2011). According to Lease (1998) as cited in Neog and Barua (2014:305) "Employees who have higher job satisfaction are usually less absent, less likely to leave, more productive, more likely to display organizational commitment and even more likely to be satisfied with their lives." Robbins (2003) also notes that organizations with more satisfied workers are more effective than those with less satisfied workers.

2.4. Organizational Factors

The organizational climate has a major influence on employee performance through its impact on employees' attitudes (Butt, Buhitoo, & Abass, 2013). The perception of employees regarding their organizational climate has significant consequences for both public servants and public organizations. It has profound impact on the work behavior of public servants in public organizations (Afolabi, 2005; Metle, 2001). It is a key variable in successful organizations because organizations that are able to create environments which employees perceive to be considerate and in which they are able to achieve their full potential are regarded as a key source of competitive advantage (Brown & Leigh, 1996; Castro, 2008; Haritha & Subrahmanyam, 2013). Correspondingly, in high-performing organizations, organizational climates have particular measurable characteristics of performance that directly account for up to 30 percent of the variance in key business performance measures (Watkin & Hubbard, 2003). Pittigrew, cited in Al-Kasawneh (2013) has also suggested that organizational climate is crucially important for organizational excellence and is the basis for organizational success.

The organizational climate is the set of characteristics that describe an organization and distinguish it from others while influencing the behavior

Figure 1: Organizational climate dimensions

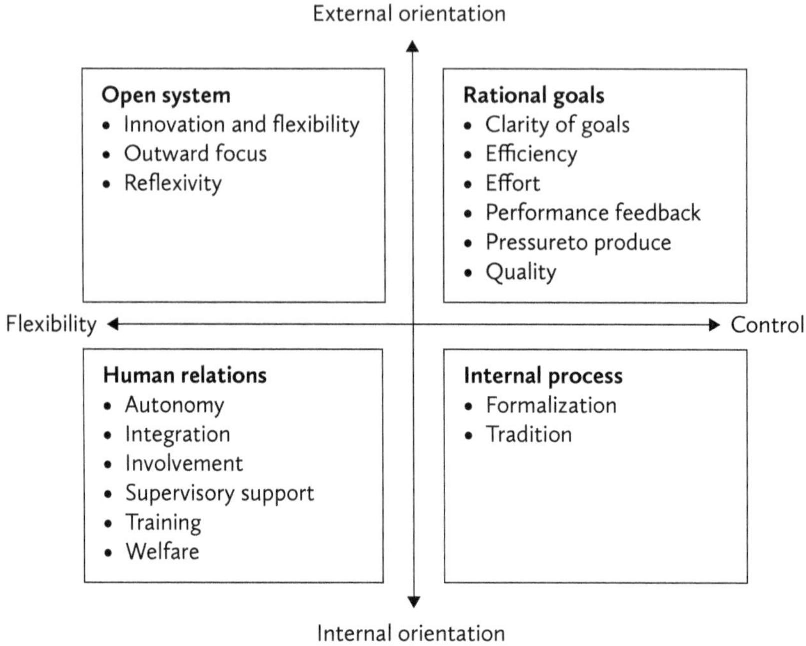

Source: Patterson et al. (2005)

of people iwithin its walls (Farooqui, 2012). Most researchers agree that organizational climate is multidimensional. For example, Patterson et al. (2005) divided organizational climate in to four dimensions that consists of seventeen scales.

In the case of Ethiopia, few studies have been undertaken on organizational climate and job satisfaction. Moreover, these prior studies lack comprehensiveness: for instance the investigation by Bekele Serbasa (2014) focused only on six dimensions of organizational climate (autonomy, trust, team work /cohesion, rewards and recognition, fairness, and organizational/supervisory support); similarly, Fekadu Abdissa (2015) used only ten dimensions of organizational climate (training and development, communication, performance management, team work, salary package, work load, leadership, administrative styles, role clarity, quality of service, and rules, regulations and policies).These limitations mean that there is a deficiency in our understanding of very important organizational dimensions such as integration, involvement, formalization, tradition, innovation and flexibility, outward focus, reflexivity, efficiency, effort, and pressure to produce. Therefore, the researchers believe that this study will fill the gap by considering Paterson et al.'s (2005) seventeen dimensions of organizational climate, which they developed and categorized into four quadrants, namely human relations, internal process, open system, and rational goals.

2.5. Individual Factors

Individual factors affecting public servants performance included in this research are: 1) Job Selection, the way in which the public servant is selected for his/her job or position; 2) Employee Competence, the ability of the public servant to do his/her job; 3) Employee Incentives/Rewards, – inducements (either financial or nonfinancial)that stimulate one to action in a desired direction; 4) Employee' Commitment, the measure of the employee's willingness to remain with the organization in the future, which often reflects the employee's belief in the mission and goals of the organization, willingness to expend effort in their accomplishment, and intentions to continue working in the organization; and 5) Turnover Intention, a measurement of whether a public servant plans to leave his/her job or position.

2.6. Empirical Evidence on Ethiopian Public Service

Since 1991, the Ethiopian government has embarked on a series of reform programs associated with the ideological shift from a command economy to a free market economy. In the early 1990s, the government launched a Structural Adjustment program, which included a Civil Service Reform Program (CSRP) as one of the components to be undertaken in phases. The first phase of the reform (1991-1996) focused on the restructuring of government institutions and a retrenchment program. The second phase of CSRP was launched in 1996 and comprised five subprograms, namely, the top management system, expenditure management and control, human resource management, service delivery, and ethics. The su-programs were further split into various projects (Eshete, 2007; Mesfin, 2009).

Six projects were designed under the umbrella of the Service Delivery SubProgram. These included the development of a service delivery policy, grievance handling directives, an award system in the civil service, methods integrating related public service, and preparation of technical directives for improving civil service delivery and service delivery standard directives. However, the actual implementation performance of these projects did not meet expectations (Capacity Building Strategy paper, 2001). This result may be attributed to many factors, such as too much focus on technical aspects rather than on changing the attitudes of the workforce, an impulsive start to implementation, a and lack of committed political leadership (Mesfin, 2009).

The Ethio-Eritrean War and the split of the EPRDF party was followed by "Tehadiso," otherwise known as the party Renaissance, in which it took the initiative to critically evaluate the implementation of CSRP reform. Having evaluated the pros and cons of CSRP performance during 1996-2001, the government found a huge implementation capacity gap. Consequently, the Ministry of Capacity Building was established in 2002 to take charge of capacity building activities that had been fragmented previously, and to give centralized directives and leadership to public organizations at various levels (Mesfin, 2009; MoFED, 2012). Next, in 2004, a new program emerged titled the Public Sector Capacity Building Program (PSCAP) emerged, comprising six programs: Civil Service Reform, Tax System Reform, Justice System Reform, District level Decentralization, Urban Management Capacity Building, and Information and Communication Technology Development. It aimed at improving the scale, efficiency, and responsiveness of public service delivery at the federal, regional, and local level, empowering citizens' self-development, and promoting good governance and accountability (Mesfin, 2009). 2012). However, the Ministry of Capacity Building was soon merged with Federal Civil Service Agency in 2010, into a new institution named the Ministry of Civil Service (MoFED, 2012).The establishment of the Ministry of Civil Service necessitated a revision of PSCAP to reflect the duties and responsibilities of the ministry (MoFED,2012). Despite this, the expected performance improvement in the civil service did not materialize. (Ibid).

Consequently, changes in the implementation of CSRP manifested themselves in a series of trainings on change management, performance management, management by objectives, strategic planning management, business process re-engineering, and balanced score card among other topics (Mesfin, 2009). In February 2012, the Ministry of Civil Service even launched a Citizens' Charter, with the aim of enabling civil servants to serve the community in an improved way. However, the development and reformation of programs and management tools in the country became a fashion rather than resulting in real change in the service delivery system.

According to the World Bank (2008), Ethiopia's experience with the introduction of a handful of performance related systems, namely the BPR and BSC, signalled the need for a coherent and consistent plan to avoid confusion and conflicting priorities during implementation.

Despite the reform efforts of the government in transforming the public sector in service of the improved socioeconomic development of the new Ethiopia, the country has experienced a syndrome of on again, off again reform measures. A copious literature indicates that the implementation of the civil service reforms in Ethiopia has faced the lack of a properly integrated and sequential approach (Mesfin, 2009), the lack of accountability in the performance management system (Solomon, 2007), inconsistency in the performance evaluation system (Teka, Fiseha, & Solomon, 2007), civil servants' resistance to change (Emnet & Habtamu, 2011; Eshete, 2007; Tesfaye, 2007; Tilaye, 2007), the lack of a well-designed and implemented remuneration system (Tilaye, 2007), the lack of awareness on the service seekers' side on their duties and responsibilities (Mesfin & Taye, 2011), poor communication, poor sense of ownership, inefficient technological readiness, and a weak team work culture (Emnet & Habtamu, 2011).

The researchers assume that institutional and behavioral issues are primarily responsible for this major gap between public expectations and actual performance in service provision. These may include both economic and noneconomic reasons together with ever-changing market conditions. The question now is, what are these factors, how can we measure them quantitatively for concrete decision-making, and what implications can we derive for emerging Ethiopia? Thus, the current study critically assesses the factors that actually determine public servants' performance within selected federal public institutions by developing a simple analytical model and hypothesis as indicated below.

3. Conceptual Framework, Research Design, and Methods

3.1. Conceptual Framework of the Study

As described in figure 2, both organizational and individual factors determine public servants' performance either directly or via attitudinal change.

Figure 2: Conceptual framework of the study

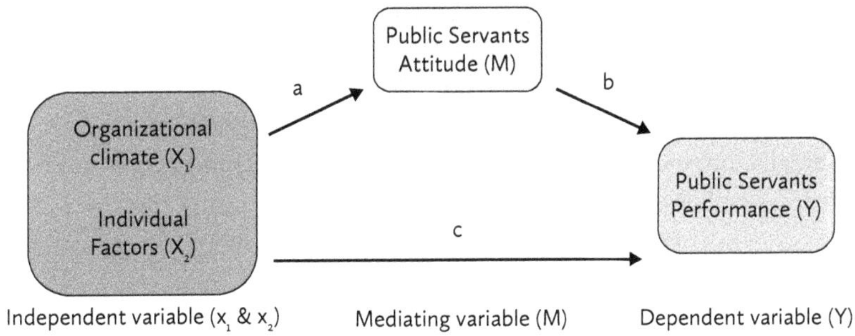

Source: Researchers' own construction path model

A series of single and multiple regression analyses (path analysis) were used to explore the mediating effect of public servants' attitude on the relationships between organizational climate, individual factors, and public servants' performance. For this purpose, we established three regression models as follows:

Model 1: $Y = \beta_0 + \beta_1 X_1 + \beta_2 X_2 + \varepsilon_1$ Equation (1)

Model 2: $M = \alpha_o + a X_1 + b X_{2+} \varepsilon_3$ Equation (2)

Model 3: $Y = \beta'_0 + \beta'_1 X_1 + \beta'_2 X_2 + \beta_3 M + \varepsilon_2$ Equation (3)

Where:

Y is the outcome variable = public servants' performance,

X_1 and X_2 are independent variables = organizational climate and individual factors respectively,

M is the mediator = public servants' attitude,

β_1 and β_2 are the total effects = that demonstrates the zero-order correlation between X_1 and X_2 and Y (ignoring M) in the first equation,

β'_1 and β'_2 is direct effect = that demonstrates the Beta coefficient relating the independent (X_1 and X_2) to the outcome (Y) adjusted for the effects of the mediator(M), in the second equation,

a and b = is the coefficient that demonstrate the zero-order correlation between X_1 and X_2 and M (ignoring Y), in the third equation,

ε_1, ε_2 and ε_3 code unexplained variability of equations (1), (2), and (3) respectively, and

β_0, α_o and β'_0 are the intercepts of equations (1), (2), and (3) respectively

Specifically, the study assesses public servants' attitude as a mediating factor. The argument here is that an employee with a positive attitude toward their job or career as well as to the organization's vision will likely prove to be a more productive, motivated, and reliable employee than one harboring negative attitudes (Burns & Burns, 2008). In the literature, Kagaari et al. (2010) found that there was significant positive relationship between employees' attitude and performance. In this study, we investigated the relationship as stated in figure 2.

Hypothesis

Hypothesis 1 stated that "organizational climate and individual factors have a significant and positive effect on public servants' job performance" and has been confirmed in this study.

Hypothesis 2 was "organizational climate and individual factors have a significant and positive effect on public servants' attitudes" and was also confirmed.

Hypothesis 3 stated that "public servants' attitudes significantly mediate on the relationship between predictors and public servants' job performance" and was confirmed with variation.

3.2. Research Design and Methods

This research was a mixed method design that combines both quantitative and qualitative approaches due to the very nature of the study objectives related to public servants performance and the expected outputs identified by the federal public service sectors.

Population and Sampling

The target populations for this study were public servants in the federal public service sector. The federal public sector was classified in to three categories: 1) **Civil Service** (Ministry of Education, Ministry of Health, Ministry of Agriculture, Ministry of Public Service and Human Resource Development, Ministry of Finance and Cooperation, etc.), 2) **Public Enterprises** (Ethiopian Airlines, Commercial Bank, Telecommunication, Hydropower, etc.), and 3) **Political Institutions** (the Parliament Office, the Prime Minster's Office, Office of the President, House of Federation, etc.).

Sample Design: A total of fourteen public institutions from the three categories were included in this study. This included ten organizations from the Civil Service: 1) Ministry of Education, 2) Ministry of Health, 3) Ministry of Agriculture, 4) Ministry of Public Service and Human Resource Development, 5) Ministry of Finance and Economic Cooperation, 6) Ministry of Urban Development and Construction, 7) Ministry of Trade, 8) Ministry of Industry, 9) Addis Ababa University, and 10) Ethiopian Civil Service University; three public enterprises: 1) Ethiopian Airlines, 2) Ethiopian Telecommunication Corporation, and 3) the Ethiopian Electric Power Corporation; and the Parliament Office (of the House of People's Representative) from among the political institutions

Once the institutions were selected, sample public servants (both managers and employees) were selected based on proportional a random sampling technique across the selected organizations, providing all respondents with an equal chance of being included in the sample. The sampling frames were the lists of public servants in these selected federal public service institutions.

Sample Size: A sample size should be statistically representative and ensure that the sample is disaggregated based on the selected institutions. The standard sampling frame formula that was used to estimate the sample size is Kish, Leslie (1965):

$$n = \frac{z^{2*}p^*(1-p)}{c^2}$$

The following parameters are assumed in estimating the sample size: n = sample size, Z = Z value (e.g. 2.054 for 96% confidence level), p = prevalence, if prior information is not known. In this case we took 0.5, thus for this study a conservative estimate of 0.5 will be used to get the maximum sample size and c = confidence interval, expressed as a decimal (0.05).

$n = (2.064)^2 * 0.5 * (1-0.5)/(0.05)^2$
$n = 422$

There are over eighty federal public institutions in Ethiopia. However, this study was carried out in fourteen federal public institutions located in Addis Ababa. The sample size presented in line with the selected institutions.

Table 1: Number of employees and sample size of each institution

Branch name	Number of permanent public servants	Sample size	response
Ministry of Education	1155	33	33
Ministry of Public Service and Human Development	1015	29	29
House of People's Representatives	1015	29	29
Ministry of Urban Development and Construction	1225	35	35
Addis Ababa University	1190	34	34
Ministry of Finance and Economic Cooperation	1330	38	38
Ministry of Agriculture	1330	38	38
Ministry of Industry	910	26	26
Ethio-Telecomm	945	27	27
Ethiopian Civil Service University	770	22	22
Ministry of Trade	1120	32	32
Electric Power Corporation	1120	32	32
Ethiopian Airlines	735	21	21
Ministry of Health	910	26	20
Total	14770	422	416

3.3. Data Collection Methods

In this study, both quantitative and qualitative data were collected from secondary and primary sources.

Secondary Data /Documents Review/

The study began by reviewing the selected public service institutions' policy documents, reports, published and unpublished documents, website data, CSA data, Ministry of Public Service and Human Development data, and any documents related to the public service. Secondary data on the bureaucratic heritage of the public service were collected from the literature. Moreover, the concepts of public service reform, public servants, etc. were reviewed and used as a data collection and analysis tool. In addition, to this, literature that can inform international best practices in the study and support of the public service was reviewed.

Survey and Key Informants Interviews

The data collection was carried out at the institutional level (federal public service institutions) and individual public servants' level. At the institutional level, key informant interviews were undertaken with ministers, department leaders, and experts. This typeof interview permits the researcher to obtain rich, detailed information regarding the bureaucratic heritage and factors affecting employees' performance in a flexible way. At the individual level, a survey was conducted of public servants in different hierarchies of the selected federal public service institutions. This survey data, which was based on a structured questionnaire identifying the key determinant factors affecting the performance of public servants, allowed the researchers to do quantitative analysis.

The questionnaire had five main sections. The first comprised seven questions dealing with respondents' general information, whereas the second, which covered the major area of this study (organizational climate) comprised eighty-two questions under four broad categorical dimensions. The third part, which comprised six broad categories, addressed the individual factors determining public servants' performance. The fourth part focused on public servants' attitude, via twelve items. The final section addressed employee performance and included thirteen questions.

Standard tools developed by Paterson et al. (2005) for measuring organizational climate and by Halim (2013) for measuring employee's performance were employed. The researchers developed their own tools for measuring individual factors and attitudes. The level of agreement in the questionnaire used a 5-point Likert scale that scored 1 to 5 as follows: Strongly disagree = 1, disagree = 2, neutral = 3, agree = 4, strongly agree = 5 for positive questions, and scored reveresely in SPSS for negative questions.

Eight key informants were interviewed to supplement the survey data. In addition, five focus group discussions were conducted with experts and public servants' representatives in five selected public institutions.

3.4. Data Analysis and Presentation

Both descriptive and inferential statistical techniques were used to analyze the quantitative data. Data collected from the public servants' survey and different secondary sources were analyzed and presented in tabular or graphic form, while qualitative information was incorporated in the report to support the quantitative data in thematic summaries on the basis of determinant factors. The data analysis technique was supported by the SPSS software program.

Data gathered through the structured questionnaires were processed and analyzed using SPSS version 20. Accordingly, descriptive statistics (frequency, percentage, mean, standard deviation) was used to describe the data. Next, inferential statistics, such as correlation and regression analyses, were employed. Inferential statistics allow the researcher to draw conclusions about a population from the sample of a particular study (Cooper & Schindler, 2006). Moreover, inferential statistics make it possible to test hypotheses by determining the statistical likelihood that the data reveal true differences. The Pearson product-moment correlation coefficient was used to examine the relationship between organizational climate, individual factors, attitude, and performance. Next, regression assumptions tests like the normality test and multicollinearity test were undertaken. AFinally, a series of multiple regression analyses were conducted to determine the mediating effect of public servants' attitude in the relationship between organizational climate, individual factors, and public servants performance.

Reliability Statistics

The reliability test is an instrument used to measure the items in a questionnaire that act as the indicators of the variables. Nunually (1978) has suggested that the Cronbach's alpha coefficient of a scale must be greater than 0.7. Reliability analysis tells us whether the items included in the model are realizable proxies of variables. Table 2 shows reliability statistics as follows.

Table 2: Reliability statistics

Scale	Cronbach's alpha coefficients (standardized)	No. of Items
Organizational factors	0.897	75
Individual factors	0.829	30
Attitude	0.926	13
Performance	0.895	14

Source: Computed from survey data

The value of Cronbach's Alpha coefficient (based on standardized items) for organizational factors is 0.8970, which clearly indicates that the results are reliable. Similarly, Cronbach's Alpha coefficient for individual factors, attitude, and performance is 0.829, 0.626, and 0.895 respectively. Since the reliability value for the dependent, independent, and mediator variables is greater than 0.7, the results in this study are viable.

4. Results and Discussion

This section presents the findings of the study obtained from descriptive and econometric analysis. It aims to analyze the factors that affect the performance of employees at Ethiopian federal public institutions. The data (primary and secondary) was collected, organized, coded, and analyzed systematically using a mixed approach. The Likert scale data was analyzed quantitatively while data from interviews and document review was analyzed descriptively.

The descriptive part includes: the characteristics of respondents, the major factors of employee performance, how employee attitudes affect their performance, the actual performance of employees and their interrelationship presented in tables and figures. Finally, the quantitative analysis is based on the three multiple regression models indicated above. Generally, our result reveal how organizational and individual factors (causal factors) affect employee attitudes, how the employee attitudes (casual mechanisms) affect their performance, and how both the casual factors and attitude affect employees' performance.

4.1. Characteristics of Respondents

As depicted in figure 3, the total number of respondents is 416, with a maximum and minimum respondents of 38 and 20 respectively from each sample organization. These respondents were drawn randomly from nested work units. They filled out standardized questionnaires having 136 specific items, 24 sub-dimensions, and 7 main dimensions. The questionnaire design involves standard grid measurements used to collect five-level Likert scale data. The index of each variable was computed using SPSS/STATA to obtain the weighted mean values for each subdimension, which in turn was indexed to generate weighted mean value for the major dimensions, namely, organizational, individual, attitudinal, and performance values.

This approach is supported by O'Reilly et al. (1996), who proposed the "Organizational Culture Profile (OCP)," the most widely cited survey instrument in the organizational culture literature. In addition, Boone Jr. & Boone, 2012) have successfully demonstrated how Likert scale data can be analyzed quantitatively.

Figure 3: Number of respondents in sectors

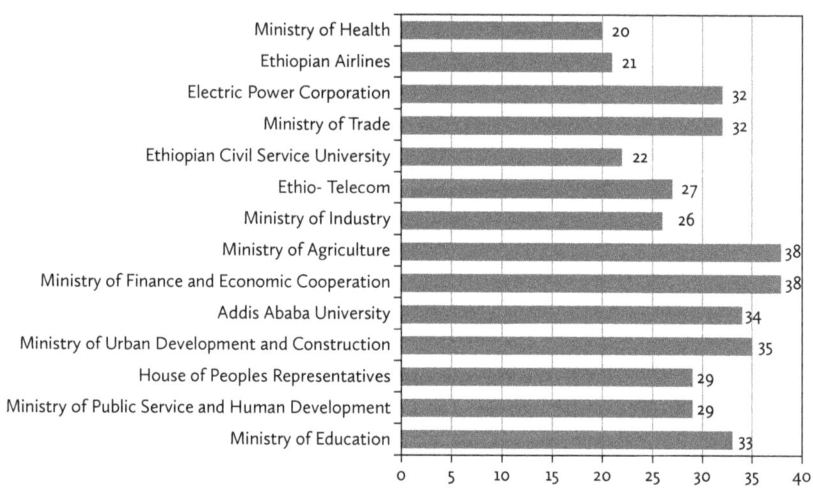

Respondents' composition by sex indicated that 311 (about 75 percent) of federal public workers in the selected organizations are males and 105 (25 percent) are female. This implies that the workforce in the public service sector is still predominantly occupied by males and that females are marginalized for different reasons (individual and organizational).

The education level of respondents has implication for performance. In this study, about 60 percent of the respondents hold the first degree, 35 percent hold the second, and 2.6 percent hold PhDs. At the same time, 2.4 percent hold diplomas, about 0.5 percent completed grade 10, and 0.2 percent; left school between grades 7 and 8 (second cycle primary school). Although it is difficult to draw a conclusion about the entire country based on this sample survey, the result indicates that there is improvement in the human resource composition of the federal public sector.

4.2. Descriptive Analysis

In this subsection, we analyze the basic determinants of employees' performance by using summary statistical figures and correlation of variables. As described above, the five-point Likert type data is systematically estimated to obtain the weighted mean for each variable/factor in order to analyze the Likert scale data quantitatively. As indicated on the conceptual framework, public servants' performance is broadly determined by organizational and individual factors through attitudinal factors. The organizational dimension in turn is proxied by four major dimensions, namely, human relations, internal process, open systems, and rational goals. Furthermore, these four dimensions involve seventeen subdimensions and eight-one individual items or factors. The five-point Likert scale captures: strongly disagree (1), disagree (2), indifferent (3), agree (4), and strongly agree (5), with corresponding codes. The descriptive statistics for these major dimensions are presented in tables and analyzed in that order as follows. According to Zaidatol and Bagheri (2009), a mean score of <= 3.39 is low, from 3.40 up to 3.79 is moderate, and > 3.80 is high. We use these parameters to compare the scores obtained.

Table 3 shows that the average response of the respondents to the statement "human relation interventions highly improve the performance of federal public servants" was "indifferent." This implies that there was neither disagreement nor agreement about the role of human relations on employees' performance. This might be because the do not have adequate information about the variable or the result is mixed (positive or negative). Therefore, actual workers' involvement and autonomy in decision-making, supervisory support by the management, work-related integration, training and welfare activities does not determine the performance of employees at in the federal public sector of Ethiopia.

Theoretically, the existence and practice of a merit system respecting cultural values within an organization is expected to contribute to the attainment of goals. However, the results (see table 3) nullify this assumption,

Table 3: Descriptive statistics of organizational and individual factors

Items/Variables	Obs.	Mean		Std. Deviation	Variance
	Statistic	Statistic	Std. Error	Statistic	Statistic
Human relations dimension					
Involvement	416	2.903	.027	.565	.320
Autonomy	416	2.981	.032	.655	.430
Supervisory support	416	3.045	.044	.899	.810
Integration	416	2.982	.032	.655	.429
Training	416	2.959	.032	.670	.449
Welfare	416	2.935	.037	.763	.583
Internal process dimension					
Formalization	416	2.803	.030	.621	.386
Tradition	416	3.087	.045	.937	.879
Open systems dimension					
Innovation & flexibility	416	2.774	.042	.866	.751
Outward focus	416	2.819	.037	.773	.598
Reflexivity	416	3.036	.041	.836	.700
Rational goals dimension					
Pressure to produce	416	2.929	.036	.742	.551
Clarity of organizational goals	416	3.041	.036	.751	.565
Performance feedback	416	2.890	.031	.642	.413
Quality	416	3.034	.041	.836	.700
Efficiency	416	3.434	.038	.782	.612
Effort	416	3.069	.033	.689	.475
Individual Factors					
Job selection	416	3.082	.037	.760	.578
Employee competence	416	3.835	.040	.820	.673
Employee incentives	416	3.034	.035	.732	.537
Employee's commitment	416	3.313	.038	.775	.601
Turnover intention	416	3.004	.040	.817	.668
Attitude	416	2.965	.038	.789	.624
Performance	416	3.500	.03194	.651	.424

Source: Computed from survey data

since the estimated score is about 3, similarly to the human relations case. Indeed, with little autonomy, poor relations, and mutual values among workers and managers, realizing the intended target would be unlikely. Thus, we can conclude that internal process dimensions do not necessarily affect the performance of public servants.

Although the standard deviation for the three variables is large, the mean value is nearly 3. However, the mean scores of innovation and flexibility/outward focus are low, indicating that the system is not as open as it should be. Unless sufficient opportunity is provided for innovation, employees will not be creative and visionary, leading to a deterioration in their performance. This "indifferent" response indicates that the organizational system is neither closed nor open but falls between the two.

Rationality may refer to those decisions that maximize common benefit. The actual relationship between RGD and workers' performance is depicted in table 3. In comparison to the internal process dimension, the rational goals dimension marginally affects performance of government employees working at federal institutions. However, the entire mean estimate falls around 3, approaching the neutral point on the scale. Given this fact, the value of efficiency and effort slightly exceeds 3, meaning that respondents fairy agree that efficiency and effort (see table 3) contribute to the outcome variable. Still, one cannot conclude that RGD significantly determines workers' performance.

The individual employees' factors remain an importance source of their performance. What are these and how large they are? Table 3 shows the individual variables that influence work performance. The indicators of the individual dimension are: job selection, employee competence, employee incentives (rewards), employee's commitment, and turnover intention.

The employee competence estimate promises to raise individuals' performance among other individual factors; these latter were found by respondents to be unconvincing. However, the employee's commitment score is 3.31, which slightly falls above the neutral scale. Despite poor statistical evidence of individual factors, still the individual dimension is better when compared to organizational factors. Generally, this dimension is found to be inconclusive, and may call for an eclectic reform in the public sector of Ethiopia. Fundamental changes such as enforcing the rule of law and professionalism, providing recognition and autonomy for employees, and treating the public service and politics separately are equally important.

Among others, attitude plays a key role in realizing certain endeavors. While a positive attitude leads to better results, a negative attitude leads to poor outcomes. Although attitude is a qualitative variable, it is measured by many items and its weighted index is taken as single figure. The quantitative estimate is given in Table 3.

As shown by these statistics, workers' attitude toward their roles, organization, and managers is neither positive nor negative but indifferent. However, since attitude is a linking variable (casual mechanism) in our model, its effect on performance depends on other casual variables (organizational and individual factors). In order to change the attitude of workers, various institutional and individual positive interventions might be needed on a continuous basis.

Best performance is associated with organizational goal achievement. As presented in table 3, the composite index of employee's performance statistics reveals an acceptable level (3.5) of achievement.

Despite the small statistic for basic determinants as seen above, the aggregate performance estimate is attractive. The standard error is also very small, indicating that the majority of the respondents fall around the mean value. Furthermore, a detailed explanation will be made from econometric analysis below.

4.3. Econometric Analysis

In this subsection, a quantitative analysis is made from multiple regression models. The correlation and reliability analysis, model adequacy tests, and the regression results are presented and analyzed.

Correlation Analysis

Correlation between variables is said to be significant when the value is less than 0.05. The correlation along explanatory, mediator, and outcome variables is statistically significant at less than 1 percent level of significance (0.00). Table 4 presents the correlation of variables included in the model.

Table 4: Correlation statistics

Variables	Org factor	Ind factor	Attitude	Perform
Org factor	1.000			
Ind factor	.521**	1.000		
Attitude	.517**	.494**	1.000	
Perform	.389**	.537**	.372**	1.000

Source: Computed from survey data

From this table, it is clear that organizational factors have a good correlation with individual factors (0.52) and attitude (0.52) but are poorly correlated with performance (0.39). While individual factors yield acceptable levels of correlation with organizational issues and performance, they show weak correlation with attitude. Similarly, there is weak correlation between attitude and performance (0.37) and moderate correlation between attitude and the other two variables. Finally, performance is correlated with individual factors (0.54) but has weak correlation with organizational factors (0.39) and attitude (0.37). Generally, correlation analyses allow us to make a simple assertion, while regression results are more robust, as will be seen below.

Regression Analysis

The first model analyzes the basic determinants against employees' performance. The result of multiple regressions is depicted in table 5 below.

Table 5: Regression results

	Model 1*	Model 2*	Model 3*
(Constant)			
Indfactor	.483**	.323**	.442**
Orgfactor	.102*	.354**	.056
Attitude	-		.128*
Level of education	.113**	-.104*	.127**
Work experience	-.084*	.042	-.089*

1* Dependent variable: Perform
2* Dependent variable: Attitude
3* Dependent variable: Perform
Source: Computed from survey data

The weighted mean of these explanatory variables was taken, regressed, and the estimators presented. This stylized novel result is analyzed hereunder. The finding indicates that both the organizational and individual factors have a positive and significant impact on employees' performance. However, neither all the organizational variables nor all the individual ones are significant. For instance, factors such as involvement, autonomy, supervision, welfare, innovation, formalization, tradition, outward focus, performance feedback, clarity of goals, etc. are statistically insignificant variables. The basic reason behind this is that a motivation and merit-based reward system is lacking in public institutions. The other two control variables, level of education and work experience, are also important factors. But experience is inversely related to employee performance.

When coefficients are considered, the constant term is positive but statistically insignificant. This implies that, in the absence of collective and individual roles, performance cannot be assumed. Despite the direct relation and significance of organizational factors, its magnitude is small (for a unit role of OGF, employee perform would improve by 0.18 roles). This small magnitude implies that much work is required in order to raise the employees' performance. Meanwhile, a unit increase in individual role/intervention would lead to an increase in 0.707 units of workers' performance. This value is relatively adequate, indicating that an individual's role is vital to task performance. Put differently, individual roles are more important than institutional roles in determining performance. Important variables here include job selection, employee competence, employee incentives (or rewards), and employee's commitment. The more motivated the employee, the more productive he/she will be and hence his/her organization too.

The second model considers attitude as a dependent variable and organizational and individual factors as well as the control variables as explanatory variables. Table 5 model 2 shows the regression estimators of attitude.

This composite variable consists of twelve scaled items (reflecting individual, organizational culture, value, goals, and mixed roles). Although the variable is more subjective, we have systematically quantified it to see both its direction and magnitude of influence. As presented in Table 5, all the indicated factors have significant (1 percent & 5 percent levels of significant) role on attitude. While the level of education and individual factors influence attitude at 1 percent levels of significance; work experience and organizational factors fit at 5 percent. In addition, work experience is negatively related to attitude, which means the longer an employee stays at a given organization, the lower his/her attitude toward common ends.

The third model in Table 5 analyzes the effect of organizational, individual, and attitudinal factors on employee performance. The regression result is presented as follows:

While the individual factor and attitude significantly affect public servants' achievement, the organizational factor does not. This implies that organizational interventions are too small to influence employees' performance, or that the approach might be not convincing. Use of inappropriate intervention strategies and poor leadership and the availability of a centralized decision-making system may be responsible for such results. For a unit increase in individual and attitudinal factors, employees' performance is improved by a value of 0.646 and 0.105 units respectively. If one compares the coefficient of individual factors in model 1, 2 and 3, the direction of influence is similar. However, the magnitude of individual factor in model 1 is higher, followed by model 3 and then model 2.

The interesting implication here is that optimal employee performance can be achieved if and only if the cumulative effects of all basic determinants are in their normal states. Put differently, if one or more of organizational and attitudinal variables are missing, these conditions are expected to pull down the effect of individual factors on performance, ultimately decreasing the performance value. Thus, to achieve best organizational goals, public institutions need to work on individual factors, organizational factors, and attitudinal factors simultaneously.

5. Summary, Conclusions, and Recommendations

5.1. Summary

A total of 422 questionnaires were distributed to employees of selected federal public institutions in Addis Ababa. From the distributed questionnaire, 416 (98.6%) were collected and used in the data analysis. Reliability test was conducted and the result was acceptable for further analysis. Since each construct was affected by other constructs, a regression analysis was conducted, using employee performance as the dependent variable, attitude as the mediator variable and organizational climate and individual factors as independent variables. This was done to get the best linear combinations of the constructs as well as to obtain the predictive value of individual predictors for testing the hypotheses proposed. The researchers applied a quantitative approach, in the form of descriptive statistics to assess the level of employee perception on organizational culture, individual factors, attitude, and employee performance; inferential statistics involving the Pearson correlation in describing the relationship between organizational culture, individual factors, attitude, and employee performance; and path analysis in evaluating the mediating effect of attitude on the relationship between organizational climate, individual factors, and employee performance. In section 4, the primary data was analysed and interpreted in relation with the statement of the problem and objectives of the study. Finally, in this section, the conclusions reached on employee perception of organizational climate, individual factors, attitude, and employee performance were assessed and presented.

5.2. Conclusion

This research was conducted at Addis Ababa with the intent of critically assessing employees' perception of organizational climate, individual factors, attitude, and employee performance in the federal public sector of Ethiopia. Based on the objectives and findings of the study, the following conclusions are worth highlighting.

The results of the study enable us to conclude that both organizational climate and individual factors determine public servants' attitude and performance in federal public organizations in Ethiopia. The Pearson correlation results of this study indicate that there is a significant relationship between organizational climate, individual factors, attitude, and employee performance in the studied areas. In terms of mediating effect, the study shows that attitude significantly mediates the relationship between individual factors and employee performance in the federal public sector. However, attitude does not mediate the relationship between organizational climate and employee performance.

5.3. Recommendations

- It is recommended that the federal public sector should work on both the organizational factors (human relations dimension, rationale goals dimension, open systems dimension, and internal process dimensions) and individual factors (job selection, employee competence, employee incentives [rewards], employee's commitment and turnover intention) and find ways to improve the perception of public servants, since their perception toward these factors is either low or moderate.
- The federal public sector should provide due emphasis to individual factors to facilitate positive attitudes in order to enhance employee performance
- An attitude is based on many factors that an employee brings to the workplace. When a public servant reports to work, his/her attitude affects his/her work performance. Public servant with good attitudes demonstrate stronger performance, while workers with poor attitudes exhibit less-than-superior performance. It is up to managers to monitor employee attitudes and address attitude problems.
- Management can assess whether an employee's poor performance reflects an attitude problem or factors such as job satisfaction, an inability to handle work tasks, training needs, problems with the work environment, or personal problems. Upon closer examination, managers may find that an employee struggles to perform because of a combination of these

or other factors. Therefore, it is important to approach an employee's performance problems with care, because they may or may not be related to his/her attitude.

- Management should encourage and recognize employees with positive attitudes and satisfactory or above-average performance. These employees contribute to a positive workplace and positively impact workplace morale. They are often unnoticed because people with negative attitudes or weak performance demand more of a manager's time. Recognition reinforces their positive attributes and promotes continued achievement.
- Management should empower the executives and believe in the ability of their people and give them the support they need to achieve organizational goals. Management should provide freedom to employees to decide how to deliver the required results through innovation, decisiveness, and action.
- It is optimal for federal public institutions to enhance public servants' performance by investing more in incentives, training, and development programs. Employees need up-to-date knowledge and skills to perform well, because training continually nourishes their work attitude and behaviour.
- Finally, further research should investigate in depth how public servants' performance within the federal public sector varies over time. Panel data econometric modelling might be used to explain the determinants of performance across time. Similarly, future empirical research in the area in question will be helpful in considering the space-time differences in explaining determinants of public servants' performance.

Acknowledgements

We are indebted to the anonymous reviewers who provided critical comments and constructive suggestions that helped us to improve the chapter.

References

Ahmad, H., Ahmad, K., & Syah, I. A. (2010) Relationship between Job Satisfaction, Job performance Attitude towards Work and Organizational Commitment, *European Journal of Social Sciences*, 18(2), 257-267.

Allport, G. W. (1935) Attitudes. In C. Murchison (ed.), *Handbook of Social Psychology* (pp. 798-884) Worcester, MA: Clark University Press.

Altrasi, M. A. (2014). Determinants of Performance among Public Sector Managers in Saudi Arabia: An Analysis of the Organizational Factors and Job Attitudes. *Middle-East Journal of Scientific Research* 22(3), 409-416.

Boone, Jr., H. N., & Boone, D. A. (2012). Analyzing Likert Data. *Journal of Extension*, 50(2), Article Number 2TOT2.

Carpenter, M., Talya, B., & Erdogan, B. (2009.) *Principles of Management*. New York: Flat World Knowledge

Catherine, D. (2009). *Introduction to Research Methods: A Practical Guide for Any One Undertaking a Research Project*, 4th ed. United Kingdom: Books Ltd.

Coase, R. (1937). The Nature of the Firm. *Economica, New Series*, 1937, 4(16), 386-405.

Kagaari, J., Munene, J.C., & Ntaayi, J. M. (2010). Performance Management Practices, Employee Attitudes and Managed Performance. *International Journal of Educational Management*, 24(6), 507-530.

Kish, Leslie. (1965). *Survey Sampling*. New York: Wiley.

Knight, F. (1965). *Risk, Uncertainty, and Profit*. New York: Harper and Row.

Korir Salome, C. R., Rotich, J., & Bengat, J. (2015). Performance Management and Public Service Delivery in Kenya. *European Journal of Research and Reflection in Management Sciences*, 3(4),, ISSN 2056-5992.

Marchand A., Haines III V. Y., & Dextras-Gauthier J. (2013). Quantitative Analysis of Organizational Culture in Occupational Health Research: a Theory-based Validation in 30 Workplaces of the Organizational Culture Profile Instrument. *BMC Public Health*, 13, 443. http://www.biomedcentral.com/1471-2458/13/443.

Ministry of Civil Service/MoCS/. (2013). The Civil Service Reform Program in Ethiopia: a Brief Summary. Addis Ababa: Ministry of Civil service.

Muda, I., Rafiki, A., & Harahap, M. R. (2014). Factors Influencing Employees' Performance: A Study on the Islamic Banks in Indonesia. *International Journal of Business and Social Science*, 5(2). Center for Promoting Ideas, www.ijbssnet.com.

O'Reilly, C. A, & Chatman, J. A. (1996). Culture as Social Control: Corporations, Cults and Commitment. *Res Organ Behav*, 18, 157-200.

Pollitt, C. & Bouckaert, G. (2011). *Public Management Reform: A Comparative Analysis—New Public Management, Governance, and the Neo-Weberian State*, 3rd ed. New York: Oxford University Press.

Rauch, J. E., & Evens, P. B (2000). Bureaucratic Structure and Bureaucratic Performance in Less Developed Countries. *Journal of Public Economics*, 75(1),49-71.

Recanatini, F., Alessandro, P. & Guido, T. (2005). Why Are Some Public Agencies Less Corrupt than Others? Lessons for Institutional Reform from Survey Data. Working Paper Prepared for the Sixth IMF Jacques Polak Annual Research Conference. Washington, DC.

Riketta, M. (2009). The Causal Relation between Job Attitudes and Performance: A Meta-analysis of Panel Studies. *Journal of Applied Psychology*, 93 (2), 472-481.

Rodrik, D., Subramanian, A., & Trebbi, F. (2004). Institutions Rule: The Primacy of Institutions over Geography and Integration in Economic Development. *Journal of Economic Growth*, 9, 131-165.

Saunders, M., Lewis, P., & Thornhill, A. (2009). *Research Methods for Business Students*, 5th ed. London: Pearson Education Ltd.

Taehee, K. (2014). Performance Appraisal: Determinants of Public Employees' Acceptance. PhD Thesis, State University of New Jersey, Rutgers.

Williamson, O. (2002). The Theory of the Firm as Governance Structure: From Choice to Contract. *Journal of Economic Perspectives*, 16(3), 171-195.

World Bank. (2003). Understanding Public Sector Performance in Transition Countries (an Empirical Contribution.) Washington, DC: Poverty Reduction and Economic Management Unit of the World Bank.

V.1

EDUCATION

20

Institutional Autonomy of Ethiopian Public Universities: An Application of the European University Autonomy Scorecard Methodology

Solomon Gebreyohans Gebru, Annie Hondeghem, and Bruno Broucker

Box 1: Key points of the chapter

- ✓ There are various approaches/perspectives used to assess/measure universities' level of IA;
- ✓ The level of IA of Ethiopian public universities is quite low when evaluated through the EUAS methodology; and
- ✓ Though it has its own limitations and contextualizing that warrant serious attention, the EUAS could serve as a useful tool in evaluating and improving the IA of public universities in Ethiopia.

Box 2: Reading this chapter will give an insight about

- ✓ The concept of IA (including its types, the rationale for it, and how it is measured / assessed); and
- ✓ Ethiopian public universities' current levels of (a) organizational; (b) academic; (c) staffing; and (d) financial autonomy.

Box 3: Abbreviations

EUA = European University Association
EUAS = European University Autonomy Scorecard
FCSC = Federal Civil Service Commission
FDRE = Federal Democratic Republic of Ethiopia
HE = Higher Education
HEIs = Higher Education Institutions
HEP = Higher Education Proclamation
HERQA = Higher Education Relevance and Quality Agency
HESs = Higher Education Systems

HESC = Higher Education Strategy Center
HPR = House of Peoples' Representatives
IA = Institutional Autonomy
MoSHE = Ministry of Science and Higher Education
MU = Mekelle University
QA = Quality Assurance

1. Background

Since the end of the twentieth century, the rapid expansion of higher education (HE); the growing complexity of higher education institutions (HEIs); and the emergence of the knowledge-based global economy (which has led to growing expectations from HEIs to contribute to national economic development), have resulted in a demand for states to give more autonomy to HEIs (Marmolejo, 2016). Consequently, a significant reduction in state regulation of HEIs and a substantial increase in the latter's autonomy have become characteristic features of higher education systems (HESs) in the twenty-first century. In the context of HE, Mora (2001) defines autonomy as "the ability of universities to organize their own affairs without interference from the state" (p. 102, cited in Tamrat, 2012, p.2). Here, it is noteworthy that institutional autonomy (IA) does not imply the absence of external regulation. For example, states can regulate HEIs to ensure quality and fairness (Pruvot & Estermann, 2017). Further, IA is defined not only in terms of the state-university relationship but also in terms of the universities' independence from the market and non-state actors.

So far, however, the questions of the pertinent areas/dimensions of autonomy, how much autonomy should be granted, and how autonomy is measured in the context of HE remain debated among scholars and practitioners alike. For example, historical and traditional practices as well as political and societal culture ideals, norms, and beliefs usually dictate the question how much autonomy should be offered to institutions. This is so because countries have different legal frameworks and historical and cultural settings that shape universities' IA (Pruvot & Estermann, 2017). This makes comparison among HESs difficult. Cognizant of this, the European University Association (EUA) launched a European University Autonomy Scorecard (EUAS) in 2011 and developed, for the first time, a methodology to score and compare data on university autonomy in Europe (Estermann & Pruvot, 2018). In 2017, the EUA produced an updated version of the EUAS, published with the title "The University Autonomy in Europe-III: The Scorecard 2017," which includes the autonomy profile of twenty-nine European HESs and an interactive online tool demonstrating the level of autonomy in each system. The EUA claims that the EUAS allows for benchmarking and can serve as a reference and tool of analysis within and beyond Europe (Pruvot & Estermann, 2017). In fact, Matei & Iwinska (2018) argue that the EUAS "is the only such tool allowing for benchmarking of autonomy available in Europe and probably in the world" (p. 363). This study thus intends to apply the EUAS to Africa, taking Ethiopia as a case study.

Ethiopia is an interesting case study because, on the one hand, the number of HEIs (both public and private) has grown rapidly over the last two decades. The number of public universities and the number of private HEIs (universities, university colleges, colleges, and institutes) increased from barely two public universities before 2000 to forty-five and from zero private institutions to two hundred twenty-one in 2019, respectively (HERQA, 2019; MoSHE, 2019). This rapid expansion has made it difficult, if not impossible, for the state to regulate HEIs directly. On the other hand, the Ethiopian HES is characterized by poor performance in terms of quality of teaching, quality and productivity of research outputs, and level of engagement with the local community and industry (Akalu, 2014; Woldegiyorgis, 2014). Although there could be several other factors (including lack of the necessary inputs/resources) for the low performance, it could partially be attributed to lack of sufficient autonomy. This is so because recent studies have identified governance, with autonomy as its core component, as among the key determinant factors that influence the performance of HEIs (Aghion et al., 2010; Fiszbein & Ringold, 2012). More specifically, a study by Aghion, *et al.* (2010) found a strong relationship between universities' level of autonomy and their performance on research. Autonomy enables HEIs to respond flexibly to emerging market and societal demands (Fiszbein & Ringold, 2012). Generally, although other factors are equally necessary, "institutional autonomy is a crucial precondition that enables universities to achieve their missions in the best possible way" (Estermann & Steinel, 2011:87). Today, as HEIs are increasingly affected by both government regulations and market mechanisms, university autonomy has become a key area of focus for HES.

Thus far, there are only a few studies (see for example, Akalu, 2014; Asgedom & Hagos, 2015; Gebru, 2013; Tamrat, 2012) focusing on the IA of Ethiopian public HEIs, and none of them employed comprehensive autonomy indicators such as the EUAS. Gebru (2013) rightly observes that the "academic literature on university autonomy in Ethiopia is scanty" (p.278). Thus, the present study fills this gap by applying the EUAS methodology. Pruvot and Estermann, the crafters of the EUAS, claim that the EUAS "contributes to raising awareness in the university sector of the changes needed to create a regulatory environment favorable to university autonomy." Therefore, a study that applies the EUAS methodology, a tool devised to drive "the modernization of European higher education" (Pruvot & Estermann, 2017:7) to Ethiopia, could motivate the concerned bodies to either adapt the EUAS methodology as a tool to modernize Ethiopia's HE system or develop an alternative tool. Here, it is noteworthy that, so far, Ethiopia has no tool or methodology designed to assess the IA of its public universities. Thus, this chapter intends to: (1) examine the concept of IA; and (2) asses/measure the level of (a) organizational (b) academic (c) staffing, and (d) financial autonomy of Ethiopian public universities using the EUAS methodology.

The next section presents a literature review. While the third section offers the methodology adopted, the fourth one assesses/measures the level of IA of Ethiopian public universities using the EUAS methodology. The chapter ends with a discussion and concluding remarks.

2. Literature Review

2.1. The Concept of Institutional Autonomy

IA is a multidimensional concept (Matei & Iwinska, 2018; Pruvot & Estermann, 2017). It denotes "to the ability of [HEIs] to set and implement their own policies and priorities for teaching and research, perhaps also other aspects of their mission, such as community service" (Bergan et al., 2016:3). In a recent publication, Matei (2017, in Matei & Iwinska, 2018) provided a similar definition, wherein IA is defined as "the right of the university to determine its organization and administrative structures, to decide on priorities, manage its budget, hire personnel and admit students, decide on the content and form of its teaching and research"(p. 349). IA involves the "freedom to exercise control over staffing, student, curriculum and teaching, academic standards, research, leader selection, administration, and finance" (Gebru, 2013:279).

IA is not a static concept. Accordingly, Estermann (2015) defines IA "as constantly changing relations between the state and universities and the differing degree of control exerted by public authorities, which are dependent on particular national contexts and circumstances" (p. 28). Similarly, Berdahl (1990) argues that unlike academic freedom, whose contents are supposed to be a universal value, IA is a relative value and may justifiably vary in its contents from place to place and from time to time. Thus, HESs can give more freedom to certain dimensions of autonomy and less to other dimensions depending on several factors (Gebru, 2013). All these definitions imply that IA is not absolute. In this chapter, we adopted the following definition provided by the International Association of Universities (IAU):

> *The principle of institutional autonomy can be defined as the necessary degree of independence from external interference that the University requires in respect of its internal organization and governance, the internal distribution of financial resources and the generation of income from non public sources, the recruitment of its staff, the setting of the conditions of study and, finally, the freedom to conduct teaching and research (IAU, 1998: n.p).*

2.2. What is the Need for Institutional Autonomy?

Universities need "exceptional" freedom "because they provide or contribute to the provision of an exceptional public good or service to society: knowledge" (Marginson, 2016 cited in Matei & Iwinska, 2018, p. 348). A recent joint statement by All European Academies, EUA, and Science Europe (April 2019) asserts, "Research can only contribute to a prosperous and sustainable future if it is conducted according to [the principles of academic freedom and IA]" (n.p). Similarly, a special statement on academic freedom from a 1992 UNESCO conference in Romania warns, "History has shown that violations of academic freedom and institutional autonomy have high costs in intellectual regression, social alienation and economic stagnation" (Matei & Iwinska, 2014:22). In sum, autonomy is at the heart of intellectual dynamism, scientific development, and innovation (King, 2007 cited in Gebru, 2013).

Generally, two broad perspectives may be distinguished: the *non-instrumentalist* and *instrumentalist perspectives*. From a non-instrumentalist perspective, universities need distinctive autonomy to serve as a social conscience in pursuit of truth and articulation of universal values (Moses, 2007) and to play a pivotal role in nurturing democratic culture and progressive values (King, 2007 cited in Gebru, 2013). From an instrumentalist perspective, universities need autonomy to enhance their performance (Aghion, et al., 2010; Choi, 2019; Estermann; 2015; Varghese & Martin, 2013).

2.3. Types of Institutional Autonomy

Broadly, IA is classified into two major types: *substantive* and *procedural*. While substantive autonomy refers to determining institutional goals and programs, procedural autonomy concerns the right of universities to determine the means of achieving the goals and implanting the programs (Berdahl, 1990). According to Raze (2009, cited in Tamrat, 2012), in the context of HE, while substantive autonomy involves academic issues (which include curriculum design, research policy, setting entrance standards, academic staff appointment, awarding degrees, etc.), procedural autonomy deals with the nonacademic aspects of the university (such as budgeting, financial management, purchasing, etc.).

2.4. Measuring Institutional Autonomy

Since the notion and perception of IA varies from country to county, so far it remains difficult to come up with a standardized way of measuring/assessing the level of IA that could be applicable across HESs.

Having said this, three approaches to assessing/measuring IA are noticeable in the current literature. One is represented by Beiter et al. (2016, cited in Choi, 2019), and approaches IA from a non-instrumentalist perspective. Based on this perspective, Beiter et al., "developed a scorecard that measures the degree of protection of institutional autonomy using indicators such as provision on institutional autonomy in legislation, organizational autonomy, financial autonomy, staffing autonomy, academic autonomy, extent of government intervention, and institutional independence from private interests" (Choi, 2019, p.19).

The second approach is represented, principally, by the EUA, which tackles IA from an instrumentalist point of view. In 2011 the EUA developed a relatively comprehensive quantitative methodology, the EUAS, to measure and rank university autonomy in Europe in a comparative perspective (Pruvot & Estermann, 2017).

Finally, Choi (2019) recently developed an IA assessment framework that combines the instrumentalist and non-instrumentalist perspective. Choi identified indicators based on universities' stakeholders, which are grouped into six categories: (1) academic staff, (2) administrators, (3) students, (4) governments, (5) industries, and (6) society at large (p. 21). Using this perspective, Choi identified autonomy indicators for each stakeholder. For example, the autonomy indicators for academic staff include the "right to speak on institutional issues, representation in university governance, autonomy in curriculum design, and legal provision for the protection of academic speech" (p. 25). Choi's approach is interesting but may need further investigation and validation.

In general, it should be noted that, as rightly claimed by Pruvot & Estermann (2017), "autonomy cannot be measured objectively" (p.13) and thus selection of indicators and the values of importance attributed to each indicator are determined normatively. Further, some regulations are not considered as restrictions. For example, the EUA does not consider regulations meant to ensure quality of services and fairness of employment as restrictions. However, if HEIs are not allowed, for example, to freely choose quality assurance mechanisms and providers, it may be seen as a restriction.

3. Methodology

The concept of IA is usually approached from an institutional perspective. Thus, the EUAS takes public universities as its unit of analysis (Pruvot & Estermann, 2017). This study adopted the EUAS approach to measuring IA. The EUAS "focuses on regulatory frameworks" (Estermann & Pruvot, 2018:3) because constraints to autonomy usually stem from proclamations, presidential decrees or regulations, directives, and circular letters, etc. Accordingly, data for this study are mainly generated from Ethiopia's regulatory frameworks pertinent to the HE sector.

However, to further understand the interpretations and practical applications of the regulatory framework, we studied Mekelle University (MU), one of Ethiopia's large public universities. The reason for selecting only one university is that Ethiopia's public universities, large or small, old or new, are (re)established by the Council of Ministers' Regulation as equal autonomous entities (see HPR, 2019). Thus, they are not legally differentiated in terms of autonomy, notwithstanding the recent attempt for differentiation[1] (which has not yet been implemented,). Moreover, the EUAS does not account for the peculiarity of institutions available within a given HE system. For example, it may be assumed that research universities may have more autonomy (in some respects) than comprehensive universities in a given HE system. The EUAS does not entertain this, albeit the EUA sees this as a limitation.

Although the EUAS measures autonomy from an institutional perspective, its focus is on developing a country profile on university autonomy. Finally, the reason for selecting MU has to do with convenience. One of the researchers is a faculty member of this university, which makes accessing data relatively easier. Moreover, his lived experience, including as Institutional Reform Team member and Institutional Reform Director in this university, is an asset for this project.

The EUA separates autonomy dimensions into four categories: *organizational, academic, staffing, and financial,* each of them composed of several indicators (thirty-eight in total) (Estermann & Pruvot, 2018), each indicator having relative weights within each dimension of autonomy (Pruvot & Estermann, 2017:60). For example, organizational autonomy consists of eight indicators and a value is allocated to each indicator based on relative importance. For instance, from the eight indicators of organizational autonomy, the highest value is allocated to the indicator called "capacity to decide on academic structure" (15 percent). However, unlike indicators, the dimensions of autonomy are not rated based on their relative importance and thus each dimension is assumed to have equal value.

For the purpose of simplicity, the EUA also uses a non-weighted rating. By this approach, "Each restriction on university autonomy [is] assigned a deduction value based on how restrictive a particular rule or regulation [is] seen to be. A score of 100% indicates full institutional autonomy; a score of 0% means that an issue is entirely regulated by an external authority" (Pruvot & Estermann, 2017:10). To take the above indicators as an example, if central law determines a university's academic structure, the indicator would be rated as 0 percent; if it is internally determined, it would receive 100 percent; and if it were to be negotiated with external authority, it would be around 60 percent. Another example is the selection procedure of a university executive head. If the selection of a university executive head is externally verified, the indicator receives 0 percent, if it is determined internally, then the score becomes 100 percent.

In this study, we adopted the unweighted system because the weighted system[2] is developed based on the relative importance of indicators, considering Europe's context. Second, we did not consult stakeholders such as the Ministry of Science and Higher Education (MoSHE), Higher Education Relevance and Quality Agency (HERQA), Higher Education Strategy Center (HESC),[3] or university presidents, etc. The EUA determined the weighted value after conducting several round discussions with concerned stakeholders, such as with the Rectors' Association of European Universities (Pruvot & Estermann, 2017).

The unweighted system of the EUAS online tool enables assigning unweighted value for each indicator, thereby determining the level of autonomy for each dimension. For example, according to the online interactive tool, if the selection of the executive head is not validated by an external authority, then the indicator receives 100 percent. If external validation is required, however, it will receive 0 percent regardless of how much the university is involved in the selection of the executive head (see EUA, 2020). This is so because external validation could imply rejection of the university community's preferred candidates.

We introduced two minor modifications in adopting the EUAS methodology. First, under the staffing dimension, the EUAS limits the indicators to senior academic and senior administrative staff. However, since there is not much difference between senior and junior staff in the context of Ethiopia, except in the case of promotion to full professorship, we decided to simply use the term staff (for both academic and administrative). Second, under financial dimension, there is an indicator for the "ability to charge tuition fees for non-EU students" (Pruvot & Estermann, 2017, p. 70). For the case of Ethiopia, international or non-Ethiopian students replace the "non-EU" students in the original methodology.

The EUAS assumes that for universities to be considered as fully autonomous entities, all issues represented by each indicator should be decided/ handled internally. In order to facilitate comparisons, the EUA clusters the level of autonomy of HESs as follows:

Table 1: Autonomy clusters

Cluster	Level
High	100%-81%
Medium high	80%-61%
Medium low	60%-41%
Low	40%-0%

Source: Pruvot & Estermann, 2017

Finally, based on the four dimensions of autonomy identified by the EUA, we purposefully selected the following key informants from MU: vice-president for academics; budget and planning director; quality assurance head; human resource officers; and finance officers. Semi structured interviews were conducted from December 11 to 13, 2019. Interview results were analyzed against each indicator. Consent for an interview was obtained in exchange for anonymity. Hence, interviewees are cited in the text anonymously.

4. Assessing the Level of Institutional Autonomy of Ethiopian Public Universities

In this section, we assess the level of IA of Ethiopian public universities. To put it into a comparative perspective, we compared it with several European HESs, whose level of IA is measured using the EUAS. The comparison is made based on the 2017 EUA report that covers the autonomy profile of twenty-nine European HESs. Under annex 1, we present the autonomy scorecard of twenty-nine European HESs. Table 2 presents the actual values generated for each indicator as well as the overall and each dimension's score of IA in Ethiopia. Each of the dimensions and indicators are discussed.

Table 2: Level of higher education institutional autonomy in Ethiopia

Dimension	Unweighted score (100%)	Cluster[4]
Organizational	***24.4***	***Low***
Selection procedure for the executive head	0	
Selection criteria for the executive head	75	
Dismissal of the executive head	0	
Term of office of the executive head	0	
Inclusion of external members in university governing bodies	30	
Selection of external members in university governing bodies	30	
Capacity to decide on academic structures	0	
Capacity to create legal entities	60	
Academic	***24.3***	***Low***
Capacity to decide on overall student numbers	60	
Capacity to select students	30	
Capacity to introduce and terminate	0	
Capacity to choose the language of instruction	0	
Capacity to select QA mechanisms	0	
Capacity to select QA providers	0	
Capacity to design content of degree programs	80	
Staffing	***39.4***	***Low***
Capacity to decide on recruitment procedures (academic staff)	80	
Capacity to decide on recruitment procedures (administrative staff)	0	
Capacity to decide on salaries (academic staff)	0	
Capacity to decide on salaries (administrative staff)	0	

Dimension	Unweighted score (100%)	Cluster[4]
Capacity to decide on dismissals (academic staff)	100	
Capacity to decide on dismissals (administrative staff)	60	
Capacity to decide on promotions (academic staff)	50	
Capacity to decide on promotions (administrative staff)	25	
Financial	***42***	***Medium low***
Length of public funding	60	
Type of public funding	60	
Ability to keep surplus	0	
Ability to borrow money	0	
Ability to own buildings	0	
Ability to charge tuition fees for Ethiopian students	75	
Ability to charge tuition fees for non-Ethiopian students	100	
Overall	***32.3***	***Low***

Adopted from Pruvot & Estermann, 2017.

4.1. Organizational Autonomy

Selection Procedure for the Executive Head (the President)

The Ministry of Science and Higher Education (MoSHE) is the main regulatory body of the HE sector. All universities have governing and advisory bodies, which include a board (composed of external members and mandated with supervising and monitoring the overall operation of the university), a president and vice-presidents, senate (composed of internal members and mandated mainly with academic affairs), etc. (HPR, 2019). The board nominates and the Minister of MoSHE (if the university is under the federal government) or the head of the appropriate regional state agency (if the university is under a regional government) appoints the president of a public university. Selection procedures for the president are stringently stated by the country's current Higher Education law (HEP, Proc.No. 1152/2019) (see HPR, 2019, art. 52) and by the "Directive on Selection and Appointment of Leaders and Managers in Higher Education Institutions" (here after the Directive) (MoSHE, 2018). According to the Directive, the nominees are first selected by a "Search and Selection Committee," which is composed of representatives (one each) from the board, senate, academic staff, and administrative staff and students' union. After screening candidates, the committee submits five nominees to the board.

The board conducts additional evaluation and recommends three nominees for appointment to the minister of MoSHE. Although the board and senate representatives have a say in rating presidential candidates, the minister has a final say in selecting the president from among the three nominees. The fact that Ethiopian universities are fully dependent on state for funding may justify the appointment of their presidents by external authority. However, it could also emanate from the country's political culture, which is known for power centralization. Usually, executive heads are either elected (for example by electoral body or governing body) or appointed (by the board or the senate or external authority). In either case, the selection of the executive head may need external verification (like in Ethiopia), which undermines IA since external verification could imply rejection of preferred nominees or elected candidates. According to the 2017 EUA report, in Europe too, external validation for the appointment of the rector is required in twelve out of the twenty-nine HESs considered.

Selection Criteria for the Executive Head

Similar to the selection procedure, detailed criteria for presidential candidates and their weights are listed under the Directive. For example, presidential candidates are required to have a doctorate degree or its equivalent, albeit exceptions are allowed. However, candidates are not required to hold academic positions. Accordingly, candidates can come both from within and outside the university (MoSHE, 2018). This gives universities the opportunity to choose their president from a wide range of candidates, within the given law. This is in line with the designation of the president as "chief executive" by the HEP (HPR, 2019), which shows the focus on managerial quality rather than academic excellence. Thus, the president can be someone with a good managerial background from other sectors. Although some HESs are still exercising the traditional rectorship, particularly in Southern and Eastern Europe, Europe has shifted towards the CEO type (Estermann, 2015). Stating the qualification for candidates in the national law remains dominant in Europe too, where two-third (nineteen) of the twenty-nine HESs fall under this model. Unlike Ethiopia, fourteen of these nineteen HESs also require presidential candidates to hold academic positions in the university. In this regard, thus, there is more flexibility in Ethiopia, although this may not be necessarily for the good.

Term of Office and Dismissal of the Executive head

The term of office for the president as stated both in the HEP and in the Directive is six years and can be renewed once. Thus, universities do not have the freedom to determine the term of office of their presidents. This seems in common with many European states, where the term of office of the executive is stated in the law in nearly 80 percent of the twenty-nine HESs (Pruvot & Estermann, 2017). The dismissal of the executive head is also strictly regulated by law and it is the minister of MoSHE or the concerned regional state agency, as the case may be, who relieves her/him from power. The conditions for dismissal are also plainly stated in the HEP. The HEP also allows the board to remove or cause the removal of the president under certain circumstances (HPR, 2019). In Europe too, rectors' terms of office are stated in the law in nearly 80 percent (twenty-three) of cases, and rector's dismissal is strictly regulated by law in almost two thirds (eighteen) of the twenty-nine HESs.

Determining Internal Academic Structure

Ethiopia's HEP grants universities the autonomy to "set up their organizational structure and enact and implement [their] internal rules and procedures" (HPR, 2019:11456). Yet, this autonomy is highly restricted by the same proclamation. The HEP prescribes the list of governing and advisory bodies that must be constituted in universities. They include: board, president and vice-presidents, senate, managing council, university council, academic unit council, academic unit managing council, and department council. Moreover, the constitution, composition, power, and responsibilities of the first five bodies are already stipulated by the HEP. Although determining the composition, constitution, responsibilities, and decision making process of the last three bodies is left to universities, this requires an approval from the board. The board, senate or the university council can establish other advisory or specialized committees. The HEP also obliges universities to establish academic units in a hierarchical governance structure, even though determining the level of the hierarchy is left to universities.

The names of the academic units are also already prescribed by the HEP and include college, faculty, school, institute, department, and center, although the law does not specify the number of academic units to be established. Moreover, the HEP requires that the governing and managing bodies of academic units be approved by the board. Here, it is noteworthy that the board is usually seen as an external body (see for example, Gebru, 2013) since all its members, except the president, are external and since it is established by and directly accountable to MoSHE (HPR, 2019). Generally, therefore, much of the internal academic structure and the governing and managing bodies of universities is centrally prescribed, leaving less freedom to universities. Only in less than a third of the twenty-nine HESs is internal academic structure determined by external law in Europe, which implies Ethiopia is lagging behind on this indicator.

Creating Legal Entities

This indicator concerns whether HEIs have the autonomy to establish both not-for-profit and for-profit legal entities to support their mission. Ethiopia's current HEP allows universities to establish an income generating enterprise, which operates like any business organization, albeit this needs approval from the board (HPR, 2019). Although this may seem formally less restrictive, again the fact that all board members, except the president, are external to universities may make establishing income-generating enterprises difficult. Moreover, the sources of income that enterprises may generate are restricted by the HEP. Here, the board is expected to play a political role by preventing universities from engaging in income generating areas that would negate their main mission and negatively affect the interest of other businesses. Universities are also required to report to the Ministry of Finance and MoSHE "receipt of funds from third parties and its investment incomes" (HPR, 2019:1150). This could result in restrictive consequences. Finally, the new HEP states that a directive shall determine details about income generating enterprises, which has not yet been issued. While Ethiopia is ahead of two European HESs, which allow establishing only not-for-profit entities, it is lagging behind nineteen HESs, which allow creating legal entities without specific constraints.

Inclusion and Selection of External Members in University Governing Bodies

This indicator assumes that HEIs should have the autonomy to include or not to include external members in their governing bodies, and that if they have the right to include external members, they should have the autonomy to select them by themselves (Pruvot & Estermann, 2017). However, the types of governing bodies depend on the type of governance structure. There is no common nomenclature among HESs and institutions. The international trend shows the presence of two main types of governance structures in terms of governing bodies: dual and unitary. In a dual structure, there are mainly two types of governing bodies: board/council and senate. Although the scope and division of responsibilities varies from system to system, they usually have clearly divided competencies. In countries with unitary governance structure, there is only one governing body, which may be known as the senate, council or by other names, responsible for all major decisions (Pruvot & Estermann, 2017).

Ethiopia's HEP lists several governing and advisory bodies for universities (HPR, 2019). However, in common with the international trend, here we shall focus on two governing bodies: board and senate and evaluate whether universities have the right to include, or not, external members in these bodies. The board, composed of seven voting members, is the "supreme governing body" (p.11482) in public universities. All members of the board, except the president, who is a nonvoting member, are centrally decided to be external and thus universities do not have the autonomy to decide on this issue. The board is mainly entrusted with administrative, financial, and strategic matters. The senate is the leading body for academic matters. According to the HEP, membership to the senate and its size is left to be determined by the establishing law of the university, and the latter is not prohibited from including external members to this body. Nonetheless, the HEP clearly states that the majority of the members of the senate should come from the academic staff. Upon advice by the president, the board is entitled to modify or change senate membership, number, and terms of office. In Europe, there has been a trend toward the inclusion of external members, especially in HESs or HEIs with dual governance structures. The purpose is not only to ensure accountability but also to foster links with industries and other sectors (Estermann, 2015). In Ethiopia, however, members of the board have been dominantly drawn from the government (more specifically from the ruling party). One key informant judges the board as a "club of politicians" (interview, December 11, 2019).

Regarding selection of the board, while public universities have only the right to be consulted in appointing three members, the MoSHE directly appoints four members. The HEP also prescribes the profiles of the individuals to be nominated to board membership. Ethiopia's current HEP shows a trend of recentralization in the nomination of board members. In the previous HEP (Proc. no. 650/2009), the president, in consultation with the senate and university council, had the power to nominate three members (see HPR, 2009). Today, this power is reduced only to being consulted. When it comes to the senate, the president is authorized to appoint a majority of the members, who should come from academic staff. The HEP does not prescribe as regards to the appointment of the remaining members.

Generally, compared to the senate, the board has a plethora of powers and responsibilities (such as determining policies regarding employment, promotions, discipline, salary, allowance, payments related to education, and other benefits, etc. (HPR, 2019, see art. 45). Thus, the fact that board members are external and their composition and appointment, predominantly drawn from top government officials, is externally decided is a severe restriction for public universities compared to a self-governing institution (Moses, 2007). In Europe, the situation with regard to selection and inclusion of external members in universities' governing bodies is highly divided. In some HESs, universities can appoint external members, in others they cannot appoint but can make proposals, still in others they can neither appoint nor propose (and thus it is done externally), and finally, in other systems they can appoint some of the external members. With regard to inclusion, while three HESs prohibit universities from including external members, many HESs determine the threshold for/proportion of external members to be included (Pruvot & Estermann, 2017).

4.2. Academic Autonomy

Autonomy to Decide on Overall Student Numbers

In Ethiopia, according to the HEP, MoSHE determines student placement in public institutions, based on university intake capacity proposed by academic units and the availability of facilities (such as dormitories), universities' proposal of the overall number of undergraduate students they would be able to accommodate, and in consultation with universities. However, if the number of deserving students exceeds the demand offered by the universities, then MoSHE negotiates with each university. Yet, the HEP does not make it clear whether MoSHE determines student placement for all levels of academic programs (bachelor, master's, and doctorate) and for fee-paying students. In practice, so far, MoSHE decides only on the placement of state-funded undergraduate students in consultation with universities. Meanwhile, universities have been freely determining the overall number of regular master's and doctorate programs, except for those assigned by MoSHE (former MoE) and self-paying non-regular graduate and undergraduate students (interview, December 12, 2019), although the HEP does not prohibits MoSHE from determining the overall number of applicants, in consultation with universities (HPR, 2019). In Europe, from the twenty-nine HESs, "only in a minority of systems are institutions entirely free to decide on their student intake" (Pruvot & Estermann, 2017:34).

Generally, however, the trend in Europe seems to be moving toward a negotiation-based approach (which is the case in Ethiopia too). Universities exclusively decide about the overall number of students in seven HESs; decide only on fee-paying students in four HESs (while the number of state-funded students is determined externally); negotiate with external authority in eleven HESs; have no say in one HES; and admission is free in six HESs.

Autonomy to Select Students

a) Undergraduate Students

In Europe, twelve out of the twenty-nine HESs follow a co-regulated model at the undergraduate level. In Ethiopia, the HEP and MoSHE determine admission criteria for undergraduate students. According to the HEP, admission to the undergraduate program requires accomplishing secondary school and passing entrance exams set by individual universities. The HEP also allows graduates of TVET with level 4 qualification and two years' experience to enroll in undergraduate programs (HPR, 2019). So far, students who passed secondary school with the score above the cut-off point set by MoSHE (annually) have been allowed to enroll in undergraduate programs, with no entrance exam from the university side. Thus, universities do not have any say in determining the admission criteria for undergraduate students (interview, December 1,1, 2019). Finally, until the 2019/20 academic year, universities were required to place 70 percent of their students in engineering and natural science and 30 percent in humanities and social sciences. Recently, the ratio has been changed to 60 percent and 40 percent, respectively. Since public universities are fully dependent on state funding and since the state sees the value of HE from an instrumentalist point of view (producing working force, reducing poverty, bringing economic structural change, and ensuring global competitiveness, etc.,) (see for example, MoF, 2015; NPC, 2016), this kind of regulation is not unexpected.

b) Graduate Students

Similarly, the HEP dictates the minimum requirements needed for joining graduate programs. However, it also allows universities to set their own requirements and determine the content of entrance exams. For a master's degree, students are required to accomplish undergraduate studies with adequate academic results and pass entrance exams given by the individual universities. For the doctorate level, candidates are required to accomplish a second degree and obtain academic results required by the individual university (HPR, 2019). Therefore, formally, universities have the autonomy to select second- and third- degree applicants. However, until recent years, the government was requiring universities (particularly those which run graduate programs) to enroll some second- and third-degree applicants without requiring them to take entrance exams. This was so because, following the rapid expansion of HE, the government was aggressively looking for academic staff for its newly established universities. This was perceived by the academic community as a violation of autonomy and as damaging to the quality of education (Akalu, 2014). At the graduate level, officially, Ethiopia seems in line with the European trend where admission is entirely regulated by universities in twenty-seven HESs, except in "the French-speaking community of Belgium and in Switzerland" (Pruvot & Estermann, 2017:36).

c) Special Admission

Ethiopia's HEP also allows for special admission procedures for disadvantaged citizens. The Council of Ministers determines such a procedure. Universities can also admit adults under a special admission procedure determined by MoSHE and the senate of individual universities.

Autonomy to Introduce and Terminate Academic Programs

Universities can open new and close existing degree programs at all levels (bachelor, master's and doctorate) and all modalities (regular, distance, evening, etc.) but only with the approval of the board and MoSHE (HPR, 2019). Thus, external approval is required for opening and closing academic programs. Although not explicitly mentioned in the HEP, this approval serves as accreditation, because students who received degree awards from academic programs not recognized by MoSHE are not allowed to enter the market. Getting approval also implies getting funds. So far, external approval remains more formal than substantive (interview, December 12, 2019). Previously, public universities followed a self-accreditation approach, where the senate was the highest body responsible. So far, although universities conduct course or curriculum evaluation, academic programs at public universities are not legally subject to external accreditation, be it from professional associations or HERQA. Finally, although it has been positively received, the government has been pressuring (or encouraging) universities to diversify academic programs vertically and horizontally.

In relation to the introduction and termination of academic programs, the situation in Europe is complex and divided. In some HESs for example, the "state determines the academic field, or educational remit, of universities" (Pruvot & Estermann, 2017:37), while other HESs require regular periodic accreditation of academic programs. Generally, there are four varieties. In eight HESs, opening a new program does not require pre-accreditation; pre-accreditation is necessary for public funding in four HESs, introducing any new program requires accreditation in nine HESs and other restrictions apply in eight HESs. Thus, the freedom to open academic programs without accreditation or other restrictions seems limited to only a few HESs.

Autonomy to Design Content of Degree Programs

Ethiopia's HEP states that HEIs "shall enjoy the liberty of developing curricula for all of [their] academic programs" (HPR, 2019:11459). On the other side, the HEP authorizes MoSHE to "coordinate curricula development common to public institutions". Besides, the HEP authorizes MoSHE, HERQA, and HESC to guide curriculum development through a national qualification framework. Practically, curriculum development for undergraduate students is highly centralized or homogenized. One key informant at MU had to say the following in relation to this:

> *Almost a decade ago, most undergraduate curriculums were harmonized, under the patronage of MoSHE [formerly MoE], and both old and newly established public universities have been adopting them. During the harmonization process, representatives from many public universities participated in shaping curriculums and a 10%-20% margin was allowed for each university to shape its curriculum in its own interest. Generally, nonetheless, course/curriculum contents were designed in the form of one size fits all. Moreover, the worst is coming with the adoption of the New Education Roadmap[5] in 2019. The Roadmap reintroduced freshman courses for newly enrolled undergraduate students. These courses were directly sent from MoSHE to all public universities, in the beginning of this academic year [2019/20) and we already recognized that they have problems. We are not certain what will happen to the other undergraduate courses. Finally, I would say, designing the content of curriculums/courses for graduate programs [master and doctorate] remains under the prerogative of each university* (interview, December 12,2019).

Generally, however, although the experience of undergraduate programs demonstrates the opposite, legally, universities have the right to design the content of their curriculum, albeit with some restrictions (HPR, 2019). This means that universities have the right to reject a centrally imposed curriculum if it is imposed against their consent, provided there is independent leadership from the university side. In Europe, in twenty-six of the twenty-nine HESs, "Universities can design the content of their degree programs/courses (other than for the regulated professions) without constraints" (Pruvot & Estermann, 2017:39).

Capacity to Choose the Language of Instruction

In Ethiopia, universities do not have the autonomy to determine the language of instruction. English is made to be the medium of instruction, albeit exceptions to use local languages are allowed (HPR, 2019). This has mainly to do with historical traditions, wherein British and American experts dominated the HE sector of the country. In contrast, although the degree varies between bachelor and master's programs, universities are free to choose their language of instruction in twenty out of the twenty-nine HESs in Europe, which shows that Ethiopia is lagging behind, although there could be an acceptable justification for this.

Autonomy to Select Quality Assurance (QA) Mechanisms and QA Providers

Ethiopia's HEP prescribes the mechanisms that may be used to ensure quality, although universities are neither allowed nor prohibited from using other QA mechanisms and providers.

Two main mechanisms are prescribed: accreditation and quality audit. While institutional accreditation so far remains applicable only to private HEIs, both private and public HEIs are subject to internal and external quality audit. The exemption of public HEIs from accreditation could be associated with the fact that, unlike private HEIs, they are established by regulation as autonomous entities (HPR, 2019). At the program level, however, the power to accredit academic programs in public HEIs is given to the senate, although its decisions require consent from the board and MoSHE. According to the EUA, program accreditation is seen as restrictive and instead institutional accreditation is recommended (Pruvot & Estermann, 2017).

As mentioned earlier, although the HEP does not prohibit universities from using other QA providers, HERQA is the national agency mandated with accreditation and quality audit. HERQA "evaluates [HEIs] to ensure their compliance with the standards of relevance and quality of education set forth [in the HEP]" (HPR, 2019:11517). Thus, being accredited (for private HEIs) and audited (for private and public HEIs) by this agency is mandatory, even though universities can employ other QA providers. Moreover, universities are required to establish an internal quality control unit, which carries out quality audit and enhancement measures, and to submit the results of their internal quality audit to HERQA for review (HPR, 2019). Internal quality audit is usually accompanied by external audit, which is done by HERQA. Even internal quality audits are carried out based on the standards prescribed by HERQA. The approach adopted by HERQA for quality audit, so far, has been a peer review, where most of the members of the quality audit team are selected from similar institutions. So far, HERQA has conducted quality audits in the eight relatively large and old universities (interview, December 13, 2019).

Generally, universities cannot ignore the above QA mechanisms and provider and choose freely according to their needs, but they can employ more mechanisms and providers, including from abroad. Accordingly, for example,

MU has recently initiated ISO-17025 to standardize (internationalize) its laboratories, and it is the Ethiopian National Accreditation Office that awards the accreditation (interview, December 13, 2019). With regard to choosing QA mechanisms and providers, the practice in Ethiopia seems no different from Europe. Pruvot & Estermann (2017) concluded that except in Germany (the three states), "It is rare for universities to be able to select quality assurance mechanisms freely and according to their needs."

4.3. Staffing Autonomy

According to the EUAS, staffing autonomy involves the capacity to decide on recruitment procedure and criteria, salaries, promotion, and dismissal of staff (Pruvot & Estermann, 2017). In HEIs, staff is broadly categorized as academic and administrative (even though there could be medical and other types of staff in universities that run hospitals), and the level of autonomy of HEIs in making decisions about their staff may vary depending on the type of staff. In Ethiopia, the HEP classifies the staff of HEIs into four categories: (a) academic staff, (b) academic technical staff, (c) administrative staff, and (d) professionals in teaching hospitals (HPR, 2019). Generally, Ethiopian universities are entitled to "recruit and administer their personnel in accordance with the [HEP] and other applicable laws" (HPR, 2019:11451). The HEP also permits the Board to issue directives that regulate administrative staff, albeit this should comply with the applicable civil service laws (HPR, 2019). However, the level of autonomy granted to universities in relation to staff administration varies depending on the type of staff. For the purpose of this study, we focus on the two dominant categories of staff: academic and administrative.

Autonomy to Decide on Staff Recruitment

Broadly, restrictions in relation to staff recruitment include external confirmation of appointment, controlling the number of posts externally, and carrying out recruitment externally (Pruvot & Estermann, 2017). Universities in Ethiopia are free to determine the number of academic posts and recruit their academic staff. However, while determining the number of academic posts and recruitment for academic staff and setting criteria for the recruitment of senior (PhD holders and above) is left to universities, the recruitment procedures and criteria for recruiting academic staff below the rank of assistant professor or non-PhD holders is highly regulated by an external law, i.e., by the "Academic Staff Recruitment Directive" (MoE, 2018). This Directive includes procedures, criteria, and the value assigned to each criteria for recruiting academic staff. Moreover, the type and level of academic ranks/

positions and the type of employment are determined by the HEP (HPR, 2019). In Europe, only twelve out of the twenty-nine HESs allow universities to decide freely on the recruitment of senior academic staff, which shows Ethiopia is in a better position in this indicator.

Compared to academic staff, recruitment for administrative staff is more restricted. First, officially, MoSHE, together with universities, is authorized to determine the optimum number of administrative staff of universities (HPR, 2019). Second, the number of posts for administrative staff needs approval from the Federal Civil Service Commission (FCSC). Third, the Civil Service Law (Proc.1064/2017) (HPR, 2017), determines the recruitment procedure and criteria for administrative staff. Once the number and level of posts are approved by the FCSC, however, the law allows universities to freely recruit their administrative staff for each post based on the criteria set by civil service laws and regulations. Therefore, recruitment procedure, criteria, and number of posts is externally controlled. In contrast, in Europe, as opposed to senior academic staff, around 70 percent (nineteen) of the HESs allow universities to freely decide the recruitment of senior administrative staff.

Autonomy to Set Staff Salary

The HEP allocates the power to determine staff salary neither to external authority nor to universities. So far, however, the salary of both academic and administrative staff of universities has been externally determined. Although MoSHE is consulted about the salary scale of academic staff, salary scales are proposed by the FCSC and decided by the Council of Ministers (HPR, 2017; interview, December 12, 2019). Unlike administrative staff (who are treated as civil servants), academic staff is recruited on "contractual basis" (HPR, 2019), which assumes that their scale would be determined differently. Nevertheless, like any other civil servant, their salary is centrally determined, and they are entitled to government pensions (interview, December 12, 2019). The government introduced a new salary scale in 2019, which also determined the salary scale of federal universities' employees, including for academic staff (FCSC, 2019). To wind up, therefore, universities do not have the right to set salary or to link salary with performance. There are more than six options when it comes to determining the salary of senior staff in the twenty-nine European HESs and only in less than a third of HESs are universities allowed to set salaries for their senior staff.

Staff Dismissal

Again, the HEP does not explicitly mention whether universities are free to dismiss their academic staff. Nevertheless, there are different provisions under the HEP that would enable universities to dismiss their academic staff internally. First, employment to academic positions is on a "contractual basis and one contract term is two years" (HPR, 2019:11466). In principle, this should give universities the prerogative to fire their academic staff if they are not satisfied during the two years' service. Second, the HEP stipulates that "academic staff shall have job security, and may not be dismissed from his position unless he has committed a serious breach of discipline as stipulated by the senate statutes of the public institution" (p.11469). This implies that universities are allowed to dismiss their academic staff based on their internal rules. Academic staff have the right to appeal to the court or other appropriate external bodies (interview, December 12, 2019). In contrast, dismissal of administrative staff is seen as highly restrictive by universities (interview, December 12, 2019). Unlike academic staff, universities are required to strictly follow civil service laws and rules in dismissing their administrative staff (see CM, 2002; HPR, 2017), where staff can easily take the issue into an administrative court, hosted by the FCSC. There have been scenarios where the FCSC reversed the decision of universities. In Europe too, dismissal is strictly regulated in the majority of the HESs considered, where universities are required to comply with civil service or other specific regulation (Pruvot & Estermann, 2017).

Staff Promotion

MoSHE is authorized to determine directives concerning the promotion of academic staff (HPR, 2019). Consequently, MoSHE has recently produced a "Guideline for Academic Publishing and Promotion" (currently under discussion), which determines the requirements for promotion to all levels of academic ranks (MoSHE, 2019). Previously, universities determined their academic staff promotion based on their senate legislation/internal regulation (interview, December 12, 2019). If the guideline is approved, however, universities' freedom will be limited to promoting their academic staff based on the guideline. Contrary to the case of administrative staff, however, they do not need to wait for open posts. The promotion to the rank of professorship requires an approval from the board (HPR, 2019). Though this may be considered as an internal matter, as pointed out earlier, it may still restrict the freedom of universities, particularly because all members of the board are external. While HEIs have the autonomy to decide about the promotion of their administrative staff, they can only do so when there are open posts, and only using the criteria set by civil service laws. This indicates universities do not have the freedom to determine the procedure and criteria and to promote their administrative staff even if the requirements are fulfilled (interview, December 12, 2019). In Europe too, only twelve and fourteen HESs (of the twenty-nine) allow universities to freely determine the promotion of their senior academic and administrative staff, respectively.

4.4. Financial Autonomy

Length and Type of Public Funding

In Ethiopia, universities are required to develop a strategic plan for five years in agreement with MoSHE. The strategic plan is expected to include an indicative block grant for five years and for every year of the strategic period. However, the HEP prescribes that the fiscal year of universities is the same as the fiscal year of the government (HPR, 2019), which is one year. This requires universities to settle all advance payments made for research and other projects by the end of the year. It is also noteworthy that budgets are released on a quarter basis (after quarterly reports are submitted to the Minister of Finance, and all other concerned bodies) and not on an annual basis. However, funds not utilized during a given year are rolled over into the following year (interview, December 11, 2019).

In contrast to a line item budget, a block grant is considered as a mechanism that enables HEIs to flexibly utilize their budget. With regard to funding type, in principle, Ethiopia introduced block grants for universities in 2003. The current HEP also allows for "block-grant system based on strategic plan agreement" (HPR, 2019:11498). Despite this, however, the Program Budgeting system that the country follows has been applicable to universities.

According to this system, the government sets a budget ceiling for each university. Then, each university may prepare its budget within this ceiling for its different programs (like research, teaching, etc.). Here, there are two restrictions in using the budget. First, universities are required to categorize their budget into recurrent and capital types. In this regard, universities do not have the autonomy to move capital budget to recurrent and vice versa. Second, according to the Program Budgeting formula, the budget is distributed among the following four programs: teaching, research, community service, and administration. Once the budget for each program is approved, although universities can freely allocate funds internally within the scope of each program, they do not have the freedom to transfer funds from one program to another without the approval of the minister of finance (interview, December 11, 2019). Further, funding is accompanied by other restrictions when it comes to internal spending. For example, it is very difficult or even impossible for universities to reward best-performing staff from their budget (even from the internal budget) and to provide sponsorships (interview,

December 11, 2019). In fact, universities have been recently prohibited from providing sponsorship by a directive from the Ministry of Finance (see MoFEC, 2018). In Europe, by far, the most common funding period remains one year. However, in most HE systems (sixteen of the twenty-nine), funding is provided in a lump sum and universities can internally allocate funds without restrictions (which is not the case in Ethiopia). According to the EUA 2017 Report, of the twenty-nine HESs, only one HES follows a line item budgeting approach.

Ability to Borrow Money, Keep Surplus, and Own Buildings

Although EUA treats the ability to borrow money, keep surplus, and own buildings separately (see Pruvot & Estermann, 2017), they are here combined simply because there is no difference among these criteria when they are applied to Ethiopia. In Ethiopia, universities are either not allowed to borrow money or own and sell land and buildings or need external approval to do so (HPR, 2019). Unlike the current HEP, the 2003 HEP allowed universities to get loans and to transfer, buy, lease, or mortgage their property. In the current HEP this is neither allowed nor prohibited. Universities can keep a surplus (unspent budget) but this needs to be integrated with the next annual budget (interview, December 11, 2019). In Europe too, twenty-six of the twenty-nine HE system can keep surplus (with or without restriction). Ethiopia seems also not exceptional when it comes to borrowing money, whereby universities in over 70 percent of the twenty-nine European HESs are either not allowed to or face restrictions to borrow money. Twenty-two of the twenty-nine HESs allow universities to own buildings but only a third allow selling buildings without restriction. In Ethiopia, where universities are fully dependent on state funding and where land is supplied and buildings are fully funded by the state, the restriction is expected.

Ability to Set Tuition Fees for National and International Students

Universities are allowed to charge tuition fees, although the board determines the kind, amount, and manner of payment. However, the law does not specify which kind of students universities may charge tuition fees (HPR, 2019). Practically, Ethiopia follows the split system. All regular undergraduate (bachelor) students in public universities are state-funded and their tuition fees are externally determined. However, universities are fully free to charge tuition fees on part-time undergraduate and graduate students as well as on self-paying or institution-sponsored regular graduate students (interview:, December 11, 2019). Ethiopian universities are also free to set tuition fees for international students at the bachelor, master's and doctorate levels (interview,

December 11, 2019). In Europe, the situation is also divided. Only a few HESs (four out of twenty-nine) can set tuition fees freely, others need to cooperate with external authorities, others can set fees under an externally set ceiling, in some others fees are determined externally, and finally, in some systems, universities may not charge fees (Pruvot & Estermann, 2017).

5. Conclusion and Implications

5.1. Conclusions

This chapter assessed Ethiopian public universities' level of IA using the EUAS methodology. The result shows that Ethiopian universities' level of IA is quite low both in absolute terms (see also Gebru, 2013; Tamrat and Teferra, 2018; Woldegiyorgis 2014) and compared with many European HESs. This implies that Ethiopia is following the "state-centered/controlled" governance approach, which contradicts the international trend, i.e., a shift toward the "state supervision" or "steering from a distance" model (see Dobbins & Knill, 2014). In fact, based on studies on the state-university relationship or the HE governance model pursued since the emergence of HE in Ethiopia, Hailu (2018) and Gebremeskel & Feleke (2016) concluded that Ethiopia's HE governance model over the last six decades is best characterized as a "state-centered" model.

Although Ethiopia's HEIs are legally established as autonomous entities, the ruling party has been exerting considerable influence with a strong presence in universities. It is public knowledge that the ruling party infiltrates universities not only through its internal members but also by assigning its members externally to each university. Generally, party control has been a salient element of university governance (interview, December 11, 2019). The degree of external influence depends on the strength of university leaders. Capable presidents/rectors usually exercise IA to the maximum possible and to the best interest of the university (Varghese & Martin, 2013). In Ethiopia, some universities' presidents were submissive and collaborative to external intervention (Akalu, 2014). Further, for university presidents, "their association with political leaders and affiliation with local politics is more important than merit" (Anteneh, 2016 cited in Hailu, 2018, p.46).

Ethiopia's HEP stipulates that among others the purpose of HEIs is to produce graduates "with competence to support Peace, Democracy and National development that make the country internationally competitive" (HPR, 2019:11448). According to Mosese (2007), realizing such a golden objective requires a minimalist intervention from the state. Thus, based on the pertinent literature and the findings of this study, any desire to augment HE performance would require Ethiopia to initiate reforms that boost the IA of its universities. In this regard, Ethiopian universities could opt or push their government to allow them to join the Magna Charta Universitatum, which has been signed by 904 universities from 88 countries to defend and promote academic freedom and IA (Matei & Iwinska, 2018). The government on its side may need to plan whether it wants to enhance the IA of all public universities simultaneously or selectively. The country's recent move toward HE differentiation could be of help in this regard. For instance, the government can start by offering more autonomy to one of the categories (for example research universities) and evaluate the impact of this reform before conferring the same level of autonomy to other groups. Similarly, the government may need to decide on whether to increase the IA of universities in all dimensions of autonomy or selectively. This study could serve as an input on this issue. For example, the government could start with the dimensions of autonomy, which are exceptionally low both in absolute and relative terms (for example compared to the European HESs referred to in this study).

Generally, the findings are expected to inspire the leaders of public HEIs to initiate discussions among themselves and all other concerned bodies to reform the regulatory environment in a way that augments the IA of public HEIs.

The study demonstrates that the EUAS methodology is a useful analytical tool. It enables evaluating not only the overall level of HE institutional autonomy but also that of each dimension of autonomy and each indicator within the various dimensions of autonomy. However, there are five remarks that warrant attention in adopting the EUAS to the context of Ethiopia.

First, the relative importance of the value attributed to each indicator, based on Europe's context, needs contextualization.

Second, one can clearly recognize that the indicators under the "academic autonomy" dimension in the EUAS focus on teaching or education. Thus, as the EUA itself admits, the EUAS ignores research and engagement (with community or industry).

Third, the EUAS is meant to aid the promotion of university autonomy. Nonetheless, as Aghion et al. (2010) warn, greater autonomy needs to be accompanied by disciplined competition and a strong system of accountability. In other words, since autonomy could be prone to abuse, a strong accountability framework composed of various mechanisms and tools should accompany adopting the EUAS.

Fourth, as the EUA rightly acknowledges (Pruvot & Estermann, 2017), it is worth noting that the EUAS, as a methodology, does not entertain the diverse and complex situations found in each HE system.

Finally, the EUAS follows a quantitative approach and in this regard, scholars warn of the problem of excessive quantification in assessing IA. Further, scholars argue that any attempt to promote and measure IA should include academic freedom, because universities can optimally achieve their mission when the two are equally protected. Some even argue that the EUAS as a methodology "sacrifices academic freedom altogether on the altar of [IA)" (Beiter et al. 2016, in Matei & Iwinska, 2018, 358). Thus, the EUAS is biased toward the instrumentalist perspective of autonomy, wherein autonomy is seen as a performance enhancer rather than as a right. Cognizant of this, Choi (2019) recommends developing a methodology that views IA both "as an instrument for academic freedom and as a performance enhancer" (p.20).

Generally, however, we believe that the attempt to apply the EUAS to the context of Ethiopia could motivate other (Ethiopian) researchers to examine the EUAS methodology, refine it, and either contextualize it to the country or develop an alternative methodology.

5.2. Limitations

This study has limitations. First, as the name indicates, the EUAS is Eurocentric (and even there it is not sensitive to institutional diversity), is biased toward the instrumentalist perspective of IA, and its indicators do not say much about research and engagement. Second, the study found that Ethiopia's IA is low but did not try to explain much about the underlying cause as to why this is the case. For example, this low autonomy could be attributed to the historical legacies and modes of establishment of public HEIs; the political culture and level of economic development of the country; the degree of compatibility between HE reforms and the regulatory laws, etc. Fourth, the state-of-the-art literature demonstrates that there is a positive relationship between level of autonomy and the performance of HEIs. Thus, analyzing empirically the effect of the current low level of autonomy on the actual performance of Ethiopia's public HEIs would be of interest to policy makers and academia. Fifth, the study heavily depends on regulatory frameworks (laws, policies, etc.), using empirical data from only one public university (MU), even though the country's public HEIs are equally autonomous by law. Finally, the study focused only on public HEIs despite the presence of both public and private providers in the country. Axiomatically, therefore, we recommend future research to look into these issues. Despite the limitations, this study can serve as a springboard for other researchers and as an input for policy makers in relation to IA in general and to the level of IA in Ethiopia in particular.

Notes

1. Ethiopia has recently (January 2020) differentiated its public universities into research universities (eight), applied (fifteen), specialized (three) and comprehensive (twenty-one) (Ethiopian Press Agency, January 4, 2020).
2. For example, the eight indicators of *organizational autonomy* are weighted as follows: *selection procedure for the executive head (14%); selection criteria for the executive head (14%); dismissal of the executive head (12%); term of office of the executive head (9%); inclusion of external members in university governing bodies (12%); selection of external members in university governing bodies (12%); capacity to decide on academic structures (15%); and capacity to create legal entities (12%)* (Pruvot & Estermann, 2017:70).
3. While MoSHE is the main regulatory body of HE, HERQA is in charge of accreditation (so far private HEIs) and external quality audit, while HESC is mandated with developing HE policies and strategies and funding formulas.
4. Based on the score obtained, HE systems are clustered as follows: high (100%-81%); medium high (80%-61%); medium low (60%-41%); and low (40%-0%) (Pruvot & Estermann (2017).
5. The Education and Training Policy adopted in 1994 had been the core policy from which all education strategies and plans were developed and implemented. In 2019, however, Ethiopia adopted a new education policy called Education Development Roadmap (2018-2030) (MoE, 2018b).

References

Academic Freedom and Institutional Autonomy: Commitments Must be Followed by Action (2019). Joint statement by All European Academies, EUA and Science Europe. https://eua.eu/downloads/content/academic%20freedom%20statement%20april%202019.pdf.

Aghion, P., Dewatripont, M., Hoxby, C., Mas-Colell, A., & Sapir, A. (2010). The Governance and Performance of Universities: Evidence from Europe and the US. *Economic Policy*, 25(61), 7-59.

Akalu, G. A. (2014). Higher Education in Ethiopia: Expansion, Quality Assurance and Institutional Autonomy. *Higher Education Quarterly*, 68(4), 394-415.

Asgedom, A., & Hagos, T. (2015). Governance Reforms in Higher Education in Africa: The Case of Autonomy and Accountability in Ethiopian Higher Education. In N. V. Varghese (ed.), *Reforms and Changes in Governance of Higher Education in Africa*. Paris: IIEP.

Asgedom, A., & Hagos, T. (2015). Governance Reforms in Higher Education of Ethiopia : The Case of Autonomy and Accountability. *Ethiopian Journal of Development Research*, 37(1), 1-40.

Berdahl, R. (1990). Academic Freedom, Autonomy and Accountability in British Universities. *Studies in Higher Education*, 15(2), 16-180.

Bergan, S., Egron-Polak, E., Noorda, S., & Pol, P. (2016). Academic Freedom and Institutional Autonomy – What Role in and for the EHEA ? Background document for the thematic session at the meeting of the Bologna Follow-Up Group. Bratislava, December 8 to 9, 2016.

Choi, S. (2019). Identifying Indicators of University Autonomy According to Stakeholders' Interests. *Tertiary Education and Management*, 25(1), 17-29.

CM (Council of Ministers, FDRE). (2002). "Federal Civil Servants Disciplinary and Grievance Procedure Council of Ministers Regulations No. 77/2002."*Negarit Gazeta*, Addis Ababa.

Dobbins, M., & Knill, C. (2014). *Higher Education Governance and Policy Change in Western Europe: International Challenges to Historical Institutions*. England: Palgrave Macmillan.

Estermann, T. (2015). University Autonomy in Europe. *University Education*, 3, 28-32.

Estermann, T., & Pruvot, E. B. (2018). Institutional Autonomy in Higher Education. In Shin, J. C., & Teixeira, P. (eds.), *Encyclopedia of International Higher Education Systems and Institutions* (pp. 1-8). Dordrecht: Springer Science+Business Media.

Estermann, T., & Steinel, M. (2011). University Autonomy in Europe. *Beiträge Zur Hochschulforschung*, 33, 86-91.

EUA (European University Association). (2020). University Autonomy in Europe. https://www.university-autonomy.eu/.

FCSC (Federal Civil Service Commission, FDRE). (2019). New Salary Scale Implementation Directive no. 1/2012. Addis Ababa, Ethiopia.

Fiszbein, A., & Ringold, D. (2012). *Benchmarking the Governance of Tertiary Education Systems*. Washington, DC: World Bank Group.

Gebremeskel, H. H., & Feleke, K. M. (2016). Exploring the Context of Ethiopian Higher Education System Using Clark's Triangle of Coordination. *Tertiary Education and Management*, 22(2), 99-120.

Gebru, D. A. (2013). University Autonomy: The Ethiopian Experience. *International Journal of Educational Reform*, 22(3), 271-288.

Hailu, M. (2018). Models of Higher Education Governance: Rethinking the Ethiopian Experience. *The Ethiopian Journal of Higher Education*, 5(1), 31-56.

HERQA (Higher Education Relevance and Quality Agency). (2019). List of Accredited and Re-accredited Private Higher Education Institutions for 2019/2020 Academic Year (Amharic version). Addis Ababa: unpublished.

HPR (House of Peoples' Representatives, FDRE). (2019). Higher Education Proclamation no. 1152/2019. Addis Ababa: Berhanena Selam Printing Enterprise.

HPR. (2017). Federal Civil Service Proclamation, no. 1064/2017. Addis Ababa: Berhanena Selam Printing Enterprise.

HPR. (2009). Higher Education Proclamation no. 650/2009. Addis Ababa: Berhanena Selam Printing Enterprise.

HPR. (2003). Higher Education Proclamation no. 351/2003. Addis Ababa: Berhanena Selam Printing Enterprise.

IAU (International Association of Universities). (1998). Academic Freedom, University Autonomy and Social Responsibility. IAU Policy Statement. https://iau-aiu.net/IMG/pdf/academic_freedom_policy_statement.pdf.

Marmolejo, F. (2016). What Matters Most for Tertiary Education Systems: A Framework Paper (SABER Working Paper Series Number 11).Washington, DC: World Bank.

Matei, L., & Iwinska, J. (2014). *Autonomy –A Practical Handbook*. Budapest: Central European University, Yehuda Elkana Center for Higher Education.

Matei, L., & Iwinska, J. (2018). Diverging Paths ? Institutional Autonomy and Academic Freedom in the European Higher Education Area. In Curaj, A., et al. (eds.), *European Higher Education Area: The Impact of Past and Future Policies* (pp. 345-368). Cham: Springer.

MoE (Ministry of Education, FDRE). (2018). Academic Staff Recruitment and Development in Public Higher Education Institutions, Directive no. 03/2010. (Amharic version). Addis Ababa.

MoE. (2018b). *Ethiopian Education Development Roadmap: An integrated Executive Summary (2018-2030)*. Addis Ababa: Unpublished.

MoE. (2017). Higher Education Indicative Plan for 2017/18 Academic Year (Amharic version). Addis Ababa, unpublished.

MoE. (2015). *Education Sector Development Programme V (ESDP-V) (2015/16 – 2019/20)*. Program Action Plan. Addis Ababa: MoE.

MoE, F. (2017). *Education Statistics Annual Abstract* (2016/17). Addis Ababa: MoE, Education Management Information System (EMIS) and ICT Directorate.

MoFEC (Ministry of Finance and Economic Cooperation, FDRE). (2018). Circular letter (no. 1/1/8) Prohibiting Higher Education Institutions from Providing Support and Sponsorship to Outsiders (Amharic version). Addis Ababa.

Moses, I. (2007). Institutional Autonomy Revisited: Autonomy Justified and Accounted. *Higher Education Policy*, 20(3), 261-274.

MoSHE (Ministry of Science and Higher Education, FDRE). (2019) Guideline for Academic Publishing and Promotion (under discussion). Addis Ababa: unpublished.

MoSHE. (2019b). Higher Education Indicative Plan, 2019/20. Addis Ababa: unpublished.

MoSHE. (2018). Directive on Selection and Appointment of Leaders and Managers in Public Higher Education Institutions: Directive 002/2018. Addis Ababa.

NPC (National Planning Commission, FDRE). (2016). Growth and Transformation Plan-II (2015/16-2019/20) Volume I : Main Text. Addis Ababa: NPC.

Pruvot, E. B., & Estermann, T. (2017). *University Autonomy in Europe – III: The Scorecard 2017*. Brussels: European University Association.

Pruvot, E. B., & Estermann, T. (2018). University Governance : Autonomy, Structures and Inclusiveness. In Curaj A., Deca L., Pricopie R. (eds) European Higher Education Area: The Impact of Past and Future Policies (pp. 619-638). Springer, Cham.

Tamrat, W. (2012). University Governance in Ethiopia: Trends, Challenges and Options. *The Teacher*, 5(10), 1-12.

Tamrat, W. & Teferra, D. (2018). Government-University Relations–A Troubled Matrimony. *University World News*, October 12. https://www.universityworldnews.com/post.php?story=20181009144147891.

Varghese, N. V., & Martin, M. (2013). *Governance Reforms and University Autonomy in Asia. IIEP Research Papers*. Paris: International Institute for Educational Planning.

Woldegiyorgis, A. A. (2014). Ethiopia. In Pausits, A., Zheng, G., & Abebe, R. (eds.), *New Public Management in Higher Education-International Overview and Analysis* (pp. 84-100). Krems: Edition Danube University Krems.

Appendix 1: Level of (university) institutional autonomy in Europe (unweighted score)

	Dimensions of autonomy					Cluster (by level)			
Countries	Organizational (%)	Financial (%)	Staffing (%)	Academic (%)	Total score (%)	High (100%-81%)	Medium high (80%-61%)	Medium low (60%-41%)	Low (40%-0%)
Austria	77	44	72	72	66.25		✓		
Belgium - Flanders	70	68	75	34	46.25			✓	
Belgium - Wallonia	94	44	43	31	53			✓	
Croatia	62	65	35	49	52.75			✓	
Denmark	94	53	86	75	77		✓		
Estonia	82	69	100	95	86.5	✓			
Finland	91	51	92	88	80.5		✓		
France	56	33	42	39	42.5			✓	
Hungary	60	44	49	52	51.25			✓	
Germany (Branden-burg)	55	31	57	83	56.5		✓		
Germany (Hessen (y)	75	24	62	87	62		✓		

	Dimensions of autonomy					Cluster (by level)			
Countries	Organizational (%)	Financial (%)	Staffing (%)	Academic (%)	Total score (%)	High (100%-81%)	Medium high (80%-61%)	Medium low (60%-41%)	Low (40%-0%)
Germany (North Rhine-Westphalia)	69	31	62	87	62.25		✓		
Iceland	45	55	67	77	61		✓		
Ireland	71	71	42	92	69		✓		
Italy	59	62	42	55	54.5			✓	
Latvia	56	93	89	50	72		✓		
Lithuania	82	73	89	44	72		✓		
Luxembourg	35	93	95	92	78.75		✓		
The Netherlands	76	78	72	57	70.75		✓		
Norway	72	29	62	87	62.5		✓		
Poland	64	47	84	78	68.25		✓		
Portugal	74	75	62	52	65.75		✓		
Slovakia	40	64	59	55	54.5			✓	
Slovenia	68	55	42	41	51.4			✓	
Spain	60	40	47	58	51.25			✓	
Serbia	53	60	58	44	53.75			✓	
Sweden	62	44	96	72	68.5		✓		
Switzerland	56	62	95	75	72		✓		
United Kingdom	100	90	96	92	94.5	✓			

Source: European University Association. Online: https://www.university-autonomy.eu/

21
Outcomes and Challenges of the 1994 Ethiopian Education and Training Policy Reform

Challa Amdissa Jiru

Box 1: Key points of this chapter

- ✓ The 1994 education policy reform was part of the political, economic, and social reforms that took place in Ethiopia in 1991.
- ✓ The goals of the 1994 education policy were to correct the acute shortage and inequitable access, inefficiency, low quality, low relevance, and undemocratic nature of Ethiopian education system.
- ✓ This policy was implemented for about twenty-five years and achieved mixed results.
- ✓ Any future education program should focus on improving the quality and sustaining the current pace of expansion in access to education.

Box 2: Reading this chapter will give you insights in

- ✓ The driving forces for the formulation of 1994 Education Policy of Ethiopia;
- ✓ The major changes introduced by the 1994 education and training policy reform;
- ✓ The achievements in access, equity, efficiency, quality, relevance, and democratization goals of the education system; and
- ✓ The challenges ahead.

Box 3: Abbreviations

EPRDF = Ethiopian Peoples' Revolutionary Democratic Front
ESDP = Education Sector Development Programs
GER = Gross Enrolment Rate
NIR = Net Intake Ratio

1. Introduction :Political Context of the 1994 Education Policy and the Problem Statement

The 1994 Education Policy of Ethiopia was part of the systemic changes in political, economic, and social order in Ethiopia following the regime change in 1991 (Demeke, 2011). Therefore, to understand the political environment within which the education policy was formulated, it is essential to highlight the country's macroeconomic policy and the political and institutional reforms of the 1990s. May 1991 is a turning point in Ethiopian history, as it marked the end of the two decades of internal war and civil strife that led to the secession of Eritrea. The Ethiopian Peoples' Revolutionary Democratic Front (EPRDF) took control of state power in May 1991 and formed the Transitional Government in July of the same year. Upon seizing control, the EPRDF immediately started radically restructuring the political system of the country to establish a country with a new order that differs significantly from its predecessors.

The political reform of the 1990s transformed the old centralized unitary state system into a federal state arrangement, while the economic reform put into effect privatization, deregulation, denationalization, and other liberalization measures. Besides the liberalization of the economy and regionalization of the state structure, new social sector polices such as women, population, education, health, and disaster prevention and preparedness were formulated (Tewodaj, Gezahegn, & Zelekawork, 2008). Among these social policies, the subject of this chapter is the 1994 Education and Training Policy of Ethiopia. This policy remained in place until the endorsement of a new education road map in 2019.

Criticisms of the policy by different stakeholders were often heard ever since its commencement in 1994. For example, at the HR Development summit, held at the United Nations Conference center at Addis Ababa from August 30 to 31, 2017, employers' representatives noted that they were facing challenges due to the incapability of the education system to produce candidates with employable skills. According to views reflected at the summit, the graduates of the Ethiopian education institutions do not have reliable competence that the employers need; as a result, employers face challenges in finding skillful candidates in the local labor market to fill their job vacancies. Since poor labor productivity will make the country uncompetitive in attracting foreign investments, the participants of this summit warned the government to rethink its policy (HRD Africa, 2017).

In addition to lack of competence, the current generation of graduates is also criticized for lacking acceptable moral and ethical behaviors. For instance, the prime minister of Ethiopia, Abiy Ahmed, claimed at a meeting in Assosa that the Ethiopian education system is unable to produce graduates who could serve the interest of their family and the interest of their country, particularly from the moral and ethical perspective. Similar to this view (Demeke, 2011) indicates that there are groups who conceive of Ethiopians who have passed through the school system as disrespectful to their society and institutions.

The professionals in the education sector have also been known to criticize the appropriateness of the existing education policy of Ethiopia. This group shares the concern over the deterioration of education quality in Ethiopia and links the problem among other factors with the 1994 reform policy's reduction of four-year degree programs to three-years. Meanwhile, students and parents blame the education policy of the country for poor prospects injob opportunities for school graduates.

Thus, the appropriateness of the Ethiopian educational policy has been challenged by many stakeholders from different perspectives. It is true that the policy has many shortcomings; nevertheless, most of the criticisms of the education system of Ethiopia were not research based. The few available studies are incomplete in balancing both the achievements and the failures of the policy across all aspects of the policy goals. In addition to the scarcity of research evidence, the neutrality of the critics is also questionable as most of them are ideologically driven. The author of this chapter argues that the criticism of education policy has some basis but is mostly not supported by research evidence and not balanced in revealing both the success and failures of the policy. Policy analysis requires a good understanding of policy intentions, adequate analysis of policy environments, and assessment of the policy outcomes in relation to desired goals. In this regard, research conducted so far on the 1994 education and training policy of Ethiopia is insufficient to reveal the lessons to be taken from the past experience.

This study is motivated by such critical limitations in research on education policy. The objective here is to evaluate the effectiveness of the 1994 education policy of Ethiopia in terms of its achievement in access, equity, efficiency, democratization, relevance, and quality goals. More specifically, the study tries to address the following research questions:

1. What were the driving forces for the formulation of 1994 Education Policy of Ethiopia?
2. What major changes were introduced by the implementation of the 1994 education policy reform?
3. How well has Ethiopia achieved the education goals established by 1994 education policy and what are the challenges ahead?

Analysis of these questions is important if we are to derive lessons from the success and failure of the 1994 education policy and to provide policy inputs for future initiatives. Accordingly, by shedding lights on the policy aspect of the Ethiopian education system, this chapter identifies the achievements and failures of the policy and suggests ideas that will help to overcome the challenges faced by the country's education system. Furthermore, this research shows avenues for future research on education policy of Ethiopia. Guided by these questions, the remaining part of this chapter presents consecutively data sources and methodology, literature, discussions, and conclusions.

2. Data Sources and Methods of Data Analysis

A mixed research approach was chosen to take advantage of combining quantitative and qualitative techniques of analysis and to make use of data of different forms. Different secondary sources, which include the official data of government, the World Bank database, government education sector plans and reports and statistical abstracts, were used to analyze policy driving forces, policy goals, policy outcomes and new challenges. The problems of the Ethiopian education system prior to 1994 and the policies pursued by the current government to solve them were analyzed based on a review of government policy statements and other publications of Ministry of Education. Different reform plans and implementation reports were reviewed to determine the changes introduced in the education system by the government, so as to identify the major departure of the 1994 policy from the past. The effectiveness of the education policy was assessed by comparing policy goals and policy achievements. Finally, new challenges not covered by the existing policy are explored based on the views of experts as shown in different statistics, research reports, and media. In order to ensure the reliability and validity of the research, the study used data from official sources, after careful inspection of their relevance to the topic. Because of the nature of the data at hand, the descriptive method of analysis was chosen.

The next part of the chapter presents performance indicators in education policy analysis, participation in the 1994 education policy formulation process, the driving force for policy change, and major changes in the 1994 education policy of Ethiopia. It then analyzes the achievements of education policy in terms of access, equity, efficiency, relevance, and quality and democratization. Finally, the discussion part highlights the challenges not properly addressed by the 1994 Education and Training Policy of Ethiopia.

3. Indicators of Performances in Education Policy Analysis

As education is a complex social undertaking, analysis of education policy is also complex; however, it is worth doing as education is also a determinant of development. Education has become the most powerful tool in providing solutions to various challenges (Semela, 2011) and it plays a key role in the globalized world. The many dimensions of social and economic objectives that education policies aim to achieve are complex to understand, nevertheless, conducting study on education policy is a necessary task.

One of the important indicators of education policy is its attention to educational inputs. The better-endowed schools tend to produce better results, as measured by such indicators as student achievement and schooling careers. As teachers typically represent the single most important component of educational inputs, managing the resources they embody warrants especially close attention (Mingat, Tan, & Sosale, 2003). Achievement on the basis of input measurement focuses on education expenditures, for example on the expenditure on primary education as (a) percentage of GNP and (b) as per pupil, or as a percentage of GNP per capita and as a percentage of total public expenditure on education (Norelius & Mendes, 2003).

Another element of education policy is the issue of equity and access that affirms the need to ensure equitable access and participation of all groups, particularly of vulnerable and disadvantaged children, as well as adults. Equity may be assessed from the perspective of gender, geography/region, and place of residence (urban/rural) (Mingat, Tan, & Sosale, 2003). Equity in education attracts interest in public policy for several reasons. In most countries the government subsidizes education, so access to education determines who benefits from the subsidies. Because spending on education represents a substantial share of government budgets in both industrial and developing countries, the education system effectively is a major conduit for the distribution of public subsidies. Furthermore, education affects people's life chances as adults in terms of their earning capability as well as social mobility. Equity in educational opportunity therefore influences the future distribution of income, wealth, and status in society. Beyond its economic significance, education is viewed widely as a good in itself, and indeed a basic human right with regard to the lower levels of education. For this reason too, equity in education is often a focus of public policy debate.

With regard to methods for analyzing access and equity in education, several approaches are suggested by the vast literature on the subject (Norelius & Mendes, 2003). This chapter uses comparison of differences in access to a specific level or type of education across population groups, using such indicators as relative rates of entry, transition, and completion. This approach of equity analysis assumes that education is a good in itself without elaborating on the specific nature or value of the benefits.

Besides inputs and equity, there are many measurements of achievements in education policy analysis (Norelius & Mendes, 2003). Achievement in access to education can be measured along indicators such as: gross enrolment in early childhood development programs, as a percentage of the official age group concerned, if any, otherwise in the age group three to five; percentage of new entrants to primary grade 1 who have attended some form of organized early childhood development program; apparent (gross) intake rate (new entrants in primary grade 1 as a percentage of the population of official entry age); net intake rate (new entrants to primary grade 1 who are of the official primary school entrance age as a percentage of the corresponding population); gross enrolment ratio; and net enrolment ratio.

When it comes to assessing quality aspects, indicators like percentage of primary school teachers having the required academic qualifications; percentage of primary school teachers certified to teach according to national standards; and the pupil-teacher ratio are widely used.

Widely used indicators of achievement in relation to efficiency are the repetition rate; the survival rate to grade 5; the coefficient of efficiency; and percentage of pupils having reached at least grade 4 of primary schooling who have mastered a set of nationally defined basic learning competencies. Literacy rate of fifteen to twenty-four-year-olds; adult literacy rate; and the Gender Parity Index can also be used as indicators of education achievement (Norelius & Mendes, 2003).

Indicators are related to goals and targets (Norelius & Mendes, 2003). For instance, some targets of the UN millennium development goals and associated indicators are presented in the table below:

Table 1: Millennium development goals and targets

Goals	Targets	Indicators
Achieve universal primary education	Ensure that, by 2015, children everywhere, boys and girls alike, will be able to complete a full course of primary schooling	- Net enrollment ratio in primary education - Proportion of pupils starting grade 1 who reach grade 5 - Literacy rate of 15- to 24-year-olds

Goals	Targets	Indicators
Promote gender equality and empower women	Eliminate gender disparity in primary and secondary education preferably by 2005 and in all levels of education no later than 2015	- Ratio of girls to boys in primary, secondary, and tertiary education - Ratio of literate females to males among 15- to 24-year-olds - Share of women in wage employment in the nonagricultural sector. - Proportion of seats held by women in national parliament.

One of the seventeen goals of the 2030 Agenda for Sustainable Development is to ensure inclusive and equitable quality education and promote lifelong learning opportunities for all. The indicators of this goal among others are to ensure access to free, equitable, and quality primary and secondary education; quality early childhood development, care and preprimary education; affordable and quality technical, vocational, and tertiary education; increase the number of youth and adults who have relevant skills, including technical and vocational skills, for employment, decent jobs, and entrepreneurship. Furthermore, the global actors agreed by 2030 to eliminate gender disparities; achieve literacy and numeracy; and substantially increase the supply of qualified teachers.

The Education and Training Policy of 1994 has been the inspiration for five medium-term Education Sector Development Programs (ESDP). Each ESDP has its own goals and specific targets. For instance ESDP I aimed at increasing access, improving quality, increasing effectiveness, achieving equity, and expanding finance at all levels of education in Ethiopia (Martin, Riitta, & Tuomas, 2000). The ESDP V is the fifth medium-term plan, which serves as the central strategy document for educational development in Ethiopia from 2015/16 to 2019/20. Its major goals are to provide equal opportunities and participation for all; deliver quality education that meets diverse learning needs, develop competent citizens; promote effective leadership, management, and governance at all levels; and to assist citizens to share common values and experiences and to embrace diversity.

4. Participations in the Process of Framing the 1994 Education Policy

The process of policy formulation requires consultations with the stakeholders. Policymakers in education are responsible for developing a vision and strategy for educational development and mobilizing support and cooperation for implementing the former from a wide range of stakeholders. The key stakeholders of the education sector may include ministers in other sectors, nongovernment organizations that provide resources, teachers, and school administrators; students and their families who are the immediate beneficiaries of the services provided; and employers and the public at large. Thus, this section overviews the participation of these stakeholders in the 1994 Education and Training Policy formulation process.

A taskforce composed of eleven members from various institutions was formed under the coordination of the prime minister's office to study key educational issues and come up with policy recommendations. The taskforce studied six policy issues: teacher training, teaching methods, professional development, and working conditions; educational measurement and evaluation; language in education; educational organization, management and finance; and educational materials and support inputs (Martin, Riitta, & Tuomas, 2000). In order to assess the above issues a technical committee composed of six study teams from various ministries, research organizations, the teachers' association, and institutions of higher learning was formed. All in all, forty national organizations and three hundred experts participated in the study. Moreover, public consultation on the draft policy document was conducted at the central, regional, zonal, Woreda, and school levels throughout the country. For instance, schools in Addis Ababa were closed for a day to discuss the Education and Training Policy (Martin, Riitta, & Tuomas, 2000).

In the development of the different educational policy documents, the MoE and the Social and Administration Sub-Sector of the Office of the Prime Minister were key players. Additionally, the regional education bureaus, higher education institutions, and international organizations such as Sida, UNDP, UNESCO, etc. took part in the policy development process (Martin, Riitta, & Tuomas, 2000).

Despite the attempt to involve these stakeholders, commentators describe the government as having a make-or-break role while other stakeholders had a symbolic role in the policy formulation process. As described by Alemu & Tekleselassie (2006), though discussions were held with stakeholders, no input provided by teachers was incorporated in the final policy. Worse, people who reflected different views on the policy proposal were threatened by the government. Alemu & Tekleselassie (2006) further found that the worst outcome of participation in consultations was the split of the Ethiopian Teachers' Union into two opposing factions (one pro-EPRDF/government and the other independent). The level of the government's involvement in the Ethiopian higher education system is very high (Yohannes, 2016). The amount of financial contributions affects the influence of various donor groups. Additionally, in countries (such as Ethiopia) following macroeconomic structural adjustment programs, general policy conditionality agreed on between the government and the World Bank/IMF is significant in framing educational policy (Martin, Riitta, & Tuomas, 2000).

5. The Driving Forces for Change and the 1994 Education Policy Goals

As the twentieth century drew to a close, Ethiopia found itself with an education system that was regimented in its management, conservative in its intellectual orientation, limited in its autonomy, short of experienced doctorates among academic staff, concerned about declining educational quality, weak in its research output, and poorly connected with the intellectual currents of the international higher education community (Saint, 2004). The reform pressures that had begun to build in the 1960s were suppressed by the Dergue in the 1970s and1980s (Saint, 2004). The seizure of state power by EPRDF in 1991returned the reform of the education system to the fore of the government's concerns.

At the time when the education and training policy of Ethiopia was framed, the Ethiopian government was embarking on establishing a new order to transform the command economy of the military regime into a market economy. The new policy direction in the education sector was motivated by the need to destroy the vestiges of the military regime and replace it with the new order. For example, the policy study sponsored by Ministry of Education confirms that it was necessary to replace the educational system that served the old discarded order with a new one (Ministry of Education, 2002). Similarly, Teshome (2003) also notes that Ethiopia engaged in reform to realign its higher education system in more direct support of its national strategy for economic growth and poverty reduction.

As shown in (Ministry of Education, 2002), the government justified a reform and a new policy direction because of the many problems of the previous education system. EPRDF held the belief that the past regime never had a clear policy by which education and training would be guided and evaluated(Ministry of Education, 2002). EPRDF questioned the objective of education under the previous regime, which aimed to produce trained manpower for the emergent government bureaucracy. It also denounced the ambition of the students, which was securing government employment.

It should be noted that, at a time where the country depended on expatriates who were working at various levels in public offices and schools, seeking to produce manpower for the government bureaucracy and replacing expatriates with Ethiopian nationals should not be criticized as a mistaken objective. Similarly, in the absence of a private sector that would have provided employment opportunities for those who left schools without capital and without necessary entrepreneurial background, students should not be expected to aspire to anything other than securing employment in the public sector. Devising a policy reform simply to avoid the heritage of the past regime is not convincing.

The dismantling of the institutional systems of the Dergue regime was however not the only motive of the EPRDF government in formulating the new education and training policy for Ethiopia. A study by the Ministry of Education (2002) identifies the long-standing problems associated with the Ethiopian education system, which were related to limited and inequitable access, lack of quality and relevance, and continuous decline in quality and standards. These problems are further discussed in detail.

a) Limited Access: **While** many African countries that are generally considered to be poor had 60 to70 percent of their school-age children enrolled in elementary schools, only 20 percent of school-age children had the opportunity to attend first- to sixth-grade education in Ethiopia. As (Ministry of Education, 2002) shows, in 1993 only 277 high schools, 2 universities, 5 junior colleges, and 16 vocational and technical schools were found in the country. Similarly, there were only about thirteen teacher training centers and sixteen technical and vocational schools, with a very limited enrollment capacity that had never exceeded 2,500 per year. Towards the end of the Dergue period, enrollment was even declining, which is thought to be attributed to the prolonged effects of war and instability. Table 2 depicts vividly the decreasing trend recorded between 1988/89 and 1992/93, particularly at the primary level (Martin, Riitta, & Tuomas, 2000).

Table 2: Gross enrollment ratio at primary (1-6) level (1985/86 - 1993/94)

Year	Gross Enrolment Ratio	Year	Gross Enrolment Ratio
1985/86	37.4	1990/91	32.7
1986/87	40.8	1991/92	26.5
1987/88	41.9	1992/93	23.1
1988/89	40.3	1993/94	27.5
1989/90	36.5		

b) Inequitable Distribution of School Services: The beneficiaries of the limited educational opportunities were the children of urban dwellers and the rich. The tuition-free primary, secondary, and higher education created an unfair benefit, whereby the poor and the rural population was forced to contribute to the construction of educational facilities to which their own children had no access. This inequity had also created educational opportunity gaps between regions, residents of urban and rural areas, and between genders as well (Ministry of Education, 2002).

c) Problem of Efficiency: In the old system, according to (Ministry of Education, 2002), the high repetition rate was considered as an indication of the educational system's academic rigor and excellence. A high rate of dropouts and repeaters came to be considered an indicator of the inefficiency of the educational system.

d) Lack of Quality and Relevance: The other driving forces for the formulation of the 1994 policy were the lack of focus on mathematics, science, and engineering; insufficient vocational education both at the high school and college levels; and a poor supply of educational inputs, such as poor laboratory facilities, poor library service, unmotivated teachers, a shortage of books, and limited opportunity to involve in practical learning. These constraints in educational inputs together with lack of focus on the "more important fields of study," according to the government, had reduced the quality and relevance of education (Ministry of Education, 2002). Low employability of the graduates was also taken as an attribute of the poor quality of the pre-1994 education system of Ethiopia. The government also considered the twelve years of education necessary to leave high school and four years of university education as irrelevant and wasteful.

e)Problem of School Language: In Ethiopia before 1991, the principle that every child should, at least in primary school, learn in the child's native language was totally ignored. In addition to being a violation of the right to language, every aspect of the contents of the old education system glorified the attributes, contributions, customs, culture, and history of one group and reinforced its domination over the others(Ministry of Education, 2002).

Together with ideological change, the above problems drove education policy revisions in Ethiopia in 1994. When critically evaluated, the meager access to education was well shown by comparing the enrollment with other African countries, but the study by the Ministry of Education did not clearly indicate the repetition rate, the dropout rate, and the level of equity in education. The low education quality and relevance was indicated by a lack of focus on mathematics, science, and engineering, as well as by insufficient vocational education and inadequacy of inputs. Hence progress can be measured by the proportion of students enrolled in science and in vocational fields, and improvements in educational inputs. Moreover, since the government associates a low education quality with the high unemployment of school alumni, change in employment opportunity is another indicator for measuring the success of the 1994 education and training policy.

Motivated by radically changing the policies of the preceding regime and the need to correct the problem of low access, high dropout and repetition, inequitable access, undemocratic content, and poor quality and relevance, the government of Ethiopia launched an education and training policy and began its implementation in 1994. The 1994 Education and Training Policy of Ethiopia set educational goals as describe below:

- Expanding Educational Opportunity and Ensuring Its Equity: The government aspired to create access of education to all nations and nationalities, urban and rural residents, the poor and the rich, male and female. It intended to ensure equity in order to reduce the gaps that existed since the introduction of modern education in Ethiopia.
- Democratization of the Administration and Content of Education: The 1994 policy aspires to foster the use of mother-tongue languages in order to reduce the difficulty of students learning in the lower primary schools. The decentralized system of government is considered helpful to materialize the use of different languages as medium of instruction in different regions and to increase community participation in education.
- Provision of Quality and Relevant Educational Services: Government-revised curricula were intended to make the education relevant to the needs of society and to make the curriculum career-oriented. The policy also established a quality and standards authority to ensure schools and colleges would provide quality education.
- Ensuring Efficiency: The government intended to increase the completion rate by keeping repetition and dropout rates at lower levels than they had been under the previous regime.

6. Major Changes Introduced by the 1994 Education Policy of Ethiopia

The 1994 policy redefined primary education as grades 1– 8 and eliminated standardized testing prior to grade 8. It placed new emphasis on the expansion of technical and vocational education and training and the use of mother tongue languages for primary instruction (Tewodaj, Gezahegn, & Zelekawork, 2008).

Other initiatives included harmonizing curricula for all of the undergraduate programs, adopting a modular approach for course delivery so as to enhance active learning, instituting quality assurance offices at each university, and trying to equip libraries and laboratories. Bachelor degree courses were reduced from four to three years in length, with much of the former "freshman" year subject matter being transferred to the secondary school level (Yohannes, 2016).

Graduate program enrollments are rising rapidly in an effort to boost the supply of academic staff for the expanding system. All existing diploma programs (50 percent of public enrollments in 2003) were transferred to technical colleges to make universities concentrate on the bachelor level and above. A revision of university curricula has added courses like civics, ethics, communication skills, and entrepreneurship, among others. Anew oversight agency was mandated to monitor both the quality and the relevance of academic programs. To shore up quality in the classroom, national and local pedagogical resource centers were set up to encourage instructional innovation and to assist less experienced lecturers (Saint, 2004).

Education expenditure also increased as a proportion of the overall government budget, from 9.5 percent to 16.8 per cent. Such increases still fall short of reaching the general range of 20 percent to 25 percent seen in most developing countries (Saint, 2004), suggesting the need for further increasing the financing efforts. Expenditure per student was very low and seemed likely to be pushed lower by rapid expansion (Saint, 2004).To reduce the burden on the government budget as a result of expanding the education sector at all levels, the government introduced user charges through a cost sharing program in September 2003.

The proclamation of 2003 (No.351/2003) awards some autonomy to universities. Autonomy is granted in the administration of personnel, finances, internal organization, and in establishing linkages with internal and international organizations, etc. All nonacademic staff is classified as civil servants managed by the national civil service system (Saint, 2004). Strategic planning, income diversification, and information and communications technology development are being encouraged to meet the fiscal, space, and instructional requirements of the on-going expansion (Saint, 2004). The Higher Education Proclamation No.650/2009 also grants universities autonomy to administer and govern their core activities. According to this proclamation, universities are free to set up their organizational structures and to introduce reform programs and activities that support academic and research excellence (Yohannes, 2016).

However, in the view of some critics, persistent violations of academic freedom make effective institutional autonomy a difficult proposition. The study by Saint (2004) uncovers that the government has sought to inject political criteria into the academic staff evaluation process and directly appoint universities' presidents and vice presidents. The government ordered all public higher education institutions to implement BPR, BSC, and other business model management techniques as part of the nationwide reform process since 2008 (Kahsay, 2012).

7. The Performance of Education Policy

7.1. Performance in Expansion of Access

As discussed in the previous section, one of the critical problems of the education system during the formulation of the 1994 education policy was very low coverage, even in comparison with achievements in other poor countries. To reverse this situation, the education policy of the EPRDF-led government has aimed to improve access to education. In line with this policy goal, the government made tremendous efforts to expand educational opportunity at all levels and has achieved remarkable success. The government has implemented five consecutive education sector development plans since it began implementation of the 1994 education and training policy.

This research relies on the ESDP IV, because the data of ESDP V is expected to be compiled only after the end of the planning period. At the end of ESDP IV in 2014, the Gross Enrollment Rate (GER) for preprimary education reach 34 percent, of which around a quarter is in three-year kindergarten and the remainder one-year O-Class and Child-to-Child instruction (Ministry of Education, 2015).

In the 1971 to 1972 education review, the year 2000 was set as the year when Ethiopia would extend universal primary education to all its citizens (Demeke, 2011). However, Ethiopia was far from achieving universal primary education in 1994 when the education policy was put to effect. The EPRDF government has planned to achieve universal primary education in line with the "Education for All" goals. By the end of ESDP IV, the number of primary schools had risen from 11,000 to 32,048 and student enrollment at this level had grown from less than 3 million to over 18 million. In 2015, the supply of schools allows for full intake of students into Grade 1 when they reach the age of seven years. As of 2013/14, the Net Intake Ratio (NIR) was 106 percent, compared to the target of 100 percent.

Rates of more than 100 percent are technically impossible, but happened in the measure of NIR. Such an irregular measure arises due to imprecise population figures and challenges in measurement of student age at the point of entry due to lack of uniform birth registration. Such a situation makes the precision of educational performance measure less reliable. GER ratios indicate the capacity of each level of the education system, but a high ratio may reflect a substantial number of overage children enrolled in each grade because of repetition or late entry rather than a successful education system. Table 3 depicts the comparison of primary school enrollment.

Table 3: Primary school enrollment, (% gross)

Countries	1990	2000	2010	2011	2012	2013	2014	2015
Ethiopia	35.3	54.7	91.7	94.3	94.3		99.3	101.0
Sub-Saharan Africa	72.6	82.1	97.4	98.8	99.6	99.8	99.4	98.0
Low income	62.2	75.4	102.8	103.2	104.1	103.4	103.6	102.4
High income	102.4	100.8	101.9	101.6	101.7	102.2	101.9	102.1
World	99.7	98.8	103.2	103.5	104.2	104.0	102.8	102.5

Source: World Development Indicators, 2019

Comparison of educational access in Ethiopia with other countries is one way of measuring educational achievement. Table 3 compares performance of Ethiopia in primary school enrollment with Sub-Saharan Africa, with low income countries, and with the world. As depicted in the table, in 1990 Ethiopia performed the lowest of all groups being presented for comparison. After twenty-five years of expansion of education service, Ethiopia had able to exceed the average primary school enrollment of Sub-Saharan African countries.

Secondary school enrolment has also expanded rapidly, roughly increasing five-fold, from an enrolled population of 371,000 in 1994/95 to almost 2 million in 2013/14. However, the achievement in secondary school enrollment was lower than the achievement in primary school, due to low primary completion (flow through the system). The GER in Grades 9–10 has changed from 39.1 percent to 39.3 percent, against a target of 62 percent. Other factors that influence low achievement in secondary education were poverty, lack of transport, the need to work (time and economic restrictions), early marriage, gender biases, lack of accommodation near schools (financial, cultural and social), and disability (Ministry of Education, 2015).

Still, the government has demonstrated a continued commitment to expanding equitable access to higher education. As a result, the number of public higher education institutions has increased to thirty-six at the end of ESDP IV (and now reached forty-five), distributed across all regions of the country. Private higher education institutions have also expanded, reaching ninety-eight institutions in total, accommodating around 15 percent of all student enrollment by the end of the ESDP IV period (Ministry of Education, 2015). This extra capacity has allowed rapid increases in intake. Undergraduate enrollment (government and private) rose from 447,693 in 2010/11 to 593,571 in 2013/14. Of total enrollment, 57 percent of students now participate in regular undergraduate classes and 43 percent in a combination of distance, summer, and extension courses. Likewise, total masters' enrolment in public higher education institutions increased from 7,211 in 2007/08 to 27,643 in 2013/14. Recently private institutions began enrolling postgraduate students and in 2015 they accommodated 3,000 master's students.

7.2. Performance of Education Policy in Ensuring Efficiency and Equity

Despite the dramatic achievement in policy goals pertaining to access to education, the Ethiopian education policy did not achieve equivalent success in efficiency and equity goals. Grade 8 completion rate was only 47 percent in 2015.The overall GER and NER in the second cycle stand at 64 percent(63 percent for girls and 65 percent for boys) and 50 percent (50 percent for girls and 49 percent for boys) respectively in 2013/14. These are against targets of 100 percent and 80 percent, respectively. As a result of inefficiency in primary school education, expansion of secondary school was constrained to remain below the planned target. For both boys and girls, the target set in ESDP IV for dropout was 1 percent in all primary grades and the target set for repetition was 1 percent in all primary grades. But, as ESDP V begins, repetition rates persist at around 8 percent and dropout remains at 22 percent in grade 1 and 11 percent thereafter. Both repetition and dropout rates are approximately the same for girls and boys.

Ensuring equity goal in terms of area of residence (between urban and rural), region, and gender remains unattained. Access to secondary schools is uneven, with supply favoring urban areas. Enrollment rates vary from less than 10 percent in Afar to more than 100 percent in Addis Ababa (Ministry of Education, 2015).

7.3. Performance of Education Policy in Ensuring Quality and Relevance Goals

The 1994 Education and Training policy outcome was envisioned as the improvement of education relevance and quality in terms of improving educational inputs, the achievement of 70 percent of students joining the science and vocational field, and the increase in job opportunities for the school and university graduates. This section presents the data and evidence of education quality in higher education and in general education, while the next section will discuss job opportunities.

Quality in Higher Education

The effort to improve education quality by increasing educational inputs has been challenged by the rapid expansion of higher education institutions. Arega (2016) argues the rapid expansion in the number of higher education institutions and student population, with inadequate human and investment capital, negatively affected education quality of in Ethiopia. This view was shared by the World Bank (2005), which warned that rapid enrollment expansion in Ethiopia is inevitably bringing progressively less qualified student into the system. A similar view was reflected by Negash (2006), who stated that the most fundamental cause for the decline of education is the uncontrolled expansion of the sector in relation to available material resources and job opportunities.

According to Arega (2016), the poor and declining quality of education is likely not a misperception by the public or the media; rather it is a real phenomenon occurring in the education system of Ethiopia. He strongly argued that rapid expansion of schools for the sake of opening access to education despite inadequate infrastructure and resources has negatively affected the quality of education in Ethiopia. Arega (2016) calls for action, as he believed that the quality of education should be a real concern both for the institutions involved and for the nation at large.

Contrary to the objective of the education policy, the poor quality in higher education is still caused by a low inputs system. Arega (2016) identified some of inputs-related shortcomings as follows:

(a) Serious academic staff shortages with quality implications, such as huge teaching loads, eventually leading to the discontinuation of tutorials (The teacher-regular student ratio was 1:16 in 2014 [when students of regular and non-regular classes are considered, the ratio rises to 1:23]). This is against the international standards of a 1:19 ratio and without consideration of excessive moonlighting.

(b) Employment of unqualified personnel. Given the target of 0:70:30 (Bachelor: Master's: Doctorate degree holders, respectively), so far only a ratio of 27:58:15 has been achieved.

Bolton and Foster (2014) observe quality constraints due to poor infrastructure. In their assessment, universities still report insufficient supplies of text and reference books, laboratory and workshop equipment, and access to information and communications technology facilities. The country has suffered from regular rolling blackouts, and few universities have generators to keep technical infrastructure operational during power cuts. The construction of classroom space, expansion of library collections, addition of computer labs, and the development of electronic networks lag behind enrollment expansion (Bolton & Foste, 2014).

Many students have joined higher education institutions with results below the 50 percent threshold in the higher education entrance examinations. Students' behaviors and attributes, such as poor communication skills, resistance to active learning, and absenteeism, were seen as major challenges by internal leadership. Another serious challenge was associated with negative behavior and attributes of instructors, such as low levels of academic qualification, lack of dedication, excessive moonlighting, and lack of pedagogical skills (Arega, 2016).

Financial support for research is low. In 2011/12, the research allocation of all universities accounted for only 1 percent of their total budget. In addition, there are limited numbers of personnel available to conduct high quality research and higher education research is conducted predominantly by postgraduate students.

The government has achieved its goal of increasing the ratio of students studying in the science fields but has been unable to provide resources to achieve quality education. Apart from input aspects, the competence of graduates is also an indicator of education quality. Measuring quality of education in this aspect, Arega (2016) argues there is stakeholders dissatisfaction with the quality of graduates, which can be explained by a large number of graduates who cannot be productive without being retrained to meet applied technical skill and communication skill requirements.

Quality in General Education

The performance of education and training policy in ensuring quality is assessed using the results of students at different grades. Examinations were administered by the government in order to get feedback on the quality of education. Table 4 shows baselines for oral reading fluency in seven languages, at grade 2, and table 5 shows the targeted and achieved examination results. The data in both tables clearly show the poor quality of general education in Ethiopia.

Table 4: Baselines for oral reading fluency in seven languages, at grade 2 (%)

Language	Proficiency level			
	Proficient	Basic	Below basic	None
Afan Oromo	5	20	21	54
Af-Somali	34	27	13	26
Amharic	6	21	48	25
Hadiyyisa	4	7	13	76
Sidaamu Afoo	3	13	15	69
Tigrinya	2	33	34	31
Wolayttatto	12	20	18	50

"Proficient": Reading fluently with full comprehension
"Basic": Reading with some fluency and comprehension
"Below Basic": Reading slowly with limited comprehension
None: Non-reader
Source: National Learning Assessments (Ministry of Education, 2017)

Table 4 shows that students with proficient and basic oral reading fluency constitute more than half of the students only among those who use the Somali language. In all the rest, students who are proficient and basic in their oral reading fluency comprise less than 35 percent. Surprisingly, students who cannot read at grade 2 are as high as 76 percent in Hadiya and 69 percent in Sidamu. The figure is a good warning signal for the government to take appropriate measures to improve education quality in the lower grades.

Every four years a National Learning Assessment is conducted in grades 4, 8, 10 and 12. For ESDP IV, the shares of students scoring at least 50 percent and 75 percent in National Learning Assessments were set as targets. But the gaps between what was planned and what was achieved at all levels were huge (see table 5).

The data in table 4 and in table 5 show similar results with other research findings. Modern education in Ethiopia has been criticized for failing to provide students with depth of understanding, an ability to interpret and apply information, the habit of critical thinking-reflection, the ability to form opinions and to value the expression of diverse opinions, and the ability to apply school knowledge to realities of personal experiences and the problems of everyday life (Demeke, 2011).

At the outset, the 1994 education policy masked quality with what it calls relevance (allocation of students in different fields). It attempted to improve the investment of resources but the resources supply was challenged by rapid expansions. Tewodaj et al.(2008) argue that the improvement in coverage of education in Ethiopia has been accompanied by a sustained deterioration in quality of education. As evidence to support their argument, the Pupil-to-Teacher Ratio, which was thirty-two in rural areas and thirty-four in urban areas in 1994, had reached seventy-three in rural areas and forty-eight in urban areas by the year 2001. This chapter concludes that quality never get due attention in the Ethiopian education sector reform programs of the period.

Table 5: National Learning Assessment results against targets set in ESDP IV (%)

Grade (Assessment Year)	4 (2012)		8 (2012)		10 (2014)		12 (2014)	
Benchmark	Target	Achieved	Target	Achieved	Target	Achieved	Target	Achieved
Scoring 50% or above	75	25	70	7.5	70	23	70	34
Scoring 75% or above	25	2.3	25	0.1	25	3	25	4

Source: (Education Statistics Annual Abstract, 2008 E.C. (2015/16), 2017)

7.4. Performance in Correcting the Undemocratic Content of the Previous Education System

In the political context of Ethiopia, the issue of language as a medium of instruction in schools is hotly debated. Studies on language policy (Ramachandran, 2012; Trudell, 2016) unanimously confirm that using a language spoken by the pupil has comparative advantage over using one that is not. Trudell (2016) indicates that the language of instruction has positive impacts on students' learning outcomes, their overall learning experience, as well as on the wider community as well. A study by Ramachandran (2012) shows that the provision of mother tongue instruction could increase the percentage of the population completing primary schooling by as much as 15 percentage points. Beyond its effect on educational attainment, the mother tongue is important for effective transmission of knowledge, participation, and division of power in society (Ramachandran, 2012). On the other hand, choosing a language that the learners do not master has high costs in terms of poor uptake of the curriculum content, poor performance on examinations, increased dropout rates, and the marginalization of populations that do not control the language of instruction (Trudell, 2016).

Providing education in mother tongues has been considered as part of democratizing the education system of Ethiopia (Ministry of Education, 2002). In this regard, the government has seen are markable achievement in protecting and fulfilling language rights of Ethiopian nations and nationalities. By the year 2013, the number of languages used as a medium of instruction in primary schools reached thirteen in the most ethnically diversified region of SNNP. While the Amhara region provides education in four alternative languages, Harari, Dire Dawa, and Gambela use three mediums of instruction, as shown in table 6. Similarly, Somali, Afar, and Oromia are offering primary education using two languages. In 2013 Tigray, Benishangul, and Addis Ababa were using a single language as medium of instruction in schools, but more recently Benishangula Gumz and Addis Ababa started providing education in Afan Oromo. Further study is required to know the level of representation of values, cultures, and history of nations and nationalities in the education curriculum.

Table 6: Number of local languages used in primary education in 2007 and percentage of people with mother tongue other than the official language in 2007

Regions /City Admin	No. of local languages used in primary education in 2007	% of people with mother tongue other than the official language
1. Addis Ababa	1	29%
2. Afar	2	-
3. Amhara	4	7
4. Benishangul Gumuz	1	-
5. Dire Dawa	3	-
6. Gambela	3	-
7. Harari	3	-
8. Oromia	2	13
9. SNNP	13	-
10. Somali	2	3
11. Tigray	1	5
Total	35	

Source: compiled from (Vujcich, 2013)

7.5. Limited Job Opportunity Remain a Challenge

Toward the end of the imperial regime, the public sector could no longer absorb secondary school graduates produced by a continuously growing number of schools. Hence, as early as 1973, up to 25 percent of the secondary school graduates were unemployed (Demeke, 2011). This huge level of unemployment continued to be a problem during the Dergue and the EPRDF regimes. Though EPRDF associated the problem of low employment opportunity for students who leave high school with the quality of education in the past, in the end this government itself produced even larger number of graduates who cannot find job.

The EPRDF-led government criticized the past regime due to a high number of youths that completed grade 12 and could not be employed by the government. However, the problems of unemployment have become worsen and now even university graduates are challenged to find jobs. Saint (2004) correctly understood the problem of limited job opportunity for university graduates as early as the problem became apparent. He states that the Ethiopian labor market for university graduates will remain limited in an economy where 80 percent of the labor force is engaged in agriculture and in which the civil service appears amply staffed.

Only steady economic growth will provide the financing required to improve opportunities for gainful employment for the rising numbers of graduates (Saint, 2004). Furthermore, he notes that roughly a century ago, many of Europe's industrialized countries had tertiary enrolment ratios similar to those of Ethiopia today. In contrast to Ethiopia, however, they (with the exceptions of Italy and Russia) already had less than 50 percent of their labor force engaged in agriculture and had all achieved universal primary education (Fredriksen, 1984). The implication is that a rapid expansion of access to education at all levels may not by itself stimulate economic growth unless it is accompanied by productivity-driven structural changes in the economy. The latter is yet to occur in Ethiopia (Saint, 2004).

At present the government has accepted the fact that the existing job opportunities will not absorb all graduates of universities. In its ESDP V, the government has planned to increase the share of graduates with degree-relevant employment within twelvemonths after graduation to 80 percent. This means that even if the plan will be 100percent successful, 20 percent of the graduates will not find a job within a period of one year. Improving the quality of education and expanding job opportunities will continue to be on the agenda in future education policy change initiatives.

8. Conclusions and Implication for Future Research

The education policy of Ethiopia was developed as part of the impetus to replace past legacies with a new order and as a response to acute shortage in equitable access to education, inefficiency in using limited supply of resources due to high repetition and dropout rates, low quality, low relevance, and limitation in upholding democratic values. The 1994 education policy did not receive wide acceptance among stakeholders due to the unbalanced power of the ruling party in the formulation process, but implemented for about 25 years regard less of those criticism. This analysis shows the policy has achieved mixed results. Above all, Ethiopia has been most successful in addressing the problem of low access to education while still struggling to address the problem of inequity and inefficiency. The promotion of the use of mother tongue as a medium of instruction in schools has been successful, while other attempts to democratize the education system as stipulated in the policy goals need further studies. Likewise, the education policy under the EPRDF regime has completely failed in improving the quality of education, particularly from the perspective of the competence of graduates. All the assessed evidence suggests the challenge of low quality is valid at all levels of education, from preprimary to higher education. This chapter argues that whatever reform programs may be introduced, if they have no positive effect on quality of education, then they have little relevance.

Unbalanced growth in the job market with the supply of graduates has been a persistent problem for about half a century. The government severely criticized its predecessor on the basis of the failure of education system to provide adequate job opportunity to those who leave schools, but has ended by exacerbating the problem of unemployment. Whether related to the quality of education or other socioeconomic factors, the shortage of job opportunities for those who leave school has only become worse. Based on these conclusions, the author recommends the central focus of education program should be on achieving quality and the employability of graduates, while sustaining the current pace of expansion and creating equitable access to education.

Though the chapter discusses relevant policy issues using secondary data, there are a number of limitations that must be considered in future research. In a bid to cover achievements in all policy goals, this research has compromised elements of depth. Thus, future researchers will benefit in producing further insights by concentrating on one goal of the education policy and one level of education instead of covering the whole education policy at a glance. For example it is essential to study in depth the educational inputs, competence and motivations of teachers, school facilities, and pedagogical issues. Furthermore, future study is required to know the level of the representation of values, cultures, and the history of nations and nationalities in the educational curriculum.

Acknowledgement

The author would like to thank Worku Negash and Mihret Ayenew for initiating me to undertake this policy analysis, reviewers and editors for comments on earlier drafts and assistance in improving the final version, and Bacha Kebede Debela for facilitating the presentation of the paper at the Ethiopian Public Administration Professional Association annual conference.

References

Alemu, D. S., & Tekleselassie, A. A. (2006). Instructional Language Policy in Ethiopia: Motivated by Politics or the Educational Needs of Children?. *Planning and Changing*, 37, 151-168.

Arega, Y. (2016). Quality of Education in Private Higher Institutions in Ethiopia: The Role of Governance. *SAGE Open* (https://us.sagepub.com/en-us/nam/open-access-at-sage), 1-12.

Bolton, L., & Foste. (2014). *Higher Education Reform. Helpdesk Report.* British Government Department For International Development

Demeke, Y. (2011). Ethiopian Education Policy Analysis: Using Foucault's Genealogy.

HRD Afirica. (2017, August 30 and 31). Employability and Skills Development: Building at National and Enterprise Level. *First Annual Conference on Human Capital Development in Africa*, pp. 1-43.

Kahsay, M. N. (2012). Quality and Quality Assurance in Ethiopian Higher Education: Critical Issues and Practical Implications. University of Twente

Martin, J., Riitta, O., & Tuomas, T. (2000). *Preparation of the Education Sector Development Program in Ethiopia.* Paris, France: Association for the Development of Education in Africa (ADEA) ISBN 92-9178-021-0.

Mingat, A., Tan, J.-P., & Sosale, W. S. (2003). *Tools for Education Policy Analysis.* Washington, DC 20433: World Bank.

Ministry of Education. (2002). *The Education and Training Policy and Its Implimentation.* Addis Ababa: Ministry of Education.

Ministry of Education. (2015). *Education Sector Development Program (ESDP V) (2008 – 2012 E.C.) (2015/16 – 2019/20 G.C.).* Addis Ababa: Ministry of Education of Federal Democratic Republic of Ethiopia.

Ministry of Education. (2017). *Education Statistics Annual Abstract, 2008 E.C. (2015/16).* Addis Ababa: MINISTRY OF EDUCATION.

Ministry of Education, Federal Democratic Republic of Ethiopia. (2015). *Education Sector Development Program V (ESDP V) 2015/16 – 2019/20.* Addis Ababa.

Ramachandran, R. (2012). Language Use in Education and Primary Schooling Attainment: Evidence from a Natural Experiment in Ethiopia. IEB Working Paper 2012/34.

Saint, W. (2004). Higher Education in Ethiopia: The Vision and Its Challenges. *Journal of Higher Education in Africa / Revue de l'enseignement supérieur en Afrique* 2(3), 83-113.

Nigussa, F. (2013). Reconsidering Civil Service Reform in Ethiopia. Civil Service Commission Government of Ethiopia

Norelius, C. G., & Mendes, S. (2003). *NEW EDUCATION DIVISION DOCUMENTS NO. 15 Institute of International Education Stockholm University Progress and Result Indicators and Their Relevance for Educational Policy Analysis Final Report.*

Semela, T. (2011). Breakneck Expansion and Quality Assurance in Ethiopian Higher Education: Ideological Rationales and Economic Impediments. *Higher Education Policy,* 24(3), 399-425.

Teshome, Y. (2003). *Transformations in Higher Education: Experiences with Reform and Expansion in Ethiopian Higher Education System.* Ghana, Accra: unpublished.

Tewodaj, M., Gezahegn, A., & Zelekawork, P. (2008). *The Bang for the Birr Public Expenditures and Rural Welfare in Ethiopia.* International Food Policy Research Institute (IFPRI).

Trudell, B. (2016). Language Choice and Education Quality in Eastern and Southern Africa: A Review. *Comparative Education,* 52(3), 281-293.

The World Bank. (2005). *Education in Ethiopia: Strengthening the Foundation for Sustainable Progress: A World Bank Country Study.* Washington DC: The International Bank for Reconstruction and Development /World Bank.

Vujcich, D. (2013). *Policy and Practice on Language of Instruction in Ethiopian Schools: Findings from the Young Lives School Survey.* Working paper. Oxford UK: Young Lives School an International study of Child poverty.

Yohannes, H. M. (2016). *Governance Reform in the Ethiopian Higher Education System; Organisational Responses to Business Management Tools in the Case of Mekelle University.* Tamperensis: Acta Universitatis Tamperensis.

22
Catch-up Trails: Public Administration Education and Professionalization Trajectories in Ethiopia

Kiflie Worku Angaw

Box 1: Key Points of the chapter

- ✓ The chapter studied the Ethiopian public administration education and the labor market.
- ✓ Public administration education is important for achieving values of economy, efficiency, effectiveness, and social equity of bureaucracies.
- ✓ Strengthening public administration education leads to strengthening the public sector's institutional executive (policymaking and implementation) capacities.
- ✓ Professionalization of public administration is crucial to the success of local, federal, regional, and supranational institutions.
- ✓ Ethiopian public administration education and professionalization has faced bottlenecked challenges.

Box 2: Lesson drawn from the chapter

- ✓ Readers will be able to understand the path and trend of Ethiopian public administration education.
- ✓ Readers will be able to underscore the importance of strengthening public administration to the contemporary governance spectrum.
- ✓ Readers will understand public administration graduates' experiences in the labor market.
- ✓ Readers will understand the indispensable role of public administration at the micro and macro (local, national, and supranational) levels.

Box 3: Abbreviations

AU = African Union
GTP = Growth and Transformational Plan
MoSHE = Ministry of Science and Higher Education
MTPA = Management and Public Administration

NGOs = Nongovernmental Organizations
PADM = Public Administration and Development Management
SDGs = Sustainable Development Goals
UN = United Nations

1. Introduction

The origin of public administration as a practice traces back to ancient human civilization and emerges as an academic body of knowledge after Wilson's article "The Study of Administration" in 1887. Thus, as an academic arena, it is a relatively young field of study.

The professionalization of public administration provides the latter with capable diligent socioeconomic and politically responsible experts, who are the building blocks for carrying out public policies for national development in the contemporary world. In the real world, these experts advise politicians, providing crucial assistance in policy-making and implementation at different levels of government, i.e., local administrations, regional agencies, central government ministries/agencies (Hustedt et al., 2020), as well as within supranational bureaucracies, i.e., the United Nations, African Union, European Union, and so forth. For instance, the paramount role of public administration has been clearly reflected in the Agenda 2063 goals of Pan-Africanism, which envision the strengthening the continent's well-being and prosperity via a clear roadmap through which Africa aspires to achieve inclusive growth and sustainable development, continental integration, and political unity aimed at improving African governance for Africa's renaissance (Agenda 2063, 2017).

Supranational agencies' efforts/policies responding to complex societal challenges are meant to be realized through public governance across a spectrum of partnerships between multiple actors. The UN is typical in this respect, as seen in the UN Sustainable Development Goals (SDGs) #8, 11, 16, and 17, which highlight the following expertise areas of public administration: promoting sustained, inclusive, and sustainable economic growth, full and productive employment and decent work for all (corresponding to the social security policy concern of public administration); making cities and human settlements inclusive, safe, resilient, and sustainable (corresponding to the public services and urban governance areas of public administration); promoting peaceful and inclusive societies for sustainable development through strong institutions (public sector capacity building); and strengthening the means of implementation and revitalizing global partnerships (partnership with multiple actors) (UN, 2015). Bouckaert (2020) also underlines the indispensable role of public administration in the achievement of the above UN goals, as they may be achieved by moving to concrete principles of effective SDG governance through public administration, wherein the UN envisions the provision of safe and nutritious food, affordable drinking water, universal access to education, physical, mental and social well-being, granting equal opportunities and permitting the full realization of human potential in promoting shared prosperity (Bouckaert, 2020).

Public administration education has become extremely important these days because public services are expected to provide value for public money (Kwaku Ohemeng 2014), with careful consideration of the following public administration values/pillars: economy, efficiency, effectiveness, and social equity (Norman-Major, 2011). In the context of developing economies and Africa in particular, effective public governance is called upon to respond to numerous developmental challenges while taking into consideration the explicit normative dimensions of public service values and administration (Bouchaert, 2020). In Ethiopia, public administration is expected to contribute to the success of the Ethiopian national development policy, i.e., the implementation of the strategic pillars of the Growth and Transformational Plan (GTP), specifically, fostering the governance and management of rapid urbanization to accelerate economic growth and building democracy and ensuring good governance through enhancing the implementation capacity of public institutions (National Planning Commission, 2015).

Taking all of the above into consideration, this chapter seeks to explain the history of Ethiopian public administration education and the country's labor market trajectories using empirical evidence. In this chapter, readers will able to understand the path and trend of Ethiopian public administration education in Ethiopia since its inception in the 1960s to the present time. The chapter also provides insight into the experiences of public administration graduates in the labor market. Furthermore, the chapter posits that the importance of strengthening public administration education lies in strengthening executive agencies for effective policy formulation and implementation at both the micro and macro levels of local, national, and supranational institutions.

2. The Study Setting and Problem Context

The relevance of public administration education in the contemporary world is vital, as it provides employees of public organizations with the knowledge and skills that they should possess as competent and qualified public servants

(Blace, 2015). Its scientific inquiry and study domain are characterized by often competing paradigmatic perspectives and seemingly endless teaching modalities that differ from other applied social sciences (Van der Waldt 2014). As Nadia (2016) stated, the evolution and current status of public administration education is well developed and documented in the Western world but less clear and underdeveloped in developing countries in general and Africa in particular. According to Pal and Clark (2016), the hypothetical assumption of public administration education is that those who do better have been taught better, and that quality education in this field enables graduates to deal effectively with real life problems, acting as social physicians via effective public policy-making and execution.

Quality public administration education can potentially improve the quality of government and governance through nurturing responsible graduates who build effective civil service systems imbued with high rates of commitment to civic virtues (Rubaii & Pliscoff, 2014), enabling government officials and civil servants to demonstrate and adhere to higher levels of professionalism. The implementation of the Ethiopian development plan (GTP-II) requires strong institutional capacities. Strategic pillars of the GTP include building democratic and developmental good governance through enhancing the implementation capacity of public institutions and actively engaging the citizens, fostering the governance and management of rapid urbanization to accelerate economic growth (National Planning Commission, 2015). Besides the GTP, the success of different public sector reform tools (Business Process Re-engineering, Balanced Score Card, and Kaizen) introduced and others to be introduced in the future in Ethiopia largely relies on public administration.

The inability of educational institutions to provide quality training and education of public administrators and civil servants has resulted in ineffective policymaking and execution (Barabashev and Kastrel, 2013). This situation is embodied in inadequate curricula, which often copy courses from Western programs without adapting it to the specific country's' realities. As a result, public administration education has failed to grow, a deficiency that is exacerbated by merging public administration with business management, underestimation by labor markets, lack of educational competences, and pedagogical limitations (Barabashev and Kastrel, 2013; Ewoh, 2014).

The management of public affairs is a complex activity that entails the balancing of various and/or contradictory objectives. Thus, public administration education is necessary for equipping public administrators with the tools to deal with often complex tasks and sensitive situations (Antwi-Boasiako, 2015). Furthermore, the complexities and changes in the political, social, and economic landscape and functions of the government and public agencies manifest the need for excellence in public administration education (Blace, 2015). The complexities that public administrators face in the contemporary world the preparation of qualified graduates who can deal effectively with highly complex issues involving very complicated issues related socioeconomic development. According to Henry (2005), the education of public administrators comprises an understanding of the ecology of public agencies function, including the questions of how they function, what they do, and why they do it. A public administration education that provides students with a body of knowledge while ensuring practical experience is expected to contribute to the creation of a better government, better public agencies, and therefore to the realization of a better and egalitarian society, in which the body of knowledge acquired through rigorous research methodologies ranges from simple observations to complex modeling (Blace, 2015).

Public administration education trains future public administrators for mid-career, senior, and managerial positions in the areas of management, organizational leadership, personnel administration, budgeting and financial management, public policy, program evaluation, project & program management, and administrative functions, who will work within government, nonprofit organizations, and the private sectors (Blace, 2015; Pal and Clark, 2016). Students may pursue either the academic field of study (public administration theory and research) or practical studies, such as executing the policy of public administration in practice and learning about administrative structures with their functional responsibilities (Antwi-Boasiako, 2015).

Education and curricula in this field should adequately prepare public management to be aware of the political processes that characterize the work of government officials. Unfortunately, most of the time government appointees critically lack this required training, hindering them from functioning and performing as expected (Antwi-Boasiako, 2015). European countries' public administration education systems may be classified in in three clusters; legal (strong emphasis on administrative law), public (unique public and political character) and corporate or managerial (business management techniques) (Hajnal, 2003). The main characteristics of public administration education differ in different political and social contexts, as well as depending on historical factors that have influenced the selection and training of graduates (Cepiku, 2013).

Fred (1962) argues that public administration as education and practice will not achieve its goal if it fails to consider the country's specific context in applying the prismatic model and structural functionalism. Public administration education in Ethiopia began soon after the introduction of the higher education system in Ethiopia during the regime of Emperor Haile Selassie I, in the 1950s. Since then the discipline has been producing experts and practitioners in the field. However, as far as this author knows, there has been little research on public administration education and professional growth trajectories in Ethiopia. To this end, this chapter tried to answer: What are the public administration education trajectories in Ethiopia? How does the labor market accommodate public administration graduates?

Ultimately, this chapter seeks to contribute as a springboard work on public administration education and professional development trajectories, as it provides empirical evidence on Ethiopian public administration education and professionalization endeavors while solving the problem of the constraints stemming from the paucity of available literature.

3. Methods and Materials

The study applied an exploratory type of research using the mixed research approach. The study used both primary and secondary data sources. Fundamentally, the primary data of the study were public administration scholars' profiles obtained from Ethiopian public universities and labor market data. The Ethiopian public administration scholars' (researchers and academicians) profiles were collected from different Ethiopian public universities: Addis Ababa, Ambo, Dilla, Kotebe Metropolitan, Dire Dawa, and Wolayta Sodo Universities. The data were collected in two ways (departments' database and the online Survey Monkey tool). In the online Survey Monkey tool, scholars were asked to click on the questionnaire link through their email address, fill in the survey questionnaire, and return it back to the researcher. In all, sixty-five public administration scholars' profiles were collected using the two mentioned data collection mechanisms.

In terms of the labor market and professionalization, data were collected from the well-known Ethiopian job advertising newspaper *Addis Zemen*, which publishes on a daily basis. Two months' worth (sixty-one days) of open positions/vacancies were collected, as published in *Addis Zemen* from June 1, 2019, to July 31, 2019. All vacancies published in the newspaper were collected; subsequently, positions unrelated to the professional domain of public administration were automatically filtered out. After this filtering, 142 vacancies remained for analysis within the public administration domain, all of which were related to the current curriculum of public administration education in Ethiopia. In theory, graduates could effectively discharge the required functions and adhere to the job responsibilities, demonstrating their professional competencies on the assignments to be given them by these employers and advertised vacancies.

Furthermore, the author used the following secondary data: published works (scientific articles/journals, book chapters, and books) and policy documents, such as the new Ethiopian education development policy roadmap, the Growth and Transformational Plan (GTP I&II), the harmonized public administration curriculum, the Pan-African University strategic plan, the African Agenda 2063, and the UN SDGs, among others. Finally, the data were analyzed using narrative, descriptive and explanatory data analysis methods. The study used path dependency (historical institutionalism) theory as the framework of analysis. Readers should note that in addition to the universities studied here, other public sector capacity development institutions include civil service universities (federal and regional), Meles Zenawi leadership academies, and Ethiopian management institute (on job training institute). However, due to different limitations and institutional setups, the structures and curricula they are using differ from those of the Ethiopian higher education institutions (universities). For this reason, those institutions were excluded from the study as sources of data.

4. Result and Discussion

4.1. Public Administration Education in Ethiopia

The African education systems are largely dominated by Western educational ideologies, particularly those of the former colonial powers (Ewoh, 2014; Haruna, 2004). Consequently public administration education in Africa has narrowly focused on the need to respond to the pressures of global forces, Western theories, multinational corporations, and nongovernmental organizations, without paying considerable attention to the uniqueness of the social, economic, and political experiences of the African context.

As highlighted earlier, public administration education in Ethiopia as an independent academic discipline is sixty years old. In 1961, public administration began to be offered as an independent department within the faculty of Arts at Addis Ababa University (the then Haile Selassie I University). From 1977-1981 it was placed under the department of political science and government, and subsequently under the department of management at the college of business administration. In 1982, management (business administration) and public administration were merged together into the department of management and public Administration (MTPA) and stayed that way for more than two decades (National Harmonized Curriculum, 2013). In 2004, public administration was established as an independent department (public administration and development management (PADM)) and placed in the faculty of business and economics, taking into consideration the global and national demands for skill and knowledge within its curriculum (National Harmonized Curriculum, 2013). Here we can understand the instability of the discipline, buffeted by institutional systemic changes over time.

From the point of view of historical institutionalism or path dependency theory, it may be observed that the institutions already created in the context of public administration education in Ethiopia are disincentives (Stuteville and Jumara, 2010) for change (clear and long-lasting) in the field of the study through the creation of self-reliant schools or faculty, because so much is already invested in the existing institutions. Patterns of timing and sequence matters are in favor of incremental changes (Stuteville and Jumara, 2010) instead of building new systems, introducing new designs, and new institutional change platforms that consider institutions (public administration teaching universities) as structural variables (Trouvé et al., 2010) from which stem arrangements of ideas, interests (public administration placement faculty), and powers (among public administration and other disciplines' academicians). The historical institutionalism analytical framework considers institutions as structural variables from which stem arrangements of ideas, interests, and powers that affects the system (Steinmo et at., 1992). The theory starts from the premise that organizations and actors are part of institutions that structure and channel their behavioral standards and activities along established paths. The path taken highlights a historical dynamic that dictates that once a path is chosen, it is difficult to change it because the processes become institutionalized and are reinforced over time (Trouvé et al., 2010). It becomes increasingly difficult to reverse past institutional choices because not following the rules and standards established by previous choices (*exit option*) and building up new systems might incur inconveniencies. These paths are made up of institutional structures determined by previous choices that impose constraints on institutional development processes. That is why existing institutions are usually modified and not replaced despite their less than optimal nature and institutional inertia (Steinmo et at., 1992; Trouvé et al., 2010).

Currently, several public universities in Ethiopia offer an undergraduate program in public administration even though private colleges and universities haven't yet offered it as a field of study in their programs. This might be due to the low demands for public administration graduates in the job market (Antwi-Boasiako, 2015). The job market and public administration graduates will be discussed later on. Within public universities, till now Ethiopian public administration education remains disbursed in different faculties throughout the Ethiopian public universities, such as under the college of business and economics in more than ten public universities; under the school of law (Bahir Dar and Jimma Universities); in the college of social sciences (Hawassa University); and within the school of management (University of Gondar and Kotebe Metropolitan University), with related names like governance and development studies, etc. Even though the discipline has had different names, such as public administration, public policy/policy science, public management, and public governance (Bouckaert and Jann, 2020; Verheijen and Connaughton, 2003), the nomenclature is unstable and will likely see unending renovation in the years to come. In this context, clear distinctions and borderlines must provide to distinguish academic program of public administration from public administration as an interdisciplinary/transdisciplinary program or as a public administration specialization integrated with other programs (Verheijen and Connaughton, 2003), in order to maintain its specific identity.

Because of different actors' interests (public administration teaching institutions and scholars), Ethiopian public administration education follows the path dependency theory based on the premise that organizations and actors are part of institutions channeled along established paths (Trouvé et al., 2010). These paths are made up of institutions (with their interests, standards, and rules) determined by previous choices that impose constraints on the development of public administration education. It's difficult to change since the processes become institutionalized and are reinforced over time (; Stuteville and Jumara, 2010; Trouvé et al., 2010).

Thus, the placement of the field within the university system remains contentious. With regards to its identity crisis, Rasmussen and Callan (2016) argue that it stems from the absence of a public administration epistemic community that would serve as a gatekeeper/owner society guarding the profession, as seen in law, economics, medicine, engineering, and other professional fields of studies. As Van der Waldt (2017) has pointed out, because of the lack of clear disciplinary border lines, the Ghanaian public administration education overwhelmingly accepts the superiority of business administration education curricula in its curriculum (Kwaku Ohemeng, 2014).

Similarly, the Italian public administration educational cluster covers three major areas: public (includes programs whose disciplinary orientation is political science, as well as sociology or economics), legal (covers programs whose disciplinary orientation is law), and corporate (programs whose disciplinary orientation is management as well as communication)

(Cepiku, 2013). The Ghanaian public administration education also has no single system; rather it varies based on national size, the interest of tertiary institution/diversity, political system structures, and the role of the central government. Furthermore, in the Ghanaian case, the influence of former colonial (Britain's) legacies is an associational factor on public administration education (Antwi-Boasiako, 2015; Stuteville and Jumara, 2010). More importantly, (Cepiku, 2013) argues that the concept and tradition of the state has a direct impact on the development of public administration education.

The identity crisis of public administration as an academic and professional label, combined with its multidisciplinary and interdisciplinary character and the continuously evolving nature of government and government-society relations, disallows the development of a unified body of theory. This lack of unified identity is evident in Europe, Asia, the US, and Africa as well (Cepiku, 2013).The survival of public administration as a distinct field of study and areas of professional expertise will depend on the ability of scholars to develop relevant techniques, concepts, methodologies, theories, and practices (Cepiku, 2013).

Because of the above-mentioned factors and disciplinary development trajectories, public administration borrows theories and methodologies from other disciplines, a fact that has been at the center of debate since the first days of its self-awareness as a field of study. Indeed, the field owes its theories and methodologies to other disciplines like economics, law, and political science, due to the necessity of relevant methodologies to test theories (Onder & Brower, 2013) and hypothetical assumptions/problems and the association of practicability with disciplinary development and self-sufficiency. In this regard, Van der Waldt (2017) presented public administration as an interdisciplinary field of study entailing the convergence different disciplinary theories. Meanwhile, according to Pollitt (cited in Van der Waldt, 2017) "public administration suffers from multiple personality disorder," is characterized by diversity, and finds its origin in various theoretical schools of thought instead constructing its own theories and methodologies.

I argue here that, while keeping in mind it's interdisciplinary, multidisciplinary, and transdisciplinary characteristics, public administration education has a peculiar identity and unique mode of scientific inquiry that should be maintained in Ethiopia via the creation of independent schools/institutes and/or the establishment of unique departments. Indeed, this is done in the United States (Harris School of Public Policy, American University School of Public Affairs, and others), Republic of South Korea (Korean Development Institute School of Public Policy and Management, Korea Institute of Public Administration, and others), Hungary (School of Public Policy at the Central

European University, National University of Public Service and others), Singapore (Lee Kuan Yew School of Public Policy), and in other countries around the world. While this is not an easy task to accomplish, above all, public administration scholars must come together and design methods and theories applicable to the discipline of public administration.

This is due to the importance of public administration education, which is increasing as never before. According to Rosenbaum (2015), the 21st century's growing demand for effective public governance make it clear that the demands on the next generation of public administrators will be great and the demands on those who train them will be even greater (quality and quantity). Since the demands and needs of contemporary society continue to grow, the tools and technologies with which public administrators need to work have become increasingly sophisticated.

4.2. Ethiopian Public Administration Scholars Profile

The academic and professional profile of scholars of a certain discipline has a remarkable contribution to the development and embracing of disciplinary self-sufficiency. In this regard, (Rosenbaun, 2015) clearly stated that the commitment and quality (the highest standards of teaching, training and research and community services) of the faculty members of public administration is central to the achievement of program goals in all areas of activity.

In this study, we observe the disciplinary backgrounds of the Ethiopian public administration scholars, both researchers and academicians, who are responsible for teaching-learning assignments in public universities, both at the undergraduate and postgraduate level, engaging in research undertakings and discharging community services. As the faculty members' profiles revealed, significant numbers of scholars have non-public administration backgrounds (undergraduate and postgraduate degrees). Graph 11 below presents the statistics of public administration faculty members' profiles. 30.77 percent of the scholars selected in this study have business management/administration undergraduate degrees, 23.07 percent have other (civics and ethical studies, political science, law, language, cooperative and administrative sciences) undergraduate/bachelor degrees, and only 46.15 percent of the scholars have public administration undergraduate degree backgrounds.

In a similar vein, more than 10 percent of the staff postgraduate (MSc/MA) degrees are either in business administration, globalization studies, gender studies or international economics. From this we can surmise that large number scholars might lack the theoretical foundations and fundamental background knowledge of public administration, which increases the probability of their being influenced by their prior background knowledge, which in turn affects the curricula, teaching pedagogy, research activities, and community service, all of which cumulatively influences public administration students'/graduates' knowledge, competency, and skills. Even though public administration education should involve a pragmatist approach to enable students to comprehend sensitive contexts (structural functionalism and prismatic modeling), it also involves focusing on uncertainties and teaching students to decide on issues after sensing, reflecting, and acting on their outcomes using their discipline distinctive methods. In this regard Rubaii & Pliscoff (2014) argue public administration education programs must prepare graduates with a full range of competencies knowledge, skills, and public service values (economy, efficiency, effectiveness, and social equity), and they must do so in ways that are relevant to their national culture and context, which is greatly faculty members profiles (Rubaii & Pliscoff, 2014). The overall effects of this have presented (Mitiku, 2018) the Ethiopian public service systems with serious challenges involving serious technical and tactical institutional incompetence, skill inadequacies, and methodological disorientations of public values. Public administration as an academic and practice will contribute to the expected result when a considerable investment is assigned to its education system. This was confirmed by Bouchaert and Jann (2020), who have pointed out that strengthening public administration means strengthening academic research outputs and teaching activities.

Therefore, these scenarios are highly likely to affect students' professional competencies, expertise knowledge, as well as skill acquisition. According to Barabashev & Kastrel (2013), public administration education might be influenced by institutional development (higher education systems), educational curricula of higher education, government standards, and the job market demand for graduates. Similarly, the interrelationship between academicians and practitioners' collaborative research and interoperability plays an underpinning role in disciplinary development. As Onder & Brower (2013) point out, a public administration education system and practitioners' productivity have direct associations. This spillover effect also expands to industry: for instance, Turkish public administration practitioners' engagement in research undertakings and article publication declined from 18.9 percent to 8.5 percent in the 1990-2009 period (Rubaii & Pliscoff, 2014).

As (Barabashev & Kastrel, 2013) have stated, public administration education is influenced by faculty members' qualifications and level of professionalism (publication tracks and scientific research undertakings related to societal problems and solution provision in an academic forum where scholars come together and interact with state authorities). In relation to this, nevertheless,

Graph 1: Disciplinary background of Ethiopian public administration scholars

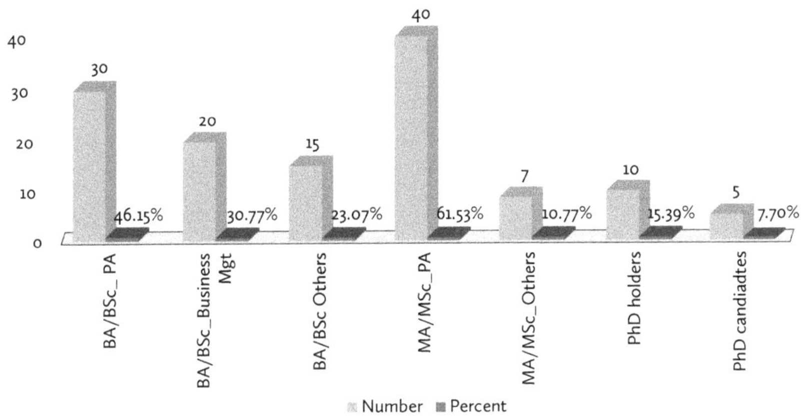

Source: Survey (2019)

even though public administration education began in Ethiopia with the introduction of higher education in Ethiopia in 1960s, for more than fifty years it stayed without a professional organization comparable to other disciplines. Interestingly, the Ethiopian Public Administration Association (EPAA) was established in 2016, as a platform for research undertakings, dialogue, and exchange, as well as a forum for the professionalization of Ethiopian public administration. However, in this chapter, it's difficult to evaluate the professional organization's performance due to its recent establishment.

In regard to the general academic rank of public administration scholars as presented below, it is at the infant stage of development. As shown in graph 2, more than 78 percent of the scholars surveyed in this research have a rank of lecturer (MA/MSc degree holders), less than 16 percent are assistant professors (Ph.D. degrees and research assistantship), 7.77 percent are Ph.D. candidates, 4.61 percent are assistant lecturers (BA/BSc holders), and only 1.54 percent hold associate professorships. However, the government of Ethiopia and the Ministry of Science and Higher Education (MoSHE) declare the public universities staff ratio should, as a general principle, reflect a 0-30-70 basis (zero percent undergraduate, 30 percent MA/MSc holders, and 70 percent Ph.D. holders). In contrast, the dominant number (more than 78 percent) of public administration faculty members are still MA/MSc holders. We can deduce that this scenario significantly affects the disciplinary development of public administration as a field of study and professional areas of expertise. This is due to the limitation of postgraduate programs, specifically research degrees or Ph.D. programs in public administration

Graph 2: Academic rank of Ethiopian public administration scholars

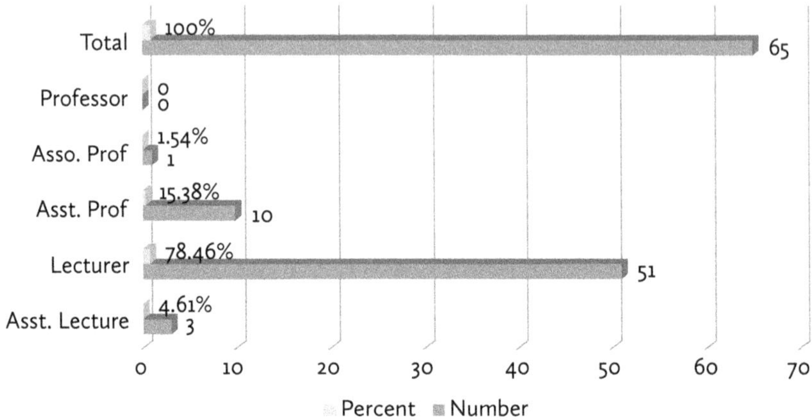

Source: Survey (2019)

in Ethiopian universities. This is the critical challenge of departmental staff development as well as for the development of the field of study more generally. Addis Ababa University is the only university that has a Ph.D. program in public management and policy but at present there are no regularly enrolled Ph.D. candidates in this program.

4.3. Professionalization of Public Administration and Labor Market in Ethiopia

Public administration education potentially nurtures graduates capable of carrying out government functions with normative and pragmatic approaches that seek the general public's interests. According to Henry (2005), the government (at all levels i.e., federal to local) is the biggest employer of public administration graduates in areas of public administration professional domain and expertise.

The Ethiopian public administration field of study foundational document and national harmonized curriculum clearly state that the professional profile of graduates of public administration should allow them to effectively discharge responsibilities as experts and team leaders and assume managerial positions in areas of human resource administration, policymaking and implementations, leadership and strategic lesions, diplomacy, public relations and governance, project/program and development, public service provisions, finance administrations as they pursue careers in the public sector (federal, regional and local constituents) working in the realm of public interests, nongovernmental organizations, associations, civil society organizations, international organizations, and development partners (UN agencies, AU, regional and international organizations) as experts in project management, strategic management, human resource development and management, technical advisors, consultants, and researchers (National Harmonized Curriculum, 2013).

While this sounds impressive on paper, the present study has found that public administration graduates are having difficulty finding jobs in the above-mentioned areas of expertise and organizations. As table 1 shows, among thirty-four vacancies in human resource administration (managerial and expert level) offered by public sectors, private companies, public enterprises, NGOs, and think tank organizations, public administration graduates are excluded from applying to seventeen (50 percent). This is despite the fact that graduates had studied human resources administration in a seven-hour lecture module comprising human resources administration and personnel administration courses. Only fourteen (41 percent) of open human resources vacancies invited them to apply.

Furthermore, among twenty-six positions open in project/program management nineteen (73 percent) vacancies automatically excluded public administration graduates from applying for competitions, and only three invited them to apply. This is in spite of the fact that students routinely take courses related to these vacancies, counting twenty hours lecture hours' courses in project planning and administration, strategic management, macroeconomics and microeconomics, and entrepreneurship. Moreover, among twenty-six open vacancies offered by different organizations in the areas of budgeting/planning and finance administration eighteen (69 percent) excluded public administration graduates from applying and only five (19 percent) indirectly invited them to do so. In fact, public administration graduates have taken a twelve lecture hour's module entitled Public Finance Administration, which is composed of relevant courses (public finance and taxation, public budgeting and financial administration, and principles of accounting). For detailed information on the labor market and public administration graduate career opportunities, see annex 1 at the end of this chapter. The role of public administration education in strengthening public sectors is clearly stipulated in GTP-II, which emphasizes building democratic and developmental good governance through enhancing the implementation capacity of public institutions (National Planning Commission, 2015) as a strategic pillar of GTP-II. Without hiring/attracting the public administration graduates into the public sector, how will this development plan be successfully implemented?

As other scholars argue, (Blace, 2015; Henry, 2005; Pal & Clark, 2016), the government is the biggest employer of public administration graduates, specifically in the areas of budgeting and financial management, public policy, and program evaluation. Furthermore Evans et al. (2019) has highlighted that public affairs education schools primarily anticipate and build the immediate and long-term skills needed by students entering public service leadership roles. The new Ethiopian education policy roadmap document also confirms that the higher education curricula are not geared toward the development of employability and other lifelong learning skills among graduates. Ethiopian universities did not seem to have strategies and tactics to prepare programs requiring intensive use of IT and emerging technologies/theories within the discipline (Tefera et al., 2018).

As the study confirmed and labor market data reveals, the domestic job market of Ethiopia does not yet consider and treat public administration graduates as a competent, potential, and qualified workforce for vacant positions in the main areas of graduates' expertise offered by the public sector (federal to local), public enterprises, private companies, NGOs, and development partners, regardless of the graduates' professional profile, professional domain, and the Ethiopian public administration curriculum own stated main areas of expertise. Surprisingly, candidates from other fields who are less likely to have expertise in the areas required by the market are often invited to directly apply to these same positions/vacancies directly (see annex 1) while public administration graduates are still excluded from applying.

Of the other sixty-four vacancies/positions used for analysis, twenty-five were public/customer service positions, nine covered crosscutting issues (gender experts and youth affairs exerts), ten offered general manager, executive director, country representative, public relations, and directorship positions, and the remaining twenty positions were others, like secretary-general, office coordinator, team leader, and cost-sharing expert positions offered by the public sector, public enterprises, financial institutions, and NGOs. Still, more than 90 percent of those job offers don't invite public administration graduates to apply for competition (see annex 1), even though public administration graduates are equipped with the essential competencies and skills of the job specifications and job analysis of those offered jobs requirements. Public administration graduates have gained the required knowledge, skill, and competencies for these vacancies and positions during their study at university from public administration modules, namely, development management, management of public enterprises and NGOs, foundations of public administration, government and governance, and public finance administration, all of which includes different comprehensive courses within each module specifically with the required knowledge, skills, and competencies required by the above job vacancies.

Table 1: Job market and public administration graduates career opportunities

S. No	Open Vacancy Category		Total No of Vacant positions	Open Positions Level		Jobs offered by Organizations					Public Administration Graduates Invitation Status		
				Expert	Managerial	Gov't	Pvt*	Public Enterprise	NGO	RI**	Directly	Indirectly	Not Invited
1	Human Resource Administration	No	34	15	18	8	15	6	2	3	14	3	17
		%	100	44.11%	53%	23.5%	44.11%	17.65%	5.9%	8.8%	41.17%	8.8%	50%
2	Project/Program Management	No	26	13	13	8	2	5	7	3	4	3	19
		%	100	50%	50%	30.7%	7.69%	19%	26.9%	11.5%	15.38%	11.5%	73.07%
3	Budgeting/Planning and Finance Admin	No	26	18	8	15	5	3	2	1	3	5	18
		%	100	69.03%	30.7%	57.7%	19 %	11.5%	7.69%	3.8%	11.5%	19%	69.03%%

* Private organizations
** Research Institutes/think tank
Source: Survey (2019)

This situation urges us to raise questions as to why public administration graduates are excluded from the job market to this extent? One might argue this is because of the subject matter and because the discipline is a young field of study. The appropriateness of this argument is questionable since the beginning of public administration as a field of study has traced back to the introduction of higher education in Ethiopia since the 1960s. The other two arguments might be that, first, the discipline doesn't market itself to the job market (particularly to the domestic) and second, the job market might not have enough information on the professional domain, qualification, competencies, and potential areas of expertise of public administration as a field of study and the professional aptitudes of the graduates. I believe both these arguments may be valid, affecting the labor market and the professionalization of the discipline in Ethiopia. In this regard Barabashev & Kastrel (2013) argue that the information employers have on graduates' profiles greatly affects employment opportunities. Furthermore, Pan African University's strategic plan document clearly envisions the projection of its graduates' employability rate to at least 80 percent (PAU, n.d); meanwhile, the Ethiopia public administration education curriculum says nothing about its graduates' employability rate, nor is such a target found in the strategic plan.

Consequently, I argue that public administration graduates face fragile labor market development and/or opportunities in Ethiopia due to information asymmetry in which employers lack a clear understanding of what professional competencies they need from their employees/graduates and analytical segments of the market as well. Likewise, there are no clear employment prospects after graduation and even employers and government authorities may have no idea what specialists they require (Barabashev & Kastrel, 2013; Van, 2014).

Even though public administration graduates rigorously studied the required modules and are equipped with necessary competencies, financial institutions discriminate against them in competition for offered jobs. Surprisingly, the public sector and public enterprises don't offer public administration graduates the opportunity to apply to vacancies regardless of the fact that the graduates' main domain of studies is related to those organizations (see annex 1). Besharov & Oser (2013) argue that to the challenges public administration graduates face in career opportunities around the world, combined with a narrowing job market that does not address the needs of students planning to work elsewhere, the study of public administration is restrained. In this regard, the undergraduate program of public administration is not the priority choice of students as they apply to universities.

5. Implications and Concluding Remarks

In this chapter, we came to understand that public administration education is worthwhile. It adds value to public interest and ensuring the general welfare, value for public service and money, and strengthens the executive (policymaking and implementation) capacity of institutions at the local, regional, federal, and/or supranational organizational levels. Public administration education enables the public governance and leadership to comprehend the complexity of emerging societal challenges and responds proactively in appropriate ways.

As the Ethiopian GTP-I performance report evidenced, institutional capacity constraints were major challenges to implementing the development plan (National Planning Commission, 2015). To this end, public administration education plays a significant role in strengthening public sector institutional capacity building. Thus, the government and universities teaching public administration should work jointly to overcome these institutional capacity constraints. Therefore, strengthening public administration education may be equated to strengthening public sector institutional executive (policymaking and implementation) capacities. To do so, due attention is required from concerned stakeholders (government, universities, and industries) as well.

The chapter also assessed the Ethiopian public administration education and its professional development, which is now nearly sixty years old. As the study makes evident, there have been different efforts to integrate it into the Ethiopian higher education system. During this period, the discipline has passed through different development routes. Even though its inception coincided with the introduction of the higher education system in Ethiopia, public administration's disciplinary development is immature and its place within the system is still debated. The implication of this situation is a long-lasting challenge for public administration education development and disciplinary growth as well as professionalism in Ethiopia.

Furthermore, its graduates experience serious challenges in the job market (labor industries) despite the fact that available vacancies fit with their major areas of expertise; this probably negatively affects the ability of public administration programs to attract outstanding prospective students. In a similar vein, public administration instructors" profile still remain poor and a significant number of faculty are from related fields of studies that directly negatively affect the disciplinary and professional development of public administration. The limitation of postgraduate and research degrees, especially Ph.D. programs in Ethiopia public universities, like other disciplines greatly affects the academic profile of the scholars teaching these subjects, contributing to the inadequate disciplinary development and professional growth of Ethiopian public administration.

Therefore, considerable attention should be given by concerned bodies to market the discipline, improving its ability to sell itself to job markets through job fairs and internships, and launching/expanding postgraduate/research degrees to improve scholars' academic profile. As Kwaku Ohemeng (2014) has pointed out, marketing of public administration is a breaking-through strategy into the labor market and expansion of graduate programs development is extremely promising due to its education (quality and relevance). Because public administration is applied science (Rosenbaun, 2015), universities that teach it should make commitments to the integration of theory and practice (the highest quality of research and the most outstanding practical experience, i.e., facilitate internship [students'] as well as externships [faculty members]). Programs should be actively engaged through their teaching, training, research, and community service activities with all of their stakeholders from the local, regional, federal institutions and with the global community (scholarship) spectrum at large.

Finally, I want to inform the readers that the study has certain limitations. Due to different constraints the study was limited in its ability to assess the public administration education program course contents, curriculum and pedagogical methodologies, as well as instructional techniques and public administration graduates' (employed) efficiency and effectiveness on the assigned positions/jobs. Therefore, these are the remaining potential areas for potential future research into the Ethiopian public administration education system.

Acknowledgment

I want to express appreciation for the great support of different individuals who contributed to the publication of this chapter. I am first of all extremely grateful to anonymous reviewers who provided constructive comments that greatly enriched the draft chapter. I thank Bacha Kebede Debela (EPAA, president) for his unreserved encouragement and endless reminders and I am indebted to the editors for their inputs. Thank you all.

References

Africa Union Commission. (2017). *Agenda 2063-The Africa We Want.*

Antwi-Boasiako, K. B. (2015). The (Un) Identical Twins: Public Administration and Public Management: Toward Improving Education and Training for Effective Governance in Ghana. *Journal of African Studies and Development*, 7(6), 148-161.

Barabashev, A., & Kastrel, T. (2013). Education in Public Administration in Russia: New Standards and Trends. *Hrvatska i komparativna javna uprava: časopis za teoriju i praksu javne uprave*, 13(1), 105-121.

Besharov, D. J., & Oser, J. (2013). Teaching in today's Global Classroom: Policy Analysis in Cross-national Settings. *Journal of Public Affairs Education*, 19(3), 381-387.

Blace, N. P (2015). The Relevance of Public Administration Education: Towards Professional Development of Men and Women in Public Organizations. *Public Administration Research*, 2(4). doi:10.5539/par.v4n2p52

Bouckaert, G. (2020). From Public Administration in Utopia to Utopia in Public Administration. In Bouckaert & Jann, *European Perspectives for Public Administration*, 71.

Bouckaert, G., & Jann, W. (Eds.). (2020). *European Perspectives for Public Administration: The Way Forward.* Leuven University Press.

Cepiku, D. (2013). Embracing Disciplinary Diversity: Public Administration Education in Italy. *Hrvatska i komparativna javna uprava: časopis za teoriju i praksu javne uprave*, 13(1), 71-104.

Evans, A. M., Morrison, J. K., & Auer, M. R. (2019). The Crisis of Policy Education in Turbulent Times: Are Schools of Public Affairs in Danger of Becoming Irrelevant? *Journal of Public Affairs Education*, 25(3), 285-295.

Ewoh, A. I. (2014). Public Administration Education and Training in Nigeria: Problems, Challenges, and Prospects. *Journal of Public Affairs Education*, 20(4), 455-468.

Haruna, P. F. (2004). Training Public Administrators in Africa: A Case Study of Civil Service Employees in Ghana. *International Journal of Public Administration*, 27(3-4), 171-195.

Henry N. (2005). Public Administration and Public Affairs, 9th ed. Upper Saddle River, NJ: Pearson Educational, Inc.

Hustedt, T., Randma-Liiv, T., & Savi, R. (2020). Public Administration and Disciplines. In Bouckaert & Jann, *European Perspectives for Public Administration*, 129.

Kwaku Ohemeng, F. L. (2014). Challenges and Prospects of Public Administration Education and Training in Africa: The Case of Ghana. *Journal of Public Affairs Education*, 20(4), 469-486.

Mitiku, A. A. (2018). *The Ethiopian Public Sector Leadership Profile Unveiled: Determining the Leadership Profile of the Ethiopian Federal Civil Service Organizations.* Leuven: KU Leuven Public Governance Institute (Printed by Acco).

National Harmonized Curriculum (2013). Nationally Harmonized Modular Curriculum for Bachelor of Arts Degree in Public Administration and Development Management. Addis Ababa.

National Planning Commission. (2015). The Second Growth and Transformation Plan (GTP-II) (2015/16-2019/20) (Draft). Addis Ababa: The Federal Democratic Republic of Ethiopia.

Norman-Major, K. (2011). Balancing the Four Es; or Can We Achieve Equity for Social Equity in Public Administration? *Journal of Public Affairs Education*, 17(2), 233-252.

Onder, M., & Brower, R. S. (2013). Public Administration Theory, Research, and Teaching: How Does Turkish Public Administration Differ? *Journal of Public Affairs Education*, 19(1), 117-139.

Pal, L. A., & Clark, I. D. (2016). Teaching Public Policy: Global Convergence or Difference? *Policy and Society*, 35(4), 283-297.

Pan African University (PAU, n.d). Strategic Plan 2020-2024.

Rasmussen, K., & Callan, D. (2016). Schools of Public Policy and Executive Education: An Opportunity Missed? *Policy and Society*, 35(4), 397-411.

Rosenbaum, A. (2015). Public Administration Education and Training in a Turbulent Time. *In Quest of Excellence: Approaches to Enhancing the Quality of Public Administration Education and Training*, 27. Division for Public Administration and Development Management, United Nations Department of Economic and Social Affairs, New York, USA: United Nations, 2015

Rubaii, N. M., & Pliscoff, C. (2013). Public Administration Education in Latin America Understanding Teaching in Context: An Introduction to the Symposium. *Journal of Public Affairs Education*, 19(4), 585-589.

Steinmo, S., Thelen, K. A., & Longstreth, F. (1992). *Structuring Politics: Historical Institutionalism in Comparative Analysis*. Cambridge, UK: Cambridge University Press.

Stuteville, R., & Jumara, J. (2010). The Role of Path-Dependency in Public Administration and Economics and Implications for the Future. A Paper Presented at the Annual Conference of the National Association of Schools of Public Affairs and Administration, Las Vegas, Nevada.

Teferra T., Asgedom. A, Oumer J., W/hanna T., Dalelo A., & Assefa B. (2018). Ethiopian Education Development Roadmap (2018-30): An Integrated Executive Summary, Ministry of Education, Education Strategy Center (ESC), Draft for Discussion.

Trouvé, H., Couturier, Y., Etheridge, F., Saint-Jean, O., & Somme, D. (2010). The Path Dependency Theory: Analytical Framework to Study Institutional Integration. The Case of France. *International Journal of Integrated Care*, 10 (2) http://doi.org/10.5334/ijic.544

United Nations (UN, 2015). Transforming Our World: The 2030 Agenda for Sustainable Development:

Van der Waldt, G. (2014). Public Administration Teaching and Interdisciplinary: Considering the Consequences. *Teaching Public Administration*, 32(2): 169-193.

Van der Waldt, G. (2017). Theories for Research in Public Administration. *African Journal of Public Affairs*, 9(9), 183-202.

Verheijen T., and Connaughton B., (2003). Public Administration Education and Europeanization: Prospects for the Emancipation of a Discipline? *Public Administration*, 81(4), 833-851.

Annex 1: Public Administration Graduates & Job Market

S. No	Vacancy Title	Organization Type (Gov't, Pvt, Pbc Entp's, NGOs, Research Institutes)	Qualification Required	PA_ Graduate Invitation status (Directly, Indirectly or Not Applicable)	Vacancy Relation to PA_ Discipline (Directly, Indirectly or Not Related	Vacancy relation to specific module) in PA	Month Vacancy Posted (2019)
1	Social Policy Researcher	Research Institute	Dev't Eco, Public Policy, sociology	Directly invited	Directly		June
2	Human Resource Researcher	Research Institute	Labor economic, HRM, Public Policy	Directly invited	Directly		June
3	Project Manager	NGO	Social science, Political science, Dev't studies	NA	Directly	Project Mgt and Program Mgt	June
4	Reform and good governance expert	Gov't	Management, sociology, political science	Indirectly Invited	Directly		June
5	Program Team leader	Gov't	Economics, Management	NA	Directly		June
6	Training officer	Pvt	Management and related	Indirectly Invited	Directly	HRA	June

S. No	Vacancy Title	Organization Type (Gov't, Pvt, Pbc Entp's, NGOs, Research Institutes)	Qualification Required	PA_ Graduate Invitation status (Directly, Indirectly or Not Applicable)	Vacancy Relation to PA_ Discipline (Directly, Indirectly or Not Related	Vacancy relation to specific module) in PA	Month Vacancy Posted (2019)
7	Human Resource team leader	Pvt	HRM, Management or Public Administration and related	Directly invited	Directly		June
8	Human Resource Director	Pvt	Mgt, Bus's Mgt, HRM, PA	Directly invited	Directly		June
9	Planning and Budgeting Expert	Gov't	AcFn, Mgt, Eco, LSCM, Mktg and related	NA	Directly	Public finance Admn	June
10	Grievance Handling Expert	Gov't	Law, Mgt, and related	NA	Directly	Public Service	June
11	HRM and procurement Admn	Pvt	Eco, Mgt, Bu's admn	NA	Directly	HRM	June
12	Administration and Finance Services	Pvt	AcFn, Mgt, and Bu's Admn	NA	Directly	Public Finance	June
13	Manager and Public IR	Pvt	Eco, Mgt, Bu's admn and Language	NA	Directly	Public Service, Admn Comn	June
14	Planning and Budgeting Expert	Gov't	Mktg, Mgt, Eco and Related	Indirectly Invited	Directly	Public finance Admn	June

S. No	Vacancy Title	Organization Type (Gov't, Pvt, Pbc Entp's, NGOs, Research Institutes)	Qualification Required	PA_ Graduate Invitation status (Directly, Indirectly or Not Applicable)	Vacancy Relation to PA_ Discipline (Directly, Indirectly or Not Related	Vacancy relation to specific module) in PA	Month Vacancy Posted (2019)
15	General Public Services	Gov't	Mgt, Eco, and related	Indirectly Invited	Directly	Public Service	June
16	Program Monitoring & Evaluation	Gov't	EdPM or related	Indirectly Invited	Directly	Progrma Mgt	June
17	Personnel admin Officer	Pvt	Mgt, HRM	NA	Directly	HRA	June
18	HRM officer	NGO	Mgt, HRM and Related	NA	Directly	HRA	June
19	Project Administrator	Pvt	Mgt, Eco or Bus's Mgt	NA	Directly	Project Mgt	June
20	HRM and Leadership Trainer	Gov't	HRM, Leadership and Change Mgt	Indirectly Invited	Directly	HRM, leadership	June
21	Project Coordinator	Pvt	Eco, Mgt, Sociology and Social Science	NA	Directly	Program Mgt	June
22	HRM officer	Gov't	PA or Related	Directly invited	Directly	HRA	June
23	HRM Expert	Gov't	Mgt, HRM, PA, PSIR, Sociology…	Directly invited	Directly		June

S. No	Vacancy Title	Organization Type (Gov't, Pvt, Pbc Entp's, NGOs, Research Institutes)	Qualification Required	PA_ Graduate Invitation status (Directly, Indirectly or Not Applicable)	Vacancy Relation to PA_ Discipline (Directly, Indirectly or Not Related	Vacancy relation to specific module) in PA	Month Vacancy Posted (2019)
24	Youth Affairs Expert	Gov't	Eco, Sociology, Dev't studies, PSIR and related	Indirectly Invited	Directly	Dev't Mgt	June
25	HRM Manager	Gov't	Mgt, HRM and Bus's admn	NA	Directly	HRA and Personnel Admn	June
26	Public safety Expert	Gov't	LSCM, Mgt, Eco, Bus's Mgt, and EdPM	NA	Directly	Public Services	June
27	Education and Training Expert	Gov't	Mgt, PA, PSIR, and EdPM	Directly invited	Directly		June
28	Tax information admn Expert	Gov't	AcFn, Mgt, PA, LSCM, Mktg and related	Directly invited	Directly		June
29	HRM Manager	Pvt	Mgt, and Bus't admn	NA	Directly	HRA & Program Mgt	June
30	Public Services and Development	NGO	Mgt, Project Mgt ...	NA	Directly		June
31	HRM President	Public Enterprise	Eco, Mgt, AcFn and related	NA	Directly		June

S. No	Vacancy Title	Organization Type (Gov't, Pvt, Pbc Entp's, NGOs, Research Institutes)	Qualification Required	PA_ Graduate Invitation status (Directly, Indirectly or Not Applicable)	Vacancy Relation to PA_ Discipline (Directly, Indirectly or Not Related	Vacancy relation to specific module) in PA	Month Vacancy Posted (2019)
32	HRM officer	Gov't	HRM, Personnel, PA, and Mgt	Directly invited	Directly		June
33	General Manager	Pvt	Mgt, Project Mgt, Eco and related	NA	Directly		June
34	Program Management Officer	NGO	AcFn, Admn Mgt, Project Mgt, Bu's Admn	NA	Directly	Program Mgt	June
35	Personnel admn Officer	Pvt	Mgt, PA and Related	Directly invited	Directly		June
36	Project Admn and Finance Head	Pvt	Eco, AcFn, Mgt	NA	Directly	Project Mgt and Public Finance	June
37	Finance and Admtve Asst	NGO	Bus's admn, AcFn and Related	NA	Directly	Public Finance & Taxation	June
38	Administration and Finance Officer	Gov't	AcFn, Mgt	NA	Directly	Public finance and Taxation	June
39	Property Mgt officer	Gov't	AcFn, Mgt, Dev't Mgt, Eco and related	Indirectly Invited	Directly	HRA	June

S. No	Vacancy Title	Organization Type (Gov't, Pvt, Pbc Entp's, NGOs, Research Institutes)	Qualification Required	PA_ Graduate Invitation status (Directly, Indirectly or Not Applicable)	Vacancy Relation to PA_ Discipline (Directly, Indirectly or Not Related	Vacancy relation to specific module) in PA	Month Vacancy Posted (2019)
40	HR Officer	Gov't	Mgt, HRM, Bus's Mgt, PM/A	Directly invited	Directly		June
41	HR Officer	Public Enterprise	HRM, Mgt, PA, Bus's Admn	Directly invited	Directly		June
42	HRM Head	Pvt	Mgt	NA	Directly		June
43	Assistant Supervisor	Pvt	Mgt, Bus's Mgt, HRM	NA	Directly		June
44	Reform and good governance expert	Gov't	Mgt, PA, Sociology, PSIR	Directly invited	Directly		June
45	Planning and Budgeting Expert	Gov't	Eco, Mgt, Bu's Mgt, Statistics	NA	Directly	Public finance Admn	June
46	Program Expert	Gov't	Mgt, EDPM, Bu's Mgt	NA	Directly	Program Mgt	June
47	Education and Training Expert	Gov't	Mgt, Dev't studies, HRM, EDPM	Indirectly Invited	Directly		June
48	Cost Sharing Expert	Gov't	AcFn, Mgt, Bu's Mgt	NA	Directly		June
49	HRM head	Pvt	Mgt, HRM	NA	Directly		June
50	Team leader	Embassy		NA	Directly		June

S. No	Vacancy Title	Organization Type (Gov't, Pvt, Pbc Entp's, NGOs, Research Institutes)	Qualification Required	PA_ Graduate Invitation status (Directly, Indirectly or Not Applicable)	Vacancy Relation to PA_ Discipline (Directly, Indirectly or Not Related	Vacancy relation to specific module) in PA	Month Vacancy Posted (2019)
51	Management Representative officer	Pvt	Mgt and Related	NA	Directly		June
52	Foreign and Commonwealth Officer	Embassy	Accounting	NA	Directly	Foreign Policy and Diplomacy	July
53	Administrative Assistant	NGO	Office Mgt, Secretary Science	NA	Directly		July
54	Executive Director, Dialogue Africa	Think Tank	Econ, Law, Social Science, Bu's admn, PA…	Directly invited	Directly		July
55	Deputy Manager	Pvt	Mgt, Bu's admn, EDPM	NA	Directly		July
56	Project Office	NGO	Mgt, Social Science, Public health	Indirectly Invited	Directly	Project Mgt	July
57	HR and Property Admn officer	Pvt	Bus's admn, Mgt, EdPM	NA	Directly		July
58	Project Coordinator	Gov't	Eco, Sociology, Mgt, Social Work	NA	Directly	Program Management	July

S. No	Vacancy Title	Organization Type (Gov't, Pvt, Pbc Entp's, NGOs, Research Institutes)	Qualification Required	PA_ Graduate Invitation status (Directly, Indirectly or Not Applicable)	Vacancy Relation to PA_ Discipline (Directly, Indirectly or Not Related	Vacancy relation to specific module) in PA	Month Vacancy Posted (2019)
59	Office Coordinator	Gov't	Law, Mgt, Eco, Mktg, AcFn	NA	Directly		July
60	Monitoring & Evaluation Officer	Gov't	Law, Mgt, Eco, Mktg, AcFn	NA	Directly		July
61	HR Officer	Pvt	Mgt, Bu's admn, and Personnel Admn	NA	Directly		July
62	Project Admn and Finance Head	Pvt	Mgt, and AcFn	NA	Directly	Pgm Mgt and Public Finance	July
63	Project Personnel officer	Pvt	Mgt	NA	Directly	Project Mgt	July
64	Shift Manager	Public Enterprise	Risk Mgt, Dev't Mgt, Urban Mgt, Mgt, Env'tal Science	NA	Directly		July
65	HRA Head	Pvt	Mgt, Bu's Mgt	NA	Directly	HRA and PA	July
66	Office Manager	Pvt	AcFn, Office Mgt, Bu's Mgt, Computer science	NA	Directly		July

S. No	Vacancy Title	Organization Type (Gov't, Pvt, Pbc Entp's, NGOs, Research Institutes)	Qualification Required	PA_ Graduate Invitation status (Directly, Indirectly or Not Applicable)	Vacancy Relation to PA_ Discipline (Directly, Indirectly or Not Related	Vacancy relation to specific module) in PA	Month Vacancy Posted (2019)
67	Case Manager	Pvt	AcFn, Bu's Mgt, PR, Computer Science	NA	Directly		July
68	Creative Communication Expert	Public Enterprise	Eco, Mgt, Bu's Mgt, Journalism, language and literature, Theatrical art, AcFn	NA	Directly	Public Enterprise Mgt	July
69	Digital Mktg Communication Expert	Public Enterprise	Eco Mgt, Bu's Mgt, Bu's Admn, Journalism, language and literature, Theatrical art ...	NA	Directly	Public Enterprise Mgt, Public Service	July
70	Social and Economic Reintegration	NGO/ Consultancy	Social Science, Dev't Studies	Indirectly Invited	Directly	Dev't Mgt	July
71	Deputy Project Coordinator	NGO	Social Science, Dev't Studies, Public Health	Indirectly Invited	Directly	Program Mgt	July
72	General Manager	Pvt	Mgt	NA	Directly		July
73	Project on Climate Change	Gov't	Bu's Admn. AcFn, Mgt	NA	Directly	Program Mgt	July

S. No	Vacancy Title	Organization Type (Gov't, Pvt, Pbc Entp's, NGOs, Research Institutes)	Qualification Required	PA_ Graduate Invitation status (Directly, Indirectly or Not Applicable)	Vacancy Relation to PA_ Discipline (Directly, Indirectly or Not Related	Vacancy relation to specific module) in PA	Month Vacancy Posted (2019)
74	General Manager	Pvt	Bu's Admn. AcFn, Mgt and Eco	NA	Directly		July
75	Project Coordinator	Think Tank	Law, PA, Eco	Directly invited	Directly		July
76	HR Head	Think Tank	Law, PA, Sociology, Journalism, Psychol-ogy, International Relation	Directly invited	Directly		July
77	Human Rights Officer	Think Tank	Law, PA, PSIR, Sociology	Direct invited	Directly		July
78	Finance and Admn Manager	Think Tank	AcFn	NA	Directly	Public finance admn	July
79	Deputy Program Manager	NGO	Mgt, Bu's Admn, Eco	NA	Directly	Program Mgt	July
80	Program officer	NGO	Mgt, Bu's Admn, Eco	NA	Directly	Program Mgt	July
81	Implementation of Competitiveness and Job Creation	Public Enterprise (Consultancy)	Bu's admn, Bu's Mgt, Eco	NA	Directly	Public Enterprise	July

S. No	Vacancy Title	Organization Type (Gov't, Pvt, Pbc Entp's, NGOs, Research Institutes)	Qualification Required	PA_ Graduate Invitation status (Directly, Indirectly or Not Applicable)	Vacancy Relation to PA_ Discipline (Directly, Indirectly or Not Related	Vacancy relation to specific module) in PA	Month Vacancy Posted (2019)
82	General Services & Property Admn	Public Enterprise	PA, Bu's Admn, HR, Property Admn, and Transport operation	Directly invited	Directly	Public Service, and Public Finance Administration	July
83	Customer Service Manager	Financial Institution	Mgt, Eco, AcFn	NA	Directly		July
84	Branch Manager	Financial Institution	Mgt, Eco, AcFn	NA	Directly		July
85	Underwriter Trainee	Financial Institution	Eco, Mgt, AcFn	NA	Directly		July
86	Customer Service Manager	Financial Institution	Bu's admn, Bu's Mgt, Eco, AcFn	NA	Directly		July
87	Workflow Exert	Financial Institution	Bu's admn, Bu's Mgt, Eco, AcFn	NA	Directly		July
88	Bank Trainee	Financial Institution	AcFn, Eco, Bu's Mgt, Mktg,...	NA	Directly		July
89	Customer Service officer	Financial Institution	AcFn, Bu's Mgt, Eco...	NA	Directly		July

S. No	Vacancy Title	Organization Type (Gov't, Pvt, Pbc Entp's, NGOs, Research Institutes)	Qualification Required	PA_ Graduate Invitation status (Directly, Indirectly or Not Applicable)	Vacancy Relation to PA_ Discipline (Directly, Indirectly or Not Related	Vacancy relation to specific module) in PA	Month Vacancy Posted (2019)
90	Property Admn officer	Public Enterprise	Mgt, Property Admn.	NA	Directly		July
91	Customer Service Expert	Financial Institution	Eco, Mgt, Bu's admn, AcFn...	NA	Directly	Public Service	July
92	Water Supply, Sanitation and Hygiene	Gov't (Consultancy)	Water Mgt and Related	NA	Directly	Public Service and Urban Governance	July
93	Secretariat Assistant	NGO	Secretarian science, Mgt, office Mgt	NA	Directly		July
94	Livelihood Expert	NGO	Agr Eco, Cooperative, Mgt	NA	Directly	Dev't Mgt	July
95	Project Manager	Gov't	Mgt, Eco, Bu's Mgt, Development Studies,	Indirectly Invited	Directly	Project Mgt	July
96	Project Monitoring & Evaluation	Gov't	Eco, Mgt	NA	Directly	Project Mgt	July
97	Team Leader Monitoring & Evaluation	Financial Institution	Mgt, Police Academy, Eco, leadership, AcFn,	NA	Directly		July
98	Manager Command Center	Financial Institution	Police Academy, Mgt, Leadership	NA	Directly	Leadership and Change Mgt	July

S. No	Vacancy Title	Organization Type (Gov't, Pvt, Pbc Entp's, NGOs, Research Institutes)	Qualification Required	PA_ Graduate Invitation status (Directly, Indirectly or Not Applicable)	Vacancy Relation to PA_ Discipline (Directly, Indirectly or Not Related	Vacancy relation to specific module) in PA	Month Vacancy Posted (2019)
99	Customer Service officer	Financial Institution	AcFn, Mgt, Eco, ...	NA	Directly	Service Delivery	July
100	Tax Admn Expert	Gov't	AcFn, Mgt, Eco, PA, Tax Admn...	Directly invited	Directly		July
101	HRM Head	Pvt	HR, Mgt	NA	Directly		July
102	Risk Management Officer	Financial Institution	AcFn, Eco, Mgt...	NA	Directly		July
103	Customer Service officer	Financial Institution	AcFn, Mgt, Eco..	NA	Directly	Service Delivery	July
104	Assistant Manager	Financial Institution	Mgt, AcF, Bu's Mgt	NA	Directly		July
105	Program Manager	Public Enterprise	Social sciences	Indirectly Invited	Directly	Pgm Mgt	July
106	Project Manager	Public Enterprise	EdPM, Social Work, Mgt	NA	Directly	Pgm Mgt	July
107	Project Coordinator	Public Enterprise	Education, Social Science	NA	Directly	Pgm Mgt	July

S. No	Vacancy Title	Organization Type (Gov't, Pvt, Pbc Entp's, NGOs, Research Institutes)	Qualification Required	PA_ Graduate Invitation status (Directly, Indirectly or Not Applicable)	Vacancy Relation to PA_ Discipline (Directly, Indirectly or Not Related	Vacancy relation to specific module) in PA	Month Vacancy Posted (2019)
108	Executive Secretary	Public Enterprise	Bu's Admn	NA	Directly	Public Enterprise Admn	July
109	Customer Service Expert	Financial Institution	Bu's Mgt, AcFn, Eco...	NA	Directly		July
110	Customer Service Manager	Financial Institution	Mkt, Mgt, Eco...	NA	Directly		July
111	Humanitarian Program Manager	NGO	Social sciences, Dev't, Agr, Agri Eco.	Indirectly Invited	Directly	Mgt of NGOs	July
112	HR Head	Public Enterprise	Mgt, ACFn, Bu's Admn, Eco	NA	Directly		July
113	Finance & Admn Officer	NGO	AcFn, Mgt...	Indirectly Invited	Directly		July
114	Executive Director	Think Tank	Law	NA	Directly	Pgm Mgt	July
115	HR Head	Pvt	HR, Mgt,	NA	Directly		July
116	Deputy Manager	Pvt	Mgt	NA	Directly		July
117	Property Admn officer	Gov't	Procurement Admn, AcFn, Mgt, Eco	NA	Directly		July

S. No	Vacancy Title	Organization Type (Gov't, Pvt, Pbc Entp's, NGOs, Research Institutes)	Qualification Required	PA_ Graduate Invitation status (Directly, Indirectly or Not Applicable)	Vacancy Relation to PA_ Discipline (Directly, Indirectly or Not Related	Vacancy relation to specific module) in PA	Month Vacancy Posted (2019)
118	Recruitment Officer	Gov't	PA, Bu's Admn, HRM	Directly invited	Directly		July
119	Cost Sharring Expert	Gov't	AcFn, Eco, ICT, Mgt	NA	Directly		July
120	HRM Expert	Gov't	HRM, PA, EdPM, Mgt	Directly invited	Directly		July
121	Emergency Project Officer	NGO	Risk Mgt, Dev't Studies, NaRM,	Indirectly Invited	Directly	Pgm Mgt	July
122	Peace & Security Coordinator	NGO	Social Sciences	Indirectly Invited	Directly		July
123	HR Head	Pvt	HRM, Mgt,	NA	Directly		July
124	HR Admn	Pvt	HRM, Mgt	NA	Directly		July
125	Service Center Controller	Think Tank	Mgt	NA	Directly	Pbc Service	July
126	Personnel Affairs Expert	Public Enterprise	HRM, Mgt, Bu's Admn	NA	Directly		July
127	Gender Affairs Director	Public Enterprise	Gender studies, Anthropology, Dev't studies, Sociology	Indirectly Invited	Directly	Gender and Dev't	July

S. No	Vacancy Title	Organization Type (Gov't, Pvt, Pbc Entp's, NGOs, Research Institutes)	Qualification Required	PA_ Graduate Invitation status (Directly, Indirectly or Not Applicable)	Vacancy Relation to PA_ Discipline (Directly, Indirectly or Not Related	Vacancy relation to specific module) in PA	Month Vacancy Posted (2019)
128	Case Manager	Pvt	Law, Journalism, IR	NA	Directly		July
129	General Service	NGO		NA	Directly		July
130	Chief Case handler	Pvt	Law, PSIR, Journalism	NA	Directly		July
131	PA Lecturer	Education	PA, MBA	Directly invited	Directly		July
132	Reform Officer Head	Gov't	Mgt, HRM, PSIR, PA, Bu's Mgt, Dev't studies, Leadership	Directly invited	Directly		July
133	HR Expert	Gov't	Mgt, PA, Bu's Mgt, PSIR	Directly invited	Directly		July
134	HR Expert	Public Enterprise	Mgt, PA, HRA	Directly invited	Directly		July
135	Gender Affairs Head	Public Enterprise	PSIR, Dev't studies, Sociology, PA, Leadership...	Directly invited	Directly		July
136	Youth Affairs Expert	Public Enterprise	PSIR, Dev't studies, Sociology, PA, Leadership, Public Policy	Directly invited	Directly		July

S. No	Vacancy Title	Organization Type (Gov't, Pvt, Pbc Entp's, NGOs, Research Institutes)	Qualificat on Required	PA_ Graduate Invitation status (Directly, Indirectly or Not Applicable)	Vacancy Relation to PA_ Discipline (Directly, Indirectly or Not Related	Vacancy relation to specific module) in PA	Month Vacancy Posted (2019)
137	Administrative Officer	Embassy	HR	NA	Directly		July
138	Customer Service officer	Financial Institution	AcFn, Mgt, Eco, ...	NA	Directly	Service Delivery	July
139	Branch Manager	Financial Institution	AcFn, Mgt, Eco...	NA	Directly		July
140	Early warning Expert	Public Enterprise	AcFn, Mgt, HR....	NA	Directly		July
141	Team Leader	Public Enterprise	Mgt, HRA, Urban Mgt,	NA	Directly		July
142	Program Manager	NGO	Mgt, Bu's Mgt, Mgt, PSIR	NA	Directly		July

V.2

POLICING

23
The Implementation of Community Policing in Addis Ababa City, Ethiopia

Wondem Meuriaw Ayalew

Box 1: Key messages of the chapter

- ✓ AAPC has organized community policing geographically and assigned community policing officers for a long period of time at the "ketena" level.
- ✓ AAPC is a moderately formed community partnership to prevent crime in the city.
- ✓ The commission is partially applying problem-solving techniques and devolution of authority and responsibility to frontline officers.
- ✓ Major obstacles to community policing include the organization of the commission and awareness gaps among residents, officers, and managers.

Box 2: Reading this chapter will give insight in

- ✓ The practice of community policing in the city
- ✓ The structure of community policing in the city
- ✓ The level of implementation of community policing in the city
- ✓ Major challenges facing the implementation of community policing

Box 3: Abbreviations

AAPC = Addis Ababa Police Commission
AEO = African Economic Outlook.
EFPC = Ethiopian Federal Police Commission
EPRDF = Ethiopia Peoples' Revolutionary Democratic Front
FDRE = Federal Democratic Republic of Ethiopia
LI = Level of implementation
MoFED = Ministry of Finance and Economic Development
NPM = New Public Management
PASDEP = A Plan for Accelerated and Sustained Development to End Poverty.
TQM = Total Quality Management

1. Introduction

Ethiopia has registered remarkable economic growth and improvement in the human development index in the last decade (Molina & Purse, 2010). This economic growth enhances the overall welfare of the citizens, but it does not guarantee a decent quality of life (Bekele *et al.*, 2012). Thus, it is vital to strengthen the capacity of law enforcement institutions to promote human security by protecting citizens' entitlements (Bekele, et. al., 2012). The absence of peace and order disrupts commerce, provision of public services, and all economic activities, plunging people into destitution and poverty. Therefore, efforts to sustain economic growth should be accompanied by building durable institutions capable of upholding lasting peace and order (Bekele et.al, 2012).

The police department is a law enforcement institution charged with ensuring safety and security. In Ethiopia, the modern police force was established during the reign of Emperor Menelik II in 1913, under the name "*Yeketema Zebegna*" or the City's Guard. Since its establishment, the police department has undergone several reforms to meet the demands of the time (EFPC, 2017).

To adjust to the current situation, the Ethiopia police department was re-established by Ethiopian Federal Police Commission establishment proclamation no. 720/2011. The proclamation reorganized the Addis Ababa Police Commission (AAPC) under the Ethiopian Federal Police Commission (EFPC) in order to ensure better institutional capabilities. According to the proclamation, the objectives of the commission are ensuring and maintaining peace and security of the public and state through the active participation of the public (FDRE, 2011).

To strengthen the institutional capacity of the commission, the government of Ethiopia planned to implement a justice system reform plan, particularly community policing, in the 2006-2010 national five-year development plan, i.e. in the Plan for Accelerated and Sustained Development to End Poverty (PASDEP) (MoFED, 2006). One of the objectives of the justice system reform program is building the capacity of law enforcement institutions to improve efficiency and effectiveness (MoFED, 2006). AAPC commenced community policing to improve the institutional capacity to maintain peace and order in the city (Mulat, 2015).

Community policing, as its name implies, involves the community in policing efforts, in identifying problems and conditions that give rise to crime, and providing solutions proactively (Diamond & Weiss, 2016). The core idea of community policing is the police and community should work together to identify and solve community problems before they cause crime (Community Policing Consortium, 1994).

Community policing was launched by the Addis Ababa Police Commission regulation no.1/2010. The regulation states that the structure of community policing in Addis Ababa stretches from the City to the community level. The formal structures include the City, Sub-city, Woreda, and village/ "Ketena" structures (AAPC, 2010). However, block level and household level community structures are voluntary and managed by a selected committee with the help of a community policing officer. According to AAPC (2010), there are consultative councils at each level of community policing and the councils are chaired by the mayor, sub-city chief administrator, and chief woreda administrator, respectively. The consultative councils are tasked with solving problems proactively to prevent crime and reduce fear of crime.

The structures below the "Ketena" level are led by committee with the assistance of the assigned community policing officer. The structures enable the community to participate. Every household has a family police member who is a representative of the family and is obliged to control the actions of his/her family members (AAPC, 2010).

However, there has been no research conducted on how effectively community policing has been implemented in Addis Ababa City, with the exception of Legesse *et al.* (2016). They have researched the specific subpart of Addis Ketema Sub-city of Addis Ababa city. However, they did not clearly show the level of community policing implementation either in their specific study area or in the city at large.

Community policing emphasizes the value of individual community policing officers. Frontline community policing officers, in community policing, are responsible for managing every activity that concerns community policing. They are also responsible for delivering policing service to the neighborhood. Therefore, the shifting of responsibility to line officers requires organizational changes in terms of the management style, organizational structure, human resource management practices, and information system of the police department. In consideration of the importance of police service, the government of Ethiopia has introduced several reforms, of which the justice system reform program and service delivery reform program are perhaps the most significant (MOFED, 2006). These reforms have been introduced to make police organization fit with new philosophy, i.e., the community policing system. In doing so, AAPC has made some adjustment in police organizations in line with the federal government's system. However, how far these reforms support community policing system has not been assessed.

Community policing demands smooth relations with and support from the community to be effectively implemented. Alpert et.al (2001) and Skogan (1995) insist that without the support of the community that knows the neighborhood well the police will hardly be able to effectively implement community policing. Against this assertion and the missions and vision of the police, Ethiopian police, particularly Addis Ababa police, were engaged in political activities. As Nunzio (2014) and Woldekidan (2016) have explained, under both the previous and current regimes, Addis Ababa police were politically partial and advocated the political agenda of the ruling party instead of upholding the constitution. This unconstitutional experience damaged the image of the police and resulted in negative community memories. Yet, as has already been said, community policing demands smooth relations with the community and the creation of a partnership with it. Wilson and Kelling (1982) strengthen the argument that the success of community policing relies on community partnerships (Alpert, Flynn, & Piquero, 2001). Without the support of the community who knows the neighborhood well, police will be unable to maintain peace and order (Skogan, 1995). Thus, how these bad experiences with the police affects the effective implementation of community policing remains to be examined.

Against this backdrop, the study answers the following research questions:

- How far has the commission been transformed to adopt community policing?
- What are the practices of community policing in Addis Ababa City?
- What is the level of implementation of community policing in Addis Ababa City?
- What are the challenges of community policing in Addis Ababa City?

2. Literature Review

2.1. Introduction

In the 1960s and 1970s, the Western governments were challenged by a financial crisis, public discontent on inflexible public sector bureaucracy, and low public trust (Pollitt *et al.*, 2007). These issues brought a historic shift toward the neoliberal movement in industrial countries, especially in the USA and UK. The ideology rejects the welfare state, opposes large bureaucracy, doubts the capacity of the government, blames public bureaucracy for inefficiency and ineffectiveness, advocates adapting the private sector management and operating system into the public sector, and focuses on the private sectors like service delivery (Pollitt *et al.*, 2007).

This ideological turn was reinforced by new managerialism thinking, called New Public Management (NPM), which supports adopting of the organizational principles, leadership styles, and other experiences of the private sector into the public sector (Gruening, 2001). It also focuses on structural devolution and management principles and efficiency (Christensen and Lægreid, 2011). Sozar (2008) argues that Total Quality Management (TQM) also gave momentum to the new movement. TQM is a management approach that advocates continuous improvement with the participation of all employees in an organization with the aim of achieving customer satisfaction (Kim, 2016).

In addition, the end of 1990s saw the emergence of post-New Public Management (post NPM). This approach focuses more on central capacity and control, coordination within and between sectors, and value-based management (Christensen and Lægreid, 2011). These paradigm shifts have compelled public service delivery institutions to consider the quality of service and public satisfaction (Sozer, 2008). As police departments are by their nature a public service delivery institution, they also became worried about efficiency, effectiveness, quality of service, and public satisfaction.

Particularly, in the 1960s street riots, the civil right movement, and the rise of crime and fear of crime put police departments at the center of the maelstrom (Uchida, 1993). Between the 1960s and 1970s, the crime rate in the United States doubled. In addition, the continuous civil right movement exerted another pressure on the police department (Uchida, 1993). Moore and Trojanowicz (1986) posit that the fear of crime had been increasing continuously since the 1960s. Finally, the local police departments were faced with a budget imbalance as they sought to tackle the growing problem (Community policing consortium, 1994).

The circumstances of the 1960s compelled politicians, police, and policymakers to reassess the situation of law enforcement organizations. Scholars were also invited to study the effort of policing and police organization from several perspectives and brought into question the effectiveness of professional policing. According to Walker (1977), on the one hand, the situation revolves around the level of training, recruitment, efficiency, and the level of service. On the other side, despite improvements in these areas, the problems in society remained the same or increased (Uchida, 1993). Furthermore, professional policing views police officers as experts in crime prevention, considering police as the experts who have all the answers, which undermines the capacity and contributions of the community in policing efforts. It, therefore, limited and weaken the relationship between police and community (Community Policing Consortium, 1994). In short, traditional policing disregarded the contribution of community to the police service and concentrated on the top-down approach while remaining reactive in nature. This approach has, in effect, failed to cope with the complex and dynamic nature of crime and fear of crime (Chan, 2008).

The main objective of traditional policing is reducing crime and gives little emphasis to fear of crime, public satisfaction, and disorder (Bucqueroux and Trojanowicz, 1990). Furthermore, it focuses on "serious" crimes rather than on disorder. It deals with crimes through rapid response and undercover operations. In conclusion, professional policing limits the capacity of police in the crime fighting effort (Community Policing Consortium, 1994) and as such is no longer considered an effective strategy in crime prevention (Kusow, Wilson and Martin 1997). Research has revealed that the tactics of professional policing have had little or no contribution to preventing or minimizing crime and fear of crime in society (Uchida, 1993).

These problems compel the government to innovate a new policing which would the weakness of traditional policing strategies. In the 1990s, the police department brought community policing into the police department to tackle the elevated crime and fear of crime. Community policing has been developed as an alternative solution to the failed efforts of professional policing to effectively deal with crimes.

2.2. The Rationales of Community Policing in Ethiopia

Like Western countries, Ethiopia faced a similar situation in preventing crime and delivering quality police service to the community. In 2001 and 2005 young citizens were rioting in support of the opposition political parties. However, arguably, such riots were labelled by the ruling Ethiopian Peoples' Revolutionary Democratic Front (EPRDF) as a dangerous alliance between opposition politicians and ordinary street crime and named participants "gangsters and dangerous vagrants." In labeling the youths as vagrants and unemployed, the government was able to frame their behavior as a sign of disorder and crime. In addition, from 2001 to 2004, there was an intensive youth group conflict over a simple and an irrelevant reason, which created tension in the community and fertile ground for offenders to commit crime (Di Nunzio, 2014).

Another influential factor that compels police reform is the centrality of crime prevention and community policing in the current political discourse of African countries. Western development aid came up with conditionality, which is a governance system used to overcome the challenges related to growth and security. It also focuses on extensions of best practices to the role of the state and local community, and commitment to cost-effectiveness and accountability (World Bank, 1989). Therefore, to get international development aid, African countries, including Ethiopia, consider adopting reforms proposed by donor agencies. For instance, the Department of International

Development of the UK allocated more than 20 million euro for community policing programs in Ethiopia. The government of Ethiopia was externally induced to implement and indeed implemented community policing in Addis Ababa City (Di Nunzio, 2014).

Abebe (2002) rationalized that the demand for responsive, transparent, accountable, and customer-oriented police service; the inability of professional policing to maintain peace and order in the city; and increasing awareness that police alone cannot maintain or prevent crime gave momentum to the Ethiopian government to question the policing system.

Indeed, the inability of the police department to maintain peace and order in the city concerns the government, especially since Ethiopia is a developmental state that encourages state intervention to correct social and economic injustice (Bayeh, 2018). In its view, building a strong and competent professional bureaucracy and creating a public private partnership (major features of developmental state) are important panacea for the problems of law and order. Therefore, the government of Ethiopia implemented the justice service reform program in law enforcement institutions, especially the police commission, in part through introducing community policing into the police department (Abebe, 2002; FDRE, 2006).

The government attempting to restructure the police commission and trained officers by relying on community policing science to provide customized and quality service to the community. Besides, the government has created an opportunity for the community (residents and other stakeholders who have concern for the community) to participate and shoulder the policing service along with the government in order to reduce budget burden and provide effective and inclusive service. The reform focuses on the governance system and making police public service more citizen centric (Stebek, 2018).

2.3. Community Policing

Community policing is a governance system in the police department that promotes partnership with multiple actors; applies problem-solving techniques to address problems that lead to crime and disorder; and changes the organization to support such efforts (Diamond & Weiss, 2009). COPS (2014) defines it as a philosophy that encourages organizational change that backs the systematic utilization of public partnership and problem-solving practices, to proactively solve problems that compromise the safety of the community. Community policing has three interrelated core elements, namely organizational transformation, community partnership, and problem-solving (Lawrence & McCarthy, 2013).

2.4. Elements of Community Policing

In community policing, frontline officers are responsible for all policing tasks and deliver police service to the neighborhood. Hence, the enhanced role of the officers requires changes in the structure, management, operation, and information system (Community Policing Consortium, 1994). One of the changes in the police department entails reorganizing the department geographically and assigning frontline officers for a long period of time at the neighborhood level. It facilitates close and frequent contact with the community. The officers also get opportunities to identify local priorities, problems, and resources available within the community, to address issues before they cause crime and disorder (Lawrence & McCarthy, 2013). Under community policing, frontline officers are given the discretion to decide what, how, when, and where should be done in the area where they are in charge. Thus, community policing requires the devolution of authority and discretion (Community Policing Consortium, 1994).

Community policing officers should be recruited and hired in the spirit of service provision rather than adventure. In addition, they should be trained and encouraged to develop creative thinking, communication, proactive orientation, and analytical skills, and techniques for dealing with community issues. Moreover, change changes in departmental information systems is required to facilitate access to quality information. Accurate and timely data make problem-solving effective in proactively addressing issues (COPS, 2014).

Community policing invites the community to participate in the quest for crime control and prevention and exploit the community's resources to address priorities. A strong community partnership helps to pinpoint and alleviate the underline causes of crime and disorder (Community Policing Consortium, 1994). Additionally, the community has the right to participate in community policing, since citizens have the right to a voice in any decision that affects their lives. Thus, police should develop a positive and strong partnership with the community (encompassing residents, public and private agencies, nongovernmental organizations, religious institutions, local government offices, hospitals, schools, etc.)

Problem-solving is a process of systematically identifying and analyzing specific community problems that can give rise to crime, fear of crime, and disorder, and providing proactive solutions and evaluating the outcome of the solutions (Diamond & Weiss, 2009). It transformations the police department's approach from reactive and incidence-driven policing to proactive or preventive policing (Lawrence, and McCarthy, 2013). The assumption of problem-solving relies on minimizing crime and disorder by systematically studying the characteristics of a definite geographical area's problems and then providing area-specific solutions (Community Policing Consortium, 1994).

Community policing changes the structure and practices of an organization in terms of organizational transformation, community policing, and problem-solving. Therefore, this study has measured the level of implementation of community policing from the perspectives of such changes.

3. Research Methods

3.1. Research Design and Approach

The purpose of this study is measuring the effectiveness of implementation of community policing in Addis Ababa City. A descriptive research design is appropriate to achieve the objectives. Such a research design serves to describe the characteristics of community policing and states the practice of community policing as it is.

A mixed research approach is used to address the objectives. Both qualitative and qualitative data are used. Quantitative methods show the level of implementation of community policing in Addis Ababa City. On the other hands, qualitative methods help to identify challenges that hinder the effective implementation of community policing in the city.

3.2. Types and Sources of Data

The study used both primary and secondary data. Primary data were collected through a questionnaire and interviews. The questionnaire emphasized the implementation of community policing and was distributed to frontline officers. The interviews were conducted with middle and higher officials of community policing. They focused on the overall implementation of community policing and challenges that inhibit community policing from being effective.

Secondary data consulted included unpublished documents available from authoritative and authenticated organizations such as AAPC. The data therein is utilized to substantiate the survey results.

3.3. Sampling Methods and Procedures

The study used different procedures to select respondents for the questionnaire and interviews. Since Addis Ababa City Administration is too vast to

Table 1: Sample sub-cities, "ketenas," and community policing officers for the questionnaire

Sampled sub-cities	Number of woredas	Number of "keternas"	Sampled officers
Bole	14	75	50
Arada	10	65	44
Kolfe Keranio	15	128	85
Gullele	10	68	45
Lideta	10	54	36
Total	59	390	260

Source: Author's Survey, 2018

Table 2: Interview respondents

Community policing structure	Sub-cities	Number of interviewees
Commission level		2
Sub city level		4
	Bole 1sub-city	3
	Arada sub-city	3
Woreda level	Kolfe Keranio sub-city	3
	Gullele sub-city	3
	Ledita	3
Total		22

Source: Author's Survey, 2018

cover all areas, the study took 50 percent of sub-cities as a sample. Addis Ababa City Administration is divided into 10 sub-cities and/or 116 woredas (Addis Ababa City Administration, 2018). Out of ten sub cities, five sub-cities were taken as a sample study area. Sample areas included Bole, Arada, Kolfe Keranio, Gullele and Lideta sub-cities. The sample sub-cities were selected by lottery method.

To determine how far community policing is successfully implemented in the neighborhood, a questionnaire was distributed to community policing officers. The target population (community policing officers) of the study is found on the "ketena" level. In each "ketena," one community policing officers is assigned. To sample these officers, the study used a two-stage sampling technique.

Interview respondents comprised community policing coordinators at the woreda, sub-city, and commission level. The study interviewed twenty-two community policing officers to obtain information about the overall community policing activity of Addis Ababa. The respondents of the interview were selected purposefully.

3.4. Sample Size Determination

The study should have include an optimum sample size for efficiency, representative, reliability, and flexibility. Hence, the sampling procedure and sample size should be determined based on logical processes (Kothari, 2004). The study used the Krejcie and Morgan (1970) sample size determination formula.

$$S = \frac{X^2NP(1-P)}{d^2(N-1)+X^2P(1-P)}$$

Where:
S= Required sample size
X= The degree of freedom at the desired level of confidence Z value (1.96)
N= Population size
P= Population proportion (assumed to be 0.5, which would give maximum sample size)
d=Degree of accuracy marginal error

Out of 816 community policing officers, 261 community policing officers responded to the second questionnaire.

3.5. Data Analysis

The data collected through a review of documents, questionnaire, and interviews were analyzed within the framework of the study objectives. The data collected through the questionnaire was coded and entered in SPSS version 21. Subsequently, the data were analyzed using descriptive statistics: mean, percentage and frequency. Data collected from the interviews were analyzed and interpreted to get a real picture of the system. Data obtained from secondary sources were utilized to enrich, illustrate, and elaborate on the quantitative and qualitative findings.

Since community policing has three core interdependent elements, it requires the implementation of each element. These core elements are expressed in the activities of community policing activities. Hence, twenty community policing activities were developed to represent all core elements of community policing. Activities were developed and adopted from the AAPC (2010), Mwachidudu and Likaka (2014), and Maguire and Katz (2002).

The sampled officers were asked to indicate the activities performed by AAPC. The activities were coded "0" if the activities are not performed by the commission and coded as "1" if the activity is performed by the commission.

The level of implementation of community policing is obtained by the total score of the twenty community policing activities for the ith respondent by the sum of the most desirable score of all community policing activities, thereby reducing the level of implementation to a scale of $0 \leq \text{LICO} \leq 1$ (Asante et al., 2012).

$$LICP = \frac{\Sigma A_{1i} A_{2i} A_{3i} A_{4i} A_{5i} \ldots A_{20i}}{T}$$

Where:
LICO= Level of implementation of community policing
A_{1i} to A_{20i}= Community policing activities
T= The sum of the most desirable score of all community policing activities

The threshold value of the additive index is 0 to 0.33 considered as "low," 0.34 to 0.66 as "moderate," and 0.66 to above labeled as "high" (Asante et al., 2012). Based on this decision rule, the level of community policing implementation is determined.

4. Findings and Discussions

Off 252 frontline community policing officers who participated in the study, 248 are male and rest 4 frontline officers are female. The age of frontline officers falls in the age category between 18 to 29. The experience of frontline officers in community policing is on average 1.58 years.

4.1. The Implementation of Community Policing

Community policing promotes problem-solving partnership between police and the community to proactively identify and address the problems that could lead to compromising the safety of the public. It advocates geographical organization of the police department and provides decentralized services suited to local conditions. In addition, it empowers frontline officers' discretion and authority to manage everything concerning policing in the area where the officers are in charge (Community Policing Consortium, 1994). Thus, it requires organizational structure and practices.

Table 3: Level of organizational change made in Addis Ababa police commission.

Activities related to organizational change	N	Frequency	Percent
The structure of community policing decentralized to community level, i.e., "ketena" level	252	251	99.6
The commission decentralized decision making power to community policing officers	252	172	68
Community policing officers are assigned to beat permanently	252	240	95
Community policing centers are constructed in each "ketena"	252	151	60
Frontline officers are recruited, hired, and trained in the spirit of community policing	252	21	08
Community awareness training provides for the last 12 months	252	156	62
Community policing officers have facilities such as a cell phone that help to communicate with the community.	252	119	47
The commission developed specific evaluation criteria for community policing.	252	233	92

Source: Author's survey, (2018)

AAPC has been successful in restructuring the commission and making community policing closer to the community (99.6 percent), assigning of frontline community policing officers at the neighborhood level for a long period of time (95 percent), and developing specific performance evaluation criteria for community policing (92 percent) (table 3).

On the other hand, the commission does not recruit, hire, and train officers for community policing. Table 3 reveals that only 8 percent of the officers believed that the commission is recruiting, hiring, and training in line with the community policing philosophy.

The commission's structural transformations are not enough for the effectiveness of community policing. It requires changes in the philosophy and practices in terms of problem solving and partnership.

Table 4: Activities related to problem solving and community partnership of community policing.

Activities related to problem solving and partnership	N	Frequency	Percent
There is a regular meeting with the community to identify problems that need solutions	252	101	40
Community policing officers are encouraged to provide creative and innovative solutions to the problems	252	211	84
Community policing officers' conduct crime analysis in the assigned areas (e.g., keeping records of crimes and the types of request for help)	252	128	51
Consultative councils regularly hold meetings to provide solutions for the identified problems	252	85	34
Consultative councils are formed at each level of community policing	252	182	72
Community policing works with other governmental organizations to solve community problems	252	103	41
Citizens serve voluntarily in patrols coordinated by community police officers	252	141	56
Citizens participate in the neighborhood watch committee	252	140	56
Develop a partnership with schools to combat crime	252	144	57
Develop a partnership with neighborhood associations to combat crime	252	142	56

Source: Author's Survey, 2018

Table 4 reveals that 84 percent of community policing officers believe that the commission encourages the officers to utilize innovative and creative solutions to problems. 72 percent of the officers also attested that consultative councils, in which all stakeholders propose solutions to the problems above the jurisdiction of line officers, were formed, but only 34 percent officers believed that the councils are regularly in session. In general, the commission has been limited in the implementation of activities related to problem-solving and community partnership.

4.2. The Challenges of Community Policing in Addis Ababa City.

Coordinators of community policing at woreda, sub-city and city level were interviewed. They identified the challenges affecting the community, community police officer, and Addis Ababa Police Commission levels of the present study.

The respondents pointed out that the Ethiopian Federal Police establishment proclamation no. 720/2011 to reorganize AAPC is under the federal police commission (FDRE, 2011). The proclamation indirectly mandates that the peace and security issues of Addis Ababa City are the responsibility of the federal government and the city administration in general and the mayor, in particular, do not have the power or police personnel to maintain peace and order in the city. Hence, maintaining this peace and order is not the responsibility of the mayor and chief executives.

On the other hand, the mayor and chief executives at the sub-city and woreda level are key people in creating partnerships with the community. This paradox creates a gap in implementing community policing functions as planned. As a result, the heads of the councils call meetings either at the instigation of the mayor and chief executives or when there are current and urgent security issues where they are in charge. In addition, the structure creates a challenge for transparency and accountability. Since policing is not the responsibility of the city administration, the mayor and chief executives are not responsible for the failure of policing in the city.

Another challenge affecting the performance of community policing is low community participation. The community is reluctant to participate in community policing efforts. Historically, Ethiopian police, especially the Addis Ababa police, were politically partial and worked for the ruling party instead of upholding the constitution, which is one of the missions of the commission. The police were highly involved in political activities in current and previous regimes. Besides, the current ruling party used community policing as a political tool to spy on the members of rival political parties and terrorizing the public into not supporting opposition parties. These unconstitutional acts have made it difficult for community members to enter into an active alliance with the police. In addition, the interviewees have pointed to the inability of community policing officers to mobilize the community. The departure of experienced community policing officers either through resignation or transfer to another division along with insufficient training about community policing results low community participation.

Weak relations between community policing officers and the community is another challenge that inhibits the effective implementation of community policing. The task of community policing depends on the level of relations built between the officers and the community. However, the commission have not trusted community policing officers to have closer relations with the community. This is manifested in the fact that the commission does not devolve decision-making power to frontline community officers and suspects community policing officers of being corrupt when they have good relations with the community. Secondly, senior and experienced community policing officers have left the division and the low commitment of the existing officers also creates a gap in terms of building strong relationships between police and the community. Thirdly, AAPC was involved in political activity and serving the ruling party instead of upholding the constitution in the recent past national elections, a partial political activity that has hindered the police from having a good relationship with the community. Finally, the confusion and mixing of the role of community policing and pre-crime prevention officers is also creating a challenge to building strong relation. Pre-crime prevention officers are involved in apprehending criminals, using force if necessary, and escorting criminals, and are trained in the spirit of adventure. These features of pre-crime officers affect the good will of community policing officers and in turn harm the relationship between community policing and the community. At the end of the day, low levels of trust in the community police/community relationship have hindered the practice from reaching its effective potential.

The effectiveness of community policing depends on the ability to provide solutions to existing problems. Community policing officers and/or consultative council are the bodies responsible for providing solutions for identified problems. The councils provide solutions when the identified problems demand the involvement of a third party and the officers are unable to provide solutions in their personal capacity. However, only 9 percent and 6 percent of consultative councils are functional at the woreda and sub cities level, respectively (AAPCCPD, 2017). This malfunction of the councils hinders the effective implementation of community policing in the city.

Another formidable challenge facing community policing is the high turnover of community policing officers. The activities of community policing are too vast and require a high level of commitment from community officers. Conversely, the salary of community policing officers is too small to cover their basic needs. In addition, the absence of incentives forces community policing officers either to transfer to another division or leave the commission. The number of officers who leave the commission has increased every year. In 2010, the number of officers who left the commission was 823 and reached 2026 in 2014/15 (figure 1).

AAPC (2010) states that all "ketenas" should have community policing centers where in community policing officers reside and deliver service. AAPC (2010) also stipulates that each center should be constructed with community participation. The commission does not have a budget for the construction of community policing canters. The construction of the centers depends on the ability of community policing officers and development committee to mobilize the community and on the willingness of the sub-cities

Figure 1: The Trends of the turnover in Addis Ababa Police Commission

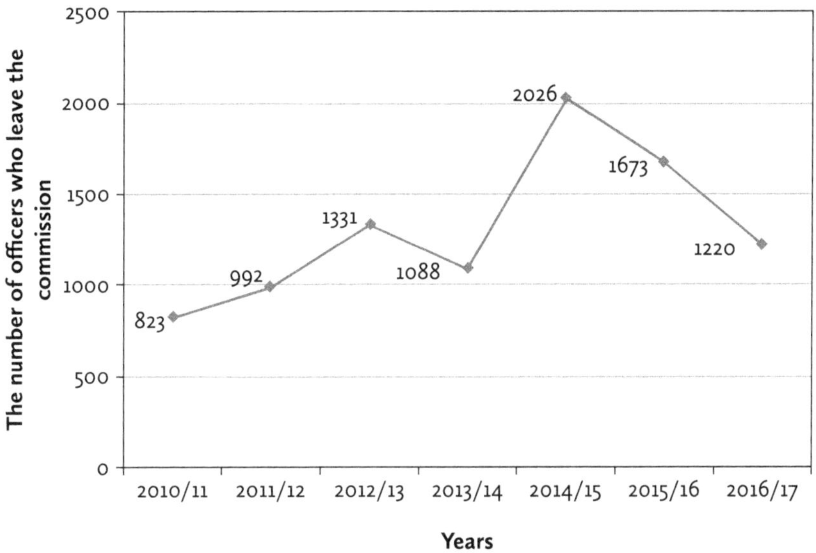

Source: Addis Ababa Police Commission (2010/11-2017)

land administration to give land for construction. Currently, the coverage of community policing centers does not exceed 46 percent (Addis Ababa Police Commission Community Policing Division, 2017). This informal and inconsistent work creates a challenge for community policing.

Another formidable challenge to the effective implementation of community policing involves awareness gaps in the coordination of community policing. The coordinators pointed out that community policing officers and managers of police stations have awareness gaps about community policing. This is manifest in the fact that they assign community policing officers as pre-crime prevention officers, which is against the philosophy of community policing. Additionally, the coordinators discourage the committed and energetic community policing officers by labelling them as corrupted and rent seekers. In addition, they compel the officers to focus on process instead of being result-oriented. They further elaborate that community and community partners, namely neighborhood associations, private organizations, nongovernmental organizations, and religious institutions have an incorrect perception, which is that the peace and security of the city is vested merely in the police. These awareness gaps of the community are created/creating obstacles to the proper implementation and functioning of community policing.

One of the problems that poses a tough challenge is budget constraints. The interviewees revealed that community policing officers are faced with a serious budget shortage to run the activities of community policing. The proclamation in article 20 sub article 2 arguably states that the budget of the commission is allocated by the city administration council (FDRE, 2011). The city administration council appropriates the budget for the organization, which is not under its jurisdiction. Since the commission is under the federal police commission, it does not follow the budget request and allocation format. This creates a huge gap between the demand and the appropriate budget to run community policing. Hence, the efforts of community policing are financed by the contribution of the community and the personal capacity of the chief administrators at the woreda and sub-city levels, respectively.

The last but not least challenge to the success of community policing is competency of community policing. One of the assumptions of community policing is that each specific geographic area has unique problems that require area specific solutions (Cordner, 1997). Community policing focuses on delivering personalized and tailored policing service. Therefore, the officers have a pivotal role in managing all community policing efforts and delivering police service in the area they are in charge of and should have appropriate competencies that fit with the philosophy. However, community policing officers do not have appropriate training to carry out the task. Even though community policing officers are expected to develop specific area strategies to deliver personalized service, only 9 percent and 8 percent of sub cities and woreda have area specific plans, respectively (AAPCPD, 2017).

4.3. The Implementation Index of Community Policing

The commission has been implementing justice service reform, particularly community policing, to make police service customer-oriented in a way that satisfies the public. The essence of the reform is building durable institutions that are capable of delivering quality service. The reform focuses on organizational transformation, community partnership, and providing effective and quality service. Organizational transformation focuses more on devolution of authority and structure, information systems, and other aspects that enable the commission to create a governance system. On the other side, community partnership deals with inviting multiple actors from multiple sectors to participate in delivering police service. It also applies a problem-solving approach to provide decentralized, personalized, and tailored service that fits the norm and value of the community. Hence, to measure the level of implementation, measurement indexes have been developed by the commission from these perspectives. The implementation index was adapted from Maguire and Katz (2002) and Mwachidudu and Likaka (2014) and contextualized into the Addis Ababa community policing context.

Table 5: Level of implementation of community policing in Addis Ababa City.

Indicators	N	Index	Decision
Level of organization change	252	.6662	High
Level of problem solving	252	.5208	Moderate
Level of community partnership	252	.5635	Moderate
Level of community policing implementation	252	.5835	Moderate

Source: Author's survey, 2018

Table 5 reveals that the level of problem-solving and community partnership is moderately implemented whereas, the level of organizational transformation implementation is high, based on the index of Asante *et.al* (2012). Additionally, the result shows that the overall level of community policing implementation in Addis Ababa city is moderate (table 5).

5. Conclusions

Community policing is a policing philosophy that promotes problem-solving partnerships to proactively identify problems that cause crime and disorder and addresses them in creative and innovative ways (Diamond & Weiss, 2009). It assumes that each area has a specific type of problem that requires specific solutions that fit the norms and values of the community (Cordner, 1997). Hence, it promotes decentralized and personalized policing that suits the local context (Cordner, 1997). Community policing requires active community involvement in policing and gives autonomy, discretion, and responsibility to the frontline community policing officers to manage the whole activity of community policing and deliver police service in the area where they are assigned (Community Policing Consortium, 1994). Existing organizational structure, management style, and information systems are obsolete when it comes to carrying out the new policing philosophy (Community Policing Consortium, 1994).

Therefore, community policing requires changes in the police department in terms of management style, structure, personnel, and information system

(Lawrence & McCarthy, 2013). These changes empower frontline community policing officers and create an opportunity for community participation (Community Policing Consortium, 1994). In considering these factors, the commission has made organizational changes to support partnership with the community and problem-solving techniques.

The commission has restructured the structure of the commission and organized operations based on geography, assigned community policing officers at the "ketena" level for a long period of time, and developed performance evaluation criteria specific to community policing and the officers involved. The establishment of neighborhood community policing centers and fulfilling facilities, and devolution of authority and responsibility to the frontline officers have been partially implemented.

Even though community policing officers should be recruited, hired, and trained in the spirit of community policing the commission does not perform such practices. Rather, it assigns pre-crime prevention officers as community policing officers with three days orientation. In general, the Addis Ababa Police Commission has tried to implement organizational change to support community partnership and problem-solving techniques. There is moderately implemented organizational change in the commission in terms of carrying out the new philosophy.

Community policing underlines the importance of community partnership in pursuit of achieving the mission and vision of the commission. Community policing is a type of policing that considers community as a major partner and involves it in the effort of prevent crime and reduce fear of crime (Community Policing Consortium, 1994). Additionally, involving the community in policing efforts is not a privilege, rather it is the right of the community to have a voice in any decision which affects residents' lives (Skogan, 1995). Hence, involving the community in policing efforts is mandatory. In consideration of this fact, the federal police establishment Proclamation no. 720/2011 states that active participation of the community is required in the efforts of crime prevention (FDRE, 2011). As a result, consultative councils, one of the main methods of community participation, are formed at each level of the structure of community policing (AAPC, 2010). The members of the councils are a representative of all stakeholders who have an interest in the peace and security of the community. Private organizations, religious institutions, the representatives of the residents, non-governmental organizations, government officers, community associations, i.e., "Eders" and other neighborhood institutions are represented in the councils (Addis Ababa Police Commission [AAPC], 2010). The councils are responsible for providing solutions to the identified problems and evaluating the effectiveness of the solutions. However, the functionality of the councils merely depends on the assent of the head of the councils. The heads of the councils are the mayor, chief administrator of the city, and the sub-cities and the woreda, respectively. There is no law that compels the councils to be in operation. As a result, fewer than 10 percent of the councils are operational. To sum up, the evaluation of community policing officers and households shows that there is a moderate level of partnership between police and the community.

The third core element of community policing is problem-solving. Problem-solving is a process of proactively identifying and analyzing problems from which crime rise, examining them systematically, and putting forward solutions that will be evaluated (AAPC, 2010). Cordner (1997) has elaborated that each geographic area has a unique problem, which requires a unique strategy that fits with the values and norms of the community. Hence, frontline officers have the discretion and responsibility to provide appropriate solutions (Community Policing Consortium, 1994). The solutions should be designed by considering the resources, norms, and values of the community. However, Addis Ababa community policing has applied almost a uniform style of solution to all areas. Despite the effectiveness of the problem-solving techniques, AAPC only moderately implemented problem-solving techniques in the city. In general, Addis Ababa Police Commission has moderately implemented community policing in the city.

To summarize, AAPC has been moderately effective in implementing community policing in the city to prevent crime, reduce fear of crime, and improve public satisfaction with police. However, there are several challenges that hinder the commission from effectively implementing community policing.

- The problem of the organization of AAPC under the Federal Police Commission instead of under Addis Ababa City Administration creates various problems in accountability, mobilizing the community, applying problem-solving techniques to solve problems that compromise the safety of the community, and providing incentives to the officers.
- The history of the political partiality of Ethiopian police limits the community's desire to actively participate in policing efforts.
- Awareness gap between the community, community policing officers, and coordinators of community policing about the methods and benefits of community policing.
- Shortage of budget at the "ketena" level affects effective implementation.
- High turnover of community policing officers
- Low community interest in participating in community policing.
- There is no legal mechanism that forces stakeholders to participate in policing efforts.

6. Implications

- Community policing is implemented to improve efficiency and effectiveness, increase community participation and improve police legitimacy in the community. These objectives are achieved when the structure of the commission is decentralized and accessible to all stakeholders. However, the structure of the commission is under the Federal Police Commission, which is more centralized and more hierarchal, depriving the community of a voice in the affairs that affect them, which is against the basic feature of the developmental state, which promotes strong community partnership. Thus, the participation of community in policing efforts is low. To enhance the participation of the community in policing service, the structure of the commission should be decentralized and accessible to the community. This would increase the opportunity of the community to have a voice in decisions that concern them and enable the commission to provide personalized and tailored public service that fits the norms and value of the constituency. This implies that the structure of public administration is crucial in creating a real governance system and making government more citizen centric.
- One of the challenges that affects the effectiveness of the commission in implementation of community policing is the political partiality of the commission, which is against the basic features of developmental state. State machinery should not be mixed with party politics and the bureaucracy should be competent and professional. Even though FDRE proclamation 720/11 clearly states that police involvement in political activity is strictly prohibited, the Addis Ababa Police Commission was involved in political activity in recent past national elections of 2010 and 2015. In addition, police were engaged in arresting and terrorizing people based on their political ideology and opinion (Di Nunzio, 2014). These activities damaged the efforts of community policing. Therefore, the effectiveness of the developmental state depends on a neutral and professional bureaucracy. Thus, public institutions should be competent and impartial from party politics in principle as well as in action. Unless the public administration is professional and neutral in regard to party politics, a formidable challenge to implementing reforms in the public sector will remain.
- The community has the right to a voice in any decision that affects their lives. In addition, Reddy (2002) points out that the community has the capacity participate in decision-making in setting goals and how resources are utilized, contributing in ideas, financial support, material

and labor, working together to benefit the whole community and creating a long-term partnership. On the other hand, police alone neither maintain nor prevent peace and order in the community. The community should shoulder policing efforts along with the police to reduce the budget burden of the government (Community Policing Consortium, 1994). Thus, community participation is crucial to providing customer-oriented, effective, responsive, transparent, and accountable public police service.
- Community policing is a governance system that invites the participation of multiple actors from multiple sectors to address the problems that could compromise the safety of the community. As a result, community policing is organized geographically to make the service more accessible and inclusive. However, the commission does not devolve authorities and responsibilities to the grassroot level and limits the frontline officers' ability to mobilize the community and participate in policing efforts. The governance system helps to provide customer-driven service, where the public interest is defined and enables the provision of customer-oriented, responsive, transparent, and accountable police service. Therefore, decentralization of the structure and tasks to the grassroot level is a basic imperative in the creation of creating the commission's governance system.

7. Limitations

The current study has contributed by giving insights into the concept and importance of community policing and contributed to the literature of community policing. However, this chapter has limitations that should be acknowledged, as well as suggestions for future research.
- Since the concept of community policing is amorphous and varies depending on country context, there is no comprehensive model that is used to measure the level of implementation of community policing. If someone would replicate the measurement and the model on the regional and country level, this would provide good input for policy analysts and the commission to improve the measurement of the implementation of community policing.
- There are insufficient empirical findings in the context of developing countries, especially in Africa context. Since the concept of community policing is new for developing countries, it proved impossible to obtain empirical findings that would allow a comparison of implementation levels.

- The study relied on cross-sectional data to measure the level of implementation of community policing. It was impossible to obtain documentation of the progress of implementation of community policing in the city. Hence, the study shows only the level of implementation at the time of data collection and is limited in its ability to predict future progress.

Acknowledgements

I am indebted to the anonymous reviewers who provided critical comments and constructive suggestions that helped me in improving the chapter.

References

Abebe, M. (2002). Community Policing and Ethics. MA thesis, Addis Ababa University.

Addis Ababa Police Commission (AAPC). (2010). Community Policing Manual. Addis Ababa, Ethiopia. (Unpublished Document).

AAPC (2010). Addis Ababa Police Commission Regulation no. 1/2010. Addis Ababa. (Unpublished Document).

Addis Ababa Police Commission Community Policing Division. (2017). Annual Community Policing Performance Evaluation Report of 2017. Addis Ababa Police Commission. Addis Ababa (Unpublished Document).

Alpert, G. P., Flynn, D., & Piquero, A. R. (2001). Effective Community Policing Performance Measures. *Justice Research and Policy*, 3(2), 79-94.

Asante, F. A., Boakye, A. A., Egyir, I. S., & Jatoe, J. B. (2012). Climate Change and Farmers' Adaptive Capacity to Strategic Innovations: The Case of Northern Ghana. *International Journal of Development and Sustainability*, 1(3), 766-784.

Bekele, S., Mekonnen, F., & Ayangafac, C. (2012). *Towards a Comprehensive Peace-building Policy and Strategy for Ethiopia* (No. 4). UNDP Ethiopia. 4-5.

Bayeh, E. (2018). Developmental State of Ethiopia: Reflections on the Benefits Obtained and the Costs Incurred. *Ethiopian Journal of the Social Sciences and Humanities (EJOSSAH)*, 14(2): 72-92. DOI: https://dx.doi.org/10.4314/ejossah.v14i2.3.

Bucqueroux, B., & Trojanowicz, R. (1990). *Community Policing: A Contemporary Perspective*. Cincinnati, OH. Anderson Publishing Company.

Chan, Y. L. (2008). Community Policing in Hong Kong: An Implementation in Kwai Tsing District. *HKU Theses Online (HKUTO)*. Retrieved from http://dx.doi.org/10.5353/th_b4101445: 114.

Christensen, T., & Lægreid, P. (2011). Democracy and Administrative Policy: Contrasting Clements of New Public Management (NPM) and Post-NPM. *European Political Science Review*, 3(1), 125-146.

Community Policing Consortium. (1994). *Understanding Community Policing: A Framework for Action*. Washington, DC: Bureau of Justice Assistance.

Cordner, G. W. (1997). Community Policing: Elements and Effects. *Critical Issues in Policing: Contemporary Readings*, 5, 401-418.

Denney, L., & Jenkins, S. (2013). Securing Communities: The What and the How of Community Policing. Overseas Development Institute Background Paper PhD thesis. Dept. of Economics. Adelaide University.

Di Nunzio, M. (2014). Thugs, Spies and Vigilantes: Community Policing and Street Politics in Inner City Addis Ababa. *Africa*, 84(3), 444-465.

Diamond, D., & Weiss, D. M. (2009). Advancing Community Policing through Community Governance: A Framework Document. US Department of Justice, Department of Community Oriented Policing Services.

FDRE. (2011). Ethiopia Federal Police Establishment Proclamation no. 720/2011, Addis Ababa, Ethiopia. 6214-6216.

Federal Police Commission. (2017). How the Ethiopian Police Was Founded. http://www.federalpolice.gov.et/web/guest/background-information, accessed March 24, 2017.

Gray Molina, G., & Purser, M. (2010). Human Development Trends since 1970: A Social Convergence Story. *UNDP-HDRO Occasional Papers* (2010/2).

Gruening, G. (2001). Origin and Theoretical Basis of New Public Management. *International Public Management Journal*, 4(1), 1-25.

Kim, Gye-Soo. (2016): Effect of Total Quality Management on Customer Satisfaction. *International Journal of Engineering Sciences & Research Technology*, 5(6), 507-514.

Kothari, C. R. (2004). *Research Methodology: Methods and Techniques*. New Delhi, New Age International.

Krejcie, R. V., & Morgan, D.W. (1970). Determining Sample Size for Research Activities. *Educational and Psychological Measurement*, 30, 607-610.

Kusow, A. M., Wilson, L. C., & Martin, D. E. (1997). Determinants of Citizen Satisfaction with the Police. *Policing: An International Journal of Police Strategies & Management*, 20(4), 655-664.

Larsen, J. E., & Blair, J. P. (2009). The Importance of Police Performance as a Determinant of Satisfaction with Police. *American Journal of Economics and Business Administration*, 1(1), 1.

Lawrence, S., & McCarthy, B. (2013). What Works in Community Policing: A Best Practices Context for Measure Y Efforts. The Chief Justice Earl Warren Institute on Law and Social Policy.

Legesse, F. M., Mekonen, K. D., and Genetu, Y. P. (2016). The Implementation of Community Policing in Slum Neighborhoods of Addis Ababa, Ethiopia. *International Journal of Current Research Research*, 8 (7), 35358-35366.

Maguire, E. R., & Katz, C. M. (2002). Community Policing, Loose Coupling, and Sensemaking in American Police Agencies. *Justice Quarterly*, 19(3), 503-536.

Ministry of Finance and Economic Development (MoFED). (2006). Ethiopia: *Building on Progress: A Plan for Accelerated and Sustained Development to End Poverty (PASDEP), Federal Democratic Republic of Ethiopia*. Addis Ababa: FDRE.

Moore, M. H., & Trojanowicz, R. C. (1988). *Policing and the Fear of Crime* (no. 3). US Department of Justice, National Institute of Justice.

Mulat, F. (2015) An Assessment of Challenges and Prospects of the Implementation of Community Policing: the Case study of Bole Sub-city. PhD thesis, Addis Ababa University.

Mwachidudu, C. J., & Likaka, L. (2014). Community Policing Implementation by Security Agencies in Njoro Sub-County, Nakuru, Kenya. *International Journal of Research in Social Sciences*, 4(8), 23-31.

Office of Community Oriented Policing Services (COPS). (2014). *Community Policing Defined*. Washington, DC http://ric-zai-inc.com/Publications/cops-p157-pub.pdf, accessed March 19, 2018.

Palmiotto, M. J., Birzer, M. L., & Unnithan, N. P. (2000). Training in Community Policing. *Policing: An International Journal of Police Strategies & Management*, 23(1): 8-21.

Pollitt, C., Thiel S. V., & Homburg, V. (2007). *New Public Management in Europe*. Basingstoke: Palgrave Macmillan.

Ponsaers, Paul. (2001): Reading about "Community (Oriented) Policing" and Police Models. *Policing: An International Journal of Police Strategies & Management*, 24(4), 470-497.

Reddy, G. N. (2002). *Building Capacities for Sustainable Development*. New Delhi, Kanishka Publishers.

Skogan, Wesley G., (1995). *Community Participation and Community Policing*. Evanston, IL: Center for Urban Affairs and Policy Research, North-western University.

Sozer, M. A. (2008). *Assessing the Performance of Community Policing: The Effect of Community Policing Practices on Crime Rates*. Indiana, PA: Indiana University of Pennsylvania.

Stebek, E. N. (2018). Ethiopia's Justice System Reform at Crossroads: Impediments Relating to Institutional Continuity, Ethnic Politics, and the Land Regime. *Mizan Law Review*, 12(2), 259-302.

Uchida, C. D. (1993). The Development of the American Police: An Historical Overview. In Dunham, R. G. & Alpert, G. P. (eds), *Critical Issues in Policing: Contemporary Readings* (pp. 16-32). IIlinois, US. Waveland.

Woldekidan, W. G. (2016). *An Analysis of the Influence of Politics on Policing in Ethiopia*. PhD thesis, University of South Africa.

World Bank. (1989). *Sub-Saharan Africa from Crises to Sustainable Growth: A Long-term Perspective Study*. Washington, DC: The World Bank.

Zhao, J., Thurman, Q. C., & Lovrich, N. P. (1995). Community Oriented Policing across the US: Facilitators and Impediment to Implementation. *Am. J. Police*, 14, 11.

V.3

DATA ANALYSIS

24
The Practices and Challenges of Community Policing in Reducing Crime: The Case of Adama City Administration

Dessalegn Kebede Kedida

Box 1: Key points of this chapter

- ✓ There is little practice and a lack of skilled community policing officers in the area studied
- ✓ There is no clear strategy for community policing in the area studied
- ✓ There is a lack of concern about implementing community policing in Adama (Oromia), Ethiopia.
- ✓ Citizens' reluctance to participate is the major challenge of community policing.

Box 2: The readers will have insight into

- ✓ The role of community policing in reducing crime in Adama (Oromia), Ethiopia
- ✓ Elaborating the practice and challenges of community policing in Adama (Oromia), Ethiopia.
- ✓ Organizational changes in community policing: organizational structure, organizational culture, and management style.
- ✓ Methods/Processes of problem solving (SARA model).

Box 3: Abbreviations

CP = Community policing
FGD = Focus Group Discussion
OPC = Oromia Police Commission
SARA = Scanning, analyzing, response, and assessment

1. Introduction

Community policing is a substantive reform in police institutions. It is a dramatic change in the philosophy that determines the way police agencies engage the public. It incorporates a philosophy that broadens the police mission from a narrow focus on crime and law enforcement to a mandate encouraging the exploration of creative solutions for a host of community concerns, including crime, fear of crime, perceptions of disorder, quality of life, and neighborhood conditions (Trajanowicz et al., 2002).

This philosophical shift has occurred over the past decade in the nation‘s thinking about policing, the role of police officers, and their relationship to the communities they serve. This implies that new strategies are needed to increase police department effectiveness and community connectedness (Harris 2001). Hence, it can be argued that community policing models have their roots in the failure of previous models of professional policing to address community concerns (Wilson, 2006).

Community policing is a philosophy and organizational strategy that promotes a partnership based, collaborative effort between the police and the community to more effectively and efficiently identify, prevent, and solve problems of crime, the fear of crime, physical and social disorder, and neighborhood decay in order to improve the quality of life for everyone (Force, 2017).

Community policing was a paradigm shift established on the bedrock of community partnership in creating safe and secure environment for all. It was envisioned as policing whereby the people would take active part in their own affairs; the would not be seen as a problem or stranger whose presence stands for danger but as partners in development; and members of the community would be coproducers of justice and a quality police service. This fact indicates the need of involving the community, the local government, and the police to work together to tackle crime. One rationale for public involvement was the belief that police alone can neither create nor maintain safe communities. Therefore, community policing has emerged as a major issue in the development of public safety in many countries in the world. For example, England, Singapore, Canada, Israel, and the Scandinavian countries (i.e., Norway, Sweden, Denmark, and Finland), had already variously introduced some form of community policing by 2000. Community policing has seen worldwide growth. Indeed, “Police in previous times were brutal in their actions. We used to run when we saw them. Now the changes are dramatic … developing the mentality of serving the community was always on the mind of police officers” (Di Nunzio, 2014).

Developmental state doctrine and its emphasis on bureaucracy as the basis of the developmental state led to the creation of an alliance between politics and the economy, which materialized in the establishment of a specialized bureaucratic apparatus that had ample powers and coordinated the developmental efforts, at least in their initial stages (Esteban, 2008). This is directly related to the concept of community policing and police sector reform.

In practice, as Baker (2009, 2013) points out, community policing in Africa has been interpreted as the creation, recognition, and incorporation of alternative security providers with a wide variation in terms of their capability, legitimacy, and links to the state police. It is also a conceptualization that has become engrained within security sector reform approaches more broadly, with the advocacy of "multi-layered" approaches to security that recognize nonstate actors as "the primary purveyors of day-to-day service delivery" (OECD, 2007:7). This was partly a pragmatic recognition of the reality on the ground, namely, the lack of resources available to the police preventing coverage, particularly in rural areas (Baker and Scheye, 2007). It also puts the African state in a permanent state of negotiation or mediation (Menkhaus, 2006) with nonstate providers and a hybrid political system (Boege et al., 2008). The state is now only one provider among many, and boundaries between state and nonstate actors are problematized by complex interactions and interpenetration of providers following different logics and drawing on varying sources of power (Luckham & Kirk, 2012).

Community policing is a new type of police service provision, in which officers cooperate with the community to proactively identify problems and provide a solutions in advance to minimize crime (Community Oriented Policing Service, 2014). In the other words, it is a type of policing in which the police provides police services in combination with the community. The aim of the community policing system is to improve the living quality of the community by reducing crime and disorder and promoting safety (Community Policing Consortium 1994, quoted in Fridell, 2004). In consideration of the above, the government of Ethiopia in general and in Oromia regional state, Adama City Administration in particular commenced a community policing system in the country since 2005, in an effort to make service accessible and responsive to the community (Abebe, 2009).

This entailed several changes within the police system. The first was the restructuring of the police organization and bringing the previously centralized police service closer to the people. Secondly, it required building community policing officers' capacity to do multiple tasks and change their orientation toward service provision. Additionally, community policing officers were supposed to be generalists capable of carrying out multiple responsibilities and taking a team approach to collaborative problem solving and partnership with the community. Thirdly, the organization had to decentralize and commit resources and finances in fulfilling necessary facilities such as offices, communication infrastructures, and other facilities to make the system continuous and effective (Community Oriented Policing Service, 2014). In pursuit of this objective, the Adama City administration has undertaken an adjustment in the organization of the local police force. However, how effective the reforms have been in supporting police services remains a debatable issue. Against the backdrop of the above-mentioned issues and arguments, therefore, the study tries to close the gap in our knowledge of the situation in Adama City by investigating the practices and challenges of community policing in reducing crime.

Specific objectives

- To assess the practice of community policing in reducing crime in Adama City,
- To examine the role of community policing in reducing crime in Adama City,
- To assess the attitudes of local residents toward community policing in reducing crime in Adama city, and
- To identify the challenges of community policing for reducing crime in the area studied.

Research questions

- What is the current practice of community policing in reducing crime in Adama City ?
- What challenges are faced in implementing community policing in reducing crime in Adama City?
- What has been the role of community policing in reducing crime in Adama City?
- What have been the attitudes of local residents and police officers toward community policing in Adama City ?

2. Review of Related Literature

2.1. The Concept of Community Policing

Community: Some conceive community as a geographic area while others look at community as an area of common life. The following definitions show the essence of community. According to the UN Office on Drugs and Crime, "community" can refer to small neighborhoods, areas within a city, or small villages or towns, or in some cases groups of citizens with particular concerns.

In addition, as Taye Kejila (2015) has stated in his dissertation, a community may be defined as any group of people which is "likely to have a number of characteristics in common, such as geographical area, occupation, ethnicity, economic status, shared government, and a common cultural and historical heritage." Moreover, as stated by Oliver, "community was the term that refers to a group of people who share three things: they live in a geographically distinct area (such as a city or town), they share cultural characteristics, attitudes and lifestyles and they interact with one another on a sustained basis."

The Bureau of Justice Assistance (BJA, 1994) states: "Community policing was democracy in action. It requires the active participation of local government, civic and business leaders, public and private agencies, residents, churches, schools, and hospitals. All who share a concern for the welfare of the neighborhood should work together with Police officers. The above-mentioned bodies must take a unified stand against crime, violence, and disregard for the law and must make a commitment to increasing crime prevention and intervention activities."

It is also helpful to better understand the relationship between the police and the community they serve. For this reason, this study has been strongly driven by the imperative to investigate the concept and practice of community policing.

Community policing may be concisely defined as "the Nine P's of Community Policing." Community policing is a philosophy of full-service personalized policing, where the same officer patrols and works in the same area on a permanent basis, from a decentralized place, working in a proactive partnership with citizens to identify and solve problems (Wycoff, 1999).

2.2. The Practices of Community Policing

In 1984, the Office of Justice Programs (OJP) was created to provide federal leadership in the United States with assistance in developing the nation's capacity to prevent and control crime, administer justice, and assist crime victims (US Department of Justice, 2001). OJP pursues its mission by forming partnerships with other federal, state, and local agencies as well as with national and community-based organizations to develop, operate, and evaluate a wide range of criminal and juvenile justice programs. OJP is dedicated to comprehensive approaches that empower communities to address crime, break the cycle of substance abuse and crime, combat family violence, address youth crime, hold offenders accountable, protect and support crime victims, enhance law enforcement initiatives, respond to terrorism, and support advancements in adjudication.

OJP also works to reduce crime in Native-American communities, enhance technologies within the criminal and juvenile justice systems, and support state and local efforts through technical assistance and training (US Department of Justice, 2001).

2.3. The Role of Community Policing for Crime Prevention

The lack of a concrete definition for community policing and vague measures of success have contributed to the difficulties in determining its effectiveness. In addition, the complex nature of community policing limits the ability to provide sufficient evidence of either success or failure. However, the literature shows a number of benefits of implementing community policing. According to the New Zealand Police, for example, the (perceived) benefits of community policing include "improving Police community relationships and community perceptions of Police; increasing community capacity to deal with issues; changing officers' attitudes and behaviors; increasing perceptions of safety; and reducing crime, disorder and anti-social behavior" (Thurman & McGarrell, 2005).

Generally, implementation issues that have not been identified or resolved can affect the overall success of a community policing initiative. Indeed, a range of barriers to successful implementation could negatively affect the potential benefits of community policing. Some of the possible consequences of poor implementation include: lack of control, flexibility, and tailoring at neighborhood level; not recognizing the historical lack of trust between police and certain communities; and lack of good quality information about crime provided to communities.

More specifically, on the side of police officers, they may work independently of the community in identifying and solving problems; training in problem solving and community engagement may be neglected; and community police officers may lack performance measures. On the part of the residents/ communities, problems may include: their ambiguity with respect to different values and expectations; agencies' promotion of conflicting values; ownership of problems often allocated to police rather than the whole community; low participation resulting from individualism and lack of social capital; and limited community voice given to the vocal minority. With respect to police culture, resistance to community policing has been attributed to the perception it is a move away from traditional law enforcement practices to a "softer" style of policing; at the same time, the community can be disempowered when offering solutions if police dominate as the crime and disorder experts. Indeed, police are still reluctant to share information with the community. Other challenges also emanate from specialized units. As a result, the isolation of officers can limit effectiveness while allocation of extra resources to community policing teams and special conditions of work can create internal friction.

2.4. Pillars of Community Policing

Community policing system is an organization strategy that helps to identify causes that potentially increase fear of crime and social disorder and take remedial actions through community partnership and problem-solving tactics. (Chene, 2012).The system has three key elements (Community Oriented Policing Service, 2014). These are:

Community Partnerships Aspect of Community Policing
One of the core components of the system is a strong police community partnership. Within this system, it is understood that police should not be the sole responsible body in maintaining peace and security. The community, i.e., the local government, civic and business leaders, public and private agencies, residents, churches, schools, and hospitals should also participate in ensuring safety and security of society (Bureau of Justice Assistance, 1994). Unlike traditional policing, community policing takes community involvement as an advantage in ensuring community safety and wellness (Fridel, 2004).

To build a strong community partnership, police must have a good relationship with the community, putting it in a position for better crime control and prevention and mobilizing the resources of the community to solve its priority issues (Bureau of Justice Assistance, 1994). This partnership may be challenged if a community shows resistance to the partnership as a result of low awareness, poor community relations with the police, and low participation of community in police services, among other problems (New Zealand Police, 2008).

Problem Solving Aspect of Community Policing System
This aspect focuses on the process of identifying problems of community and systematic examination of identified problems to take effective response measures by both the community and police (Community Oriented Policing Service, 2014). The major objectives of community policing are carefully studying the characteristics of crime and a neighborhood's problems and taking remedial action accordingly (Bureau of Justice Assistance, 1994).

In problem solving, both community and police are engaged in ensuring community peace and order. Police officers engage in coordination and mobilization of the community in identifying and solving problems to enhance their well-being. On the other hands, the community also takes an active role, sharing the burden with police. This type of mutual benefit enhances the police-community relationship and increases the responsiveness of the police (Chene, 2012.) According to Skogan (1995), it is hardly possible to create and maintain a safe community without community participation because every problem is created and committed within the community. Therefore, the community is a resource, support group, and source of information (Murphy, 1993, quoted in Skogan, 1995). In order to have active participation from the community, it is crucial to increase the awareness level of the community. Community participation depends on the level of community awareness about the program (Skogan, 1995).

Organizational Transformation

It is important that the structure of police institutions be transformed to ensure community involvement and empower officers to make decisions and make them accountable (Community Oriented Policing System, 2014). Organizational transformation focuses on restructuring the organization in a way that promotes people's participation and proactive problem solving. However, mere restructuring of the organization doesn't bring about the desired result. The process should also empower the community policing officers in terms of building their capacity, fulfilling basic communication facilities, delegating decision-making authority, and ensuring an equitable ordering of community resources (Community Oriented Policing Service, 2014). Effective community partnership and problem solving require the capacity of community policing officers to adopt a flexible management style and perform the decentralized responsibilities (Bureau of Justice Assistance, 1994).

Community policing cannot succeed without essential alterations inside the organization of police agencies. It not only requires a philosophical shift regarding police mission but also requires a commitment to alter the organization and its structure (Sozer, 2008). Organizational changes in this context refer to three areas: organizational structure, organizational culture, and management style.

2.5. Problem-Oriented Policing

Problem-oriented policing (POP) is an approach to policing in which discrete pieces of police business (each consisting of a cluster of similar incidents, whether crime or acts of disorder, that the police are expected to handle) are subject to microscopic examination (drawing on the especially honed skills of crime analysts and the accumulated experience of operating field personnel) in hopes that what is freshly learned about each problem will lead to discovering a new and more effective strategy for dealing with it. Problem-oriented policing places a high value on new responses that are preventive in nature, that are not dependent on the use of the criminal justice system, and that engage other public agencies, the community and the private sector when their involvement has the potential for significantly contributing to the reduction of the problem. Problem-oriented policing carries a commitment to implementing the new strategy, rigorously evaluating its effectiveness, and, subsequently, reporting the results in ways that will benefit other police agencies and that will ultimately contribute to building a body of knowledge that supports the further professionalization of the police (Herman, 2001).

In other words, crime is not just a police problem; it's a community problem. POP is a way of looking at community problems through the lens of a police agency, figuring out what to do about that problem, and bringing all resources/ stakeholders to the table to work together on the problem. It doesn't mean that deputies will do all of the work, but it does require deputies to play a significant role in the scanning, analysis, response, and assessment of problems and to be actively engaged in solutions (Herman, 2001).

The SARA Model

A commonly used problem-solving method is the SARA model (scanning, analysis, response, and assessment).

While the SARA model is useful as a way of organizing the approach to recurring problems, it is often very difficult to figure out just exactly what the real problem is. The problem analysis triangle (sometimes referred to as the crime triangle) provides a way of thinking about recurring problems of crime and disorder. This idea assumes that crime or disorder results when (1) likely offenders and (2) suitable targets come together in (3) time and space, in the absence of capable guardians for that target. A simple version of a problem analysis triangle looks like this:

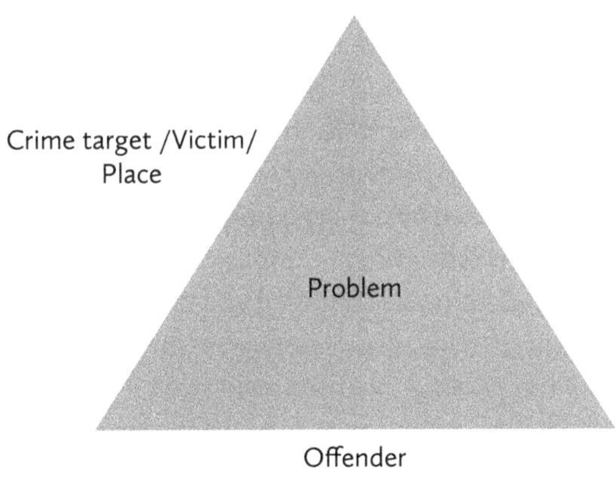

3. Research Methodology

3.1. Research Design

Research design is the blueprint (strategy) for fulfilling research objectives and answering the research questions (Creswell, 2009). The research design selected for this study was descriptive. This was an ideal methodology when collecting information about people's attitudes, opinions, habits, or any of a variety of social issues (Orodho & Kombo 2002).The reason for using descriptive research as a research design is to describe the existing practice and identify the major hindering factors of community policing in reducing crime.

3.2. Research Approach

This research will apply the sequential mixed methods procedure throughout data collection and report presentation to keep consistency. First, the quantitative data was collected, and based upon the results, the interview questions were developed, interviews were conducted and findings are presented in the same manner. The findings are mixed throughout the discussion section.

3.3. Study Population, Sample, and Sampling Techniques

A study population encompasses the total collection of all units of analysis about which the researcher wishes to make specific conclusions. The population of the study for quantitative purposes was the aggregate of Adama regular police members of all ranks working in all the six sub-city administrations. The total population of Adama City regular Police is 678 in number. Hence the researcher attempted to conduct the study of practices and challenges of Adama City community policing in reducing crime on a selected representative sample of the study population.

At present, Adama City administration police comprise six sub-cities police stations, namely the Dabe, Bole, Abba Geda, Dembela, Boku, and Lugo sub-cities police. The six sub-cities of city administration police are organized in the form of the six components of city administration police command. The researcher used a random sampling techniques to frame the sample. After the location of study population was identified and the proper size of the sample was determined by proportionality, sampling techniques were applied to keep the proportionality of participants from each sub-city. This population was manageable and the data collection process easy, smooth, and manageable.

The sample size was calculated by using Taro Yamane's (Yamane, 1967) formula with 93 percent confidence level. (According to an Adama City police official report of September 2019, the total population from the selected sub-cities was 380.) The calculation formula of Taro Yamane is presented as follows:

$$n = \frac{N}{1+N(e)^2}$$

Whereas:
n =Sample size,
N =Population size,
e =Level of precision given that 93% confidence level and P = ±7% are assumed.

$$n = \frac{380}{1+380(0.07)^2} = 204$$

n= 204

The researcher used 204 respondents as a sample. In addition, the selection of respondents was made by simple random sampling (probability sampling).

Table 1: Sample size

Source (Place)	Total no. of female police offices	Percentage (%)	Sample size	Remark
City Police depnt	73	0.192	39	
Bole sub city	112	0.2947	60	
Lugo sub city	80	0.210	43	
Abba Gada sub city	115	0.3026	62	
Total	**380**	**100%**	**204**	

Source: Author

A purposive sampling technique was used to select key informants from Bole, Lugo, and Abba Gada sub-city community policing board members, city administration, prosecutors, and city administration police command leaders. Purposive sampling leads to greater depth of information from a smaller number of carefully selected units (Patton, 2002). A purposive sampling technique was applied based on the high rank and leadership experience of police officers and members of the community policing board. Accordingly four police leaders, two prosecutors, two judges of the city administration, two security and administration leaders, three religious leaders, and four community policing board members were selected for the study, for a total of seventeen key informants, following the principle that –fifteen to thirty-five participants are adequate for key informant interviews (Janet 1999; USAID 1996). For a focus group discussion (FGD) one group (six to eight people) of police customers who were currently (conveniently) came for service was selected and discussion was conducted. This enabled the researcher to gather data in an efficient manner.

3.4. Tools of Data Collection

The researcher used data collection tools including a questionnaire, key informant interviews, FGD, observation, and document analysis.

3.5. Techniques of Data Analysis

The quantitative data, which was collected via questionnaires, was presented using tables and charts to describe the results in relation to the research questions. The findings of the study were analyzed using descriptive statistics. Descriptive statistics were obtained by feeding the quantitative data into the statistical software program SPSS version 20 and analyzing the frequency and percentage to examine the occurrence and variation by chart and table.

The qualitative data obtained from documents, observation, and semi-structured interviews was transcribed, edited, and organized around the subtopics derived from the research questions. Furthermore the data from the interviews, observation, and documents was triangulated, checked against the quantitative data. In addition the findings were discussed and interpreted in relation to the relevant literature.

4. Results and Discussion

4.1. The Current Practice of Community Policing

To understand the practice of community policing, community policing officers in their respective sub-cities were asked.

As indicated in table 2, with respect to the question of the usefulness of mini-stations located within the tribal community areas to improve officer access by the community in the respective sub-cities, about 55.9 percent of respondents indicated that the availability of community service police station for delivering service was adequate.

As it can be observed from table 2, 88.64% of the respondents disagree that community policing is adequately practiced in Adama City administration.

Table 2: Community policing practice

Questions and Filters	N	Strongly agree		Agree		Neutral		Disagree		Strongly disagree	
		F	%	F	%	F	%	F	%	F	%
Mini stations located within the tribe's community areas to improve officer access by the community.	203	90	44.1	**113**	**55.9**						
Community-based outreach programs to share crime prevention and public safety information.	203			167	82.2.	36	17.8				
Use of a Community Safety Survey to identify tribal community perceptions.	203	158	75.4	45	24.6						
Use of service calls classification and prioritization to reduce the number of calls to which field personnel are immediately dispatched.	203			108	57.7	95	48.3				
Officer input applied to targeted deployment plan and strategies.	203	70	31.4	75	33.9	58	26.3				
Officers attend community-based meetings, community advisory groups, etc.	203					105	50.8	98	49.2		

Questions and Filters	N	Level of agreement									
		Strongly agree		Agree		Neutral		Disagree		Strongly disagree	
		F	%	F	%	F	%	F	%	F	%
Citizen complaint process is in place, reviewed regularly, and used to train/ evaluate officers.	203							203	100		
Officers are recognized for problem solving or supporting community policing strategies.	203					20	14.4	183	85.6		
A victim assistance program is available to provide victim support on-scene and/or after a crime.	203									203	100
Crime analysis is used to determine problem areas and/or the most effective deployment of resources.	203					**112**	**58 5**	**91**	**41.5**		
Community members are engaged through crime and safety surveys to better inform the police and involve citizens in crime prevention.	203							163	78.8	40	21.2

Source: Researcher's Field Survey, September 2019

Table 3: Respondents' views on the adequacy of community policing officers

Level of agreement/disagreement	Frequency	Percent
strongly agree	3	1.478
Agree	20	9.85
Disagree	132	65.02
Strongly disagree	48	23.64
Total	**203**	**100**

Source: Researcher's Field Survey, September 2019

What Activities Are Expected to Be Implemented in Community Policing?

Community policing requires discussion between society and police, and active participation is expected from all residents. Assessing the potential crime areas is also another activity that falls under the umbrella of community policing. Almost all research participants informed that the structures formed for community policing are not working in those situations that require close follow-up. On the other hand, focus group members from the Adama City administrative police indicated that the number of community policing officers is kept deliberately small in order to facilitate supervision of whether the structures of community policing are working according to the theoretical framework. On the other side, even providing job opportunities to the unemployed is one activity that may minimize the potential crime rates. Identification of the potential causes of crime is also crucial.

Different respondents explained that the practice of community policing varies between the rural and urban areas. FGD participants in the Adama City administrative police department explained that the structure and way of implementing the strategy can vary greatly, being most effective in rural areas where residents are effectively using it to prevent crime alleviate security concerns. In contrast, it is not as effectively implemented in the urban area due to the unstable nature of the residents and other constraints.

4.2. Structure of Community Policing

The community policing officer is responsible for creating the structures and training participants. Each structure has its own duties and responsibilities, wherein all the structures are mainly formed and monitored by the CP officer assigned in the city kebele. This shows that the officers are constantly with society, and are in a position to improve these structures and identify the potential causes of crime and making society more confident in terms of security issues.

Nonetheless, the crime statistics of Adama City are increasing, demonstrating that the implementation of community policing is far from fully successful.

Table 4: Five year crime statistics in Adama City

	Number of crimes recorded
2015	1,123
2016	1,104
2017	1,645
2018	2,871
2019	3,556
Total	**10,299**

Source: Adama city police dep. five years Crime statistics report (June,2019)

4.3. Challenges of Implementing Community Policing

In an attempt to understand the challenges of implementing community policing, this research investigated issues related to the level of participation of community members in community policing activities; whether the culture of public disclosure of community policing has increased after its implementation; whether research participants as members of the society took community policing trainings and the frequency with which these trainings are offered; and the knowledge of community members on community policing and their views on their participation in community policing activities. Findings obtained on each of these aspects are described below.

However, prior to discussing the aforementioned issues related to the challenges of implementing community policing, an attempt was made to examine whether there are in fact challenges of implementing community policing. The result shows that while 68.3 percent of the respondents argued in favor of the existence of challenges to implementing community policing, the remaining 31.7 percent argued that there are no challenges in implementing it.

Table 5: Challenges of implementing community policing

	Frequency	Percent
Yes	157	68.3
No	45	31.7
Total	203	100

Source: Researcher's Field Survey, April 2019

Table 6: Whether respondents took community policing officer training

	Frequency	Percent
Yes	99	49.8
No	104	50.2
Total	**203**	**100**

Source: Own survey, 2019

Similarly, in regards with the frequency of trainings, while 49.8 percent of respondents reported undergoing only once, a sizable number (50.2 percent) of the respondents had undergone no training at all.

Table 7: Who participates in community policing

Participants	Frequency	Percent
Residents	2	1.7
Members of the police	12	10.2
Kebele administrators and Militia	3	2.5
Other authorities	5	4.2
All	181	81.4
Total	203	100

Source: Own survey, 2019

Data collected from qualitative methods also showed that community policing officers participated in training. Yet, many respondents mentioned its short-term nature, usually lasting from two to five days; they also pointed to its irregular nature and recycling of similar content for the last five or more years. In related fashion, community policing officer focus group discussants in Adama City revealed that since they are not motivated by educational opportunities, they will leave their positions as new opportunities arise, after which new officers will come in and begin work as new community policing trainees.

Table 8: Implementation of community policing versus public disclosure of crime

Degree of agreement	Frequency	Percent
strongly agree	25	11.9
Agree	96	47.5
Disagree	64	31.4
Strongly disagree	18	9.3
Total	**203**	**100**

Source: Researcher's field survey, 2019

This study also sought to find out whether new problems may crop up as a result of implementing community policing. A four-level response rate was offered to respondents to indicate their levels of agreement or disagreement. The findings shows that while more that 38 percent of the respondents responded that they agree or strongly agree, the remaining more than 61 percent disagree or strongly disagree on the subject.

The term "community partnerships" can mean different things in different jurisdictions. In those in which there are the most examples of community policing strategies at work, relationships are created between police and community groups, such as faith-based organizations, tenant councils, business groups, local government agencies, social service providers, schools, and local businesses.

These partnerships are ongoing projects rather than periodic neighborhood watch meetings and have the objective of developing interaction between police and the community. Indeed, some of the most successful examples of community policing strategies are when police services are provided or co-located with other civic services, such as paying utility bills or obtaining parking permits.

In addition to the above quantitative data on the challenges of implementing community policing, researchers have also made use of qualitative data. The findings showed a number of challenges for implementing the community policing philosophy in the study areas. One of these is the lack of qualified human resources, as police officers lacked skill on how to manage/handle, investigate, and proactively prevent the potential occurrence of crime. Though advanced crimes were found to be committed in the study areas, almost none of community policing officers has computer skills. As one discussant in FGD held in Adama City stated, "there is no any police who even knows how a computer is opened and closed." It is also found a high level of turnover of police officers as a result of low salary, a very low incentive system, and the challenging and tiresome nature of the work.

Indeed, the study also found that incentives for police officers for this type of work are very low despite the routine and tiresome work community policing officers perform twenty-four/seven. Furthermore, though implementing community policing in rural areas was found very effective because the residents know each other; are homogenous and have residences, in urban areas, it was found to be challenging because of the instability of the population, which includes b street children, university students, college students, daily laborers, and prostitutes, to list a few. Yet, it is also found that even in urban areas, community policing officers are not only engaged with other tasks but also become too busy to implement community policing. For instance, officers are engaged with current tasks/activities to be done, like meetings, sports races, new students' arrival, students graduation ceremonies, etc. Furthermore, while the work by itself is routine and very tiresome, no budget is allocated for the implementation of the community policing program; and finally, low societal contribution to the budget has variously challenged its implementation.

4.4. The Role of Community Policing in Crime Prevention

To examine the role of community policing, data were collected on issues related to its role in crime prevention as well as other roles it may have played. With respect to the role of community policing in crime prevention, data were collected to understand the views of respondents on the role of community policing, whether community policing has reduced crime rate; to understand their levels of agreement about changes brought after the implementation of community policing; and other roles of community policing.

Many community policing officers defined community policing as the prevention of crime via the active participation of the society and the police, in an area which was previously viewed as the sole responsibility of the police. It has also improved the relationship between society and police officers, where previously the two were seen as antagonistic.

Regarding the question on whether community policing has a role in crime prevention, the finding shows that while 87.3 percent indicated its positive role, the remaining 12.7 percent said that it has no role.

Table 9: The role of community policing for crime prevention

		Frequency	Percent
	Yes	177	87.3
Valid	No	26	12.7
	Total	203	100

Source: Researcher's field survey, 2019

Data collected using qualitative methods also supports the survey results. While almost all of the interviewees and focus group discussants expressed the existence of challenges for implementing community policing in their respective sub-cities, they explained it as an essential tool for minimizing crime incidence. Many also indicated their concern with levels of crime and that they feel more secure after the implementation of the program in their local area. They also highlighted that the introduction of community policing has not only broken down the long-lived view that crime is the sole purview of the police, it also minimized the number of crimes from year to year. As an additional role, implementation of community policing goes beyond identification of criminals to providing them with job opportunities and frequent advice and follow-up with the intent of helping them change their lives for the better.

4.5. Attitudes of Local Residents and Police Officers toward Community Policing

The attitude of local residents and police officers about community policing was assessed. Focus group discussants in Adama City explained that residents support the work of the police, and that rural area residents are especially actively engaging in community policing work Residents' support can take the form of providing office materials, building houses and offices, and cooperating with the officers to prevent crime. Especially in the rural area, the construction of houses for officers, material support, and providing information when necessary increased after the introduction of community policing. This collaborative work and active involvement of the community is one indicator of the residents' positive attitude toward community policing.

As far as the police officers are concerned, despite the fact that they are working in a challenging environment, and even though the turnover of police officers high, they generally have a positive attitude toward the strategy itself, pointing in particular to the role and relevance of community policing in minimizing the occurrence of crime.

According to a FGD discussant, community partnerships are ongoing projects rather than periodic neighborhood watch meetings; furthermore, they have the objective of developing interaction between police and the community. Indeed, some of the most successful examples of community policing strategies at work are when police services are provided or co-located with other civic services, such as paying utility bills or obtaining parking permits.

Building on the organizational transformation above, much of the police interaction at co-location venues is provided by civilians or local volunteers, which helps with the identification of localized problems and the means of solving them. They also provide a good opportunity for law enforcement agencies to engage with neighborhood watch groups and share crime prevention tips.

Shared Problem Solving

The biggest consequence of organizational transformation and community partnerships has been the success of shared problem solving. Police departments with the most successful examples of community policing strategies train officers to focus on creative and active problem solving in the community and with the help of community members rather than simply react to crime or disorder.

One of the most common approaches to shared problem solving in community policing is the "SARA Model." SARA stands for scanning, analysis, response, and assessment and involves recurring issues in the community being identified and analyzed, and community members being consulted, in order to determine the root causes of the issues and find long-term solutions to address them.

Evidence suggests shared problem solving based on the SARA Model can achieve significant reduction in crime over traditional response models. A 2017 review of Adama City police found proactive problem solving had a significant impact on improving public safety and that the shift from reactive crime response had resulted in specific social issues being resolved and crimes being prevented before they happen.

But these improvements in community policing outcomes in the Adama City context were somewhat dampened by constraints in the availability of technology and the immature levels of community partnership, social awareness, and police officers' commitment.

5. Conclusions and Recommendations

5.1. Conclusion

The positive contribution of community policing to crime prevention and crime investigation is direct. There is no other strategy as significant as implementing community policing if the police organization as a whole is to prevent and control crime. Crime and disorders are fundamentally societal products, implying that community participation in crime prevention and crime investigation is of paramount importance. It should be accepted that traditional police methods alone are no longer capable of managing crime prevention and crime investigation. However, implementing community policing is challenging. Institutionalizing the community policing philosophy involves value system changes at all levels of police organization and the public in general. Implementation of community policing requires new ways of thinking and establishing a new organizational culture. It is about changing the entrenched beliefs from a traditional approach to crime control and law enforcement to a proactive approach to crime prevention and disorder. It is about focusing on the causes of crime and disorder more than on treating incidences and symptoms. It is not only about law enforcement but also about behavioral disorders.

Hence, the implementation of community policing strategy demands addressing both systemic and operational aspects of problems that police organizations face. From a systemic point of view, it is highly important to restructure police organizations, their legal frameworks, policies, strategies, and organizational culture. To this end, the commitment and the will of the government and high-level officials are indispensable.

The operational perspective focuses on the implementation aspect of community policing. Day-to-day follow up plays a critical role in the success of the community policing strategy. Hence, designing proper monitoring and evaluation mechanisms should be prioritized. The monitoring and evaluation mechanisms should identify strengths, weaknesses, challenges, and best experiences that should be scaled up to other areas.

Constructive feedback should be given to concerned bodies based on the results of monitoring and evaluation and so help in bridging the skill and knowledge gaps. Designing and implementing trainings based on the practical gaps would be very helpful. Designing and implementing continuous communication strategies also plays a pivotal role in implementing the community policing strategy. Communication plays a critical role in changing entrenched beliefs regarding the traditional approach to crime control and law enforcement.

Above all, trust building is important. The community can participate in crime prevention and crime investigation only when the community trusts the police organization. To this end, as much as possible police organizations and individual police members should refrain from any activity that can undermine their images. Within the theoretical and practical contexts of community policing, it is possible to roughly assess the status of Oromia police commission in terms of implementing community policing strategy, as the police commission has taken serious initiatives in designing and implementing community policing strategies.

Namely, it has tried to restructure its organizational setups, designed special incentives for community policing officers, built a number of offices that offer community policing services, deployed its community police officers to kebeles, and organized different training programs for police personnel, community, and other stakeholders. It has also mobilized the community and resources in crime prevention and crime control.

However, these positive efforts seem to have encountered serious obstacles. The community policing strategy has lacked continuous supervision of its implementation status. Support from the top seems to have deteriorated. Logistics and other related challenges seem to have obstructed implementation. The deeply entrenched beliefs regarding traditional approaches to crime prevention and law enforcement have not shifted to a proactive approach to crime prevention. There is no significant shift of value system or organizational culture. Some practice shows that police in Oromia continue to focus on dealing with incidents and symptoms of crimes than focusing on the root causes of the same. All these weaknesses and facts imply that the attempted fundamental departure from a traditional approach to crime prevention and crime control is not commensurate with the current level of crime. These suggest that Oromia police commission should fundamentally evaluate its performance regarding the whole processes of designing and the implementing community policing with the view to learn from the processes and to organize itself afresh to properly implement the same.

The research results also revealed that currently the practice of community policing implementation is low and mostly ineffective, as are the awareness of community and society about community policing.

From the findings of this study the following major conclusions may be made. The old system of crime prevention and the relationship between the police force and society changed with the coming and functioning of community policing. The philosophy of community policing as indicated in different literatures allows proactive prevention, collaborative work, and developing a sense of ownership of society on security issues in general.

Community policing as a strategy for crime prevention involves collaborative work between society and the police. Its achievement requires the formation of different structures, which were indeed formed and currently operate in the area studied in this chapter. The implementation of community policing in Oromia state began in 1998 as a pilot project and was later expanded in all sub-cities and city administrations of Adama. The theory behind community policing and actual practice, however, do not match in this case. Whereas the strategy requires trained and skilled police officers whose job involves actively organizing and effectively mobilizing society to actively engage on security issues, in our study the police officers are not exclusively assigned and working to implement and follow the strategy. Most police officers in Adama City who are placed to the position of community policing do not work in their position; instead the officers are expected to do tasks which may not be related to the specific position they hold.

All research participants in this study expressed a clear understanding of the central role and significance of community policing in crime prevention. People's level of consciousness and concern with crime issues has improved after the implementation of community policing.

A low level of societal concern and participation is the major challenge of community policing. In the philosophy of community policing society is the main actor and without its involvement it cannot function. Other challenges include limited human resources for coordinating community policing activities, unmotivated police officers, decreased attention from the government to the program, and high turnover of police officers.

The attitude of the police officers and the community about the program was assessed in this study, and officers explained that they have a positive attitude toward the strategy despite working in an environment replete with challenges and problems. Officers strongly emphasized the continuity and relevance of community policing to overcome crime and to increase the community's sense of security. Especially in rural areas, residents are effectively using this system to prevent crime, as well as actively engaging on community policing discussions and reporting crime incidence.

5.2. Recommendations

Based on the findings of the study and the conclusions drawn on the practice and challenges of community policing in reducing crème in Adama City, the following recommendations have been compiled:

1. To effectively implement community policing, the Oromia police commission should assign adequate number of police officers in each area. On the job training must be given to update and scale up police officers' knowledge and skill on crime reducing management issues in general and community policing implementation in particular. The government of Oromia and any concerned body must give emphasis to the community policing program. A sufficient budget and adequate supply of essential materials to community policing officers is fundamental for the successful implementation of community policing.
2. Traditional society associations like the Gada system, Jigi, and Afosha must be used as one structure in the community policing strategy since accessing people is possible through these community associations.
3. Increasing awareness and mobilizing society toward peace and security-building and crime prevention must be consistent and should not be a one-time activity; instead, it must be done frequently and in an organized and pre-scheduled manner.
4. Community policing must be taught in Oromia Police College in detail, with maximum hours to provide police officers with basic police skills.
5. Due to their geographical proximity, the public universities in Oromia and Oromia Police College must work to strengthen the strategy by providing training to the police officers in order to fill the knowledge gap, conducting research to further strengthen the community policing program in the region.
6. The Adama city administration's police department should implement the Gada system and Taajoo in conflict resolution and to improve community engagement and participation in community policing.

Acknowledgement

I want to express my gratitude to editors and reviewers for their constructive comments and encouragement to successfully complete this book chapter. Next, I would like to express my deepest thank to Dr. Bacha Kebede Debela for his scholarly encouragement and guidance.

References

Admasssie, Y. (2010) *Social Research Methods: Teaching Material for Postgraduate Programme.* Addis Ababa: Addis Ababa University.

Benishanguel Gumuz Regional State Police Commission. (2014). *Benishanguel Gumuz Regional State Community Policing Strategic Document.* Assosa, Ethiopia.

Caldentey, E. P. (2008), Developmental State Doctrine and Its bureaucratic Fundamentals in Malaysia. *International Journal of Political Economy,* 37(3), 27-53.

Community Oriented Policing Service. (2014). Community Policing Defined. Washington, DC: US Department of Justice. http://ric-zai-inc.com/Publications/cops-p157-pub.pdf.

Coquilhat, J. (2008). *Community Policing: An International Literature Review.* Wellington, NZ: New Zealand Police. http://www.ccsenet.org/journal/index.php/jsd/article/download/7769/6790, accessed September 28, 2016.

Creswell, J.W. (2009). Research Design Qualitative, Quantitative, and Mixed Methods Approaches, 3rd (ed.) SAGE Publications Ltd USA.

Degu, Y. (2014). *Community Policing or Policing the Community? The Emerging Police Practice in Ethiopia.* Mekelle, Ethiopia: Mekelle University.

Denney, L., & Kassaye, D. (2013). *Securing Communities for Development Community Policing in Ethiopia's Amhara National Regional State.* https://www.odi.org/sites/odi.org.uk/files/odiassets/publications-opinion-files/8656.pdf.

Di Nunzio, M. (2014). Thugs, Spies and Vigilantes: Community Policing and Street Politics in inner City Addis Ababa. *Africa,* 84(3), 444-465.

Friedman, R. R. (1992). *Community Policing: Comparative Perspectives and Prospects.* New York: Harvester Wheatsheaf.

Trajanowicz, R, Kappeler, V.E., and Gaines, L.K., (2002). *Community Policing: A Contemporary Perspective,* 3rd (ed.) US: Matthew Bender & Company, Inc.

Jeremy, W. M. (2006). *Community Policing in America.* New York: Routledge Taylor and Francis Group.

Kalof, L., Dan, A., & Dietz, T. (2008). *Essentials of Social Research.* London: McGraw-Hill Education.

Kothari, C. R. (2004). *Research Methodology, Methods and Techniques,* 2nd rev. ed. New Delhi: New Age International.

Lisa, D. & Kassaye, D. (2013). *Securing Communities for Development: Community Policing in Ethiopia's Amhara National Regional State. Odi.org. UK.*

Oromia Police Commission. (2015). *Growth and Transformation Plan of Five Years Report.* Addis Ababa, Ethiopia.

Organization for Social Science Research in Eastern and Southern Africa, (2011). Gender Issues Research Report Series – no. 22 ISSN 1608-6295: Kenya.

Patton, M. Q. (1990). *Qualitative Evaluation and Research Methods.* SAGE Publications, Inc. Newbury Park, California.

Rue, H., & Held, L. (2005). *Gaussian Markov Random Fields: Theory and Applications*. CRC press. London

Sekaran, U. (2000). *Research Methods for Business: A Skill-building Approach*, 3rd ed. New York: John Wiley & Sons, Inc., p. 288.

Thurman, Q. C., & McGarrell, E. F. (2005). *Community Policing in a Rural Setting*, 2nd ed. Cincinnati, OH: Anderson Publishing Co.

Walker S., Walker, C., & McDavid, J. (1992). *The Victoria Community Police Stations: A Three Point Evaluation*. Ottawa: Canadian Police College.

Wilson, J. M. (2006). *Community Policing in the United States*. London: Routledge.

Wycoff, M. (1999). *Community Policing: Past, Present, and Future*. Washington, DC: Police Executive Research Forum.

VI

CONCLUSIONS AND IMPLICATIONS

25
Conclusions and Implications

Bacha Kebede Debela, Geert Bouckaert, Meheret Ayenew Warota, and Dereje Terefe Gemechu

Introduction

The contributions in this handbook have unveiled several interesting findings enabling us to address the research question "*How can we describe and explain the contexts, the processes and the results of the post-1990 politico-administrative reforms in Ethiopia and what are the implications for sustainable development?*" Interestingly, although each contribution has unique features, they are increasingly complementary. In this chapter, we draw conclusions and implications. We also connect the conclusions with SDGs, specifically with Goals 11, 16, and 17, and with PA teaching and research in Ethiopia.

Conclusions

Five conclusions could be drawn from the contributions on governance, participation, and institutions. First, it is apparent that improving democratic quality is a precondition to improving public trust in government and has a positive influence on citizens' life satisfaction. Yet, it should be noted that for the sustenance of democratization and better governance, both the processes and results of democratic elections are equally important. Second, in the Ethiopian context, the contributions show that historical factors, and the endorsement of the Developmental State doctrine, have not only stalled the democratization process and progress towards good governance and multi-stakeholders' participation in public service delivery (e.g., health service) but have also restricted citizens' participation and empowerment in development processes. Third, the inadequate institutional capacity of the government, the issue of legitimacy of the legislature, particularly since 2005, and the overarching power of the executive branch of the government have further increased the intractability of problems in the area under discussion. Partly due to inadequate institutional capacity and politico-administrative and cultural factors, and partly due to the trade-offs between private (efficiency) and public values (such as impartiality and equity) (Lapuente & Van de Walle, 2020; Pollitt & Bouckaert, 2017), the net effect of NPM types of reform appears low. Fourth, although the representation of women in national parliament has been increasing, the glass ceiling and glass walls continue to constrain women from holding political executive leadership and managerial positions, particularly at local government levels. This holds true even in local governments with 50 percent women councilors. Fifth, interestingly and remarkably, the findings show that there is a significant difference between the indigenous Gadaa system and Western democratic systems in terms of democratic values and processes. Simply put, in Ethiopia multiple factors appeared to significantly increase citizen distrust in government and public administration. Consequently, therefore, the country was hit by public protests between 2014 and the first quarter of 2018. Distrust in government and public administration has continuously resurfaced despite the patchy official politico-administrative reforms.

We have also drawn five conclusions from the contributions on people as human resources. The first key conclusion is that structural and instrumental politico-administrative reforms introduced since mid the 1990s have changed many aspects of HRM at the federal, regional, and local government levels. The second key conclusion is that due to historical, sociological, and political factors, human resource recruitment, career development, and promotion in the civil service include a mix of meritocratic and political patronage. The third crucial conclusion is that historical and sociological factors, as well as top-down structural and instrumental politico-administrative reforms, have reinforced the allegiance of civil servants to the political executives. The fourth conclusion is that it appears that middle-level managers have played a substantial mediating role in institutionalizing the quasi-meritocratic civil service to a certain degree. Finally and importantly, politico-administrative and sociological contexts define the leadership contexts, which in turn have streamlined the relevance of pragmatic leadership, although authoritarian leadership remains deeply entrenched.

Concerning the contributions on performance and quality, we draw four conclusions. Urban local governments encounter trade-offs between economic, social, and ecological objectives in providing drinking water services. Second, the cost and time performance of the Ethiopian mega sugar construction projects were significantly weak, having substantial socioeconomic and political implications. The other plausible conclusion, which is perhaps strongly connected to all the conclusions in this handbook, is that Ethiopia's performance on good governance indicators is inconsistent with trends on voice and accountability, a particularly worrisome outcome. Third, it appears that improving organizational and individual factors may help to enhance civil servants' attitudes toward their performance. This suggests a promising potential for future reform programs in Ethiopia.

The contribution on the governance of policies enabled us to draw four conclusions. First, despite NPM-type reform programs, which have also adversely hit higher education in Ethiopia and its legal autonomy, the institutional autonomy of the Ethiopian higher public education was significantly low, particularly when compared with European universities. This is partly due to the fact that the ruling party uses the structural-instrumental institutional arrangements and legal instruments to control universities to a considerable degree. In addition, the influence of historical and sociological factors appears to be strong. Second, the institutional capacity of Ethiopian universities is in general inadequate for quality teaching and research. An emblematic example relates to the challenges of public administration teaching and research in Ethiopian higher institutions. The inadequate institutionalization of PA teaching and research, combined with the lack of a strong connection between PA academia and practitioners and the non-PA graduate groups/individuals who appear to act as the "gatekeepers," has constrained not only the professionalization of PA but also the employability of PA graduates, particularly those with bachelor credentials. Third, student enrollment in primary and secondary schools as well as in higher education institutions has been substantial. However, the quality of education and gender inequality at all levels of education requires significant attention. Fourth, contrary to popular assumptions and despite weak institutional capacity, the ruling party has substantially used community policing to control citizens at the grass-roots level instead of co-producing peace and order, which has been a brake on promoting good governance and trust in government.

Implications

Against the above overreaching conclusions, we now draw implications for the Sustainable Development Goals and PA teaching and research in Ethiopia. To this end, we organize our implication points into four major clusters. These clusters are inclusive, resilient, and sustainable cities (SDG 11); effective, accountable, and inclusive institutions (SDG 16); effective partnerships (SDG 17); and PA teaching and research (present and future). We also connect with other SDGs whenever necessary, because all seventeen SDGs cannot be realized without effective public administration in place.

Inclusive, Resilient, and Sustainable cities

The UN's SDG 11, among others, specifies inclusive and economically, socially, and environmentally resilient cities. These cities should be able to substantially minimize the trade-offs between economic, social, and ecological goals in development programs and public services. In this connection, all contributions in this handbook have revealed that the progress of Ethiopian cities toward achieving the UN's envisioned cities of 2030 is constrained due to the following: (1) trade-offs between the dimensions of the "Triple Bottom Line" for drinking water supply (UN Goal 6 as well as Goal 11); (2) community policing that is allegedly used as a political instrument for exercising control over citizens rather than ensuring inclusive, resilient, and sustainable cities; (3) inadequate government performance on good governance indicators, particularly the declining trend on voice and accountability; (4) an overtly politicized civil service; (5) lack of adequate citizen empowerment and participation, as well as widespread corruption; and (6) a strong glass ceiling and glass wall that have obstructed women from holding political executive and managerial jobs (SDG Goal 5). Moreover, the effects of the deep-seated historical and sociological factors, politico-administrative culture, and the culture of top-down planning are equally significant. However, taking all factors into context, it might be crucial to develop an inter-organizational bench-learning platform for institutional innovation and pragmatic leadership to design strategic solutions.

Effective, Accountable, and Inclusive Institutions (SDG-Goal 16)

The findings in this handbook also zoom in on SDG 16, which underscores the necessity to develop effective, accountable, and inclusive institutions at all levels. The first implication is that, despite many reforms and capacity building programs, some findings suggest that Ethiopian public administration remains weak and ineffective at all levels (federal, regional, and local). Furthermore, the reform programs and reform tools used to disproportionately tilt the allegiance of civil servants to the political executives, and in the worst case to sideline or remove competent civil servants instead of improving the effectiveness and efficiency of the civil service and the institutional capacity of public administration. The second important implication is that the vision to develop inclusive institutions at all levels could be substantially hampered because of: (1) the non-inclusiveness of the parliament; (2) the gender-based occupational segregation in the civil service and political executive and managerial positions; (3) the limited space for vibrant citizen participation in the development and governance processes, and the increasing inequality generated due to political historical and sociological factors; (4) the longstanding problem of educational quality (primary to higher education levels); (5) and gender parity challenges as regards access to education at all levels. The third implication is the decreasing levels of voice and accountability and the inconsistent performance on other dimensions of governance, which may increasingly constrain the accountability of institutions at all levels. The incompatibility of the indigenous governance system with the Western democratic system, if not properly reconciled, may also increase the trade-offs between different values.

Effective Partnerships (SDG Goal 17)

The UN specifies that achieving all SDGs requires a partnership between actors at all levels and the participation of stakeholders, including the community, and all people (UN, 2015). Effective partnership requires effective vertical and horizontal interaction and mutual interdependence and collective accountability for performance at all levels (Bouckaert & Halligan, 2008). As revealed by the contributions in this handbook, however, the power relation between state and other actors, including state-citizen interactions, are not optimal but rather significantly unequal. The Ethiopian hierarchical governance approach has constrained effective multi-stakeholder development and participative governance and development. The formal multi-stakeholder partnerships, such as community policing, are largely used to control actors instead of institutionalizing genuine participation at all levels. Often, the voices of stakeholders and citizens are either unheard or systematically suppressed. Indeed, the regime in power seems to use the multi-stakeholder approach for mobilizing resources. However, it is believed that learning and unlearning from historical factors and effectively building on the existing egalitarian culture, indigenous institutions, and pragmatic leadership could be helpful in balancing the top-down development planning and political culture. This would widen and increase the space for inclusive dialogue and interactive participation for the co-production of sustainable development.

PA Teaching and Research

The role of higher education in achieving sustainable development goals is indisputable (Pinheiro et al., 2018). More specifically, as noted in the introductory chapter, effective and context-appropriate PA teaching and research are crucial to strengthen public institutions, enhance public service motivation and public interest, and solve societal problems (Bouckaert, 2020; Newcomer & Allen, 2015; Ongaro, 2020; Rosenbaum, 2015). Therefore, it is not a coincidence that the themes of Ethiopian PA conferences focused on strengthening institutions for sustainable development.

It also holds true that effective PA teaching and research need an effective institutional framework and governance system. However, as revealed in this handbook, the institutional autonomy of Ethiopian universities is weak. Recently, an initiative to ensure the quality and relevance of educational programs has been launched. The country's Higher Education Relevance and Quality Agency (HERQA) is responsible for conducting internal program audits for public universities and accrediting private universities. But being a governmental institution, its professional autonomy may be doubted.

Concerning PA research and teaching, a contribution in this book has brought out the fact that Ethiopian PA universities and departments have inadequate institutional capacity for ensuring quality in PA teaching and research. In addition, although PA teaching and research should closely be connected to PA practice (Pollitt, 2020) in order to improve both theory and practice (Ongaro, 2020), the link between PA departments and the public sector for teaching and research has been found to be inadequate. In this regard, it is worth mentioning that the Ethiopian Public Administration Association (EPAA) was established in 2016, after over five decades of PA teaching in the country, to partially remedy this undesirable state of affairs. Moreover, while the politico-administrative contexts and cultural factors are significantly different, PA teaching in Ethiopia predominantly relies on Western models and books/journals authored by Western scholars, often without contextualization of the Ethiopian reality. Moreover, although the qualities of all program graduates are comparable, graduates in the PA field face institutional barriers in employment and the broad areas of career and professional development.

It is appropriate to observe that this first Ethiopian PA handbook means not only to reduce overreliance on the Western model in PA teaching but also to serve as a steppingstone to develop the Ethiopian PA model. Among other things, Ethiopian PA may be able to develop a model that reconciles the indigenous institutions and Western PA models. Interestingly enough, the contributors of this handbook are from different PA universities as well as para-academics (representativeness), which may contribute to the achievement of this goal. We hope that the circle and network of academics and practitioners will further increase and lead to the coproduction of PA theory and practice as well as helping to address the employability challenges of PA graduates. The accreditation of PA programs is also crucial, as the many Ethiopian PA programs are not accredited thus far. Ongaro (2020) rightly claims that enlightened knowledge (theoretical knowledge), problem-orientated knowledge, and practice-extrapolation knowledge are crucial for the development of the practice of PA. This in turn strengthens a two-way interaction between academia and practitioners and helps to bridge the gap between theory and practice (Bouckaert, 2010; Saporito, 2020), permitting the coproduction of relevant knowledge that fits the purposes and demands of the present and the future (Bouckaert, 2019; Bouckaert & Jann, 2020). The three types of knowledge are important in the context of Ethiopia because the contributions in this handbook have revealed gaps in the existing PA teaching and research and revealed unjust citizen-state interaction that should profoundly change if we are to address existing and future problems and shortcomings in this regard. In addition, it is to be noted that Ethiopian PA should be informed by historical and sociological factors, as well as future scenarios. Bouckaert (2010) argues that PA research should not be only retrospective but should also focus on some aspects of the future. Furthermore, as rightly pointed out by Joyce (2020) in his recommendations on European PA, Ethiopian PA academics should be duty bound to contribute to the democratization process, strengthen public institutions, and improve the well-being of citizens. Indeed, this requires both learning and unlearning.

Interestingly, the EPAA, which comprises academics and practitioners, engages in the three types of knowledge identified by Ongaro (2020). In addition, the EPAA study groups comprise of Public Policy Analysis study group; Performance Management, and Trust Study Group; Leadership Study Group; Partnership Management/ co-Production Study Group; Multilevel Governance, and Democracy Study Group; Teaching Public Administration Study Group; and Indigenous Institutions and Development Study group. Once these different groups take off and begin functioning, they will leverage the dynamics of PA practice, teaching, and research in Ethiopia.

The contributions in this handbook also fit with the three complementary angles for research: theory/model, method, and data as developed by Bouckaert (2019). While two of the contributions were deductive theory/model-driven, three were purely data-driven, and the remaining were a combination of elements of the three angles. However the proportions of the mix vary considerably. Furthermore, the majority of the contributions rely on primary and secondary data sources and mixed research design approaches. The other novelty of the studies in this handbook is that they build on the PhD studies and conference papers written by Ethiopian academics (supply) and para-academics/practitioners (demand). This does not only bridges the supply and demand sides of knowledge production (Bouckaert, 2019) but also allows enhancing research and practice-driven PA teaching, as well as ensuring the relevance and quality of PA education and research to advance public interest and improve public services.

Finally, it needs to be underscored that this handbook has not only uncovered the "wicked" problems facing Ethiopian public administration but also provides relevant context and steppingstones for PA teaching and research in Ethiopia. We also hope that EPAA will continue to facilitate debate and dialogue between different actors, including academia and practitioners and to play a significant role in creating space to address the crucial problems of the lack of accommodating diversity and effective participation of the relevant stakeholders. Furthermore, we also hope EPAA can help us to overcome "the power of the few; the powerlessness of many" and ultimately enhance the "collective power of the people to demand change" (UNDP, 2019: iii) and build the envisioned utopian, but achievable, sustainable future. We also hope EPAA will have the capacity to dialogue with international peers, which would enhance international cooperation and understanding toward positive goals that we all cherish.

References

Bouckaert, G. (2010). Research in Public Administration for the Future. *Society and Economy. In Central and Eastern Europe | Journal of the Corvinus University of Budapest*, 32(1), 3-15.

Bouckaert, G. (2019). Dissemination of Scientific Knowledge on Reforming Public Administration: Some Changing Mechanisms. *Hrvatska i komparativna javna uprava: časopis za teoriju i praksu javne uprave*, 19(1), 9-22.

Bouckaert, G. (2020). From Public Administration in Utopia to Utopia in Public Administration. In Bouckaert and Jann (eds.), *European Perspectives for Public Administration: The Way Forward* (pp. 71-84). Leuven: Leuven University Press.

Bouckaert, G., & Halligan, J. (2008). *Managing Performance: International Comparisons*. London: Routledge Taylor & Francis Group.

Bouckaert, G., & Jann, W. (2020b). Lessons and Next Steps. In Bouckaert and Jann, European *Perspectives for Public Administration* (pp. 455-465). Leuven: Leuven University Press.

Joyce, P. (2020). Governing for the Future: Means, Ends and Disconnects. In G. Bouckaert and Jann (eds). European Perspectives for Public Administration (pp. 85-102). Leuven: Leuven University Press.

Lapuente, V., & Van de Walle, S. (2020). The effects of new public management on the quality of public services. *Governance*, Special Issue, pp, 461-475. https://onlinelibrary.wiley.com/journal/14680491

Newcomer, K. & Allen, H. (2015). Public Administration Education: Adding Value in the Public Service. In Rosenbaum (ed.), In *Quest for Excellence: Approaches to Enhancing the Quality of Public Administration Education and Training*. United Nation and IASIA/IIAS, pp. 43-59.

Ongaro, E. (2020). Forms of Knowledge for the Practice of Public Administration. In Bouckaert and Jann, *European Perspectives for Public Administration*, 273-282.

Pinheiro, R., Šima, K., Young, M., & Kohoutek, J. (2018). University Complexity and Regional Development in the Periphery. In Pinheiro, R. Young, M. and Šima, K (ed.) *Higher Education and Regional Development* (pp. 1-20). Cham: Palgrave Macmillan.

Pollitt, C. (2020). Shadowland: The Poorly-Mapped, Underdiscussed Yet Vital Interface between Public Administration Research and Practice. In G. Bouckaert and Jann (eds). *European Perspectives for Public Administration* (pp. 249-272). Leuven: Leuven University Press.

Pollitt, C., & Bouckaert, G. (2017). *Public Management Reform: A Comparative Analysis – Into the Age of Austerity*, 4th ed. New York: Oxford University Press

Saporito, R. (2020) Do We Practise What We Preach When We Teach (and Research) Public Administration? In G. Bouckaert and Jann (eds). *European Perspectives for Public Administration* (pp. 293-316). Leuven: Leuven University Press.

UNDP. (2019). Human Development Report 2019. Beyond Income, beyond Averages, beyond Today: Inequalities in Human Development in the 21st Century. New York: United Nations.

United Nations (UN). (2015). Transforming Our World: The 2030 Agenda for Sustainable Development. General Assembly (70/1). New York: United Nations.

www.ingramcontent.com/pod-product-compliance
Ingram Content Group UK Ltd.
Pitfield, Milton Keynes, MK11 3LW, UK
UKHW021012120926
8556IPUK00039B/1075

9 789462 702561